The Family in the New Millennium

THE FAMILY IN THE NEW MILLENNIUM

WORLD VOICES SUPPORTING THE "NATURAL" CLAN

VOLUME 2

MARRIAGE AND HUMAN DIGNITY

Edited by A. Scott Loveless and
Thomas B. Holman

PRAEGER PERSPECTIVES

Westport, Connecticut
London

Library of Congress Cataloging-in-Publication Data

Loveless, A. Scott and Holman, Thomas B.
The Family in the new millennium : world voices supporting the "natural" clan / edited by A. Scott Loveless and Thomas B. Holman.
    p. cm.
  Includes bibliographical references and index.
  ISBN 0–275–99239–X (set : alk. paper) — ISBN 0–275–99240–3 (v. 1 : alk. paper) — ISBN 0–275–99241–1 (v. 2 : alk. paper) — ISBN 0–275–99242–X (v. 3 : alk. paper) 1. Family. 2. Marriage. 3. Family policy. I. Loveless, A. Scott. II. Holman, Thomas. III. Title
  HQ519.F37 2007
  306.85—dc22   2006031055

British Library Cataloguing in Publication Data is available.

Library of Congress Catalog Card Number: 2006031055
ISBN: 0–275–99239–X (set) (alk. paper)
        0–275–99240–3 (vol. 1)
        0–275–99241–1 (vol. 2)
        0–275–99242–X (vol. 3)

First published in 2007

Praeger Publishers, 88 Post Road West, Westport, CT 06881
An imprint of Greenwood Publishing Group, Inc.
www.praeger.com
Printed in the United States of America

The paper used in this book complies with the Permanent Paper Standard issued by the National Information Standards Organization (Z39.48-1984).

10 9 8 7 6 5 4 3 2 1

These volumes are not published or endorsed by the United Nations System.

Every reasonable effort has been made to trace the owners of copyrighted materials in this book, but in some instances this has proven impossible. The authors and publisher will be glad to receive information leading to more complete acknowledgments in subsequent printings of the book and in the meantime extend their apologies for any omissions.

Contents

Preface of Her Highness Sheikha Mozah Bint Nasser Al-Missned

In the Name of God, the Most Gracious, the Most Merciful:

We are pleased to publish this collection of international scholarship, gathered during the 2004 Doha International Conference for the Family. The Conference culminated on 29–30 November 2004 in Doha, Qatar. This gathering, held to celebrate the Tenth Anniversary of the International Year of the Family, was preceded by a series of conferences and meetings held in various cities and continents around the world. Those meetings reaffirmed the importance and vitality of the family, regardless of cultural, social, and national backgrounds and interests.

There is no common denominator better able to bridge the gap between different people from around the world, despite conflicts and diversity, than a firm belief in the sacred nature of the family. All divine laws have blessed this sacred institution, which forges a strong bond between males and females, a bond which conforms to human nature in bearing and raising new generations that, in turn, contribute to building civilization.

The Doha International Conference for the Family emphasized the ongoing need to re-energize the role of the family in public life. These volumes provide a new opportunity for global society to discuss the role of the family and to participate in promoting the family as the fundamental pillar of society and repository for values and high ideals. As shown in these volumes, the family plays an important role as a safety valve to reduce social pressures on the individual—pressures that have rapidly increased in the modern world. By performing this, and other functions, the family safeguards social stability and security.

I praise the fact that these volumes address various issues of paramount importance confronting the family in the New Millennium. The modern family faces serious challenges that should be addressed, without delay, by serious thought and action. The concept of the family, as we all know, has been defined at times in a manner contrary to established social norms, religious values, and basic concepts of human consciousness. We should resist these notions, especially those that are promoted solely under the guise of modernity. Modernity cannot be accepted as a pretext to bypass social, cultural, and religious values that have long shielded and maintained the family.

The family in the New Millennium is charged with new responsibilities, including social progress and development, which must be discharged effectively. An enlightened, strong, and stable family not only provides a safety net for men, women, and children, it also safeguards society. By properly fulfilling its fundamental role of bearing, rearing, and teaching children, the family contributes to strengthening intercultural dialogue and forgiveness, as it remains the first institution where we form first impressions of the world and develop the art of building relationships with others.

The importance of the family as a school encourages further emphasis on its proper functioning, so that it can train and prepare enlightened and open-minded people who will accept rational thought, be open to dialogue with others, and learn from differences in opinion, rather than accept extreme views without proof. This process strengthens national entities and promotes the culture of democracy, in accordance with ongoing calls for intercultural dialogue and peaceful coexistence among nations. National and international organizations should work hand in hand for the family at the outset of this New Millennium to overcome all legal, political, economic, and social barriers that threaten the family or prevent it from performing its basic roles and duties.

It is not possible to guarantee the safety of the family—or prevent social disintegration—by assuming that the "real problems" faced by the modern world are merely clusters of separate questions such as poverty and illiteracy. These and other issues indeed present serious challenges. But they cannot be addressed or solved without using the family as a strategic tool for social reconstruction and development.

It is imperative to coordinate national and international family programs in order to guarantee that the family, as the basic social unit, receives the widest possible protection and assistance by society and the state. As a practical matter, it is impossible to deal with family issues and problems by means of individual programs or separate systems. Rather, what is needed are comprehensive national and international approaches that are capable of dealing with all tasks, issues, duties, and challenges related to the family— all of which now go beyond any limited view of social responsibility and awareness.

Safeguarding the family, as noted in Article 16(3) of the Universal Declaration of Human Rights, is a prerequisite for promoting national progress and supporting a spirit of universal cooperation. Accordingly, there is an urgent need for a new mentality that sees the family as part of the solution rather than part of the problem. In other words, what is required is a mentality that does not treat the family as an impediment to social progress and development, but rather as the driving force behind it.

Such an approach, in my opinion, requires adoption of references and standards that will safeguard the rights of the family and ensure its integration as an effective and constructive factor in all national, regional, and international development programs. The Doha Declaration, adopted at the end of the Doha International Conference and subsequently noted by the United Nations General Assembly in December 2004, sets out such references and standards.

But, despite its importance, The Doha Declaration on its own is not sufficient. Global society must work together to research, explore, and implement the references, standards, and goals set out in the Declaration. For this reason,

I have organized The Doha International Institute for Family Studies and Development. The Institute has been charged with the responsibility of inviting the international community to undertake constructive and cooperative efforts to research, coordinate, and implement effective family policies at the national, regional, and international levels. The Institute will achieve these goals by completing and supporting academic research, organizing forums, publishing family scholarship, and supporting other family-based initiatives that will place the family within a complementary national and global framework and as the pivot around which all plans for development revolve.

It is my pleasure to present these volumes as an initial step in this process. I am confident that the diverse and rich religious, political, intellectual, and practical experience contained in these volumes will be of immense help in beginning further discussions and analysis of the family in the New Millennium. These volumes begin an important international effort to create concrete and practical policies and practices that will strengthen the family as "the natural and fundamental group unit of society." (*Paragraph 3, The Doha Declaration, reaffirming Article 16(3) of the Universal Declaration of Human Rights.*)

Peace and blessings be upon you.

Her Highness Sheikha Mozah Bint Nasser Al-Missned, Consort of His Highness the Emir of Qatar; President of the Supreme Council for Family Affairs, State of Qatar; Chair of the Board of Directors, The Qatar Foundation; and Founder of The Doha International Institute for Family Studies and Development

Preface of the NGO Working Committee

I am honored to write a short preface to these volumes on behalf of the NGO Working Committee who assisted Her Highness Sheikha Mozah Bint Nasser Al-Missned, Consort of His Highness the Emir of Qatar, in organizing the Doha International Conference for the Family.

The NGO Working Committee included Mr. Charlie Colchester of CARE, Dr. William Saunders of the Family Research Council, Dr. Douglas Sylva and Dr. Lea Sevcik of the Catholic Family and Human Rights Institute, and myself (as Managing Director of The World Family Policy Center). The NGO Working Committee is grateful for the vision of Her Highness and the hard work of the many scholars and experts around the world, who have made publication of these volumes possible. We also express our gratitude to Dr. A. Scott Loveless, Acting Managing Director of the World Family Policy Center, and Dr. Thomas B. Holman, Professor of Marriage, Family, and Human Development, both of Brigham Young University, for their yeoman service as editors of these volumes.

In early 2004, the NGO Working Committee circulated a worldwide call for papers, seeking the finest available scholarship addressing modern family life. The response was overwhelming. During regional dialogues convened in Mexico City, Stockholm, Geneva, and Kuala Lumpur, a broad range of scholars—including sociologists, demographers, lawyers, philosophers, and social historians, among others—gathered from Africa; Asia; Australia; North, Central, and South America; and Europe. These volumes present only a portion of the scholarship gathered during this process.

Some commentators have described a supposedly unavoidable clash of civilizations. The Doha International Conference for the Family, however, underscored the fundamental values and beliefs that unify (rather than divide) the world. The Conference process brought together a unique group of international actors from strikingly diverse cultures, political systems, and faiths. The extensive evidence developed during the yearlong processes of the Doha Conference suggests that increasing levels of cultural conflict are far from inevitable. The chapters in these volumes—representing a rich variety of cultures, political systems, and faiths—demonstrate that all peoples and cultures of the world are united by shared understandings related to the natural family. Building on these shared understandings, now reflected in The Doha Declaration, these volumes can prompt local, national, and international actions that will not only protect and fortify the family but also build a secure and peaceful world.

Article 16(3) of the Universal Declaration of Human Rights embodies fundamental truths that, for too long, have not been given their deserved attention and respect. The Article declares that "the family is the natural and fundamental group unit of society and is entitled to protection by society and the state." This short assertion expertly reflects wisdom distilled from the entire course of human history.

As reflected in the precise and elegant terms of the Universal Declaration, the family is not merely a construct of human will or imagination. The family has a profoundly important connection to nature. This connection begins with the realities of reproduction (underscored by recent studies which demonstrate that children thrive best when raised by married biological parents) and extends to the forces that shape civilization itself. It encompasses, among other things, the positive personal, social, cultural, and economic outcomes that current research suggests flow from a man learning to live with a woman (and a woman learning to live with a man) in a committed marital relationship. The family, in short, is the "natural and fundamental group unit of society" precisely because mounting evidence attests that the survival of society depends on the positive outcomes derived from the natural union of a man and a woman.

These volumes provide a unique, new starting point for future cooperative efforts by governments, nongovernmental organizations, research institutions, academicians, faith communities, and members of civil society. The extensive, interlocking activities of the Doha International Conference for the Family provided all actors in the international community with important opportunities for recommitment to "the natural and fundamental group unit of society." *(Paragraph 3, The Doha Declaration, reaffirming Article 16(3), Universal Declaration of Human Rights.)* The data, scholarship, legal analysis, and ideas presented here point to hopeful new policies for the world's men, women, and—most importantly—children.

Dr. Richard G. Wilkins
Managing Director, The Doha International Institute for
Family Studies and Development, Doha, Qatar

Acknowledgments

The Family in the New Millennium: Protecting the Natural and Fundamental Group Unit of Society presents papers selected from more than 3,000 pages of scholarship collected during the 2004 Doha International Conference for the Family (the "Conference"). The Conference, as well as publication of these volumes, was possible because of the vision and support of Her Highness Sheikha Mozah Bint Nasser Al-Missned, Consort of His Highness the Emir of Qatar, President of the Supreme Council for Family Affairs, and Founder of The Doha International Institute for Family Studies and Development. The Conference was convened by Her Highness with the assistance of Her Excellency Sheikha Hessa Bint Khalifa Bin Hamad Al-Thani, Vice President of the Supreme Council for Family Affairs. An Executive Committee, chaired by His Excellency Abdullah Bin Nasser Al-Khalifa, Secretary General of the Supreme Council for Family Affairs, State of Qatar, whose members included Dr. Abduljalil M. Lahmanate, Special Advisor to the Office of Her Highness the Emir's Consort, coordinated the Conference's various events. His Excellency Nassir Bin Abdulaziz Al-Nasser, Ambassador and Permanent Representative of the State of Qatar to the United Nations, who also served as Chair of the Group of 77 during 2004, together with Mr. Abdulla Al-Sulaiti, First Secretary to the Mission of the State of Qatar to the United Nations, coordinated the UN and intergovernmental aspects of the Conference.

Preparatory events for the Conference were organized by an NGO Working Committee comprising Dr. Richard G. Wilkins, Managing Director of the World Family Policy Center, Brigham Young University, Provo, Utah; Mr. Charles Colchester, Executive Director, CARE, London, England; Dr. William L. Saunders, Senior Fellow in Human Life Studies, The Family Research Council, Washington, D.C.; and Dr. Douglas Sylva and Dr. Lea Sevcik of the Catholic Family and Human Rights Institute ("C-Fam"), New York, New York. Governmental and nongovernmental organizations around the world —including members of the Swedish, Latvian, and New Zealand Parliaments; the Population and Family Development Board of the State of Malaysia; the Permanent Mission of Benin to the United Nations; and family action groups in Africa, Latin America, Southeast Asia, and Europe— provided invaluable assistance to the NGO Working Committee. Mr. and Mrs. Gary (Joy) Lundberg assisted the Committee in organizing (and collecting reports from) more than 200 civil society meetings convened in 34 nations during 2004.

The enormous task of selecting and finalizing the papers contained in these volumes was undertaken and completed by two distinguished editors, Dr. A. Scott Loveless, Acting Managing Director of the World Family Policy Center, J. Reuben Clark School of Law, Brigham Young University, and Dr.

Thomas B. Holman, Professor of Marriage, Family, and Human Development, Brigham Young University. Dr. Loveless and Dr. Holman have spent hundreds of hours ensuring that these volumes include the most significant and up-to-date research relevant to the norms and principles underlying The Doha Declaration.

The editors express their gratitude for the invaluable editorial assistance provided by Dr. Marya Reed, Jake Black, Sacha Bikhazi, Erica Krueger, Rachel Swim, Cheri Loveless, Emily Hardman, Eric Walker, Tracy Schofield, Kimmy Edmon, Emily Parks, Sarah Stewart, and Elena Starovoitova.

Section 1

MARRIAGE

1

Marriage in the Western Legal Tradition: A Product of Natural Law or a Creature of the State?

Charles J. Reid, Jr. (USA)
Associate Professor of Law
University of St. Thomas, Minneapolis, USA

I. Introduction

The propositions that marriage has a transcendent dimension and is the product of natural law; that marriage came into being before the state itself and is the foundation upon which state and society is constructed; and that marriage consists of a series of interlocking rights and duties in which the public has an interest and which the parties are not free contractually to alter have been understood to be at the heart of legal definitions of marriage for most of the last millenium of Western history.

Only in the last four decades has it been decisively asserted by the courts that marriage is a creation of the state. Only in the last four decades has natural law been derided as a source of marital obligation. Only in the last four decades has the judiciary come to label as irrational traditional efforts to distinguish legally between the rights of married partners and the rights of the unmarried in matters of responsibility for children or norms for sexual conduct. The roots of these ideas can be found as far back as the 1870s and 1880s, but they have carried the day only in the last forty years.

A number of decisions of the American Supreme Court in the early and middle 1970s eroded the special status of marriage at law. *Stanley v. Illinois* (1972) spoke of "those family relationships unlegitimated by a marriage ceremony."[1] *Eisenstadt v. Baird* (1972) wrote of "the right of the *individual*, married or single, to be free from unwarranted governmental intrusion into matters so fundamentally affecting a person as the decision whether to bear or beget a child."[2] *Planned Parenthood of Central Missouri v. Danforth* (1976), for its part, denied to fathers any legal interest in the lives of children they have fathered in the context of the mother's decision to abort.[3] Marriage, on this analysis, seems stripped of all its traditional reasons for existence: legally cognizable interests can be created without reference to marriage (*Stanley*).

The right of privacy is made into an individual, not a marital, right (*Eisenstadt*). And no room is made for the father's interest in abortion cases (*Danforth*).

The same-sex marriage decisions can be seen as representing a further stage of this development. Marriage, deprived of its traditional reasons for existence, has come to be understood in the same-sex marriage cases as reducible to a "lowest-common denominator" type of analysis in which state-conferred economic and property benefits are seen as the most important aspect of the marital relationship. Marriage, according to the Hawaii Supreme Court, is nothing more than "a partnership to which both parties bring their financial resources as well as their individual energies and efforts."[4]

The Massachusetts Supreme Judicial Court, in *Goodridge v. Department of Public Health,* took only a slightly more sophisticated view of marriage: "Tangible as well as intangible benefits flow from marriage," the *Goodridge* Court wrote.[5] And what are these benefits? Property rights, inheritance rights, and the numerous rights and benefits of the modern social-welfare state become the new goods of marriage: everything from insurance benefits, to holding property in joint tenancy, to filing joint income tax returns were mentioned.[6] The Court added, with little in the way of serious analysis and no evident sense of irony, that: "[i]t is undoubtedly for these concrete reasons, as well as for its intimate personal significance, that civil marriage has long been termed a 'civil right.'"[7]

The idea that great public goods might be served by marriage, that marital rights exist in correlation with solemn marital duties, and that these benefits and responsibilities have a foundation outside the reach of state power escaped the notice of the *Goodridge* Court. Indeed, when the Court spoke of the married couple's decision to have children, it viewed this choice not as the fulfillment of some public obligation but as the occasion for the conferral of additional state benefits: "Where a married couple has children, their children are also directly or indirectly, but no less auspiciously, the recipients of the special legal and economic protections obtained by civil marriage."[8]

Marriage, the Massachusetts Supreme Judicial Court further taught, was not the parent of society, or the source of civic obligation. It did not exist anterior to the state. It was not the creature of natural law that the state might legitimately regulate but not dominate. Rather, the *Goodridge* Court wrote, "Simply put, the government creates civil marriage."[9] So, on the authority of the Massachusetts Supreme Judicial Court, marriage became one more state-created channel for distributing the largesse of the state.

This way of viewing marriage might be seen as the final product of the philosophical liberalism that has come to prevail as a kind of quasi-official American public philosophy. Agnostic about ultimate purposes, modern liberal thought exalts proceduralist values as its ultimate good. We should all be free, on liberal thought, to pursue our "projects," provided that they do not interfere with the ability of others to pursue their own projects.[10] On this account, the decision to marry, to have children, and to assume family obligations is simply one more among many projects that one might choose to undertake, of no greater or lesser value than a range of other activities. As one commentator crisply put it: "Here is one view: Marriage is an essentially private, intimate, emotional relationship created by two people for their own personal well-being. Marriage is created by the couple, for the couple."[11]

This view, regrettably, has come to prevail in many quarters—both in the legal academy and at the level of popular understanding—at the expense of an understanding of marriage that prevailed literally for most of the last two millenia. My purpose in this chapter is to describe in outline form some of the salient characteristics of that older view of marriage. I focus on two periods that seem at first glance quite remote from one another: the Christian middle ages of the eleventh through fifteenth centuries and the world of nineteenth-century judicial thought.

These periods are not as unrelated as they seem. The canon lawyers of the middle ages gave to marriage its essential legal form. As mediated by the Anglican canon lawyers of the seventeenth and eighteenth centuries, the canonistic forms were brought to American shores and applied by American judges. A great continuity thus binds us to the Christian middle ages and the legal structures of that early period.

In particular, I focus on three elements of that medieval synthesis that survived into the twentieth century: the belief that marriage was the product of natural law; that it has an existence independent from and anterior to the state; and that it confers public rights and duties on the parties of which the parties are not free to divest themselves.

II. The Medieval Synthesis

A. Pope Leo XIII

Pope Leo XIII reigned as pope from 1878 to 1903. He is respected today as a conservative innovator, simultaneously faithful to the Church's medieval tradition and responsive to the new social needs of the late nineteenth-century industrial world, who put the "social question" on the Church's agenda with encyclicals like *Rerum Novarum* (1891). In this famous encyclical, Leo argued both for the legal protection of the rights of labor and for the protection of property rights. In effect, he created the matrix out of which later popes, like John Paul II, have brought forth much rich fruit.

Our concern today, however, is with Leo's contribution to marriage. As with the cause of social justice, so also with marriage, the writings of Leo XIII mark a new departure even while they imbibe the rich tradition of scholastic philosophy and canon law. His great encyclical on marriage, *Arcanum Divinae Sapientiae*—"The Secret of Divine Wisdom"—was published in 1880.[12] Marriage, Leo asserted, was established at the beginning of time by God. It was the "source and origin" (*fons et origo*) of the family and of all human society.[13] Marriage in this sense was not only the product of the natural law, but came before the state. It would have been ludicrous, so Pope Leo claimed, for St. Paul to have taught about marriage in the name of the Roman emperors of his day: Tiberius, Caligula, and Nero.[14] Marriage was divinely instituted, not the creation of the state or its rulers. Among Christians and non-Christians alike, Leo asserted, marriage existed to serve fundamental purposes: Man and wife should come together for the sake of producing and raising the next generation, but they should also join together in order to provide "a better and more blessed life" for one another.[15]

Furthermore, Leo asserted, marriage was a bundle of rights, the *ius matrimonii*.[16] This marital right was intended to establish a fundamental equality between man and woman. Writing of ancient Rome, with his own day also firmly in view, Leo condemned men who took concubines or mistresses, or who failed to respect their wives. They exercised dominion over their households without a corresponding sense of responsibility. They availed themselves of divorce, blithely disregarding the enduring obligations they agreed to undertake. In short, the rights of the wife have been ignored in favor of a disordered freedom on the part of the male. But, with the coming of Jesus Christ, Leo continued, female as much as male enjoyed the right to mutual affection and the right to expect marital duties be fulfilled. Christ, Leo taught, both "asserted and vindicated the dignity of women."[17]

B. The Middle Ages: Peter Lombard and the Canonist Hostiensis

1. Peter Lombard   Although Leo XIII clearly represented a new synthesis, he drew from an old and venerable tradition. One might begin with Peter Lombard, the twelfth-century theologian who is generally considered the starting point of the scholastic tradition. It would be Peter's major work of theology, his "Four Books of Sentences" (*Libri Quattuor Sententiae*) that would form the foundation of theological instruction in the later middle ages.[18] Peter's view of theological doctrine, whether on marriage, or on the other sacraments, or on other issues, would become the starting point of future analysis, even where his views ultimately were refined or ultimately did not prevail.

Marriage, Peter argued, was no mere relationship of convenience, nor was it the creation of the state. It was founded by God, as attested in both the Old and New Testaments. God the Father blessed marriage at the time he created Adam and Eve. This blessing was renewed by Jesus Christ at the marriage feast of Cana. Christ, in fact, spoke of marriage as making the parties "two in one flesh."[19]

Marriage, so understood, served three large purposes, or goods. The first of these purposes, and the most exalted, was its existence as a sacrament. As such, Peter asserted, marriage was "a sacred sign of a sacred thing"—the union of Christ with the Church.[20] It was the task of the parties to represent this union in their lives together.

But this was not the only purpose for which marriage was created. Using Aristotelian terminology, Peter asserted that marriage had a "final cause," an immediate and direct purpose as we might say today. And that purpose was the procreation of children: "For it was because of this that God instituted marriage when He told them, 'Increase and Multiply....'"[21] It was not necessary, Peter stated, that all marriages were fruitful, or that every party to a marriage had the direct intention of having children. Parties might marry out of a desire to avoid the crime of fornication or to cement a political alliance that their parents had arranged or to provide comfort and support in their old age.[22] What mattered in all these cases, however, was that the final cause of marriage—procreation—not be affirmatively frustrated, whatever the parties' subjective motivations might have been.[23]

Marriage had yet another purpose in Peter's estimation: the good of the spouses coupled with the parties' lifelong faithfulness to one another. Borrowing heavily from St. Augustine, as he had throughout his treatment of marriage, Peter noted that marriage served not only as a sacramental sign and as the means by which children were brought into the world but marriage also served the well-being of the married partners themselves. So long as the spouses treated one another with "marital affection," so long as they remained available to tend to one another's needs, they should be accounted as married, Peter asserted. This was so even where they have not had children, provided that they have not had recourse to contraceptives or had abortions to frustrate the good of children.[24]

Both men and women had rights within marriage, Peter asserted. Quoting from St. Augustine, Peter noted that so long as both parties remained alive, they retained "the rights of marriage" (*iura nuptiarum*) that they had when the marriage first commenced.[25] Fundamentally, marital rights were understood as embracing the conjugal debt, namely, the mutual obligation to be open to the sexual requests of the other party. In most respects, Peter acknowledged, the man was understood to be the "head" of the woman. In the matter of the conjugal debt, however, male and female were equal in rights.[26] For support, Peter looked to patristic sources that had in their turn relied on St. Paul's admonition that a wife had no power over her body, but her husband, and that a husband had no power over his body, but his wife.[27] This biblical teaching, scholastic writers generally agreed, constituted an equal and reciprocal right, a power that each party had by which sexual relations might be legitimately claimed.[28]

2. Hostiensis   Peter's *Sentences,* given its exalted status as the obligatory starting point for theological commentary in the later middle ages, established the basic principles that would dominate scholastic thought for the succeeding eight centuries. But this sort of theological speculation did not occur in splendid isolation. It had, as it were, real-world consequences, which were felt through its practical application by the canon lawyers. In the twelfth century, canon law had not yet fully differentiated itself from theology. Important early canonists still thought of themselves as practical theologians, not as lawyers.[29] But when one turns to thirteenth century, one finds a well-established legal profession with its own specialized books, its own conditions and terms of entry, and its own ethical standards by which to judge who might or might not be called a canonist in good standing.[30]

I would like to consider briefly the marriage teaching of a leading thirteenth-century canonist, Henry of Susa, more commonly known as "Hostiensis," the "Cardinal of Ostia." Hostiensis taught briefly at the University of Paris, but spent most of his career in the active service of the Church—he was a diplomatic envoy to England in the mid-thirteenth century, then served as bishop in three different sees, the last being Ostia, the ancient port-city adjacent to Rome. Hostiensis authored two of the most influential canonistic works of the middle ages, a *Summa,* intended as a comprehensive restatement of canonistic principles, and a *Lectura,* or commentary on the legislation of Pope Gregory IX. Born around the year 1200, Hostiensis might have been elected pope at the conclave of 1270, had he not taken ill. He died in 1271.[31]

Hostiensis, of course, agreed with the main lines of Peter's analysis of marriage, as did most of the theological and canonistic writers of the later middle ages. Peter Lombard's work, after all, represented what we, in modern parlance, might call "mainstream" thought. I would like to focus on two aspects of Hostiensis's conception of marriage, his notion of marriage's naturalness and his belief that marriage stood apart from and anterior to the state.

Hostiensis stressed the naturalness of marriage. Looking in part to Scripture, in part to Roman law, Hostiensis defined marriage as "the joining of male and female in a unified way of life that participates in divine and human affairs."[32] He stressed that marriage could happen only between a man and a woman and supported this assertion with two lines of argument. The first argument was drawn from the Bible: God did not, at the beginning, create two men or two women, but a single man and a single woman, who were expected to cooperate in propagating the human race.[33]

And, Hostiensis continued, marriage had to be between a man and a woman for a second reason as well: the sexual relations of the spouses had to reflect and represent the union of Christ and His Church.[34] To understand what this theological doctrine must have meant to someone like Hostiensis, one must appreciate the dualities at stake. Jesus Christ had a dual nature, being both true God and true man. Christ mystically united himself with an institution, the Church, that also had a dual character, with both earthly and heavenly dimensions. Monogamous marriage between one man and one woman, being itself a synthesis of dualities in its union of male and female, thus reflected these larger dualities that were at the heart of Christian belief.

Hostiensis followed this statement of principle with a careful parsing of his definition of the naturalness of marriage: Marriage, he stressed, involved not only physical coupling, but a unity of hearts and minds—a *commixtio corporum* ("a joining of bodies") and also a *coniunctio animorum* ("a union of minds").[35] This fundamental fact about marriage set human marital relations apart from the sort of coupling one sees among animals. Indeed, Hostiensis asserted, one can distinguish between two types of natural law, the natural law common to animals and "brutes," and a "rational" natural law, which governs the affairs of the human person.[36]

Like other medieval writers, Hostiensis also maintained that marriage did not belong to the state. Indeed, Hostiensis was willing to explore this proposition more systematically and more radically than many of his contemporaries. He did so in the context of his commentary on a decretal of Pope Innocent III known as *Per venerabilem*.[37] Today, *Per venerabilem* and the commentaries upon it are known to historians of political thought and constitutional theory for their insights into the legal relations of the pope and the crowned heads of Europe.[38] The implications of this material for ecclesiastical teaching on marriage have been left relatively underexplored.

Per venerabilem involved an appeal by a French nobleman, William of Montpellier, to the court of Innocent III (who reigned in the years 1198–1216). William, whose feudal overlord was the king of France and whose marital history might euphemistically be described as checkered, fathered children by a sexual partner not his wife. He sought to have the pope legitimize his children, not for ecclesiastical preferment, which all conceded the pope might do, but for secular preferment, which was a more politically risky step, since it involved an intrusion on the prerogatives of the king of France. Innocent, who entertained an exalted view of his divine responsibilities as vicar of Christ,[39] handled the matter with expert delicacy. He declined to consider William's petition because it lacked the good faith that might justify extraordinary ecclesiastical intervention on the ground that William's disregard for the sanctity of marriage could not be rewarded. But, Innocent also did not want to miss an opportunity to expand the bounds of papal power. Where the demands of justice and the exceptional circumstances of the case so required, Innocent made clear, the pope might legitimize even for secular purposes.

Early canonistic commentators on this text attempted to limit the reach of Pope Innocent III's teaching by invoking the notion of voluntary jurisdiction. Only where all the parties to be affected by a petition for legitimation agreed in advance to be bound by the pope's decision might this extraordinary power be exercised.[40] Such a reading was modest and nonthreatening to the established order. Royal rights could not be violated on this reading of the text, since the monarch had to agree to be bound by the pope's decision.

Hostiensis, however, chose to return to the theoretical boldness of Innocent III. "With all due regard" (*salva reverentia*), Hostiensis commenced his commentary on the text, his predecessors had missed the essential issue.[41] The power to legitimize, whether for secular or ecclesiastical purposes, belonged to the church alone because marriage itself was so completely a spiritual matter that a secular judge could not claim power over it, even incidentally.[42]

In his *Lectura*, Hostiensis amplified this theme by looking to the natural law for further support. The natural law, Hostiensis asserted, was fundamentally different from the positive law, which can be laid down or removed by the will of the ruler.[43] In the realm of positive law, Hostiensis grimly noted, it is often the case that "will stands for reason," by which he meant that earthly rulers grounded their law on exertions of raw power, not on the reason that belongs to the natural law.[44] Marriage, however, belonged to the rational natural law, over which the Pope, acting as guardian and interpreter, exercised supreme authority. The pope might assume responsibility over temporalities where there has been a failure of justice. By how much more, Hostiensis argued, did the pope therefore have responsibility over a spiritual matter like marriage?[45]

In advancing these claims, Hostiensis gave further intellectual justification to the belief that marriage was not the province of the state. It was a natural phenomenon, an institution brought into being by God at the time of creation and used by human beings for reproduction and companionship and the good of society itself. Emperors, kings, judges, and the state itself could not alter the basic framework of the divine and natural law.

III. The Great Continuity: The Survival of these Conceptions in American Jurisprudence

It is the contention of this chapter that a great continuity binds American jurisprudence to the Christian middle ages. The propositions examined above—that marriage is the product of natural law and confers certain inalienable rights on the parties and that it exists anterior to the state—continued to exercise a powerful hold on the imagination of the American legal community until well into the twentieth century. We now consider American legal treatment of these propositions.

A. Marriage as the Product of Natural Law

Early American jurists routinely wrote of marriage as the product of the natural law. One can take Chancellor James Kent as an example of this disposition. Kent (1769–1847), who as Chancellor of New York and later as professor of law at Columbia University authored one of the most influential commentaries on American law, was born into a family deeply conversant with Protestant Christianity. His grandfather, Elisha, was a Presbyterian minister who took an active role in the Great Awakening of the middle eighteenth century.[46] His grandmother was the daughter of a leading Connecticut pastor.[47] A recent French biography of Kent notes that the future Chancellor's father broke with family tradition when he did not pursue a career in the ministry, opting instead for law.[48]

Kent was, not surprisingly, quite traditional and orthodox in his views on marriage and its relationship to natural law. Marriage, he wrote, "has its foundation in nature, and is the only lawful relation by which Providence has permitted the continuance of the human race."[49] "The basis of the marriage contract," Kent added, was "consent."[50] And this requirement in turn was also the product of the *ius gentium,* the law of nations, which Kent treated as coterminous with the natural law.[51] The sources Kent furnished for this last observation were Hugo Grotius, the seventeenth-century Dutch jurist, and

Henry Bracton, the foremost of the thirteenth-century English legal writers.[52] Clearly, Chancellor Kent viewed himself as working within a tradition that stretched centuries back in time. He was one with Peter Lombard and Hostiensis in viewing marriage as grounded on a divine plan and reflecting natural justice.

Nor was Kent's a lonely voice. Joseph Story (1779–1845), Supreme Court Justice, Harvard Law School professor, and the great organizer and systematizer of early American law, wrote, regarding the origin of the marriage contract:

> Marriage is treated by all civilized nations as a peculiar and favored contract. It is in its origin a contract of natural law....In civil society it becomes a civil contract, regulated and prescribed by law, and endowed with civil consequences.[53]

For his part, John Bouvier, in his *Institutes of American Law,* published in 1851, wrote that "[m]arriage owes its institution to the law of nature, and its perfection to the municipal or civil law."[54] In describing marriage in these terms, Bouvier echoed an essentially scholastic understanding of the relationship between the natural law and the positive law of the state. Natural law, on the scholastic account, had to be mediated and made particular through the positive law of the state.[55] This was Bouvier's point in describing the civil law as "perfecting" the natural law. It was through the civil law that the natural institution of marriage was adapted to particular needs and given specific application.

Commentators as late as the 1920s continued to ground claims about marriage on natural law. In 1921, in the sixth edition of his commentary on marriage law, James Schouler could still write:

> Man, in a state of nature and alone, was subject to no civil restrictions. He was independent of all laws, except those of God. But when man united with woman, both were brought under certain restraints for their mutual well-being. The propagation of offspring afforded the only means whereby society could hope to grow into a permanent and compact system. Hence the sexual cravings of nature were speedily brought under wholesome regulations; as otherwise the human race must have perished in the cradle. Natural law, or the teachings of a Divine Providence, supplied these regulations.[56]

As recently as 1959, the New York Surrogate's Court invoked the idea of natural law to determine the validity of a proxy marriage entered into by a couple in Italy.[57] The context was a contest over a deceased husband's estate. The Surrogate's Court, charged with probate responsibilities in New York, observed that the state's highest judicial authority, the Court of Appeals, permitted the judiciary to invalidate marriages contracted outside the jurisdiction found to violate the natural law.[58] The Court reviewed the history of proxy marriages: such marriages had been authorized by medieval canon law and were permitted in England until the eighteenth century.[59] The Surrogate's Court thus concluded that the proxy marriage in question could not be held invalid as a matter of natural law and allowed the distribution of the deceased husband's estate to go forward.[60]

B. Marriage as Independent of and Prior to the State

Like their medieval ancestors, many jurists during the first 150 years of the American Republic tended to agree that marriage existed prior to the state and that the state was dependent upon marriage to a greater or lesser extent. This argument, in the American context, differed in at least one fundamental respect from the medieval claims of a writer like Hostiensis, or even from the claims of eighteenth-century English canonists: Because of the existence of ecclesiastical courts—alike in thirteenth-century Europe and eighteenth-century England—and because of the monopoly of jurisdiction these courts enjoyed over matrimonial matters, the independence of marriage from the state was a real and lived reality. There were, on the other hand, no ecclesiastical courts in the United States from the founding of the new nation. This fact set nineteenth-century America apart not only from the medieval experience, but from contemporary England, where ecclesiastical courts continued to exercise coercive jurisdiction over marriage well into the nineteenth century. Hence American jurists were required to confront a paradox that was unknown to their sources: jurists and judges at one and the same time proclaimed the independence and priority of marriage from state control and nevertheless exercised judicial power over all of its attributes.

Despite the absence of ecclesiastical courts, American jurists tended to look to English parallels as a principal source for their theoretical understanding of the marital relationship. And English writers were emphatic in stressing that marriage remained an institution fundamentally apart in some ways from state control. Leonard Shelford, for instance, wrote of "[t]he liberty of marriage [as] a natural right inherent in mankind, confirmed and enforced by the Holy Scriptures."[61] Marriage, in Shelford's mind, was a "divine institution."[62] It belonged to the state to regulate this institution, but not to dominate it. Shelford carefully explained what was entailed by this human legislative responsibility for a sacred relationship:

> [H]uman legislatures have very properly assumed the power of regulating the exercise of the right of marriage, on account of its leading to relations, duties, and consequences materially affecting the welfare and peace of society. It has been the policy of legislators, proceeding on the ground that marriage is the origin of all relations, and consequently the first element of all social duties, to preserve the sacred nature of this contract.[63]

This sort of argument came to be replicated on American shores. Joseph Story asserted that marriage came not only before the state but before organized society:

> [Marriage] may exist between two individuals of different sexes, although no third person existed in the world, as happened in the case of the common ancestors of mankind. It is the parent and not the child of society; *principium*

urbis et quasi seminarium reipublicae ["the cornerstone of the city and, as it were, the school of the republic"].[64]

Elsewhere, Story added: "The contract of marriage is the most important of all human transactions. It is the very basis of the whole fabric of civilized society."[65] Because of this transcendent origin, because of its fundamental importance, the law of "civilized nations" is generally unanimous in the way the marital relationship ought to be structured.[66] Story singled out in particular two elements—the indissolubility of the marital contract, at least at the motion of the parties, and the requirement that marriage be formed by the consent of the parties—as components of marriage adhered to by every nation and so part of the natural structure of marriage.[67] One sees at work in Story's treatment of the relationship of marriage and the state a delicate interplay: marriage came into being before society itself and educated society on the requirements of successful self-governance. In turn, the state was charged with regulating marriage, but was obliged nevertheless to retain its basic framework.[68]

Chancellor Kent made similar points. Marriage, according to Kent,

> is one of the chief foundations of social order. We may justly place to the credit of the institution of marriage, a great share of the blessings which flow from the refinement of manners, the education of children, the sense of justice, and the cultivation of the liberal arts.[69]

American case law from the nineteenth and twentieth centuries consistently agreed with this philosophical premise. A federal court in Illinois wrote in 1890: "The relation of marriage is a sacred and important relation. It is the foundation of family life and social happiness, and the family is, in an important sense, the foundation of the state in free and enlightened countries."[70] An Ohio court wrote in 1906: "The family is the foundation of the state. Marriage is the basis upon which the family rests."[71] The Illinois Supreme Court wrote in 1930: "[the marital] relation is the foundation stone of modern society in civilized countries, and we think sound public policy dictates that the relation should not be allowed to be interfered with."[72] This language was repeated by an Illinois appeals court as recently as 1974.[73] A West Virginia federal court wrote in 1918: "The marriage contract is *sui generis*. It is the very foundation of society."[74] Echoing Joseph Story, the Maryland Court of Appeals declared that "[m]arriage...the most important contract into which individuals can enter, [is] the parent, not the child, of civil society. The great basis of human society throughout the civilized world, is found on marriages and legitimate offspring."[75] The Oklahoma Supreme Court described "the marriage relation as the foundation of the home and the state."[76] In these, and in many other such opinions, the primacy of the marital relation and its anteriority to the state was recognized.

C. Marital Rights

It was the common opinion among jurists and judges that parties to a marriage were possessed of certain rights but that these were rights of a public, not a private character. Joseph Story thus made clear that while marriage was a contract that arose from the consent of the parties, marriage "differ[ed] from other contracts in this, that the rights, obligations, or duties arising from it, are not left entirely to be regulated by the agreement of the parties, but are, to a certain extent, matters of municipal regulation, over which the parties have no control, by any declaration of their will."[77]

A treatise written on marital rights in Texas law but influential outside that state, published in 1916, set forth a comprehensive listing of marital rights.[78] The treatise, by Ocie Speer, began by grounding marital rights on the Bible. "Through the pages of profane and Bible history, we find that mankind has always existed in families. It is God's chosen plan for the promotion of the well-being, peace, and comfort of man, and the protection and happiness of woman."[79] In florid language that makes painful reading even when considered solely as an historical artifact, Speer described the man as the natural head and woman as the natural "helpmeet" in marriage.[80]

Despite his ringing endorsement of a male-dominated view of marriage, Speer simultaneously denounced the doctrine of female coverture.[81] Coverture, the legal doctrine that held that a wife's legal personality was essentially merged with her husband's to form a single juridic entity was, Speer asserted, a product of the common law and at variance with the historical experience of Texas.[82] Texas law had been influenced by Spanish law, which had always acknowledged the separate legal personality of the wife and her capacity to own property in her own name, and it is Spanish law, Speer insisted, that should be followed.[83]

Speer commented at length on the affective dimension of marital rights and obligations. In an attempt to define the entire range of marital rights and the correlation of marital rights with duties, he wrote:

> Upon marriage each party to the pact necessarily recognizes and assumes the obligation towards the other, of those duties, services, aids, and the like usual to married persons. This includes the personal services, the care, attention, and affections of the parties, the nurture, care, and support of their children, and, in short, all those things usually enjoyed by married persons. The husband's or the wife's interest in the society of the other is most frequently expressed by the word "consortium," which signifies generally the right to the conjugal fellowship, company, co-operation, aid, and affection in every conjugal relation. The term is very broad, and includes infinitely more than mere physical labor or services of the partners in and about the domestic affairs.[84]

This expansive understanding of conjugal rights can be found replicated in the case law. Clearly, sexual relations were considered an important aspect of conjugal rights, not only in medieval law but also in nineteenth- and twentieth-century case law. Thus in a case decided in 1921, the California Court of Appeals referred to a spouse's "refusal of marital rights" as the equivalent of a refusal to engage in sexual relations.[85] And the Missouri Court of Appeals, in an action of divorce on the basis of the wife's refusal to have sexual relations, wrote: "Marriage is the union of opposite sexes and sexual intercourse is the distinguishing feature of the union."[86] The Kentucky Supreme Court added: "The text-books establish the doctrine that, 'without sexual intercourse, the ends of marriage, the pro-creation of children and the pleasures and enjoyments of matrimony, cannot be attained.'"[87]

But the term "marital rights" or its synonym "conjugal rights" involved more than claims to sexual privileges.[88] The Iowa Supreme Court asserted as recently as 1969:

> The conjugal rights of married persons include the enjoyment of association, sympathy, confidence, domestic happiness, the comforts of dwelling together in the same habitation, eating meals at the same table and profiting by the joint property rights as well as the intimacies of domestic relations.[89]

And this expanded notion of marital rights was also seen to be grounded on naturalist premises. Thus the District of Columbia Circuit Court of Appeals of Appeals, in an opinion authored by Bennett Champ Clark, a former United States Senator from Missouri appointed to the federal bench by Harry Truman, declared that rights of consortium, broadly understood, belonged equally to male and female, both by "natural right" and by "legal right arising out of the marriage relation."[90]

IV. Conclusion

The purpose of this chapter has been to trace three great continuities in the western law of marriage. Historically, marriage has been considered the creation of natural law. It was understood as existing prior to the state. Indeed, state and society alike were seen as the products of marriage. And marriage conferred rights and privileges, as well as obligations, on the parties, which the parties were not free to discard.

This model of marriage was already being criticized at the end of the nineteenth century. A new individualism was making itself felt at the jurisprudential level, and this individualism in turn influenced conceptions of marriage. A Kansas case from 1887 illustrated the sort of challenge that the future would bring. Two parties entered into a union that they described as "autonomistic" marriage, by which they meant a marriage freed of the classic rights and obligations of marriage. The parties proclaimed themselves free to set their own terms and conditions of married life, without interference from state and society. They understood themselves free to come and go as they pleased and treated marriage as purely a matter of private ordering.[91] The parties were convicted for violating the state's Marriage Act, a conviction that the Kansas Supreme Court upheld.

What has occurred in the eighty years between the 1880s and the 1960s, has been the triumph of this individualistic conception of marriage. Parties are now free to set the terms of their unions. Marriage has been transformed from the most exalted of all contracts to an agreement terminable at the will of one of the parties—that is, marriage has now become something less than any other contract. It is this triumph of the will of the individual that has become enshrined in Supreme Court decisions like *Stanley, Eisenstadt,* and *Danforth.*

Presented at the Asia/Pacific Dialogue
Kuala Lumpur, Malaysia, October 2004.

Endnotes

1. *Stanley v. Illinois,* 405 U.S. 645, 651 (1972).

2. *Eisenstadt v. Baird,* 404 U.S. 438, 453 (1972) (emphasis in original).

3. *Planned Parenthood of Central Missouri v. Danforth,* 428 U.S. 52 (1976).

4. *Baehr v. Lewin,* 852 P. 2d 44, 58 [quoting *Gussin v. Gussin,* 73 Haw. 470, 483, 836 P. 2d 484, 491 (1992)].

5. *Goodridge v. Department of Public Health,* 440 Mass. 309, 322, 798 N.E. 2d 941, 955 (2003).

6. *Id.,* 440 Mass. 323–325; 798 N.E. 2d at 957.

7. *Id.,* 440 Mass. at 325; 798 N.E. at 957.

8. *Id.,* 440 Mass. at 325; 798 N.E. at 956.

9. *Id.,* 440 Mass. at 321; 798 N.E. 2d at 954.

10. One liberal writer has explained the relationship of marriage and liberal theory in the following terms:

> Liberalism dictates official neutrality among the projects to which individuals might come to commit themselves, but a polity can be liberal and yet recognize that patterns of attachment widespread within the community can create a legitimate demand for the creation of social structures within which these attachments can achieve fitting expression. For many individuals, the attachments that are most forceful and ripe with meaning are not to abstract ideas or to artifacts of one's own creation or to large-scale social and political movements but to particular persons. Loren E. Lomasky, *Persons, Rights, and the Moral Community* (New York: Oxford University Press, 1987), 167.

11. Maggie Gallagher, "What Is Marriage For? The Public Purposes of Marriage Law," *Louisiana Law Review* 62 (2002), 773, 775. It must be noted that Gallagher is criticizing, not endorsing, the view expressed.

12. Leo XIII, *Arcanum Divinae Sapientiae,* reprinted in *De Matrimonio Christiano* (Rome: Pontificia Universitas Gregoriana, 1942), 15.

13. *Id.,* II.10.21, 16.

14. *Id.,* II.11.23, 18.

15. *Id.,* II.14, 27, 21 ("meliorem vitam coniugem beatioremque efficiant").

16. *Id.,* I.5.13, 11–12.

17. *Id.,* I.9.19, 15 ("adserta et vindicata mulierum dignitas").

18. For a helpful review of the gradual acceptance of Peter's text as foundational to medieval theological instruction, see Nancy Spatz, "Approaches and Attitudes to a New Theology Textbook: The *Sentences of Peter Lombard,*" in *The Intellectual Climate of the Early University: Essays in Honor of Otto Gründler,* ed. Nancy van Deusen (Kalamazoo, MI: Western Michigan University, 1997), 27–52.

19. Peter Lombard, *Sententiae In IV Libris Distinctae* (Rome: College of St. Bonaventure, 1981), Bk. IV, dist. 26, cc. 5 and 6, vol. II, pp. 419–420.

20. *Id.*, Bk. IV, dist. 26, c. 6, vol. II, p. 419.

21. *Id.*, Bk. IV, dist. 30, c. 3, vol. 441.

22. *Id.*

23. *Id.* Cf. Bk. IV, dist. 31, c. 3 (condemning those who procure the "poisons of sterility" and c. 4, on judging those who commit abortions to be "homicides"). See vol. II, pp. 445–446.

24. *Id.*, Bk. IV, dist. 31, c. 2, p. 445.

25. *Id.*, Bk. IV, dist. 81, c. 2, vol. II, p. 443. (Quoting St. Augustine's *De nuptiis et concupiscentia*, 1.10.11, *CSEL* vol. 42, p. 223.)

26. *Id.*, Bk. IV, dist. 82, c. 1, p. 451.

27. *Id.*, Bk. IV, dist. 82, c. 1, vol. 2, p. 452 (looking to St. Augustine and the work of the Ambrosiaster, which Peter took to be the genuine writing of St. Ambrose). On the Ambrosiaster, see generally Alexander Souter, *A Study of Ambrosiaster* (Nendeln: Kraus Reprints, 1967) (reprint of 1905 volume). Cf. 1 Corinthians 7:4 (citing the relevant text by St. Paul).

28. See Charles J. Reid, Jr., *Power Over the Body, Equality in the Family: Rights and Domestic Relations in Medieval Canon Law* (Ann Arbor: Eerdmans, 2004), 103–116 (exploring the transformation of St. Paul's exhortation into a rights-based moral and legal category).

29. See John van Engen, "From Practical Theology to Divine Law: The Work and Mind of Medieval Canonists," *Proceedings of the Ninth International Congress of Medieval Canon Law* (Vatican City: Biblioteca Apostolica Vaticana, 1997), 873–874.

30. On the rise of canon law as a distinct profession, see generally James A. Brundage, *The Profession and Practice of Medieval Canon Law* (Aldershot, NH: Ashgate, 2004).

31. For biographical detail, see James A. Brundage, *Medieval Canon Law* (London: Longman, 1995), 214, and the sources cited therein.

32. Hostiensis, *Summa* (Lyon, 1537) (reprinted, Aalen: Scientia Verlag, 1962), Bk. IV, *De matrimoniis*, sec. 2. Hostiensis's definition of the naturalness of marriage is an adaption of Justinian's *Institutes*, Bk. I.9 (on paternal power).

33. *Id.*

34. *Id.*

35. *Id.*

36. *Id.*

37. The decretal is found at X.4.17.13.

38. Two important studies of the political implications of this letter and the commentaries upon it are the following: Brian Tierney, "*Tria quippe distinguit iudicia:* A Note on Innocent III's *Per venerabilem*," *Speculum* 37 (1962): 48–59; and Kenneth Pennington, "Pope Innocent III's Views on Church and State: A Gloss to *Per venerabilem*," in *Law, Church, and Society: Essays in Honor of Stephan Kuttner*, ed. Kenneth Pennington and Robert C. Somerville (Philadelphia: University of Pennsylvania Press, 1977), 49–67.

39. A recent study notes that Innocent III, to a degree remarkable even by medieval standards, considered his pontificate a providential event. See Brenda

Bolton, "Signposts from the Past: Reflections on Innocent III's Providential Path," in *Innocenzo III: Urbs et Orbis*, ed. Andrea Sommerlichner (Rome: Dell'istituto Palazzo Borromini, 2003), vol. I, pp. 21–55.

40. Pennington, "Pope Innocent III's Views on Church and State," 55, 65, and note 41.

41. Hostiensis, *Summa*, Bk. IV, *Qui filii sint legitimi*, sec. 11.

42. *Id.* ("cum enim causa matrimonialis spiritualiter pertineat ad ecclesiam adeo, quod secularis iudex de ipsa cognoscere non potest etiam si inciderit").

43. Hostiensis, *Lectura* (Turin: Bottega d'Erasmo, 1965), X. 4.17.13, v. *testamento*.

44. *Id.* On the history of the phrase *pro ratione voluntas* ("will standing for reason"), see Kenneth Pennington, *Pope and Bishops: The Papal Monarchy in the Twelfth and Thirteenth Centuries* (Philadelphia: University of Pennsylvania Press, 1984), 17–20, 34–38, and the older sources cited therein.

45. Hostiensis, *Lectura*, X. 4.17.13, v. *causis*.

46. John Theodore Horton, *James Kent: A Study in Conservatism, 1763–1847* (New York: Da Capo Press, 1969) (reprint of 1939 volume), pp. 7–8.

47. *Id.*, 7.

48. Jacques de Cazotte, *De révolution réussie: le Juge James Kent, 1763–1847: A l'aube de la nation américaine* (Paris: Maionneuve et Larose, 1995), 23.

49. James Kent, *Commentaries on American Law* (New York: E.B. Clayton, 1836), vol. II, p. 73.

50. *Id.*, 76.

51. *Id.*, 86.

52. *Id.*

53. Joseph Story, *Commentaries on the Conflict of Laws* (Boston: Hilliard, Gray, and Company, 1834), 100.

54. John Bouvier, *Institutes of American Law* (Philadelphia: Robert E. Peterson, 1851), vol. I, p. 101.

55. It has been said about Thomas Aquinas's theory of the relationship of natural and positive law: "Laws and rights are necessary to particularize the natural law, to apply it, and to determine the manifold relations between private individuals (positive private law) and the relations between the state and its members (positive public law)." Hans Meyer, *The Philosophy of Thomas Aquinas* (St. Louis, MO: B. Herder Book Company, 1944), 500–501.

56. James Shouler, *A Treatise on the Law of Marriage, Divorce, Separation, and Domestic Relations*, 6th ed. (Albany, NY: Matthew Bender and Company, 1921), vol. I, pp. 3–4.

57. *In the Matter of the Probate of the Will of Donato Valente*, 18 Misc. 2d 701, 188 N.Y.S. 2d 732 (Surr. Ct., 1959).

58. *Id.*, 18 Misc. 2d at 704, 108 N.Y.s. 2d at 735. Cf. *In re Estate of May*, 305 N.Y. 486, 114 N.E. 2d 4 (1953).

59. *Will of Valente*, 18 Misc. 2d at 704, 188 N.Y.s. 2d at 736.

60. *Id.*, 18 Misc. 2d at 705, 188 N.Y.S. 2d at 737.

61. Leonard Shelford, *A Practical Treatise on the Law of Marriage and Divorce* (London: S. Sweet, 1841), 4.

62. *Id.*

63. *Id.*

64. Story, *The Conflict of Laws,* 100. The phrase *principium urbis et quasi seminarium reipublicae* is traceable to Cicero's *De Officiis,* sec. I.17.

65. *Id.,* 101.

66. *Id.,* 101–102.

67. *Id.*

68. This reading of Story is in keeping with other elements of his jurisprudence. Generally speaking, one can state that Story strongly rejected the positivist understanding of the state as a theoretically all-powerful force. Story's notion of the state as naturally limited in competence is on display in his treatment of the First Amendment as creating a zone of freedom in which state power was incompetent to intrude. See Charles J. Reid, Jr., "The Religious Conscience and the State in U.S. Constitutional Law, 1789–2001," in *Religion Returns to the Public Square,* ed. Hugh Heclo and Wilfred M. McClay (Baltimore: Johns Hopkins University Press, 2003), 63, 68.

69. Kent, *Commentaries,* vol. II, p. 74.

70. *Waldron v. Waldron,* 45 F. 315, 317 (Cir. Ct., N.D. Ill., 1890).

71. *Bates v. State,* 9 Ohio C.C. 273, 281 (1906).

72. *Tripp v. Payne,* 339 Ill. 178, 182, 171 N.E. 131, 133 (Ill., 1930).

73. *In re Estate of Gerbing,* 22 Ill. App. 3d 454, 462, 318 N.E. 2d 117, 124 (Ct. App., Ill., 1974).

74. *Hastings v. Douglass,* 249 F. 378, 381 (N.D. W. Va., 1918).

75. *Le Brun v. Le Brun,* 55 Md. 496, 503 (1881). The Maryland Court here was closely tracking the language of the United States Supreme Court, in *Gaines v. Relf,* 53 U.S. (12 How.) 472, 534 (1852).

76. *Wooden v. Wooden,* 113 Okla. 81, 83, 239 P. 231, 233 (1925).

77. Story, *The Conflict of Laws,* 101.

78. Ocie Speer, *A Treatise on the Law of Marital Rights in Texas* (Rochester, NY: Lawyers' Co-operative Publishing Company, 1916).

79. *Id.,* 85.

80. *Id.* "Man, physically strong, courageous, bold, capable of planning, providing, protecting; woman, delicate, affectionate, confiding, dependent; the one a born ruler, the other a helpmeet; the former the natural head of the family, whose right is to govern and whose duty is to provide; the latter a dependent whose right is maintenance and protection, and whose duty is obedience and helpfulness."

81. Coverture, Speer insisted, was a "foolish fiction" and "little less than slavery." *Id.,* 90. It must be noted, *pace* Speer, that Texas developed a system of *femme covert* closely modeled on the common law.

82. *Id.,* 90–91.

83. *Id.* Speer again, it must be noted, was arguing against Texas precedent at this point.

84. *Id.,* 121.

85. *Lemberger v. Lemberger,* 55 Cal. App. 231, 234, 203 P. 2d 786, 787 (Ct. App., 1921).

86. *Williams v. Williams,* 121 Mo. App. 349, 355 (1907) (quoting an authority identified only as "Nelson," probably William Nelson's treatise on Divorce and Separation, first published in 1895).

87. *Shackleford v. Hamilton,* 93 Ky. 80, 87 (1892).

88. Thus a Delaware court wrote, "Marital intercourse is only one marital right or duty. There are many other important rights and duties." *A. v. A.,* 43 A. 2d 251, 252 (Super. Ct., Del., 1945).

89. *Lovett v. Lovett,* 164 N.W. 2d 793, 802 (1969).

90. *Hitaffer v. Argonne Company,* 183 F. 2d 811, 816 (D.C. Cir., 1950). Judge Clark was here quoting from an early New York decision, *Bennett v. Bennett,* 116 N.Y. 584, 590 (1889).

91. *State v. Walker,* 36 Kan. 297, 13 P. 279 (1887). This case is discussed in Hal D. Sears, *The Sex Radicals: Free Love in High Victorian America* (Lawrence, KS: The Regents' Press of Kansas, 1977), 80–96.

2

Supporting the Institution of Marriage: Ideological, Research, and Ecological Perspectives[1]

William J. Doherty (USA)
Professor and Director, Marriage and Family Therapy
University of Minnesota, USA

Jason S. Carroll (USA)
Assistant Professor of Marriage, Family, and Human Development
Brigham Young University, Provo, USA

Linda J. Waite (USA)
Professor of Sociology and of the Social Sciences
Alfred P. Sloan Center on Parents, Children and Work
University of Chicago, Chicago, USA

Introduction

Marriage in the contemporary world is a social institution and a legal contract between two individuals to form a sexual, productive, and reproductive union. This union is recognized by family, society, religious institutions, and the legal system. Marriage defines the relationship of the two individuals to each other, to any children they might have, to their extended families, to shared property and assets, and to society generally. It recognizes the paternity of the father and defines his responsibilities to the mother and child. It also defines the relationship of others, including social institutions, toward the married couple.

In recent decades, this idea of marriage as a social institution and central legal contract has been challenged by the view that marriage should be seen as a personal lifestyle entered and exited freely. From this perspective, parenthood should not necessarily be linked to marriage, and marriage should not be privileged or promoted over other adult intimate arrangements (Doherty & Carroll, 2002a). In addition to libertarian ideological grounds, this view of marriage has been based on two empirical assumptions that we challenge in this chapter. First is the idea that marriage does not contribute to the well-being of married people—women in particular. Second is the idea that the collective well-being of children can be disentangled from marriage.

It is striking how in recent decades family professionals[2] from a variety of disciplines (e.g., therapy, education, public policy, law, medicine, ministry, etc.) have accepted these assumptions and therefore have grown cautious, even skeptical, about marriage as a social institution. Partly this stems from the uncovering, in the 1970s and 1980s, of the dark underbelly of marriage through the feminist analysis of gender-based power differentials and abuse. Partly this comes from the appreciation of the strengths and resilience of many family forms, including single-parent families, that are not based on marriage. And recently some have decried the fact that legal marriage has excluded gay and lesbian couples. The result is that many professionals and policy makers emphasize the "shadow side" of marriage and are suspicious of the burgeoning marriage movement in the United States.

In this chapter we offer a brief overview of the marriage movement and present a model for understanding different ideological views on marriage. We suggest a way for family professionals and policy makers to be constructively but critically "pro-marriage." We then review the empirical research on the benefits of marriage for spouses and their children. We conclude with an ecological model of marital health that articulates how good marriages benefit individuals, families, communities, and society, and with a call for family professionals to become players in the contemporary marriage movement and not skeptical bystanders.

The Marriage Movement

The marriage movement is a widespread cultural trend, at multiple levels and with various constituencies, to revive the institution of marriage and promote healthy marriages. Think tanks are devoting their energies to marriage (notably David Blankenhorn's Institute for American Values, David Popenoe's and Barbara Dafoe Whitehead's National Marriage Project, and Theodora Oom's Marriage Project within the Center for Law and Social Policy). State legislatures and governors are getting involved in initiatives to support premarital education, covenant marriage, and relationship education in high schools. States such as Oklahoma are using TANF (Temporary Assistance to Needy Families) funds for marriage education at the community level. Community initiatives such as First Things First in Chattanooga, Tennessee, and Healthy Marriages Grand Rapids (Michigan) are mobilizing local communities in support of healthy marriages. The federal government is funding healthy community marriage initiatives with a special focus on low-income couples. Religious bodies in the United States have declared their support for reviving marriage and preventing divorce. There are stirrings of a movement in the African American community to restore marriage to a position it held in the past. Even the current debate about gay marriage can be seen as an indicator of strong contemporary interest in marriage as a social institution that is so important that a new group wants entry. Another symbol of changing cultural times was the wedding of feminist Gloria Steinem in 2000. At a presentation to family therapists in 2001, she said she was bringing the news that getting married can be a radical countercultural act and that she used to see marriage as "limiting," but now she sees having someone in your corner for life as "limitless."

Some family professionals are skeptical about the marriage movement out of concern that it represents a right-wing religious backlash against the gains of women in the workforce and against egalitarian marriages. Indeed, there are religiously conservative leaders in the marriage movement and some proponents of traditional gender roles. However, the marriage movement also has many leaders who consider themselves politically progressive and profeminist. To try to bring some clarity to the ideological issues in the marriage movement and among its critics, Doherty and Carroll (2002a) developed a typology (which we adapt here) of ideological stances towards marriage: the noncritical pro-marriage stance; the neutral/skeptical stance; and the critical pro-marriage stance (see Table 2.1).

A Typology of Ideological Perspectives on Marriage

In struggling to understand and address the splits and controversies in the professions about marriage, we have developed a typology of ideological stances. The stances shown in Table 2.1 represent ideal types rather than fully developed models, and in practice individuals and groups might hold to aspects of more than one type. The three types represent a dialectic process, with the third offering a synthesis of the first two opposing approaches to marriage. The noncritical pro-marriage perspective has characterized much of Western thinking about marriage until the last third of the twentieth century. The neutral/skeptical perspective then emerged as an antithetical perspective focusing on individual autonomy and the dangers of traditional marriage. We believe it continues to hold sway in the social sciences and among many family professionals and policy makers. The critical pro-marriage perspective is a recent effort to retain the pro-marriage, pro-commitment, and communal dimensions of the noncritical pro-marriage position but with sensitivities to the critiques of the neutral/skeptical proponents.

In this section we briefly review the core philosophies of these ideological perspectives and present a comparative analysis of how they differ on several crucial issues that are debated in the current cultural and professional dialogue on marriage. We give particular attention to articulating the critical pro-marriage stance that has emerged within the current marriage movement and in the writings of Don Browning and his colleagues (2003; see also Browning, Miller-McLemore, Couture, Lyon, & Franklin, 1997). One payoff from this typology is a way to address the fears of neutral/skeptical advocates that any pro-marriage stance is tantamount to a return to a patriarchal,

Table 2.1 Contemporary Ideologies about Marriage

	Noncritical Pro-Marriage	Neutral/Skeptical	Critical Pro-Marriage
Core philosophy	Authoritarian	Libertarian	Communitarian
Value of marital commitment and stability	Absolute value, few exceptions	An individual choice, based on personal values	An ideal to be promoted, but not feasible in every case
Decision to divorce	Divorce stigmatized, except for adultery, abuse, or abandonment	Divorce equally valued with staying married, based on personal choice	Divorce tragic, to be prevented if possible, but sometimes unavoidable
Two-parent versus one-parent families	Two-parent families always preferable	No privileging of two-parent families over one-parent	Two-parent ideal, but one-parent families preferable to high-conflict two-parent families
Cohabitation	Condemned	Equally valued with marriage as lifestyle option	Valued less than marriage, viewed with caution
Same-sex marriage	Strongly opposed	Strongly in favor	Divided—some supportive, some opposed
Marriage education	Viewed cautiously; commitment should be enough	Viewed cautiously; concerned about traditional gender roles, divorce prevention	Strongly encouraged to promote both satisfaction and stability
Feminism	Not embraced	Embraced enthusiastically; concern about male power and women's well-being; skepticism about marriage	Gender equality embraced, but not feminism's emphasis on male power and skepticism about marriage
Religion versus social science	Religion strongly preferred; social science viewed warily	Religion viewed warily, social science embraced with feminist and multicultural slant	Religion and social science both valued, but critically

Sacrifice versus personal satisfaction	Sacrifice emphasized more strongly	Personal satisfaction emphasized; sacrifice seen as dangerous	Satisfaction and sacrifice both valued and mutually intertwined
Public versus private emphasis	Public face of marriage emphasized	Private face of marriage emphasized	Private and public emphasized

prefeminist view of marriage. Instead, we see the critical pro-marriage perspective as embracing the best of both of the previous models.

The Noncritical Pro-marriage Stance

The dominant view of marriage until the last third of the twentieth century, still held among some conservative religious groups, is the noncritical pro-marriage perspective. In this view, marriage is a permanent bond between man and woman and a centrally important institution for the well-being of adults, children, and society. Depending on the theological tradition, marriage is viewed as a natural institution governed by natural law as well as a divinely ordained institution governed by religious doctrines (Witte, 2002).

We label this stance "noncritical" for three reasons: (a) the virtues of marriage are largely assumed and celebrated via an understanding of the natural order and the divine order; (b) problematic features of marriage such as patriarchal authority patterns and physical, sexual, and emotional abuse are not examined or are deemphasized; and (c) the tension between individual well-being and marital stability is not dealt with in a systematic fashion. This is not to say that religious beliefs that view marriage as a natural or divinely ordained institution are inherently noncritical in their orientation, but historically these beliefs have been filtered through cultural norms and practices that support a hierarchy of male privilege in the familial and social realms. For this reason, until recently even sophisticated theological and philosophical discussions of marriage have lacked a critical discussion of marriage.

The noncritical pro-marriage perspective is not confined to religious world views. The structural functionalist school of family sociology, dominant in the mid-twentieth century, can be characterized as having a noncritical stance toward marriage because it largely assumes the functional "goods" of marriage and of contemporary marital roles, it accepts traditional gender roles as part of the natural order of social relations, and it ignores the dark side of marriage that could create tensions between individual health and marital stability (Kingsbury & Scanzoni, 1993; Parson, 1965).

It is important to stress that scholars who have taken a noncritical pro-marriage position are not necessarily simplistic thinkers. Thomas Aquinas and Talcott Parsons can hardly be accused of lacking analytical skill. But their views of marriage can still be labeled "noncritical" for the reasons listed above. Indeed, it was what many saw as the critical blind spots of conservative theological and structural-functional views of marriage that fueled the backlash of the neutral/skeptical perspective.

The Neutral/Skeptical Stance

The social movements of the late 1960s, 1970s, and 1980s ushered in feminism, multiculturalism, and postmodernism, all of which offered profound criticisms of conventional ways to think about marriage, family life, and social relations in general. Feminism in particular shone a bright light on the dark underbelly of marriage: the prevalence of physical and sexual abuse, the gap between egalitarian norms for marriage and the actual division of labor and decision making between the sexes in the family, women's assumed greater responsibility for the quality of marriage and parenting, the impact of the greater earning power of husbands relative to wives, and the stigmatization of single mothers. Thus emerged the neutral/skeptical stance towards marriage, which is now prevalent in the professions.

At best, this stance views marriage in neutral terms and regards it as one of a number of viable lifestyle arrangements an individual can personally chose, with the marriage-based, two-parent family form being neither more nor less deserving of support from professional and community resources. Marriage is seen ultimately as a personal lifestyle choice and, as such, should be regarded as a private contract whose terms should be set by only the partners themselves. At a policy level, being neutral about marriage means treating all coupling forms as equal—in particular cohabiting couples and gay and lesbian couples, who are currently denied access to legal marriage—and treating the decision to divorce as a strictly personal decision that should not be encumbered by outside pressures. As a well-known therapist colleague of ours likes to say, "The good marriage, the good divorce—it matters not."

Some professionals move past neutrality to open skepticism about marriage relationships and worry that efforts to promote marriage and prevent divorce may be inflicting more harm than good for individuals. Those espousing this position point out that the reality of marriage relationships often departs significantly from the idealized notions portrayed in noncritical pro-marriage dialogue. This position is wary of the potential dark side of marriage and questions if marriage, as traditionally defined, is an inherently hierarchical institution that oppresses women and serves to reinforce patriarchal power structures in our society. Those who hold this view see marriage as a major context in which sexism, heterosexism, and racism are fostered and reinforced (Baber & Allen, 1992; Oswald, Blume, & Marks, 2005). They therefore oppose efforts to support marriage as a social institution and are wary of interventions for married couples that do not focus on power inequities.

The Critical Pro-Marriage Stance

The third and most recent ideological perspective on marriage is the critical pro-marriage stance. For its formulation, we owe a debt to work by Browning et al. (1997) on developing a model of "critical pro-familism" and to the artic-ulation by Amitai Etzioni and colleagues (Elshtain et al., 1992) of a communi-tarian approach to marriage and the family. If the noncritical pro-marriage stance has authoritarian philosophical roots (in culturally based interpreta-tions of natural law or divine revelation) and the neutral/skeptical stance has roots in social libertarianism (individuals are free to choose their lifestyle), the critical pro-marriage stance is communitarian (trying to balance individ-ual needs and society's needs).

This perspective has the pro-marriage elements of the noncritical pro-marriage stance. Marriage is viewed as an ethical vocation, not just a lifestyle choice. Marriage promotes social and communal goods in addition to per-sonal goods. But, having learned from the neutral/skeptical critique of mar-riage, it is also "critical" because it acknowledges the historical injustices of marriage for women and the prevalence of abuse and inequality. It goes beyond both previous perspectives by acknowledging the inevitability of ten-sion at times between the needs of individuals for autonomy and personal happiness and their marital, family, and community obligations. In the critical pro-marriage perspective, this tension is not resolved by saying either "do your duty" or "do your own thing." Both sides of the dialectic are held, along with an attempt to resolve them by showing how duty and autonomy are mutually intertwined in the complexities of married life.

We next discuss how these three perspectives deal with certain core aspects of marriage.

Marital Commitment and Divorce

Much of the current marriage debate has emerged in response to varied interpretations of the causes and consequences of the high rates of divorce of the last three decades. Within a noncritical pro-marriage perspective, mari-tal stability is a near-absolute value. Divorce is often stigmatized, except for cases of adultery, abuse, or abandonment. In some religious communities, divorce is not recognized or seen as a viable option, leaving divorced individ-uals feeling like second-class citizens, even if they have remarried. There is lit-tle attention paid to the problem of the stable but highly conflicted marriage or to the social and economic consequences of the stigmatization of divorce, especially for women. The current high divorce rates are seen as disastrous for families and society.

Within the neutral/skeptical perspective, divorce is equally valued with staying married, as long as individuals have made free choices. While the ending of a relationship might be seen as regrettable, the decision to divorce is ultimately made on the basis of whether the marriage meets the needs and expectations of the spouses. No one should be legally or psychologically pressured into staying in an unsatisfactory marriage out of a sense of duty or responsibility. Historically high divorce rates are not viewed as a sign of decline, rather as an evolution in family patterns that have resulted from removing barriers that kept individuals of past generations trapped in unsuccessful relationships. In the realm of therapy, the neutral position comes down solidly on the side of promoting individual happiness as opposed to the institution of marriage. Arnold Lazarus (1981) writes: "For me, the worth of a marriage is weighed solely in terms of human happiness. Marriage is not a sacred entity to be preserved for its own sake" (p. 20). Some scholars move past this neutral stance toward divorce to posit that high divorce rates are a confirming sign that "the traditional institution of marriage is deeply, if not fatally, flawed" (Baber & Allen, 1992, p. 34).

Within the critical pro-marriage position, permanent marital commitment is seen as very important for marriage to promote the well-being of individuals, couples, children, extended families, and communities. This is particularly true when the role of wife or husband is intertwined with the role of mother or father. Divorce is seen as tragic and to be prevented if at all possible. But the critical pro-marriage perspective recognizes that some marriages cannot and should not be salvaged, especially when there is danger and harm to spouses or children. This perspective is reflected in a communitarian statement on marriage, which notes that "though divorces are necessary in some situations, many are avoidable and are not in the interest of the children, the community, and probably not of most adults either" (Communitarian Network, 2000, p. 4). Staying married is clearly held as a more desirable outcome than divorce. Divorce can be viewed like an amputation—something to be prevented and avoided with all vigor and persistence and embraced only after all other solutions have been attempted, but sometimes unavoidable for survival (Doherty, 1995).

Two-Parent Versus One-Parent Families

Another issue that distinguishes ideological perspectives on marriage is how they regard single-parent families versus two-parent families. Within the noncritical pro-marriage perspective, two-parent families are seen as always being a preferable arrangement for raising children. This is the natural order of family life and, from some theological perspectives, the divinely ordained order. Not infrequently single-parent families are assigned responsibility for a host of social ills, but the pathologies of two-parent families are not emphasized.

As we noted previously, neutral/skeptical perspectives hold that no family form or arrangement should be privileged above others. Therefore, there is strong opposition to the privileging of two-parent families over one-parent families. For those with a neutral view of marriage, there is concern that promoting marriage and two-parent families stigmatizes single and divorced parents, many of whom are raising children under difficult circumstances. Likewise, since single parents are more prevalent in African American communities, a pro-marriage agenda may seem particularly insensitive to their concerns and realities (Ooms, 1998). Those who move past neutrality to skepticism about marriage often embrace and promote intentional single parenting, a stance that only a generation or so back would have been seen as unthinkable. In this way of thinking, getting married and becoming a parent are separate and unconnected life decisions, each to be made on its own merits as seen by the individual.

Within the critical pro-marriage stance, there is a two-parent family ideal but also a recognition that in particular cases one parent is preferable to two parents when the family environment is emotionally, verbally, and physically hostile. The ideal is held because marriage is seen as the best environment for the raising of children psychologically, economically, and socially. Marriage is also valued because it promotes responsible fathering (Waite & Doherty, 2006). Most proponents of the critical pro-marriage stance support social programs for single-parent families, since many children grow up in these households, but they insist on maintaining the ideal of a married, two-parent family and believe that society should promote the viability of this family form.

Cohabitation

Based generally on religious beliefs, the noncritical pro-marriage stance sees cohabitation as one of the primary indictors of marriage decline. This living arrangement is morally inappropriate and condemned because it violates natural and theological laws about the proper place for sexual behavior. Generally, distinctions are not made as to the motive for the cohabitation or the nature of the commitment between the partners.

Holding to the principle that no family form should be privileged above others, neutral/skeptical perspectives view cohabitation as a personal lifestyle option equally valued with marriage. Some even hold up the flexibility and freedom of cohabitation as virtues of the lifestyle arrangement and see the rise in rates of cohabitation as a sign of progress, especially for women, who are regarded as having been traditionally limited within obligations of marital relationships.

Within the critical pro-marriage perspective, cohabitation is viewed with caution and skepticism but is not condemned. Drawing on the research literature, advocates of this perspective are concerned with the association of cohabitation with later divorce and poorer marital quality. It is particularly seen as a bad arrangement for children. Another concern is that since many religions disapprove of cohabitation, couples who choose this form of union are distanced from organized religious communities, which are potentially strong support networks for their relationship and family (Waite, 2000). It should be noted that there is some variance on views of cohabitation among the critical pro-marriage stance. Citing the research literature on the differential impact of different kinds of cohabitation, some make a distinction between prenuptial or engaged cohabitation, in which the couple has a solid commitment and a planned wedding date, and cohabitation in which the couple lives together without a permanent commitment. Others see all types of cohabitation as ultimately an inferior imitation of marriage and something to be discouraged.

Same-Sex Marriage

Cultural discussions about the legal definition of marriage and whether or not the institution of marriage should be extended to include same-sex couples has emerged as a divisive ideological issue in the contemporary discussion of marriage. Advocates of the noncritical pro-marriage perspective promote a traditional definition of marriage and are strongly opposed to the legalization of same-sex marriage on religious and moral grounds, as well as because they believe that it will hurt children. Those endorsing the neutral/ skeptical view are strongly in favor of expanding the definition of marriage to same-sex couples on equal rights grounds, holding that it is discriminatory to privilege one type of couple relationship above others. The critical pro-marriage perspective is divided on this issue. There are some who favor same-sex marriage because they believe that marriage will be as good for homosexual couples as it is for heterosexual couples and will strengthen the status of marriage in society. Others oppose legally redefining marriage because they believe that same-sex marriage will further weaken the institution of marriage and will further marginalize fathers from the lives of their children by indicating that the married, mother-father family is not the cornerstone of family life.

Marital Therapy and Education

The noncritical pro-marriage perspective is cautious about secular approaches to assisting marital relationships, preferring to focus on biblical and other theological perspectives. Recently, however, the challenge of high divorce rates in all faith communities has moved conservative faith communities to develop initiatives to prepare couples for marriage, to support married couples, and to help troubled couples. However, there is still wariness in many circles about adopting secular models of marriage education and therapy. It should be noted that there are grounds for this wariness, given the historical skepticism of social scientists and therapists about religion.

The neutral/skeptical perspective takes a generally positive view of marital therapy, as long as the therapist is neutral on marital stability versus divorce and is attentive to problems of abuse and inequality for women in marriage. Therapy is seen as a way to clarify individual desires and to promote communication and problem-solving skills to allow couples to overcome their problems and shape their marriage in a more egalitarian direction. When it comes to marriage education, however, neutral/skeptical advocates are wary of the pro-commitment stance of many marriage educators, and they criticize the absence of an explicitly egalitarian stance toward marital roles in most of the marriage education movement.

The critical pro-marriage stance is strongly supportive of marital therapy and marriage education, both before and after marriage, as a way to promote both stability and satisfaction in marriage. It differs here from the noncritical pro-marriage perspective on marriage education by positing that even couples who are religious and deeply committed to their relationship need to be intentional in growing their marriage by developing good communication and problem-solving skills. The critical pro-marriage perspective joins the skeptical/neutral perspective in recognizing that equality and mutual regard are necessary to have satisfying marriages in the contemporary world, and that marital therapy can be helpful. It differs from the neutral/skeptical stance by being more positive about marriage education's emphasis on stability. It also differs in ideas about marital therapy, having the opposite concern that therapists are often not supportive enough of couples' commitment. Finally, the critical pro-marriage perspective has a unique emphasis on the larger community's responsibilities in promoting lifelong marriage education and support for troubled couples.

Feminism

With regard to feminism, the noncritical pro-marriage perspective historically has been skeptical, for reasons that should be clear. The neutral/skeptical stance has been enthusiastic about the contributions of feminism to the understanding of marriage, while the critical pro-marriage stance embraces feminism's emphasis on gender equality but does not emphasize patriarchy and male power as priority areas for discussion and intervention. The critical pro-marriage stance also does not embrace feminism's skepticism about marriage.

Religion Versus Social Science

As mentioned before, the noncritical pro-marriage stance has historically been wary of social science, especially when its moral neutrality is seen as threatening the institution of marriage. The neutral/skeptical perspective, for its part, views religion warily and embraces social science, especially social science that has feminist and multicultural emphases. The critical pro-marriage perspective values both religion and social science but takes a critical stance toward both: each is viewed as making important contributions, but each has limitations and blind spots when it comes to understanding and supporting marriage. Stated simplistically, religion is strong on the issues of commitment and the public dimension of marriage but tends to lack sophisticated ways to understand and promote the well-being of modern companionate marriages. Social science is strong on understanding contemporary marital relationships but is generally poorer in the areas of commitment and community in marriage.

Sacrifice Versus Personal Satisfaction

The notion of self-sacrifice in marriage is a key dividing point among the three ideological views of marriage. Sacrifice for the good of the marriage is at the heart of the noncritical pro-marriage perspective, while it is an anathema to the neutral/skeptical perspective because sacrifice is seen as compromising individual well-being. The critical pro-marriage perspective values both sacrifice and individual satisfaction and sees them as necessarily interconnected. This stance is reflected in the following quote from Browning and colleagues (1997), in which the ideas of sacrifice and equal regard or mutuality are viewed as intertwined: "One of the great tasks of our time is to create a spirituality of marriage which links sacrificial love and the experience of the transcendent in ways that reinforce a steadfast love in the service of equal regard and mutuality" (p. 292).

Public Versus Private Emphasis

The noncritical pro-marriage perspective has a strong emphasis on the institutional, community dimension of marriage, which views personal relationships as strongly connected with public purposes. The personal side of marriage was often less strongly emphasized in these traditions, but in recent decades it has come into greater prominence as conservative churches have become more active in promoting marriage. The neutral/skeptical perspective, reflecting its social libertarianism, strongly emphasizes the private side of marriage over the public. The critical pro-marriage perspective, once again, attempts to embrace both the private dimension of marriage and the public dimension. Marriage is a highly personal relationship to be shaped by spouses, and it is also a relationship that is embedded in two-way influences with community. Communities support or undermine marriage, and the quality and stability of marriages build or detract from community.

In conclusion, we believe that many family professionals have stayed aloof from the marriage movement because they identify it with the noncritical pro-marriage perspective. We believe that the critical pro-marriage stance reflects the desired ideals of the vast majority of families and couples and is growing in prominence as the ideological stance in the marriage movement.

Research on the Benefits of Marriage

Now we move from the domain of ideology and values to that of empirical research. The summary below is adapted from a chapter by Waite and Doherty (2006). Practitioners in the helping professions are typically aware of the negative health consequences of distressed marriages, but they are often unaware that married people tend to have better physical and emotional health than single people, at least in part because they are married (Mirowksy & Ross, 2003; Waite & Gallagher, 2000). The social support provided by a spouse, combined with the economic resources produced by the marriage, facilitate both the production and maintenance of health. The specialization, economies of scale, and insurance functions of marriage all increase the economic well-being of family members, and the increase is typically quite substantial. Generally, married people produce more and accumulate more assets than unmarried people (Lupton & Smith, 2003). And children raised by their married parents experience better outcomes, on average, than those raised in other situations (Parke, 2003).

Next, we describe the benefits provided by marriage on each of these dimensions and discuss possible explanations for the better outcomes shown by married people.

Emotional Health

Mental and emotional well-being are important components of health and necessary ingredients to a happy life. And these advantages seem to accrue more often to those who are married than to those who are single. Married men and married women show better emotional health than those who are not married, on average, reporting less depression, less anxiety, and lower levels of other types of psychological distress than those who are single, divorced, or widowed (Mirowsky & Ross, 2003). When social observers first noted this pattern, they wondered whether simply living with another person—which almost all married persons do—was the source of the psychological health of the married. Perhaps living alone causes distress, and those unmarried men and women living with others get the psychological benefits of marriage. Gove and Hughes (1979) tested this idea by comparing married adults and unmarried adults who lived alone with those who lived with someone else; they found that living with someone did not provide the same boost in psychological well-being as being married. Single adults were more depressed than married adults, and living with others did not solve the problem.

A number of recent studies have attempted to assess the mental health consequences of marriage and divorce and to separate these from the selection of emotionally healthy individuals getting into marriage and distressed or unhealthy individuals getting out. These studies followed individuals over time as some married, some divorced, and some retained their previous marital status. Consistently, transitions into marriage improved mental health, on average, for both men and women, and transitions out of marriage decreased it (Horwitz, White, & Howell-White, 1996; Marks & Lambert, 1998; Simon, 2002). Simon (2002) found that divorce increased symptoms of emotional distress among both women and men, but that women showed greater increases than men in depressive symptoms following divorce. Both men and women who divorced reported a significant increase in alcohol abuse. Simon also found that men and women who divorced reported more depression and more alcohol problems earlier than those who remained married, which she interprets as evidence that low levels of emotional well-being are both a cause and a consequence of disruption.

The better emotional health of married people results, at least in part, from the social support marriage offers. Almost by definition, married people share their lives with their spouses to a much greater extent than single adults share their lives with the people they live with. Roommates, parents, and adult children all have their own separate lives to a much greater extent than spouses do. Even parents and children are supposed to be relatively independent of each other emotionally and financially—at least once they are all adults—than we expect husbands and wives to be. So in marriages that are working reasonably well, husbands and wives have a built-in confidant to offer them support to an extent not generally available to those who are single. Good marriages provide the partners with a sense of being cared for, esteemed, loved, and valued as a person. And no matter what else is going on in life, these feelings make problems easier to handle.

But the psychological benefits of marriage come only from *good-enough* marriages—those rated by the individual as "happy" or "very happy." A bad marriage—one rated as "not too happy" or "not at all happy"—actually makes things worse. Not surprisingly, men and women in the relatively small number of unhappy marriages show *more* psychological distress than single individuals.[3] People who say that their relationships are unhappy, that they would like to change many aspects of their relationship, and that they often consider leaving their spouse or partner have higher distress levels than people without partners at all (Ross, 1995). If a good marriage is a source of support and intimacy, an unhappy marriage is a source of pain and self-doubt.

Physical Health and Longevity

People in good physical health feel fit and energetic, without pain, disability, or symptoms of disease. Good health means more than just the absence of disease or its symptoms; it means feeling robust and strong. Good health is a resource. It gives people access to activities and achievements that they value. And most people sincerely want to be free from pain, fatigue, and symptoms of disease. But men and women who are married are more likely to get the benefits of good physical health than are the unmarried. For example, Waite and Hughes (1999) found that, among men and women at midlife, those who were married and living only with a spouse (and, perhaps, children) reported significantly better physical health and were less likely to have a condition that limited their mobility than unmarried adults and those in more complicated living arrangements.

Married people, especially married men, showed better health behaviors than those who were not married. One out of four young single men reported in a recent national survey that they drink enough to cause them problems at work or problems with aggression. Young married men the same age—who were also similar in level of education and race—showed substantially fewer problems with alcohol. Single men no doubt see more problems from drinking because they drink more—almost twice as much as married men. One out of four married men drink so little that they qualify as "abstainers"; only one out of six or seven single men drink this little (Miller-Tutzauer, Leonard, & Windle, 1991). Divorced and widowed men also show substantially more problems with alcohol than married men (Umberson, 1987).

Single men do not just drink more than married men. They also are more likely to drink and drive, more likely to get into fights, and more likely to take risks that increase the chances of accidents and injuries (Bachman, Wadsworth, O'Malley, Johnson, & Schulenberg, 1997; Ross, Mirowksy, &

Goldsteen, 1990; Umberson, 1987). Alcohol plays a role in many of these behaviors. People drink and drive when they need to get home after an evening of drinking somewhere else. And excessive drinking can precipitate fights, arguments, and accidents. Some people drink to deal with depression, anxiety, or other emotional problems; heavy drinking reduces depression in the short run but increases it in the long run (Parker, Parker, Harford, & Farmer, 1987).

Marriage seems to discourage these unhealthy behaviors. Single men who are heading toward marriage reduce their drinking up to a year before the ceremony, so that, although they start with the same heavy drinking patterns as their friends who stay single, by the time they marry they drink much less than they did a year earlier. At the same time, the alcohol consumption of young men who stay single remains high, and they continue to experience problems from drinking. Young men who were light drinkers, moderate drinkers, and heavy drinkers prior to marrying *all* drank less after they married than they did before (Bachman et al., 1997; Miller-Tutzauer et al., 1991). Marriage also seems to benefit women during the young adult years, when they are most likely to smoke, drink heavily, and use drugs. Although young women less often drink or drink heavily than young men, and less often use cocaine or marijuana, those who marry reduce these negative behaviors dramatically compared to those who stay single (Bachman et al., 1997).

One important avenue through which marriage improves women's health and longevity appears to be income. Women with income in excess of their own rate their health as better than women without these extra financial resources (Hahn, 1993). And married women's longer lives seem to result in large part from the greater financial resources that husbands bring (Lillard & Waite, 1995).

Marriage also gives women access to private health insurance, an increasingly precious commodity in the contemporary United States. Hahn (1993) showed that just over half of divorced, widowed, and never-married women had private health insurance, compared to 83 percent of married women. Women with private health insurance rate their health significantly higher than women without private health insurance. Insurance coverage improves health directly, by giving women access to health care services, and it improves psychological health by giving women a sense of security about their health care (Hahn, 1993).

Catherine Ross and her colleagues (1990) summed up the evidence on the relationship between marital status and longevity: "Compared to married people, the nonmarried...have higher rates of mortality than the married: about 50% higher among women and 250% higher among men." The unmarried face especially high mortality rates for causes of death that have a large behavioral component, such as suicide (Smith, Mercy, & Conn, 1988), accidents, lung cancer, and cirrhosis.

All marriages are not equal. The quality of the relationship between the spouses makes a difference. Couples whose marriages improve over time also see improvements in the physical health of husband and wife, primarily through the improvements in psychological well-being that accompany better marriage quality (Wickrama, Lorenz, Conger, & Elder, 1997).

Career Success

Married men earn substantially more than otherwise similar unmarried men. The wage premium married men receive is one of the most well-documented phenomena in social science, in this country and in many others. Married men earn at least 10 percent more than single men and perhaps as high as 40 percent more. Economists call this the "marriage premium." Women get no wage premium and pay no wage penalty for being married (Waldfogel, 1997). Although high-earning men are more likely than others to get married, marriage itself seems to increase earnings (Daniel, 1995).

The longer a man is married, the greater the wage premium he receives. One recent study of younger men, for example, found that married men in their twenties and early thirties earned $11.33 an hour, while single men earned $10.38 and divorced or separated men earned $9.61 (Gray, 1997). For older men, the wage gap between husbands and bachelors is even larger. A study of men aged fifty-five to sixty-four found that married men earned 20 to 32 percent more than their nonmarried counterparts (Bartlett & Callahan, 1984). A rigorous and very thorough statistical analysis by Korenman and Neumark (1991) reports that married white men earn 11 percent more than their never-married counterparts, controlling for all the standard human capital variables. Between 50 and 80 percent of the effect remains, depending on the specification, after correcting for selectivity into marriage based on characteristics such as attractiveness or personality, which researchers do not observe but potential partners certainly do.

Economists generally agree that the greater productivity of married men plays a substantial role in their higher earnings. This productivity boost comes with the more settled, stable lifestyle of marriage, with its regular hours, adequate sleep, and decent meals. It also may come directly from the productivity-enhancing efforts of the wife herself, assisting her husband with his tasks for work, giving advice, or taking on other household duties that allow him to focus on his job (Grossbard-Shechtman, 1993).

Wealth

Married people have, on average, substantially greater assets and wealth than people with similar levels of education and earnings who are not married. Economists Joseph Lupton and James Smith (2003) estimated wealth and assets for individuals in their early 50s through early 60s who were interviewed as part of a large national survey, the *Health and Retirement Survey.* They included real assets such as a house or apartment, second home, farm or ranch, or mobile home. They also included other real estate; vehicles; business equity; IRA or Keogh; stocks, trusts, or mutual funds; checking, saving, or money market funds; CDs; government savings bonds or treasury bills; other bonds; and other savings and assets. They deducted the value of first and second mortgages, home equity loans, mortgages on second homes, and other debt.

Lupton and Smith (2003) found that, on average, married couples' net worth is substantially greater than that of unmarried people. Since there are two adults in married-couple families and only one unmarried adult in non-marital families, we might expect greater wealth simply because married couples pool resources. But even when Lupton and Smith divided the assets of married couples in half, their wealth still exceeded that of all other types of unmarried adults. For example, married couples in their study had a median net worth of $132,200, which amounts to $66,100 per person. Separated adults, who had a median net worth of only $7,600, were the worst off of all unmarried adults. But even widowed people, with a median net worth of $47,275, had substantially lower wealth than married people who were similar to them in other ways.

Some of the greater wealth of married couples results from their higher earnings, but not all of it. Even at the same level of earnings, married couples have more assets because they *save* more. Lupton and Smith (2003) also found that people who divorced lost assets. For example, a married head of household who divorced lost about a third of his net wealth over a five-year period, whereas a divorced person who married doubled his or her wealth over the same period. This research also showed what the authors call "shockingly low" net worth among both separated and never-married black and Hispanic adults and point to the low levels of marriage among blacks and Puerto Ricans as one cause of the very substantial racial and ethnic disparities in financial well-being.

The legally enforceable lifetime agreement that underlies marriage gives partners the long time horizon needed to allow them to specialize, splitting life's tasks between them to maximize efficiency. This specialization allows married adults to produce more, working together, than they would if each of them did everything alone. Married couples also get the economies of scale that come from sharing a house or apartment. The most recent estimates suggest that two people can live as cheaply as 1.65 people if they live together. Of course, the economies of scale that come with marriage accrue to roommates, cohabiting partners, or siblings who live together. But most people are unenthusiastic about sharing a bathroom and kitchen with someone of whom they are not particularly fond or do not know fairly well, limiting the availability of the economies of scale from shared living arrangements.

Married people are also much more likely than unmarried people to receive money from family, perhaps because parents and in-laws see married couples as a stable unit and cohabiting partners as not really members of the family. Marriage also increases wealth by increasing savings; Lupton and Smith (2003) found that even at the same level of family income, married adults accumulated assets at a much faster rate than otherwise similar unmarried people. Something about being married encourages saving and asset accumulation.

Finally, spouses act as a small insurance pool, protecting each other from the full effect of life's uncertainties. If one becomes ill or disabled, the other can often provide care and take over more of the household duties. If one spouse becomes unemployed, the other may work more to help out. Kotlikoff and Spivak (1981) calculated how much spouses gain from pooling their risks in marriage. Just getting married creates an annuity value that is equal to increasing one's wealth by 12 to 14 percent at age thirty and by 30 percent at age seventy-five, compared to staying single. We do not count these windfalls in wealth from marriage in any official statistics, so the astoundingly greater wealth of the married that we noted earlier is really even bigger than it looks.

The Well-Being of Children

Over the past twenty years, a body of research has developed on how changes in patterns of family structure affect children. Most researchers now agree that together these studies support the notion that, on average, children do best when raised by their two married, biological parents who have low-conflict relationships (Parke, 2003). In particular, children raised by their own married parents do better across a range of outcomes than children who grow up in other living arrangements. There is evidence that the former are less likely to die as infants (Bennett, Braveman, Egerter, & Kiely, 1994), have better health during childhood (Angel & Worobey, 1988), and even survive longer into old age (Tucker, Friedman, Schwartz, & Criqui, 1997). They are less likely to drop out of high school, complete more years of schooling, are less likely to be idle as young adults, and are less likely to have a child as an unmarried teen (McLanahan & Sandefur, 1994). Children who grow up in stable homes also tend to have better mental health than their counterparts who have gone through the experience of a parental divorce. Using seventeen-year longitudinal data from two generations, Amato and Sobolewski (2001) found that the weaker parent-child bonds that resulted from marital discord mediated most of the association between divorce and the subsequent mental health outcomes of children.

Cherlin, Chase-Lansdale, and McRae (1998) found that children whose parents would later divorce already showed evidence of more emotional problems even prior to the divorce, suggesting that marriage dissolution tends to occur in families that are troubled to begin with. However, the authors also found that the gap continued to widen subsequent to the divorce, suggesting a causal effect of family breakup on mental health. Summing up his overall assessment of the studies in this field, Cherlin (1999) concludes that growing up in a nonintact family can be associated with short- and long-term problems, partly due to the effects of family structure on the child's mental health, and partly due to inherited characteristics and their interaction with the environment. However, while the increased risks faced by children raised without both parents are certainly reason for concern, the majority of children in single-parent families grow up without serious problems (Parke, 2003).

There continues to be debate about how much of the disadvantages children experience in a nonmarital environment are attributable to poverty versus family structure. Children living with single mothers are five times as likely to be poor as those in two-parent families (Parke, 2003). While it is difficult to disentangle the effects of income and family structure, the relationship clearly operates in both directions: poverty is both a cause and an effect of single parenthood. Given the data available on the benefits of marriage for career success, wealth, and other measures of economic well-being, it is likely that marriage benefits children directly in emotional and social ways as well as indirectly through economic provision.

Do Married People Do Well Because Successful People Get Married?

Cross-sectional differences in both emotional and physical health, wealth, and career accomplishments between the married and divorced are sizeable, but they may result from the selection of the healthy and successful into marriage and the unhealthy failures out of marriage. Many recent studies have addressed this selection by following individuals over time to assess the relationship between changes in marital status and changes in their well-being. These studies consistently find that selection into or out of marriage does not account for the better physical (Lillard & Panis, 1996) or psychological (Horwitz et al., 1996; Marks & Lambert, 1998; Simon, 2002) health of married men or married women. It accounts for about half of the higher earnings of married men (Daniel, 1995). It appears that there is something about being married and something about being unmarried that affects health and well-being.

In particular, there is something about the key features of institutional marriage that promotes health and well-being for spouses and children. Permanence, joint production, coresidence, and the social recognition of a sexual and child-rearing union are, perhaps, the most important characteristics of the institution of marriage (Waite & Gallagher, 2000). These features lead to some of the other defining characteristics of marriage. Because two adults make a legally binding promise to live and work together for their joint well-being—and to do so, ideally, for the rest of their lives—they tend to specialize, dividing between them the labor required to maintain the family. This specialization allows married men and women to produce more than they would if they did not specialize. The coresidence and resource sharing of married couples lead to substantial economies of scale; at any standard of living it costs much less for people to live together than it would if they lived separately. These economies of scale and the specialization of spouses both tend to increase the economic well-being of family members living together.

The institution of marriage also assumes the sharing of economic and social resources and coinsurance. Spouses act as a small insurance pool against life's uncertainties, reducing their need to protect themselves by themselves against unexpected events. Marriage also connects spouses and family members to a larger network of help, support, and obligation through their extended family, friends, and others. The insurance function of marriage increases the economic well-being of family members (Kotlikoff & Spivak, 1981). The support function of marriage improves their emotional well-being (Mirowsky & Ross, 2003). The institution of marriage also builds on and fosters trust. Since spouses share social and economic resources, and expect to do so over the long term, both gain when the family unit gains. This reduces the need for family members to monitor the behavior of other members, increasing efficiency (Becker, 1991).

The Ecology of Marriage

This discussion of ideological models and empirical research findings of marriage sets the stage for the following discussion of marriage, health, and the professions. As noted, many family professionals have critiqued contemporary efforts to promote and uphold the social institution of marriage as exclusionary and lacking appropriate sensitivity to the diversity of modern family life. Many scholars and writers have become neutral/skeptical towards marriage, for the most part avoiding the term "marriage" in books, articles, and conference presentations. In so doing, professionals by and large have adopted the "thin view" of individual and marital health (Wall & Miller-McLemore, 2002). That is, health is viewed as a private, personal good, and marriage is viewed as a private, skilled relationship aimed at promoting personal well-being. The good marriage, from this perspective, is one that "works" for the two individuals involved. Other voices have emerged in recent years to present a more communitarian view of health and marital well-being (Carroll, Knapp, & Holman, 2005; Doherty, 1995; Fowers, 2000; Stanley, 1998).

Recently, Wall and Miller-McLemore (2002) called for an expanded perspective of "marital health" that encompasses "the wider range of social goods that evolve from good marriages" and defines the health benefits of marriage in individual, relational, and social terms (p. 187). We concur with this call and also agree with Wall and Miller-McLemore's assertion that an important task for family professionals is to explore each marriage's implicit and explicit dependencies on larger social institutions and how these relations contribute to a marriage's greater fulfillment and meaning. The ecological view of marriage that we present here is consistent with the critical pro-marriage perspective described above. It goes beyond standard models in the family professions by emphasizing the institutional as well as relational dimensions of marriage and the interplay of influence between marriage and its ecology.

An Ecological Model of Marital Health

Ultimately, an expanded perspective of marital health entails recognizing and appreciating the ecology of marriage and the *moral stakeholders* who both benefit from and support marriage relationships at each level of the system. As marital therapists and educators, we have found that an effective way to expand clients' views of marital health is to ask about and discuss the moral stakeholders whose well-being is intertwined with their marital relationship. This type of dialogue illuminates the *moral ecology of marriage* and encourages couples to view their relationship as a community-based covenant rather than as a private, contractual relationship that involves only their personal well-being. It is our experience that as individuals and couples think about the various levels of moral stakeholders of marriage, they are ultimately challenged to expand their considerations of what is truly involved in assessing marital health. Marital health becomes not only one's personal fulfillment or well-being but ultimately the well-being of a network of interconnected and interdependent stakeholders who all benefit from and provide certain goods to the marriage relationship. The promotion of marital health by professionals and policy makers is then defined as an ongoing process of balancing the mutually interdependent needs of the moral stakeholders in the marital ecosystem.

We conceptualize "marital health" at four ecological levels: (1) the individual level, (2) the family level, (3) the community level, and (4) the societal level (see Table 2.2). Each level is composed of various moral stakeholders whose well-being both influences and is influenced by the marriage relationship. In the individual and family levels, this bidirectional influence is often explicit and direct (e.g., children's welfare, personal health), but in the community and society levels it is more implicit and indirect in nature (e.g., social goods, financial productivity, the well-being of future grandchildren, and so on).

A core principle of this model is the idea that the health and well-being of the stakeholders at the various levels are interconnected and interdependent. Therefore, when viewed with an ecological lens, the promotion of individual health or community well-being should benefit the other stakeholders in the ecosystem and vice versa. Like all ecological systems, the goods of various levels exist in tension, and at times compete with each other. Rather than trying to avoid this tension by focusing on only one level or by telling ourselves that what is good at one level automatically becomes what is good for another (e.g., "if a parent is happy, that is what is best for the child"), true ecological health involves balancing the needs of all of the stakeholders at all of the levels. (This is why our perspective is "critical" in its pro-marriage perspective.) Marriage and family life involve moral decisions that, at times, will involve prioritizing some stakeholders' needs over others. But such decisions should be made with a conscious recognition of the consequences of such choices. Not acknowledging the moral ecology of marriage has short-term consequences that appear to free individuals to make unfettered, self-interested choices, but it ultimately limits the horizon of significance of marriage itself in human life. No marriage is an island.

Table 2.2   An Ecological Model of Marital Health

Ecological Level	Moral Stakeholders	Benefits: "What marriage gives"	Provisions: "What marriage receives"
Society Level	Civic institutions	Productive citizens	Policy support
	Corporate institutions	Productive employee	Financial support
	Educational institutions	Productive students	Education
	Criminal justice system	Less crime/ delinquency	Protection/security
	Religious organizations	Moral socialization	Spiritual guidance
Community Level	Neighborhoods	Shared support	Role models
	Faith communities	Shared support	Community network
	Children's Peers	Socialization	Friendship
Family Level	Children	Secure environment	Purpose/meaning
			Socialization
			Financial security
			Parental involvement
	Extended family	Strong kin network	Child care
	Children's marriages	Trust—Inst. of marriage	Family ties
	Future grandchildren	Sense of heritage	
Individual Level	Spouse	Physical health	Purpose/meaning
	Self	Mental health	Sense of belonging
		Spiritual health	Emotional support
		Personal growth	Sense of community

Table 2.2 outlines some of the two-way influences in the ecology of marriage. It is intended to exemplify some of the major influences involved, and not to be exhaustive. One difference between this ecological model and traditional top-down, structural-functional models is that we see the decisions of married couples as influencing their larger environment and not just their microenvironment. For each ecological level we specify the moral

stakeholders and describe the benefits that marriage potentially offers and the benefits that marriage potentially receives. Of course, these reciprocal influences can also be negative, as when social institutions undermine marriage through legal provisions, such as a marriage tax penalty. The table does not show indirect influences that can also be important, such as when marital breakdown influences certain societal norms that contribute to the deterioration of local community bonds.

Toward a Conceptual Ethic of Marriage Promotion

We are concerned that unless professionals and policy makers incorporate an expanded perspective of marital ethics and health into their professional identities they will continue to contribute to the contemporary crisis in the meaning and purposes of marriage. To this end, we believe that all family professions (e.g., therapy, education, policy, law, business, ministry, and so on) would be greatly benefited by the development and articulation of a conceptual ethic of marriage promotion. Dollahite and Hawkins (1998) define a *conceptual ethic* as "a framework intended not primarily to model or describe reality—although it may do that—but mainly to suggest what is possible and desirable" (p. 111). Such an ethic could provide a vision for professional and policy support of marriage and define an ideal to be promoted. We realize that the development of a conceptual ethic that is widely accepted may be difficult to achieve in our diverse society, but we feel that even the process of engaging in such a discussion could prove very beneficial. This process may be seen as an ongoing discussion that is never complete. But we believe that some common ground is possible, as exemplified by our own coauthoring process involving individuals with diverse ideological, religious, and political perspectives. Based on the foregoing analysis in this chapter, we propose several central components of a conceptual ethic of marriage promotion.

1. *Family professionals and policy makers should be guided by an ethical vision of marriage that is rooted in the moral responsibilities of spouses to each other, their children, and the other stakeholders of their marriage relationship.* Family professionals need to develop a deeper vision of what constitutes a good marriage in order to move beyond current views that predominately emphasize personal fulfillment and satisfaction as the foundation criteria of worthwhile marriage (Carroll et al., 2005). What is needed are conceptualizations of marriage that transcend individual experience and emphasize the moral companionship of marriage. In short, family professionals and policy makers should foster a vision of marriage as an ethical vocation rooted in concepts of covenant, self-sacrifice, mutual regard, and child-centeredness (Cere, 2000). Within the last several years there have been a handful of solid examples of attempts to define such an ethical vision of marriage. Drawing from a Christian critical familism perspective, Browning and colleagues (1997) have proposed an "equal regard marriage" ethic of marriage life that is based in equal regard of spouses, self-sacrifice in the service of mutuality, and the subordination of families to the larger social good. Fowers (2000) has promoted a vision of

"partnership marriage" based in appropriate expectations of marriage, meaningful shared visions and goals, and the virtues or character strengths of spouses. Drawing on Mormon theology of marriage, Hawkins and colleagues (2001) have articulated an "equal partnership" ethic of marriage based in shared family leadership, personal growth, and the interdependence of father and mother roles. There is a need to infuse these and other ethical views of marriage into professional and public discourse.

2. *Family professionals and policy makers should embrace their role as moral consultants in promoting a marriage ideal and moral responsibility in marriage.* Caught in the current neutral/skeptical ideology of our time, many professionals fear that promoting a marriage ideal and moral responsibility in marriage is beyond the scope of their profession. This is true even when they highly value marriage in their personal lives, often holding deep spiritual beliefs about the importance of marriage. As a result of this value-neutral ideology, the helping professions are currently dominated by a reflexive morality that ultimately reflects the individualistic and consumer orientation of contemporary society. Doherty (1995) has developed a model for therapists and others to move beyond value neutrality in working with marriage and other issues. Professionals become moral consultants who work sensitively to help clients unearth and examine their moral sensibilities about issues of commitment, justice, truthfulness, and social responsibility.

3. *Family professionals and policy makers need to view marriage in more expansive terms than as a network of communicative techniques.* As noted by Wall and Miller-McLemore (2002), much of our direct professional and social support for families is based in a private or individual conception of marriage that views a good marriage as one in which partners have sufficient mastery of communicative techniques to negotiate their own goals and purposes of marriage, and thus to achieve personal happiness. In support of this perspective, the last twenty-five years of marital research has consisted primarily of descriptive studies that have focused on observable conflict-oriented behavior in a relatively atheoretical way (Fincham & Beach, 1999). Although this line of research has yielded valuable insights and important behavioral tools for enhancing marriage, its paradigm is based on a skills-deficit perspective that assumes that marriage difficulties are primarily the result of marriage partners' inadequate communication and conflict resolution skills. This approach has recently been critiqued (Burelson & Denton, 1997), and a call has gone out for new models of marital functioning that include a broader array of psychological, interpersonal, and moral dimensions (Carroll et al., 2005; Fincham & Beach, 1999). Family professionals will need to deepen their ideas of what is required to develop and maintain successful marriage relationships. For example, without moral commitment to spouse and marriage, communication skills are likely to falter as a basis for long-term marriage, and without the virtue of justice or fairness, marital problem-solving skills can descend into business negotiations between two self-interested parties.

4. Family professionals and policy makers need to define the health benefits of mar-riage in individual, relational, and social terms and should seek to promote marriage from all of the levels within the ecology of marriage. The ecological nature of mar-riage has several implications for family professionals and policy makers. First, professionals should help clients see how their behavior and choices in marriage have consequences for others. Identifying and articulating the impacts of marital decision making on the stakeholders of the marriage is the heart of the moral aspect of professional promotion of marriage. Second, when seen through an ecological lens, strengthening marriage needs to take place at all levels of the ecosystem of marriage, as described below.

Individual Level: Promote Marital Competence. Many models of marriage pro-motion focus almost exclusively on couple negotiation in some form or another and operate on the assumption that all people, more or less, have equal capacity for developing and maintaining a strong marriage relation-ship. These assumptions seem shortsighted in that they do not adequately emphasize the personal virtues needed to practice such skills and to sustain a relationship during the inevitable times of miscommunication. At the indi-vidual level, therapists and educators should strive to promote marital com-petence in current or prospective spouses. Carroll and colleagues (in press) recently proposed a developmental model of marital competence that includes the promotion of (1) marriage virtues and character strengths, such as commitment, generosity, and fairness (Fowers, 2000); (2) personal develop-ment and maturation, such as personal security, identity development, and self validation (L'Abate, 1997; Schnarch, 1991); and (3) marriage skills, such as effective communication skills, consensus building, and problem solving. The development of marital competence also requires attention to the promo-tion of capacities in the areas of sustainable employment, responsible parent-ing, personal health and well-being, violence prevention, and other life skills needed for the creation of healthy marriage relationships.

Couple Level: Promote Partnership in Marriage. The benefits of marriage are most profound when couples can develop a sense of partnership in marriage. At the couple level, family professionals should promote ethical partnership in marriage. This should include helping couples develop a partnership based in shared goals and projects, a common commitment to equity, couple communication skills, mutual growth, and the successful navigation of life transitions.

Community Level: Promote Pro-Marriage Communities. At the community level, family professionals and policy makers should find ways to actively promote communities that support marriage. We have become interested in the role professionals can take in developing partnerships and tapping the natural, existing resources of communities. We believe that this type of com-munity work presents a new paradigm for family professionals. Doherty and colleagues (Doherty, 2000; Doherty & Anderson, 2004; Doherty & Beaton, 2000; Doherty & Carroll, 2002b) have begun to articulate a families and democracy model that could serve as the basis for professionals to involve themselves in grassroots efforts to build communities that are deeply nurturing of marriage.

Societal Level: Promote a Pro-Marriage Culture. Family professionals should take an active role in promoting social policy, corporate policy, and other measures that will promote a pro-marriage culture. Marriage is not only a private relationship, but it is also a social institution. A strong institution of marriage supports important government purposes. Professionals and policy makers can play a critical role in creating a funding priority for marriage-oriented research and services, encouraging couple formation services for economically disadvantaged families, and facilitating wider public awareness of and involvement in marriage education services. Family professionals and policy makers need to embrace marriage as a public health issue and participate in efforts to generate public awareness around issues that are critical to health at all levels of the marital ecosystem (see Hawkins, Carroll, Doherty, & Willoughby, 2004 for a discussion of these issues).

5. Family professionals and policy makers should take a life-course perspective that recognizes the importance of marriage promotion at the various stages of development. Marriage education is currently concentrated at the premarital stage, where it is often mandatory. The knowledge, skills, and virtues needed for a marriage after the birth of a first child or in the middle years may differ in kind or intensity from those needed by newlyweds. Likewise, adequate preparation for marriage requires age-appropriate learning throughout childhood, adolescence, and young adulthood. Different kinds of community supports aimed at marriage promotion should be linked together across the life span.

Conclusion

Family professionals and policy makers are at new crossroads as American culture changes from a focus on individual welfare, narrowly construed, to a more communitarian perspective that transcends individualism and embraces the moral stakeholders in marriage but maintains contact with the important critiques of marriage that emerged in the 1960s and 1970s. The emerging communitarian or critical pro-marriage perspective on marriage is fully consistent with the implicit personal values of most individuals and couples, even those whose explicit statements reflect neutrality about issues such as marital commitment.

Value neutrality about marriage has been exposed as the disguised embrace of individual self-interest. As professionals and policy makers, we cannot be intellectually honest or professionally responsible unless we openly grapple with the deeper moral, spiritual, and communal meaning of marriage. We believe that the creative futures of the family professions lie in the synthesis of three powerful elements: knowledge emerging from social science about the psychosocial ingredients of healthy marriage; traditional religious views of marriage as a sacred covenant and central social institution;

and a contemporary ethic of equality and mutual regard in marriage, an ethic that looks squarely at the dark side of marriage without lapsing into neutrality or skepticism and that sees the revival and reformation of marriage as perhaps the central challenge facing the next generation.

Endnotes

1. This chapter is an adaptation and expansion on our previous work (Doherty & Carroll, 2002a; Waite & Doherty, in press), which has been supported in part by the Alfred P. Sloan Center for Parents, Children, and Work at the University of Chicago; the Agricultural Experimentation Station, University of Minnesota; and the Family Studies Center, Brigham Young University.

2. We use the term "family professionals" as a broad and inclusive term referring to service professionals whose work impacts the well-being of families, both individually and collectively. This term includes, but is not limited to, professionals such as marriage and family therapists and other professional counselors, family life educators, family lawyers, family-practice physicians, family nurses and other health care professionals, ministers and clergy, and other professionals whose efforts influence families directly and indirectly.

3. About 3 percent of respondents to the *General Social Survey* between 1972 and 2000 rate their marriage as "not too happy," with 97 percent rating their marriage as "somewhat" or "very" happy.

Bibliography

Amato, P.R., & Sobolewski, J. (2001). The effects of divorce and marital discord on adult children's psychological well-being. *American Sociological Review, 66*, 900–921.

Angel, R., & Worobey, J.L. (1988). Single motherhood and children's health. *Journal of Health and Social Behavior, 29*, 38–52.

Baber, K.M., & Allen, K.R. (1992). *Women and families: Feminist reconstructions.* New York: Guilford Press.

Bachman, J.G., Wadsworth, K.N., O'Malley, P.M., Johnson, L.D., & Schulenberg, J.E. (1997). *Smoking, drinking, and drug use in young adulthood.* Mahwah, NJ: Lawrence Erlbaum.

Bartlett, R.L., & Callahan, C. (1984). Wage determination and marital status: Another look. *Industrial Relations, 23*, 90–96.

Becker, G.S. (1991). *A treatise on the family.* Cambridge, MA: Harvard University Press.

Bennett, T., Braveman, P., Egerter, S., & Kiely, J.L. (1994). Maternal marital status as a risk factor for infant mortality. *Family Planning Perspectives, 26*, 252–256, 271.

Browning, D. (2003). *Marriage and modernization.* Grand Rapids, MI: Eerdmans.

Browning, D.S., Miller-McLemore, B.J., Couture, P.D., Lyon, K.B., & Franklin, R.M. (1997). *From culture wars to common ground: Religion and the American family debate.* Louisville, KY: Westminster John Knox Press.

Burleson, B.B., & Denton, W.H. (1997). The relationship between communication skill and marital satisfaction: Some moderating effects. *The Journal of Marriage and the Family, 59,* 884–902.

Carroll, J.S., Badger, S., & Yang, C. (in press). The ability to negotiate or the ability to love? Evaluating the developmental domains of marital competence. *Journal of Family Issues.*

Carroll, J.S., Knapp, S.J., & Holman, T.B. (2005). Theorizing about marriage. In V. Bengston, A. Acock, K. Allen, P. Dilworth-Anderson, and D. Klein (Eds.), *Sourcebook of family theories and methods: An interactive approach* (pp. 263–288). Thousand Oaks, CA: Sage Publications.

Cere, D. (2000). *The experts story of courtship.* New York: Institute for American Values.

Cherlin, A.J. (1999). Going to extremes: Family structure, children's well-being, and social science. *Demography, 36,* 421–428.

Cherlin, A.J., Chase-Lansdale, L., & McRae, C. (1998). Effects of parental divorce on mental health throughout the life course. *American Sociological Review, 63,* 239–249.

Communitarian Network. (2000). *Responsive Communitarian platform.* Retrieved April 10, 2006, from http://www.gwu.edu/~ccps/platformtext.html

Daniel, K. (1995). The marriage premium. In M. Tommasi & K. Ierulli (Eds.), *The new economics of human behavior* (pp. 113–125). Cambridge: Cambridge University Press.

Doherty, W.J. (1995). *Soul searching: Why psychotherapy must promote moral responsibility.* New York: Basic Books.

Doherty, W.J. (2000). Family science and family citizenship: Toward a model of community partnership with families. *Family Relations, 49,* 319–325.

Doherty, W.J., & Anderson, J.R. (2004). Community marriage initiatives. *Family Relations, 53,* 425–432.

Doherty, W.J., & Beaton, J.M. (2000). Family therapists, community, and civic renewal. *Family Process, 39,* 149–161.

Doherty, W.J., & Carroll, J.S. (2002a). Health and the ethics of marital therapy and education. In J. Wall, D. Browning, W.J. Doherty, and S. Post (Eds.), *Marriage, health, and the professions: If marriage is good for you what does this mean for law, medicine, ministry, therapy, and business* (pp. 208–232). Grand Rapids, MI: William B. Eerdmans.

Doherty, W.J., & Carroll, J.S. (2002b). The families and democracy project. *Family Process, 41,* 579–589.

Dollahite, D.C., & Hawkins, A.J. (1998). A conceptual ethic of generative fathering. *Journal of Men's Studies, 7*(1), 109–32.

Elshtain, J.B., Enola, A., Etzioni, A., Glaston, W., Glendon, M., Minow, M., et al. (1992). *A Communitarian position paper on the family.* Retrieved April 10, 2006, from http://www.gwu.edu/~ccps/pop_fam.html

Fincham, F.D., & Beach, S.R. (1999). Conflict in marriage: Implications for working with couples. *Annual Review of Psychology, 50,* 47–77.

Fowers, B.J. (2000). *Beyond the myth of marital happiness.* San Francisco, CA: Jossey-Bass.

Gove, W.R., & Hughes, M. (1979). Possible causes of the apparent sex differences in physical health: An empirical investigation. *American Sociological Review, 44,* 126–146.

Gray, J.S. (1997). The fall in men's return to marriage: Declining productivity effects or changing selection. *Journal of Human Resources, 32,* 481–504.

Grossbard-Shechtman, S. (1993). *On the economics of marriage: A theory of marriage, labor and divorce.* Boulder, CO: Westview Press.

Hahn, B.A. (1993). Marital status and women's health: The effect of economic marital acquisitions. *Journal of Marriage and the Family, 55,* 495–504.

Hawkins, A.J., Carroll, J.S., Doherty, W.J., & Willoughby, B. (2004). A comprehensive framework for marriage education. *Family Relations, 53,* 547–558.

Hawkins, A.J., et al. (2001). Equal partnership and the sacred roles of mothers and fathers. In D.C. Dollahite (Ed.), *Strengthening our families: An in-depth look at the Proclamation on the Family* (pp. 63–82). Salt Lake City, UT: Bookcraft.

Horwitz, A.V., White, H.R., & Howell-White, S. (1996). Becoming married and mental health: A longitudinal study of a cohort of young adults. *Journal of Marriage and the Family, 58,* 895–907.

Kingsbury, N., & Scanzoni, J. (1993). Structure-functionalism. In P. Boss, W.J. Doherty, R. Rossa, W. Schumm, & S. Steinmetz (Eds.), *Sourcebook of family theories and methods: A contextual approach* (pp. 195–217). New York: Plenum.

Korenman, S., & Neumark, D. (1991). Does marriage really make men more productive? *Journal of Human Resources, 26,* 282–307.

Kotlikoff, L.J., & Spivak, A. (1981). The family as an incomplete annuities market. *Journal of Political Economy, 89,* 372–391.

L'Abate, L. (1997). *The self in the family: A classification of personality, criminality, and psychopathology.* New York: John Wiley & Sons.

Larzarus, A.A. (1981). Divorce counseling or marital therapy: A therapeutic option. *Journal of Marital and Family Therapy, 7,* 15–20.

Lillard, L.A., & Panis, C. (1996). Marital status and mortality: The role of health. *Demography, 33,* 313–327.

Lillard, L.A., & Waite, L.J. (1995). 'Til death do us part: Marital disruption and mortality. *American Journal of Sociology, 100,* 1131–1156.

Lupton, J., & Smith, J.P. (2003). Marriage, assets, and savings. In S. Grossbard-Shechtman (Ed.), *Marriage and the economy* (pp.129–152). Cambridge: Cambridge University Press.

Marks, N.F., & Lambert, J.D. (1998). Marital status continuity and change among young and midlife adults: Longitudinal effects on psychological well-being. *Journal of Family Issues, 19,* 652–686.

McLanahan, S., & Sandefur, G.D. (1994). *Growing up with a single parent: What hurts, what helps.* Cambridge, MA: Harvard University.

Miller-Tutzauer, C., Leonard, K.E., & Windle, M. (1991). Marriage and alcohol use: A longitudinal study of "maturing out." *Journal of Studies on Alcohol, 52,* 434–440.

Mirowksy, J., & Ross, C. (2003). *Social causes of psychological distress.* New York: Aldine De Gruyter.

Ooms, T. (1998). *Toward more perfect unions: Putting marriage on the public agenda.* Washington, DC: Family Impact Seminar.

Oswald, R.F., Blume, L.B., & Marks, S.R. (2005). Decentering heteronormativity: A model for family studies. In V. Bengston, A. Acock, K. Allen, P. Dilworth-Anderson, & D. Klein (Eds.), *Sourcebook of family theories and methods: An interactive approach* (pp. 143–165). Thousand Oaks, CA: Sage Publications.

Parke, M. (2003, May). *Are married parents really better for children? What research says about the effects of family structure on child well-being* (Policy Brief No. 3). Washington, DC: Center for Law and Social Policy.

Parker, D.A., Parker, E.S., Harford, T.C., & Farmer, G.C. (1987). Alcohol use and depression symptoms among employed men and women. *American Journal of Public Health, 77*, 704–707.

Parsons, T. (1965). The normal American family. In S. Farber, P. Mustacchi, & R. Wilson (Eds.), *Man and civilization: The family search for survival* (pp. 31–50). New York: McGraw-Hill.

Ross, C.E. (1995). Reconceptualizing marital status as a continuum of social attachment. *Journal of Marriage and the Family, 57*, 129–140.

Ross, C.E., Mirowksy, J., & Goldsteen, K. (1990). The impact of the family on health: Decade in review. *Journal of Marriage and the Family, 52*, 1059–1078.

Schnarch, D.M. (1991). *Constructing the sexual crucible: An integration of sexual and marital therapy.* New York: Norton.

Simon, R.W. (2002). Revisiting the relationship among gender, marital status, and mental health. *American Journal of Sociology, 107*, 1065–1096.

Smith, J.C., Mercy, J.A., & Conn, J.M. (1988). Marital status and the risk of suicide. *American Journal of Public Health, 78*, 78–80.

Stanley, S. (1998). *The heart of commitment.* Nashville, TN: Thomas Nelson.

Tucker, J.S., Friedman, H.S., Schwartz, J.E., & Criqui, M.H. (1997). Parental divorce: Effects on individual behavior and longevity. *Journal of Personality and Social Psychology, 73*, 381–391.

Umberson, D. (1987). Family status and health behaviors: Social control as a dimension of social integration. *Journal of Health and Social Behavior, 28*, 306–319.

Waite, L.J. (2000). *Cohabitation: A communitarian perspective.* Retrieved April 10, 2006, from http://www.gwu.edu/~ccps/Waite.html.

Waite, L.J., & Doherty, W.J. (2006). Marriage and responsible fatherhood: The social science case and thoughts about a theological case. In S.M. Tipton and J. Witte (Eds.), *Family Transformed: Religion, Values, and Society in American Life* (pp. 143–167). Washington DC: Georgetown University Press.

Waite, L.J., & Gallagher, M. (2000). *The case for marriage: Why married people are happier, healthier and better off financially.* New York: Doubleday.

Waite, L.J., & Hughes, M.E. (1999). At risk on the cusp of old age: Living arrangements and functional status among black, white, and hispanic adults. *Journal of Gerontology: Social Sciences, 54B*, S136–S144.

Waldfogel, J. (1997). The effect of children on women's wages. *American Sociological Review, 62*, 209–217.

Wall, J., & Miller-McLemore, B. (2002). Health, Christian marriage traditions, and the ethics of marital therapy. In J. Wall, D. Browning, W.J. Doherty, & S. Post (Eds.), *Marriage, health, and the professions: If marriage is good for you what does this mean for law, medicine, ministry, therapy, and business* (pp. 186–207). Grand Rapids, MI: William B. Eerdmans.

Wickrama, K.A.S., Lorenz, F.O., Conger, R.D., & Elder, G.H. (1997). Marital quality and physical illness: A latent growth curve analysis. *Journal of Marriage and the Family, 59,* 143–155.

Witte, J. (2002). The goods and goals of marriage: The health paradigm in historical perspective. In J. Wall, D. Browning, W.J. Doherty, & S. Post (Eds.), *Marriage, health, and the professions: If marriage is good for you what does this mean for law, medicine, ministry, therapy, and business* (pp. 49–89). Grand Rapids, MI: William B. Eerdmans.

3

Marriage in 21st Century Britain and Europe: Setting the Research Agenda

Samantha Callan (UK)
Sociologist and Senior Researcher, Care for the Family
Cardiff, UK

The main theme of this chapter is the state of the British and European research scene with regard to marriage *per se*. Social scientific research on the family has increasingly come to focus on family breakdown; for example, the incidence and process of divorce has received extensive treatment (Cummings and Davies 2002; Smart 2000; Wu and Penning 1997). There is also a growing body of work on nontraditional family forms, including cohabitation, lone parenting, and same-sex couples (Smart and Silva 1999; Prinz 1995; Simons 1996). Although leading social scientists predict that the early twenty-first century will continue "to be distinguished by greater family diversity, increasingly endorsed by formal legal codes" (Hantrais 2004:1), aspirations remain high for marriage. British surveys consistently report high scores (over 80 percent) for young people who wish to get married at some time in the future,[1] and an on-line survey conducted by a teen magazine this year found that 92 percent believed in marriage and 60 percent felt it was best for couples to marry before having children.[2] These aspirations coexist with declining marriage rates, high divorce rates, and a diversity of other family forms. The social context in which they are played out is highly ambivalent about marriage. In British national politics, for example, mixed messages are sent. A senior cabinet member recently said, "What's most important to people is their personal relationships; what makes most people happiest is a good marriage, a good family life,"[3] but when it comes to tangible measures for supporting the family, the British Labour government's efforts cluster around the core concern of reducing child poverty. However, although married couples seem to build more wealth on average than do single or cohabiting ones (Lupton & Smith 2002), married men earn more money than do single men with similar education and job histories (Gray & Vanderhart 2000), and divorce and unmarried childbearing increase poverty for both children and mothers (Smock 1999; McLanahan 2000), the explicit promotion of healthy marriage is considered to be a policy anathema.

Currently the majority view of politicians across the political spectrum in the United Kingdom is that policies have to reflect the undisputed diversity of family formations. This is similar to the position of the German government as stated by one representative who said that "we do not put up a model for the family, but orientate our policies towards what exists."[4] However, as Professor Linda Hantrais of the European Research Centre at Loughborough University states,

> Families, in the plural, do not form and develop in isolation from wider societal contexts. Rather, they are socially, economically, culturally and, it is argued, politically constructed by the environments within which they evolve, and where policies are formulated and implemented. Moreover, families are not simply passive recipients and beneficiaries of policy measures, they are also agents and actors in the policy process. Their behaviour, in terms of family formation, development and dissolution, and their attitudes concerning the legitimacy and acceptability of public policy can influence the decisions of politicians. (Hantrais 2004:2)

This does not support the premise stated by the German politician earlier that policy merely reflects demography; rather it describes more accurately the process of cocreation of policy between families and policy makers. However, we contend that this cocreative process is not always allowed to take place and that if it were there would be greater recognition of the importance of marriage at the policy level, given the facts that over half of the population of the United Kingdom are married[5] and 60 percent of households with dependent children are headed by a married couple. The enduring popularity of marriage, despite our high divorce rates (53 per hundred marriages, second highest in Europe behind Sweden),[6] is also evident in people's willingness to remarry (in 2000, remarriages accounted for two-fifths of all marriages in the United Kingdom).[7]

The pathologising imperative that drives much British research in the sociology of relationships and the family, and that focuses on their fragility, is, we contend, one reason why this cocreative process does not take place. However, sociology has always asked the taken-for-granted questions. In relation to family research, we need to understand why married couples continue to stay together in a high-divorce society, and what values seem to underpin marriage when other forms of living are also gaining social and legal acceptance. Professor Andrew Oswald[8] concluded recently that "Marriage causes a physiological benefit that enhances mental and physical well-being and helps to prolong life...exactly how marriage works its magic remains mysterious. It is important that a new generation of tests be designed to find the answer." The processes underlying his results, which support the longer tradition of work on marital status and health (which suggest a protective effect, especially for married men), require qualitative investigation and need to be put in the context of both the nature of married partnerships and wider social relationships and networks. Dr. Robin Gutteridge, a psychologist who specializes in marriage among older people, agrees that studies of marriage and marital quality may be informative about family and social well-being and that society benefits when strong and enduring marriages are created, thus justifying research into marriage as "marriage is still a little-understood relationship, we don't understand the mechanics of the relationship over time" (Gutteridge 2003), and there have been relatively few studies of the *changes* that have taken place in marriage. Returning to the issue of social policy, if the importance of marriage is to be factored into key national decisions regarding the funding and nature of programs intended to promote health and well-being, the policy-making process has to be informed by a substantial body of research on what contributes to healthy and enduring marriage.

Moreover, although the statistics indicate that marriage is still the partnership formation of choice, this is not reflected in media representations of the family, which rarely portray couples striving to make their marriages work in times of crisis. Theories of social ecology (Huston 2000) stress the importance of studying marriage from a macrosocial perspective. There is social (ecological) pressure on people to terminate their relationships prematurely or to avoid commitment, because of the perceived inevitability of dissolution.[9] This resonates with Bradbury, Fincham, and Beach's call for more large-scale longitudinal research that links marital processes with sociocultural contexts, for research that directly guides preventive, clinical, and policy-level interventions. They argue that there are two key themes which together represent a thorough understanding in marital satisfaction (Bradbury, Fincham, & Beach 2000). These are the interpersonal processes operating within marriage and the sociocultural ecologies and contexts within which marriages operate. Marriages are not contracted and enacted in an environment that is conducive to their longevity. As the sociologist Norman Denzin (2002) states,

> We inhabit a second-hand world, one already mediated by cinema, television and other apparatuses of the post-modern society. We have no direct access to this world; we experience and study only its representations...members of the post-modern world know themselves through the reflected images and narratives of cinema and television.

Well-disseminated research, which draws attention to the benefits of marriage, as well as to the kinds of behaviours that will contribute to high quality and longevity of relationships, is essential in the present climate.

The first and main part of this chapter focuses on British society and marriage research, but there are, we believe, implications from our experience for advocates of marriage across the wider European scene. It sketches out the most influential British research and the omissions that a research agenda with an emphasis on marriage should seek to fill. Some initial, though significant, steps have already been taken to make up what is lacking in the field of marriage research, and these also receive attention. The two UK national charities that I represent (Care for the Family and CARE) have sought to work collaboratively with prominent and respected academics in order to ensure that adequate funding is made available for marriage research and that dissemination is given an appropriate priority, so that it is brought to the attention of policy makers and the media, in order to redress the current situation in which marriage is unsupported in popular culture and the political environment.

Findings from the research projects that we have funded and helped to promote are discussed, as is the importance of engagement and collaboration with mainstream academic bodies. An articulation with these is vital if adequate attention is to be paid to findings by gatekeepers to public policy and popular culture. Areas for future development of this research agenda are also considered.

Finally, attention turns to research in the wider European context, which seems to be marked by a similar lack of research on marriage. Although differences between the many countries that make up the European Union will not be trivialized, it is our contention that a similar collaborative process may be necessary both in individual countries and at the level of the Commission itself in order to make explicit the benefits of marriage and long-term committed relationships.

British Research on Marriage since 1980

What follows is by no means an exclusive list of research projects and publications, but it sketches out some of the work that has proved to be most influential in the early part of the twenty-first century. Before going into detail, however, it is important to make explicit the ideological divide that has characterised the family studies community, but that may finally be breaking down to a certain extent. The observation from Dr. Jon Bernardes from the University of Wolverhampton[10] that "there does, in the UK, seem to be an entrenched divide between those who are pro-diversity and those who are pro-marriage" is well drawn in the following quotes:

> Diversity is not interpreted as a sign of decline or immorality. Rather, change is understood in relation to evolving employment patterns, shifting gender relations and increasing options in sexual orientation.... The family...is seen as transforming itself...to wider social trends and sometimes is seen as a source of change itself which prompts changes to occur in public policy and provision.

Moreover, however, the

> framing of how families should be is often juxtaposed with statistics on divorce and one-parent households...to produce a picture of the family in decline or as disintegrating, with a range of disastrous consequences for the rest of society. (Smart and Silva 1999:1)

When we first began to consider commissioning research on marriage, in 2001, this divide seemed to be firmly in place, but we and others have begun to notice a shift in the entrenchment, as conscious efforts have been made to work collaboratively across traditional boundaries. At the turn of the century, however, according to this typification, it would not be unreasonable to state that most recognised social scientists were firmly in the pro-diversity camp, for understandable reasons. To be "pro-marriage" meant to be dismissive of all other family forms as being somehow inferior to those headed by a married couple. Sociology and the other social science disciplines are suspicious of such normative prescriptions and are concerned with describing and explaining social phenomena rather than with considering how to engineer some form of desirable social world.[11] Rather than assuming that changing family forms and the rise of individualism are indicative of declining commitment and heightened selfishness, they are concerned to elucidate how values are still lived out in a social context in which the *institution* of marriage is less structurally established. Oxford academics Eekelaar and Maclean (forthcoming) state in this vein that "the moral basis which underpins people's personal relationships is complex and does not correspond in a simple way with formal, external, social categories" and refer extensively to Jane Lewis's recent research on marriage (see also Maclean & Eekelaar 2004).

Lewis (2003) contends that the advent of individualism "does not mean that there will be no consciousness of 'ought,' but it is no longer imposed but has to be negotiated." To discover more about such negotiation, she interviewed 17 married couples with children and 17 unmarried couples with children, aged between 27 and 50. In order to provide a generational perspective, 72 of their parents were also interviewed. Like most qualitative research, this was clearly not a "representative" sample of the general population, and was not intended to be, because one of the main objectives was to explore areas "likely to reveal the balance between attention to self, as opposed to attention to other and to the relationship," and the sample was designed to further that objective. However, some further questions (but not interviews) were posed to 777 people drawn from an Omnibus Survey by the Office for National Statistics, which *was* representative. Lewis describes the central issue as revolving around the idea of "commitment." The unmarried had tended to "drift" into long-term unmarried cohabitation. They had lived together for so long they saw little point in marrying. They saw their "commitment" as being "private" rather than "public." Half of the unmarried and one quarter of the married said they had no obligations to one another, or had not thought about them; but the rest saw obligation as coming from "within" and not externally imposed. "The crucial thing...was seen to be the existence of commitment rather than its manifestation. Given that...it is not surprising that most people in the sample also felt that it was proper to treat married and cohabiting parents the same." The picture is one of pragmatic compromise and, although Lewis herself does not emphasize the concept, a sense of the importance of mutual respect.

Jane Lewis pointed out that in the United Kingdom there had been only one major in-depth qualitative study of intact marital relationships in the last two decades of the century, which had been carried out by Janet Askham in 1984. Interestingly, even in 1984, Askham was lamenting the lack of systematic evidence of ordinary marriage, and her small-scale study of 20 couples from Aberdeen (Askham 1984) was intended to address this lack. She problematised the notion that marriage is an identity-validating, and identity-creating, relationship but also a stability-enhancing relationship, taking as her starting point the work of Berger and Kellner, which discussed the importance of identity and stability formation in marriage, but which did not adequately treat their different and conflicting natures. The conclusion from her research was that marriage is a relationship embodying a contradiction between identity and stability pursuits. In other words, both of these things are constantly going on inside marriage, but there will be times when the emphasis on one process will be to the detriment of the other. So in times of change (e.g., when one partner's career is really taking off), that individual's personal identity creation may be happening at a cost to stability in the relationship.

This paradox is a central part of marriage. In order to give us the certainty that the world and our own identity within it really are as we ourselves see them, we need the knowledge that other people see them in the same way. It is through interaction with other people that "validation" of the social world is carried out. Validation of one's own personal identity and place in the world can be carried out only through interaction with truly significant others (that is, those with whom we have an important or close relationship), in a continuing conversation. Marriage is therefore an identity-building relationship, but at the same time stability is part of the equation, because the relationship is grounded in norms and expectations—in other words, the relationship's *status quo*. For marriage to be a comfortable place, the status quo needs to be maintained; but for individuals to grow in their identity, this will occasionally involve a shift in the status quo that may be an uncomfortable experience for both partners. The wider social emphasis on self-development and fulfilment has shifted the dynamics in marriage towards marriage as an identity-building relationship, but the latter truly functions only when stability is seen as a high priority.

One of Askham's concluding comments is that social trends or change should be assessed in terms of their influence upon the behaviour of married couples in their search for identity and stability maintenance. For example, periods of economic growth may lead to longer working hours, an increase in the employment of married women and, therefore, an increase in the time spouses spend apart. Physical and, indeed, psychological separation threatens stability. At the same time, an increased emphasis on self-fulfilment and promotion of one's own identity will lead to an increase in divorce and a decline in marriage. Considering that this was written twenty years ago, such remarks seem to have been somewhat prescient.

Another important contribution to the research literature was the 1988 Mansfield and Collard study that looked at the ways in which marriage marked the beginning of adult life. However, although it was written less than twenty years ago, the pace of social change has been such that it, like Janet Finch's 1983 research on wives enhancing their husbands' employment prospects, reads more like a work of social history than contemporary sociology. This is recognized by the authors who are in the process of updating the work. More recent research on marriage has been carried out at Exeter University and is ongoing. Dr. Carole Burgoyne has received government funding to investigate the efficacy of marriage preparation courses in making marriages more stable, especially in the first few years of married life. Dr. Burgoyne (who specializes in economic and consumer psychology) is also studying couples' conceptions of commitment to marital relationships and the extent to which this may be reflected in the financial arrangements couples make in the first year of marriage. She has found that couples still aspire to permanence and this is bound up with their making a commitment and wanting to formalize or "seal" their relationship by making a public declaration of intent through marriage. Couples she studied described how this act enabled them to move on, develop, and explore their relationship. They reported that marriage in certain ways acted as a *constraint* on their lives. In common with participants in our own study described below, her sample found it hard to describe what commitment meant to them, but it was clear that a large majority expressed it most strongly in relation to the other person, whereas others described it more in the context of marriage's role in society. There continues to be, therefore, an appreciation of the importance of marriage as an institution as well as a relationship.

Parental values were important in the decision to marry: many couples wanted to wed because their parents were still together. When looking specifically at financial arrangements, the marital commitment seemed to come before, rather than at the same time as, a sense of financial partnership that is, for a significant period, in a state of transition. The merging of bank accounts, for example, is by no means automatic and often requires a catalyst beyond the act of getting married (such as the joint purchase of a house).

Recently published is the quantitative study commissioned by the British Government's Department of Work and Pensions and conducted by Alan Marsh and Jane Perry at the Policy Studies Institute (Marsh and Perry 2003). Although this is not an explicit study on marriage, but charts family change in the wider sense, it provides some interesting data on attitudes towards the permanence of marriage and other relationships and on breakup risks across different partnership formations. The authors addressed the debate about family structure by conducting a regression analysis to find out if socioeconomic factors alone were entirely responsible for family breakdown. After controlling for hardship and other factors, five characteristics or statuses were independently significant in predicting higher breakup risk: cohabiting couples, postdated couples (who married/cohabited after conceiving a child), ex-lone parent couples, male unemployment, and race.

However, although such studies challenge the assumption that marriages are longer lasting (and happier, healthier, and wealthier) because of selection effects (that is, people who get married are already happier, healthier, wealthier, and more disposed to work at a relationship), as a research-commissioning body we were disinclined to take part in what is now seen as a fruitless debate. In considering how to set a research agenda that would recognise the continuing value of marriage for social and individual well-being, we decided it would be counterproductive (and unrepresentative of the full gamut of our concerns as organisations that support families) to adopt an explicitly pro-marriage position. The debate on marriage versus cohabitation has become markedly sterile and unproductive in the United Kingdom at this time. As there are significant differences between mutual and contingent commitments in cohabiting relationships (the former works in a very similar way to an idealised marital commitment, whereas there is in the latter no presumption that the relationship will last), it is inaccurate to treat *all* cohabitation as essentially short-lived [although Marsh and Perry (2003:141) found that these relationships are characterised by far higher fragility than marital ones].

The charities I represent are concerned with the quality of relationships and the bolstering of commitment within families. Our services are used by cohabitees, and some are specifically targeted to assist lone parents although we are unapologetic about our belief that *healthy* marriage provides the best foundation for the family. We were, therefore, concerned to fund and promote research that would emphasise the benefits which accrue to marriage *per se* without doing so in a context that was explicitly antagonistic to the practice of cohabitation. Research that is respected by gatekeepers to policy and popular culture should not be ideologically aligned in its design or intent, and we were at every stage concerned to produce work of unimpeachable integrity. Our intention was to bridge this unfruitful divide between the pro-marriage and pro-diversity camps, to build links with academics and departments who were, in fact, *genuinely* pro-diversity: in other words, with researchers who were interested in marriage as well as in other modes of partnership formation.

Moreover, we recognise the changing status and meanings of contemporary marriage and concur with writers who, like Askham (1995), suggest that marriage will more effectively be studied within the postmodernist perspective. This framework acknowledges diversity *within* marriage and emphasises the development of self over the maintenance of social and institutional structures. To reiterate, we did not wish to pursue an explicitly "pro-marriage" research agenda that does not concern itself with the richness of diversity.

Commissioning Positive Research on Marriage

We therefore approached two highly respected academic departments in the United Kingdom and commissioned research on the nature of marriage in the twenty-first century. The first project was an exploratory study carried out by the Centre for Research in Social Policy (CRSP) at Loughborough University, which adopted a focus group methodology. It collected the views of married people about intramarital behavior and attitudes that might contribute to the stability and duration of marriages in the present day. The aim of the research was to contribute to "filling the gaps" in our knowledge of how marriages are, and have been, made to work and to last. Participants were typically in their first marriage and had been married for different lengths of time (between five and over fifty years), and this allowed researchers to explore and compare differences in attitudes towards marriages, the effects of time-varying social and cultural influences, and changing patterns of behavior inside marriage. They also came from households with varying incomes, to reflect potentially different levels of need, financial dependence between partners, and different cultural values, which might have affected their marriages and their perceptions of marriage. (See Table 3.1 below.)

Participants felt that being married was an important part of their life and identity, but also that the present generation, and society in general, did not value marriage to the same extent as they did. Marriage was perceived as an act of great symbolic importance and a public statement of commitment. The study also found that there is still a strong link between parenting and marriage, especially for the women in the sample.[12] They considered that marriage constituted an element of stability, that it provided a concrete sense of identity for their children, and that sharing one surname contributed to their sense that the family was one unit.

> Yes, I'm sure there are a lot of very successful people co-habiting and bringing up very well-balanced kids. But at the end of the day there's the open door, it's there for people to drift in and out very easily. Whereas if you've actually gone through the proper process, I don't know how to phrase it really, of signing, marriage vows etc., does mean that you have to think more carefully and have to go through more things to get out of it. So hopefully, it would be more secure for the children, etc., rather than being able to come and go freely with one and another.
>
> (Woman, medium/high income group, married for sixteen years)

Moreover, the values of their own parents were very evident all the way through the sample, although it was clear that the older generation was also learning from their married sons and daughters. Women described how their

Table 3.1   Focus Group Composition (CRSP 482 Study: Marriage in the Twenty-first Century)

| | Income Group | | Length of Marriage | | |
Gender	Low Income Group	Medium/ High Income	5–10 yrs	10–30 yrs	More than 30 yrs
Male	14	18	6	18	8
Female	13	15	4	14	10
Total	27	33	10	32	18

daughters had shown them "how not to be a doormat," and they recognised that younger couples increasingly shared responsibilities and roles were more blurred than in the past. Future research might therefore study, in more depth, how "modern" norms and values affect older relationships and how modern values can be, and are, used to stabilise (or, indeed, undermine) these relationships. "Medium-age" relationships, for whom dealing with the break between traditional and modern values may be most problematic, should be included in this. The researchers also recommended studies that compare the role and understanding of changing social rules among couples whose marriage ends in separation or divorce. Men and women participants often gave very different accounts of their relationships or their perceptions of marriage as an institution. Women appeared to display a more inward-looking, marriage-focused perspective, whereas men's perceptions appeared more strongly oriented towards events or behaviors external to a marriage. Women spoke openly of manipulating their husbands' behavior and employing strategies to achieve their personal objectives; men did not, or much less so. Future research might investigate and compare the use of symbolic as well as verbal communication strategies between husbands and wives, their awareness of the partner's use of such strategies and their own responses. It might ask whether these strategies really work as intended or whether their effectiveness is random or, indeed, imagined.

People struggled to describe commitment, and there were interesting intergenerational differences in what commitment meant for couples. Older participants stressed the more outward and public commitment, the institutional aspect of marriage, whilst those who were still in the first ten years or so of marriage emphasised the personal, relational dimensions of commitment. Despite differing emphases, however, both public and private commitment were considered to be important by all in the sample, so it would be wrong to infer a sharp dichotomy between private, relational commitment and public, institutional commitment on the basis of age. Another intergenerational difference was noted in the area of expectations. Most participants expressed the view that both men and women had higher *material* expectations at the beginning of married life than those married between twenty and thirty years ago. This, it was felt, posed an added strain on relationships. Some younger participants, from both income group categories, felt that social expectations had risen, as had the cost of living, and older participants went so far as to say that their children's generation "wanted to have everything now"; their expectations were too high.

Participants regarded the ability and willingness to communicate or "talk through problems" to resolve outstanding issues or arguments as vitally important to their marriages. Some of the most problematic periods in marriages that participants recalled were having and bringing up children, coping with redundancy, illness, death, or retirement, and becoming stepparents. However, besides such significant and far-reaching events, there were many day-to-day issues or potential disputes whose resolution required effective communication. Marriage in our study had survived despite intermittent disagreement, conflict, or disputes; and many participants had employed threats and manipulations to achieve or enforce settlements. From a more positive angle, participants stressed the importance of *both* partners in a marriage wishing to maintain the relationship for such strategies to be successful. Future research might explore the validity of this assertion and, in particular, the nature and stability of mutual commitment in situations of "marital stress."[13]

Finally, marriage in the twenty-first century was perceived to be changing mainly because of increased opportunities and expectations. The rigid norms that structured society thirty or forty years ago and constrained choice and opportunity, in particular for women, had broken down. This has resulted in more fluid roles for both men and women within the home and has brought about new forms of conflict, requiring patience, tolerance, and negotiation, if marriages are to survive. Moreover, group participants repeatedly emphasised the changing nature of their own relationships, of their stresses and harmonies, and of the means of negotiation and communication that are employed to make relationships workable. The researchers concluded that more detail is necessary to understand fully the interactions between, and responses of, couples/partners to these changes, including, as suggested by more than one participant, the role of developing shared future goals. In particular, the use of "give and take" strategies over time would benefit from more research.

This elaboration and "testing" of marriage negotiations and strategies would require a different research setting, most notably a one-to-one interview (or couple-interviewer) situation. The second piece of research that we have funded (jointly with the British government's Economic and Social Research Council) will take up this recommendation. A doctoral student based at the Centre for Research in Families and Relationships at Edinburgh University will take as his research focus the everyday practices, meanings, and values embedded in partnership maintenance and view these in the context of both the nature of married partnerships and wider social relationships and networks. In order to examine meanings and practices, multiple, qualitative, in-depth interviews will be the main research method. Each couple will be interviewed separately and jointly, resulting in three interviews within each couple unit over a six-month period. This will enable the different perspectives of men and women and changes over time to be elicited. The interviews themselves will have a retrospective, current, and future component. This will help to generate narratives embedded in the history of the partnership, locate values and meanings in the context of everyday practices, and consider future aspirations. By cofunding this PhD, we have made it possible for much-needed primary research into marriage *per se* to be conducted (although it will be a strength of this research design that a control group of cohabitees will also be included).

Collaborating with research centres and other family and relationship organisations to produce and disseminate research has been, and will continue to be, essential if we are to identify key aspects of marriages that remain intact over time and the factors, behaviours, and attitudes that engender and sustain marriage as a long-term committed relationship. Also, there is no doubting the respect that Care for the Family especially commands as a service provider. Bodies like the National Family and Parenting Institute and this research centre at Edinburgh University acknowledge that we are "at the coalface" with families, in the community and putting tools in people's hands to equip them to face the challenges of their family life, whatever shape or size that family comes in. This year we were able to announce that a quarter of a million people, from a very wide range of social backgrounds and family contexts, had attended a Care for the Family event.

Identifying and Disseminating "Positive" Marriage Research

As our research did not explicitly privilege marriage over cohabitation, we were able to cohost an influential dissemination event with the two leading family organisations in the United Kingdom, both of which receive substantial amounts of government funding and are highly regarded by the research and policy communities. We share with them the concern to strengthen all family relationships, and the event went under the rubric of supporting couples for the long term. Its aim was to broaden the focus of recent policy debate from parenting and the parent-child relationship by disseminating recent research findings on marriage and long-term relationships, examining the well-being of couple relationships, and debating implications for policy on family support. The research centres and family services organizations with whom we work were unanimous in their support for research that focuses on the nature of the committed couple relationship, acknowledging as they did the paucity of recent British research in this area and the need to redress an excessive emphasis on parenting at the policy level. This event undoubtedly raised the profile of this issue by bringing to the fore several pieces of new research, two of which I will discuss briefly here. They have a high degree of salience for the overarching concern of this chapter, which is that positive rather than pathologically driven research is carried out.

Dr. Janet Reibstein's (2006) work on couples with "happy" and long-term relationships is explicitly in the tradition of positive psychology established by Martin Seligman and Mihaly Csikszentmihalyi (Seligman 1990; Csikszentmihalyi 1990). The latter's work is especially influential in Reibstein's approach as she focuses on what can be learned from successful couples' pasts to move them and others forward toward the future. The strengths that have been demonstrated in the past and the lessons learned from things that have not worked are used in order to make progress in the future. (She carried out eighteen intensive one- to two-day-long interviews with U.S. and U.K. couples and analysed more than ninety relationship "stories" written specifically for the study.) Csikszentmihalyi's studies on "successful" people identified that they could be described as having "autotelic" personalities. They found ways to get engaged in their work, identified the levers within their situation, and used them creatively to become *engaged* in work and to fit their skills to its demands. This results in a state of what he called "optimal functioning" or "flow." Reibstein found that characteristics of those with autotelic personalities and contributors to flow or optimal experiences are strongly indicated in what she found in the stories of couples from her study, confirming some central tenets of positive psychology. This was not unsurprising as she had in her sample selected couples marked by "happiness," a target goal of positive psychology. However, in substantiation, she found accounts that suggest, as Csikszentmihalyi's research did in the field of work, that people who achieve the flow or optimal experience of relationship are people with qualities suggested by his autotelic personalities. Such people proactively look for the *fit* between their aspirations and their circumstances, instead of concentrating on the *lack*. Such partners are therefore attuned and responsive to each other, accepting of each other's influence, and this becomes evident when relationship stories are recounted. The focus of happy and successful couples' stories is positive; the communication that takes place within the marriage results in "his" and "hers" stories that match, even when told separately. Couples consciously and unconsciously seek to dovetail their stories together. She found that this contrasted with couples who were not "open" to each other and who were unwilling to consider alternative versions of events, the partner's perspective, for example. Such openness could be a way in which a partner's uncongenial actions and attitudes became explicable to the discontented other, and through adopting an empathic stance, a story might be reconstructed in a way that accentuated the positives rather than being perceived as one more instance of relational dysfunction or a lack of harmony.

Methodologically, this approach itself finds a fit with the current trend in psychological therapy, which seeks to help people create stories that recast events in an alternative and positive light or that, at the very least, suggest that another version is possible and plausible. She describes how unhappy people are limited by an orientation towards the present, whereas those with autotelic personalities are concerned with the past, the present, and the future. They seek to learn from the past in order to be better equipped for the future, so setbacks, difficulties, and relational "misfires" are not the focus; instead, emphasis is placed on the ways in which these difficulties prepare for and positively influence the future.

Although she and others (Burgess 1981) would concur that the oldest tradition in the systematic analysis of marriage and the family is sociological, the approach of positive psychology parallels the positive approach to marriage research that we are advocating. It is also the underlying motif to Dr. Robin Gutteridge's (2003) work, which was also presented at the dissemination seminar. She, like others (Askham, 1995; Schwartz & Olds, 2000; Bachand &

Caron, 2001), had concluded that marriage is an underresearched and little-understood relationship with relevance to social and individual well-being and found very little British research that took as its focus the positive aspects of marriage and the ways in which long-standing couples worked to maintain a healthy and positive image of each other, even at the worst times in the relationship. Her research asked how long-lasting marriages evolve over time, how older people in long-lasting marriages themselves evaluate their marriage, how couples manage changing needs and expectations in their long-lasting marriage, and how couples make their relationship work over time. She conducted a retrospective, modified longitudinal study, using biographical interviews with the couple jointly and individually, which afforded her the opportunity to access "his," "hers," and "our" perspectives on the marital relationship as it changed over time.

She concluded that factors such as intimacy and power are negotiated, constructed, and continuously reappraised by the couple over time (which is consistent with sociocognitive perspectives, but acknowledges that there is so far little other empirical work against which to challenge her own). Overall, this research strongly suggests that individuals actively use their marriage to construct and maintain a sense of personal meaning, identity, and security over time and within a changing social context. She notes that the experiences of the marriage are different for men and women, in terms of divisions of labor, authority, and power. However, there was little evidence to suggest that spouses held different views about the centrality of the marital relationship, the importance of jointly achieved marital satisfaction, or the meaning attached to shared intimacy. There were indications that men had taken more time to recognise the scope and importance of intimacy in a long-lasting relationship. She maintains that marital relationships change and evolve over time, and three blended phases of development were identified, each with key tasks and priorities. In each phase, of testing, building, and maturing, successful achievement of key tasks helped ease the transition towards the next phase. Individuals enter marriage separately, each with idealised expectations. During the first phase of testing, couples jointly construct an image of their marriage, which serves as a benchmark for the future. Through the remaining phases of their shared and individual lives, couples attempt to realise their jointly constructed image by actively managing fluctuations above and below this baseline. As the marriage evolves, the couple seek to harmonise different sets of identity needs and manage tensions arising by applying adjustment mechanisms to maintain expected marital satisfaction. As the tasks of each phase and a mature, integrated blend of identities are achieved, the relationship becomes a resource to facilitate coping, as well as an entity requiring investment. In the construction and maintenance of marital satisfaction over time, past, present, and future were inextricably linked in a continuum of development. Over two decades ago, Burgess (1981:179) observed that "we tend to have an idealised conception of marriage and the family. It is often portrayed as a romantic and intimate oasis. In reality, it is often an intimate battleground....Mutual investment in one another generates its own risks and pains." Gutteridge makes the same point, describing "successful" (in terms of its quality and length of duration) married life as often markedly "unromantic, pragmatic and negotiated." It was clear across the sample that "marriage is hard work but it is worth it if this coexists with the spark, the joy...."[14] As with Reibstein's work, Gutteridge is concerned that one outcome of her research is that skills are disseminated which enable people to work at their marriages in full knowledge that "hard work" may be necessary but ultimately fruitful. The next stage of her research will consist of her testing her theories with couples who have experienced relationship dissolution to see what factors were present or absent.

This section has considered some of the research presented at a seminar we cohosted, which was intended to cast marriage and long-term committed relationships in a positive light, with a view to strengthening couples for the long term. The success of the event can be measured in terms of the positive media interest it generated, as well as in the attendance of key figures from the government and other policy-making bodies. Substantively, it was clear that further empirical work must be carried out in disciplines such as sociology, psychology, and social psychology, which will examine the characteristic processes of intact marriages (and families) in a context in which, as Janet Askham (1995:10) maintains,

> traditional values and norms are breaking down, leaving individuals to use the relationship to construct and maintain their own sense of identity and security. This change has been described as one from marriage as an institution to marriage as a relationship. A post-modern sociology must therefore increasingly be concerned with how a sense of personal meaning, identity and security are developed...and with...relationships within the private sphere. Because of their central position in post-modern society *such relationships should not be peripheral but should be part of mainstream study* (emphasis added).

As a funding organisation, we turn our attention to the interplay between fathering and partnering, looking at possible links between paternal involvement, attitudes towards marriage and fathers' roles, and marital duration. This could be undertaken partly by using quantitative methods, such as analysing material that has already been collected and lies in the data sets of existing and highly reputable cohort studies. We are also interested in building on existing research on the impact of atypical working hours on family life. Nearly 60 percent of working families fall within this category, which was the subject of an extensive and well-cited study carried out by the UK's National Centre for Social Research. Shift or serial parenting is one response to the labour market's requirement for 24/7 working, with dual-earner parents sharing child care. Many are effectively parenting in shifts, returning from work and relieving the other partner of child care responsibilities so that he or she can in turn perform paid work (mainly) outside the home. The partnering relationship of these parents is being conducted in a situation of time famine, and we are interested in how marriage has adapted to such constraints in an era marked by the high expectations surrounding relationship quality.

European Research on Marriage

The balance of this chapter is concerned with the wider European research scene with regard to marriage. In many ways this can be only a rough outline as, in common with many British and Anglo-Saxon researchers, I do not consider myself to be at the "heart of Europe" and fully apprised of the trends in this research domain. In fact, Professor Linda Hantrais suggests a "disconnect" between the UK and European research in many areas,[15] as academics and politicians prefer to look to the Anglo-Saxon world, rather than to Europe, for comparisons. Although many would argue that Britain is a great deal more similar to European social democracies than to the liberal democracies of the United States and Canada, the stereotype of our commonality with these two countries remains fairly unchallenged. This assessment of a disconnect was borne out in my consideration of the literature on studies of marriage and the family. The key journal, the *Journal for Marriage and the Family* (published in the United States by the National Council on Family Relations) is not considered by academics to shed light on the European scene. Very occasionally, a Dutch paper is included (and the designation of LAT, or living apart together, relationship originated in this country and is gaining currency in Britain and elsewhere).[16] This is not necessarily because of a lack of submissions from European researchers, but perhaps, again, a result of an implicit disjuncture between Anglo-Saxon and other geographically bounded research communities, which is surely anachronistic in a global Internet age. I looked at the decadal reviews of the literature published in the November 2000 issue of the journal, and the isolated examples of referenced articles that were not from the United States, the United Kingdom, Canada, or Australia are included in the appendix. In Britain, we are very familiar with publications and researchers from bodies such as the Australian Institute for Family Studies, and, again, systematic reviews of the literature on marriage such as that written by Robyn Parker (2002) make no reference to European research. Obviously, this might also indicate a lack of European work on marriage, and this is something I will return to later.

A Brief Discussion of European Demography

First, however, it is important to point out the heterogeneity of Europe. There are 46 countries in Europe,[17] so this is to be expected. However, there are key similarities and regional patterns that I will sketch out very briefly here. In terms of similarities, Billari (2004) characterises the unifying direction with the key word of *postponement.* In general, with some exceptions, key demographic events, and more specifically events leading to the formation of new households and families, have been postponed in the lives of women and men. In the new millennium, leaving the parental home, forming a new union, getting married, and becoming a parent are experienced on average later than before. Although there is a convergence in terms of postponing key demographic transitions in early adulthood, some countries (mostly in Southern Europe) have been characterized by extreme levels of postponement, experiencing the so-called *latest-late* pattern of transition to adulthood. Some of the events, like the transition to motherhood, have been postponed to ages that have not been observed in the past. Within reproductive ages, Billari also states that the general trend towards postponement is accompanied by an increasing *destandardisation* of life courses, with varying speed.

Berthoud and Iacovou (2002) describe the strong regional patterns that are evident in the study of living arrangements. These do not correspond precisely to a "regional" classification, so they used a hybrid system to define three groups of countries in which the Netherlands is attached to its Scandinavian neighbors because it shares their social democratic policy regime, and Ireland is attached to the southern group of countries because it shares their Catholicism. This produces the following three groups, which together, these authors claim, provide an excellent typology for many (though not all) aspects of family formation.

> *Nordic* Finland; Sweden; Denmark; the Netherlands
> *North/Central* UK; Belgium; Luxembourg; France; Germany; Austria
> *Southern/Catholic* Ireland; Portugal; Spain; Italy; Greece

There are two main sources of between-country variation in partnerships. First, the speed with which young people move into partnerships varies by country, in a way that does not necessarily match the rate at which they leave home. Second, the type of partnership varies: formal marriage is the norm in some parts of Europe, and nonmarital cohabitation is more common in others. Certain features of partnership formation are common to all countries. The proportion of people living in partnerships is virtually zero below the age of eighteen in all countries, and this proportion rises rapidly through the twenties. The increase begins earliest (around age eighteen) in the "Nordic" countries and latest (around age twenty-two) in the "southern/Catholic" countries. The increase in the proportion living with partners trails off around age thirty in the Nordic countries and around age thirty-five in the southern/Catholic countries. In all countries, the proportion of individuals living in partnerships remains essentially stable between ages thirty-five and sixty-five. From a comparative perspective, most of the "action" as far as partnerships are concerned is in the twenty through thirty-five age group. This is the time when partnership status is changing most rapidly, and it is also the time when there are the widest differences between countries. At age twenty-five, only 8 percent of Italian men are in partnerships, while 48 percent of Finnish men are in partnerships: thus, Finnish men are six times more likely to be living in a partnership at age twenty-five than Italian men. These huge differences are not seen at any other age.

In all countries, nonmarital cohabitation is about three times more common among people in their twenties than among those in their thirties, and nearly twice as common in the thirties as in the forties. Among women in their twenties who live with a partner, the proportion who are cohabiting rather than formally married is well under 10 percent in southern/Catholic countries; between 20 percent and 50 percent in Austria, Germany, France, Belgium, and the United Kingdom; and between 60 percent and 75 percent in the Nordic countries. Among women in their forties, the range is much narrower: under 1 percent in Greece and Italy, and over 10 percent only in Denmark, Finland, and Sweden. Several factors are responsible for this marked difference between the generations. First, there is a cohort effect: cohabitation has become more common over the past half-century, and men and women now in middle age and beyond would have been very unlikely to cohabit even when they were in their twenties. Second, there is an age effect, with younger people preferring to live in informal cohabitations and moving later towards formal marriage. The age effect is linked to the birth of children, since couples with children are more likely to be married: this is particularly true in the Netherlands, where cohabitation is extremely common among childless couples, but very uncommon among couples with children—as uncommon as it is in southern countries.

The fragility of cohabitation across Europe is noted by scholars such as Kiernan who states that cross-nationally, children born within marriage are less likely to see their parents separate than those born into a cohabiting union (Kiernan 1999, 2002). Data collected from the Danish National Institute of Social Research has shown that the children of cohabiting parents have a risk of their family being dissolved that is twice as high as in the "traditional family."[18] However, Kiernan also states that if their parents subsequently married, the story is more nuanced. In Sweden, Norway, Austria and West Germany, the chances of children experiencing the breakup of their parents' marriage by a fifth birthday were similar whether parents were married or had cohabited and subsequently married. However, in France and Switzerland, and particularly in Great Britain, children born into marital unions were more likely to see their parents remain together until the child's fifth birthday than those children born into a cohabiting union that converted into a marriage.[19] (See Figure 3.1.)

Other ways of presenting the wider European picture should be noted. Biggart et al. (2002) distinguish different family models in Europe according to the level of deinstitutionalisation of the traditional concept of family. Accordingly, one can differentiate between traditional or conventional family patterns and nonconventional or postnuclear family patterns, representing opposite extremes on a continuum. As expected, nonconventional family formations tend to be concentrated in Northern Europe, while the traditional family model remains very much to the fore in Southern Europe and Ireland. Intermediate arrangements are typically associated with Continental Europe (France, Germany, the Netherlands, and Belgium).

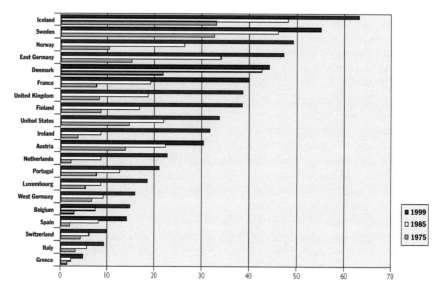

Figure 3.1   Percentage of births outside of marriage.

Source: One Plus One, *The Bulletin,* vol. 6, no. 4 (October 2002).

Implications for European Family Policy

Biggart et al. (2002) go on to state that when looking at family policies in the European Union, according to Bahle et al. (1998), a broad definition of family policy includes all policy measures directed at the family as a social group and at individuals in their roles as family members. This involves explicit as well as implicit family measures. Explicit family measures indicate that the family has been the subject of political debates and that there are explicit goals relating to it. Implicit family policies lack explicit goals concerning families. Instead, they deal with other issues, which have an indirect impact on families. Usually, explicit family policies constitute only a small part of government policies relating to the family. Thus family policy represents a cross-sectional rather than a clear-cut social policy area (Bahle & Maucher, 1998). Family policy concepts differ among the various countries of the European Union due to their divergent social values, aims, and normative concepts. In each member state, family policy has followed different paths. In France, Belgium, and Luxembourg, family policy was institutionalised before the Second World War, while the United Kingdom and the Netherlands have never had explicit family policies. In Italy and Germany, family policies were introduced by the fascist and national socialist regimes as "population" policies during the 1930s and 1940s. Subsequently, in both countries, family politics declined immediately after the War and were only hesitantly built up again subsequently. In Scandinavia, some family-related measures were introduced during the 1930s and 1940s, where the emphasis was placed upon family-related issues (e.g., provision for women and children) rather than on explicit family measures. Spain resembled Italy, in that family policy lost its favored position in the welfare state after the 1950s (Bahle et al., 1998). Today, family provision across the European Union remains highly heterogeneous, and no attempt has been made to coordinate the various concepts and measures at the European level. Moreover, the European Union does not have the necessary competencies to intervene in the field of family; i.e., it lacks the legal basis to design and implement family policies at the European level. However, interest in the field of family policies has increased in past decades as a result of changing family structures and their implications for social policies. Therefore, initiatives to analyse and monitor family policies have been started at the national as well as at the European level. At the European level, the institution in charge of monitoring family and family-related measures is the European Observatory on the Social Situation, Demography and Family. The Observatory was established by the European Commission in 1989 and has, since 1998, been coordinated by the Austrian Institute for Family Studies in Vienna.

Attitudes Towards Marriage and the Family

When looking at attitudes towards marriage and the family, it is clear that, although there is again variation between and within countries, the family and marriage itself are highly valued across the continent. The legitimacy of marriage as a social institution is recognised by large majorities within each country. Anthony Abela from the IPROSEC research project[20] found that the greatest support for the institution of marriage is recorded in Malta, closely followed by post-communist EU candidate countries, the other neighbouring Mediterranean countries, and Sweden (Abela 2003). Slightly less support is found in EU continental countries, Ireland, and the United Kingdom. With the exception of Sweden, most respondents from the other European countries think that a long-term relationship is important for a happy life and that children need both parents to grow up happily. Abela concludes that "the values of marriage and the family, or alternative long-lasting stable family-type relationships, thus serve as a foundation for solidarity and conviviality among people with different lifestyles in Europe." (See Table 3.2.)

Implications for a Marriage-Oriented Research Agenda

Returning again to the subject of research, if marriage is still considered to be a valid institution and is the basis for statistically more durable unions, it might be expected to be the subject of numerous research projects across the continent. After an initial trawl of the literature and discussions with leading European researchers, I have concluded that the paucity of research into intact marriage which characterises the United Kingdom is writ large in Europe as a whole. The European Sociological Association's database

Table 3.2 Marriage and Family Relations in IPROSEC Countries, in percent

EU accession wave:	1 Continental	2 British Isles	3 Mediterranean	4 Nordic	5a Eastern	5b Malta	Total IPROSEC 11EC
Marriage valid institution	77	76	85	80	86	93	80
Long-term relationship to be happy	63	35	70	41	77	64	60
Children need both parents	88	64	89	56	95	92	82
Immediate family							
Concerned about	89	75	94	97	93	96	88
Willing to help	95	93	96	98	93	99	94
Parent-child relationships							
Do utmost for children	68	78	75	67	65	92	70
No sacrifice of well-being	21	13	15	22	21	5	18
Neither	11	9	10	10	14	3	11
Child-parent relationships							
Always love parents	69	71	78	44	81	92	72
Parents have to earn respect	31	29	22	56	19	8	28

Source: Abela 2003.

of research contains very few references to marriage apart from a few single-nation studies on Portugal and Russia, and on births outside marriage. Similarly, when looking through the papers presented at the annual meetings of the International Sociological Association, it is clear that marriage *per se* is very rarely the subject of research in Europe, and where it is the focus of interest is in the decreasing popularity of marriage. (Relevant European papers presented in this forum over the last three years are listed in the Appendix, alongside a limited collection of other European papers and sources.)

Research commissioning bodies such as the European Commission's Directorate General for Research and the Directorate General for Employment and Social Affairs are not directly interested in relationships in families. Their policy reviews of research funded under the Framework programs reveal an emphasis on changing family structures, demographic change, and policy responses to these, as well as on poverty. Again, research appears to be focussed on dissolution and its consequences, rather than on marriage's beneficial effects and the way factors present in intact marriages can be identified and disseminated in order to tackle the causes of family breakdown. As the European Commission funds such a wide variety of social programs, the lack of this kind of research, which has an underlying preventative rationale, is an omission in need of attention. This has to be set in the context of the relative infancy of family research in many EU countries. Again, there is wide variation across the continent in the level of recognition afforded to "family studies" by academic elites. Countries such as Italy, Belgium, Holland, and Norway all have family studies modules in universities, and its status as an academic discipline is unquestioned. However, even in these countries (with the exception of Holland) overviews of research are characterised by a lack of attention to marriage.[21]

Finally, discerning the trends in marriage and relationship research across Europe is not an easy task, in the absence of systematic reviews and meta-analyses on these subjects. Professor Michael Wagner at the University of Cologne is in the process of writing a meta-analysis of European divorce research, but to his knowledge no meta-analyses of marriage or divorce research that really include European studies currently exist.

The generation of a significant body of European research on intact marriage would seem to be a priority. It is possible that some of the lessons we have learned in setting the research agenda in the British context might be transferable to the wider European scene, notwithstanding the significant differences that exist between the many different countries. The ideological divide between those who are "pro-marriage' and those who are "pro-diversity," which characterised Britain until fairly recently, may not pertain to the same extent across the Continent. Indeed, countries like Belgium have long-standing family councils that represent the many and often divergent interests of families. These councils are coalitions of different interest groups where the British "divide" is not apparent. A different approach may be necessary in the context of political systems, which are predicated on a far higher degree of cooperation than the more confrontational British order. However, the common starting point in all countries would surely be to conduct an initial and thorough exploration of the existing literature on marriage and family research in order to gain a more rigorous understanding of the predispositions of funders and researchers in the field. In each country or region there may be different intellectual disciplines that are better suited to conducting research in this field. As stated earlier, although the oldest tradition in the systematic analysis of marriage and the family is sociological, this chapter has made it clear that there are important contemporary British studies which are psychological in approach. In other countries, the literature of social psychology might reveal a greater interest in marriage. Systematic reviews and meta-analyses of marriage and family research must be carried out in such a way that the contributions and subtle differences of approach of different disciplines are recognised.

Conclusion

This chapter has focused on the state of the British and European research scene with regard to marriage *per se*. It is posited that the lack of research which was recently identified in Britain, and which we and others are attempting to address, also pertains in the wider research community of Europe. A research agenda that emphasises important trends such as the rise in cohabitation, divorce, and extramarital childbearing does not, however, make explicit at a policy level the continuing salience of marriage for the majority of individuals. Without overprivileging marriage as a topic for research (or as a living arrangement), we would argue that the currently underresearched status of marriage is preventing the institution and relationship from being understood in all its richness and subtlety. Research on marriage may indicate factors that equip partners to forge and maintain committed and durable relationships and that provide a secure context for childbearing. Identifying and testing such factors are important research objectives in postindustrial societies that are looking for anchor points in social relations in the context of constant change. We recommend that a program of research be designed that draws on existing work both across disciplines and across geographical research communities, forging a greater degree of connection between the Anglo-Saxon and European traditions. Comparative and within-country studies are both required, and research areas suggested earlier in this chapter for the British scene are offered as potential starting points to organizations and researchers who are, in common with ourselves, concerned with understanding the role marriage plays in social well-being at the microlevel of the individual family, as well as at the macrolevel of national society.

Presented at the European Regional Dialogue
Geneva, Switzerland, August 2004.

Endnotes

1. MORI Polls and Surveys (1999), *Family and Marriage Polls* (Mori Corporate Communications).

2. The Young People's Survey of Great Britain, commissioned by *Bliss* magazine, 2004.

3. *Daily Telegraph* (London), 15 October 2003.

4. TIME International, 17 September 2001.

5. Social Trends 33, ONS.

6. Eurostat, 2004.

7. Social Trends 33, ONS.

8. See Clark & Oswald 2002.

9. A major British government research project found that only 17 percent of women in cohabiting couples thought couples in difficulty should always try to stay together compared with 31 percent of those in married couples (see Marsh & Perry, 2003).

10. Private conversation with Dr. Bernardes, 7 September 2001.

11. This point is eloquently made by ex-British cabinet member Robin Cook about academics in general (see Cook 2003:97):

> The problem with academics is that they can be ruthlessly frank. If a professional politician was half as honest he would not be praised for talking from the heart, but accused of committing a "gaffe." Nor are they under any obligation, like politicians, to pretend that a problem has a solution...it is a social phenomenon, not a problem. The discussion therefore, was not, as they would say in Downing Street, solution-orientated. There were pointers to things that would help, but they appeared modest against the awesome tide of social revolution around us.

12. A detailed summary of findings is included in the Appendix.

13. Increased and new responsibilities and, for older women in particular, the experience of isolation as they took on the role of the housekeeper, were described as the main causes of stress and tension in marriage. Inside married life, the presence of children was widely acknowledged as a frequent source of stress and conflict as well as of harmony and happiness. The risk of stress and conflict appeared greatest during the period before and just after the birth of a child because of the changes in the division of labor within the household, which accompanied childbirth.

14. Private conversation with Gutteridge, August 2004.

15. Private conversation with L.H. She does note that there are exceptions to this, such as the ardent Europeanists, for example, in the social policy area (see *European Journal of Social Policy*).

16. The phenomenon of LAT (living apart together) relationships was first recognised by a Dutch journalist, who wrote an article in a daily newspaper about it in 1978. A LAT relationship pertains when a couple, not sharing the same residence, having two separate households, define themselves as a couple and are defined by their social surroundings as a couple. The two partners in a LAT relationship can be married to each other or not.

17. Worldatlas.com

18. TIME International, 17 September 2001.

19. "One Plus One," *The Bulletin*, 6, no. 4 (October 2002).

20. The IPROSEC—Improving Policy Responses and Outcomes to Socio-Economic Challenges—research project was funded by the EC within the Framework Programme 5 key action for "Improving the Socio-Economic Knowledge Base."

21. The Family Observer No. 2/2000 review of Family Research in Europe included no entries on studies on marriage, intact or otherwise.

Bibliography

Abela, A.M. (2003). Changing family structure in Europe: New challenges for public policy. In *Changing Family Structures, Policy and Practice*. Cross-National Research Papers Sixth Series: Improving Policy Responses and Outcomes to Socio-Economic Challenges.

Askham, J. (1984). *Identity and Stability in Marriage*. Cambridge: Cambridge University Press.

Askham, J. (1995). The Married Lives of Older People. In *Connecting Gender and Ageing*. S. Arber & J. Ginn (Eds.). Buckingham: Open University Press.

Bachand, L., & Caron, S. (2001). Ties that bind: A qualitative study of happy long-term marriages. *Contemporary Family Therapy* 23(1) (March 2001): 105–121.

Bahle, T., & Maucher, M. (1998). EURODATA newsletter no. 6: Research groups and projects: The Mannheim international family policy project. Mannheim: The Family Policy Database.

Bahle, T., & Maucher, M., with contributions by Fuduli, K., and Holzer, B. (1998). Developing a family policy database for Europe. Working Paper. Mannheim: Mannheimer Zentrum für Europäische Sozialforschung.

Berthoud, R., & Iacovou, M. (2002). *Diverse Europe: Mapping patterns of social change across the EU*. ESRC.

Biggart, A., Bendit, R., Cairns, D., Hein, K., & Mörch S. (2002). *Families and transitions in Europe: State of the art report* (HPSE-CT2001-00079). European Commission's 5th Framework Programme.

Billari, F.C. (2004). Choices, opportunities and constraints of partnership, childbearing and parenting: The patterns in the 1990s. Background paper for the European Population Forum 2004 (Population Challenges and Policy Responses) session on International migration: promoting management and integration.

Bradbury, T.N., Fincham, F.D., & Beach, S.R.H. (2000). Research on the nature and determinants of marital satisfaction: A decade in review. *Journal of Marriage and the Family* 62(4), 964–980.

Burgess, R.L. (1981). Relationships in marriage and the family. In *Personal Relationships 1: Studying Personal Relationships*. S. Duck & R. Gilmour (Eds.). New York: Academic Press Inc.

Clark, A.E., & Oswald, A.J. (2002). A simple statistical method for measuring how life events affect happiness. *International Journal of Epidemiology 31*, 1139–1144.

Cook, R. (2003). *The point of departure.* New York: Simon and Schuster.

Csikszentmihalyi, M. (1990). *Flow = The psychology of optimal experience.* New York: Harper and Row.

Cummings, E.M., & Davies, P.T. (2002). Effects of marital conflict on children: Recent advances and emerging themes in process-oriented research. *Journal of Child Psychology and Psychiatry 43*(1), 31–63.

Denzin, N. (2002). The cinematic society and the reflexive interview. In *Handbook of Interview research—context and method.* J.F. Gubrium & J.A. Holstein (Eds.). Thousand Oaks, London, New Delhi: Sage.

Eekelaar, J., & Maclean, M. (forthcoming). Marriage and the moral basis of personal relationships. OXFLAP Working paper.

Finch, J. (1983). *Married to the job—Wives' Incorporation in men's work.* London: George Allen and Unwin.

Gray, J.S., & Vanderhart, M.J. (2000). The determination of wages: Does marriage matter? In *The ties that bind: Perspectives on marriage and cohabitation.* L.J. Waite et al. (Eds.). New York: Aldine de Gruyter, 356–367.

Gutteridge, R. (2003). *Enduring relationships: The evolution of long-lasting marriage.* Unpublished PhD thesis, Keele University, Staffs, UK.

Hantrais, L. (2004). *Family policy matters—Responding to family change in Europe.* Bristol, UK: Policy Press.

Huston, T.L. (2000). The social ecology of marriage and other intimate unions. *Journal of Marriage and the Family 62*(2) (May 2000): 298–321.

Kiernan, K. (1999). Childbearing outside marriage in western Europe. *Population Trends 98,* 1–20.

Kiernan, K. (2002). Divorce and cohabitation across nations and generations. In *Potential for change across lives and generations: multidisciplinary perspectives.* P.L. Chase-Lansdale, K. Kiernan, & R. Friedman (Eds.). Cambridge: Cambridge University Press.

Lewis, J. (2003). *The end of marriage? Intimacy and individual relations.* Cheltenham: Edward Elgar.

Lupton, J., & Smith, J.P. (2002). Marriage, Assets and Savings. In *Marriage and the economy.* S. Grossbard-Schectman (Ed.). Cambridge: Cambridge University Press.

Maclean, M., & Eekelaar, J. (2004). The obligations and expectations of couples within families: Three modes of interaction. *Journal of Social Welfare and Family Law, 26*(2) (July 2004): 117–130.

Mansfield, P., & Collard, J. (1988). *The beginning of the rest of your life: A portrait of newlywed marriage.* London: MacMillan.

Marsh, A., & Perry, J. (2003). *Family change 1999 to 2001.* Department for Work and Pensions Research Report No. 180.

McLanahan, S. (2000). Family, state and child well-being. In *Annual Review of Sociology 26*(1), 703–706.

Parker, R. (2002). Why marriages last: a discussion of the literature. AIFS Research Paper No. 28.

Prinz, C. (1995). *Cohabiting, married or single? Portraying, analysing and modelling new living arrangements in the changing societies of Europe.* Hampshire: Avebury.

Reibstein, J. (forthcoming). *The best kept secret.* London: Bloomsbury.

Schwartz, R.S., & Olds, J.P.B. (2000). *Marriage in motion: The natural ebb and flow of lasting relationships.* Cambridge, MA: Perseus.

Seligman, M.E.P. (1990). *Learned optimism.* New York: Knopf.

Simons, R.L., et al. (1996). *Understanding Differences between divorced and intact families: Stress, interaction and child outcome.* London: Sage.

Smart, C. (2000). *Divorce in England 1950–2000.* Centre for Research on Family, Kinship and Childhood Working paper 20.

Smart, C., & Silva, E. (Eds.). (1999). *The new family.* London: Sage.

Smock, P.J., et al. (1999). The effect of marriage and divorce on women's economic well-being. *American Sociological Review 64,* 794–812.

Wu, Z. & Penning, M.J. (1997). Marital instability after midlife. *Family Issues, 18,* 459–478.

Appendix

European Research
Specific papers

- Bodenmann, G., Kauer, A., Hahlweg, K., & Fehm-Wolfsdorf, G. (1998). Communication patterns during marital conflict: a cross cultural replication. *Personal Relationships 5,* 343–356.

- Gierveld, J. (2004). Remarriage, unmarried cohabitation, LAT: Partner relationships following bereavement or divorce. *Journal of Marriage and Families, 66*(1), 236–243.

- Hahlweg, K., Markham, H.J., Thurmaier, F., Engl, J., & Eckert, V. (1998). Prevention of marital distress: Results of a German prospective longitudinal study. *Journal of Family Psychology, 12,* 543–556.

- Kalmijn, M., de Graaf, P.M., & Poortman, A-R. (2004). Interactions between cultural and economic determinants of divorce in the Netherlands. *Journal of Marriage and Families, 66*(1), 75–89.

- Stack, S., & Eshleman, J.R. (1998). Marital status and happiness: A 17 nation study. *Journal of Marriage and Families, 60*(2), 527–536.

- Wagner, M., & Weiss, B. (2003). Bilanz der deutschen Scheidungsforschung. Versuch einer Meta-Analyse [A Meta-Analysis of German Research on Divorce Risks]. *Zeitschrift für Soziologie, 32,* 1, 29–49.

- Weigel, D.J., & Ballard-Reisch, D.S. (2002). Investigating the behavioural indicators of relational commitment. *Journal of Social and Personal Relationships, 19,* 3, 403–423.

Further sources

- Proceedings from the Irish Presidency Conference 2004, Families, Change and Social Policy in Europe, Dublin Castle, Dublin, Ireland, 13–14 May 2004, http://www.welfare.ie/topics/eu_pres04/fam_conf/.

- Looking at the International Sociological Association's annual meetings, it is clear that marriage *per se* is rarely the subject of research in Europe and where it is, the focus of interest is in the decreasing popularity of marriage. The following European papers were presented over the past three years:

  - Spouse selection: Heterogamy during marriage and divorce risk. Jacques Jenssen, University of Nijmegen, The Netherlands.

  - For the child's sake. Parents and social workers discuss conflict-filled parental relations after a divorce. Margareta Hyden, Stockholm University, Sweden.

  - Structural and social causes of the decrease in the number of marriages in the Czech Republic. Tomáš Katrák, Faculty of Social Studies, Masaryk University, Brno, Czech Republic.

  - Comparative perspectives on LAT relationships. Örjan Hultåker, SKOP, Stockholm, Sweden. Irene Levin, Oslo University College, Oslo, Norway. Jessica Mjöberg, Uppsala University, Uppsala, Sweden. Jan Trost, Uppsala University, Uppsala, Sweden.

  - The Framing of Marriage and the Risk to Divorce. Hartmut Essen, University of Mannheim, Germany.

Summary of CRSP 482, Marriage in the 21st Century (September 2003)

This report summarizes the findings of eight focus groups conducted to explore married people's perceptions of the attitudes and behaviors that helped marriages to last, rather than end in separation or divorce. The eight focus groups involved sixty participants from medium/high- and low-income households recruited from two areas in an East Midlands (UK) city. Participants were married for between five and over fifty years and, with the exception of four women, were in their first marriages.

Findings

The focus group discussions showed that

- Participants felt that being married was an important part of their life and identity, but also that the present generation and society in general did not value marriage to the same extent as they did;

- Attitudes towards marriage were strongly influenced by the values, which participants had acquired from their parents, and the social norms prevailing in society and within the extended family at the time of marriage;

- The presence of, or the desire to have, children strongly influenced women's positive attitude towards marriage;

- Marriage was perceived as an act of great symbolic importance and a public statement of commitment;

- Modern social values, new opportunities, choices and expectations, and an equalization of career aspirations of men and women were thought to have resulted in more fluid gender roles within the home, which may create new areas of conflict;

- In particular, older group participants perceived these changes as threatening the foundations that may help marriages to last;

- Participants believed that a readiness to "work at a relationship" and the desire to make relationships work, even when a marriage might experience situations of duress, were essential to a lasting marriage;

- Commitment was seen as critical to a successful marriage, although participants found it hard to describe the substance of commitment;

- In addition, love, emotional stability and support, financial security, and a mutual recognition of the need to "give and take" were described as the key ingredients to a "good" marriage;

- Participants stressed that marital relationships changed with time, and so did the stresses and harmonies associated with them;

- They viewed communication, in particular, an ability and willingness to "talk through problems" and to listen to each other, as vitally important, but also recognized the practical limitations of frequent communication;

- Separate, as well as joined, activities and gestures (for instance, sending Valentine cards) were perceived to be essential to strengthening married life;

- Participants also used forms of manipulation, which they thought would help to avoid, limit, or reduce conflict (for instance, "going deaf") or to ensure their views were heard, recognized, and accepted (for instance, threats or temporarily leaving the home);

- There was some indication that women were more likely to use manipulation in marriage or, at least, were more willing to acknowledge its use than men were.

4

Marriage and Modernity: Some Evidence from the United States

Norval D. Glenn (USA)
Professor of Sociology, The University of Texas, Austin, USA

Modern societies are faced with a dilemma. The core functions performed by the institution of marriage are as crucial for the health and viability of these societies as they are for more traditional societies, and yet influences associated with modernity tend to undermine marriage. For instance, a decline in the economic interdependency of spouses tends to make marriages less stable, and the expressive individualism associated with modernity tends to weaken all social institutions. No modern society has yet dealt in a very satisfactory manner with this dilemma, though some have arguably done better than others. My own society, the United States, has been characterized by a great deal of discussion of the dilemma but a notable lack of agreement as to how to deal with it. There has been movement toward a consensus in academic and policy circles that the dilemma exists, although a few influential intellectuals still deny its existence.

I have devoted a great deal of time and effort during the past two decades to trying to understand the nature of this dilemma in the United States. I am a sociologist and demographer who analyzes data from large-scale surveys and who designs surveys, and thus I have concentrated on survey data about marriage related attitudes and behaviors. This kind of evidence has definite limitations and must be interpreted with caution and in conjunction with evidence of other kinds. Nevertheless, it has considerable utility for the task at hand. My latest effort along this line was to design a national telephone survey on marriage for the National Fatherhood Initiative (the NFIMS). The interviews, with 1,503 persons representative of the American adult population, were conducted early this year by the Office of Survey Research at my university, and I have prepared a draft report of the findings for the NFI. In my presentation today, I draw largely upon these findings.

If the respondents to the NFIMS and similar surveys are to be believed, Americans, in general, value marriage very highly and have at least moderately traditional attitudes about the institution. According to the NFIMS, an amazing 98 percent of Americans age eighteen and older either are married, have been married, or aspire to be married. The only large segment of the population that does not wish for marriage in its future consists of older (age sixty and older) divorced and widowed persons, up to four-fifths of whom seem to have a "been-there-done-that" attitude toward marriage. However, these persons who do not aspire to marriage for themselves are almost unanimous in saying that marriage is important for society and for children, and at least in the case of the women, the lack of a desire to marry may be an adaptation to very restricted opportunities for marriage.

Anyone who judges American attitudes toward marriage by mass media content and by what is said by intellectuals and academicians who write for a mass audience is likely to believe that Americans have generally rejected the traditional institution of marriage that includes the ideal of marital permanence and strong obligations associated with being married. Such a person would probably believe, for instance, that most Americans believe that fathers are not important for the socialization of children, that divorced parents can parent as effectively as married ones, and that it is unrealistic to expect couples to remain married for life now that people are living so long.

In fact, however, such attitudes and beliefs are held by only a small minority of the American public. For instance, only 3 percent of the respondents to the NFIMS disagreed with the statement that "Fathers are as important as mothers for the proper development of children," and only 12 percent disagreed that "Couples who marry should make a lifelong commitment to one another, to be broken only under rare circumstances." In view of the fact that all of the fifty United States have either *de jure* or *de facto* unilateral no fault divorce, it is interesting that only 29 percent of the NFIMS respondents agreed that "Either spouse should be allowed to terminate a marriage at any time for any reason."

In spite of the prevalence of these traditional, pro-marriage attitudes, the state of American marriage, it is well known, leaves much to be desired. For instance, if recent duration-specific divorce rates and age-specific death rates were to continue indefinitely into the future, more than 40 percent of marriages recently entered into in the Unites States would eventually end in divorce. Only about 60 percent of American adults are currently married, and as marital quality is rather crudely measured on the NFIMS, only about 40 percent are in marriages of reasonably high quality. About a third of the babies born in the United States are born to unmarried mothers, and in contrast to Western European countries with high out-of-wedlock birth rates, most unmarried mothers in the United States do not have a continuing close relationship with the fathers of their children. Up to half of all children in the United States spend part of their preadult years in a single-parent family or living with neither biological parent. Clearly, the widespread expression of traditional attitudes about marriage is not sufficient to ensure the health of the institution of marriage.

One reason, almost certainly, is that a good many persons parrot traditional attitudes in their responses to survey questions but do not act in accordance with them. Some of these persons really believe what they say about marriage but also have attitudes and values, such as consumerism and personal ambition, that override the influence of pro-marriage attitudes when crucial personal decisions are made.

Another reason often given for the coexistence of pro-marriage attitudes and widespread marital failure is that the latter results not from bad attitudes or values but from external circumstances over which persons have no control. According to this view, people want to do the right thing but are prevented from doing so by "structural impediments." The impediments cited are usually economic ones, such as a lack of good jobs. These impediments do exist for a good many people, but as an explanation for the great increase in marital failure in the United States in recent decades, they fail, because that increase came during a period of unprecedented prosperity. There is no doubt that financial problems underlie a good many divorces, but when the ever-divorced respondents to the NFIMS were asked to choose from a list of twelve possible reasons for their divorce (first divorce), "financial problems" ranked ninth, being given much less frequently than such reasons as "lack of commitment," "infidelity," "unrealistic expectations," and "married too young."

I am convinced that one of the main reasons for high rates of marital failure in the United States and in other modern societies is the influence of expressive individualism, whereby a relatively unfettered pursuit of personal gratification is encouraged and given precedence over loyalty and commitment to others, including other family members. The main purpose of marriage becomes the happiness and satisfaction of the married individuals, who come to expect more and more from marriage while often becoming less willing to sacrifice for their marriages. Although the fact that marriage "requires a lot of hard work" is given lip service by almost everyone, it is likely that a large percentage of newly married persons in modern societies underestimate the sacrifice and adaptation that marriage requires.

I recently have become convinced that another reason for the high rate of marital failure in modern societies is simply the range of choice that persons in such societies have in selecting spouses. In traditional societies, the range of choice is much more restricted, often with marriages being arranged by parents and other relatives and with the individuals to be married having veto power at most. Even in the United States of a hundred years ago, marital choice was much more restricted than it is today, if only because most people lived in small towns and rural areas where the number of prospective spouses with whom they could connect was rather small. In contrast, in America today, many young persons have hundreds if not thousands of persons whom they have a chance to meet and potentially could marry, and there is cultural encouragement to find a "soul mate"—one who will meet all of their emotional, sexual, and companionship needs—among all of those persons.

Some persons, those whom psychologists call "satisfiers," will find an acceptable mate among all of the possible choices, make a strong commitment to that person, and not reconsider their choice. Other persons, those whom psychologists call "maximizers," will choose a mate and almost immediately begin to wonder if they have made the best possible choice. They will wonder if there is someone out there among the many other potential spouses who would be a better soul mate than the one they have chosen. Some psychologists believe that the superabundance of choices in modern societies—of goods and services, of kinds of work to do, of recreational activities and entertainment, as well as of personal relationships—tends to create the maximizing personality. Whatever its source may be, this personality characteristic tends to make persons dissatisfied with their marriages and tends to prevent them from making strong commitments to, and investments in, their marriages— at least when divorce is readily available and the social penalties for ending marriages are not severe.

I have no information on what percentage of Americans are maximizers, but data from the NFIMS indicate that many spouses fail to make a strong commitment to their marriages, for whatever reason. Just under three-fourths (73 percent) of the ever-divorced respondents gave "lack of commitment by one or both persons to make it work" as a major reason for the failure of their marriage. This was by a large margin the most frequently given reason, followed by "too much conflict and arguing" (56 percent) and "infidelity, extramarital affairs" (55 percent). Similar percentages have been found by surveys conducted in specific states, such as Oklahoma and Utah.

A few commentators on American marriage have claimed that most couples who divorce do so only after doing their best to make their marriage work. The data reported above cast doubt on that claim, as do the responses to two questions asked of ever-divorced respondents to the NFIMS that asked whether or not they wished they and their spouses had worked harder to save the marriage. Sixty-two percent of both ex-husbands and ex-wives said they wished their spouses had worked harder, and 35 percent of the ex-husbands and 21 percent of the ex-wives said they wished they, themselves, had worked harder. Fewer than a third of the respondents said that both they and their ex-spouses had worked hard enough.

These and similar data from other surveys strongly suggest that problems with American marriages reside to a large extent with the personal characteristics of married persons rather than with structural impediments external to those persons. If so, individual-level interventions, such as the marriage education being offered by marriage initiatives in several of the states, are appropriate means to try to strengthen marriages and marriage as an institution, though the overall efficacy of such efforts is as yet unknown. We do not know, for instance, how effective such education is in transforming maximizers into satisficers.

It is important to add that there is at least one important segment of the American population for whom the structural impediments to good marriages are undoubtedly very real. Among African Americans, who constitute about 13 percent of the American population, there is a scarcity of marriageable males, there being only about 72 males per 100 females among unmarried African Americans age eighteen and older. When age and the fact that many of the unmarried African American males are incarcerated are taken into account, I estimate that only about half of all unmarried African American women have potential African American spouses. Obviously, so long as the greatly unbalanced African American sex ratio exists and so long as marriage remains largely racially endogamous, the prospects for African American women to enter into good marriages will not be very good.

Overall, however, any long-term solutions to the problem of maintaining a strong institution of marriage under conditions of modernity seem to lie in the realm of attitudes, values, skills, knowledge, and personality dispositions. There is now a movement afoot in the United States to change these characteristics, and there are similar, though less active, marriage movements in other modern societies, including Australia and the United Kingdom. When the next International Year of the Family is commemorated ten years from now, we will know a great deal more than we know now about how successful such movements can be.

Presented at the Doha International Conference for the Family
Doha, Qatar, 29–30 November 2004.

5

The Positive Impact of Marriage on Society: The Case for Public Policy

Steven L. Nock (USA)
Professor of Sociology, University of Virginia, USA

I wish to make a case for the proposition that marriage is an important public health and safety issue. It is a legitimate concern of all governments, and they should make every effort to promote and protect it. But they should do more than encourage it. Marriage should be privileged in law and public policy.

Married people are doing something for their societies when they care for their families, provide for, protect, and control their children. They are doing something by protecting their health. They are doing something by maintaining stable and orderly lives. If they were not doing all these things, then their governments would have to, and their nations would be weakened. The evidence is clear that married people do these things better than unmarried people. The promotion of marriage, therefore, is a legitimate interest of all governments.

Many in the United States are now beginning to recognize this. Following several decades of sweeping demographic, social, and legal changes that have minimized the importance of marriage in U.S. society, a wide-ranging assortment of Americans is now conspicuously promoting marriage. Some public policy makers in the United States promote stable marriages and discourage unmarried births. And Congress has declared out-of-wedlock births, reliance on welfare assistance for raising children, and single-mother families contrary to the national interest. But this effort faces daunting challenges.

Throughout the West, demographic, legal, and social changes have made marriage less distinct from other forms of intimate partnerships. There are fewer privileges associated with being married and increasingly more accepted alternatives.

Demographic Trends

The demographic trends are well known. First, people now postpone marriage to later ages. They often live in their parents' homes, with friends, or with unmarried partners, thus increasing the time adults spend unmarried.

Second, more couples now live together without getting married, either as a precursor to or alternative to marriage or as an alternative to living alone. The availability of such alternatives naturally makes marriage less central to domestic life. Third, high divorce rates and births to unmarried mothers leave more households headed by single parents, increasing the time both adults and children spend outside of married-couple families. Fourth, because more women, especially more married women, are in the labor force, the prevalence of one-wage-earner, two-parent families—what has been called the "traditional" family—has declined. Finally, delayed and declining fertility and declining mortality result in fewer children, smaller families, and longer lives, adding to the time parents spend "postchildren" and to the number of married couples without children.[1]

These five demographic trends reflect other important social and economic changes, including the increasing equality between the sexes, the legalization of abortion, increasing tolerance for diverse life-styles, and liberalized laws governing divorce. Perhaps the most important change, however, has been the development of effective birth control.

The centrality of marriage in culture and law can be understood, in part, as a consequence of *poorly controlled fertility*.[2] As long as sexual intercourse naturally resulted in births, marriage (or engagement) was the only permissible venue for sex. Marriage was an institutional and societal arrangement that allocated responsibility for children. No alternative civil or religious arrangement could accomplish that task except in extraordinary circumstances. By restricting sex to marriage, communities were able to reduce births of children for whom no male kin was obviously and legitimately responsible.

But once effective contraception uncoupled sex from fertility, this social justification for marriage became less compelling. The convention of "shotgun" weddings, for example, has almost disappeared.[3] Prior to the advent of effective contraception and legal abortion, a wedding to avoid the stigma of an illegitimate birth typically followed a premarital pregnancy. That it no longer does so illustrates the changing understanding of the importance of marriage for births.

The birth control pill became available in 1960. Within a decade, six in ten American married women were using medical, effective, non-coitus-related methods of birth control. This pattern of very rapid adoption of contraception is typical.[4] Demographers describe these technological innovations in birth control as a "contraceptive revolution" or a "reproductive technology shock" because of their profound implications for social customs and norms.

Effective birth control helped redefine sexual relations as *private* matters and essentially removed them from state control. A series of U.S. Supreme Court decisions during the 1960s had major implications for the legal and cultural meaning of sex and childbearing. In the most important case, *Griswald v. Connecticut* (1965), the court declared unconstitutional a state law forbidding the use of contraceptive devices, even by married couples. Writing for the court majority, Justice William O. Douglas explained that various guarantees of the Bill of Rights "create zones of privacy," making "the very idea of prohibiting the practice of birth control...repulsive to the notions of privacy surrounding the marriage relationship." *Griswald* and subsequent court decisions established a constitutional right to privacy in matters of sexual behavior among consenting adults, married or single, and most recently heterosexual or homosexual.[5]

Before *Griswald,* sexual matters had never been completely private because of their potential public consequences. Communities prohibited sexual freedoms because adultery and illegitimacy disrupted family lines, sometimes creating collective obligations for the care of offspring. Premarital and extramarital sexual intercourse was illegal. The ability to separate intercourse from reproduction removed much of the rationale for such regulations.

Prior to the development of effective contraception, sexual intercourse was the legal symbolic core of marriage; consummation defined its *de facto* creation. Sexual exclusivity was the basis for a range of legal restrictions surrounding marriage. Adultery, for example, provided grounds for lawsuits by the aggrieved spouse. A married person's *consortium,* the legally protected emotional stakes a spouse has in his or her marriage, was protected in family law.

Such legal claims are now more a curiosity than a conspicuous feature of domestic relations law except when physical injury is involved. Most jurisdictions have abolished, or limited, such suits. That such actions are now pursued so infrequently (in the few remaining states where they are still permitted) attests to the declining legal significance of sexual exclusivity in marriage.[6] Similarly, the rapid spread of no-fault divorce laws since 1970 has effectively eliminated adultery as a condition for divorce.

Culturally, once sexual relations came to be viewed as private decisions unrelated to marriage, so did reproduction choices. In other words, once *sex and procreation* could be separated, so could *sex and marriage.* But so, too, of course, could reproduction and marriage, as they increasingly have been.

Both the social stigma and the legal consequences of having an "illegitimate" child have virtually vanished in recent years. In a series of decisions between 1968 and 1978, the U.S. Supreme Court declared unconstitutional the legal distinctions associated with the marital status of a child's parents.[7] In this, as in most areas of domestic relations, American family law has shifted its primary focus from the married couple to the individual.[8] The marital status of parents is legally irrelevant from the perspective of either generation.

In short, now that fertility can be controlled, parenthood and marriage are less institutionalized and much less predictably connected. A once near-universal insistence on an adult social script governing marriage has given way to an expanding range of acceptable, though less traditional, life course options, such as cohabitation. Living together in a sexual relationship, once taboo, is now so acceptable that a majority of Americans cohabit before they marry.[9] And yet the practice is still so novel that it lacks a vernacular name.

Nor, importantly, do norms or explicit laws yet govern it. Like many social changes fostered by sexual freedom, cohabitation is not yet institutionalized, not yet integrated fully into our culture or law.[10]

The old rules have changed, yet new standards have yet to emerge. Nonmarital living arrangements are often incompatible with old customs and conventions. Even more vexing, the new arrangements offer fewer traditional solutions when problems arise because many of the problems themselves are the result of nontraditional arrangements. Cohabiting couples, for example, have little tradition to follow when dealing with the informal equivalent of their "in laws." Relations with the older generation are strained, as a result.[11]

Scientific evidence suggests that children and adults benefit from satisfying and stable marriages. For well over a century, researchers have known that married people are generally better off than their unmarried counterparts. As early as 1897, sociologist Emile Durkheim was theorizing about why married adults have lower suicide rates. In a recent survey David Ribar notes that links between marriage and better health in children and adults "have been documented in hundreds of quantitative studies covering different time periods and different countries."[12]

The accumulated research shows that married people are typically healthier, live longer, earn more, have better mental health, have better sex lives, and are happier than their unmarried counterparts. They have lower rates of suicide, fatal accidents, acute and chronic illness, alcoholism, and depression.[13] Part of the reason is that healthier and happier people are more likely to be married.[14] But part of the reason appears to be that marriage actually causes people to change.[15]

Even if we believe that marriage is the cause of better outcomes for adults and children, we must ask *why*. What theory would predict or explain such differences? A variety of such explanations exists and can be grouped under three broad themes: specialization, the domesticating role of marriage, and marriage as a social institution.

The first theory about why married people might differ from unmarried people is specialization. When two people marry, they tend to develop an efficient division of labor. To the extent that spouses have different skills, preferences, or abilities, marriage allows each to concentrate on those in which he or she has a relative advantage. Even in contemporary marriages, where both partners tend to be employed at comparable wages, efficiencies from a division of labor still arise. For example, married parents with young children have been shown to stagger their work hours to permit one to deliver children to school, and another to be home when school is out. This simple strategy reduces the demand for expensive day care.[16] As couples refine their division of tasks, the household benefits to the extent that each partner's productivity increases. Such specialization produces greater interdependencies and lower divorce rates.[17] These interdependencies also have economic value ("marriage-specific capital") and have been protected in tort law as *consortium*.[18] Cohabiting couples are less likely to specialize.

The second theory about differences between married and unmarried people involves marriage's domesticating role. Men are thought to change more when they marry than women because unmarried men live unhealthier lives than unmarried women and therefore have more room in their lives for positive change. Specifically, once men are married, they are much less likely to engage in risky behaviors such as drinking heavily, driving dangerously, or using drugs. They are also more likely to work regularly, help others more, volunteer more, and attend religious services more frequently. Others have made similar arguments about how marriage "domesticates" men by fostering a sense of responsibility for their families, producing a future orientation that makes them sensitive to the long-term consequences of their actions, and providing someone to offer advice, schedule medical appointments, or encourage pro-social behaviors (the so-called "nagging" factor).[19]

Both of these perspectives are based on the idea that marriage is a special kind of *relationship*. Both focus on the individuals in a marriage. But marriage is much more than a relationship.

The third perspective views marriage as a social institution. The institutional perspective argues that marriage changes individuals both to the extent that others treat them differently and to the extent that they come to view themselves differently.[20] The marital relationship carries with it legal, moral, and conventional assumptions about what is right and proper. It is, in other words, institutionalized and defined by social norms. It is culturally patterned and integrated into other basic social institutions like education, the economy, and politics. In this sense, married individuals have a tradition of solutions to rely on when they confront problems. For many matters in domestic life, marriage supplies a template.

In marriage, there are things that husbands and wives should and should not do *because they are married* . . . not simply because they are men and women, or because they live together in a relationship, or because they have children together.

Others will treat married people differently because of these cultural assumptions made about husbands and wives. Employers may prefer married to unmarried workers, for example, or may reward married employees with greater opportunities and benefits. Insurers may discount policies for married people. And the law gives married partners legal rights vis-à-vis each other that are not granted to unmarried people.[21] Economists refer to this aspect of marriage as its "signaling" function. Economic signals are activities or attributes of a person that convey information to others. The most effective economic signals are those that involve significant cost to the sender. A classic example is a college degree, which transmits, for example to an employer, valuable information about the sender. Because marriage, like a college degree, has significant costs attached, it serves as an economic signal of those things culturally associated with marriage: commitment, stability, and maturity, among other things. Friends, relatives, and employers will be inclined to assume such things about married people. To the extent they do, married people will benefit.[22] Because cohabitation is relatively costless (in signaling theory, cohabitation is "cheap talk"), it does not convey the same positive signal marriage does. Thus, for example, it is not surprising that cohabiting men earn more once they are married, even when other aspects of their relationships are similar.[23] Regardless of what marriage may mean to an individual in a relationship, it has broader implications in what it implies to others. This is a core assumption of the institutional argument about marriage.

Marriage as a Social Institution

The cultural assumptions made about married people, and that partners themselves adopt, are what define marriage as an institution. I want to briefly consider six of the core expectations that define the institution of marriage as it is found throughout the West.[24]

1. *The first is the expectation that the choice of a partner is a free choice and based on love—presumably for life.* Increasingly and universally, marriage is based on love. This does not mean that parents and others are uninvolved. It simply means that the two individuals are the most important ones in more and more societies today.

Love is associated with feelings of security, comfort, and companionship. Ideally, love lasts a lifetime and lovers stay committed forever. To the extent that marriage and love are associated, marriage also implies security, companionship, and lifelong commitment. These things expected from love are also expected from marriage.

My research shows that married couples experience love differently than do unmarried couples. Married partners have a shared past together but also a long imagined future together. The present is now interpreted in light of that past and future. This makes problems in the present less important. Unmarried couples are less likely to share a commitment to a shared future. Current problems are more damaging as a result.

As a consequence, *marriages last longer than other types of relationships, and they tend to endure even when problems arise.*

2. *The second expectation about marriage pertains to maturity.* Most societies have laws or customs that define how old one should be before getting married. Societies presume that married people can execute contracts, conduct business, and be held responsible. Once people are married, they are expected to behave as adults. They are no longer excused from immature decisions.

Marriage has always been an important rite of passage into adulthood. It is a sign of maturity. For men, it is also a demonstration of masculine identity because heterosexuality is an implicit assumption about married people (see below).

As a consequence, *married people behave more maturely than unmarried people. They are less likely to commit crimes or break important rules.*

One challenge to marriage in many societies today is the trend to postpone it to later and later ages. Throughout the West, a new stage of life is emerging between the time people leave their parents' home and when they start their own families. This now lasts almost ten years in some societies such as America. There are no rules that apply in this stage of life and there are troubling implications as more and more children are now born to unmarried individuals in this stage of life. Another troubling implication is that more women now postpone childbearing during this stage of life, thereby missing the most advantageous reproductive years of their lives. The result of this new stage of life is both an increase in the number of births to unmarried individuals and a decline in the overall birth rate.

3. *The third expectation about marriage is that married couples will collaborate economically for the sake of their family.* This norm accounts for the specialization found among married couples.

The large majority of married wives, and especially married mothers, work outside the home. But even when both spouses earn money, there are differences in who does what in married households. This specialization is a hallmark of the efficiency of married households. The expectation of equality in marriage does not mean the absence of gender differences. Most married couples specialize as a way of collaborating economically.

As a consequence, *married couples earn more, save more, and produce more. More generally, specialization counters excessive individualism by creating joint dependencies.*

4. *The fourth expectation about marriage is that partners will be faithful to each other.* In law and religion, sexual intimacy is the symbolic core of marriage and defines it in obvious and restrictive ways. Sexual intimacy in marriage is actually a form of *property.*

Property is a social relationship among individuals who agree how to behave toward a particular thing. To own something means that (1) you have a right to use it; (2) other people do not have the right to use it; and (3) you can call on the rest of society to enforce your rights. Intimacy in marriage satisfies these three conditions: husbands and wives have a right to have sexual relations with one another, other people do not have a right to sexual relations with either of them while they are married, and either spouse can enlist the assistance of society to enforce his or her sexual rights (e.g., divorce or adultery charges).

As a consequence, *married couples are less likely to be promiscuous. Their sex lives are better, and their health benefits from their fidelity.*

5. *The fifth expectation about marriage is that it is a heterosexual arrangement.* Historically, people of the same sex have been forbidden to marry. This is now changing as some countries and one American state (Massachusetts) now permit such marriages. In addition, several American states currently recognize same-sex *civil unions* that carry the same legal obligations and privileges that marriage does. The recognition of legal unions between people of the same sex has attracted more public reaction than any other trend in family

life in recent times. Conservatives fear and liberals hope that this experiment will lead to a general redefinition of marriage. It is much too soon to know. But personally, I consider it unlikely that legal imprimatur for same-sex marriage could successfully alter the long-standing place of heterosexual marriage in our societies. Almost all people see marriage as a social and/or religious institution rather than a purely legal arrangement. Perhaps the ultimate question involves social values, mores, and morals, rather than marriage *per se.* So while there is growing tolerance for homosexuality in general, public support for homosexual marriage has not followed. Regardless of what state or federal courts may decide, marriage is still primarily defined by convention and tradition. Heterosexuality is still central to the traditional conception of it. Whether legal changes will alter conventional understandings is not at all certain. To the extent that men are expected to publicly express suitable masculinity, marriage is the primary way most will be able to do so. Masculine identity is a central component of married men's character.

As a consequence, *married men are rewarded for supporting others and providing for their families.*

6. *The final expectation I will mention is that married people are expected to become parents.* The obligations for support and care of children must be assigned to someone if the state is not to become responsible. Marriage has traditionally served this objective by making some male and female responsible for every child.

Parents of any child born to a married couple are responsible for that child. Thus, the only action that a man must take to be a child's father is to be married to the mother when that child is born. Childbirth clearly resolves the question of who a child's mother is. But marriage solves the more complex issue of paternity. In this sense, marriage is the most elementary method of connecting every child with an adult male who becomes responsible for him or her.

As a consequence, *children of married couples are treated better and enjoy superior lives.*

Conclusion

With respect to their marriages, men and women are increasingly viewed as separate individuals with their own identities. Likewise, unmarried people are increasingly treated the same as married people in law. Throughout the West, it is increasingly true that individual spouses are protected in law without concern for their marriages.

Family law now embodies a more marriage-neutral view of relationships. This means that marriage is less central as an identity for people. Law is not the sole cause of such trends, as I have shown. But it is a good reflection of the direction we are heading.

As I have argued, the expectations associated with marriage are one of the main reasons for the enormous benefits produced for individuals and societies. If we abolish this distinction, then all people become soloists.

I am a musician, and I can assure you that two soloists produce a poor duet. Any society needs strong groups to care for one another and for children. The opposite happens when we emphasize individuals and minimize the importance of their marriages.

There are those who would argue that marriage should not be privileged in law or elsewhere. And, as I have suggested, we are moving quickly in this direction. I would like to conclude with some very brief thoughts about the implications of such trends.

Regardless of the details of the particular relationship involved, married men and women derive significant benefits from their status. Were this not so, unmarried cohabiting individuals would be similar to married people. A decade of research has convincingly shown this not to be so.

I think it is remarkable how much we have learned about marriage from seeing the alternatives.

- We have learned that when people live together before getting married, they have higher divorce rates, not lower as many had predicted.

- We have learned that women are more often the victims of domestic violence when they live with a man who is not their husband.

- We have learned that unmarried couples do not accumulate and save as much.

- We have learned that unmarried couples are not as generous to others.

But most importantly, cohabitation illustrates my basic point about marriage as an institution. The problems with a very simple sentence illustrate much about the challenges we now confront in matters of alternative living arrangements. Tell me how you would complete this introduction of your cohabiting partner when we first meet: "Steve, I would like you to meet my ?????" It is not simply the lack of a term for such a person that is so telling. Rather, the fact that we cannot even agree on what to call our cohabiting partners is clear evidence that we have not yet come to agree about what cohabitation is or what it should be. We simply have no agreed-upon understandings of what such a relationship is or implies. Like many social changes fostered by sexual freedom, cohabitation is not yet integrated fully into our culture or law. It is not a social institution. The same can be said for many contemporary family issues.

There is a collective cost we pay, as a society, for the weakening of marriage. The economic costs of remaining unmarried for *individuals* are already well known: lower earnings, higher rates of poverty, higher need for public assistance, and so on. If we were able to estimate the economic costs of divorce, unmarried childbearing, and lower marriage rates *for a society*, we would discover that we pay an enormous price for the retreat from marriage.

There are strong egalitarian arguments in support of treating all adults and children alike. According to this view, unmarried people are no less entitled to the prerogatives of civic life than husbands and wives. At the same time, this amounts to a significant challenge to traditional assumptions embodied in the social institution of marriage.

Quite simply, there is no way to treat all adults the same without weakening marriage. How then are we to justify any legal distinction between married and unmarried people? First, we must recognize the *collective benefits* all people enjoy because couples get married. Second, we must recognize that married people morally *deserve* legal privileges in return for the sacrifices they make in their personal lives.

Married people are justifiably entitled to different treatment in law because marriage requires different behaviors. At a minimum, married people voluntarily limit their personal autonomy in many ways. The norms that define the institution of marriage are, essentially, self-imposed limits on behavior, or sacrifices of personal autonomy. These sacrifices are sufficient grounds for differential treatment in law. They may be regarded as a form of social control, voluntarily accepted by most spouses as part of their marriage vows. Unless we discover an equally effective and economical form of social control and caring, or until we are willing to accept the collective costs of such crucial social functions, we should reward those who accept the obligations of marriage.

Presented at the World Family Policy Forum
Brigham Young University, July 2005.

Endnotes

1. Julie DaVanzo and M. Amar Rahman, "American Families: Trends and Correlates," *Population Index* 59 (1993): 350–86; Sara S. McLanahan and Lynne M. Casper, "Growing Diversity and Inequality in the American Family," in *State of the Union: America in the 1990s*, vol. 2, *Social Trends*, ed. Reynolds Farley (New York: Russell Sage Foundation, 1995), 1–45; Lynne M. Casper and Suzanne M. Bianchi, *Continuity and Change in the American Family* (Thousand Oaks, CA: Sage, 2002), 7–8.

2. Steven Nock, "The Divorce of Marriage and Parenthood," *Journal of Family Therapy* 22, no. 2 (2000): 245–63; Hendrick Hertog, *Man and Wife in America: A History* (Cambridge, MA: Harvard University Press, 2000).

3. John D'Emilio and Estelle B. Freedman, *Intimate Matters: A History of Sexuality in America* (New York: Harper and Row, 1988), 251; George A. Akerlof and Janet L. Yellen, "An analysis of out-of-wedlock childbearing in the United States," *Quarterly Journal of Economics*, no. 2 (1996): 277–317.

4. Charles F. Westoff and Norman B. Ryder, *The Contraceptive Revolution* (Princeton, NJ: Princeton University Press, 1977).

5. *Griswald v. Connecticut*, 381 U.S. 479; *Eisenstadt v Baird*, 405 U.S. 438 (1972); *Roe v. Wade*, 410 U.S. 113 (1973); *Lawrence v. Texas* (Docket No. 02-102) (2002).

6. Mary Ann Glendon, *The Transformation of Family Law* (Chicago: University of Chicago Press, 1989), 96; Harry D. Krause and David D. Meyer, *Family Law* (St. Paul, MN: Thomson/West Publishers, 2003), 96.

7. *Levy v. Louisiana*, 391 U.S. 68 (1968); *Glona v. American Guarantee and Liability Insurance Co.*, 391 U.S. 73 (1968); *Weber v. Aetna Casualty and Surety Co.*, 406 U.S. (1972); *Gomes v. Perez*, 209 U.S. 535 (1973); *Jiminez v Weinberger*, 417 U.S. 628 (1974); *Matthews v Lucas*, 427 U.S. 495 (1976); *Trimble v. Gordon*, 430 U.S. 762 (1977); *Fiallo v Bell*, 430 U.S. 787 (1977); *Lalli v. Lalli*, 439 U.S. 259 (1978).

8. Hendrick Hertog, *Man and Wife in America: A History* (Cambridge, MA: Harvard University Press, 2000), see note 4.

9. Larry L. Bumpass and Hsien-Hen Lu, "Trends in Cohabitation and Implications for Children's Family Contexts in the United States," *Population Studies* 43 (2000): 29–41.

10. Steven L. Nock, "A Comparison of Marriages and Cohabiting Relationships," *Journal of Family Issues* 16 (1995): 53–76.

11. Ibid.

12. Emile Durkheim, *Suicide: A Study in Sociology*, trans. John A. Spaulding and George Simpson, ed. with an introduction by George Simpson (New York: Free Press, 1997), see note 12; David C. Ribar, "What Do Social Scientists Know about the Benefits of Marriage? A Review of Quantitative Methodologies," Office of Planning, Research, and Evaluation, Administration for Children and Families (U.S. Department of Health and Human Services, 2003), 1.

13. Linda J. Waite, "Does Marriage Matter?" *Demography* 32 (1995): 483–507; Linda J. Waite and Maggie Gallagher, *The Case for Marriage: Why Married People are Happier, Healthier, and Better Off Financially* (New York: Doubleday, 2000).

14. Noreen Goldman, "Marriage Selection and Mortality Patterns: Inferences and Fallacies," *Demography* 30, no. 2 (1993): 189–208; Ribar, "What Do Social Scientists Know?" (see note 13).

15. Reviews are found in John E. Murray, "Marital Protection and Marital Selection: Evidence from a Historical-Prospective Sample of American Men," *Demography* 37, no. 4 (2000): 511–21; Lee Lillard and Constantijn Panis, "Marital Status and Mortality: The Role of Health," *Demography* 33 (1996): 313–27.

16. Steven L. Nock and Paul W. Kingston, "The Family Work Day," *Journal of Marriage and the Family* 46 (1984): 333–43.

17. Steven L. Nock and Margaret F. Brinig, "Weak Men and Disorderly Women: Divorce and the Division of Labor," in *The Law and Economics of Marriage and Divorce*, ed. Antony W. Dnes and Robert Rowthorn (Cambridge, UK: Cambridge University Press, 2002); Steven L. Nock, "The Marriages of Equally Dependent Spouses," *Journal of Family Issues* 22, no. 6 (2001): 755–75.

18. Gary S. Becker, *A Treatise on the Family* (Cambridge, MA: Harvard University Press, 1981); Margaret F. Brinig, Carl E. Schneider, and Lee E. Teitlebaum, *Family Law in Action: A Reader* (Cincinnati: Anderson Publishing Company, 1999).

19. Durkheim, *Suicide* (see note 12); Steven L. Nock, *Marriage in Men's Lives* (New York: Oxford University Press, 1998) (see note 17); Steven L. Nock. "Time and Gender in Marriage," *Virginia Law Review* 86, no. 8 (2000): 1971–87; Waite and Gallagher, *The Case for Marriage* (see note 14).

20. Nock, *Marriage in Men's Lives*.

21. Waite and Gallagher, *The Case for Marriage* (see note 14).

22. Antony W. Dnes, "Marriage as a Signal," in *The Law and Economics of Marriage and Divorce,* ed. A.W. Dnes & R. Rowthorn (Eds.) (New York: Oxford University Press, 2002).

23. Philip N. Cohen, "Cohabitation and the Declining Marriage Premium for Men," *Work and Occupations* 29 (August 2002): 346–63.

24. These ideas are developed fully in Steven L. Nock, *Marriage in Men's Lives* (New York: Oxford University Press, 1998).

Bibliography

Casper, Lynne M., and Suzanne M. Bianchi. *Continuity and Change in the American Family.* Thousand Oaks, CA: Sage, 2002. Two family demographers explain the current trends in households and families in the United States. An excellent source for data about changing patterns of union formation, marriage, divorce, childbearing, and labor-force issues.

Nock, Steven L. *Marriage in Men's Lives.* New York: Oxford University, 1998. Nock fully develops the concept of marriage as a social institution. He shows that the institution of marriage creates measurable benefits for men because it is a rite of passage into adult masculine identity.

Waite, Linda J., and Maggie Gallagher. *The Case for Marriage: Why Married People are Happier, Healthier, and Better Off Financially.* New York: Doubleday, 2000. The authors review and summarize a vast literature on the effects of marriage for men and women.

6

The Formless City of Plato's *Republic:* How the Legal and Social Promotion of Divorce and Same-Sex Marriage Contravenes the Philosophy and Undermines the Projects of the Universal Declaration of Human Rights

Scott FitzGibbon (USA)
Professor of Law, Boston College Law School, Boston, USA[1]

The family is the natural and fundamental group unit of society and is entitled to protection by society and the State.

—Universal Declaration of Human Rights, Article 16(3)[2]

Everyone is entitled to a social order in which the rights and freedoms set forth in this Declaration can be fully realized.

—Universal Declaration of Human Rights, Article 28[3]

It depends on what each of us does, what we consider freedom in a democracy means.

—Eleanor Roosevelt, "Freedom and Human Rights"[4]

The advent of no-fault divorce law, the promotion of a "divorce culture," the licensing of "marriages" between two men or two women, and the promotion of homosexual couplings as a basis for the rearing of children represent as drastic a revision or deconstruction as has ever been attempted of the institution of the family. It is not an exaggeration to say that the United States, and much of the world, at least the Western world, is involved in a struggle of considerable scope as regards the nature and meaning of marriage and the family. This chapter presents the view that the purposes and principles of the Universal Declaration of Human Rights invite us to join this struggle and to oppose the initiatives of revision and deconstruction.[5]

The Universal Declaration of Human Rights (hereinafter referred to as the "Declaration") takes special care to protect the family and to identify its role.

Article 16(3) states that "[t]he family is the natural and fundamental group unit of society and is entitled to protection by society and the State." Article 12 provides that "[n]o one shall be subjected to arbitrary interference with his... family."[6] Articles 23 and 25 contain protections for the family's economic status and for motherhood and childhood.[7] The Declaration's references to "family" allude to a nexus of committed affiliations rather than transient ones, and the Declaration's references to "marriage" allude to a solemn, committed, and lasting bond between a man and a woman. That is what those terms meant to those involved with preparing and adopting the Declaration and what they mean in most of the world today.

More fundamentally, the Declaration proposes an order of basic international ethics that conflicts with the ideologies underlying recent movements to revise or deconstruct the family. It is a major purpose of this chapter to bring this fundamental conflict to light.

I. The Philosophy and Purposes of the Universal Declaration of Human Rights

A. The Declaration's Philosophical Orientation and "Voice"

The Declaration displays, through its history[8] and in its language, four fundamental characteristics. The first is moral objectivism. The Declaration is founded on belief in an objective moral order above and beyond the "positive" orders of rules and principles invented by states and cultures. Thus the Declaration involves the rejection of ethical skepticism and ethical subjectivism: rejection, that is, of the opinion, widespread during the middle of the twentieth century, that there is no objective ethical truth applicable across the barriers of nation, culture, and civilization.[9]

Subjectivist or relativist views were proposed to the drafters of the Declaration in a submission from the American Anthropological Association, which asserted that "[s]tandards and values are relative to the culture from which they derive."[10] The anthropologists recommended that the Declaration therefore include "a statement of the right of men to live in terms of their own traditions" and warned that precepts for worldwide applicability must be based on the understanding that "man is free only when he lives as his society defines freedom, that his rights are those he recognizes as a member of his society...."[11]

The leading drafters were not subjectivists or relativists, and the Declaration bristles with provisions that repudiate this sort of thinking.[12] The most vivid examples appear in provisions in the early parts that base the Declaration on conscience: the second "whereas" clause notes that "disregard and contempt for human rights have resulted in barbarous acts which have outraged the conscience of mankind" and Article 1 states that "[a]ll human beings...are endowed with reason and conscience." A leading scholar of the Declaration, Johannes Morsink, observes:

[F]or Hitler conscience was nothing but a "Jewish invention."...The drafters' view of "conscience" was very different. They adopted numerous
articles and clauses precisely because they were collectively outraged by
what Hitler had done....By using the phrase "the conscience of mankind"
the drafters generalized their own feelings over the rest of humanity. Taking
a position diametrically opposed to Hitler's, they believed that any morally
healthy human being would have been similarly outraged when placed in
similar circumstances.[13]

The Declaration proposes, in opposition to the statement of the anthropologists, that the practices and policies of the governments and institutions of
the world, and also their ethics of freedom, rights, and duties, should be
tested by reference to a wider moral order.

The second fundamental characteristic exhibited by the history and text of
the Declaration is an attitude of aspiration. Its aspirational character is most
obvious in its first passage just after its "whereas" clauses, where it refers to
"striving" and to "progressive measures":

> *The General Assembly, Proclaims* this Universal Declaration of Human Rights
> as a common standard of achievement for all peoples and all nations, to the
> end that every individual and every organ of society, keeping this Declara-
> tion constantly in mind, shall strive by teaching and education to promote
> respect for these rights and freedoms and by progressive measures, national
> and international, to secure their universal and effective recognition and ob-
> servance.[14]

In its call for "progressive" measures the Declaration reflects the hopeful
longings of many of the world's people just after the Second World War, and
especially those articulated by the governments and leaders most influential
over the drafting of the document: the Roosevelt administration (whose "four
freedoms" are clearly echoed in the Declaration), the moderate socialist
government of Great Britain, the Liberal government of Canada, socially
progressive governments in Latin America, and the government of the
Republic of China, which thought of itself as in many ways a progressive
insurgency.[15] Similarly, many of the leading drafters were very progressive
people: Canada's principal representative, the very influential John Humphrey, was a moderate socialist, and China's representative, Peng-Chun
Chang, also a very influential drafter, had a progressive cast of mind.[16]
Catholic representatives felt the currents of social justice that were running
strongly in the papal encyclicals, notably *Rerum Novarum*[17] and *Quadragessimo
Anno.*[18]

Eleanor Roosevelt above all, the Chair of the United Nations Commission
on Human Rights, which prepared the Declaration, deserves her characterization as a progressive, the "First Lady of American Liberalism."[19] One of her
grandsons observes:

> There was a common thread running throughout Grandmere's life...her
> ever-present inquisitiveness, which questioned the bounds of society's status
> quo and challenged what was thought to be sacrosanct. Why were the

laws and traditions that reinforced social injustice and economic imbalance perpetuated?. . .

That the conditions of some people within the family of humankind were intolerable not by their own fault but by societal strictures was an unacceptable condition of the status quo, and Grandmere was completely undeterred in her determination to make changes.[20]

The Declaration's aspirational character is reflected in the fact that the Declaration does not present itself as a manual nor a legalistic code; the better future towards which it gestures is not presented in blueprint form. The Declaration invites the peoples of the world to reach towards a future that is only in part spelled out. This quality reflects a strain in the writings of some of the major drafters, who were mature persons acutely aware of the limitations of their own powers—of all human powers—to discern the future and develop complete answers to the greater questions of life. John Humphrey, for example, wrote during this period, "I. . .cling to my intellect as my surest if imperfect guide."[21] Here is Eleanor Roosevelt to similar effect:

[B]eing oneself to the utmost & yet being related to the great upward struggles, all that one loves, human beings, nature, ideals, kinship with God & man add to the sense of relatedness. There is a point beyond which one cannot explain or think thro [sic]; one can only feel & believe.. . .

. . .Christ. . .said we had to be like little children because he knew just thinking alone never solved the riddle which at some time preoccupies us all.[22]

If reading of its open-minded aspirationalism leaves the reader with the impression that the drafters of the Declaration were on a journey to Disneyland or had their feet planted on the yellow brick road, this impression must be corrected.

The third fundamental characteristic exhibited by the history and text of the Declaration is an attitude of personal self-criticism, national self-criticism, self-sacrifice, and commitment to duty. Unlike many people, in her era or any other, Eleanor Roosevelt unflinchingly confessed to doubts as to her capacities to fulfill her responsibilities. Marital difficulties in the form of Franklin's infidelity elicited these traits in her to the highest degree. Late in her life, she wrote the following painful words:

Perhaps one of the most difficult things any of us has to do is to be able to say clearly, "This is a limitation in me. Here is a case where, because of some lack of experience or some personal incapacity, I cannot meet a situation; I cannot meet the need of someone whom I dearly love, my husband or my children.". . .

Life teaches you that you cannot attain real maturity until you are ready to accept this harsh knowledge, this limitation in yourself, and make the difficult adjustment. Either you must learn to allow someone else to meet the need, without bitterness or envy, and accept it; or somehow you must make yourself learn to meet it.. . .There is another ingredient of the maturing process that is almost as painful as accepting your own limitations and the knowledge of what you are unable to give. That is learning to accept what other people are unable to give. You must learn not to demand the impossible or to be upset when you do not get it.[23]

Marital difficulties among her children, some of whom saw their marriages end in divorce during the 1940s, elicited in Eleanor Roosevelt the inclination to put the blame on herself.[24] In her thinking, candor compelled self-criticism and personal failings elicited a renewed commitment to duty. On the occasion of the failure of her daughter's marriage and the illness of one of the family, Eleanor wrote:

> Perhaps when things like this happen which seem just too much to bear, we are being given a lesson in values. There is no use trying to teach the weak but the strong are worth training. When a child is ill you know that the other losses were of little importance, his life & happiness is all that counts. You work to repay money losses to others because you have a sense of integrity & responsibility. You work for some future security so as not to be a burden on the young but you learn that the satisfactions that come are in doing the work well & in making those you love happy.[25]

Similarly in political affairs:

> Many of the boys I saw in hospitals are now leading happy and useful lives, but they carry with them, day after day, the results of the war. If we do not achieve the ends for which they sacrificed—a peaceful world in which there exists freedom from fear of both aggression and want—we have failed. We shall not have paid our debt until these ends are achieved.[26]
>
> Among the people Eleanor invited to Hyde Park that summer [1944] to use the cottage and the pool were two veterans who had lost their legs overseas. Watching these young men swim in the pool despite their amputated legs caused Eleanor to burst forth, as she often did.... "If we don't make this a more decent world to live in, I don't see how we can look these boys in the eyes. They are going to fight their handicaps all their lives & what for, if the world is the same cruel, stupid place."[27]

Like many progressives—Humphrey, perhaps Chang,[28]—Roosevelt was unflinching about the defects in her own country.[29] Like many people of all stripes in the aftermath of the Second World War, living amid a sense of its horrors and an increasing awareness of the Holocaust, the drafters experienced a strong sense of moral onus.

As a result, the Declaration and its history display a certain sense of firmness and determination. The social order that appears on the horizon of the Declaration is precisely that—an *order*. In this respect the Declaration differs from aspirational writings of a utopian nature. It not only hopes, it also regrets and perhaps fears. It not only promises, it demands.

The drafters were people who placed duty front and center in their moral thought. For Catholic participants, the influence of Thomist thought pressed that way, since Thomist ethics is a system of virtues and duties rather than rights.[30] For Latin American participants, the contemporaneous work that was being done during 1947 and 1948 on the American Declaration of the

Rights and Duties of Man pressed that way, since this document (the "Bogota Declaration") repeatedly emphasized duties as well as rights, prominently stating, for example:

> The fulfillment of duty by each individual is a prerequisite to the rights of all. Rights and duties are interrelated in every social and political activity of man. While rights exalt individual liberty, duties express the dignity of that liberty.[31]

For Chinese participants, rights were a controverted modern concept; their Confucian heritage pointed instead towards responsibilities and the possession of excellence of character.[32] Chang was a vigorous supporter of references to duties in the Declaration.[33]

In the moving final passage of his important essay on the document, René Cassin, the leading French representative, characterized the Declaration as having presented a "common moral code" to all members of human society.[34] The Declaration states in Article 29(1) that "[e]veryone has duties to the community in which alone the free and full development of his personality is possible."[35]

The fourth fundamental characteristic exhibited by the history and text of the Declaration is that the drafters apply their objectivist, duty-embracing progressivism not only to the state and the individual but also to associations, communities, and families. The Declaration speaks directly to social institutions. It exhorts "every organ of society"—"keeping this Declaration constantly in mind"—to strive to "promote respect" for the Declaration and secure its "recognition and observance." It recognizes a right everyone has to a "social order"[36] in which the aims of the Declaration can be realized.[37] René Cassin underlined the importance of "marriage, family, household, vocation, city, [and] nation."[38] Eleanor Roosevelt eloquently referred to the Declaration's solicitude for the "small places, close to home":

> Where, after all, do universal human rights begin? In small places, close to home—so close and so small that they cannot be seen on any map of the world. Yet they *are* the world of the individual person: the neighborhood he lives in; the school or college he attends; the factory, farm or office where he works. . . .Unless these rights have meaning there, they have little meaning anywhere. Without concerted citizen action to uphold them close to home, we shall look in vain for progress in the larger world.
>
> Thus we believe that the destiny of human rights is in the hands of all our citizens in all our communities.[39]

The drafters influenced by Catholicism—Charles Malik[40] and the large Latin American contingent—were heirs to the Aristotelean understanding that man is a political animal,[41] a partnership-forming creature, and a "household-maintaining animal,"[42] insights transmitted to modern Catholicism through Thomas Aquinas,[43] whose perennial authority was reinvigorated by an encyclical from Leo XIII in 1879.[44] This social philosophy had recently been rededicated to the goods of the family, marriage, and workplace association by two encyclicals issued by Pius XI in 1930 and 1931. One, *Quadragesimo Anno,* recognized a "natural right to form associations"[45] and deplored the circumstance that:

> things have come to such a pass through the evil of what we have termed "individualism" that, following upon the overthrow and near extinction of that rich social life which was once highly developed through associations of various kinds, there remain virtually only individuals and the State.[46]

The other, *Casti Connubi,* emphasized "conjugal honour" and the indissolubility of marriage.[47]

The emphasis on associations rested in part upon the insight that social organizations and especially the family support and nourish the political community, the state, and the moral order of rights and duties contemplated by the Declaration. Eleanor Roosevelt wrote: "The principles of democratic citizenship are taught in the home and the example is given there of the responsibility assured to the individual under a democratic form of government."[48]

Quadragesimo Anno stated that "the more perfectly a graduated order is kept among the various associations...the stronger social authority and effectiveness will be [and] the happier and more prosperous the condition of the State."[49] *Casti Connubii* stated that:

> [T]he prosperity of the State and the temporal happiness of its citizens cannot remain safe and sound where the foundation on which they are established, which is the moral order, is weakened and where the very fountainhead from which the State draws its life, namely, wedlock and the family, is obstructed....[50]

Peng-Chun Chang stated:

> In order to bring peace to the world, there must be order in the different countries. In order to bring order to the countries, the family (social relations) must be regulated. In order to regulate the family (social relations) individuals must be cultivated. In order to cultivate the individuals, their hearts must be rectified. In order to rectify their hearts, their thoughts must be made sincere. In order to make their thoughts sincere, they must extend their knowledge. In order to extend their knowledge, they must go to things as they are.[51]

Dr. Chang there quoted from one of the most important works in the Confucian tradition, called the *Great Learning,* which continues:

> It is only when things are investigated that knowledge is extended; when knowledge is extended that thoughts become sincere; when thoughts become sincere that the mind is rectified; when the mind is rectified that the person is cultivated; when the person is cultivated that order is brought to the family; when order is brought to the family that the state is well governed; when the state is well governed that peace is brought to the world.[52]

An emphasis on associations implies an emphasis on the duties of their members. Eleanor Roosevelt's commitment to the preeminence of duty in marriage was emphasized in an article she published in 1931:

> It takes, time, trouble, patience to make a marriage go. You must *grow* along with it. It is a relationship that must be looked after....
>
> Unquestionably there are many unnecessary divorces. As a people, I think we are softer than we used to be. Many of us lack the stamina to face and see uncomfortable situations through. Today many seem to think that marriage is like a position in employment, which one can leave when everything does not go well. We *should* think of it as a permanent, lifetime job.[53]

The American Declaration of the Rights and Duties of Man includes an article stating that "[i]t is the duty of every person to aid, support, educate and protect his minor children, and it is the duty of children to honour their parents always and to aid, support and protect them when they need it."[54] *Casti Connubi* emphasized the "firmness" and "indissolubility" of the marriage bond,[55] the "bonds of love," and the "order of love,"[56] and it deplored that "exaggerated liberty, which cares not for the good of the family."[57]

An emphasis on associations implies a duty to protect them and help them flourish. It implies the principle of "subsidiarity" articulated in *Quadragesimo Anno*:

> Just as it is gravely wrong to take from individuals what they can accomplish by their own initiative and industry and give it to the community, so also it is an injustice and at the same time a grave evil and a disturbance of right order to assign to a greater and higher association what lesser and subordinate organizations can do. For every social activity ought of its very nature to furnish help to the members of the body social, and never destroy and absorb them.[58]

B. The Declaration's Purposes and Moral Commitments

1. Prohibiting Barbarous Acts Against Individuals   Reacting against "barbarous acts which have outraged the conscience of mankind,"[59] the Declaration prohibits torture, slavery, arbitrary arrest, arbitrary deprivation of property, and other actions characteristic of the Nazi regime.[60] This reflects the Declaration's most noticeable strategy: that of identifying and condemning wrongs committed by the State against individuals.

2. Prohibiting Barbarous Acts Against the Family   The Declaration is in part a reaction against attacks on the family. Nazi laws mandated involuntary sterilization and involuntary abortion in cases of persons deemed unfit to reproduce.[61] Nazi propaganda sought to remold the mother into "a Brunhilde who would target children for sterilization...or turn her daughter out of the family for dating a boy with communist or Jewish parents."[62] Nazi policies deprived German parents of their normal control over the training of their children by imposing programs of indoctrination in Nazi ideology. In occupied Europe, Nazi authorities identified certain children as possessing desirable biological characteristics, forcibly separated them from their parents, transported them to Germany, "Germanized" them, and placed them for adoption with SS families.[63] Reichsfuhrer Himmler organized institutions called *Lebensborn* whose mission was "to help combat conventional Christian-bourgeois morality" and to substitute a "new, *volkisch* morality" involving selective extramarital breeding.[64]

The Declaration prohibits such barbarities: for example, Article 12 provides that "[n]o one shall be subjected to arbitrary interference with his privacy, family, home or correspondence"; Article 16(1) provides that "[m]en and women of full age, without any limitation due to race, nationality or religion, have the right to marry and to found a family"; and Article 26(3) provides that "[p]arents have a prior right to choose the kind of education that shall be given to their children."

3. Promoting a Better Social Order   Aspiring to "promote social progress and better standards of life in larger freedom,"[65] several passages of the Declaration turn from prohibiting specific evils to commending general social goods and a just and beneficent social order. This reflects two major purposes.

In part, the Declaration seeks to prevent a return to totalitarianism. The drafters recognized that such things could be forestalled in the future only through the development and preservation of decent societies. This recognition is evident in the Declaration's third, sixth, and seventh "whereas" clauses:

> *Whereas* it is essential, if man is not to be compelled to have recourse, as a last resort, to rebellion against tyranny and oppression, that human rights should be protected by the rule of law,. . .
>
> *Whereas* Member States have pledged themselves to achieve, in co-operation with the United Nations, the promotion of universal respect for and observance of human rights and fundamental freedoms,
>
> *Whereas* a common understanding of these rights and freedoms is of the greatest importance for the full realization of this pledge.. . .

One finds a clear line of analysis here:

- to avoid tyranny and oppression or rebellion, you need:
- human rights; and to secure human rights you need:
   - the rule of law;
   - a universal respect for human rights; and
   - a common understanding of human rights.

This line of reasoning is extended in the "Now, therefore" clause:

> *Now, therefore, The General Assembly, Proclaims* this Universal Declaration of Human Rights as a common standard of achievement for all peoples and all nations, to the end that every individual and every organ of society, keeping this Declaration constantly in mind, shall strive by teaching and

education to promote respect for these rights and freedoms and by progressive measures, national and international, to secure their universal and effective recognition and observance....

The Declaration commits education to the family and provides in Article 26(2) that education "shall promote understanding, tolerance and friendship among all nations, racial or religious groups, and shall further the activities of the United Nations for the maintenance of peace."

The other major reason for some of the Declaration's provisions is the obvious one that things like freedom, reason, education, the rule of law, a sound social order, and brotherhood are good things in their own right and not only as instruments for the avoidance of barbarities.[66] Thus the Declaration's fifth "whereas" clause includes a reference to "social progress and better standards of life in larger freedom."[67] The period immediately after World War II was one of cautious optimism for a great era of beneficence and peace —the "sunny uplands" that Winston Churchill had foretold as the fruit of Allied victory; the "world made new" for which Eleanor Roosevelt nightly prayed:

> Open our eyes to simple beauty all around us and our hearts to the loveliness men hide from us because we do not try to understand them. Save us from ourselves and show us a vision of the world made new.[68]

Basic goods—resting as one commentator puts it on "deep truths rediscovered in the midst of the Holocaust"[69]—are embraced in Article I: "All human beings are born free and equal in dignity and rights. They are endowed with reason and conscience and should act towards one another in a spirit of brotherhood."

Emphatically noninstrumentalist bases for human rights were articulated in the Bogota Declaration,[70] which was influential with leading drafters of the Universal Declaration of Human Rights[71] and which closely resembles it in many respects.[72] The Bogota Declaration, noting that "[t]he American States have on repeated occasions recognized that the essential rights of man are not derived from the fact that he is a national of a certain state, but are based upon attributes of his human personality,"[73] rests on the propositions that "spiritual development is the supreme end of human existence,"[74] that "it is the duty of man to serve that end with all his strength and resources,"[75] that "culture is the highest social and historical expression of that spiritual development,"[76] that "it is the duty of man to preserve, practice and foster culture,"[77] and that "since moral conduct constitutes the noblest flowering of culture, it is the duty of every man always to hold it in high respect."[78] Rights are recognized because they "exalt individual liberty."[79] Duties "express the dignity of that liberty."[80]

When the Universal Declaration of Human Rights protects the "freedom to hold opinions" and to "receive and impart information and ideas" (Article 19) and when it mandates "[e]ducation shall be directed to the full development of the human personality" (Article 26(2)),...it goes beyond the erection of barriers against barbarism and nurtures practices that instantiate reason and conscience and thus are part of human flourishing quite aside from any further results to which they may lead. When the Declaration protects the freedom of association (Article 20), it recognizes the inherent goodness of those social connections that put the spirit of brotherhood to work.

C. Some Implications for Efforts to Reform Marriage and the Family

If Eleanor Roosevelt and the other drafters appeared among us today, they might offer several lines of commentary and criticism of our era's efforts to redefine or deconstruct the family, and remind us of how the philosophy and purposes of the Declaration are implicated.

First, they would ask us to reflect on the gravity of the matter. They would recommend that we consider, not only how much is at stake for how many people in their private lives, but also how great may be the consequences and for how long a term in public and social life. They would adjure us to bear in mind the importance of sustaining public morality in a republic and of fostering those international commonalities that ground transnational brotherhood. The family is, the Declaration reminds us in Article 16(3), the "fundamental" group unit of society. We have taken into our own hands, they might remind us, the foundation stones of those "small places, close to home . . .the world of the individual person," and placed our tools upon their support beams.

Second, the drafters would recommend that we bear in mind not only the positive law and the fashions of one country's or another's social morality and ideological fashions but also those objective, nonpositive, transcultural goods on which the family is founded and which it ought to serve. The Declaration emphasizes in Article 16(3) that the family is—not only fundamental— but also the "*natural. . .group unit of society.*"[81]

Third, the drafters would commend to us a morality of modesty, self-criticism, self-sacrifice, and respect for duty, both as to how we conduct ourselves in framing law and policy and as regards our conduct as husbands, wives, brothers, sons, and daughters. On grounds of subsidiarity, they would be suspicious of efforts to deprive marriage and the family of their proper functions, and on grounds of respect for obligation, they would be astonished by any effort to separate the theory and practice of family from the exercise of responsibility among family members or duties running from the family to the wider social order. Eleanor Roosevelt would say to our age what she wrote to her own: "I think we ought to impress on both our girls and boys that successful marriages require just as much work, just as much intelligence and just as much unselfish devotion, as they give to any position they undertake to fill on a paid basis."[82]

Fourth, the drafters would remind us of the intention behind the Declaration to preserve social forms from being molded like putty in the hands of the state or any socially dominant group. They would emphasize, as did Charles Malik, that the family is the "cradle of all human rights and liberties"[83] and that "society [is] not composed of individuals, but of groups, of which the family [is] the first and most important unit; in the family circle the fundamental human freedoms and rights [are] originally nurtured."[84] To alter the family is to revise or deconstruct the fundamental unit recognized by the Declaration as having charge of the education of the young, and thus to affect what the Declaration understands as the purpose of education: "the full development of the human personality."[85] Altering the family necessarily implicates the development of "reason and conscience."[86]

II. Plato's Formless City and the Deconstruction of Marriage and the Family

In the *Republic,* Plato depicts a deteriorated city in which each resident believes that he has license to behave just as he wishes. Each

> lives along day by day, gratifying the desire that occurs to him, at one time drinking and listening to the flute, at another downing water and reducing; now practicing gymnastic, and again idling and neglecting everything; and sometimes spending his time as though he were occupied with philosophy. Often he engages in politics and, jumping up, says and does whatever chances to come to him; and if he ever admires any soldiers, he turns in that direction; and if it's money-makers, in that one. And there is neither order nor necessity in his life...."[87]

Plato describes this condition as a stage in the decay of a city in which it descends from oligarchy into a state that could be called "formlessness." Overthrowing the rule of the oligarchs—corpulent and avaricious rich men—the people enjoy, for a time, a "rainbow hued" social situation where all sorts of differences are accepted and none is preferred:

> [There is] license in it to do whatever one wants[88]...And where there's license, it's plain that each man would organize his life in it privately just as it pleases him.
>
> . . .
>
> ...[T]he absence of any compulsion to rule in this city...even if you are competent to rule, or again to be ruled if you don't want to be, or to make war when the others are making war, or to keep peace when the others are keeping it, if you don't desire peace; and, if some law prevents you from ruling or being a judge, the absence of any compulsion keeping you from ruling or being a judge anyhow, if you long to do so—isn't such a way of passing the time divinely sweet for the moment?
>
> ...Isn't the gentleness toward some of the condemned exquisite? Or in such a regime haven't you yet seen men who have been sentenced to death or exile, nonetheless staying and carrying on right in the middle of things; and as though no one cared or saw, stalking the land like a hero?
>
> ...And [this city] spatters with mud those who are obedient, alleging that they are willing slaves of the rulers and nothings...while it praises and honors...the rulers who are like the ruled and the ruled who are like the rulers....

...[A] father...habituates himself to be like his child and fear his sons, and a son habituates himself to be like his father and to have no shame before or fear of his parents...and metic is on an equal level with townsman and townsman with metic, and similarly with the foreigner.

...

...[T]he teacher...is frightened of the pupils and fawns on them, so the students make light of their teachers....[T]he old come down to the level of the young; imitating the young, they are overflowing with facility and charm, and that's so that they won't seem to be unpleasant or despotic.

...

Then, summing up all of these things together...do you notice how tender they make the citizens' soul, so that if someone proposes anything that smacks in any way of slavery, they are irritated and can't stand it? And they end up, as you well know, by paying no attention to the laws, written or unwritten, in order that they may avoid having any master at all.[89]

Plato characterizes it as a city of "license." Professor Arlene Saxonhouse characterizes it as a city afflicted with "blurring of form" and "forgetfulness of form."[90] It is a Woodstock of a city.

The movements to reform or deconstruct marriage and the family in recent decades display several characteristics of the formless city. They display, in the first place, its denigration of law and custom. They reflect the philosophy that law is fiat and stands on no firmer basis than the will of the State or the votes of the judges. So things probably operated in the oligarchic regime that preceded the formless city; so perhaps the system functioned with many of the *ancien régime* oligarchies against which our liberal forebears rebelled; so things are alleged *always* to work by exponents of the leading school of jurisprudence in the United States and Britain during the twentieth century. So things work in the deliberations of the United States Supreme Court according to the reiterated characterization of one of its most influential twentieth century justices, a man very influential on several "progressive" family-law decisions. When asked by one of his law clerks: "Justice Brennan, what *is* the Constitution?," he responded: "Five votes...Five votes."[91]

A positivist understanding of the basis of the law of marriage was embraced by the plurality of the Supreme Judicial Court of the Commonwealth of Massachusetts in *Goodridge v. Department of Public Health* (holding that same-sex couples were entitled to the benefits of marriage): "[T]he terms of marriage—who may marry and what obligations, benefits, and liabilities attach to civil marriage—are set by the Commonwealth."[92] "[T]he government creates civil marriage."[93]

The second characteristic that recurs in elements of modern family-reform movements is ethical skepticism or nihilism and the corresponding sense that the order which structures human affiliations is malleable, subject to reconfiguration ad libitum. Ethical nihilism implies affiliational plasticity. It implies the "nonjudgmental" attitude recommended recently by a prominent sociologist:

[Policy makers] could attempt to create policies to support and help people in what ever type of social structures they create, giving equal credence and respect to divorced and married people, cohabiting and married couples, to children born out of wedlock and children born to married couples, and to married and unmarried parents.

...[S]ocial policies need to support people as they enter into, reside within, and move to whatever pair-bond structures fit their needs and goals....Social policies must be based on respect for people's right to choose—to live...within any particular pair-bond structure.[94]

A third characteristic takes a step outside of ethical nihilism and allows one kind of good as an appropriate guide to action and policy, namely the good of maximizing pleasure. On this view—the utilitarian—the marital affiliation, like associations of all sorts, is of instrumental good only, and there is therefore little reason to stabilize it in one form only. If marriage is nothing other than a means to an end, then it is surely right to recommend that society effect "a basic redefinition of family from a unit defined exclusively by blood and procreation" to a unit—actually an assortment of differing units—in which "the rights and obligations of people in the different pair-bonding structures need not...be the same."[95]

A related characteristic may involve antipathy towards duties and a mutinous attitude towards the obligational aspects of affiliation. Plato mentions a man[96] who displays a contempt for what he calls the "necessary" and an impatience with all the ties that ought to bind him: "For the sake of a newly-found lady friend and unnecessary concubine such a man will strike his old friend and necessary mother....For the sake of a newly-found and unnecessary boy friend, in the bloom of youth, he will strike his elderly and necessary father...."[97]

Such a man also repudiates, Plato could equally well have said, the bonds that connect him to his "necessary" wife.

"Necessary"—"*anankaion*"—here is used in a special sense.[98] It does not refer to what you need to keep yourself alive such as food and water. That man no longer finds his mother and father necessary for purposes like those. Rather, the term refers to a bond or tie within a friendship or a family. The root of "*anankaion*" may be "*ankon*"—"arm"—so perhaps the underlying concept is that your "necessary" people are those who grip you by the arm, obliging you to honor their wishes and to help them when they are in distress.[99] Another sense of *anankaion* makes it refer to that which is morally compulsory. An excellent person recognizes more things as morally binding than ordinary people might do, but a debased person, it appears, will acknowledge fewer.

The denizen of the formless city is unsteady. He is inconstant. He turns abruptly from pursuing this pleasure to that, from engaging in one project to engaging in another. His soul is "tender," Plato tells us, and abhors restraint.[100] A modern academic exemplar may be Henry A. Murray, a prominent figure in the study of psychology at Harvard University for several decades.[101] Professor Murray was an admirer of Herman Melville and accepted Melville's opinion that behind the institution of marriage was "the Church and the great bulk of respectable men and women with their damn rules, customs, formalities, manners, fads, proprieties, pretensions, rites, rituals, decrees, ordinances, laws, taboos, sentiments, beliefs, principles, Catechisms, creeds, and categorical negations."[102]

Professor Murray deserted his wife for his lover Christiana Morgan. She abandoned her husband, and together they conducted an affair that extended for more than forty years (1925 to 1967) and which was based on their having repudiated the "damn rules" and conventions, on an alternative ethic. "Mutual erotic love, erotic adoration, is the most natural religion,"[103] he wrote. Their relationship will "transform the world." "The whole spiritual course of man will pivot on you."[104]

A fifth attitude that recurs in modern reformist movements pertinent to the family, closely following from the fourth and the others, is affiliational dispensability.[105] If social forms are means to ends, they should be retained so long as they serve those ends and no longer. If a *marriage* is good only instrumentally, there is no reason to sustain its existence a minute longer than its serviceability may perdure. So, this same sociologist quoted above recommends: "[s]ocial science researchers need to move beyond a judgmental attitude toward divorce. Divorce needs to be viewed as a normal outcome that may be desirable... ."[106]

Today attitudes like these are promoted by a legal regime that is easy on divorce and minimalist in its protection of marriage. In the United States, adultery prosecutions are almost unheard of. The tort of alienation of affections has been widely abolished. Across the country, divorce is available merely by the consent of the parties, and indeed by the fiat of one party alone, however great his own wrongdoing and without regard to the harm that may be imposed on the other spouse. It is a regime of divorce by repudiation.

Elite media outlets that seek to guide public opinion follow and promote this line of approach to marriage. The *Boston Globe* in 2003 printed an advice column in which a man who had grown fonder of his mistress asked about the advisability of leaving his wife. His wife was a "good woman," he admitted, and they had a ten-year-old daughter. The Globe's columnist advised him to go right ahead. ("[C]hildren are quite resilient.")[107]

The denizens of Plato's formless city may come in the end to a repudiation, not only of the bonds imposed by custom, law, and morality—not only to a shaking off of the necessary ties to parents, husbands, and wives—but also to the loosening of the requirements of reason.[108] They may come to the point of rebelling even against those constraints by which a disciplined mind restricts its conclusions to those supported by the evidence and its systems of belief to those that stand up to the requirements of consistency. They may be led on to the lunatic opinion that one is not truly free until one invents one's own reality.

The Supreme Court of the United States has stated in recent decisions pertinent to family law: "At the heart of liberty is the right to define one's own concept of existence, of meaning, of the universe, and of the mystery of human life."[109]

Much in the movement towards liberty of divorce and same-sex marriage and other reformist efforts towards the family reflects these tendencies. It reflects an ideology of licentiousness. It promotes desertion of family and the practices of homosexuality in the name of freedom, an ideology of blurring of form—an ideology hostile to differentia and anxious to obliterate or ignore them—differences, for example, between men and women. In Massachusetts we are pressed by our highest court to blur one of the most fundamental distinctions of all: that between a man and his wife, on the one hand, and a man and his boyfriend, on the other.

III. Conclusion

The Universal Declaration of Human Rights commends a philosophy quite the reverse of that embraced by the denizens of Plato's formless city. The Declaration's morality, Eleanor Roosevelt's morality, of objectivism, of self-critical, conscience-driven, aspiration—and above all the embrace by Eleanor Roosevelt and the other drafters of the importance of firmness, courage, and duty—speak to our present age.

The Universal Declaration of Human Rights commends policies pertaining to the family much the contrary to those that are embraced by many modern reformers. It identifies the family as a "natural" not a positive. It defends the family against those who would try to turn it into putty in the hands of the judiciary or the legislature. It contemplates stable and lasting marriages and well-grounded and secure families. Only households with those characteristics serve the Declaration's purposes of assuring the education of children, establishing bulwarks against tyranny, and promoting the civic virtues of order and self-discipline, recognition of distinction, and respect for the necessary.

Plato's formless city morphs into a tyranny. Nothing much else could be expected. The self-indulgent life styles of the denizens make them soft and weak. (What sort of soldier will that flute player make?) Their "forgetfulness of form" deprives them of discernment. People who will not distinguish between a mother and a mistress, or between the licit and the illicit, will also fall short when it comes to distinguishing between true friend and pretended friend, true leader and false leader, democrat and tyrant. They will fail to maintain the distinctions between the judge and the advocate, the law that is unconstitutional and the law that is merely politically incorrect. They will fail to discern the difference between those who would protect authentic liberty and those who would undermine it.

The Universal Declaration of Human Rights was born out of war and reflects an aspiration for peace. It commends us to locate objective moral truths in a world that seemed then as it sometimes seems today to have lost sight of them. It commends us to a sustained and disciplined commitment to duty in a world that seems rather to prefer self-indulgence. In an age of hypertrophied men and nations, it calls us to remember the "small places"—the households and families in which each individual must thrive if he thrives at all—and to apply its order of reason and duty there as much as anywhere else. In an age of blurred vision and dissolution of form, hostility to tradition and enthusiasm for repudiation, it commends to us clear and sustained discernment and unwavering adherence to the basic obligations of personal life.

The Declaration reminds us that these projects may not be easily accomplished and that the definition and protection of marriage and the family are likely to involve, during our era, a lasting struggle.

This chapter closes with some words that Eleanor Roosevelt spoke to the men and women of her era. She might have been speaking to us on the struggle that we must endure in our own era to preserve marriage and the family:

> It depends on what each of us does, what we consider freedom in a democracy means and whether we really care about it enough to face ourselves and our prejudices and to make up our minds what we really want to be.
>
> The day we know that then we'll be moral and spiritual leaders.
>
> You are going to live in a dangerous world for quite a while I guess, but it's going to be an interesting and adventurous one. I wish you the courage to face it. I wish you the courage to face yourselves and when you know what you really want to be and when you know what you really want to fight for, not in a war, but in order to gain a peace, then I wish you imagination and understanding.
>
> God bless you. May you win.[110]

Presented at the European Dialogue
Geneva, Switzerland, August 2004.

Endnotes

1. J.D. Harvard. B.C.L., Oxford. Professor of Law, Boston College. Member of the Massachusetts Bar.

Thanks are extended to Dean John Garvey of Boston College Law School for arranging funding; to Professors Christopher Bruell, David Lowenthal, Francis McLaughlin, and Paul McNellis, S.J., of Boston College, and Professors Dean Hashimoto and Daniel Kanstroom of Boston College Law School for guidance on certain aspects of this chapter; and to Mark Sullivan, Research Librarian at the Boston College Law School Library, and Cecilia Zhang and William Stroever, students at Boston College Law School, for research assistance. Thanks are also extended, for general guidance in the world of family scholarship, to two past presidents of the International Society of Family Law: Professor Sanford Katz,

Libby Professor at Boston College Law School, and Professor Lynn Wardle, of Brigham Young University's J. Reuben Clark School of Law.

2. Universal Declaration of Human Rights, adopted December 10, 1948, G.A. Res. 217A (III), UN Doc. A/810 (1948).

3. *Id.* The words "and international" appear between the words "social" and "order."

4. *Quoted in Courage in a Dangerous World: The Political Writings of Eleanor Roosevelt* (Allida M. Black ed., 1999) (unnumbered fifth page). A fuller quotation of this passage appears at the end of this chapter.

5. Of course, to facilitate divorce is not the same thing as to promote same-sex marriage. In some intellectual environments different from our own, these projects might stand on separate philosophical bases. But at present they grow out of a single cluster of opinion; one constituted, as described in Part II below, by subjectivism as to ethics, positivism as to the law, and an emphasis on the good of pleasure and choice. It is the aim of this chapter to depict the considerable dissonance between this set of views and the purposes and principles of the Declaration.

6. "No one shall be subjected to arbitrary interference with his privacy, family, home or correspondence, nor to attacks upon his honour and reputation. Everyone has the right to the protection of the law against such interference or attacks."

7. Article 23(3) provides that "Everyone who works has the right to just and favourable remuneration ensuring for himself and his family an existence worthy of human dignity...." Article 25(1) provides that "[e]veryone has the right to a standard of living adequate for the health and well-being of himself and his family...." Article 25(2) provides that "[m]otherhood and childhood are entitled to special care and assistance." *See also* Article 26(3), which provides that "[p]arents have a prior right to choose the kind of education that shall be given to their children."

8. Besides the works reflecting the history of the Declaration discussed below, *see*, for a brief discussion of the basis of the introductory portions of the Declaration in the United Nations Charter and its history, Johannes van Aggelen, *The Preamble of the United Nations Declaration of Human Rights*, 20 Denv. J. Int'l. L. & Policy 129 (2000).

9. Or, perhaps, the rejection of the belief that moral truth can be known. For materials on ethical relativism, *see* Mohammad A. Shomali, *Ethical Relativism: An Analysis of the Foundations of Morality* (2001); *Relativism: Cognitive and Moral* (Jack W. Meiland & Michael Krausz eds., 1982). For discussions of the application of relativistic or skeptical conclusions to problems of international relations and international rights, *see Human Rights in Cross-Cultural Perspectives: A Quest for Consensus* (Abdullahi Ahmed An-Na'Im ed., 1992), and especially the editor's *Conclusion* at 427, 428–29: "all normative principles...are necessarily based on specific cultural and philosophical assumptions" and his recommendation that international standards of rights or values be based on "shared norms." For defenses of the objectivist understanding of the Declaration, *see* Mary Ann Glendon, *A World Made New: Eleanor Roosevelt and the Universal Declaration of Human Rights* (2001) (hereinafter referred to as "Glendon, *A World Made New*"), especially chapters 12 and 13; Johannes Morsink, *The Universal Declaration of Human Rights:*

Origins, Drafting & Intent (1999) (hereinafter referred to as "Morsink, *The Universal Declaration*"). *See* Mary Ann Glendon, *Foundations of Human Rights: The Unfinished Business*, 44 Am. J. Jurisprudence 1 (1999); Mary Ann Glendon, *Knowing the Universal Declaration of Human Rights*, 73 Notre Dame L. Rev. 1153 (1998); Jack Donnelly, *Unfinished Business*, in *Symposium: Free and Equal in Dignity and Rights: The Universal Declaration of Human Rights*, 31 Political Science & Pol. 530 (1998) ("Human rights are 'universal' in the sense that they are held by every person simply by virtue of being human.") For authorities as to the objective basis of the morality of the family and marriage, *see* n. 81, *infra*.. For dissent from objectivist views, *see* Tore Lindholm, *Prospects for Research on the Cultural Legitimacy of Human Rights*, in *Human Rights in Cross-Cultural Perspectives, supra*, 387 passim and especially at 397 ("the justificatory prototheory of human rights in the Universal Declaration...is that it is...an exercise in 'situated' geopolitical moral rationality").

10. Executive Board, American Anthropological Association, *Statement on Human Rights*, 49 Am. Anthropologist 539, 542 (1947) (available on jstor), *reprinted in* Morton E. Winston, *The Philosophy of Human Rights* 116, 119 (1989).

11. *Id.*, 49 Am. Anthropologist at 543, Winston, *supra*, at 199. *See id.*, 49 Am. Anthropologist at 542, Winston, *supra*, at 119: "the eternal verities only seem so because we have been taught to regard them as such...." For a discussion of this memorandum and related authorities, see Morsink, *The Universal Declaration, supra* n. 9, at ix–x.

12. Eleanor Roosevelt's position appears in the following passage from a political speech:

> [W]e believe that individual personality is endowed by God with certain inherent freedoms and therefore we have something as individuals which we can delegate to our government which gives us a stronger basis than the Communist people. As I told the [Soviet] Deputy Commissioner,...[w]hen you speak of freedom you mean something your government has given you, we mean something inherent in us as a gift of God.

"Stevenson Campaign Address," Charleston, West Virginia, October, 1956, *quoted in Courage in a Dangerous World: The Political Writings of Eleanor Roosevelt* 273, 276 (Allida M. Black ed., 1999). In her speech to the General Assembly commending the Declaration for approval, she stated:

> The central fact is that man is fundamentally a moral being....Man's status makes each individual an end in himself. No man is by nature simply the servant of the state or of another man....
>
> ...This declaration is based upon the spiritual fact that man must have freedom in which to develop his full stature and through common effort to raise the level of human dignity.

"Adoption of the Universal Declaration of Human Rights," Speech to the General Assembly of the United Nations, 9 December 1948 (quoting Gladstone Murray) (available at www.americanrhetoric.com/speeches/eleanorroosevelt declaration-humanrights.htm). Charles Malik, another leading drafter, was "by way of being a Thomist and believed in natural law." *The Memoirs of John P. Humphrey, the First Director of the United Nations Division of Human Rights*, 5 Human Rights Q. 387,

397 (1983). A UNESCO committee proposed a largely objectivist basis for the Declaration: UNESCO Committee on the Theoretical Bases of Human Rights, "The Grounds of an International Declaration of Human Rights" II, 1 (July, 1949), *reprinted in* Human Rights. Comments and Interpretations 258, 268 (UNESCO ed., 1949) ("All rights derive...from the nature of man" as well as from "the stage of development achieved by the social and political groups in which he participates.") *See* Glendon, *A World Made New, supra* n. 8, especially chapters 12 and 13; Morsink, *The Universal Declaration, supra* n. 8, especially chapter 8 ("The words 'inherent,' 'inalienable,' and 'born' in the first recital and in Article I...add up to what I shall call the inherence view of human rights. This is the view that human rights inhere in people as such...." (*id.* at 290)).

13. Morsink, *The Universal Declaration, supra* n. 8, at 90–91.

14. After the word "observance," the Declaration continues: "both among the peoples of the member States themselves, and among the peoples of the territories under their jurisdiction."

15. *See* Mayling Soong Chiang, *What China Has Faced,* in General Chiang Kai-Shek & Madam Chiang Kai-Shek, *General Chiang Kai-Shek: The Account of the Fortnight in Sian When the Fate of China Hung in the Balance* 1 (1938), reflecting the "progressive" stance of the Republic of China (p. 11); the aspiration that China will "emerge a modernized nation" (p. 59) with emancipated women (p. 58) and the capacity to "contribute vastly to the economic [and]...spiritual betterment of the world" (p. 59).

16. *See* Peng-Chun Chang, *China at the Crossroads: The Chinese Situation in Perspective* 138 (1936) (praising his government's "advance in the process of political transformation").

17. Leo XIII, *Rerum Novarum,* AAS 23 (1891) at 641 *et seq* (hereinafter referred to as "Leo XII, *Rerum Novarum*"), *reprinted in* The Papal Encyclicals 1878–1903 at 241 (Volume 2 of The Papal Encyclicals (Claudia Carlen ed., 1990)). *See generally* Jean-Yves Calvez, S.J., & Jacques Perrin, S.J., *The Church and Social Justice: The Social Teaching of the Popes from Leo XIII to Pius XII* (1961).

18. Pius XI, *Quadragesimo Anno,* AAS 23 (1931) pages 177–228 (hereinafter referred to as "Pius XI, *Quadragesimo Anno*"), translated into English as *On Reconstructing the Social Order* (Francis J. Haas & Martin R.P. McGuire, trans.), *reprinted in* The Papal Encyclicals 1903–39 at 415 (IV The Papal Encyclicals (Claudia Carlen ed., 1990)) *and also reprinted in The Companion to the Catechism of the Catholic Church: A Compendium of Texts Referred to* in *The Catechism of the Catholic Church* 641 (1994).

19. Lois Scharf, *Eleanor Roosevelt: First Lady of American Liberalism* (1987).

20. David B. Roosevelt (with Manuela Dunn-Mascetti), *Grandmère: A Personal History of Eleanor Roosevelt* 191 (2002).

21. *On the Edge of Greatness: The Diaries of John Humphrey, First Director of the United Nations Division of Human Rights* (Vol. 1: 1948–49) at 49 (A.J. Hobbins ed., 1994). Here is another passage (from *id.* at 39):

> I was impressed by the sermon which was delivered by the rector of the seminary in Quimper. The theological structure (necessity of approaching God through the Virgin, etc. etc.) was artificial and could hardly be accepted by anyone of average intelligence, but the, to me, more profound theme was unattackable. There is something, which we have learned to call the

Christian ethic…without which life is mean and egotistical. It is mainly because, putting all his faith in the achievements of Science, man has forgotten this ethic that the world has gotten itself into its present mess….Surely a world that can achieve the atomic bomb but fail in the creation of the United Nations is morally bankrupt….What we need is something like the Christian morality without the tommyrot.

22. Letter to Joseph P. Lash, 27 April 1944, *quoted in* Joseph P. Lash, A *World of Love: Eleanor Roosevelt and her Friends 1943–1962,* at 121 (1984). *See* Eleanor Roosevelt, Letter to Joseph P. Lash, 13 October 1943 *quoted in* Lash, *op. cit.,* at 83 (the foundation of the Christian religion is "the greatest of all the underground revolutions but we've allowed churches & doctrines & priests to separate us from the reality which is as real today as it ever was").

23. Eleanor Roosevelt, *You Learn by Living: Eleven Keys for a More Fulfilling Life* 66–67 (1960).

24. *See, e.g.,* Elliott Roosevelt & James Roosevelt, *Mother R.: Eleanor Roosevelt's Untold Story* 163 (1977).

25. Letter to Anna Roosevelt, 28 August 1948, *in Mother and Daughter: The Letters of Eleanor and Anna Roosevelt* 242 (Bernard Asbell ed., 1982) (Anna's marriage was failing and she had courageously assumed the debts of her and her husband's failed newspaper).

26. *The Autobiography of Eleanor Roosevelt* 261–62 (1961).

27. Letter to Joseph P. Lash, 26 August 1944, *quoted in* Joseph P. Lash, *A World of Love: Eleanor Roosevelt and her Friends 1943–1962,* at 136 (1984).

28. *See* Peng-Chun Chang, *China at the Crossroads: The Chinese Situation in Perspective* 136–49 (1936) (setting forth criticisms of Chinese society). *See also* William Theodore de Bary, *Asian Values and Human Rights: A Confucian Communitarian Perspective* 163 (1998) (characterizing the Confucian tradition as "a continuing discourse of internal self-criticism").

29. *See* Eleanor Roosevelt, *Soviet Attacks on Social Conditions in the U.S.,* Department of State Bulletin, January 19, 1953, at 116–17, *reprinted in What I Hope To Leave Behind: The Essential Essays of Eleanor Roosevelt* 613 (Allida M. Black ed., 1995) ("[S] ocial conditions in the United States are not perfect and the standard of living of large numbers of the American people is far from satisfactory. It does not require this annual shower of crocodile tears by this group of representatives to make me aware of the defects in American life. I am fully aware of these defects, for I have spent the better part of my life fighting to help correct them.").

30. *See* Mary Ann Glendon, *The Forgotten Crucible: The Latin American Influence on the Universal Human Rights Idea,* 16 Harv. Hum. Rights J. 27 (2003), for a discussion of the considerable influence exerted by Latin American political traditions on the Declaration and for the point that Thomist and other Catholic thinkers helped form a Latin American tradition in which "[t]he insistence on the correlation between human rights and duties…has been a characteristic feature." *Id.* at 37. *See* n. 44, *infra,* for a reference to the encyclical *Aeterni Patris* and quotations to passages commending Thomas's teachings as a corrective for licentiousness.

31. American Declaration of the Rights and Duties of Man, O.A.S. Res. XXX, adopted by the Ninth International Conference of American States (1948), Preamble, paragraph 2 (available in the University of Minnesota Human Rights

Library, http://www1.umn.edu/humanrts/oasinstr/zoas2dec.htm), *reprinted in* Basic Documents Pertaining to Human Rights in the Inter-American System, OEA/Ser.L.V/II.82 doc.6 rev.1 at 17 (1992), *also reprinted in* Human Rights: A Compilation of International Instruments (published by Office of the United Nations High Commissioner for Human Rights, Geneva), Vol. II: Regional Instruments 5 (1997). As to connections with the drafters of the Universal Declaration of Human Rights, see n. 70, *infra.*

32. Wang Gungwu, *Power, Rights and Duties in Chinese History,* Australian J. Chinese Affairs No. 3 at 1 (1980); Chung-Sho Lo, *Human Rights in the Chinese Tradition,* in Human Rights. Comments and Interpretations 186, 187 (UNESCO ed., 1949) (the author, a consultant to UNESCO in 1947 and a Professor of Philosophy at West-China University, states that "[t]he basic ethical concept of Chinese social political relations is the fulfillment of the duty to one's neighbour, rather than the claiming of rights."). *See* Jack Donnelly, *Human Rights and Human Dignity: An Analytic Critique of Non-Western Conceptions of Human Rights,* 76 Amer. Pol. Science Rev. 303, 308–309 (1982). *Compare* William Theodore de Bary, *Asian Values and Human Rights: A Confucian Communitarian Perspective* 24–25 (1998), referring to a "long line of Ming neo-Confucian scholars" who, "reaffirming the morally responsible and affectively responsive self," found "the conviction and courage to challenge Ming despots." De Bary observes:

> When one risks one's life in order to be true to one's own inmost self, it cannot be thought of as merely performing for others, fulfilling a social role or conforming to the values of the group. Though it would be equally inappropriate to call this self-centeredness simply a form of "individualism" (if by that one means individual freedom of choice or emancipation from social constraints), it does affirm a strong moral conscience, shaped and formed in a social, cultural process that culminates, at its best, in a sense of self-fulfillment within society and the natural order.

33. But Chang was not a pure example of Confucian thinking, having been educated largely in the United States (B.A. Clark University, 1913; Ph.D., Columbia University, 1924). *See Peng Chun Chang, 1892–1957: Biography & Collected Works* 26–27 (Ruth H.C. & Sze-Chuh Cheng eds., 1995) (privately printed).

34. *La Pensée et l'Action* 118 (1972). (The Declaration "forme la base d'un droit minimum et offre un code moral commun à chacune des personnes qui composent le societé humaine et qui veulent garder, avec leur individualité, leur indestructible vocation à la liberté de leur pensée et de leur conscience.")

35. This provision approximately parallels Article XXIX of the Bogota Declaration, *supra* n. 31: "It is the duty of the individual so to conduct himself in relation to others that each and every one may fully form and develop his personality."

36. Article 28 (including the words "and international" between "social" and "order").

37. Article 29.

38. *La Pensée et l'Action* 114 (1972). *See id.* at 110 (reporting debates, "*presque dramatique,*" over the question whether human rights were to be entirely in the care of the state or whether instead they were to be protected by various social groups such as the family).

39. "In Your Hands," Speech at the United Nations, New York, 27 March 1958 (available at www.udhr.org/history/inyour.htm). Credit accrues to Professor Glendon, who, in *The World Made New, supra* n. 9, at 239–40, brought this passage to attention.

40. For a brief identification of Charles Malik's role and background, see n. 12, *supra*.

41. *Politics* 1253a 2–9, in II *Complete Works of Aristotle* 1986, at 1987–88 (J. Barnes ed., B. Jowett trans., 1984). Aristotle also identifies man as *politikon* in *Politics* 1278b 18-20 (II *Complete Works of Aristotle, supra,* at 2029), in *Nicomachean Ethics* 1097b 12, 1162a 17–19, and 1169b 17–19 (II *Complete Works of Aristotle, supra,* 1729 at 1734, 1836 & 1848) (W.D. Ross trans.) and in *History of Animals* 488a 9–10 (I *Complete Works of Aristotle, supra,* 774, at 777) (d'A.W. Thompson trans.).

42. *koinonikon anthropos* and *oikonomikon zoon.* ("[M]an is not merely a political but also a household-maintaining animal, and his unions are not, like those of the other animals, confined to certain times, and formed with any chance partner, whether male or female; but...man has a tendency to partnership with those to whom he is by nature akin.") (elision in the text as quoted; note omitted). *Eudemian Ethics* 1242a 22–24, in II *Complete Works of Aristotle* 1922, at 1968 (J. Barnes ed., J. Solomon trans., 1984).

43. *See, e.g., Summa Theologica* I-II Q 90 a. 3 ad. 3 (I *Summa Theologica of Thomas Aquinas* 995 (Fathers of the English Dominican Province trans., 1946)). The many places in which Thomas follows Aristotle in identifying man as naturally part of a *civitas* are cited in John Finnis, *Aquinas: Moral Political and Legal Theory* 245–46 (1998). Relevant authorities on marriage and the household are cited in *id.* at 242–45. *See generally* Montague Brown, *Aristotle and Aquinas on the Family and the Political Community* (Chapter 1, Volume 3 here).

44. *Aeterni Patris,* AAS 12 (1879), at 97–115, *reprinted in The Papal Encyclicals* 1878–1903, at 17 (II *The Papal Encyclicals*) (Claudia Carlen ed., 1981), *and also reprinted in* I *Summa Theologica of Thomas Aquinas* VII (Fathers of the English Dominican Province trans., 1946) ("We exhort you, venerable brethren, in all earnestness to restore the golden wisdom of St. Thomas, and to spread it far and wide...." (paragraph 31); "[T]he teachings of Thomas on the true meaning of liberty, which at this time is running into license, on the divine origin of all authority, on laws and their force, on the paternal and just rule of princes, on obedience to the higher powers, on mutual charity one toward another...have very great and invincible force to overturn those principles of the new order which are well known to be dangerous to the peaceful order of things and to public safety." (paragraph 29)). These quotations are from the Carlen edition at 25 and 26.

45. Pius XI, *Quadragesimo Anno, supra* n. 18, paragraph 37 (at 420 in the Carlen edition).

46. *Id.,* paragraph 78 (at 427 of the Carlen edition).

47. Pius XI, *Casti Connubii,* AAS 22 (1930), at 539–92 & 604, *reprinted in The Papal Encyclicals* 1903–39, at 391 (IV The Papal Encyclicals) (Claudia Carlen ed., 1990) (hereinafter referred to as "Pius XI, *Casti Connubii*"). The phrase "conjugal honour" appears at paragraph 19 (at 394 of the Carlen edition).

48. Syndicated newspaper column, 28 March 1941, *reprinted in My Day: The Best of Eleanor Roosevelt's Acclaimed Newspaper Columns, 1936–1962,* at 53 (David

Emblidge ed., 2001). The passage continues: "Every man and woman's college should have that objective in view as part of the educational process. Without it no education is complete." This column is also reprinted in *Eleanor Roosevelt's "My Day"—Her Acclaimed Columns 1936–1945*, at 198 (Rochelle Chadakoff ed., 1989).

49. Pius XI, *Quadragesimo Anno, supra* n. 18, paragraph 80 (at 428 of the Carlen edition). *See also id.* paragraph 79 (at 427–28 of the Carlen edition): "[W]ith a structure of social governance lost, and with the taking over of all the burdens which the wrecked associations once bore, the State has been overwhelmed and crushed by almost infinite tasks and duties."

50. Pius XI, *Casti Connubi, supra* n. 47, paragraph 123 (at 412 of the Carlen edition).

51. *An address delivered by Dr. Chang to the students of Baghdad at King Faisal II Hall, March 11, in the presence of H.R.H. the Regent* (1942), *reprinted in Peng Chun Chang, 1892–1957: Biography & Collected Works* 146, 149 (Ruth H.C. & Sze-Chuh Cheng eds., 1995) (privately printed).

52. *Quoted in* I *Sources of Chinese Tradition from Earliest Times to 1600* at 331 (2d ed., Wm. Theodore de Bary & Irene Bloom, compilers, 1999). Chang quotes, in a different translation, the immediately preceding passage, not this one.

53. *Ten Rules for Success in Marriage,* Pictorial Review (December, 1931) 4, *reprinted in What I Hope To Leave Behind: The Essential Essays of Eleanor Roosevelt* 205, 206 & 213 (Allida M. Black ed., 1995).

54. The Bogota Declaration, *supra* n. 31, Article XXX.

55. Pius XI, *Casti Connubii, supra* n. 47, paragraph 32 (at 396 of the Carlen edition).

56. *Id.* paragraph 26 (at 395 of the Carlen edition).

57. *Id.* paragraph 27 (at 395 of the Carlen edition).

58. Pius XI, *Quadragesimo Anno, supra* n. 18, paragraph 79 (at 428 of the Carlen edition). Owing in part to the Declaration, the principle of subsidiarity has attained an important status in international law and international morality. Paolo G. Carozza, *Subsidiarity as a Structural Principle of International Human Rights Law,* 97 Am. J. Int'l. L. 38 (2003).

59. This phrase appears in the second "whereas" clause.

60. *See* Morsink, *The Universal Declaration, supra* n. 9, *passim* and especially ch. 2 for a discussion of the many ways in which the Declaration was a reaction against Nazism.

61. *See* Claudia Koonz, *Ethical Dilemmas and Nazi Eugenics: Single Issue Dissent in Religious Contexts,* 64 J. Modern Hist. S8, S13–S14 (1992).

62. *Id.* at S20.

63. Peter D. Stachura, untitled "Shorter Notice," in 103 English Historical Rev. 271, 272 (1988).

64. "Only after being very carefully scrutinized for their racial soundness were women permitted to have their children, who were frequently illegitimate, in the special Lebensborn Homes. Even married SS men were urged to consider extramarital procreation with suitable partners. By 1942–43 Lebensborn had about two dozen Homes scattered throughout occupied Europe...." *Id.* at 271–72 (1988) (reviewing and describing material in Goerg Lilienthal, Der "Lebensborn

E.V." Ein Instrument Nationalsocialistisher Rassenpolitik (1985)). But this line of development never became Nazi orthodoxy, as it ran into conflict with another strain of the movement that romanticized hearth and home. The Declaration cannot be confidently said to have been motivated by a reaction against the *Lebensborn* variety of Nazism because it is not clear whether the drafters ever learned much about it.

65. This phrase appears in the fifth "whereas" clause.

66. *See generally* Morsink, *The Universal Declaration of Human Rights, supra* n. 9, at 318–19 (maintaining that the drafters did not embrace an entirely instrumentalist understanding of rights).

67. Directly tracking language in the United Nations Charter, which also refers to "the promotion of the economic and social advancement of all peoples." The language appears in one of the unnumbered introductory passages, shortly before Chapter One.

68. *Quoted in* Elliott Roosevelt & James Brough, *Mother R.* 152 (1977). Thanks are extended to Professor Glendon, who brought this passage to light, prominently quoted it, and used it for the title of her book *A World Made New, supra* n. 9.

69. Morsink, *The Universal Declaration of Human Rights, supra* n. 8, at 38.

70. *Supra* n. 31.

71. *See The Memoirs of John P. Humphrey, the First Director of the United Nations Division of Human Rights,* 5 Human Rights Q. 387, 425 (1983) ("There was even a well organized attempt, under the leadership of the Cuban, Guy Perez Ciseros, to replace the Commission's text in most of its essentials by the text of the American Declaration of the Rights and Duties of Man....Since twenty out of fifty-nine delegations were from Latin America, this was no small threat."); Glendon, *A World Made New, supra* n. 9, at 141 (Santa Cruz, an influential drafter and a member of the Chilean delegation, stated that "a draft of the Bogotá Declaration had been a major source for the drafters of the Universal Declaration, and many of its provisions had found their way into the final document.") *See generally* Morsink, *The Universal Declaration of Human Rights, supra* n. 9, at 131–33.

72. Notably the first paragraph of the Preamble to the Bogota Declaration, which states that "[a]ll men are born free and equal in dignity and in rights, and, being endowed by nature with reason and conscience, they should conduct themselves as brothers one to another" and Article VI, which provides that "[e]very person has the right to establish a family, the basic element of society, and to receive protection therefor." Another important provision about the family, not closely mirrored in the Universal Declaration of Human Rights, states that "[i]t is the duty of every person to aid, support, educate and protect his minor children, and it is the duty of children to honor their parents always and to aid, support and protect them when they need it." (Article XXX).

73. This language appears in the second paragraph of the "Whereas" clauses.

74. Fourth paragraph of the Preamble.

75. *Id.*

76. Fifth paragraph of the Preamble.

77. *Id.*

78. Sixth paragraph of the Preamble.

79. Second paragraph of the Preamble.

80. *Id.*

81. Emphasis added. For some of the history of this provision, see Morsink, *The Universal Declaration of Human Rights, supra* n. 9, at 255: "The only person to speak against [Charles Malik's proposed amendment adding such language] was Bogomolov of the USSR. He did not accept Malik's definition of the 'family.' 'Various forms of marriage and family life existed in the world,' he said, 'each form corresponding to the special economic conditions of the people concerned.'" *See* Allan Carlson, *The Family is the Natural . . . Unit of Society: Evidence from the Social Sciences,* in conference materials, European Regional Dialogue in Preparation for the Doha International Conference for the Family (Geneva, Switzerland, 23–25 August 2004) (discussing some of the drafting history of this provision and identifying the natural basis of marriage in anthropological history). *See generally* Pius XI, *Casti Connubii, supra* n. 47, paragraph 5 (at 392 of the Carlen edition): "[M]atrimony was not instituted or restored by man but by God; not by man were the laws made to strengthen and confirm and elevate it but by God . . . and hence those laws cannot be subject to any human decrees or to any contrary pact even of the spouses themselves."

82. Syndicated newspaper column, 28 March 1941, *reprinted in My Day: The Best of Eleanor Roosevelt's Acclaimed Newspaper Columns, 1936–1962,* at 53 (David Emblidge ed., 2001), *also reprinted in Eleanor Roosevelt's "My Day"—Her Acclaimed Columns 1936–1945,* at 198 (Rochelle Chadakoff ed., 1989). Further material from this passage is set forth at n. 48, *supra,* and accompanying text.

83. Morsink, *The Universal Declaration of Human Rights, supra* n. 9, at 255. Charles Malik's role and his background are briefly identified in n. 12, *supra.*

84. Quoted in *id. Accord* Pius XI, *Casti Connubii, supra* n. 47, paragraph 37 (at 397 of the Carlen edition):

[U]nassailable stability in matrimony is a fruitful source of virtuous life and of habits of integrity. Where this order of things obtains, the happiness and well being of the nation is safely guarded; what the families and individuals are, so also is the State, for a body is determined by its parts.

85. Article 26(2): "Education shall be directed to the full development of the human personality.. . ."

86. Article One provides, "All human beings are born free and equal in dignity and rights. They are endowed with reason and conscience and should act towards one another in a spirit of brotherhood."

87. *The Republic of Plato* 561c-d (Alan Bloom, trans., 2d ed., 1991, at 239–40) (hereinafter referred to as "Plato, *Republic*").

88. This is actually in the form of a question in the original ("And isn't there license in it to do whatever one wants?"). But it is clear from the context that Socrates expects an affirmative answer. He receives one and builds on it.

89. Plato, *Republic, supra* n. 87, 557b–563d (Bloom translation at 235–42).

90. Arlene W. Saxonhouse, *Democracy, Equality, and Eide: A Radical View from Book 8 of Plato's Republic,* 92 Am. Pol. Sci. Rev. 273, 280 (1998). *See generally* Julia Annas, *An Introduction to Plato's Republic* 294–320 (1981) for an unimpressed reading of Plato's argument in these passages; especially her comment at 300 that Plato displays "opposition to any form of pluralism." Perhaps he may manifest this

attitude in other parts of the *Republic;* but here Plato's objection is that the denizen of the formless city distinguishes poorly rather than that he draws distinctions at all.

91. As reported in an e-mail communication to me dated 11 August 2004 from Professor Dean Hashimoto of Boston College Law School, formerly a clerk to Justice Brennan.

92. *Goodridge v. Department of Public Health,* 440 Mass. 309, 321, 798 N.E. 2d 941, 954 (2003).

93. *Id.*

94. William M. Pinsof, *The death of "till death us do part": the transformation of pair-bonding in the 20th century,* 41 Family Process 135, at 151 (2002).

95. *Id.*

96. Not necessarily a man who lives in the formless city.

97. Plato, *Republic, supra* n. 87, 574b-c (Bloom translation at 258). This assertion is actually posited as a question by Socrates, but it is clear in context that Socrates expects to receive an affirmative answer and that he approves of it once he receives it.

98. This paragraph is taken with few changes from Scott FitzGibbon, *Marriage and the Ethics of Office,* 18 Notre Dame J. of Law, Ethics & Pub. Policy 89, 100 (2004).

99. Or perhaps it refers to those whom you have grasped or embraced. *See* I Ceslas Spicq, O.P., *Theological Lexicon of the New Testament* 97–100 (James D. Ernst trans., 1994).

100. Plato, *Republic, supra* n. 87, 563d-e (Bloom translation at 242).

101. This passage is adapted from similar material in Scott FitzGibbon, *Marriage and the Good of Obligation,* 47 Am. J. Jurisprudence 41, 51–52 (2002).

102. *Quoted in* Forrest G. Robinson, *Love's Story Told: A Life of Henry A. Murray* 241 (1992). It is not entirely clear from the context whether Murray was expressing his own views directly or those of Melville; but if he was communicating Melville's views he was also clearly agreeing with them.

103. Henry A. Murray, *quoted in id.* at 381.

104. Henry A. Murray, *quoted in id.* at 170.

105. For discussions of societal trends and attitudes, especially among the elite, inimical to marriage and marital fidelity, see Linda J. Waite & Maggie Gallagher, *The Case for Marriage: Why Married People Are Happier, Healthier, and Better off Financially* ch. 1 (2000); Barbara Dafoe Whitehead, *The Divorce Culture: Rethinking our Commitments to Marriage and Family* (1998); Maggie Gallagher, *The Abolition of Marriage: How We Destroy Lasting Love* (1996); Lynn D. Wardle, *Is Marriage Obsolete?,* 10 Mich. J. Gender & L. 189 (2003), especially Section IV D.

106. William M. Pinsof, *The death of "till death us do part": the transformation of pair-bonding in the 20th century,* 41 Family Process 135, at 153 (2002).

107. "Annie's Mailbox: Because of daughter, he stays in empty marriage," Boston Globe, 30 December 2003, at E-2 col. 3. ("While divorce isn't the preferred option, children are quite resilient....If counseling doesn't help, try a legal separation.")

108. The formless city is "fair and heady." (Plato, *Republic, supra* n. 87, 563e (Bloom translation at 242)) and the inhabitant of the city is "fair and many-colored" (*id.* 561 e (Bloom translation at 240)) and perhaps dreamy (*see id.* 574 d-

e (Bloom translation at 255)) and similar to the "lovers of sights" discussed in an earlier passage of the *Republic*:

> The lovers of hearing and the lovers of sights... surely delight in fair sounds and colors and shapes and all that craft makes from such things, but their thought is unable to see and delight in the nature of the fair itself.
>
> ... Is the man who holds that there are fair things but doesn't hold that there is beauty itself and who, if someone leads him to the knowledge of it isn't able to follow—is he in your opinion, living in a dream or is he awake? Consider it. Doesn't dreaming, whether one is asleep or awake, consist in believing a likeness of something to be not a likeness, but rather the thing itself to which it is like?

Id. 476 a-c (Bloom translation at 156). Their cognition has a disordered and episodic quality. Their thinking resembles feeling. *See* Terence Irwin, Plato's Ethics 664–71 (1995) for a discussion of Plato on knowledge, dreaminess, and the sight-lovers.

109. *Planned Parenthood v. Casey*, 505 U.S. 833, 851 (1992), *quoted in Laurence v. Texas*, 539 U.S. 558, 574 (2003).

110. *Freedom and Human Rights, quoted in Courage in a Dangerous World: The Political Writings of Eleanor Roosevelt* (Allida M. Black ed., 1999) (unnumbered fifth page). Departing from normal canons, elision marks have here been omitted in three or four places. In its entirety, the first sentence reads:

> It depends on what each of us does, what we consider democracy means and what we consider freedom in a democracy means and whether we really care about it enough to face ourselves and our prejudices and to make up our minds what we really want our nation to be, and what its relationship is to be to the rest of the world.

The last two sentences are not set out as a separate paragraph in the source.

7

The Role of Marriage in Transmitting Values Between Generations

Daniel Lapin (USA)
Rabbi and Journalist, USA

Thank you very much indeed, and perhaps I can intrude on just a few moments of my precious time here this morning to express my appreciation to His Highness, the Emir of Qatar as well as the Sheikha, the President of the Supreme Council for Family Affairs, the government, and also the people of Qatar, as well as also Professor Richard Wilkins and Dr. Alan Carlson. Perhaps it would also be appropriate for me to express appreciation to the people behind the glass windows, the translators, who make it possible for us here to become a unified symphony of commitment instead of just a babble of different voices.

I am here because I do believe that this Doha conference could well become a historic line of defense for the traditional family in the face of formidable and ferocious assaults on the traditional family. And on my way here, and it was well over 20 hours of travel, on the front wall of the airplane, they depicted a map of our progress as I traversed my way halfway across the globe. I was struck by the fact that almost every frame showing our progress referred to both the origin and the destination—time at the origin, time at the destination, temperature at origin, temperature at destination. The map showed a line that steadily began to link the origin and the destination.

This is one of the great secrets of successful navigation. You need to know where you came from, and you need to know where you are trying to get to. That is also one of the great secrets of successful living. We need to know where we came from, and we need to know where to go.

The problem is that time is not intuitive to us. It is much easier to live in the present than it is to integrate our lives with the past as well as with the future. After all, children are born and grow with an almost intuitive understanding of certain dimensions. They understand length and distance very quickly. They understand the weight of an object very quickly. They even understand temperature very quickly. When things are too cold, they howl. But children do not intuitively understand time. And who can blame them, for time is the secret of relativity. We did not understand that until the beginning of the twentieth century. For children, a year can stretch forever. When you are a little older, the years fly by with frightening speed. Time is relative. It was in

1908 that the Polish mathematician, Herman Minkovsky, introduced a new and accurate understanding of time when he spoke to the German Academy of Natural Science: "From now onwards, neither time nor space can be understood separately. They need to be unified." And so our very understandings of reality through quantum mechanics and relativity theory are rooted in the complexities of time. Time—the past, the present, and the future.

Well, in the language of the Torah, there actually is not a present. There are only two times, the future and the past. The present is not a time. The present is an activity. It is a process that converts the future into the past. And so we as human beings are born, and we grow with an intuitive understanding of length and of weight and of temperature and of the present process; but if nobody teaches the future and nobody teaches us the past, we are orphans in time. And that is why most religions start by telling us where we came from and speaking of a day of glorious redemption to which we aspire. It is impossible to navigate through life without knowing where we came from and to where we are headed. As a matter of fact, virtually all we take for granted that enriches our lives would be impossible without the clear understanding and the integration of past and future. What distinguishes us from kangaroos and beavers and falcons? The difference is that animals are born with no sense, no consciousness of the past, no sensitivity to the future— merely instincts with which to function in the present.

I believe that the proposition that I place before you today, I place before the Doha Conference for the first time. I believe that one of the saddest problems to which members of this distinguished panel have already alluded is the fact that we are raising a generation of children who are orphans in time. They are incapable of integrating their past and their future. They live instinctively in an almost animal-like fashion only in the present. We as human beings, our technological advances, our medical advances, all of these things are based on knowing where we came from—knowing the background and history, knowing the mistakes that were made by the technologists and the scientists that came before us as well as a very clear indication of where it is we are trying to go. We are trying to reach greater accomplishments in medical care and health. We are trying to overcome the human limitations of space and time by improved communication. We know where we came from, and we know where we are going, but we have raised children who simply do not have the capacity to link the future, to link the past, and to build their present based upon that integration of past and future.

What is the consequence? Well, little boys who grow up with no awareness of the past become cowards. They grow up with no sense of honor. Little boys with no sense of the future become capable of impregnating women but not capable of becoming fathers. Little girls with no sense of the past run the risk of making terrible choices in men, and little girls with no sense of the future run a greater risk of destroying their lives with unplanned events that are tragic for everybody concerned.

I believe that perhaps one reason we speak of marriage as an eternal covenant is because it brings a man and a woman together in the unique capacity of unifying past and future. For instance, it is the man who is better equipped to communicate to his son and to his daughter the meaning of the past. Let me explain what I mean. Distinguished speakers before me have alluded to the threat of homosexual marriage. Well, I have been told many times by those furious at what I say that what children need is just love—it does not matter whether it comes from two men or two women. And I believe that what children need is love but also an integration with time that can only come fully from both a father and a mother, because a father is better equipped than a mother to communicate the importance of the past. That is one of the reasons that in many cultures the family name gets brought down through the father's line, not through the mother's line, because it is the father linking the children and the family to the past. In the language of the Torah and in many other languages, the word for male has a similar root to the word for memory. I understand that this is true in Arabic as well. In English, the word member, which is part of the word remember, is also used to signify the male reproductive organ, an implicit recognition that deep within English culture lies the recollection that masculinity and memory of the past are tied together.

I think that the God who created us gave us a clue, because he made one very fundamental distinction between men and women. Men are capable of producing seed in almost incomprehensibly unlimited quantity. The commodity is limitless. Women have a limited number of seeds. Women have a limited number of ova, a limited number of opportunities to bring life into the world. Sensitive women experience periodic melancholy for that reason. What is the difference? My friends, whenever you are in possession of an absolutely limitless commodity, you are not sensitized to look ahead. If you have limitless funds, you will never budget for a rainy day—you do not have to. Therefore, you are not looking forward. I believe that this explains part of the reason imbedded within us that men do not look forward as much as women. And a woman equipped so naturally by nature to be forward looking, to be concerned about the future in a very different way than a man is, and so generating between them an integrity of time, something that brings together past and future in an eternal covenant and creates an environment in which children can grow. They grow, not like young animals driven by the passions of the present, but like human beings, intent on building and maintaining civilization, by constant integration of past and future as guides to that process that shapes and molds the present.

This is why I am persuaded that one of the greatest threats to human civilization is the threat to normalize homosexual marriage. Ultimately, is it destined to produce children that are not loved? That is not true. I have seen homosexual men and women bringing up children that they have adopted or in some cases produced by artificial insemination, and I would have to tell you they lavish great love upon those children. But, my friends, once upon a time my son lavished great love upon his puppy dog. Love is a *necessary* condition for raising children. It is not an *adequate* or *sufficient* condition for raising children. Love is vital, but so is a complete integration of time. And the only way that a young boy and a young girl acquire total integration of time is from both a father who can persuasively and compellingly inject a consciousness of the past and a mother who can persuasively and compellingly inject an awareness and consciousness of the future. In that way we are able to raise children. We can produce boys who are not cowardly and without honor, but boys who proudly carry on the traditions of their families and of their fathers and of their cultures. We can raise boys who are not only capable of impregnating women, but also capable of facing a future as fathers. We can raise girls who can listen to their fathers about what men have been like in the past since time immemorial, hearing that message more clearly than they would from their mothers. Their fathers possess credibility when it comes to talking about men and the past; and they listen to their mothers about the adventures of motherhood that lie ahead of them if only they are able to integrate the totality of that time message. And in that way, my friends, I believe that it will be possible to raise children who are not orphans of history but children who themselves will be capable of growing up one day to become part of an eternal covenant of marriage and ensure that the story of civilized humanity can indeed continue.

I pray that the efforts of all of us here today should be blessed, that we should play a vital role in bringing this blessing for all of humanity. I thank you.

Remarks Presented at the Doha International Conference for the Family
Doha, Qatar, 30 November 2004.

8

Does Sex Make Babies? Legal Justifications for Marriage, Same-Sex Marriage, and the Regulation of Intimacy in a Post-*Lawrence* World*

Maggie Gallagher (USA)
President, Institute for Marriage and Public Policy

Most public arguments in favor of same-sex marriage focus on the question of "horizontal" equal protection—formal equality between same-sex and opposite-sex couples. Do same-sex couples have a right to be treated the same under the law as opposite-sex couples?[1] However, there is an even more basic question of equal protection raised by marriage law—call it "vertical" equality, or equal treatment within the category of gay and lesbian (or heterosexual) people.

In light of the U.S. Supreme Court's assertion in *Lawrence v. Texas* of a constitutional right to "private sexual conduct," what right has the government to prefer one type of relationship (permanent, faithful, twosomes) over the alternatives?[2] On what basis can the law suggest to gay and lesbian people that other kinds of intimate or sexual relationships are somehow less worthy of public concern, attention, or benefits than same-sex marriages?

E.J. Graff, same-sex marriage advocate, writes: "Western marriage today is a home for the heart: entering, furnishing, and exiting that home is your business alone. Today's marriage—from whatever angle you look—is justified by the happiness of the pair."[3]

If the public rationale of marriage is the happiness of the individuals involved, as Graff asserts, the problem of "vertical" equal protection becomes even more urgent. How can the law deny other kinds of relationships their own vision of personal happiness? By what right do we tell people, who may desire polygamous, polyamorous, or open unions—or no union at all—that their vision of happiness is wrong or defective?

For the most part, this fundamental question about marriage law has been ignored in equal protection analyses: By what right does the law intrude in intimate relationships at all, either to burden and regulate or to benefit and prefer?

When the question is about regulating intimate relationships conducted by people attracted to the opposite sex, there is a traditional answer. The state is justified in regulating sex and intimacy because the marriage relationship creates not only unique, but irreplaceable and necessary, benefits for the whole society, and (to put it another way) sexual relationships outside of marriage impose unique costs and burdens on the whole society.

In practice, this traditional legal justification for the regulation of intimacy falls into two broad categories: the necessity of babies and the importance of fathers. Society needs a next generation, and those children ought to have both their mothers and the fathers. The critical importance of discouraging unmarried childbearing and the simultaneous need to encourage childbearing in some context justified the once-exclusive sexual license granted to married couples.

But society has changed dramatically, both legally and socially, in the past forty years. Improvements in contraceptive technology, changes in social mores, and the legalization of abortion have changed the relationship between sex between men and women and pregnancy. Unmarried people who have sex no longer necessarily have children. Married people who have sex no longer necessarily have children either. As societies become more affluent, social supports from government increase, and the capacity of single mothers to give their children the basics—food, clothing, shelter, education— also increases.

Under these circumstances, is marriage as the union of male and female still rationally related to any legitimate government objective? Is the state justified in "privileging" marriage over other forms of sexual unions men and women may want and create?

In other words: The legal justification for the unique status of marriage rests on three assertions: sex makes babies, society needs babies, and children need mothers and fathers. Marriage is about uniting these three dimensions of human social life—creating the conditions under which sex between men and women can make babies safely, the fundamental interests of children in the care and protection of their own mother and father will be protected, and women receive the protections they need to compensate for the high and gendered (i.e., nonreciprocal) costs of childbearing.

Creating this social good requires a social institution that is not "narrowly tailored" but broadly promoted. Every man and woman who have sex outside of marriage increase the probability that children will be conceived in unions where the father (and possibly the mother) are unprepared and unwilling to care for them. The more men and women who are married, the fewer children will be conceived in such situations and either aborted or born out of wedlock. The more men and women who are married, the fewer children will be abandoned or disconnected from their fathers and the more mothers will enjoy the support of fathers in raising children. The more men and women who are married, the more men and women there will be who are in a good position to undertake the costly, risky, yet irreplaceable work of bearing and raising the next generation together.

Marriage cannot be coerced. But it can be privileged, promoted, and encouraged over other kinds of relationships because it unites a unique set of critical social goods. Moreover, for marriage to produce these social goods, many players besides the law need to be involved. Families, churches, and communities must raise boys and girls to become the kind of young men and women who aspire to (and can be successful at) marriage. This is another reason why marriage law, to be effective, must be broadly rather than narrowly tailored to meet this compelling state interest.

Sex makes babies. Society needs babies. Children need mothers and fathers. Together these three ideas ground the "marriage idea" as a public, legal relationship. However, each of these ideas is now contested in the public square and particularly in the academy. This chapter examines the evidence for each proposition separately asking, in essence, are these statements still sufficiently true to justify the unique legal status of marriage? Together do they continue to constitute a rational legal justification for the regulation of intimacy? Or, as some advocates of same-sex marriage have argued, have social and legal changes in sexual experience and mores of the past forty years rendered traditional public policy preferences for marriage archaic and irrational?

Does Sex Make Babies?

For most of American history, the relationship of marriage to procreation was axiomatic.[4] Marriage was society's sexual license par excellence. By authorizing, encouraging, and indeed requiring sex between a man and a woman,[5] marriage ensured the procreation of the human race as well as mutual support and the only lawful sexual satisfaction. By favoring marriage over other kinds of sexual unions, society discouraged out-of-wedlock births and encouraged procreation within marriage.

Is this still a legitimate justification for marriage? Does sex still make babies? Many scholars and other observers both right and left have concluded the answer is "No." Legalized contraception, they argue, makes traditional notions of marriage as a regulator of reproduction anachronistic at best, irrational at worst.

As one legal scholar put it:

> When in the 1960s, oral contraceptives became available, and a constitutional right to use them had been established by the Supreme Court in *Griswold v. Connecticut*, the courts retreated from this rhetoric, perhaps realizing that the survival of the species and of civilization did not depend on every sexual encounter having procreative potential.

He continues:

> The point here is that the conception of marriage as sexual, wherever found in the law, has outlived its usefulness. Unless and until we contemplate

reestablishing meaningful legal penalties for fornication, the mere existence of marriage as a legal institution cannot realistically be looked upon as a means to control sex outside of marriage, and therefore control out-of-wedlock childbirth.[6]

Nonlegal observers have come to a similar conclusion:

> Today, though, sexual intercourse is de-linked from procreation. Since the invention of the Pill some 40 years ago, human beings have for the first time been able to control reproduction with a very high degree of assurance.....[T]he causal relationships between sex, pregnancy, and marriage were severed in a fundamental way.....Sex, childbearing and marriage now have no necessary connection to one another, because the biological connection between sex and childbearing is controllable. The fundamental basis for marriage has thus been technologically obviated.[7]

When advocates of same-sex marriage charge that allowing couples who have no intention to have children to marry means that marriage no longer has an intrinsic relationship to procreation, they are making (implicitly) a version of this same argument. Indeed, court cases creating same-sex marriage or marriage equivalents have held that marriage no longer has any intrinsic relationship to the making of babies. Observing that "many opposite-sex couples marry for reasons unrelated to procreation, that some of these couples never intend to have children, and that others are incapable of having children,"[8] and again that "increasing numbers of same-sex couples are employing increasingly efficient assisted-reproductive techniques to conceive and raise children,"[9] the Vermont Supreme Court in 1999 rejected the state's assertion that marriage laws were intended to promote children, or a connection between children and their biological parents.[10] The Massachusetts Supreme Judicial Court was even more dismissive:

> It is hardly surprising that civil marriage developed historically as a means to regulate heterosexual conduct and to promote child rearing, because until very recently unassisted heterosexual relations were the only means short of adoption by which children could come into the world, and the absence of widely available and effective contraceptives made the link between heterosexual sex and procreation very strong indeed...But it is circular reasoning, not analysis, to maintain that marriage must remain a heterosexual institution because that is what it historically has been. As one dissent acknowledges, in "the modern age," "heterosexual intercourse, procreation, and child care are not necessarily conjoined."[11]

Are these analyses true? Is there no longer any rational relation between affirming marital sexual unions and preventing unmarried births?[12] Has contraceptive technology stripped sex of any intrinsic relationship to pregnancy, thus rendering the state's interest in encouraging men and women attracted to the opposite sex to get into marital unions, rather than other kinds of relationships, obsolete?

Forty years after *Griswold v. Connecticut*,[13] we now have considerable social experience testing these propositions. Is there still a rational justification for marriage, on the grounds that, when men and women enter this kind of union, the possibility of out-of-wedlock births is minimized? Or has contraceptive technology rendered this formerly rational relation obsolete? Does sex still make babies?

Yes. Sex between men and women continues to make babies on a regular basis, with or without the conscious intention of the participants. The longer men and women engage in nonmarital sexual careers, the greater the risk of a nonmarital pregnancy. Despite legal contraception, numerous studies have shown that unintended pregnancy is a common, not rare, consequence of sexual relationships between men and women.

Consider these statistics from an analysis of the 1995 National Survey of Family Growth, based on a nationally representative sample of 10,847 women between the ages of fifteen and forty-four.[14] Almost a third of all births between 1990 and 1995 were unintended.[15] Fifty-six percent of births to unmarried women were unintended (as were 19 percent of births to married women and 39 percent of births to divorced women).[16] Almost a third of births to married parents and three-fourths of births to unmarried couples were unintended by at least one of the parents.[17] About 17 million American women of childbearing age have already had an unintended birth.[18]

When considering the number of pregnancies (as opposed to births), the statistics are even more striking. Consider these data from a study in *Family Planning Perspectives*, published by the Alan Guttmacher Institute:[19] Excluding miscarriages, 49 percent of all pregnancies in 1994 were unintended.[20] Almost half of all women aged fifteen to forty-four had had at least one unplanned pregnancy in their lives.[21] By their late thirties, 60 percent of American women had had at least one unintended pregnancy.[22] Almost four in ten women aged forty to forty-four had had at least one unplanned birth.[23]

Similarly a scholarly analysis of contraceptive failure rates in actual use concluded, "About three million pregnancies in the United States (48%) were unintended in 1994. Some 53 percent of these occurred among women who were using contraceptives."[24]

Contraceptive failure rates in the first year of use varied considerably among different demographic groups but were never trivial: About 47 percent of cohabiting adolescent women experience a contraceptive failure (i.e., an unintended pregnancy) in the first year of contraceptive use, compared to 8 percent of married women age thirty and older.[25]

Another analysis of the 1995 National Survey of Family Growth concluded: "The risk of failure during typical use of reversible contraceptives in the United States is not low—overall, 9% of women become pregnant within one year of starting use. The typical woman who uses reversible methods of contraception continuously from her 15th to her 45th birthday will experience 1.8 contraceptive failures."[26] The typical woman who uses contraceptives continuously will experience almost two unintended pregnancies.[27]

Technology has not obviated the state's interest in encouraging men and women to enter marital sexual unions, as opposed to other kinds.

Contraceptive technology lowers the odds of pregnancy, but never eliminates the risk, especially for people who engage in extended nonmarital sexual careers.

Moreover, marriage helps regulate the efficacy of (among other things) contraceptives. Without a legal, shared, public category called "marriage," neither law nor culture would be able to motivate young men and women to avoid pregnancy out of wedlock. This is one reason that, while contraceptives may lower the state's interest in absolutely forbidding nonmarital sexual relations (given the high degree of intrusion on personal liberty involved), the existence of contraceptives does not eliminate the state's interest in preferring voluntary marital sexual unions between men and women to other kinds. Virtually every child born to a married couple will have a mother and a father already committed to caring for him or her. Most children conceived in sexual unions outside of marriage will not.

Sex between men and women still makes babies. By creating a clear shared public category called "marriage" and preferring marital unions as the context for sex and childbearing, the law (a) informs young people of the importance of doing whatever is necessary to delay pregnancy until marriage (as well as enabling other stakeholders, such as family, friends, and faith communities, to communicate this message), and (b) creates a clear marker for when men and women have created the kind of unions where babies can be encouraged.

Does Society Need Babies?

The second historic purpose of marriage is to encourage men and women to create the next generation. The idea that babies are a social good is now, however, widely contested. At the same time the widespread use of contraceptive technology helped spark a revolution in ideas about sex and marriage, another dramatic change in social perspective occurred: a population explosion. High birthrates in the 1950s in developed countries, combined with dramatically lower rates of infant mortality throughout the world, sparked fears that too many babies might overwhelm our economic and ecological systems.[28]

Does society still need babies? Or has the specter of overpopulation turned the tables on this state interest? Does the state still have a rational interest in encouraging marriage rooted in the need to encourage reproduction?

Relatively few American elites appear aware of the dramatic change in the factual situation of developed countries around the world. Since the 1950s, many countries, especially the industrialized democracies, have experienced a sustained drop in fertility rates that makes a population *implosion* imminent. According to American Enterprise Institute scholar Nicholas Eberstadt, eighty-three countries and territories, encompassing 44 percent of the world's population, are experiencing below-replacement fertility.[29]

Demographers define "very low fertility" as a birthrate below 1.5 children per woman.[30] Europe's total fertility rate (TFR) from 1995 to 2000 was

1.42 children per woman.[31] The UN's medium variant predicts it will rise to 1.84, while the low variant prediction is a drop to 1.34 children per woman by year 2050.[32] In 2002, twenty-eight nations experienced very low fertility including Switzerland (1.4), Germany (1.3), Austria (1.3), Italy (1.3), Spain (1.2), Greece (1.3), Japan (1.3), Russia (1.3), the Czech Republic (1.1), and most other Eastern European nations.[33]

In 2000, for the first time in human history, there were more old people (age sixty or over) than children (ages infant to fourteen) (19 percent versus 18 percent) in the developed countries of the world.[34] By 2050, the UN projects there will be twice as many elderly people as children (32 percent versus 16 percent).[35] Under the UN's "medium" projection, by the year 2050, the median aged person in Europe will be almost forty-eight years old.[36]

It could get worse. In the former East Germany, women are now, on average, having less than one child each, a level which, if continued, leads to the virtual extinction and/or replacement (e.g., through immigration) of the resident population in a few generations.[37]

How serious is the possibility of population decline? For a thought experiment, consider the effects of a total fertility rate of 1.0 babies per woman, close to what many European countries are now experiencing. At a total fertility rate of 1.0, every 100 people (50 women) in the first generation will have 50 children (the second generation). This second generation of 50 (25 women) will in turn have 25 children. This third generation of 25 will then produce just 12.5 children, shrinking the population by 87 percent in just four generations (once the older generations die off).[38]

Consider the social change that could occur in an ethnically and religiously mixed population with different fertility rates. Assume a town of 100 people composed of 90 percent native Germans with a total fertility rate of 1.0, and 10 percent Turkish immigrants with a TFR of 4 children per woman. In the first generation, the 90 Germans produce 45 ethnic German children while the 10 Turkish immigrants produce 20 ethnic Turks. In the next generation the 45 Germans produce just 22.5 ethnic German children. The 20 Turks, meanwhile, produce 40 ethnic Turks, which now compose a substantial majority of the town. With no immigration (once the older folks die off), the town has gone from 90 percent (90 of 100) German to 64 percent Turk (40 of 62.5).

In two generations, differing fertility can dramatically change the ethnic and religious composition of Europe. Of course, this is a radically simplified scenario. Immigrants tend to move towards the lower fertility of natives, making social change this swift unlikely. But the consequences of long-term below-replacement fertility are clear. As early as 1982, Kingsley Davis and a colleague warned that if "women in industrial societies today are not motivated to achieve replacement fertility...the social order that gave rise to it will be replaced by another—either one that supports traditional sex roles or some new order that rewards women adequately for reproduction."[39]

World leaders are beginning to notice. Russian President Putin sounded the alarm about population decline in his 2000 State of the Nation address, warning, "If the current trend persists, the nation's survival will be threatened."[40] In 2002, the Japanese Health Minister Chikara Sakaguchi warned that unless the nation's birthrates stop plunging, "the Japanese race will become extinct."[41] "Europe Has Every Right to Worry About Disappearing" is the headline over a Canadian university professor's op-ed:

"Will Europe Disappear??" the magazine cover bluntly asks. The question does not refer to rising waters caused by global warming...it refers to a current European obsession: depopulation. There will soon be fewer Europeans than there currently are. Moreover, Europeans will matter much less than they have during the last 200 years.[42]

A London expert warns, "The social and economic upheaval implied by depopulation on this scale would be immense....Only in the last 15 years has a serious risk arisen that the population of Europe may not be reproducing itself."[43] Kojima Akira, a professor at Keto University in Japan, echoes the same fears:

I once heard one of my friends wonder whether the last Japanese will be a man or woman. We can no longer laugh at such a joke now that rapid depopulation is becoming a reality. The decline in the number of children and the aging population is not merely an economic problem. It is a serious problem that will force changes in the social and political frameworks.[44]

A scholar at the Center for Strategic and International Studies in Washington, D.C., recognizing the military implications, stated: "As NATO grows older, there will be fewer young people to fill military roles. The shrinking of the alliance's domestic work forces is now a demographic certainty, and the competition from the private sector will make military recruitment harder than ever before. Countries with manpower shortages may prove unwilling to commit to military confrontations," raising questions about the reliability or value of the NATO alliance for the United States.[45] A reporter notes:

At first glance, Cottbus looks like an orderly and prosperous old German City...[then] you begin to wonder where all the people are. Cottbus, two hours south of Berlin in what used to be East Germany, is a dramatic victim of a phenomenon the Germans call "shrinkage," a crisis of depopulation rooted in declining birth rates that is now afflicting all Europe...."Even at the most busy times, there are not as many people here as you would expect to see in a city," said Andreas Berthold who works at a clothing shop in Cottbus's quaint but almost deserted historic center. "The fake city," as he calls it, is maintained by the government at a cost of millions.[46]

Another reporter continues:

No one is entirely sure why so many women in this quaint, cobblestoned city south of Berlin stopped having babies 10 years ago. But it does not take a degree in sociology to see the effects of the rock-bottom birthrates:...

Workers have begun to dismantle, piece by piece, dozens of vacant apartments, part of a plan to demolish 5,000 units over the next decade.[47]

"Scotland's population decline has set off alarm bells in the corridors of power....Economists warn continued slow growth and the falling population are feeding off each other to create an unstoppable dynamic of decline," reports another journalist.[48]

The proportion of governments expressing concern that their birthrates were too low increased from 11 percent in 1993 to 15 percent in 1999.[49] An even higher proportion (38 percent) of countries expressed major concern about a related demographic phenomenon—population aging—mostly developed countries in Europe with below replacement-level fertility.[50] In more developed regions, the proportion of governments with policies aimed at increasing population growth rose from 16 percent in 1993 to 23 percent in 1999.[51]

What, then, are the consequences of low fertility rates? At the 2 April 2004 meeting of the Population Association of America, UN demographer Joseph Chamie warned, "A growing number of countries view their low birth rates with the resulting population decline and ageing to be a serious crisis, jeopardizing the basic foundations of the nation and threatening its survival. Economic growth and vitality, defense, and pensions and health care for the elderly, for example, are all areas of major concern."[52]

To the author of a paper presented at a recent United Nations conference, fertility levels of 1.5 to 1.8 children per woman constitute a "strong dearth calling for deep revision of population policy....[H]igher risk of labor shortage and reduced capacity to integrate new immigrants; since the main engine of integration of foreigners is the school, this integration cannot happen if a minimal fertility is not realized among the resident population."[53]

As fertility levels fall to 1.2 to 1.5 children per woman (the European average), the result is "[h]eavy and structural contraction, which digs a deep hole at the base of the age pyramid and consequently compromises the future of the society at large...the resident population is progressively replaced by a continuous and bulky inflow of immigrants."[54]

As fertility falls to less than 1.2 children per woman, as in Spain and Italy, the situation becomes an "[e]xtreme case that is less and less rare, namely in Southern Europe and in the former Eastern bloc. A severe amputation of the base of the age pyramid is taking place under our eyes....Acute and rapid aging process; deep and longlasting migratory dependency that could be unbearable or unmanageable...."[55]

The familiar population explosion is replaced by a population implosion or "exponential decrease."[56] Financial consequences include "a growing transfer of resources for the elderly (pension and health care costs) to the detriment of younger workers," which can create a "feedback effect, creating a disincentive to fertility."[57]

An older labor force "means more rigidity, less geographical and occupational mobility, smaller capacity to adapt to economic change; this could represent a threat to innovativeness which is so important in global competition."[58] Then there is "downward pressure on the value of assets" especially the housing market. "In a shrinking and greying population, the supply of vacant houses grows faster than the demand, thus reducing the prices...family capital could melt."[59]

In Italy, at current fertility levels (1.2 children per woman), the population will fall from 57.3 million in 2000 to 36.8 million in 2050.[60] Italy is already one of the "oldest" countries in the world.[61] In 1995, children under the age of fifteen composed just under 15 percent of the population; almost 4 percent of Italians were over age eighty.[62] If current fertility rates continue, by 2050 there will be twice as many octogenarians as children in Italy.[63]

There is no agreement on the (likely complex) causes of low fertility.[64] But the move away from preference for marriage, as well as a decline in the extent to which marriage is seen as a childbearing institution, play a clear role:

> Low fertility can also be linked to the movement away from marriage, which many western European countries have experienced for the recent decades. Of course, marriage is no longer a pre-condition for childbearing in most of these populations, but it remains true that married couples have a higher fertility than non-married people, even those who live in a "marriage-like" cohabitation.[65]

Similarly, another UN analysis focused on "the interaction of marital and reproductive behaviors resulting in below-replacement fertility":

> The demographic transition from high to replacement fertility has consistently been associated with the implementation of reproductive choices within marital unions. Post-transitional developments have been driven mostly by transformations of partnership behavior. During the last decades of the twentieth century, the family as a social institution changed, obligation and commitment with regard to formal marriage eroded and new forms of partnership proliferated in many countries. The range of options for individuals expanded. These options consisted of a permanent or much more prolonged state of celibacy, and of partnership that did not assume formal contractual status and may or may not have involved childbearing. The diversification of partnership options relaxed obligations to previously strict social norms when choosing the path of union formation. Marriage and parenthood were starting to exist independently of each other....[66]

Once the social, cultural, economic, and legal changes that produce population decline are in place, they become extremely difficult to reverse, especially in democratic societies. Children do not vote and older people do. Once a population has disconnected marriage and childbearing, and the norms supporting marriage as a procreative union have weakened or disappeared, there is little political leaders can do to improve the situation for young families without creating enormous resistance. Coming up with the necessary resources to keep pension promises becomes a central preoccupation. Even as Europe begins to dwindle, "European governments were for the most part ignoring the problem, 'In practical terms nothing has been done, or just very,

very marginally,'" said Dr. Carlo De Benedetti, an Italian financier who created a foundation to study the effects of aging in Europe.[67]

Whatever the specific causes, the larger point remains: far from making marriage obsolete as a regulator of childbearing, widespread contraceptive technology (combined with profound economic changes associated with industrialization that make children an expense rather than an asset to families) may actually make more salient, not less, the traditional role of marriage in encouraging men and women to make the next generation that society needs.

As Philip Longman points out, the levels of depopulation now projected for Japan rival the levels experienced by Europe during the Black Plague:[68]

> [F]orecasts by the UN and other organizations show that, even in the absence of major wars or pandemics, the number of human beings on the planet could well start to decline within the lifetime of today's children....Long before then, many nations will shrink in absolute size, and the average age of the world's citizens will shoot up dramatically....No industrialized country still produces enough children to sustain its population over time, or to prevent rapid population aging. Germany could easily lose the equivalent of the current population of what was once East Germany over the next half-century. Russia's population is already contracting by three-quarters of a million a year. Japan's population, meanwhile, is expected to peak as early as 2005, and then to fall by as much as one-third over the next 50 years—a decline equivalent, the demographer Hideo Ibe has noted, to that experienced in medieval Europe during the plague.[69]

Relatively high birth rates in America (just below replacement level), coupled with high levels of immigration, make the American experience, to date, considerably different from the European experience. But the underlying reality is true for all societies including America: high birth rates may not be better than lower birth rates, but societies that fail to reproduce do not survive. Every society needs an institution that encourages men and women to have children if they want them.

The more legal, cultural, and technological choice individuals have about whether or not to have children, the more need there is for a social institution that encourages men and women to have babies together and creates the conditions under which those children are likely to get the best care.

As Shakespeare put it, "The world must be peopled!"[70]

Do Children Need Mothers and Fathers?

The final historic purpose of marriage is to encourage men and women to create a particular kind of family form: one where children have both their own mother and their own father in a single family. By making marriage a permanent sexual union based on the fidelity of both spouses, the state seeks to increase the likelihood that children will be raised in "intact" families. State preferences for marriage over other kinds of unions transmit a clear message to the next generation: the man and the woman who make the baby are supposed to stick around, take care of each other, and their baby too. As twelve family scholars pointed out recently,

> Marriage exists in virtually every known human society....At least since the beginning of recorded history, in all the flourishing varieties of human cultures documented by anthropologists, marriage has been a universal human institution. As a virtually universal human idea, marriage is about the reproduction of children, families, and society....[M]arriage across societies is a publicly acknowledged and supported sexual union which creates kinship obligations and sharing of resources between men, women, and the children that their sexual union may produce.[71]

I and others have written extensively elsewhere on the social science evidence on the importance of intact, married biological parents.[72] There is now an enormous body of social science evidence that supports the common wisdom of humanity, creating a broad, nonpartisan scholarly consensus that family structure matters. In the past thirty years, thousands of studies evaluating the consequences of marriage have been conducted in various disciplines (e.g., psychology, sociology, economics, and medicine). Twelve leading family scholars recently summarized the research literature this way: "Marriage is an important social good associated with an impressively broad array of positive outcomes for children and adults alike....[W]hether American society succeeds or fails in building a healthy marriage culture is clearly a matter of legitimate public concern."[73]

Among their conclusions:

- Marriage increases the likelihood that children enjoy warm, close relationships with parents.
- Cohabitation is not the functional equivalent of marriage.
- Children raised outside of intact married homes are more likely to divorce or become unwed parents themselves.
- Marriage reduces child poverty.
- Divorce increases the risk of school failure for children and reduces the likelihood that they will graduate from college and achieve high status jobs.
- Children in intact married homes are healthier, on average, than children in other family forms.
- Babies born to married parents have sharply lower rates of infant mortality.
- Children from intact married homes have lower rates of substance abuse.
- Divorce increases rates of mental illness and distress in children, including the risk of suicide.
- Boys and young men from intact married homes are less likely to commit crimes.
- Married women are less likely to experience domestic violence than cohabiting and dating women.

- Children raised outside of intact marriages are more likely to be victims of both sexual and physical child abuse.[74]

They conclude, "Marriage is more than a private emotional relationship. It is also a social good. Not every person can or should marry. And not every child raised outside of marriage is damaged as a result. But communities where good-enough marriages are common have better outcomes for children, women, and men than do communities suffering from high rates of divorce, unmarried childbearing, and high-conflict or violent marriages."[75]

Recent analyses by mainstream child research organizations confirm this consensus that family structure matters across ideological and partisan lines. For example, a *Child Trends* research brief summed up the scholarly consensus:

> Research clearly demonstrates that family structure matters for children, and the family structure that helps the most is a family headed by two-biological parents in a low-conflict marriage. Children in single-parent families, children born to unmarried mothers, and children in stepfamilies or cohabiting relationships face higher risks of poor outcomes....There is thus value for children in promoting strong, stable marriages between biological parents.[76]

An Urban Institute scholar concludes, "Even among the poor, material hardships were substantially lower among married couple families with children than among other families with children....The marriage impacts were quite huge, generally higher than the effects of education. The impacts [of marriage] were particularly high among non-Hispanic black families."[77]

A Centers for Disease Control report notes, "Marriage is associated with a variety of positive outcomes, and dissolution of marriage is associated with negative outcomes for men, women, and their children."[78]

A Center for Law and Social Policy Brief concludes, "Research indicates that, on average, children who grow up in families with both their biological parents in a low-conflict marriage are better off in a number of ways than children who grow up in single-, step-, or cohabiting-parent households."[79]

The social costs associated with alternative family forms have never been formally estimated at the national level, but are likely to be substantial. As one group of scholars and civic reformers noted:

> Divorce and unmarried childbearing create substantial public costs, paid by taxpayers. Higher rates of crime, drugs abuse, education failure, chronic illness, child abuse, domestic violence, and poverty among both adults and children bring with them higher taxpayer costs in diverse forms: more welfare expenditures; increased remedial and special education expenses; higher day-care subsidies; additional child-support collection costs; a range of increased direct court administration costs incurred in regulating.[80]

While scholars continue to disagree about the size of the marital advantage and the mechanisms by which it is conferred,[81] the weight of social science evidence strongly supports the idea that family structure matters and that the family structure that is most protective of child well-being is the intact, biological, married family.

This consensus is not, of course, a universal one. Both courts and advocates who favor same-sex marriage often argue that family structure is not very important or is unrelated to marriage. Testifying before Congress, Professor Judith Stacey argued:

> The research shows that what places children at risk is not fatherlessness, but the absence of economic and social resources that a qualified second parent can provide, whether male or female.…Moreover, the research on children raised by lesbian and gay parents demonstrates that these children do as well if not better than children raised by heterosexual parents. Specifically, the research demonstrates that children of same-sex couples are as emotionally healthy and socially adjusted and at least as educationally and socially successful as children raised by heterosexual parents.[82]

However, as the *Child Trends* brief cited above indicates, current research finds that many forms of two-parent families (cohabiting and stepfamilies, for example) compare unfavorably with the intact, married biological family in terms of promoting child well-being.[83] Existing research on children raised by same-sex couples is preliminary, and many scholars have raised serious doubts about its reliability (at this stage) as a source of guidance for public policy,[84] especially, I would argue, given the weight of evidence now existing in favor of married mothers and fathers for child well-being.

Norms attaching marriage and childbearing have certainly weakened, and this fact has been used to argue that there is no longer any rational relation between marriage and family structure. In *Goodridge,* for example, the court argued that by allowing gay and lesbians as well as single mothers to adopt, the state legislature had already decided that family structure was not important to children:

> [T]he Commonwealth affirmatively facilitates bringing children into a family regardless of whether the intended parent is married or unmarried, whether the child is adopted or born into a family, whether assistive technology was used to conceive the child, and whether the parent or her partner is heterosexual, homosexual, or bisexual.…Protecting the welfare of children is a paramount State policy. Restricting marriage to opposite-sex couples, however, cannot plausibly further this policy. "The demographic changes of the past century make it difficult to speak of an average American family. The composition of families varies greatly from household to household." Massachusetts has responded supportively to "the changing realities of the American family," and has moved vigorously to strengthen the modern family in its many variations.[85]

But adoption is the way the law helps cope with needs of children who, by definition, do not have the ideal situation, where not even one parent is able or willing to care for them. Under these circumstances, the state legislature may well be rationally concerned about getting any parent at all for a child rather than keeping children in foster care in hopes of obtaining a theoretical "ideal" family form. Such a legislative choice does not at all suggest a decision by the state legislature that family structure does not matter for children. The existence of children in many family forms may well justify widening efforts to help children in nonmarital families. But do they render legal preferences for marriage as the only generally reliable way to give children the love and care of both their mom and dad irrational or discriminatory? No.

Legal Justifications for the Regulation of Intimacy

By affirming and preferring marriage, the law is directing young men and women sexually attracted to the opposite sex into the kind of sexual unions where (a) children can be encouraged; (b) children will have mothers and fathers; and (c) women will not be handicapped by the enormous burdens of parenting alone. The more men and women who are married, the fewer nonmarital births will occur. The more stable marriages are, the safer men and women feel about having children, and the more likely that "accidental" children will be protected.

What about same-sex couples? If this analysis is correct, it is not clear what the comparable state interest in regulating same-sex relationships might be that would justify the law singling out faithful twosomes (aka "marriage") as the preferred relationship model for gay and lesbian people.

Presented at the European Regional Dialogue
Geneva, Switzerland, August 2004.

Endnotes

* Portions of this chapter originally appeared at 23 Quinnipiac L. Rev. 447 (2004), reproduced here by permission.

1. *See, e.g.,* Tanner v. Oregon Health Sciences Univ., 994 P.2d 129 (Ore. App. 1999); Levin v. Yeshiva University, 754 N.E.2d 1099 (N.Y. 2001); Cornell v. Hamilton, 791 N.E.2d 214 (Ind. App. 2003); Dean v. District of Columbia, 653 A.2d 307 (District of Columbia Court of Appeals, 19 January 1995).

2. Lawrence v. Texas, 539 U.S. 588, 123 S.Ct. 2472, 2484 (2003). ("The case does involve two adults who, with full and mutual consent from each other, engaged in sexual practices common to a homosexual lifestyle. The petitioners are entitled to respect for their private lives. The State cannot demean their existence or control their destiny by making their private sexual conduct a crime. Their right to liberty under the Due Process Clause gives them the full right to engage in their conduct without intervention of the government.")

3. E.J. Graff, *What is Marriage For?* 251 (Beacon Press 2004). ("Marriage... turned into a way to share and shore up one's dearest companion's well-being and inner fortunes. Marriage stopped being justified only by making babies—and became justified by enriching the couple's happiness and intimacy. The family...started to be seen as a careful and nurturing nest for the vulnerable young, a nest in which men and women are equally qualified to serve as financial protector or personal nurturer or both....Social order does remain one of

marriage's key purposes: the legal institution attempts to apply a just social consensus to private disputes.")

4. *See, e.g.,* Skinner v. Oklahoma, 316 U.S. 535, 541 ("Marriage and procreation are fundamental to the very existence and survival of the race."); Maynard v. Hill, 125 U.S. 190, 211. ("[Marriage] is the foundation of the family and of society, without which there would be neither civilization nor progress.")

5. Failure to consummate a marriage (*i.e.,* have sexual intercourse) traditionally made a marriage voidable. *See* Laurence Drew Borten, *Sex, Procreation, and the State Interest in Marriage,* 102 Colum. L. Rev. 1089, 1103–07 ("The law considers sexual intercourse to be an implied term of the marriage contract and will grant an annulment when one party secretly intends not to consummate it."); Gerard V. Bradley, *Same-Sex Marriage: Our Final Answer?* 14 Notre Dame J.L. Ethics & Pub. Pol'y 729, 749 (2000). ("Physical defects and incapacities which render a party unable to consummate the marriage, existing at the time of the marriage, and which are incurable are, under most statutes, grounds for annulment.") *See also* Alaska Stat. § 25.24.030 (Michie 2002); Del. Code Ann. tit. 13 § 506(a)(2) (1999); 750 Ill. Comp. Stat. § 5/301(2) (West 1999); Minn. Stat. Ann. § 518.02(b) (West 1990); Ohio Rev. Code Ann. § 3105.31(F) (Anderson 2003); Wis. Stat. Ann. § 767.03(2) (West 2003) (including inability or failure to consummate among grounds for annulment, though several also require nondisclosure of inability to consummate). Failure to have sexual relations was also considered grounds for divorce in many jurisdictions. Borton, *supra,* 102 Colum. L. Rev. 1089, 1098 ("[M]any states list impotence as a ground for divorce.") (citing Mass. Ann. Laws ch. 208, 1 (Law. Co-op. 1994); Miss. Code Ann. 93-5-1 (1994); Dolan v. Dolan, 259 A.2d 32, 36 (Me. 1969)).

6. Laurence Drew Borten, *Sex, Procreation, and the State Interest in Marriage,* 102 Columbia Law Review 1089, at 1114 and 1123 (internal citations omitted).

7. Donald Sensing, *Save Marriage? It's Too Late: The Pill Made Same-Sex Nuptials Inevitable,* The Opinion Journal (Wall Street Journal online) 15 March 2004.

8. Baker v. State, 744 A.2d 864, 881 (Vt. 1999).

9. *Id.*

10. *Id.*

11. Goodridge v. Dept. of Publ. Health, 798 N.E.2d 941, 961, n.23 (Mass. 2003) (quoting portions of Justice Cordy's dissenting opinion).

12. My own perspective on this question is somewhat biased. In the interests of full disclosure, let me state that I came of age in the middle of the sexual revolution (Yale, class of 1982), in which the claim that we had successfully severed sex and reproduction was repeatedly made to me and my peers. My own experience (I became an unwed mother at 22) as well as the experiences of many of my peers led me to investigate the scientific basis of this assertion. We may claim to have separated sex and reproduction, but unexpected pregnancy, even among highly competent and advantaged young women at elite institutions, nonetheless remains far from rare.

13. 381 U.S. 479 (1965).

14. J. Abma et al., 1997. *Fertility, family planning, and women's health: New data from the 1995 National Survey of Family Growth.* National Center for Health Statistics. Vital Health Stat 23(19).

15. *Id.* at 25 (Table 14) (69 percent of births were "intended." The remaining 31 percent of births were either unwanted (9.1 percent) or mistimed (21.6 percent)).

16. *Id.*

17. *Id.* at 28 (Table 17) (70.4 percent of births to married women were intended by both parents, compared to just 28 percent of births to unmarried mothers).

18. *Id.* at 24 (Table 13).

19. Stanley K Henshaw, 1998. *Unintended Pregnancies in the United States,* 30(1) Family Planning Perspectives 24ff.

20. *Id.* at 26 (Table 1).

21. *Id.* at 28 (Table 3) (finding 47.7 percent of women aged fifteen to forty-four had had at least one unintended pregnancy).

22. *Id.* at 28 (Table 3) (finding 60.0 percent of women aged thirty-five to thirty-nine had had at least one unintended pregnancy).

23. *Id.* at 28 (Table 3) (finding 38.1 percent of women aged forty to forty-four had had at least one unplanned birth).

24. Haishan Fu, et al., 1999. "Contraceptive Failure Rates: New Estimates from the 1995 National Survey of Family Growth," *Family Planning Perspectives* 31(2): 56–63, 56.

25. *Id.* at 56.

26. James Trussell and Barbara Vaughan, 1999. "Contraceptive Failure, Method-Related Discontinuation and Resumption of Use: Results from the 1995 National Survey of Family Growth," *Family Planning Perspectives* 31(2): 64ff, 71.

27. *Id.* ("These high pregnancy rates do not reflect the inherent efficacy of methods when used correctly and consistently...but instead reflect imperfect use (because most reversible methods are difficult to use correctly).")

28. *See, e.g.,* Paul R. Erlich, *The Population Bomb* (New York: Ballantine Books 1971).

29. Nicholas Eberstadt, *The New Trend: A Population Bust,* The Washington Post, 18 March 2001, at B7 (excerpted from Eberstadt's article entitled *The Population Implosion* in the March/April 2001 issue of Foreign Policy).

30. John C. Caldwell and Thomas Schindlmayr, *Explanation of the Fertility Crisis in Modern Societies: A Search for Commonalities,* 57(3) Population Studies 241–263, 241 (2003). "Lowest low fertility" is often defined as a total fertility rate of 1.3 or less. Hans-Peter Kohler et al., *The Emergence of Lowest-Low Fertility in Europe During the 1990's,* 28(4) Population and Development Review 641–680, 641 (2002).

31. Population Division of the Department of Economic and Social Affairs of the United Nations Secretariat (2003). World Population Prospects: The 2002 Revision. Highlights. (United Nations) (26 February 2003): 4 (Table 2). North America, by contrast has near-replacement level fertility at 2.01 children per woman. *Id.*

32. *Id.*

33. John C. Caldwell and Thomas Schindlmayr, *Explanation of the Fertility Crisis in Modern Societies: A Search for Commonalities,* 57(3) Population Studies 241–263, 242 (Table 1) (2002).

34. Population Division of the Department of Economic and Social Affairs of the United Nations Secretariat (2003). World Population Prospects: The 2002 Revision. Highlights. 15 (United Nations) (26 February 2003).

35. *Id.* Based on the medium variant, which assumes total fertility in developed nations will rise to a rate of 1.85 children per woman by the year 2050 while fertility rates in less developed countries continues to fall. *Id.* at 4 (Table 2).

36. *Id.* at 15 (Table 9) (medium variant assumes European fertility rates will rise to 1.84 by the year 2050).

37. Ron Lesthaeghe, *Europe's Demographic Issues: Fertility, Household Formation, and Replacement Migration,* paper presented to the Expert Group Meeting on Policy Responses to Population Ageing and Population Decline 5 (Population Division, Department of Economic and Social Affairs, United Nations in New York, 16–18 October 2000) (Table 1).

38. *See, e.g.,* Hans-Peter Kohler et al., 2002. *The Emergence of Lowest-Low Fertility in Europe During the 1990's,* 28(4) Population and Development Review 641–680, 642. ("[A] TFR of 1.3 also implies an annual decline of the population size by 1.5 percent....A TFR of 1.3 also implies a reduction of the birth cohort by 50 percent and a halving of the stable population size every 45 years. If the TFR declines further and persists at a level of 1.0, the annual rate of decline in the stable population rises to 2.4 percent and the halving times of population size and birth cohorts are merely 29 years.")

39. Kingsley Davis and Pietronella van der Oever, *Demographic Foundations of New Sex Roles,* 8(3) Population and Development Review 495–511, 511 (1982) (quoted in John C. Caldwell and Thomas Schindlmayr, *Explanation of the Fertility Crisis in Modern Societies: A Search for Commonalities,* 57(3) Population Studies 241–263, 244) (2003).

40. Anatoly Zoubanov, *Population Ageing and Population Decline: Government Views and Policies,* paper presented to the Expert Group Meeting on Policy Responses to Population Ageing and Population Decline 4 (Population Division, Department of Economic and Social Affairs, United Nations in New York, 16–18 October 2000).

41. Reuters, *Japanese Threatened with Extinction, Minister Says* (21 May 2002).

42. John English, *Europe Has Every Right to Worry About Disappearing,* Toronto Star, 1 September 2001: A15.

43. Tim Congdon, *The Ideas Exchange: Expert View—Babies Can Deliver Us From a Crisis,* Independent on Sunday (London), 13 January 2002: Business at 2.

44. Kojim Akira, *Depopulation in Japan,* Journal of Japanese Trade and Industry, 1 September 2002.

45. Craig Romm, 2002. *Will NATO be Defeated by Demography?* The San Diego Union-Tribune, 4 October 2002: B7.

46. Doug Saunders, *Falling Birth Rates Killing European Union Cities,* Ventura County Star (CA), 23 May 2003: A22.

47. Thomas Fuller, *Low Birthrates Pose Challenge for Europe: The Depopulation Bomb,* International Herald Tribune, 12 December 2002: 1.

48. Tom Martin, *Focus: With Falling Birthrates, Experts Warn of Crisis Ahead,* Sunday Express, 28 September 2003: 21.

49. Anatoly Zoubanov, *Population Ageing and Population Decline: Government Views and Policies,* paper presented to the Expert Group Meeting on Policy Responses to Population Ageing and Population Decline 2 (Population Division,

Department of Economic and Social Affairs, United Nations in New York, 16–18 October 2000).

50. *Id.* at 2–3.

51. *Id.* at 23 (Table 4). Note, however, the proportion committed to maintaining current population levels dropped from almost 34 percent to just over 10 percent, and the proportion committed to no intervention on population increased from 48 percent to almost 65 percent, indicating the difficulties liberal democracies have in policies that appear to interfere with the private ordering of sexual and childbearing choices, as well as the financial pressures to reduce the cost of child allowances and other fertility subsidies. As populations age, political pressures to reduce support for children might also be expected to increase, since the UN estimates that elderly cost twice as much as a child in terms of government and social supports, mostly due to high medical costs. United Nations, *Replacement Migration: Is it a Solution to Declining and Ageing Populations?* 93 (2000), http:// www.un.org/esa/population/publications/migration/migration.htm. ("A number of researchers...report that when considering the public provision of programs or taking into account private nonmedical expenses, public education expenses and medical care, the costs are roughly two and a half times greater to support an older person (aged 65 or older) than to support a young person (under 20 years of age).")

52. Joseph Chamie, *Low Fertility: Can Governments Make a Difference?* paper presented at the Annual Meeting of the Population Association of America, Boston Massachusetts, 2 April 2004.

53. Jean-Claude Chesnais, *The Inversion of the Age Pyramid and the Future Population Decline in France: Implications and Policy Responses,* paper presented at the Expert Group Meeting on Policy Responses to Populating Ageing and Population Decline in New York, 16–18 October 3 (Population Division, Department of Economic and Social Affairs, United Nations 2000).

54. *Id.*

55. *Id.*

56. *Id.* at 2.

57. *Id.* at 8.

58. *Id.* at 10.

59. *Id.*

60. Antonio Golini, *Possible Responses to Population Ageing and Population Decline: The Case of Italy,* paper presented at the Expert Group Meeting on Policy Responses to Population Ageing and Population Decline in New York, 16–18 October 2000, 2 (Population Division, Department of Economic and Social Affairs, United Nations 2000).

61. *Id.* at 2. ("Italy has now become the 'oldest' country in the world, recording the highest proportion of population aged 65 and over, and the lowest proportion of people aged under 15.")

62. Rita-Maria Testa, *Fewer and Older Italians, More Problems? Looking for Solutions to the Demographic Question,* paper presented at the Expert Group Meeting on Policy Responses to Population Ageing and Population Decline in New York, 16–18 October 2000. (Population Division, Department of Economic and Social Affairs, United Nations) (Table 1).

63. *Id.* (predicting children to comprise 8.3 percent of the population, and octogenarians 15.7 percent).

64. For a discussion of theories (and an introduction to the literature on causes of low-fertility), see John C. Caldwell and Thomas Schindlmayr, *Explanation of the Fertility Crisis in Modern Societies: A Search for Commonalities,* 57(3) Population Studies 241–263 (2003).

65. Patrick Festy, *Looking for European Demography, Desperately?* paper presented at the Expert Group Meeting on Policy Responses to Population Ageing and Population Decline in New York, 16–18 October 2000, 3 (Population Division, Department of Economic and Social Affairs, United Nations). However, "The countries with the highest TFRs, France and UK, are those in which low nuptiality has been compensated for by the rise of fertility out of marriage. In the countries with very low period fertility, the decline in marriages has been directly consequential for fertility, because marriage remains *the* place for childbearing, without any substitutes for it." *Id.* (emphasis in original).

66. Population Division, Department of Economic and Social Affairs, United Nations Secretariat, 2002. *Partnership and Reproductive Behavior in Low-Fertility Countries,* 74 Population Newsletter 4 (December) (emphasis added).

67. Fuller, *supra* note 47 at 1.

68. Philip Longman, *The Global Baby Bust,* 83(3) Foreign Affairs 64, 66 (May/June 2004).

69. *Id.* at 65–66.

70. William Shakespeare, *Much Ado About Nothing,* Act 2, Scene 3, Line 227, p. 7.

71. William J. Doherty et al., *Why Marriage Matters: Twenty-One Conclusions from the Social Sciences* 8–9 (Institute for American Values 2002).

72. Linda J. Waite and Maggie Gallagher, *The Case for Marriage: Why Married People Are Happier, Healthier, and Better Off Financially* (Doubleday 2000); Maggie Gallagher, *What is Marriage For? The Public Purposes of Marriage Law,* 62(3) LA. L. Rev. 773 (Spring 2002); Maggie Gallagher, *Rites, Rights, and Social Institutions: Why and How Should the Law Support Marriage?* 18 Notre Dame J.L. Ethics & Pub. Pol'y 225 (2004); Maggie Gallagher & Joshua K. Baker, *Do Moms and Dads Matter? Evidence from the Social Sciences on Family Structure and the Best Interests of the Child,* 4 Margins Law Journal 161 (2004); Maggie Gallagher & Joshua Baker, *Do Mothers and Fathers Matter?,* iMAPP Policy Brief (27 February 2004), www.marriagedebate.com. *See also* William J. Doherty et al., *Why Marriage Matters: Twenty-One Conclusions from the Social Sciences* 6 (Institute for American Values 2002); Paul R. Amato and Alan Booth, *A Generation at Risk: Growing Up in an Era of Family Upheaval* (Harvard University Press 1997); Sarah McLanahan & Gary Sandefur, *Growing Up With a Single Parent: What Hurts, What Helps* (Harvard University Press 1994); Kristin Anderson Moore et al., *Marriage from a Child's Perspective: How Does Family Structure Affect Children and What Can We Do About It?,* Child Trends Research Brief 1 (Child Trends June 2002) (http://www.childtrends.org/PDF/MarriageRB602.pdf); Institute for American Values, The Marriage Movement: A Statement of Principles 11 (2000) (www.marriagemovement.org).

73. Doherty, *supra* n. 71 at 6 (co-authors include William J. Doherty, William A. Galston, Norval D. Glenn, John Gottman, Barbara Markey, Howard J. Markman,

Steven Nock, David Popenoe, Gloria G. Rodriguez, Isabel V. Sawhill, Scott M. Stanley, Linda J. Waite, and Judith Wallerstein).

74. *Id.* at 6–17.

75. *Id.* at 18.

76. Kristin Anderson Moore et al., *Marriage from a Child's Perspective: How Does Family Structure Affect Children and What Can We Do About It?*, Child Trends Research Brief 1 (Child Trends June 2002) (http://www.childtrends.org/PDF/MarriageRB602.pdf). This research brief on family structure does not compare outcomes for children in same-sex couple households to children in other types of families.

77. Robert I. Lerman, *Impacts of Marital Status and Parental Presence on the Material Hardship of Families with Children,* 27 (Urban Institute July 2002) (http://www.urban.org/url.cfm?ID=410538).

78. Matthew D. Bramlett & William D. Mosher, *First Marriage Dissolution, Divorce, and Remarriage: United States,* CDC Advance Data no. 323, at 1 (31 May 2001).

79. Mary Parke, *Are Married Parents Really Better for Children? What Research Says About the Effects of Family Structure on Child Well-Being,* CLASP Policy Brief no. 3, at 6 (Center for Law and Social Policy) (May 2003). These are findings about the family structure debate in general. On the question of sexual orientation and parenting, the brief summarizes the social science this way: "Although the research on these families has limitations, the findings are consistent: children raised by same-sex parents are no more likely to exhibit poor outcomes than children raised by divorced heterosexual parents. Since many children raised by gay or lesbian parents have undergone the divorce of their parents, researchers have considered the most appropriate comparison group to be children of heterosexual divorced parents. Children of gay or lesbian parents do not look different from their counterparts raised in heterosexual divorced families regarding school performance, behavior problems, emotional problems, early pregnancy, or difficulties finding employment. However, as previously indicated, children of divorce are at higher risk for many of these problems than children of married parents." *Id.* at 5.

80. Institute for American Values, The Marriage Movement: A Statement of Principles, 2000, 11 (Institute for American Values), www.marriagemovement.org.

81. *See, e.g.,* E. Mavis Heatherington & John Kelly, *For Better or For Worse—Divorce Reconsidered* (W.W. Norton & Co. 2002).

82. *What is Needed to Defend the Bipartisan Defense of Marriage Act of 1996?: Hearing Before the Subcomm. on the Constitution, Civil Rights and Property Rights of the Senate Comm. on the Judiciary,* 108th Cong., 4 September 2003 (written statement of Professor Judith Stacey, Ph.D., Department of Sociology, New York University).

83. Kristin Anderson Moore et al., 2002. "Marriage from a Child's Perspective: How Does Family Structure Affect Children and What Can We Do About It?" *Child Trends Research Brief* (Washington, D.C.: Child Trends) (June): 1 (http://www.childtrends.org/PDF/MarriageRB602.pdf). This research brief on family structure does not compare outcomes for children in same-sex couple households to children in other types of families.

84. *See, e.g.,* Diana Baumrind, 1995. "Commentary on Sexual Orientation: Research and Social Policy Implications," *Developmental Psychology* 31 (No. 1):

130; Affidavit of Stephen Lowell Nock, Halpern v. Attorney General of Canada, No. 684/00 (Ont. Sup. Ct. of Justice); Robert Lerner & Althea K. Nagai, 2001. *No Basis: What the Studies Don't Tell Us About Same-Sex Parenting* (Washington, D.C.: Marriage Law Project). For a summary of the existing research see Maggie Gallagher & Joshua Baker, *Do Mothers and Fathers Matter?*, iMAPP Policy Brief (27 February 2004), www.marriagedebate.com.

85. Goodridge v. Dept. of Publ. Health, 798 N.E.2d 941, 962–63 (Mass. 2003) (quoting Troxel v. Granville, 530 U.S. 57, 63-64 (2000)) (internal citations omitted).

9

Theory, Tradition, and Contemporary Marriage

Camille S. Williams (USA)
Lecturer, School of Family Life
Brigham Young University, Utah, USA

The creation stories of various cultures include tales of creators and creatures both male and female;[1] the folk tales of many lands include a running battle of wits between the sexes.[2] In some respects, it is in those narratives that marriage is the combination of the respective strengths of male and female;[3] the culmination of their efforts to best each other is in marriage transformed into a joint project of best selves. While some in our contemporary cultures may view these foundational stories as little more than myth, others note that the women and men who have gone before us, our fathers and our mothers, recognized strengths and weaknesses common in the respective sexes and were wise enough to appropriately recognize the need for men and women to co-operate in all aspects of society, but most especially in the home and family. Cultural wisdom comes from learning from those who went before.

Marriage has for centuries been the image of unity despite differences and, to some degree, has reflected the belief that "neither man nor woman is perfect or complete without the other"; they are enough alike to love each other, but enough different that they need to unite their strengths and stewardships to create a whole.[4] The heterosexual union has formed an implicit norm for families and for family studies. For those who hold cultural or religious beliefs that support the traditional family founded on heterosexual marriage, or those whose lived experience of marriage has been fulfilling, a good marriage may appear to be obviously beneficial to men, to women, and to their children.

What may be less obvious, though, is how community—the ties that bind us in civil society—depends upon heterosexual marriage. As Wendell Berry notes, a community entails

> a set of arrangements between men and women. These arrangements include marriage, family structure, divisions of work and authority, and responsibility for the instruction of children and young people. These arrangements exist, in part, to reduce the volatility and the danger of sex—to preserve its energy, its beauty, and its pleasure; to preserve and clarify its power to join

not just husband and wife to one another but parents to children, families to the community, the community to nature; to ensure, so far as possible, that the inheritors of sexuality, as they come of age, will be worthy of it.[5]

Good News about the Traditional Family

Let us consider some of the arguments in favor of traditional marriage.

Heterosexual Marriage Is Good for Men and for Women

It now appears, from an analysis of two waves of data from the National Survey of Families and Households that the "emotional benefits of marriage apply equally to men and women, but that men and women respond to marital transitions with different types of emotional problems."[6]

Marriage may provide the emotional support men and women need to face life's various stressors. It may be that for many individuals, gender roles within the family may have served more as patterns against which the rising generation measures its development, rather than as cages which trap men and women and constrain their development. Marital roles invite greater knowledge of self and each other as the couple learn to love and support each other in the ordinary irritations and in the extraordinary joys of family life together. Jerrold Levinson contends, "On the assumption that gender, the difference between masculine and feminine, whatever the extent of its natural basis, marks a highly significant division in the human world...the choice of homosexual over heterosexual orientation in the sexual arena arguably counts as a suboptimal one, because it offers reduced scope for the development of certain virtues, such as courage, maturity and trust, which initiating and sustaining a heterosexual relationship calls forth. As such it represents a missed opportunity in self-development, a small failure in duty to the self."[7]

If it is the case that "the modes of being of men and women remain emotionally, bodily, and socially distinct, even in the modern world, and even as both modes exemplify personhood to the full...[then] in a sexual relationship...they are brought into contact in a way that allows for some sort of knowledge—knowledge by acquaintance, if you will—to flow across the divide."[8]

I would argue further that by virtue of loving her husband and sons, it is possible for a woman to better perceive some of the strengths, some of the concerns, and some of the vulnerabilities that she could not see in her own father or her own brothers—and that might elicit a more understanding response to the males in her family and toward males generally. Conversely, through the experience of loving his wife and daughters, a man may be able to understand his own mother and sisters better, and perhaps have more concern for women in general. Marriage and family life does positively contribute to better physical, emotional, and financial health for men and women.

The same cannot yet be said for same-sex pairing. One suboptimal aspect of same-sex pairing is that it is not psychologically healthful. It appears that there are significant differences in psychological or physical health of gays and lesbians as compared to heterosexuals. A large-scale Dutch study found, for example, that there is a "higher prevalence of substance use disorders in homosexual women and a higher prevalence of mood and anxiety disorders in homosexual men, both compared with their heterosexual counterparts."[9] The usual response to statistics like these is that social stigma associated with homosexuality causes this suffering, and that were there more social acceptance of same-sex couples, there would be greater psychological health among gays and lesbians. Given that this study was conducted in the Netherlands, arguably the society most friendly toward nonheterosexual coupling, that conclusion is difficult to sustain.

Heterosexual Marriage of the Parents Benefits Their Children

Heterosexual marriage capitalizes on the strengths of both a man and a woman, and protects against the weaknesses or vulnerabilities of either sex. Several decades of research suggest that there are differences between the sexes and that, by combining those differences in the child's behalf, the child benefits.[10] Some research, for example, indicates that mothers tend to be risk-adversive and emotionally nurturing, while fathers tend to encourage their children to try new things, but tend to be less emotionally expressive.[11] It may be that such complementarity allows for the best emotional and social development for children, by encouraging growth while protecting them from grave harms. If it is the case that a same-sex couple would, in effect, double both the strengths and weaknesses common to their sex, their child might not receive an upbringing as "balanced" as heterosexual parents could provide.[12]

Heterosexual Marriage Benefits Society

Because traditional marriage helps create a stable environment in which a child may learn of his or her physical, emotional, social, cultural, and religious heritage, the society as a whole derives a benefit. Couples who invest themselves heavily in their marriage and in the rearing of their children build human capital, the basis for any successful society.[13] Marriage requires that individuals think of someone other than themselves; marriage is bigger than the self (or even the two selves) and requires commitment to each other and to the community.[14] Each wife and each husband holds a place of honor and importance in the giving and sustaining of human life; to deliberately deprive a child of the heritage of either a mother or a father is to impoverish that child in a multitude of ways.[15] The female-male combination is more stable, more sustainable than either male-male or female-female,[16] and so provides the best environment for child-rearing.

Marriage Is the Foundation for the Multigenerational Family

The longing to know about one's "roots" appears to be universal, and the multigenerational traditional family allows a child to see how family works across generations. The small child who helps her grandmother take a plate of hot food over to her great-grandfather learns about how interesting old people are and how to treat them with respect. She begins to understand how one generation can help the next ones and is, in turn, helped by children and grandchildren. This helps her think of life not as bounded simply by her own birth and death, but as an overlapping chain of concern and commitment, of which she is a part.

The ever-growing practice of genealogical research as a hobby, as family history, and as a business illustrates the deep-felt need individuals have to find out more about their families of origin and ultimately about themselves, and much of that self-knowledge can come by watching a parent care for a younger sibling or care for an elderly grandparent, or by working with a parent or grandparent. In everyday tasks, the child is invited to see how mothers and fathers, husbands and wives, men and women approach problem solving, negotiate resolutions, find humor in everyday incidents, or comfort each other when fearful or sad. In this context, the child learns that his or her actions affect other generations of the family, and learns how the respective gifts of men and women can bless the lives of their families.

What the Data Cannot Tell Us

While a significant number of studies of the family offer support for the traditional family, it may be shortsighted to count on a compilation of data to validate a family form. Various studies in sociology, gerontology, child development, psychology, and family studies report data on sex differences, for example, but the interpretation of those data vary considerably from researcher to researcher. Some researchers characterize sex differences as "complementary" and perhaps benign; other researchers condemn the belief in complementary gender differentiation as contributing to the oppression of women.[17] While additional research is always needed to test what appear to be truisms, all research on the family is based on assumptions about the nature of human beings, the meaning of human sexuality, and the purpose of the family, and so should consider the philosophical and historical aspects of the heterosexual family, so that the data gathered reflects a clear-eyed assessment of the philosophical assumptions behind the research.[18]

All research proceeds on philosophical assumptions. Perhaps in part because so many families seem so troubled today, numerous scholars propose that we no longer view heterosexual marriage as the essential foundation for families. Rather, it is proposed that via "queer theory"[19] the heterosexual norm for families be displaced and that researchers focus on "family construction processes," rather than on the structure of the family. In a sense, then, each individual is seen as constructing his or her sexuality and family according to his or her desires. The challenge of those incorporating queer theory into family theories, is "to bracket all assumptions about what configuration of members qualifies as 'family,'" as individuals "make decisions to resist or accommodate heteronormativity."[20] As sexual minority activists seek increased political power and social acceptance, the gay and lesbian rights movement argues that "[t]he appropriation of the family model is crucial, as the family is the central place where sexual citizenship is affirmed. In contrast, a queer political strategy, born out of queer and AIDS activism of the 1980s, challenges the heterocentric model altogether."[21]

It is my belief that family theory, research, and practice will require that there be a more complete understanding of the philosophy of the family in order for the data gathered to be interpreted in ways that will help us to better understand, support, and improve what is generally termed the natural or traditional family—married biological parents and their children. I do not believe that it will be helpful to jettison heterosexual marriage as the norm or to move to a "normless" theory of family studies.

Such a proposal is inherently contradictory in that it posits a social constructionist view of heterosexuality, but accommodates an essentialist view of individual desire.[22] Moreover, queer theory faces natural, biological limits that reduce its explanatory power.[23]

Nevertheless, the proposal, though hardly new, is quite serious, appears to have been well-received, for example, at the premier conference in North America on family theory, and is likely to have a significant impact on the kind of data-gathering done about families in the years to come. Legislative proposals in many nations reflect this approach already. Family theorists Ramona Faith Oswald, Libby Balter Blume, and Stephen R. Marks, describe heteronormativity as "a vast matrix of cultural beliefs, rules, rewards, privileges, and sanctions that impel people to reproduce heterosexuality and to marginalize those who do not."[24] Their description of the binary thinking upon which they believe heterosexuality rests, appears to be an intentionally faulty description of cultural practices, which, when so described, are more open to attack from those who object to the alleged demand that individuals are required to fit into sex-stereotyped gender, sex, and family roles. While acknowledging that "evidence abounds that many individuals' lived experiences are not (and were not) as constricted as the ideological composite would suggest," they find it objectionable that heteronormativity persists as "a continuing interpretive resource that guides social action at multiple levels."[25]

This proposal reflects, first, that Gay, Lesbian, Bisexual, and Transgendered (GLBT) activists and academics do not "at any one moment," as Douglas NeJaime points out, "express a single normative vision for the GLBT community,"[26] and, second, that there is reluctance in the GLBT community for sexual norms of any kind to be recognized, because they fear that such norms may restrict them from engaging in sexual activities they desire, or may deprive those activities of the social acceptance or approval the GLBT community desires. The belief that individuals have the capacity, and the right, to define themselves and their relationships, seems to be fundamental to contemporary queering of family theory. There is an effort by researchers to "invert and subvert dualistic thinking" about men, women, and human sexuality, even as they acknowledge that norms remain central to the gathering and interpretation of data.[27] This undertaking—the deconstruction of the notion of heterosexual normality—will, they believe, give us a better understanding of heterosexuality itself, even as it is destabilized as the norm against which all other family forms are evaluated. In contrast to the traditional family structure, with its alleged binary thinking, they are interested in "complex gendering, complex sexualities, and/or complex families." In short, they study the following: ways in which "humans resist or subvert sex stereotyping"; the practices of "homosexuality and heterosexuality...[and] bisexuality, asexuality, people who change their sexual identifications, and people who refuse any sexual identification or call themselves queer, as well as other fully consensual ways of complicating sexual identities and practices"; and the ways that individuals construct families, including biological and legal ties, and ties with "chosen" family members.[28] The subtext of their proposal is that affirming the dignity, creativity, and value of marginalized persons be a salient feature of family studies.

I agree that each individual is unique, valuable; I don't think, however, that queer theory is the means to a positive transformation of the family or of family studies because:

> Queer theory is inherently contradictory.
>
> Queer theory faces natural or biological limits that reduce its explanatory power.
>
> Queer theory is likely to disadvantage women.
>
> Queer theory is likely to reinscribe the view of nonheterosexuals as abnormal.
>
> Queer theory is likely to disadvantage children.

Each of these issues is addressed in sequence below.

Queer Theory Is Inherently Contradictory

If the social construction of heteronormativity is as powerful as it is described to be, then it is unclear how sexual or gender self-definition *cannot* be socially constructed, too. It appears that Oswald et al. may represent the impulses "to reinvent" the way an individual "does" family, or "inner sensibility" in an essentialist fashion, since such impulses or sensibilities seem not to be represented as socially constructed. There is no explanation, however, of how an impulse or an inner sensibility—of all human acts or sentiments—escapes being constructed either according to heteronormativity or in resistance to heteronormativity. It may be that they are proposing a structuralist transformation: that is, by changing the structure of the family—disentangling sexuality, gender, and family configuration—desires and sensibilities will arise that are not influenced by heteronormativity. Certainly they are tracking what they see as the "potential family transformation that may lead people to queer their own patterns of doing family...."[29]

Another contradiction of queer theory is that, while it ostensibly destabilizes all categories of sexuality, it is marshaled primarily in the defense of and affirmation of categories of sexual minorities: gays, lesbians, bisexuals, transsexuals, transgendered persons, and individuals questioning their sexual identity. This would appear to be an antiessentialist theory used in support of essentialism, a contradiction of some consequence.[30]

Further, it is not apparent from the present proposal and studies based on such an approach whether destabilization of sex, gender, and family is

1. intended to continue indefinitely;

2. should continue until certain preferred sexual orientations gain legitimacy;

3. should be practiced only until all categories of sexuality appear to be equally respected in society; or

4. should continue until there are no boundaries, that is, no norms for human sexual desire or activity.

None of those outcomes seems likely.

Destabilization is unlikely to continue indefinitely because people have a stake in what is destabilized and any postdestabilization norms that arise. Decentering heteronormativity may simply shift normality to include alternative family structures or alternative sexual preferences. However, it is unclear why such a shift would necessarily improve the lives of individuals or groups, or even how it would be possible to evaluate whether the changes were good or bad.

Should destabilization of heteronorms expand far enough, a queernorm would likely arise,[31] which would then need to be destabilized, presumably by heteronorms or other norms. But the destabilizing proposed by queer theory seems unidirectional: it is intended to undermine heterosexuality. Current objections to reparative therapy demonstrate that at least some homophiliacs have little tolerance with analyses or behaviors intended to destabilize queerness, if such destabilization tends toward heterosexuality.

It is unclear how to stop the destabilization process if we want simply to help queer folk gain legitimacy or respect equal to heterosexuality. If we accept the analysis of binaries presented by Oswald[32] (and which are presumably equally applicable to triads, or quads, or quints), we would have to assume that one category would inevitably end up having more prestige or power than another, so there is no guarantee that destabilization will result in a net gain for queer individuals or groups.[33]

The real issue, then, is choosing and defending the reasons, or grounds, for esteeming one category—whether it be varieties of sexual behaviors or varieties of family structures—as more valuable than another. Those grounds have historically included tradition, religion, and sustainability. It appears that Oswald et al. propose creativity as the ground for judging family theory—either that or they are recommending a study of the family without reference to norms, other than that the family forms chosen be based on the mutual consent of adults.

Creativity as a criterion for judging the decentering project seems less than useful, since creativity is notoriously hard to measure. Is creativity in sexuality, gender, and family, by definition, present only when it challenges heteronormativity? If creativity is measured only by variation from the norm, then it ceases when the norm ceases to exist. It might be expected that over time sexual practices would pendulate between heterosexual and other categories, or that the creativity might move out of what are now considered fairly firm sexual boundaries of normality and into what are now considered immoral, illegal, or dysfunctional sexualities: necrophilia, bestiality, public lewdness, intergenerational sexual activity, incest, or coercive sexual activities. Left unexplained are what evaluative standards might be imagined as replacement(s) for a norm or norms for individual sexual behavior and family structure or process.[34]

Published research already exists on the fluidity of adult sexual identity, and it has been posited that such fluidity may actually be beneficial to children. However, we may not want to become a society of multiple sexual identities any more than we would want to become a society of multiple personalities. "Our existing society is one that depends in many circumstances on the ability to correlate a human body fairly reliably with a set of behavioral dispositions,"[35] John Dupre points out. While he concludes that "attempts at purely descriptive accounts of normal behavior can aspire only to the statistical," normative judgments of behaviors, he asserts, are culturally embedded and should not be confused with statistical norms.[36] That means that we are likely to make comparisons among "the spectrum of 'sexual lifeways,'" and judge some better than others, even if the current norm is decentered. A new norm or a norm for each subcategory is likely to arise, i.e., what is normal for heterosexuals, what is normal for nonheterosexuals.[37]

Queer Theory, Like Social Construction Theories in General, Faces Natural or Biological Limits which Reduce its Explanatory Power.
As Richard Williams has argued,

> it seems that human beings cannot "conjure." That is, we cannot, by any narrative act or any exercise of rational powers, bring into existence things in the material world. There are certain stubborn states of physical affairs—reflecting an underlying ontology—which do not adapt themselves to our narratives. We should be careful in assuming that there are no similarly stubborn...states of human affairs—reflecting an underlying ontology—which similarly do not adapt themselves to our narratives, which we must thus seek to apprehend, and to which we must give considerable deference.[38]

One reason heterosexual coupling has been dominant is that it is sustainable, it can reproduce itself, while same-sex couples cannot. For most of human history that ability to give and sustain life has been of fundamental importance, particularly to women. That such matters of material fact can be characterized as "socially constructed" is an index of our wealth and of our reliance on technology. But both are historical and cultural anomalies. Only now and only in a few countries with access to advanced medical technology can costly contemporary desires such as sex reassignment surgery or gestational surrogacy be fulfilled.

The desire to decenter the heteronormative family may be an ethnocentric project in nations where most people are rich enough not to have to worry constantly about survival. The desire to define one's self and relationships seems a romantic western notion, as contrasted to some Asian cultures which do not so privilege autonomy. As John Rothfork expresses it, "Asians feel relieved and grateful to be given a set of directions and a provisional role to play; to start (living) somewhere instead of eternally dreaming about it (in adolescence)."[39] Queer theory may have less relevance in developing nations where simply sustaining life is hard, or in cultures where the multigenerational family is more important than the nuclear, or even the "intentional" family, or family of affinity or choice.[40]

Until technology obviates the need for at least one man and one woman (suppliers of sperm and ova) in reproduction, it is highly likely that family will retain much of its heterosexual nature.[41] Human reproduction is still a cooperative process between female and male, even when mediated by medicine or contract. Thus, the normativity of the heterosexual family is not merely socially constructed, it is part of the facts of our lives and part of our collective history. There are natural, factual limits to social construction projects because there are natural, factual limits to our bodies, and likely to our minds.

Queer Theory Is Likely to Disadvantage Women

Feminist theory alleges that the family has been identified as a site of oppression for women, but feminist theory has also recognized the family as a site of power and influence for women. Because the heterosexual family is the only important social institution in which large numbers of women have always participated, and have been *necessary* participants, I am unwilling to legitimate any form of the family that excludes women or only exploits women's reproductive capacity.[42]

To some extent, intended or not, the feminisms of the past thirty years have erased the historical female role in bearing and sustaining life. To a large degree, both men and women now pursue "a fairly unsatisfying version" of the male gender role.[43] That is unfortunate and should not be replicated in the application of queer theory to family studies, lest women find that queer theory is hazardous to their social status.

The recent move to what "social critic John O'Neill calls the 'libidinal body,' the body that titillates and ravishes and is best embodied as young, thin, antimaternal, calculating, and disconnected," is, as Jean Bethke Elshtain reminds us, "deeply, and troublingly antinatal—hostile to the regenerative female body and to the symbolism of social regeneration to which this body is necessarily linked."[44]

At a minimum, we can expect in family studies, as has happened elsewhere, a collision between queer theory and feminist (especially lesbian) feminist theory. As expressed by Amy Goodloe, queer theory "privileges sexuality, in both political analysis and cultural expression, over gender, and thereby threatens to erase or reduce the gender-bound experience of lesbians as women."[45] Some lesbian feminist theorists seem to have judged queer theory as male privilege and sexuality as co-opting the work of feminists over the past three decades. Some "lesbian scholars have become acutely aware of the hegemony that queer theory threatens to hold over all studies of gender and sexuality in the academy, and have thus launched into full-scale critiques of its totalizing tendencies."[46]

Consider how the word "gay" is in widespread usage, and sometimes represents gays and lesbians, sometimes the entire queer community, even in the most unlikely contexts. It is frequently alleged that there is a significant body of research on *gay* and lesbian parents. That research (which specializes in nonsignificance) is almost entirely about *lesbian* parents.[47] Though research also shows us that the sexual and coupling behaviors of male same-sex couples differs considerably from that of female same-sex couples, lesbians seem willing to allow gays to trail them into parental legitimacy. I do not understand that apparent lesbian passivity in the social context of aggressive gayness.[48]

Queer theory claims to represent transgender and transsexual concerns, but both of those groups tend to identify a different gender or sex as being necessary or essential to their identity. That could be interpreted as a case of essentialism (of gender or of sex) reified in cross-dressing or in a sex-change operation. It might be possible to define those choices as the ultimate examples of self-created sexual identities,[49] but that would need to be sketched out so that we could distinguish between essentialism and creativity in transgendered or transsexual persons. These forms of "self-fashioning" can hardly be the expression of "random presocial desires [because they]...take place in larger political contexts." They may simply be variants of heteronormativity.[50]

Queer Theory Is Likely to Reinscribe the View of Nonheterosexuals as Abnormal

Dennis Altman notes that

"Queer theory" shares with much of contemporary postmodernism an emphasis on representation as an aesthetic rather than a political problem, a desire to deconstruct all fixed points in the interests of "destabilising" and "decentering" our preconceptions. Given the arcane language within which much such theory is written...this theory is almost totally ignored by the vast majority of people whose lives it purports to describe.[51]

Altman is unconvinced that "queer" provides a useful term for political strategy or even for understanding power relations. "Indeed," he contends, "there is a basic confusion around 'queer,' which is sometimes used to describe a particular way of being homosexual, perhaps expanded to include bisexual desires and unorthodox gender behaviour, and sometimes meant to represent the whole gamut of opposition to the sex/gender order, so that lesbian prostitutes and heterosexual, suburban sado-masochists are equally 'queer.'" At this juncture, there may be too much slippage in core concepts for the project of decentering heteronormativity to provide an insightful theory or stable base for positive social change.

Anthropologist Donald E. Brown reportedly lists traits universal to all known people across all time periods: it is the heteronormativity of "families built around a mother and children, usually the biological mother, and one or more men," what columnist John Derbyshire calls "normality at the most basic level, recognized as such by Lapp reindeer herders, Roman Senators, Turkish peasants, Chinese warlords, fishermen on Lake Chad, stallholders in the bazaars of Persia and aborigines in the Australian bush...by all human beings that have ever lived, except our enlightened selves."[52]

The destabilization approach may have the unintended effect of reinscribing a view of sexual minorities as either uncommonly driven by sexual desire or as unstable because it is difficult for the law to accommodate the destabilization of sex and gender categories. For most people arrested and taken to jail, for example, it matters whether they are searched by or housed with persons of their own biological sex or not. Currently, in our response to and our analysis of domestic violence, both sex and gender appear to be salient features. Is domestic violence theory therefore unqueerable, even though we know that both gay and lesbian couples also experience domestic violence?

In child custody cases the best interests of the child include having a stable and permanent bond with the parent; anything that destabilizes the parent's sexuality, gender, personal identity, or household may impair the stability of the parent-child bond, and negatively impact a custody decision. DSM-IV (APA 1994) recognizes as normal those who can demonstrate a stable, unitary, and consistent identity separate from other subjects.[53] Will judges consider a transsexual as stable as his/her heterosexual ex-spouse in custody cases? Given the fact that sex-reassignment surgery requires a showing of psychological distress to justify such drastic intervention, it may be that such a signifier of instability will be determinative in some cases.

One legal scholar expressed the difficulty with inconsistent or contradictory theories of queerness in discussing litigation tactics on behalf of sexual minorities: "What would you do if you were trying a class action with the most unruly of classes, like trying to herd kittens scurrying every which way [with] their theories, wants and desires?"[54]

Is queer theory a fad? Gerald Graff contends that "[r]evolutionary ideas are picked up lightly, worn for a season, and disposed of when next season's models come in. The very profusion and confusion of ideas simultaneously

competing for attention ensures that many, if not all, viewpoints will be toler-
ated while few have much impact."[55] Some theorists contend that queer
theory is being used to shore up heterosexuality by helping to create a "sense
of 'virtual equality'...based more on the appearance of acceptance by straight
America than on genuine civic parity."[56]

Queer Theory Is Likely to Disadvantage Children

Queer theory may turn family studies into a merely descriptive art, rather
than a predictive or evaluative science.[57] If there is no norm, if queering family studies affirms the capacity of all people to define themselves and their
relationships, it would seem that each individual's desires, however fluid or
capricious, would be validated, and so could be described, but not evaluated.

In a normless form of family studies, what process or criteria might be used
by a custody evaluator? What guidance can normless family studies give a
judge who must decide the fate of a child born during a heterosexual marriage and, now after her parents' divorce, must live either with her mother,
who is now a Christian polygamist, the second "spiritual" wife of a man
who is currently advertising for a third wife on the internet,[58] or her father,
who is in a polyamorous living arrangement with one woman, two men,
and their respective children (four in number). Both family forms help decenter heterosexual norms, but it is unclear how affirming the human dignity,
creativity, and autonomy of the respective parents would provide a prin-
cipled basis for evaluating the efficacy of the family forms available to this
child.

It is unsubstantiated, wishful thinking to suppose that a child caught in the
instability of her parents' fluctuating sexual identities will necessarily, like the
daughter of a lesbian and transsexual activist "father" highlighted as a success story for sexual fluidity, "emerge from her adolescence with a much better chance than most of us to select whatever form of sex and gender
expression and sexual object choice are most compatible with her inner sensibilities."[59] We do know that family instability increases a child's risk of
abuse,[60] and that "less sexually permissive family cultures" delay adolescents' sexual debut, reducing their risk of pregnancy and sexually transmitted
diseases.[61] To make the queered version of family studies useful in the law,
we would need to have a reasonable way to judge whether a child will have
a safe, stable home whether straight or queer.

The proposed queering of family studies does not give us any way of measuring the effectiveness of family forms or processes. Presumably, consent in
sexual relationships and egalitarian, nonexploitive family forms are more
desirable than their opposites, but we cannot assume that simply decentering
heterosexuality will ensure that those qualities of family will arise. Perhaps
"disentangled" desire will result in a Sartrian "insatiable desire to consume,
acquire, dominate, violate, and destroy,"[62] causing increased inequity, exploitation, or coercion. Certainly that concern is part of the subtext of the debates
about same-sex marriage, polyamory, polygamy, intergenerational sex,

pornography, and other aspects of sexual behavior outside traditional boundaries, all of which might be seen to have the potential to destabilize the heteronormative family.

Right now postmodernist feminist, lesbian, and queer theories can attribute any and every negative individual or familial trait to heteronormativity, because it is the dominant form. As researchers study creatively self-defined individuals and their sexual behaviors, and their families of choice, will the researchers have the evaluative tools to report negative outcomes, if any? If the "main goal" is decentering heterosexuality and heteronormativity, by definition, that precludes to some extent self-critical analysis, or any critique that would subvert that decentering. If queer theory does not allow a self-critical stance, all that is left for us is to appreciate "diversity" and suspend judgment about the potential impact those disorders could have on individuals and their children.

Surely a researcher would be at liberty to reread with a "straight eye" the coming out stories of gays and lesbians not as parents rejecting their children, but as children rejecting their parents, the multigenerational family, their own history, and condemning the very heterosexual relationships that brought them into being, just as queer theory rejects heteronormativity, our own history, and the relationships that brought us into being. Perhaps theorists engaged in an overt effort to destabilize heteronormativity could remain open to the possibility that their efforts could also result in individual, familial, or social ills. Presumably, they would not feel constrained to hide those ills.

To keep family theory part of an interpretative or predictive social science, it is necessary to master the individual agent's or family's self-description;[63] but that does not mean that we must adopt that individual's or family's point of view. Researchers must be willing to evaluate families, their structures, functions, aspirations, processes—at least if we want family studies to remain a relevant, applied social science.

The Donald Norman axiom that "[A]cademics get paid for being clever, not for being right"[64] ought to sober us. We do not have family theory right, yet. But queer theory may be more usefully applied to texts than to people. It does not much matter what kind of interpretation we make of *Hamlet;* we can be creative and put binary opposites into play, and, at worst, people only get bored and stop reading or listening. In contrast, a theory of the self or the family that encourages creative experimentation with sexual identities could have grave consequences for some teen questioning heteronormativity, as well as the society that may have to pick up the pieces.[65]

Philosophical Bases for the Traditional Family

I have rehearsed and critiqued[66] the proposed normless family theory at length in order to illustrate the results of a paucity of good theoretical and philosophical work in support of the natural family. There has been an erosion of what many would see as the foundation for personal identity, family structure, and society and culture generally. While we have a rich history and tradition about family life, and considerable research about family processes and dynamics, we have relatively little about the underlying justification for the heterosexual family,[67] perhaps because it seemed self-evident, or because religious and cultural tradition were more generally valued until recently.

As scholars proceed to collect data that many of us hope would be supportive of the natural or traditional family, it will be necessary for some to continue the theoretical and philosophical work as well. One fruitful area may be a reintroduction of at least some natural law concepts articulated for our own times. For example, Robert George notes that some of the most contentious issues today "are concerned with sexuality, the transmitting and taking of human life, and the place of religion and religiously informed moral judgment in public life." He argues that the positions on these issues taken by traditional Christian, Jewish, and to a large extent Islamic morality are rationally superior to the positions taken by those who have abandoned that religious world view in favor of various "isms"—"feminism, multiculturalism, gay liberationism, lifestyle liberalism," what he calls "secularist orthodoxy."[68] He also acknowledges that classical philosophy, rather than religious tradition, can form a basis for similar conclusions. The important point being that such a philosophical foundation allows a basis for a shared understanding of what constitutes a basic human good and acknowledges that there can be a consensus, rather than each individual constructing his or her own conception of what is good or moral.

George lists marriage as an intrinsic or basic human good that provides noninstrumental reasons for choice and action, thus justifying a definition of marriage and family. He argues that the heterosexual marital relationship

> mak[es] spouses truly, and not merely metaphorically, "two in one flesh." The sexual union of spouses—far from being something extrinsic to marriage or merely instrumental to procreation, pleasure, the expression of tender feelings, or anything else—is an essential aspect of marriage as an intrinsic human good. Marital acts are the biological matrix of the multi-level (bodily, emotional, dispositional, spiritual) sharing of life and commitment that marriage is.[69]

George concludes that "marital acts realize the unity of marriage, which includes the coming to be of children. In consensual nonmarital sex acts, then, people damage this unity, the integrity of the marriage, inasmuch as the body is part of the personal reality of the human being and no mere sub-personal instrument to be used and disposed of to satisfy the subjective wants of the conscious and desiring part of the 'self.'"

This is a brief introduction to the foundation George lays for heterosexual marriage and against sexual activity outside of marriage. It is an implicit refutation of homosexual marriage and could help provide the foundation for a philosophy, or a psychology, or a family theory undergirding research that would support the viability or efficacy of the traditional family. Additional work needs to be done to answer the postmodernist and feminist critiques of the traditional family, and to find legal models of the family that are more appealing than contract or economic analysis.

John Witte, Jr., reminds us that

> marriage is one of the great mediators of individuality and community, revelation and reason, tradition and modernity. Marriage is at once a harbor of the self and a harbinger of the community, a symbol of divine love and a structure of reasoned consent, an enduring ancient mystery and a constantly modern invention.[70]

As he points out

> Ideally, marriage enhances the life of a man and a woman by providing them with a community of caring and sharing, of stability and support, of nurture and welfare. Ideally, marriage also enhances the life of the child, by providing it with a chrysalis of nurture and love, with a highly individualized form of socialization and education.[71]

If we are to continue to view this ideal, if only as an aspiration, we need to draw on the resources of tradition, theory, practice, and research to present a coherent body of knowledge that makes that aspiration a genuine, living possibility.

Presented at the Asia/Pacific Family Dialogue
Kuala Lumpur, Malaysia, October 2004.

Endnotes

1. *See, e.g.,* Bernard Doyle, *Creation Myths,* Encyclopedia Mythica from Encyclopedia Mythica Online, http://www.pantheon.org/articles/c/creation_myths.html (accessed 5 October 2004).

2. *See, e.g.,* Robert Alter, *The Art of Biblical Narrative* (1981).

3. Meliss Bunce, *Happily Ever After: Folktales That Illuminate Marriage and Commitment* (August House Publishers 2003).

4. *See, e.g.,* Sheri L. Dew, *It is Not Good for Man or Woman to Be Alone,* Ensign, Nov. 2001, 12, at http://library.lds.org/nxt/gateway.dll?f=templates$fn=default.htm

5. Wendell Berry, *Sex, Economy, Freedom and Community* 120 (Pantheon Books 1993), 120–121.

6. Robin W. Simon, *Revisiting the Relationships among Gender, Marital Status, and Mental Health,* American Journal of Sociology, 107:4, 1065–1096, 1065 (January 2002).

7. Jerrold Levinson, *Sexual Perversity,* The Monist, 86:1, 30–54, at 41 (2003), referring specifically to Roger Scruton, *Sexual Desire: A Philosophical Investigation* (London: Weidenfeld and Nicolson 1986) (U.S. edition: New York Free Press 1986). Levinson is not condemning homosexual relationships, however.

8. *Id.*

9. Theo G.M. Sandfort et al., *Same-sex Sexual Behavior and Psychiatric Disorders: Findings from the Netherlands Mental Health Survey and Incidence Study (NEMESIS),* 58 Archives of General Psychiatry 85 (2001), 88–89. This large-scale study was

conducted in the country which is arguably the most gay/lesbian friendly in the world, so it is unlikely that the disorders arise from homophobia, internalized or otherwise; the authors seem to conclude that "sex-atypical levels of prenatal androgens play a major role in the causes and development of homosexuality."

10. Steven E. Rhoads, *Taking Sex Differences Seriously* (San Francisco: Encounter Books, 2004), compiles and summarizes a significant amount of the research in arguing that the differences appear to be real, and ought to be recognized by individuals and policy makers.

11. Research on gender differentiated parental approaches are summarized in Brenda Hunter, *The Power of Mother Love: Transforming Both Mother and Child* (Westbrook Press 1997), and also in Kyle D. Pruett, *Father Need: Why Father Care is as Essential as Mother Care for Your Child* 17–53 (The Free Press 2000).

12. James M. Herzog, a psychoanalyst, has examined what he calls "father hunger" among the children of divorced parents. Boys especially seem to need to have a father who is loved by the mother, showing him how to "recognize his masculinity and claim it functionally rather than succumb to its inherent capacity to disorganize and destroy." *Father Hunger* 310–311 (Hillsdale, NJ: The Analytic Press, 2001). Herzog contends that fathering is "a distinctly male form of caretaking," which he argues can only successfully occur in the presence of a mother, and is "contingent on the presence of homeostatic-attuned caregiving by the mother." At 259–260.

13. Ann Crittenden, *The Price of Motherhood* (Metropolitan Books 2001).

14. Wendell Berry, *Sex, Economy, Freedom and Community* (Pantheon Books 1993).

15. See Camille S. Williams, *Planned Parent-Deprivation: Not in the Best Interests of the Child,* Whittier Journal of Child and Family Advocacy (forthcoming).

16. *See* Janis S. Bohan, *Psychology and Sexual Orientation: Coming to Terms* 192 (Routledge 1996); Michael Shernoff, *Male Couples and their Relationship Styles,* 2 The J. of Gay & Lesbian Social Services 2 (1995), http://www.gaypsychotherapy. com/relstyle.htm; David E. Greenan, *Do Open Relationships Work? Gay Couples and the Question of Monogamy,* 27 Psychotherapy Networker 3 (May/June 2003), http://gaypsychotherapy.com/networkermonogamy.htm; Michael Shernoff and Jack Morin, *Monogamy and Gay Men: When are Open Relationships a Therapeutic Option?: Case Study and Commentary,* Family Therapy Networker (March/April, 1999), http//www.gaypsychotherapy.com/MONOGAMYCASE.htm. Also, Laumann et al., *The Social Organization of Sexuality* (1994), cautions that the sample size of persons in his study who might be classified as homosexual is too small to confidently generalize to the larger population; he also notes "the group of people with same-gender partners (or who define themselves as homosexual or bisexual) have higher average numbers of partners than the rest of the sexually active people in the sample." Laumann, at 312. "Married men and married women exhibit substantially higher rates of sexual exclusivity than do people in other marital statuses." Laumann, at 192. Laumann opines that formal recognition of same-sex relationships might provide social pressure supportive of long-term bonding for same-sex couples. Laumann, at 316.

17. See, for example, Angelamaria Loreto et al., *Equal Dignity Between Man and Woman Enhances the Value of Differences: The Keys of Conflict Resolution, Integration*

and Cooperation Are in the Brain, International Conference, Barriers to women's career in Academia: A Dialogue between social psychology and policy, Sala della Biblioteca–Palazzo della Penna, Perugia, 6 October 2001. Nuray Sakalli, links "complementary gender differentiation" to "benevolent sexism" and violence in *Beliefs About Wife Beating Among Turkish College Students: The Effects of Patriarchy, Sexism, and Sex Differences, Sex Roles: A J. of Research,* May 2001. For a religious interpretation of the complementary natures of the sexes see http://www.vision.org/jrnl/0310/feminism.html

18. This caveat is applicable to the social sciences generally. *See* Brent D. Slife and Richard N. Williams, *What's Behind the Research? Discovering Hidden Assumptions in the Behavioral Sciences* (Sage 2001).

19. "Queer" is not used here as a pejorative, but is the term selected by those advancing the theory, and is used to refer to a variety of activities or beliefs in opposition to heterosexuality. Martha M. Ertman, *Constructing Heterosexuality: Reconstructing Marriage: an InterSEXional Approach,* 75 Denver University Law Review 1215, 1226–1227 (1998), notes that "Queer Legal theory builds on the insights of poststructuralism, feminist and critical race theory, as well as critical legal studies to critique legal theory and doctrine based on their impact on gay people."

20. Ramona Faith Oswald, Libby Balter Blume, and Stephen R. Marks, *Decentering Heteronormativity: A Model for Family Studies,* in *Sourcebook of Family Theory and Research* (Vern L. Bengtson, Alan C. Acock, Katherine R. Allen, Peggye Dilworth-Anderson, David M. Klein eds., Thousand Oaks: Sage 2004), 148.

21. Keri Jacqueline Brandt, *The Skin We Live In: Explorations of Body Modification, Sexuality, and Citizenship,* Review Essay, Symbolic Interaction, 27:3, 429–436, at 430 (2004).

22. This problem has been recognized by feminist and sexual orientation theorists, who have attempted to keep, for example, "woman" from collapsing "into Aristotelian essentialism because essence is not viewed as an immutable underlying characteristic of a thing. It changes with cultural understanding which is itself informed by empirical science, but...always involves power....There is no fixed definition of woman at stake because the possibility of such a move is closed by the emphasis upon an essence that is subject to change." Janice Richardson, *Selves, Persons, Individuals: Philosophical Perspectives on Women and Legal Obligations* (Ashgate 2004), at 40 (discussing feminist nominalism and essentialism, particularly in the work of Battersby). Edward Stein, *The Mismeasure of Desire: the Science, Theory and Ethics of Sexual Orientation* (Oxford University Press 1999), describes queer theory as "the project of dredging up the heterosexist and homophobic assumptions deeply embedded in various disciplines. By exploring sexual orientation in metaphysics, science, and ethics, I have tried to break free of the tyranny of custom in thinking about sexual orientation using philosophy and queer theory." His discussion of social constructionism and essentialism includes a list of strengths and weaknesses of the theoretical perspectives he examines. Needless to say, however, his effort to free himself of the "heterosexist and homophobic assumptions" to which he refers demonstrates his own allegiance to social acceptance of homosexuality, and other alternative sexual practices.

23. See Stan J. Knapp and Camille S. Williams, *Where Does Queer Theory Take Us?*, in *Sourcebook of Family Theory and Research* (Vern L. Bengtson, Alan C. Acock, Katherine R. Allen, Peggye Dilworth-Anderson, and David M. Klein eds., Thousand Oaks: Sage 2004), 626–628

24. Ramona Faith Oswald, Libby Balter Blume, and Stephen R. Marks, *Decentering Heteronormativity: A Model for Family Studies*, in *Sourcebook of Family Theory and Research* (Vern L. Bengtson, Alan C. Acock, Katherine R. Allen, Peggye Dilworth-Anderson, and David M. Klein eds., Thousand Oaks: Sage 2004), 144 (quoting Coontz, 1992).

25. *Id.*

26. Douglas NeJaime, *Note: Marriage, Cruising, and Life in Between: Clarifying Organizational Positionalities in Pursuit of Polyvocal Gay-Based Advocacy*, 38 Harvard Civil Rights-Community Lawyering Law Review 511 (2003).

27. See Peter Hegarty and Felicia Pratto, *The Differences that Norms Make: Empiricism, Social Constructionism, and the Interpretation of Group Differences*, 50 Sex Roles (78) 445, 452 (April 2004).

28. Ramona Faith Oswald, Libby Balter Blume, and Stephen R. Marks, *Decentering Heteronormativity: A Model for Family Studies*, in *Sourcebook of Family Theory and Research* (Vern L. Bengtson, Alan C. Acock, Katherine R. Allen, Peggye Dilworth-Anderson, and David M. Klein eds., Thousand Oaks: Sage 2004), 148.

29. *Id.*, at 151.

30. *See* Charles Taylor, *Foucault on Freedom and Truth*, 178–9, in Philosophy and the Human Sciences: Philosophical Papers 2. Cambridge UP, 178–9 (1985). Charles Taylor wonders (in footnote 51) whether Foucault is trying to have it both ways with the notion of resistance arising from desire, from the body, inarticulate and unarticulated even to ourselves. This makes no sense, he says, concluding that resistance requires that there must be an articulation and an affirming of the truth of that articulation against the specious claims of the system of control. This, of course, is a much simplified fragment of both Foucault's work and Taylor's critique.

31. John Dupre, *Normal People*, Social Research 65:2, 221–249 (1998).

32. See Oswald, *et al., supra* n. 20.

33. In analogous fashion, destabilizing a totalitarian government does not necessarily result in freedom or democracy for a nation.

34. The deconstruction of heteronormativity has already begun, but it may only reinscribe the existing binary: the heterosexual and the queer. It appears that the task of deconstructing of heteronormativity could be mistaken for endorsing what Freud called "polymorphous perversities" at their most creative.

35. Dupre, *supra*, at 234. Even if the multiple sexual identities, or a fluid identity, seemed optimal to the individual, that is no guarantee that the individual's spouse would agree, or would develop a similarly fluid sexual identity accepting of the spouse's variations. This could significantly impact familial stability.

36. Dupre, *supra*. at n. 22.

37. If the deconstruction alluded to is a deconstruction of norms in general, then queer theory may have incorporated a misunderstanding of deconstruction *a la* Jacques Derrida, who notes that "deconstructing academic professional discourse doesn't mean destroying the norms or pushing these norms to utter

chaos," and cautions "I'm not in favor of disorder." Interview with Gary A. Olsen, *Jacques Derrida on Rhetoric and Composition: A Conversation,* in Interviews: Cross-Disciplinary Perspectives on Rhetoric and Literacy (Gary Olsen & Ilene Gale eds., Southern Illinois UP, 121–141, 1991), quoted in James E. Faulconer, *Deconstruction* (1998), http://jamesfaulconer.byu.edu/deconstr.htm

38. Richard N. Williams, *Psychology in the Breach: The Importance of Being Earnest,* in Theoretical Psychology: Critical Contributions, Selected Proceedings of the Ninth Biennial Conference of the International Society for Theoretical Psychology, Calgary, Alberta, Canada, 3–8 June 2001 (Niamh Stephenson, H. Lorraine Radtke, Rene' Jorna, and Henderikus J. Stam eds., Concord, Ontario: Captus University Publications, 2003), 2–3.

39. John Rothfork, *Foucault on Freedom & Truth,* Charles Taylor, Philosophical Papers 2: Questions & Answers #6 "Foucault offers us an angry, adolescent daydream of identity as uncompromised. The outrage in his tone implies that we have been victimized by the conditions of actual life." http://jan.ucc.nau.edu/~jgr6/NMT/2Tay6.html

40. For a discussion of intentional families see Kath Weston, *Families We Choose: Lesbians, Gays, Kinship* (Columbia University Press 1991).

41. We do not yet clone human beings, so the heterosexual family *is* both social and biological. Although it is unclear, apart from the many ethical concerns, what relationship the clone would have to the person cloned. It is not a child, although like a child he or she was brought into being by another person—but only one, not two persons. A delayed twin, perhaps, although can it be said that the parents of the person cloned are also the parents of the clone?

42. For example, the gay couple who use a woman as a gestational surrogate to produce for them a child biologically related to one of them.

43. See Rita M. Gross, *What Went Wrong?: Feminism and Freedom from the Prison of Gender Roles,* 8–20 Crosscurrents, 53:1 (Spring 2003).

44. Jean Bethke Elshtain, *Against Gay Marriage—II: Accepting Limits,* 686 Commonweal (22 November 1991). She quotes John O'Neill, in part.

45. Amy T. Goodloe, *Lesbian Feminism and Queer Theory: Another 'Battle of the Sexes'?* http://www2.kenyon.edu/Depts/WMNS/Projects/Porteousd/Lesbian%2 (1994). Goodloe's discussion is here in reference to Arlene Stein's 1992 article *Sisters and Queers: the Decentering of Lesbian Feminism,* 22.1 Socialist Review 33–35 (January 1992).

46. Goodloe, at 3.

47. "As is common in research on gay and lesbian parenting, more lesbian mothers (336) than gay fathers (79) volunteered to participate. This may be due to the fact that the sample included only custodial parents, and for previously married individuals, fathers are still less likely to receive custody than are mothers. Another possible explanation is that there may be fewer gay fathers than lesbian mothers in the nation, or the sample may not be representative of the true proportion of gay and lesbian parents in this country." Beverly R. King, *I Have "A Mommy, a Daddy, and a Barbara": The Psychology of Parenting as a Lesbian or Gay Man* (sic), 39(4) Journal of Sex Research, 335 (2002), describing the National Study of Gay and Lesbian Parents. See also Charlotte J. Patterson, 62 *Family Relationships of Lesbians and Gay Men,* Journal of Marriage and the Family 1052–1069 (November

2000). "Although some gay men are also becoming parents after coming out, no research has yet been reported on their children."

48. Perhaps there is some kernel of truth to the Dan Savage theory of lesbian deep-process versus gay nonprocessing (or to the old notion that changing the family structure changes family process). Dan Savage, *The Kid (What Happened After My Boyfriend and I Decided to Go Get Pregnant: An Adoption Story* (Penguin 2000). When the various females cannot make a decision about collaborating with Dan to make a baby, Dan and his lover, Terry, decide to adopt the child of a young woman they refer to as a gutterpunk. *But see* the feisty Ruthann Robson, *Resisting the Family: Repositioning Lesbians in Legal Theory,* 19:4 Signs 975 (Summer 1994), who argues that "family must be problematized as a nonessential, cognitive, and contested category," (at 979) arguing that the "domestication of lesbianism must be resisted" (at 991), and that "lesbian relations are comensurate [not to familial relations] but only to themselves" (at 993).

49. *See* Bernice L. Hausman, *Recent Transgender Theory,* 27(2) Feminist Studies, 465 (2001), quoting Pat Califia, *Sex Changes: The Politics of Transgenderism,* 224 (Cleis Press 1997). "A new sort of transgendered person has emerged, one who approaches sex reassignment with the same mind-set that they would to obtaining a piercing or a tattoo." *But see,* Cressida Heyes' discussion of Raymond and Hausman, *infra.*

50. *See* Cressida J. Heyes, *Feminist Solidarity after Queer Theory: The Case of Transgender,* 28(4) *Signs: Journal of Women in Culture and Society,* 1093 (2003), especially her discussion of the work of Janice Raymond and Bernice Hausman, at 1098–1109.

51. Dennis Altman, *On Global Queering,* Australian Humanities Review, http://www.lib.latrobe.edu.au/AHR/archive/Issue-July-1996/altman.html (1996).

52. John Derbyshire, *Situation Normal,* National Review, 11 June 2001, http://olimu.com/Journalism/Texts/Commentary/Normal.htm, quoting Brown, in part.

53. Marie Crowe, *Constructing Normality: A Discourse Analysis of the DSM-IV,* 7 *Journal of Psychiatric and Mental Health Nursing,* 71 (2000).

54. Kate Diaz et al., *Queer Law 1999: Current Issues in Lesbian, Gay, Bisexual and Transgendered Law,* 27 Fordham Urban Law Journal 279, 359 (2000).

55. Gerald Graff, *American Criticism Left and Right, Ideology and Classic American Literature,* 94 (Sacvan Bercovitch & Myra Jehlen eds., Cambridge University Press 1986), quoted by Helene Meyers, in *To Queer or Not to Queer: That's Not the Question,* 24(1) College Literature 171, at 175 (1997).

56. Urvashi Vaid, *Virtual Equality: The Mainstreaming of Gay and Lesbian Liberation* xvi (Doubleday 1995), quoted by H. Meyers, *in To Queer or Not to Queer: That's Not the Question,* 24(1) College Literature 171, at 175 (1997).

57. I understand the objections to using science as applied to human behavior, but use the term here as a short reference to what are usually termed the social sciences. "Science" also carries the sense that its knowledge claims are at least somewhat more than whimsy, desire, and self-construction.

58. The scenario is imagined, but possible. See http://www.polygamy.net and http://www.polyamorysociety.org/page6.html

59. Ramona Faith Oswald, Libby Balter Blume, and Stephen R. Marks, *Decentering Heteronormativity: A Model for Family Studies*, in *Sourcebook of Family Theory and Research* (Vern L. Bengtson, Alan C. Acock, Katherine R. Allen, Peggye Dilworth-Anderson, and David M. Klein eds., Thousand Oaks: Sage 2004), 151.

60. *See, e.g.* Robin Fretwell Wilson, *Children at Risk: The Sexual Exploitation of Female Children After Divorce*, 86 Cornell Law Review 251 (2001); and Michael N. Stiffman et al., *Household Composition and Risk of Fatal Child Maltreatment*, 109:4 Pediatrics 615–621 (2002). Unrelated adult males in the household are the most common perpetrators.

61. This is a rereading of Oswald et al.'s reading of Erin Calhoun & Lisa V. Friel, *Adolescent Sexuality: Disentangling the Effects of Family Structure and Family Context*, 63:3 Journal of Marriage & Family 669 (2001).

62. Craig Beam, *Sartre vs. Nietzsche: Will to Power, Platonism, and Pessimism*, 17 (2) The Carleton University Student Journal of Philosophy 3 (1998), http://rideau.carleton.ca/philosophy/cusjp/v17/n2/beam.html

63. Charles Taylor's caution in *Understanding and Ethnocentricity, Philosophical Papers 2* (Cambridge University Press 1985).

64. As should the article introduced by that axiom, authored by Chip Morningstar, "How to Deconstruct Almost Anything," http://www.tcp.com/~mary/decon.html, also at http://www.fudco.com/chip/deconstr.html

65. *See, e.g.,* Stephen T. Russell et al., *Same-Sex Romantic Attraction and Experiences of Violence in Adolescence*, 91:6 *American Journal of Public Health* 903 (2001); also, Laura Dean et al., *Lesbian, Gay, Bisexual, and Trans gender Health: Findings and Concerns*, 4:3 *Journal of the Gay and Lesbian Medical Association* 101 (2000). Because fecal material can carry so many pathogens, anal-genital and anal-oral sex have a high risk of infecting at least one of the participants.

Although homosexuality has been declassified as a psychological disorder for decades, the tendency of MSM [men who have sex with men] to engage in high-risk sex has led researchers to propose that in addition to educational efforts about the biological facts of high-risk sexual practices, preventative measures must also address the "psychosocial factors" which "influence sexual risk-taking." Dean, at 114.

66. A significant portion of this chapter was from my response to an earlier version of Oswald et al.'s *Decentering Heteronormativity*; both were presented at the Theory Construction and Research Methods Conference in Vancouver, B.C., November 2003.

67. There is considerable debate in law reviews, much of which relies on various philosophical or theoretical constructs, but relatively little philosophical discourse on the natural family itself, other than feminist critiques, which tend not to support the traditional family.

68. Robert George, *A Clash of Orthodoxies*, 95 First Things 33 (August/September 1999), http://print.firstthings.com/ftissues/ft9908/articles/html

69. *Id.* at 36–37.

70. John Witte, Jr., *The Meaning of Marriage*, 126 First Things 30, 30 (October 2002).

71. *Id.* at 41.

10

Liberal Cautions on Same-Sex Marriage

Don Browning (USA)
Emeritus Professor, Divinity School, University of Chicago, USA

Elizabeth Marquardt (USA)
Affiliate Scholar, The Institute for American Values, USA

The question of same-sex marriage is difficult. There are strong arguments that can be advanced in support of same-sex marriage that must be taken seriously. But before considering what can be said for or against gay marriage, we must first pose as carefully as possible the question to be addressed. Here is our formulation of the issue. Should our present society allow persons who believe that they have a homosexual orientation the privileges and responsibilities of civil marriage to members of the same sex? This formulation raises three issues that will be addressed in this essay—the character of our present society (the question of modernity), the meaning of civil marriage, and the nature of same-sex orientation.

All three of these issues have often been ignored in recent debates on same-sex marriage. First, the question of the nature of modernization and its impact on the field of intimate relations is almost completely invisible in public deliberations about gay marriage. Second, many people who are for or against same-sex marriage seldom advance careful definitions of marriage, particularly civil or legal marriage in contrast to marriage solemnized by a religious community. Finally, the question of the meaning and nature of homosexual orientation also has nearly vanished from the contemporary discussion, yet assumptions about the concept are constantly being made by all sides in the controversy.

We approach these issues as religious and political liberals. In both fields of human endeavor, we value justice and critical reflection. Although we honor tradition, we believe that the wisdom of the past must submit to a variety of critical tests. Nonetheless, these commitments, in contrast to those of many of our liberal colleagues, lead us to believe that same-sex marriage is unjust in many ways and that liberals should be cautious about endorsing it. We argue that it is most particularly an infringement on the rights of children, whose voices, it should be noted, are often neglected on this issue.

The Multiple Separations of Modernity

We examine these three issues more carefully. First, the question of same-sex marriage should not be approached as a single issue isolated from a wide range of social trends. To be for or against extending civil marriage to gay and lesbian couples is to be tacitly for or against, or at least critically reflective about, a range of other social trends. We think these trends are nicely summarized under the phenomenon of modernization. Both the demand for same-sex marriage and many of the best arguments on its behalf can be understood fully only within the context of the social and cultural transformations wrought by the processes of modernization. We define modernization, following both Max Weber and Jürgen Habermas, as the spread of technical rationality. This is the drive to bring more and more of life under the control of efficient means-end procedures, coming from either market or state bureaucracy, that accomplish short-term satisfactions.[1] The spread of technical rationality also is fueled in Western societies by individualistic cultural values, but it can be motivated almost as easily by more corporate ideals, as is the case in Eastern societies such as The People's Republic of China, South Korea, and Singapore.[2]

The processes of modernization have greatly changed the meaning of marriage. They have influenced the rise of publicly visible homosexuality and possibly certain cultural manifestations of the phenomenon as well. The subtle changes brought by modernization to the broad field of human sexuality have so transformed the meaning and dynamics of marriage in the popular mind as to render the idea of same-sex marital unions far more plausible than was the case earlier.

Modernization has influenced our experience and understanding of marriage through many social and cultural avenues. The summary result of these influences has been the introduction of a variety of separations or disjunctions into the complex range of goods that the institution of marriage legally and religiously has *intended* to integrate and hold together. The end result of these multiple separations has been to reduce the idea and reality of marriage in the minds of many people to little more than an affectionate sexual relationship (the lucky finding of a soul mate) of tentative commitment and uncertain duration.[3] The market, the areas of medicine and reproductive technology, and the sphere of law (especially family law and constitutional law) have, in different ways, mediated both technical rationality and individualism into the realms of sex, marriage, and the family. These three spheres have injected a range of disconnections among certain goods that they once worked together to integrate into the institution of marriage.

Take the world of business. Economists point out that the move in the nineteenth century from the farm to the wage economy disconnected the conjugal couple from the larger extended family.[4] In the second half of the twentieth century, women moved into the wage economy, gained new economic independence from men and partially, and in some cases completely, separated their financial well-being from the institution of marriage. In addition, since technical and functional skills have become the main qualification for job competence in the modern corporation, companies increasingly have deemphasized the marital status of employees and competed for skilled workers by extending marriage-type benefits to unmarried and same-sex couples. These moves in market and industry were paralleled by government's entrance into the family welfare field, further making women less dependent on marriage and family stability.[5] Although these economic and bureaucratic trends have had some positive effects, they also have injected marriage and family with the cost-benefit and efficiency logics of both market and government bureaucracy, weakened patterns of mutual dependency between husband and wife, and contributed to the rise of a culture of divorce, cohabitation, and nonmarriage.[6]

But these trends have been further aggravated by other modernizing developments. Take the field of reproductive technology. Reliable contraception, legal abortion, artificial insemination, in vitro fertilization, surrogacy, gamete intrafallopian transfer, zygote intrafallopian transfer, and the possibility of cloning all inject new separations into the delicate, historically marital integration of sexuality, love, childbirth, socialization of children, and mutual dependency. Although many, but not all, of these procedures can be used within the institution of marriage to enhance these integrations, many are increasingly used outside of marriage. Furthermore, some of them will doubtless be used more and more to promote childbirth by singles and same-sex couples. In fact, legalized same-sex marriage will likely spur demands for greater legal and social support for same-sex couples to have access to reproductive technologies, since only by using these technologies can they have their "own" children.

Law has contributed to these separations as well. Beginning in the 1950s and continuing to the present, American family law has replaced the central principles supporting marriage and monogamy with new ones supporting the concepts of consent and privacy. Although most people would be sympathetic to the U.S. Supreme Court's decision in *Griswald v. Connecticut* (1965) that "freed birth control for married couples from state interference," the decision did soon set the precedent for *Eisenstadt v. Baird* (1972) that "struck down a Massachusetts law that prohibited the prescription or sale of contraceptives to unmarried people."[7] As historian Nancy Cott has written,

> Rather than tying privacy in reproductive decision-making to marital intimacy the Eisenstadt decision made it a more portable, individual right: "the right of the *individual,* married or single, to be free from unwarranted governmental intrusion into matters so fundamentally affecting a person as the decision whether to bear or beget a child."[8]

As harmless as the Eisenstadt decision must have seemed at the time, it simultaneously made marriage less central to the law, set the stage for the eventual treatment of marital and nonmarital sexual and reproductive acts as equivalent before the law, and robbed the law of the grounds for restricting certain reproductive technologies to their use within marriage. The emerging emphasis on privacy and consent led to the erosion of an institutional understanding of marriage, making it a private intimate association with little public significance, yet one still deserving of the protection and legitimation of the law. Although these decisions might possibly have been justified on grounds of the impossibility of enforcing laws applying to behavior that usually takes place in private, the mode of legal reasoning clearly functioned to make law a leading contributor to the multiple separations of the goods of marriage that have occurred in recent decades. These disconnections also contributed to the precedents needed to increase the legal plausibility of same-sex civil marriage and the significant cultural redefinition of marriage that same-sex marriage entails.[9]

Alternative Responses to the Tensions between Marriage and Modernization: Four Strategies

Marriage is a complex social phenomenon and has been perceived as such throughout history in all cultures. As legal historian John Witte has pointed out, through most of the history of marriage in the West, it simultaneously has been perceived as a material institution giving expression to many natural needs and tendencies, a contractual institution requiring social control, a public institution contributing to the common good, and a religious institution seen as covenant or sacrament and witnessed and sanctioned by God.[10] Different periods of history have emphasized one or the other of these dimensions of marriage, but most of them were visible in one way or another at all times. I would add that marriage as affection, sexual exchange, and intersubjective communication—what the Roman Catholic tradition has called the "unitive" goods of marriage—were also visible.[11] The history of marriage can be seen as the growing ascendancy of the unitive values of marriage in relation to the procreative. The present controversy over same-sex marriage is in some respects about whether the so-called unitive aspects should now become almost completely separated from the procreative and yet still enjoy the legal privileges and protections of traditional marriage that held the unitive and procreative in some kind of balance. The question has become "should marriage be seen primarily as an interpersonal 'close relationship' between consenting adults, with considerations such as material dependency, the conception of children, and child-rearing responsibilities being viewed as contingent and incidental?"[12]

The dynamics of modernization have forced this question. Any solution to the problem of same-sex marriage inevitably raises additional issues about modernity's desirability and the possibility of constraining or redirecting some of its social and cultural consequences. We have identified four grand strategies for coping with the tensions between marriage and modernization. We list them now and discuss them from time to time in the remainder of this chapter.

First, there is the strategy of retrenchment. This view idealizes the divided spheres of the nineteenth century between home and paid employment and would use both religion and law to reinforce the monogamous, marriage-centered, and child-centered family built around a pronounced differentiation between the roles of men and women.[13]

A second view, advanced by legal scholar Martha Fineman, holds that modernization has already rendered the family of the married mother and father raising children as a thing of the past and that marriage therefore should be delegalized. She would then have law and public policy directed to the support of arrangements where the care of dependents is the central task—single mothers with children being the chief example.[14]

Then there is the view powerfully associated with Jonathan Rauch's argument in his *Gay Marriage* (2004). He proposes fighting the disruptions of modernization by creating a new marriage culture that would eliminate domestic partnerships and cohabitation by convincing everyone—gays and straights alike—to align affection, sex, and commitment within the institution of marriage.[15]

Finally, there is the position that we represent called "critical familism." This position tries to retain the historic alignment of sex, affection, generativity, child care, and mutual assistance accomplished by the institution of marriage. It does this, however, by advocating for a *reconstructed* view of gender and work-family relations in modern marriage, as well as an aggressive curtailment of the negative impact of modernization on the integrity and stability of the conjugal couple raising children. We hold that this position best grasps the weight of tradition on the primary purposes of marriage, best protects the interests and rights of children, best serves the common good, and best preserves the integrity of the law.

A Brief Archeology of Marriage

We now turn to the second neglected issue listed above—the meaning of marriage. It is widely thought that the history of the institution of marriage is about what religious forces, especially Judaism and Christianity, have taught and imposed on the whole of society. Nothing could be further from the truth. The theory of marriage in the West has had a religious dimension, but beneath and within the symbolism of religion can be found a variety of additional features. One can find naturalistic assumptions about human nature; Greek, Roman, and German legal theories about marriage; and philosophical perspectives from Plato, Aristotle, Kant, Locke, and Rousseau. We claim that powerful philosophical and naturalistic views of marriage can be found within the contours of what often appears to be primarily theological thinking and that this inner core of Western marriage theory is worth retaining, even as it is amended in some respects.

We argue that Western marriage theory brought both religious and legal support to the consolidation of what evolutionary psychologists today call *kin altruism*. This term refers to the care that natural parents are inclined to give to their children because they have labored to give them birth and have come to recognize them as a part of themselves that should be preserved and extended. The idea of kin altruism also implies a reciprocal identification of children with natural parents because of this labor and because children perceive the bodily continuity with those who give them life. The other goods of marriage—sexual exchange, affection, and mutual assistance—are goods in themselves but also gain their larger meaning from their integration into the having and caring for children. The covenantal and sacramental aspects of marriage provided by religion gave sacred weight and approval to these integrations as centered in the solidarities of kin altruism. In addition, the Abrahamic religions of Judaism, Christianity, and Islam added the idea that parents should love their children not only because they are extensions of themselves but also because of the deeper reason that they are also children of God and objects of God's unconditioned love.

It is a matter of cultural variability as to whether families are patriarchal, polygynous, monogamous, extended, joint, or nuclear. But within all this pluralism of family forms, there is a persistent core value that is widely cherished and protected around the world. *This is the importance of the people who give life to the infant also being, as nearly as possible, the ones who care for it.* This principle is based on the widely held assumption that people who conceive a child, when they recognize their relation to it, will on average be the most invested in its nurture and well-being. It is also based on the observation that, when other things are equal, children themselves want—indeed, often *long*— to be raised by those who gave them life.

There are various languages designed to communicate this truth. Religious and theological languages in Judaism, Christianity, and Islam used the language of divine creation and divine command. Some philosophical systems have employed a combination of biological and philosophical arguments. Then there were a surprising number of instances in which a dual language combining both religious revelation and naturalistic philosophy came together to create powerful synthetic arguments supporting the integration of kin altruism into the reinforcements of marriage.

Aristotle provided much of the naturalistic and philosophical language for the centrality of kin altruism in family theory found in Western philosophy, law, and religion. His insights were used to reinforce folk observations in Christianity, Judaism, and Islam. He had insight into what modern-day evolutionary psychologists describe as our tendency to invest ourselves more in those individuals with whom we are biologically related—those individuals who carry our genes.[16] In his *Politics,* Aristotle writes, "in common with other animals and with plants, mankind have a natural desire to leave behind them an image of themselves."[17] It was simple comparative observation that formed Aristotle's belief that humans share this impulse with other animals and that this tendency constitutes a basic framework within which behavior proceeds.

We see this idea developed more in Aristotle's critique of Plato's *Republic.* Plato tells us that Socrates believed that nepotism (the preferential treatment of kin by blood relatives) was the fundamental cause of divisiveness within a city. This factionalism could be eliminated, he believed, if the city required elite men to have offspring with women who were held in common, then having state nurses raise the infants with neither parents nor children knowing their biological ties with one another. In such a state, Plato believed that everyone would "apply the terms 'mine' and 'not mine' in the same way to the same thing"—especially to children, thereby undercutting the divisive consequences of nepotism.[18]

Aristotle, however, believed that Plato was wrong. In developing his case, we see Aristotle's theory of kin altruism amplified even more fully. He wrote,

> Whereas in a state having women and children in common, love will be watery; and the father will certainly not say "my son," or the son "my father." As a little sweet wine mingled with a great deal of water is imperceptible in the mixture, so, in this sort of community, the idea of relationship which is based upon these names will be lost; there is no reason why the so-called father should care about the son, or the son about the father, or brothers about one another. Of the two qualities which chiefly inspire regard and affection—that a thing is your own and that it is your only one—neither can exist in such a state as this.[19]

Aristotle believed that such a society would water down and undermine parental recognition and investment. Furthermore, he believed it would unleash violence because people will no longer "be afraid of committing any crimes by reason of consanguinity."[20]

The great Roman Catholic theologian Thomas Aquinas synthesized Aristotle's insights on kin altruism with the theology of creation from Judaism and Christianity. He developed a double language on marriage that was simultaneously philosophical and religious, secular and sacred, naturalistic and sacramental. It constituted the core ideas supporting one of the most powerful theories of the relation of family to the state that is available, i.e., subsidiarity theory as it functions in Roman Catholic social teachings and the secular family law of several modern nations, most notably Germany.

Aquinas called marriage in its primordial form an "office of nature." It was a matter of natural reason and natural law that both children and adults flourish better if supported by the power of marriage to integrate procreation, the socialization of children, love and commitment, and the regulation of sexual desire.[21] At this level marriage could be illuminated by the natural law, especially that aspect of it that identifies those natural inclinations that are further guided by interventions of "the free will" and "acts of virtue."[22] But marriage for Aquinas also was revealed in scripture, specifically the Genesis account of creation. In the "Supplement" to the *Summa Theologica,* he quotes Matthew 29:4, "Have ye not read that He Who made man from the beginning 'made them male and female,'" a verse which itself refers back to Genesis 1:27. Nearby he refers to Genesis 2:21 and claims that from the foundations of Creation and before the emergence of sin among humans, God "fashioned a helpmate for man out of his rib."[23] This implies what the full Genesis passage makes explicit, "It is not good that the man should be alone; I will make a helper as his partner" (Genesis 2:18).

Scripture deepens and gives ontological significance to Aquinas's philosophical view of marriage, *but his full argument does not stay at the level of scriptural interpretation.* This observation is extremely important. Religious perspectives are not always advanced on narrowly religious grounds, just as so-called secular arguments often contain in their horizons quasi-religious assumptions about the depth of human experience.[24]

Thomas Aquinas was one of the architects of the sacramental view of marriage that has so much influenced marriage theory in Christian nations in recent centuries. Yet, despite this, we should not blind ourselves to his naturalistic theory of family formation and marriage, especially in view of how similar it is to modern scientific views found in the emerging field of evolutionary psychology. Aquinas defined matrimony as the joining of the male to the primordial mother-infant family. He saw this happening for four natural reasons. First, the long period of human infant dependency makes it very difficult for mothers at the human level to raise infants by themselves. Hence, they turn for help to their male consorts.[25] Second, the fathers are much more likely to attach to their infants if they have a high degree of certainty that the infant is actually theirs and hence continuous with their own biological existence.[26] Third, males attach to their infants and consorts because of the mutual assistance and affection that they receive from the infant's mother.[27] Finally, even Aquinas realized that sexual exchange between mother and father (even though he talked about it as paying "the marital debt") helped to integrate the male to the mother-infant dyad. Of course, Aquinas could not support his biophilosophical theories with the scientific explanations that are available today. We should note, however, that these four conditions are almost perfectly parallel to those that the fields of evolutionary psychology and anthropology believe led humans, in contrast to most other mammals, to form families and long-term attachments between fathers and mothers for the care of their offspring.[28]

Kin altruism was at the heart of this naturalistic model of family formation. When Aquinas said that the human male "naturally desires to be assured of his offspring and this assurance would be altogether nullified in the case of promiscuous copulation,"[29] he was echoing Aristotle's belief that parental investment is more intense and durable between natural parents and their offspring. We see that belief again when Aquinas offers naturalistic reasons for the permanence of marriage by referring to the long period of care that is required to raise to maturity the child who is, as well, "something" of the parent.[30]

Aquinas's naturalistic theory of family formation gains consolidation and reinforcements from his theology of creation and sacrament, but can stand independently of them. Indeed, this Aristotelian-Thomistic naturalism has been a powerful force in subsequent legal and religious developments for centuries after Thomas gave them such compelling articulation in the double language of theology and philosophy. The idea that the institution of marriage should channel the investments of kin altruism for the good of both children and their parents is the grounding assumption of the Roman Catholic theory of subsidiarity—the principle that governments and markets should support (*subsidum*) the family solidarities motivated by kin altruism, but should do nothing to undermine or replace them.[31] We believe that this basic concept is one that contemporary law should recall, fine-tune for present-day circumstances, and appropriate.

It is important to notice the flexibility of Aquinas's naturalistic argument. He was fully aware that humans have conflicting natural tendencies with no single fixed aim. The world of nature is full of proximate causes. But when human sexuality is guided by the needs of child-rearing, then the inclinations toward kin altruism, reinforced by culture and religion, should have a commanding role in ordering our unstable natural tendencies. Hence, Aquinas gave us a flexible natural law argument, not a rigid one.

Aquinas's view is consistent with the images of natural law developing in the thought of contemporary philosophers and theologians, such as Mary Midgley,[32] Jean Porter,[33] Stephen Pope,[34] Larry Arnhart,[35] and Lisa Cahill.[36] Mary Midgley says it well when she writes that, in spite of our plural and flexible human desires and needs, "The central factors in us must be accepted, and the right line of human conduct must lie somewhere within the range they allow."[37] It is clear that for Aristotle, Aquinas, and much of contemporary evolutionary thought, kin altruism is a central tendency that both biology and moral sensibilities have honored as being one of these "central factors." It is our argument that it also should be the *intention of law* to honor kin altruism in its understanding of marriage.

To say this, of course, does not mean that either law or religion should allow the kin solidarities of one family to harm other families. Plato's concern with nepotism and unjust family preferences had a point. Nor do we intend to diminish the special, pro-child role of adoption in finding willing parents for children who need them. Our argument is simply that justice between families includes the idea of supporting and enhancing their kin investments, even as it resists the possibility that our kin investments might be absolutized to the point of harming other families. The good of marriage—whether seen as a philosophically conceived intrinsic good or a religious sacrament or covenant—is crucially preserved by the mutual investments of kin altruism.

Marriage for All

Until recently, it has been the intention of law to support both marriage and kin altruism. Until the 1960s and 1970s, divorce was difficult to obtain, nonmarital sex was sometimes penalized, and certain legal privileges extended only to married couples. But, as Cott points out, since that time law has relativized and decentered marriage and granted legal protections to a variety of nonmarital sexual and reproductive behaviors, all in the name of enhancing liberty and individual freedom. The journalist Jonathan Rauch agrees that the directions of modernizing societies and their family-law trends may be highly problematic. He is pro-marriage, through and through. In fact, he wants marriage for everyone—straights and gays alike. And, as the subtitle of his book *Gay Marriage* suggests, he claims it will be "good for gays, good for straights, and good for society." Rauch wants to develop a new marriage culture to resist the individualizing and isolating forces of modernization. He wants to reintegrate sexual behavior—all sexual behavior—back into marriage.[38] Furthermore, he would eliminate domestic partnerships and civil unions, not only for opposite-sex partners but same-sex partners as well. The real enemy of marriage is not, he tells us, same-sex marriage; rather it is those marital substitutes that give legal privileges and protections to new forms of "marriage-lite."[39]

Marriage, for Rauch, is primarily about mutual dependency, commitment, and intimacy. From the standpoint of the classic goods of marriage spoken about by Augustine and Aquinas, Rauch puts the accent on mutual dependency and commitment (*fedeles*).[40] Marriage is about two consenting adults committing themselves to take care of each other—in sickness or in health, whether rich or poor, whether young or old. Marriage is also, for Rauch, about kinship—about married couples becoming integrated into extended families and enjoying shared celebrations, holidays, and, once again, mutual care. His view of kinship should, however, be distinguished from the Aristotelian-evolutionary psychological view of kin altruism. His idea is not primarily about parental investment in children but, rather, the emotional enrichment and communal involvement of adults in family-like networks.

Nonetheless, Rauch does address those who believe that the institution of marriage is primarily about having and raising children. Rauch agrees: children are a fine thing. However, the goods of sexual pleasure, love, commitment, and mutual dependency are, for Rauch, plenty enough reasons for marriage. These goods can be enhanced by the good of children; the children just do not necessarily need to be one's own offspring.[41] Nor does the presence of children need to be a defining element of marriage. Same-sex marriage is like sterility. He writes, "Biologically speaking, a homosexual union is nothing but one variety of sterile union, and no different even in principle: a woman without a uterus is no more open to procreation than a man without a uterus."[42] He points out that society does not prevent infertile couples from marrying. Nor does it prohibit the elderly from marrying nor those heterosexual couples who simply do not intend to have children at all. So, he asks, why restrict gays and lesbians from marrying? The nonprocreative reasons to marry are reason enough, he says, especially the good of mutual dependency.

Rauch's understanding of marriage is serious and requires critical response. It also gives us an opportunity to tighten the definition of marriage that we advance in this chapter. Rauch would agree with the majority opinion of the Massachusetts *Goodridge v. the Department of Public Health* decision mandating same-sex marriage in that state. It defines marriage as primarily a "private," "intimate," "committed," and "exclusive" union" that is "among life's momentous acts of self-definition."[43] The majority opinion in Good-ridge says that it is "incorrect" to claim that having children is the primary purpose of marriage. Although the majority admits that, "it is certainly true that many, perhaps most, married couples have children together (assisted or unassisted)," it nonetheless asserts that "the exclusive and permanent commitment of the marriage partners to one another, not the begetting of children,...is the sine qua non of civil marriage."[44] The heavy-duty genera-tive purposes of the large majority of married couples is set aside and replaced with the idea of marriage as a sexual and affectionate friendship. The Goodridge majority acknowledges, in ways that Rauch does not, that this is a change in the definition of the institution of marriage, but asserts, in total contradiction to the historic principle of subsidiarity, that the state "creates civil marriage." The majority admits that its final definition of marriage as the "voluntary union of two persons as spouses, to the exclusion of all others" is a "reformulation" of the historic, dare we say, classic definition.[45] But it assumes that the Supreme Judicial Court, in its role as the authoritative inter-preter of the Massachusetts Constitution, has the right to contradict history, the *jus gentium,* common law definitions of marriage, and even past legal assumptions of the Commonwealth of Massachusetts. In short, the court's justifications for decentering marriage from generativity constitute an unre-flective and naïve affirmation of the blind forces of modernization and the various changes in intimate life that it has shaped.

For example, the Goodridge majority first invokes the *de facto* demographic decline of households with children. It then cites trends in Massachusetts law to respond "supportively to the changing reality of the American family" and to "strengthen the modern family in its many variations."[46] Hence, the socio-logical fact that Massachusetts *already* in its many family policies has blurred the distinction between marriage and nonmarriage and *already* has drifted toward taking lightly the childbearing features of marriage becomes the excuse to continue riding the wave, taking the final step of intentionally rede-fining marriage at the level of law, with all of the normative, cultural, and channeling implications that this act implies.

The difficulties with the position of Rauch and the Goodridge majority (shared by other articulate advocates of same-sex marriage such as Evan Wolfson and Andrew Sullivan) are multiple.[47] First, this position intention-ally aims to undermine, with the force of law, understandings of marriage and family that have already been fragmented by the modernizing forces summarized at the beginning of this chapter. In fact, their position assumes that the struggle to balance modernization with marriage is over—modernity has won. Goodridge is full of statements taking for granted that the law has already swung to the side of what Daniel Cere has called the "close relation-ship" theory of marriage.[48] Its reading of the Massachusetts Constitution is filtered through lenses of interpretation that assume the permanence of some of the current drifts in demography, reproductive practices, and the pluralism of family forms. The decision follows the logic that since these social realities have already evolved, then same-sex marriage is all the more justified. It never occurs to either Rauch or the Goodridge majority to question these trends or to envision the use of law to reinforce those forces in civil society intent on reconstructing marriage to better cope with the forces of modernity.

The *intention* of the law is the issue at stake here. It is one thing for law not to question the capacity of opposite-sex couples to have children, be they infertile, too old, uncertain, or disinterested. In the rightful name of privacy, the law does not pry, partially because things change (infertility is sometimes corrected, people sometimes change their minds), and the elderly traditionally have married to honor the child-centered view of marriage and the need to symbolically reinforce the norm of integrating sex, love, dependency, childbirth, and child-rearing into the institution of marriage. So, it is the classic intentionality of law that the Goodridge majority rejects—the intention to guide and channel the integration of this list of goods as nearly as possible. The problem with the final decision of Goodridge and the inclusive marriage program of Rauch is that they both intend a form and model of marriage that breaks the integrative goals of the institution. They both make sexual exchange, affection, and mutual dependency the center of the institution with its generative goals secondary, incidental, and even ignored.

Second, this redefinition of marriage raises to the level of public policy the rejection of the historic relation between marriage and kin altruism. It dispenses with the principle that the individuals who give life to children should be the ones who raise them in a bonded and enduring relation. We believe that the reasons implicit in this tradition, when properly identified and brought to light as we attempted to do in the middle sections of this chapter, pass the rationality standard requested by the Judicial Supreme Court of Massachusetts. Dismissing this core relation between kin altruism and marriage constitutes the ultimate injustice to children. Children have a right not only to parents and families, as the United Nations Convention on the Rights of the Child has asserted,[49] but they also have the right to expect to be raised in a society whose legal and cultural institutions attempt to maximize the possibility that they will be raised by the parents who conceived them.

The positions of the Goodridge majority and Rauch are adultocentric. They are both correct in holding that there are goods other than procreation that marriage celebrates and protects. They both fail, however, to take or even consider the point of view of children—their need and right to be raised in a society whose legal, religious, and cultural institutions intentionally promote, and do nothing to compromise, the principle that children should be raised, as nearly as possible, by the parents who conceive them.

Marquardt has studied children of divorce whose experience was almost entirely ignored as the no-fault divorce revolution took hold.[50] In the three decades during which a high divorce rate has come to be seen by many as an unavoidable fact of contemporary society, legal theorists have continued to overlook and deny the injustice forced on these children. They are required to divide their time and affections between two homes or to lose contact with their mother or father, too often in the name of the happiness of their parents. While some divorces are necessary, the fact that the majority of divorces end low-conflict marriages reinforces this question as one of social justice.

Just as no-fault divorce was ushered in with virtually no regard for the children's needs, the Goodridge decision that legalized same-sex marriage in Massachusetts brushes aside the now-large body of social-science data that indicate that children raised by their married biological parents do better, on average, than those raised by single parents or stepparents.[51] Although data sets are not sufficiently large to demonstrate anything definitive about the strengths or weaknesses of same-sex couples for child-rearing, our society's experience with other alternative family forms suggests that these families will not, on average, be able to reduplicate the investments and consolidations of marriage built on the energies of kin altruism, the consolidation of which has been in the past the primary goal of marriage.[52] To disregard the needs of children, the traditions that have understood these needs, and contemporary social-science evidence offends natural justice. That is, this wholesale dismissal offends both what is fair and what contributes to human flourishing by meeting the unique needs of the individuals in question. If our earlier summary of the disconnections introduced by modernizations into the field of generativity is correct, the legalization of same-sex marriage would not be just one more example of the drift, but the culmination that finally shifts the institutional logic of marriage and further marginalizes children from its basic meaning.

Third, the legalization of same-sex marriage is not only unjust to children, it is unjust to a wide range of other human arrangements that attempt to meet the dependency needs of the vulnerable, including those who are old, ill, or disabled. The feminist legal scholar Martha Fineman has observed that same-sex marriage extends the protections of marriage to one type of sexual family while excluding nonsexual arrangements organized around the care of dependents. These examples include single parents with children, brother caring for ailing brother, daughter taking care of aging mother, friend caring for dying neighbor, and more.[53] She believes that the forces of modernity have so radically transformed society that the "sexual family"—whether married or unmarried, gay or straight—should in the name of justice be delegalized.[54] The benefits traditionally associated with marriage should now be distributed to actual caregivers and their dependents. Although Fineman has no prejudice against homosexual couples, it is real and grave dependency that she wants to draw attention to and protect. She does not believe that the robust benefits that once went to marriage should go to the many able-bodied heterosexual and homosexual couples who are healthy, employed, and have few actual dependency needs. She thinks the new, thin, affectionate-sexual relationships at the heart of the legal norms intended by Goodridge and Rauch should be protected, at best, by privately drawn legal contracts—not the status-granting powers of actual marriage.[55] She proposes these changes in the name of justice.

Fineman's position has the virtue of showing how same-sex marriage, rather than being unambiguously just, actually can lead to new perceived injustices. We believe, however, that her proposal has additional, potentially graver problems. First, her position is a still more radical capitulation to the fragmenting forces on families of modernity and technical rationality. She assumes that the conjugal couple with children is nearly a thing of the past.[56] Her suggestion that we remove the legal protections of marriage from the sexual family will, in the end, further undermine the integration of sexual behavior, birth, and care by natural parents. She assumes that in the future neither law nor individuals need aspire to integrate these various goods. If couples want to form sexual families, they can marry as they wish, develop private contracts, and perhaps solemnize their relation before a religious body, but not receive legal marriage. Her confidence in the ability of adults to forge meaningful, long-term, child-centered bonds with only minimal social and legal supports is much greater than ours.

Instead, we would embrace a two-part solution. The first part would retain the historic child-centered view of marriage at the center of law and public policy, requiring not only the denial of legalized same-sex marriage but the consideration of other legal and cultural changes to help support marriage. The second part of our solution is the proposal to meet the dependency needs of other classes of individuals, including single parents, the ill and old, gays and lesbians, and other needy persons, through appropriately targeted legal contracts and social programs, including welfare programs, as well as child supports and adoption in cases where these instruments are relevant. Neither the radical extension of marriage as Rauch proposes nor its eradication as a legal category as Fineman advocates meets the standard of those forms of justice that aspire to promote the common good, especially for children.

Comments on the Concept of Orientation

A few words need to be added on the concept of homosexual orientation. Critical analysis of this concept is notably absent in recent discussions about same-sex marriage. Goodridge totally avoids the subject. Rauch advances what is commonly called an "essentialistic" definition of orientation.[57] This view holds that sexual orientation is a given, perhaps biologically determined, inclination that cannot be changed short of grave damage to the psyche and personhood of people with such feelings. This view is strikingly different from another powerful perspective—the "social constructivist" view that holds human sexuality is plastic and flexible. According to this view, one learns to think of oneself as gay or lesbian depending on the social context, opportunities, and language games available to read one's sexual feelings.[58] Rauch's inclusive marriage project is buttressed by his assumptions that there are basically two kinds of people, gays and straights. He is fond of repeating the statement that "homosexuality really exists."[59] He gives that statement the weight of philosophical realism by saying that for gays, homosexuality is "natural," meaning, we take it, that this is just how they are by birth or some other unchangeable reason.[60]

We do not plan to get embroiled in an assessment of the contradictory evidence from the social sciences on the nature and cause of orientation. Nor do we believe, at all, that society should try to change those who define themselves as gay or lesbian. Nor do we want persons who attribute consistent homosexual feelings to themselves to be persecuted, shunned, stigmatized, or in other ways oppressed. In fact, we want them to live in a society that fully respects them, and we know our society has not yet reached that point.

We only want to make a few points relevant to the role of law in changing the definition of marriage. First, it should be noticed that homosexual orientation is a self-attribution. In contrast to race or gender, upon which unjust discriminations have been made, homosexuality is a definition that people place on their own subjective feelings, often struggling to read them correctly and even changing their self-definitions several times throughout the life cycle.

Furthermore, the homosexual community itself is quite torn about the concept of orientation and about the advisability of legalizing gay marriage. Regarding orientation, many hold the constructivist view and advocate getting beyond the distinction between gay and straight, forming a new, liberated, sexually fluid bisexuality.[61] It is also important to realize that a significant number of influential voices on the gay left reject the idea of same-sex marriage, finding it oppressive, and tolerating it only as a transitional moment toward the eventual abolition of marriage.[62] We mention these debates internal to the gay community not to take sides but to insist that legal positions such as Goodridge or programs such as Rauch's must not act as if these debates do not exist. (The mainstream media, for instance, choose to ignore them almost entirely, routinely featuring advocates of same-sex marriage who aspire to a bourgeois, more-or-less middle-class vision of marriage.)

Acknowledging these debates within the gay community is relevant to an accurate understanding of what is happening to marriage now and what could happen in the near future. Is society being asked to include within marriage an oppressed minority whose sexual orientation is some unchanging essence, or is it being asked to change not only its definition of marriage but its entire understanding of the organization of the sexual life cycle—a change that could usher in a new flexible bisexuality that would transcend the poles of homosexual and heterosexual? Perhaps it is far too simple to say that there are two kinds of people with differing fixed sexual orientations and that what happens to one group has no implications for the other. In view of the strong impact that legal same-sex marriage would doubtless have on the major socializing institutions of our society—elementary and secondary schools, colleges and universities, social-service organizations, and even religious institutions—this question is all the more justified. Out of justice not only to children but to their parents and other adults, this discussion tries to clarify what is actually being asked for—Marriage like straights have it? Or marriage on the way to something else?—should not be prematurely stifled by the rapid creation and enforcement of same-sex marriage.

Critical Familism and Modernity

In conclusion, we reject handling the challenges of modernization to marriage by either radically changing its meaning (as do Rauch and Goodridge) or eliminating marriage as a legal category, as does Fineman. Both strategies, in the end, are uncritical capitulations to these modernizing social forces. Nor, however, should our position be confused with a traditionalism that seeks no reconstruction of traditional marriage or no redirection of modernity. Rather, we would retain the core meaning of marriage built around generativity, increase gender justice both in domestic and in public spheres, and redirect the forces of modernity to make these first two goals more feasible.

We call this position "critical familism."[63] It is familistic in that it is a pro-marriage strategy built around the equal-regard partnership between husband and wife in both the public world of employment and politics and the domestic sphere of child care and daily chores.[64] We envision marriage in the future to be more flexible on gender roles, but we do not assume all differentiations will disappear, especially those relevant to the vulnerabilities of pregnancy, birth, and caring for small children.[65] We believe that husband and wife should both have free access to the benefits and responsibilities of participation in the wage economy, but we would limit its reach into marriage and family by encouraging—perhaps mandating—the availability of more 30-hour workweeks for parents with children, more flex time, higher tax exemptions and credits for minor children, elimination of all marriage tax penalties, and creating supports similar to the GI bill for parents who leave the wage economy for a period to care for children.[66]

We believe that marriage—its definition, renewal, and reconstruction—should be primarily in the hands of the institutions of civil society. These include voluntary organizations, religious organizations, and the open legislative process permeable to the influences of people at the grassroots. A growing and increasingly more powerful marriage education movement now teaches young people, minorities, and even the poor—in schools, the military, and in churches—new communication skills and fresh understandings necessary for the strengthening of marriage in a dynamic modern society. Law and government should support, and do nothing to undercut, such initiatives rising from civil society.

Law and government must regulate marriage, but they do not create the meaning of marriage any more than they create the substance of the institutions of education or business. Critical familism is fully aware that civil marriage is based on public principles that can be rationally reviewed and tested, and we have tried to present some of these in this essay. Although religious traditions contain religious narratives that empower and consolidate their views of marriage, critical familism holds that they also contain an inner core of rationality that can contribute to public discourse and deliberation. Hence, critical familism tries to invigorate the critical retrieval of religious traditions, not only Judaism and Christianity, which have contributed so much to Western views of marriage, but other great traditions such as Islam, Buddhism, Hinduism, and Confucianism that increasingly will and should become a part of public discourse about marriage and family.[67] The law has an important part to play in systematizing and codifying these public discussions, but it is not, and must never be, permitted to become the creator of the conversation and the only player that counts.

But a full exposition of the meaning of critical familism is beyond the scope of this chapter. Much has been written about it already, and we hope the progressive, egalitarian, pro-child, and pro-marriage position we propose becomes more visible in the current national conversation about same-sex marriage.

Presented to The Witherspoon Institute
Princeton University, December 2004.[68]

Endnotes

1. Max Weber, *The Protestant Ethic and the Spirit of Capitalism* 181 (Charles Scribner's Sons 1958); Jürgen Habermas, *The Theory of Communicative Rationality II* 333 (Boston, MA: Beacon Press 1987).

2. Ralf Dahrendorf, *A Precarious Balance: Economic Opportunity, Civil Society, and Political Liberty, The Responsive Community* 28–32 (Summer 1995).

3. Barbara Dafoe Whitehead and David Popenoe, *Why Men Won't Commit: State of Our Unions: The Social Health of Marriage in America 2002,* 8 (Rutgers, The National Marriage Project 2002).

4. Gary Becker, *Treatise on the Family* 356, 357 (Harvard University Press 1991).

5. *Id.;* Charles Murray, *Losing Ground* 129–133 (Basic Books 1984).

6. For reviews of these trends in both the United States with its strong market economy and Sweden with its emphasis on the state-supported family, see David Popenoe, *Disturbing the Nest* (Aldine De Gruyter 1988); Alan Wolfe, *Whose Keeper* (University of California Press 1989).

7. Nancy Cott, *Public Vows: A History of Marriage and the Nation* 198 (Harvard University Press 2000).

8. *Id.,* at 199.

9. William N. Eskridge, *Equality Practice: Civil Unions and the Future of Gay Rights* (Routledge 2002).

10. John Witte, *From Sacrament to Contract: Marriage, Religion, and Law in the Western Tradition* 2 (Westminster John Knox Press 1997).

11. For a philosophical and theological exposition of the unitive goods of marriage, see Karol Wojtyla (the young Pope John Paul II) *Love and Responsibility* (Farrar, Straus, and Giroux 1981).

12. Daniel Cere, *Redefining Marriage and Family: Trends in North American Jurisprudence* 24 (Family Law Project, Harvard University 2003).

13. This position is often associated with the organizations called Focus on the Family and Promise Keepers. *See* James Dobson, *Dr. Dobson Answers Your Questions about Marriage and Sexuality* iii, 65–71 (Tyndale House Publishers 1974); James Dobson and Gary Bauer, *Children at Risk* 156 (Word Publishing 1990); Tony Evans, *A Man and His Integrity, Seven Promises of a Promise Keeper* 73 (Focus on the Family Publishing 1994).

14. Martha Fineman, *The Illusion of Equality* (The University of Chicago Press 1991); Martha Fineman, *The Neutered Mother, the Sexual Family, and Other Twentieth Century Tragedies* (Routledge 1994).

15. Jonathan Rauch, *Gay Marriage: Why It is Good for Gays, Good for Straights, and Good for America* (Henry Holt and Company, 2004).

16. Martin Daly and Margo Wilson, *The Evolutionary Psychology of Marriage and Divorce, The Ties that Bind* 91–110 (Aldine De Gruyter 2000).

17. Aristotle, *Politics,* in *The Basic Words of Aristotle Bk. I,* ii (Random House 1941).

18. Plato, *The Republic* (New York: Basic Books, 1968).

19. Aristotle, *supra* n. 17, at Bk. I, ii.

20. *Id.*

21. Thomas Aquinas, *Supplement, Summa Theologica III* Q. 41, A. 1 (T. and T. Washbourne 1917).

22. *Id.*

23. *Id.* at Q. 42, A. 3.

24. For a discussion of how metaphors of characterizing the ultimate context of experience unwittingly pervade the social sciences, see Don Browning, *Religious Thought and the Modern Psychologies* (Fortress Press 1987, 2004).

25. Aquinas, *supra* n. 21 at Q. 41, A. 1.

26. *Id.*

27. *Id.*

28. For a summary of these four conditions as they can be found in the literature of evolutionary psychology, see Don Browning et al., *From Culture Wars to Common Ground: Religion and the American Family Debate* 111–114 (Westminster John Knox 1997, 2000). *See also* Don Browning, *Marriage and Modernization: How Globalization Threatens Marriage and What to Do about It* 109–111 (Wm. B. Eerdmans 2003).

29. Aquinas, *Supplement, Summa Theologica, III,* at 41.

30. Aquinas, *Summa Theologica, II-II,* at Q. 10, A. 12.

31. *Rerum Novarum, in Proclaiming Justice and Peace: Papal Documents from Rerum Novarum through Centisimus Annus,* at para. 11 and 12 (Michael Walsh & Brian Davies eds., Twenty-Third Publications); Pius XI, *Casti Connubii* (The Barry Vail Corporation 1931); and Pius XI, *Quadragesimo Anno,* The Papal Encyclicals (McGrath 1981).

32. Mary Midgley, *Beast and Man* (Cornell University Press 1978).

33. Jean Porter, *Natural and Divine Law* (Saint Paul University Press 1999).

34. Stephen Pope, *The Evolution of Altruism and the Ordering of Love* (Georgetown University Press, 1994).

35. Larry Arnhart, *Darwinian Natural Right* (State University of New York 1998).

36. Lisa Sowle Cahill, *Sex, Gender and Christian Ethics* (Cambridge University Press 1996).

37. Midgley, *supra* n. 32 at 81.

38. Rauch, *supra* n. 15 at 52.

39. *Id.* at 42.

40. *Id.* at 22.

41. *Id.* at 108.

42. *Id.* at 111.

43. Goodridge v. Department of Public Health, 798 N.E.2d 941 (Mass. 2003).

44. *Id.* at 5.

45. *Id.* at 14.

46. *Id.* at 10.

47. Andrew Sullivan, *Virtually Normal* (Vintage Books 1995); Evan Wolfson, *All Together Now, Marriage and Same-Sex Unions: A Debate* 3–10 (Lynn Wardle et al. eds., Praeger 2003).

48. Cere, *supra* n. 12, at 24.

49. The United Nations Convention on the Rights of the Child, Article 7.

50. Elizabeth Marquardt's forthcoming book is based on a new, national study that includes a nationally representative telephone survey of young adults from divorced and intact families, conducted with Dr. Norval Glenn at the University of Texas-Austin. *See The Secret Inner Lives of Children of Divorce: A Generation's Childhood Turned Inside out* (Crown Publishers September 2005) Also see www.americanvalues.org, scroll down to "children of divorce" and be sure to click on "archives" in that section as well.

51. *Goodridge*, 798 N.E.2d at 10–11.

52. Marquardt asks whether children of same-sex couples could be all that different from children in every other alternative family form we have tried, in *Gay Marriage: A fine idea in principle, but what about the kids?* Chi. Trib., 7 December 2003, at 4. Also available on the www.americanvalues.org Web site.

53. Fineman's most mature theory of dependency can be found in her recent book, *The Autonomy Myth: A Theory of Dependency* (The New Press 2004).

54. Fineman, *Neutered Mother, supra* n. 14 at 143–144.

55. *Id.* at 229.

56. *Id.* at 164–166.

57. Richard Posner, *Sex and Reason* 298 (Harvard University Press 1992).

58. David Greenberg, *The Construction of Homosexuality* (The University of Chicago Press 1988).

59. Rauch, *supra* n. 15 at 129–130.

60. *Id.* at 88.

61. Richard Goldstein, *The Attack Queers: Liberal Society and the Gay Right* 35, 50–56 (Verso 2002); Richard Goldstein, *Fear of A Queer Planet* xiii (Michael Warner ed., University of Minnesota Press 1993); and Michael Warner, *The Trouble with*

Normal: Sex, Politics, and the Ethics of Queer Life 9, 22 (Harvard University Press 1999).

62. Warner, *The Trouble with Normal, supra* n. 61 at 88–89.

63. Browning et al., *Culture Wars, supra* n. 28 at 37–38.

64. *Id.* at 2.

65. *Id.* at 287–288.

66. For a fuller discussion of the practical proposals connected with critical familism, see *id.* at 307–334; *see also,* Don Browning and Gloria Rodriguez, *Reweaving the Social Tapestry: Toward a Public Philosophy and Policy of Families* (W.W. Norton 2002), especially Chaps. 6–8.

67. For a discussion about the need for an interfaith dialogue on the reconstruction of marriage, see Browning *supra* n. 28 *Marriage and Modernization,* at 223–244.

68. This paper was prepared for The Witherspoon Institute's conference, "Why Marriage is in the Public Interest," held on 16–19 December 2004, at Princeton University. It will be published as a chapter in the edited proceedings of that conference. We are grateful to republish it here with the permission of the Witherspoon Institute, 20 Nassau Street, Suite 242, Princeton, NJ 08542. All rights reserved.

Section 2

HUMAN DIGNITY

11

Human Dignity and Family Development: The Importance and Value of Older Persons for the Family and Future Generations

Astrid Stuckelberger (Switzerland)
PhD in Health Psychology and Gerontology
Lecturer and Researcher in the Master of Public Health Programme
Department of Social and Community Health of the Faculty of Medicine
University of Geneva, Switzerland
NGO representative to the United Nations in Geneva of the Society for the Psychological Studies of Social Issues and of the International Association of Gerontology

Human Development in a Context of Change

Human development has generally been approached and studied from either an individual or a societal perspective. In this context, the family is usually considered merely as the locus for the development and interaction of two generations (parent-children).

The fact that today's population architecture has dramatically changed over the past century in terms of sociodemographic composition requires that we examine the social coherence of this new situation. This chapter demonstrates this fundamental transformation by providing facts and figures about the new architecture of society and mutation of the extended family system, and will then synthesize and discuss different findings addressing intergenerational and transgenerational variables related to violence.

In order to understand the profound mutation our society has experienced and the consequences of this new architecture of society for all generations, a general overview of three major areas of this change will be described: (i) structural changes in world development, (ii) the revolution of population ageing, and (iii) the transformation of the family and of intergenerational relations.

This chapter addresses human development and ageing with dignity from a new and innovative perspective, by demonstrating the importance of ageing issues on society and the individual role and responsibility the older generation has in setting its mark for the next generations. This innovative approach is intended to make the case for considering the valuable role of older generations within the family in the contemplation of legal issues and government policies, and to offer a set of efficient and sustainable solutions to enable a long life development with dignity.

The State of our World

In 1999, the United Nations Population Fund launched their yearly report, "State of the World Population," on the theme "6 Billion: A Time for Choices," announcing an estimate of 6 billion people alive in the world and highlighting the critical decisions facing the international community as we enter the twenty-first century: "This slow demographic change calls for policy choices." This report underlines key figures intended to stand as the background evidence during the consideration of any societal or policy issues (Table 11.1).

The world no longer looks as it did to our ancestors. Not only are our statistics more and more accurate in viewing the "state of the world," but we can today easily grasp a global picture of the world population and its key trends. The youth living today live in a different world, a global world, and this reality can be the cause or the consequence of some of the behaviors we observe in them. Furthermore, when one reflects on the genealogy of youth and their complex family histories, many have relations in different parts of the world. One generation can be living in the United States, another in Europe, while the older generation lives and remains in its homeland in South America, Africa, or Asia. Many have among their ancestors and family history— whether it is conscious or not—tales of wars and violence. Thus it is important to grasp this "picture" of the major changes in the modern world. More people are living on the same territory, with fewer children, migrating to cities or different countries and living longer. When looking more closely at the data provided by reliable international sources (UNFPA 1999; UN Population Division 2000; U.S. Census Bureau 2001) and captured in the short fact sheet (Table 11.1), the following facts can be underlined:

- The world's population has quadrupled in the past 100 years and has doubled in 40 years from 3 billion in 1960 to 6 billion in 1999; one billion was added in only the past 12 years.

- The worldwide tendency is towards *fewer children per couple, but more generations.* Women have fewer children than ever before as access to family planning gives women more choices, improving and allowing more control over the number and the spacing of childbirths. Although the population is still increasing by about 78 million people per year, the actual rate of growth has slowed down from 2.4 to 1.3 percent in 30 years. The generally sustained decrease in total fertility rates in industrialized nations since at least 1900 has resulted in current levels often well below the population replacement rate of 2.1 live births per woman in most such nations. Looking at the youth/old

Table 11.1   Architecture of the World Population

In general

- Number of inhabitants...6 billion = 1st time ever; in 1960s = 3 billion; in 2000 = 6.1 billion; in 2050 = 9.3 billion.

- Annual rate growth: 1.3% per year or 77 million people/year. Six developing countries account for half of this annual growth: India (21%), China (12%), Pakistan (5%), Nigeria (4%), Bangladesh (4%), and Indonesia (3%).

- Youth (15–24): We see today the largest-ever generation of young people at 1.05 billion.

- Elderly (60+): We see today the largest-ever generation of older persons, estimated at 420 million at midyear 2000. 795,000 are added each month.

Growing number of generations

- The number of the elderly will triple from 606 million now to 2 billion in 2050, the number of nonagenarians and centenarians is increasing worldwide, the proportion of older generations is increasing. Also, those age groups are proportionally the fastest growing segment of the population.

- 4 to 5 generations living simultaneously, of which 2 to 3 can be considered in the "older persons generation" or at retirement age; each generation living with certain age-specific cohort and historical characteristics, giving rise to new situations such as

  – "digital homeless generations"—i.e., older generations who will never be technologically connected.

  – "generations of war"—i.e., young generations who have known only a life of war, and

  – "generational wipe out"—i.e., one to two successive generations the majority of whom have died due to wars or epidemics such as HIV/AIDS.

- Continuing urbanization and international migration creates policy challenges. Half of all people live in cities, compared to a third in 1960. Worldwide, cities are growing by 60 million persons per year. Today, there are 17 megacities— with 10 million people or more. The distribution by generations is unbalanced between urban and rural areas, as younger generations tend to migrate to cities to seek better job opportunities.

  → Today, the number of children under the age of 15 is less than the number of elderly.

  → By 2050, the number of young people will be half of the number of elderly people.

  → This millennium will host four to five generations living simultaneously, each with its own cultural history and pace of development.

Some key generational elements, by regional development category:

More developed regions

• Population: 1.2 billion in 2000.

• Little change over the next 50 years.

• Low fertility levels.

• Population decline: By mid-century, it is projected that 39 countries will have a smaller population than today: Japan and Germany (each 14% smaller), Italy and Hungary (each 25% smaller), and the Russian Federation, Georgia, and Ukraine (each between 28% and 40% smaller).

• Living arrangements: There is a tendency toward one-generation households, i.e., living alone.

Less-developed regions:

• Population: To increase from 4.9 billion in 2000 to 8.2 billion in 2050.

• Decline in fertility: In the absence of such declines, the population of less-developed regions would reach 11.9 billion; fertility is projected to decline markedly in the future.

• Rapid population growth is still expected among 48 countries classified as least developed; the population is expected to nearly triple from 2000 to 2050, growing from 658 million to 1.8 billion.

• Rapid urbanization: By 2015, projections state there will be 26 megacities of 10 million and more, 22 of them in less-developed regions, 18 in Asia alone.

• Living arrangements: The tendency is for older generations to live with adult children.

Source: UNFPA (1999); UN Population Division (2000); Kinsella and Velkoff, U.S. Census Bureau (2001).

generation ratio, there are more young people and older people alive than ever before: Even with the existing large numbers of young people, the elderly population (sixty and older) has already exceeded the younger generation population (below age fifteen), and at current rates by 2050 there will be two elderly persons for every child.

• Population growth has slowed down, stopped, or reversed in Europe, North America, and Japan. Today, the population growth of those countries increases only as the result of immigration and the naturalization of migrant families. International migration and continual urbanization creates policy challenges. Half of the world population today lives in cities, compared to a third in 1960. Worldwide, cities are growing by 60 million people each year, and by 2030, it is predicted that over 60 percent of people, i.e., 5 billion, will live in urban areas or megacities. Thus, in all regions, increases in the number of migrants are pushing issues of international migration closer to the top of policy agendas. Between 1965 and 1990, migration expanded from 75 million to 120 million. Migrant workers send more than $70 billion home (out of the host country) each year in remittances. More and more migrants are women. The consequences of population mobility on the development of younger generations and on the links between generations and family architecture are underestimated. They modify the transmission of culture and knowledge, the transfer of financial assets, and the systemic patterns and roles of each member of the family, as is demonstrated later in this chapter.

Why are world facts and figures relevant in addressing local or national issues? The point is that with migration, mixed marriages, and intercultural lineages, local issues are affected directly or indirectly by today's global issues, and if proposed solutions do not take the global picture into account, local solutions might have only a short-term and inadequate effect. Violence and peace are issues that concern all sectors of all societies; addressing only one while ignoring other core elements might well be like pouring water into a bucket full of holes.

In this context the theory defended in this chapter is that older generations play a crucial role in youth development, a transgenerational effect, through the perpetuation of memories and the many forms of violence or nonviolence passed to descendants, or through their causative or preventive roles as grandparent or great-grandparent. A closer look at the older persons of today is necessary in order to avoid the "ageist attitudes" too often carried about in our society. The myths surrounding the "negative image of ageing" can be overcome with scientific findings.

*One of the most important challenges the world faces in the 21st Century is respond-
ing to the economic, financial and social implications of the changing demographics
in our ageing societies.*
                                                    —Denver Summit of the 8 (G8) in 1997

The silent revolution of population and individual ageing

At the population level   Global population ageing is emerging as a phe-
nomenon never before witnessed in human history. The spectacular increase in human life expectancy associated with lowered fertility and improved health is generating growing numbers and higher proportions of an older population and extending the duration of life to exceptional ages. This mutation has been called the "Silent Revolution" or the "Age Quake," reflecting the lack of attention given it in the media and society. The effect of technology on globalization has produced the idea of a society centered more on the values of what is "new," "young," and "fast," while the far-reaching effects of the "silent revolution" are virtually ignored, despite the fact that they are already felt by every individual, family, neighborhood, and nation throughout the world.

To further draw the new architecture of the world, what portrait of the "Ageing World" can one make today?

Recent data from the Population Division, Department of Economic and Social Affairs of the United Nations (2000) and from the U.S. Census Bureau (Kinsella and Velkoff 2001), show the following situation:

- *Longevity has dramatically increased.* Global life expectancy has increased by twenty years since 1950, to sixty-six years in 1999. Life expectancy at birth exceeds seventy-eight years in twenty-eight countries. The United States will age rapidly when the Baby Boomers (people born between 1946 and 1964) begin to reach age sixty-five after the year 2010, and in the year 2050 the population aged sixty-five and over is projected to be slightly above 20 percent (compared with about 13 percent today). By contrast, in some African countries (e.g., Malawi, Swaziland, Zambia, and Zimbabwe) where the HIV/AIDS epidemic is particularly devastating, the average life expectancy at birth may be twenty-five years lower than it otherwise would have been in the absence of HIV/AIDS. Nevertheless, the proportion of older persons is still growing as the "survivors" still have a relatively high life expectancy of sixty-five years in those regions. Thus, low life expectancy at birth does not mean that the possibility of living to higher ages has eroded.

- *The numbers and proportions of older persons, potential (great-)grandparents, has increased.* Since 1950, the proportion of the worlds' population over sixty years old has changed from one in thirteen to one in ten. By the year 2050, one in five will be sixty years or older. Europe remains the "oldest region" in the world followed closely by North America. Countrywise, Italy has the highest proportion of elderly people with 18.1 percent aged sixty-five or over. By 2020, the Japanese population will be the oldest in the world, with 31 percent over sixty years of age, followed by Italy, Greece, and Switzerland. The global population aged sixty-five and over was estimated to be 420 million as of midyear 2000, an increase of 9.5 million since midyear 1999. The net balance of the world's elderly population grew by more than 795,000 people each month during that year. Projections for the year 2010 suggest that the net monthly gain will be on the order of 847,000 people. China has the largest elderly population, numbering nearly 88 million in 2000 (Kinsella and Velkoff 2001).

- *Some developing countries are ageing at a faster pace than developed countries* (Figure 11.1). By 2020, five of the ten countries with the largest populations of older persons will be in the developing world: China, India, Indonesia, Brazil and Pakistan. Although industrialized nations have higher percentages of elderly people than do most developing countries, 59 percent of the world's elderly now live in the developing countries of Africa, Asia, Latin America, the Caribbean, and Oceania. By 2020 also, the population of older persons from developing countries will rise by nearly 240 percent from the 1980 level. For example, it took only twenty-three years for the population of people sixty-five or over in countries such as Chile or Sri Lanka to rise from 7 percent to 14 percent, while it took 115 years (five times more years) for the same degree of growth to occur in France. *Striking differences exist between regions.* For example, one in five Europeans is sixty years old or older, as compared to one in twenty Africans. The older population may still be found in rural

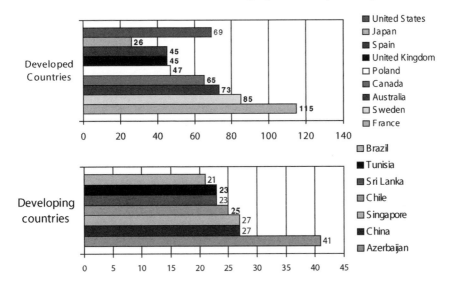

Figure 11.1 Speed of Population Aging (in years). Number of years required or expected for percentage of population aged 65+ to rise from 7 percent to 14 percent.

Source: Kinsella and Velkoff, 2001

areas, but it too is becoming increasingly urban. This point is important, as it will affect the generational structure of migrant families.

- *The older population itself is ageing.* The oldest old are the fastest-growing component of many national populations. The world's growth rate for the eighty or over population from 1999 to 2000 was 3.5 percent, while that of the world's elderly (sixty-five or over) population as a whole was 2.3 percent compared with 1.3 percent for the total population (all ages included). Currently, persons eighty years and older constitute 11 percent of the population aged sixty and above. In contrast, by 2050, 27 percent of the older population will be over eighty years old. Past population projections often have underestimated the improvement in mortality rates among the oldest old and the actual numbers of tomorrow's oldest old could be much higher than presently anticipated.

- *The majority of older persons are women (55 percent).* Among those who are eighty years or older, 65 percent are women. They make up the majority of the oldest old and the elderly widowed, and are most frequently the caregivers of the older persons in all parts of the world. Although there are more elderly women than elderly men in the vast majority of the world's countries, there are exceptions such as India, Iran, and Bangladesh. Today's generation of older women is less likely to be literate, but younger generations of women are increasing their level of education. In China in 1990, for example, only 11 percent of women aged sixty and over could read and write, compared with half of men aged sixty and over. Gender differentials in ageing have been demonstrated and reviewed in numerous studies (Stuckelberger 1996, 1997, 1998).

At the individual level   The "longer life phenomenon" is the consequence of major improvements in the ageing process of the individual. People all around the world are getting older, are in better health, and remain active longer, thus playing a longer-lasting role in the family and contributing longer to the social system (Höpflinger and Stuckelberger 1999).

The scientific findings of this past decade have revolutionized the negative model of the "irreversible decline with age." Although many stereotypes and stigmatizations of age remain, many of the prejudices and remaining myths and fictions related to ageing are being challenged today by new studies. Table 11.2 describes several scientific facts that run counter to some of the classical myths and fictions now prevalent in society. It is crucial to be aware that we have today enough scientific evidence to combat these negative stereotypes of ageing. The stereotyping and generalization of the geriatric decline model too often mislead the population to believe only the worst about ageing and to overlook the added value of life and the spiritual growth associated with ageing.

The invisible part of me is not old. In aging we gain as well as lose—our spiritual forces expand. A life of the heart and mind takes over as our physical force ebbs away.
—A 90-year-old woman

Ageing is frequently stigmatized. Discrimination against the elderly is called "ageism" and is defined as the "process of systematic stereotyping and discrimination against people because they are old, just as racism and sexism. Older people are categorized as senile, rigid in thought and manner, and old-fashioned in morality and skills" (Butler, *Encyclopedia of Ageing,* 1995). Table 11.2 shows the stereotypes often found in society, stereotypes that are today proven to be fiction by science. The majority of older persons live physically and mentally healthy lives, can maintain and improve their life condition, and live independently. The last year of life, whatever the age, is the most dependant and most costly. Other important stereotype traps that should be mentioned briefly include the following:

In statistics and data
- presenting statistics in a negative way
- hiding the real issue or generalizing physical decline to include mind/spirit decline, denying the value of experience (e.g., infantilizing the elderly)
- emphasizing or exaggerating negative findings
- focusing on the problems rather than successes

In social and interpersonal interactions
- infantilization of older persons, as in talking to them like infants

Table 11.2   Myths and Facts about Ageing

Myth / Stereotype	Evidence-based facts
"To be old is to be sick, dependant and senile"	The majority of older persons age in good mental and physical health. Statistics show that the majority of retirees, even at 80 years old, are independent and live at home. In the developed world, the younger generations of retirees have benefited from the improvement of public health and social security measures; they have better health, higher education, and sound economic situations, pursuing social activities and contacts.
"At old age, it is too late to do anything"	The newest findings show that good health can be maintained and that the process of physical and mental decline can be reversed through active measures. Interventions at higher ages can improve physical and mental health. Several studies among persons aged 75 years and above have shown that physical activity can strengthen the muscles and increase the bone mass and that mental activity can prevent mental degenerative diseases.
"The secret of ageing well is in the genes"	Our ageing process can be modulated at each stage of our lives. Twin studies with adopted and nonadopted subjects have shown that the influence of genes diminishes with age and that other factors such as life experience and culture have a stronger effect.
"The elderly can't learn anything"	At all ages, one can learn, develop, and expand knowledge and skills. Concepts such as continuous education or life-long learning are now well established. For example, Universities of 3rd Age and Seniorweb networks have flourished around the world.
"Older persons can't direct their lives, are not productive and are a burden to society"	Today, generations of retirees are healthy, active, and creative; most of them can and want to participate in society, and they have a role and responsibility in the way they use their full civil citizenship, as well as in the way they transfer their assets and memories. For example, the American Association of Retired People counts today more than 30 million members and stands as one of the strongest political lobbies in the United States.
"No cash return" when investing in the elderly	Older persons do contribute to the economy of the nation and the family through informal work and volunteering, through financial transfers to younger generations, and also as consumers. They diminish the social costs of conflict and violence in younger generations by being role models, maintaining cohesion in the family, prioritizing human values, restoring healing memories and history, and transmitting a sense of security in life.

Adapted from Rowe and Kahn, 1998

- spreading the stereotype of the difficult and rigid older person
- projecting stereotypes of a negative imprint on the family model
- considering a person only in terms of economic value and portraying beliefs that if a person does not produce or there is no cash return on investment, he or she has no social value (e.g., why invest in health if death is the end result?)
- fear of death and illness leading to denial of the value of existence, an attitude carried over to younger but also older generations.

We need to combat these myths and ageist attitudes to ensure integration, social cohesion, and a healthy human and family development. Adjusting our images of ageing with the newest realities disclosed by scientific evidence can contribute to the image we have of our own ageing, but also to the comprehension of the untapped potential of an active ageing population to participate in societal issues. Breaking "ageist" attitudes removes barriers between generations and gives a better understanding of the possible and important interactions with youth. Living longer has allowed more members of the family to be alive at the same time. We are now witnessing a multigenerational society that brings very new dynamics for younger generations, with more "older generations" than ever before in history.

Family and Genealogy in Mutation: A Multigeneration Society

The Worldwide Reality of a Four to Five Generation Society
Considering the state of the world and the spectacular increases in longevity, two key features of the new architecture of society should be emphasized:

- the extension of the intergenerational lineage and living descendants
- the restriction of intragenerational links as the fertility decline results in fewer siblings and children.

In other words, the structure, the backbone, of our society has expanded from "2 or 3 generations" during this last century to "4 to 5 generations" living at the same time, while the number of children and potential brothers and sisters has decreased, which affects family dynamics and all dimensions of life.

The potential for the existence of up to five generations living at the same time is very much a modern reality. At the population level, evidence shows that four generation families are becoming increasingly common (e.g., Lehr 1998; Soldo 1996) and the ageing of the baby boomers may produce a "great-grandparent boom" in many countries. This is true in both developed and developing countries. Population statistics show that the average growth rates of higher age groups are increasing in all regions of the world (Figure 11.2). The developing world is actually more likely to see a four or five generation structure because the average age of the mother at the birth of a first child is lower. This fact has implications when dealing with the youth of migrant families. The architecture of their families can include live grandparents and great-grandparents with specific roles. Figure 11.2 clearly shows that, even in the least developed regions, the most striking growth rate is among the age groups of eighty and over and sixty through seventy-nine— the parents, grandparents and great-grandparents of today. No longer can an increasing population of older persons be narrowly defined as a single group. The age of grandparents can now range from 35 to 123 years old, and their grandchildren from newborns to retirees. Consequently, intergenerational legal issues will become increasingly important and new legislation will be needed to address and solve conflicts between generations.

The number of centenarians is increasing worldwide (graphic 1). In 1999, 145,000 centenarians were estimated to be alive, and 2.2 million are expected in 2050, a 15-fold increase. According to researchers in Europe, the number of centenarians has doubled each decade since 1950 in industrialized countries, and developing countries seem to follow the same trend where data are available. Using reliable statistics from ten Western European countries and Japan, Vaupel and Jeune (1995) estimated that some 8,800 centenarians lived in these countries as of 1990, and that the number of centenarians was growing at an average annual rate of approximately 7 percent between the early 1950s and the late 1980s. They also estimated that, over the course of human history,

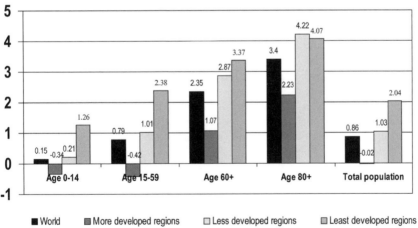

Figure 11.2   Average Annual Growth Rates

Source: UN Population Division, World Population Prospects: The 2000 Revision

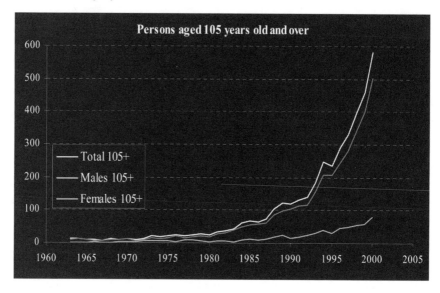

Graphic 1   Persons aged 105 years old and over.

the odds of living from birth to age 100 may have risen from one in 20 million to one in 50 for females in low-mortality nations such as Japan and Sweden. A contemporaneous study, the latest 1999 census in Vietnam, counted nearly 4,000 centenarians, which highlights the tendency for them to be a visible and significant group even in developing countries (Central Census Steering Committee 1999).

Thus we find more and more frequently *two generations at retirement age,* and the duration of "life as a retiree" is increasing in all regions of the world (Table 11.3). As an illustration, the official world record for longevity is held by a French woman, Mrs. Jeanne Calment who lived to the age of 123 in relatively good health and is known to have been bicycling at 117. Her life example requires us to contemplate the potential of six living generations with three generations at retirement age (Allard et al. 1994).

The described changes in the trends of the world population arising from the ageing of the population and the resulting four to five generation society can only convince us of the emergence of a new architecture of the world with important implications for social and family systems. But, in addition to the facts relating to structure, we can expect other important mutations in the dynamics of this multigenerational society. For example, living longer brings a higher risk of experiencing major changes or cyclical events over the course of one's life, events that can potentially affect child development in the rising generation, such as multiple employment or career changes, multiple marriages, childbearing in multiple marriages, and the magnifying effects of divorce on all of these areas.

Table 11.3   Effective Retirement Age and Duration of Retirement

Region	Effective retirement age		Expected duration of retirement	
	1950	1990	1950	1990
Japan	66.2	65.5	12.0	17.8
North America	65.9	62.6	13.1	18.1
Oceania	65.3	60.0	13.2	20.5
Northern Europe	67.2	61.9	12.2	18.7
Southern Europe	69.0	60.1	10.5	19.9
Western Europe	65.7	59.3	12.8	20.7
Central/Eastern Europe	65.0	59.2	12.8	18.6
Average W/o Central and Eastern Europe	66.5	61.8	12.4	19.0
All countries	66.0	61.0	12.5	18.9

Source: Gillion, Turner, Bailey, and Latulippe (2000). Social Security Pensions, Development and reform. International Labour Office, Geneva.

Towards Increased Complexity of Family Patterns

It is only through understanding how generations interact and evolve together that one can grasp the elements necessary to any sustainable family policy or approach in society. The difficulty is to move from a static picture, the photographic cliché of society—as presented in the first part (statistics, census, etc.)—to a more lively view, a motion picture showing us the unfolding of society (cohort and longitudinal studies, qualitative approaches). The picture enriched by a motion picture gives us a more accurate understanding of society and its dynamics. With this logic in mind, evidence-based family policy would by definition acknowledge the need for dynamic policies.

An important component of this new family architecture, shown in Table 11.4, is the transition of the traditional family structure towards heterogeneous forms of genealogies and "generation arrangements," but another is the shift from a homogeneous structure of generations within society to an increasing heterogeneity of generations.

Many factors influence this transition and give an idea of the many possible extended family systems a child can be living in today:

- *Older persons are more likely to be married or remarried than in the past and to have children at late ages.* Not only do individuals live longer, but they have more freedom than ever to be parents at any age for men and at higher ages for women. The record age for a woman giving birth is now more than sixty-seven years old (first in Italy, since repeated elsewhere), and becoming a father has reached record ages as high as 104 (in Iran). Over the last two or three decades, the marital status of the elderly has changed; there is now an increased proportion of married older men and women, and a decreased proportion of widowers. Some of the change is attributable to improved joint survival of husbands and wives (Myers 1992), but much is due to different marital experiences among birth cohorts resulting from, for example, war or disease epidemics. In most countries few elderly have never married.

- *Increase in divorce and remarriage rates at all ages.* Although current rates of divorced elderly people tend to be low, future cohorts of the elderly will have higher proportions of the divorced and/or separated. With the increase in divorce and remarriage worldwide, it becomes increasingly common to find parents who during their life course become grandparents and then parents again, breaking with the stereotype of the traditional life course of a single generation's event. Because of extended longevity, there is also a stronger potential to repeat the family cycle of "marriage-childbirth-divorce," the timing being virtually limitless for men, and this mix of timing confuses the classic genealogies. A child nowadays may experience extremely complex situations with many half brothers and sisters ranging from his age to the age of one of his parents, may have a higher number of grandparents and great-grandparents (including the "grandparents in law"), or may have a parent the age of his school friends' great-aunt or grandparents.

- *Importance of grandparents.* The importance of grandparents is not trivial and is gaining in importance. In some countries both women and men provide care for their grandchildren—from babysitting to being a custodial grandparent and primary caregiver. Survey data for the United States from the mid-1990s indicate that 9 percent of all Americans with grandchildren under age five were providing extensive care giving (minimum 30 hours/week or 90 nights/year) (Fuller-Thomson and Minkler 2001). In 1995 in the United States, 29 percent of preschool children whose parent(s) worked or were in school were cared for by a grandparent (typically the grandmother) (Smith, K. 2000). Many grandparents find themselves the sole providers of care for their grandchildren, one reason being the migration of the middle generation to urban areas to work. These "skip-generation" families are found in all regions of the world and are becoming increasingly prevalent. Another reason for the increase in the number of children living in households headed only by grandparents can be attributed to trends in several factors (e.g., divorce, HIV/AIDS, drug abuse, and child abuse). In 1997 in the United States, 3.9 million children, 5.5 percent of all children under age eighteen, lived in a household maintained by their grandparents (Casper and Bryson 1998).

- *Effect of epidemics on generations.* Today in some regions, *an entire generation may be wiped out* by crises such as epidemic and war. Children orphaned by

HIV/AIDS is a matter of great concern. Not only do the children depend on older relatives for their care, but when separated and not "brought back" to their elders or relatives, they are at an increased risk of becoming street children or entering the social assistance system and heading toward the "poorest of the poor life course." Other striking figures include the higher suicide rates among older age groups than in any younger age group (WHO 1999). This in itself could be considered a mental health disorder epidemic that might affect future generations solely due to the "role model" it provides.

- *Urbanization and migration as a "generation splitting factor."* As mentioned earlier, the tendency toward urbanization is increasing worldwide. This leads to the separation of young people from their grandparents, who previously played a role in their traditional education and socialization. It also causes new financial flows between developed and developing countries if people retire to a different country, or if working migrants return to their home country after retirement.

Finally, it appears clear today *that traditional extended families are gradually disappearing.* Recent data confirm this tendency worldwide. For example, in the Middle East, as is the case in Egypt specifically, 85 percent of all households are now nuclear families (UNFPA 2001).

The most striking mutation observed today is that *the complexity of family ties and lineages is increasing dramatically* in all corners of the world, not only with the steady decline of fertility, but with the changing patterns of women's lives in societies that allow more choices, more mobility, and higher rates of divorce at all ages. New situations arise from these changes in human society. For example, most of today's retirees did not get to know their grandparents, and they have many more brothers and sisters than the following generations. In contrast, most children today get to know their four grandparents and even their great-grandparents, and they have fewer siblings from the same father than any generation that ever lived. Many families today include halfbrothers and half-sisters living in different places, which further complicates the picture (see, e.g., the case of France, Toulemon 2001).

The mutation of traditional family patterns and the links between generations is clearly provoking a reform in classical genealogy (Table 11.4), but also in the way society and policy will have to deal with these changes without attempting to take the place of the family. It is no longer possible to build a genealogical tree without being confronted with complex situations, and the social or legal framework for solving those situations is often not yet in place. For example, the court of justice in Geneva (Switzerland) recently has reported an alarming tendency among divorced parents to resign as legal parents and request that they be released from the responsibility of having custody of their children. The motive is that their children have become "uncontrollable" and are no longer obeying the family or social rules. They address the court seeking for the state to take charge of the children, because "we no longer know what to do with them" (Tribune de Genève, March 2002).

Table 11.4   Mutation of the Genealogy and Family Pattern: from Old to New
Genealogies

Traditional architecture	Current architectural tendency
Strong mortality at all the ages	Increase of life expectancy and decrease of fertility
2 to 3 generations	4 to 5 generations
0 to 1 generation at retirement age	2 to 3 generations retirement age
Predominance of	
Intragenerational links	Intergenerational lineage increases
Many siblings	Few brothers/sisters
Numerous descent	Weak descent at each generation
Traditional family	Nuclear family or single parent
Generations living together or near	Generations living apart or abroad
Homogeneous family	Heterogeneous family—"Recomposition" of the family
One life cycle with unique events	Repetition of life cycles (divorce/ marriage, jobs, etc.)
Transmission of values	
Traditional education and socialization	Peers + new informal education (ICT,* mass media)
Shared economic management	Independent economy between generations
Genealogy-dependent survival	State-dependant survival
Women at home—Man-centered career	Men and women work outside the home
Hierarchy of age—the Elder	Multiple hierarchy (economic, technological, etc.)
Unidirectional life course	Complexities of life course pattern
Unidirectional genealogies	Multiplication of genealogies
Metamorphosis of solidarity—multiple generation society	

New programs to empower parents to apply their rights as parents will
be put in place. This is but one emerging "symptom" of a new society where
the state will have to very carefully consider its role *vis-à-vis* preserving
the responsibility of its citizens toward both their progenitors and their
descendants.

As one acknowledges the growing "complexities of traditional genealogies," the challenge ahead may be seen as lying more in the regulation and

adjustment of the dynamics between generations than in solving the challenges of old age alone. The socioeconomic interdependency of generations in building a sustainable society calls for a systematic approach with more generation-integrated or generation adjustment components. The nonadjustment of generations bears a definite risk—that of possible future conflict and clashes between generations and societal breakdown.

Interdependency of Generations

A fundamental issue when discussing the processes of generations and the family is to first clarify the concept of generation and its definitions and then to highlight research areas where psychosocial research and theories contribute to our subject, either on the intergenerational aspect or the individual development aspect.

Generation Concept: between Society and the Family

The concept of generation is similar to the methodological concept of cohort. Its significance, in essence, is that humans born and raised at different points in time experience different life events, which can have differential long-term consequences on them (Figure 11.4). Major worldwide events occurring at a specific point and place in history have profound impacts on that particular segment of the population or on that specific generation. For example, when large numbers of males are killed at relatively young ages by various wars or conflicts, the survivors become a distinct and specific group. The same must be kept in mind when considering the evolution and ageing process of a given population affected by disasters and conflicts and touching several generations at different stages of their development. Some generations of youth have known only war (e.g., the youth of Afghanistan have experienced twenty-three years of war), and other generations have survived an abrupt trauma that marks their life development (e.g., the holocaust or the Rwandan or Cambodian genocides). This aspect is fundamental when considering sustainable social and policy development for a population.

The definition of generations usually takes into account two main levels of definition:

a. *Micro level*—generation within the family context (time framework: genetic identity)
b. *Macro level*—generation within the larger context of society (time framework: sociopolitical identity)

The Micro level—The biological-family lineage generations. Based on genetic identity, a generation is defined by sequences of organisms deriving from a common ancestor, each sequence creates a generation. This is the classical concept underlying the construction of the genealogical tree.

Potential conflicts arising in the context of lineage can take many forms depending on which and how many generations are involved and the nature of the specific issue, such as interpersonal economic conflicts, family issues such as grandparent custody in the case of divorce, and transgenerational violence.

The Macro level—The sociopolitical generation. A generation is defined at the macro level in the social and cultural context as people living at a common period of time in the history of humankind and therefore sharing a degree of common historical reference points derived through personal experience. In other words, a generation in this context is defined by its sociocultural mark. This definition can be considered as belonging to a cultural-anthropological approach. Each generation comprises a composite of different individuals in society bound to common and specific social, cultural, economic, or political experiences. (Methodologically, this division of time is similar to a cohort or a period, as noted above.) The time framework of a macro generation depends on the time influence of specific events or experiences.

When considering time dynamics, the importance of lineage in generations must be underscored. It lies in the fact that there exists a mechanism of transmission of thoughts, ideas, attitudes, and values within society, which may account for variation within the larger society (Back 1995). This transmission is not so much linked to genetic factors as to psychosocial factors influencing over time the life course of both the individual and the group. Studies on generations have demonstrated that transmission of values occurs within a family (i.e., Bengston et al. 1985). Furthermore, from the psychoanalytical point of view, psychological distresses and unsolved conflicts are frequently perpetuated from one generation to another (Kaës et al. 1993). Thus, one can postulate that peace and conflict do transmit from generation to generation—at the conscious and subconscious levels—and that the role of elders is a key to perpetuating a memory and attitudes conducive of peace versus war, conflict versus reconciliation, hatred versus forgiveness, etc.

Theories on the transmission of models of behavior and values between generations have not yet been given much attention. Some researchers and anthropologists have studied this link in very different contexts. Put side-by-side in a synthetic analysis, those findings give us serious reason to say that the older generation has an impact on the younger generation. The idea here is to provide some basic reflections from scientific findings and psychosocial theories on how generations at the micro and macro levels live and interact with each other in a peaceful or conflicted way and how this affects younger and future generations.

In her famous book, *Culture and Commitment: A Study of the Generation Gap* (1970, 1971), Margaret Mead describes the evolution of links between generations in a tridimensional perspective of the past, present, and future models of interaction between or among children, parents, and grandparents. Her approach gives an interesting framework for understanding the possible developments of conflict or harmony between generations:

- *The Post-figurative Model* (traditional context): This is the traditional model where children are educated by their parents and are in contact with their grandparents, both of whom play role models for different stages of life. This model predominates in cultures with little mobility and the sense of timeless continuity and identity. Authority stems from the traditions of the past and from ancestors.

- *The Co-figurative Model* (war, migration context): This model emerges with a disruptive event—war, revolution, migration, new technologies—where children live a completely different experience from that of their parents, grandparents, and other older members of their community. In this context, the younger generations can no longer learn from their grandparents, from whom they are often separated, and must create new closer models. In this model, children do not live near or see their grandparents and great-grandparents regularly, or they see them rarely. Their parents do then maintain a dominant role. Parents look for models among their peers, while their children look for new models of grandparents they find in their surroundings.

- *The Pre-figurative Model* (today's generation gap context): Younger generations take on new authority in the unfolding of their own futures, and parents often learn from their children. Grandparents no longer play the role of transmitters of traditions. There are no or few possible links or communication between generations as parents belong to a "past" world and children to a radically "new world" that is unknown to their elders. The new generation finds its models through the mass media and modern technology. Margaret Mead emphasizes: "We know that we are facing a youth that will never experience what we have experienced and that we will never experience what they have experienced." Grandparents and even parents do not play an important role in transmitting knowledge as the speed of change and the advancement of technology do not allow sufficient time to incorporate and learn the new in order to be able to face the modified conditions of the environment. In this situation, a generation gap is clearly at hand. The "technology versus tradition" clash of generations is a risk.

Gérard Mendel also studies the relations between adolescents and older generations in a psychoanalytical approach. This author links the crisis between generations to an Oedipal-type crisis against the father figure due to the dominance of technology. The refusal of the inheritance and rejection of the father figure creates a divide, rather than a conflict, between generations and empowers youth as a political force in society (Mendel 1963). More recently, Mendel has emphasized the crisis of authority in society, especially of sacred authority. This author stresses in particular that father figures can no longer help solve the archaic anxieties brought by society and globalization (Mendel 2002). In a culture that encourages individualism, the problem is how to maintain social cohesion and a sense of social responsibility among the people. He suggests new ways to palliate the negative effects of modernization and the advancement of technology in society by humanizing and completing the psychofamilial pattern as well as by developing a new psychofamilial personality, not so much based on kinship as on social bonds, and emphasizing taking charge of one's own life with one's own values.

The sociopsychoanalytical view of Gérard Mendel, as well as the anthropologist's view of Margaret Mead, certainly bring very interesting perspectives to the development of generations, particularly with reference to the mutation from the traditional family structure to the emerging architecture of the family, and consequently to the structuring of generations. It seems quite evident that the individual can no longer be separated from the generation or from the global context in which we now live. Nowadays, assessing the world's mix of Margaret Mead's post-, co-, and pre-figurative models of generations is no doubt crucial to the decisions that will be taken for the betterment of the world and of future generations. For example, it would be worth studying whether violence and the lack of identity of youth is linked to their loss of identity with society and in particular with the older generations. In other words, the loss of one's place in the genealogy might weaken the stability or the existence of a reference system. Violent behaviors might well express the search for a role in the family and reference points in society. Several burning issues stemming from the rapid pace of modernization of our societies have already served to provoke the questioning of a common reference system between generations, which if not solved could degenerate and become a matter of major consequence and concern.

Family and Society at Risk: from Generation Gap to Generation Clash

As just described, the dynamics between generations and the mutation of the family affects how members in society live and associate, and how they develop a culture of conflict—either towards potential violence or towards conflict management and peaceful resolution. We propose to examine two examples of striking societal change and their consequences, which have been mentioned by some authors as a source of potential intergenerational conflict: (1) economy-based conflicts, and (2) technology-based conflicts.

Generation Clash through Materialism: Socioeconomic Disruption or Cohesion

According to former German Minister of Health and Professor of Gerontology, Ursula Lehr, conflicts between generations are generated not as much by demographic change as by economic constraints (1998). Today we see a variety of contrasting yet cohesive economic systems throughout the world. The increasing multigenerational social structure requires important adjustments in these social and economic systems to ensure the equal distribution of social welfare between generations. For example, the lower the age at which retirement pension benefits can be received, the longer the duration of the retirement period for which society must provide a retirement income (Table 11.3). In countries where there are limited retirement benefits or no pension system at all, the retiree will have to find other financial resources to live and survive (through his/her descendants, continuing employment, or other means). Given that the duration of retirement is increasing worldwide, the social welfare systems have started to question their own long-term viability and are pressuring the population to increase the age of retirement and/or reduce pension benefits.

In countries with strong social welfare systems, the governments are tending to slowly replace the "traditional family-based intergenerational economic system" with more individual-based financing. In this relatively new approach, the welfare state increasingly takes a key role in the management of the micro-family economy (i.e., social security, health and disability insurance, homelessness, unemployment, divorce regulation, etc.). Consequently, new forms of collective solidarity are developing (ensured by the state), and other forms of family-based solidarity are disappearing, and there is little encouragement to retain them. Ties between generations based on an "obligatory economic interdependence" are weakening, and younger generations feel less of an urge toward reciprocity than did former generations. While inheritance is still the main and universally recognized form of legalized economic transfer, today we see rising numbers of legal conflicts between or among generations, underscoring the inadequate legal framework for dealing with multigenerational conflicts.

The form of economic exchange is also changing. As life expectancy has risen, inheriting has become an event that occurs at increasingly higher ages. In developed countries, especially where social security guarantees a minimal wage to retirees, mutual exchange can take the form of kin-free and more national or global solidarity. According to German research on transfers among living kin (Kohli 1998), inheritance frequently happens at a time of life when the recipient is no longer in real need of it (i.e., to establish a household or start a family). Kohli also stresses that money transfers are part of an ongoing process of family relationships with their different dimensions of solidarity, but also with all their complications and conflicts. Nevertheless, economic transfers (inheritances) sometimes occur before death. Kohli describes the family as a component of the "new welfare mix" assuming, in the best cases, an important and complementary role the state cannot play on its own. Finally, transfers remain predominantly within the family and flow from the older to the younger members of the family, which is also the case in lower income families. The amounts passed to younger generations tend to be directly proportional to the amounts retirees receive in pensions. Poverty reduction programs would highly benefit from taking into account this dynamic dimension between generations and supporting the long term flow and preservation of financial assets and transfers among members of a family.

On the other hand, in the context of an intergenerational perspective, increased life expectancy requires that we view development not just from

Economic Inter-dependency in a 4 to 5 Generation Society

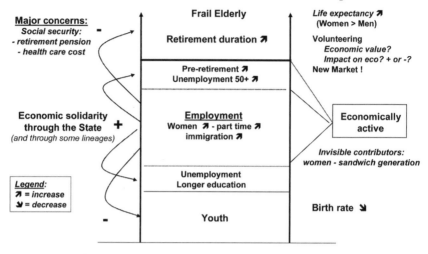

Figure 11.3   Economic Interdependency in a Four to Five Generation Society

the perspective of older people, but also from that of an extended youth period (longer period of education, marriage and family at higher ages), which is also costly to society—and from that of a reduced period of professional work—with early retirement schemes (Figure 11.3).

Today, new "symptoms" of generation mis- or maladjustment are emerging in the form of publicly expressed dissatisfaction and disputes. For example, a common argument encountered in developed countries is that the old person constitutes a "pension burden." This argument stems from a materialistic perspective and is not rationally justified, given that the elderly are not responsible for the declining birth rates of the new generations (and consequently for the declining workforce contributing to the pension system). In addition, they have put in forty to forty-five years of work while contributing to their retirement wages, had fewer choices, and a shorter education than today's active population. Another frequent criticism asserts an accountability of the older generation towards the younger generation, reproaching the elderly, for example, for leaving unwanted debts and problems to the younger generations, for which they (the younger generation) do not wish to assume responsibility. The question of accountability could well provide many future grounds for conflict and division between generations, especially resulting from situations of war and degradation of the environment. The state of the world is an issue the younger generations, as a global youth, will have to take care of, and this might well be perceived as a justified reproach that the older generation should anticipate. It is important that future economic calculations consider the time dynamics of an individual life course, as well as the cohort, generation, and period effects on social and human development.

Generation Gap through Technology: from Digital to Generation Divide

Conflicts can also emerge from the *rapid pace of technological changes and modernization* of society. The new (M)ICT society (Media Information and Communication Technology) seems on the verge of creating a new generation of "homo technicus." A recent German study found that both the young and the old felt that they were not understood by the other group (Lehr 1998). Those findings confirm the existence of the model that Margaret Mead described as the "pre-figurative model." It announces a possible cultural and technological clash between generations if care is not given to the development of a "peaceful" social cohesion while sustaining a healthy economic development within a country (Table 11.3, Figures 11.4 and 11.5). New discussions concerning the "right to development" will need to address the issue of including and addressing all ages and generations. Each generation develops at a different speed and therefore requires different policies, i.e., generation-adapted policies. Some writers and thinkers have predicted that future wars will be between the "fast" and the "slow," between the "ICT-rich" and "ICT-poor." This remark is particularly relevant when the ageing population is taken into consideration, given that the decline in the speed of performance during the ageing process is completely opposite to the increasing speed of development being imposed upon us. The same can be said about life experience; what the elders of today have lived through and experienced is very different from that of the younger generation. Let us not forget that the older generation has experienced remarkable change, having witnessed the invention of the television, radio, airplanes, phones, electronics, computers, and the Internet, while the younger generation has lived with all of these since birth. Socialization has also changed. For the older generations the mapping of the world was local-national, traveling beyond the village or the country was exceptional. Today the mixing of cultures and the open window of the media/Internet on the world is giving children a more "global" view and the awareness of living in a "global village" with a common future. Even in the arts, childrens' films are viewed internationally, from Pokémon to Harry Potter and many more. Almost all children today have access to the same information, which was not the case of the elderly as children (Figure 11.4). The generations of today's children are living with a global and universal feeling of one planet. They see through the mass media what is happening on the other side of the planet. Almost instantly, they are aware of their neighbor, whether he/she is next door or at the far end of China, Australia, Patagonia, or Iceland. With this global perspective, one can wonder how generations can communicate and what it is they can share with one another. One should also examine the value systems generations have in common, what is

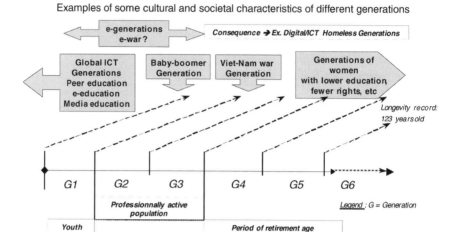

Figure 11.4   Dynamics of Generations

changing and what is continuous in time, what must be sustained, and even what should be avoided in the development of future generations. Table 11.5 summarizes these potential sources of intergenerational conflict.

Despite these described findings relating to potential conflicts between generations, other researchers have found that good relations often exist between generations today (e.g., Attias-Donfut et al. 2002; Roux et al. 1996). These contradictory results might confirm the theory of "cultural lag," formulated by Ogburn in 1922, according to which one can make the assumption that good social integration and good contacts between generations result from preexisting structural conditions in society. These findings suggest that these structural conditions, such as family ties, provide a moderating influence on the negative effects of industrialization and urbanization and at least delay the effects of these phenomena for one or two generations.

Finally, conflicts between generations can take place at different levels within society (economic, social, and cultural) and take many forms (intraindividual, in the family, within society, or at the national and international levels). What is important is to recognize that all generations are interdependent and that they must work together in order to improve the state of the world.

It is in the hands of older and younger generations to understand and grasp the opportunities to create a common vision and agenda for the future. If either the older or the younger generation were to assume sole responsibility for the agenda of society on their own, without considering the interdependency of all other generations, the risk of a generation conflict would increase. No generation can dispute that it is in everyone's interest to build a viable and sustainable future for the world, anticipating and resolving conflict and bringing or ensuring peace between generations. This perspective is a prerequisite for any sound policy or plan of action.

Table 11.5   Examples of Potential Conflicts and New Opportunities between Generations

Conflicts	Opportunities
→ *Technological clash:* information vs experience	→ *Sustainability:* transmission of skills to exist and to live
→ *ICT:* mutual ghetto of generations	→ *Younger generations as teachers of ICT*
→ *Historical culture:* local vs global (or mixed)	→ *Ageing as reference models of life/death* for youth
→ *Sociodemographic:* complexity of family ties	→ *Retiree's role and responsibility for the future:*
→ *Burning issues:*	• As promoters of peace and violence prevention
• Unequal distribution of social welfare and goods	• Protectors of the environment
• Absence of intergenerational rights	• Defenders of universal values
• "Development concept" to become generation specific	• Spiritual guides and leaders
• Retirement age as a ghetto economy	• Models of wisdom
• Employment vs free voluntary work of the retirees	→ *Older generations as contributors to youth's future*
• Health care rationing (i.e., age discrimination in access to high-tech care, transplants, etc.)	• Volunteering—time and experience available
• "Juventocracy" or "Gerontocracy": younger or older generations as leaders	• Sharing their life expertise—strategic and conflict management competencies
• Conflict of values? economy vs humanity	• Adding life networks and experience
	• Transmitting values to the children of tomorrow
	• Enhancing global solidarity—new concept of service
	• Starting a new "free" career— constraint-free

Carrying the bones of the ancestors
    Where is the common man today who offers protection to his family, people, and nation through promoting peace? Where is the common man who is committed and hardworking—who although he may be unemployed continues to work for the everyday essentials of living and for training the children, youth and young adults.

Confusion has now set in among the common man. With today's cross-cultural, high technology, choice-filled and multi-society mode of attaining more than just enough to get along in life, the common man's image has been weakened. This has often pressured him to become corrupt,...and make excuses to the point of becoming an artifact or a relic in his own world.
—Indigenous Leaders Statement, given at the Peace Summit of Religious and Spiritual Leaders, August 2000

Transgenerational Perspective on Development

What every individual indisputably has in common with all others is the life process itself, of which ageing is a part. Through life experiences each person will age and form his/her own life events and history, his/her own strategies of conflict resolution, his/her own sense of coherence in life. These "personal treasures" gathered through time are transformed into memories and values. When shared, they can have peaceful effects on the future generations, or perpetuate hatred (Figure 11.5). The personal dimensions of the individual can have tremendous effects on his/her descendants. Research has not yet measured the effect of the transmission of memories through stories or the wishes of the elderly before death, the "philosophical testimony," on to the following generations. The powerful impact of the will and wish for hatred or peace of a dying elderly person on his/her descendants—at the conscious and subconscious levels—can certainly have an impact on the behavior of one's descendants, especially in cultures with strong traditions

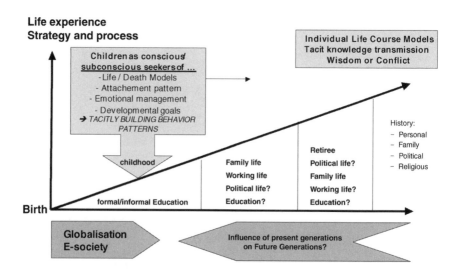

Figure 11.5   The Treasure of Time...of Life Transmitting Memories and Values

of respect toward their elders. Psychoanalytical theories have demonstrated the strong impact of nonresolved family conflicts on the ill or abnormal behaviors of both children and adults.

Research has shown that the behavior of parents affects the behavior of their children even far beyond the time of education in behaviors such as smoking, alcoholism, suicide, sexual abuse, and transgenerational violence. Much research has emphasized the importance of such transmissions between generations. Earlier writings in psychology have proposed to use the term "transgenerational perspective" to describe behavioral development and values transmission from generation to generation (Stuckelberger 2002).

Social learning theories are certainly the area of learning theory that most clearly influences current developmental thinking and research and is the most relevant in "intergenerational psychology." Watson and Skinner have become key sources of social learning theory in psychology who, like many subsequent behaviorists, had visions of a better society and humanity. If changing the environment can change behavior, there are exciting possibilities for human society. According to learning theory, personality—or the self—is a repertoire of behavior created by an organized set of contingencies. As one of the key figures of behaviorism, B. F. Skinner, wrote in 1976:

> The behavior a young person acquires in the bosom of his family composes one self; the behavior he acquires in other surroundings, say, the armed services, composes another. The two selves may exist in the same skin without conflict until the contingencies conflict—as they may, for example, if his friends from the services visit him in his home....The individual is born of society, and his indivisibility depends upon the coherence of the society which gives birth to him. "Fragmentation of a life" is said to follow "social disorganization in which a person has been ripped apart," fragmentation being defined as an "arrangement consciousness makes in response to an environment where respect is not forthcoming as a matter of course." But it is behavior, not consciousness, that is fragmented and ripped apart, and respect is only one of the disorganized reinforcers. Conflicting contingencies lead to conflicting repertoires of behavior, but they are all exhibited by one body, by one member of the human species.
>
> Skinner 1976, Chap. 10, 164–165.

Several theories of personality are classified as social learning theories. Bandura (1977) disagreed with Skinner, seeing the child as an active, thinking being who contributes in many ways to his/her own development. The child is an originating agent, free to choose the models he/she will emulate and hence will have some say about what he/she will learn from elders. In Bandura's cognitive social learning theory, observational learning requires the observer to actively attend to encode and retain the behaviors displayed by social models. Children are active information processors, who organize experience by making mental notes about their strengths and weaknesses and about the likely consequences of their behavior. For example, new findings are proving that not only do children follow implicitly throughout their life the pathological behavior of their parents, but if parents change their behavior in positive ways, the children change their behavior accordingly. A study on the cessation of smoking has proved that the cessation of smoking in parents was significantly linked to the children's pattern of taking up or quitting smoking (Farkas et al. 1999). Thus, not only do negative patterns have an impact, but positive behavior does also, which provides grounds to postulate that positive models of change of older generations do influence the behavior of younger generations—potentially enhancing their responsibility in many ways.

Bowlby, the pioneer of attachment psychology, believed that attachment theory is not only a theory of child development, but a lifelong phenomenon (e.g., Bowlby 1988). Some research shows that present thoughts about the past influence the quality of adults' relationships and attachments with their children. There is evidence for the intergenerational transfer of individual differences in patterns of attachment in different continents (see Sperling and Berman 1994 for an overview; Parkes, Stevenson-Hinde, and Morris 1991; Van Ijzendoorn 1995). These studies conclude that there is substantial intergenerational transmission of individual differences in attachment patterns. In about 75 percent of the families, the classification of the parents' mental representation of how they had attached themselves to their parents agrees with measures of the attachment relations they currently have with their infants. In about 25 percent of the families, parents classified as secure in their mental representations of the past were nevertheless diagnosed as having an insecure relationship with their infant, and vice versa. Although one can still question what is cause and what is effect, we can consider it established that we should speak in terms of degrees of intergenerational concordance or congruence, rather than simple intergenerational transmission of the quality of attachment relations (Demetriou, Doise, and van Lieshout 1999).

Understanding human life in a holistic view requires that developmental psychology include a "life course dimension" when addressing children and family issues. Furthermore, a systemic approach would also require that "linked lives" are taken into consideration, that a family is not only a children-parent dyad but the total genealogical tree, including the lives of older persons linked to those of children, grandchildren, great-grandchildren, etc. Thus, human and family development over the life span can provide explanations of many deeply engrained behaviors and patterns.

In general, human development deals with the individual throughout his/her life and studies the description, explanation, and modification of the ontogenesis of interindividual age-related change of mind and behavior from conception to death. It aims at identifying the range of conditions of individual plasticity or modifiability of development (Baltes and Smith 1995). Numerous specialties have emerged that concentrate on either age-graded periods (infancy, childhood, adolescence, adulthood, old age, centenarians) or on domains of functioning and processes (physical growth, cognitive development, memory development, personality development, social development, spiritual development, etc.). Interestingly enough, some authors have questioned the goal of development and what really develops throughout a life course (Miller 1993). Many theories have surfaced, all giving a different perspective of the course of development. Theories range from giving focus to social behaviors and personality (Freud, Jung, Erikson as well as social learning theory, ethology) to thinking and cognitive structures (Piaget, Baltes as well as information processing theories, problem solving, conflict resolution), and to perception (Gibson) or culturally constructed systems of knowledge (Vygotsky contextualism).

In the area of ageing, developmental psychology is relatively new and gerontologists have also raised questions concerning what should be considered the most important goal of ageing. Some authors have come up with the concept of "successful ageing," which combines three elements: survival (longevity), health (lack of disability), and life satisfaction (happiness) (e.g., Palmore 1979), but others have recently given more attention to the subjective appraisal of life linked to psychological mechanisms and processes such as coping, resilience, beliefs, or wisdom. A particularly interesting area of research on subjectivity has demonstrated the highly predictive power of subjective health assessment on longevity or mortality (more accurate even than medical assessments), but also on the impairment process and even on social networks. Furthermore, the greater longevity of women than men has prompted research into the process underlying personal health assessment. Subjective appraisal of health was found to operate differently between women and men as a result of their role throughout the life course. Coping mechanisms and health beliefs were the main modulators of subjective health assessment (Stuckelberger, 2000). More recently, discussions have included the process of "dying well" or the quality of the end of life as a developmental task (e.g., Lawton 2001). Findings have shown very positive aspects of ageing beyond expected ages. Individuals feel they are "survivors" and thus a certain "elite" of society, which empowers them with a sense of exception and privilege and a renewed sense of physical and psychological well-being (Perls 1995). One could actually reverse the "life time system" to a "death time system" and argue that the perception of the proximity of death is proportional to one's will or sense of being at peace with oneself and the world. Although the topic of the psychology of inner peace is not yet recognized, linking it to the ageing process would appear crucial.

Wisdom as an aspect of development has recently received increased attention. Throughout history, wisdom has been considered one of the highest forms of knowledge and personal functioning. It carries a very strong interpersonal and social aspect with regard to both its application and the consensual recognition of its existence. Wisdom is an antonym of war and violence and a synonym of peace and serenity. Research and theory on the sources and conditions associated with the development of wisdom across the life span remains one of the least developed fields of investigation in social science (Baltes and Staudinger 1993; Baltes, Smith, and Staudinger 1992). It is a difficult task to measure the increase or decrease in the wisdom of the families and nations of the world. However, the level of conflicts and wars in the world has certainly escalated, and the measurements and statistics related to violence have also increased. Sternberg and Lubart (2001) press psychologists to take the measurement of wisdom and the formulation of theories and theory-based measures of wisdom much more seriously. The work at hand is often dwarfed by work on intelligence. These authors state:

> Perhaps we even need to think about how we, as psychologists, might create experiences that would guide people to develop wisdom, much as we have been concerned in some quarters about developing intelligence. Perhaps if schools put into wisdom development even a small fraction of the effort they put into the development of an often inert knowledge base, some of the conflicts that have arisen so quickly would also quickly disappear.

From the perspective of a systemic approach to human development, one might add that family wisdom would also be an important aspect to be addressed in this pursuit.

Linked Lives: the Case of Transgenerational Violence or Peace

Of all generations living today, the older generation has been identified as the "less violent." Available evidence consistently indicates that older persons have the lowest rates of criminal acts and of getting arrested for all types of crimes. It is important to note that most crimes for which older persons are arrested are minor offenses (Cutler 1995). This provides a sound basis for involving the elderly in creating models of society or peace initiatives. This transgenerational perspective illustrates the case for the transgenerational transmission of violence and peace values.

The transgenerational model of violence against adults and elder abuse suggests that violent behavior—as perpetrator or victim—learned within the family is transmitted from one generation to the next. According to this view, abusers grow up in violent families only to reenact the parent-child cycle of violence once the dependency roles shift from child to parent (Wilber and McNeilly 2001). Such transgenerational violence conclusions are based on findings that perpetrators of domestic violence are more likely to have grown up in violent homes where they witnessed spousal abuse and/or were victims of child abuse themselves. In the same way, battered women, as well as their abusers, are more likely to batter their children. According to Quinn and Tomita (1997), the rate of transmission of abusive violence from one generation to the next is estimated at about 30 percent, compared to a 3 percent rate of abusive violence in the general population. The same pattern applies for alcoholism, suicide, and other behavioral disorders leading to "self-violence" or other forms of violence. One additional form of violence beginning to emerge is "financial elder abuse" especially in the case of patients suffering from cognitive impairment or under mental health treatment.

Today, several issues usually thought of as problems of a single generation are, in fact, of concern to all generations and indeed all of society. Violence among youth and in schools, self-inflicted violence through assisted suicide, and active euthanasia among the elderly affect all of us, not just the generation most directly affected.

Violence in Schools

Many schools throughout the world have begun to involve older generations in teaching courses, but have not yet included them as agents of conflict management or violence prevention. At the personal level, older generations might be able to achieve a better understanding and communication in cases of disruptive behavior and violence in children where direct parent or peer interactions have failed. In order to begin a process of including the transgenerational perspective, some have recently proposed a first draft of an "Intergenerational Plan of Action for Conflict and Violence Prevention in Schools," in which older generations play a significant role. This plan for schools takes into account the inner dimensions of peace as well as the outer dimension and expression of nonviolence and peace, two aspects that alone can guarantee a long-term sustainable strategy. The mutual benefit of the intergenerational component will not only benefit youth, but also the elderly by restoring their role and potential to serve society. The 2nd United Nations World Assembly on Ageing, which took place in Madrid in April 2002, offered an opportunity to address the issue of the ageing population and world peace with a proposed plan of action at the macro level to involve the elders in all efforts to (a) prevent conflict and violence, (b) promote peace at the inner and outer levels, and (c) empower future generations for peace and teach them the skills to maintain a state of peace (Stuckelberger 2002).

Self-violence or violence against others are but expressions of a dysfunctional society, a symptom of an imbalance that we all, especially older generations, have a duty to analyze and resolve. In this context, while professionally active generations are important actors, the two to three generations of retired people also play an important role as agents for improving society.

Self-Violence: the Case of Suicide, Assisted Suicide, and Active Euthanasia

Data on the elderly display two important facts relating to suicide rates and assisted-suicide legislation. The latest WHO report on suicide (WHO 1999) systematically describes from sources all around the world an increase in suicide rates with increasing age. Older men have the highest rates of suicide in the majority of countries. The social symptom reflected by those high rates of suicide in the elderly show that older age poses existential problems and exposes a deep-seated nihilism, leading people to make the decision that their life is not worth living to its natural end. This might also be the expression of other malaise or a depressive state triggered by an event such as retirement or old age.

. . .on Death. . .

Death is part of our human horizon, giving it its time and mysterious dimension. The contemporary world, especially in the West, needs to learn how to reintegrate death into the frame work of human existence.

—Pope John Paul, *The Tablet*, 1982

For nothing do we get as much preparation time as for dying. Isn't it surprising then that almost nobody is prepared for it when it's there?

—F. Hellers, 1936

Death is one of the attributes you were created with; death is part of you. Your life's continual task is to build your death.

—Montaigne

The art of living well and dying well are one.

—Epicurus

Currently, one of the most problematic issues for the family and future generations is certainly the legislation being considered and sometimes adopted by some countries allowing for assisted suicide among the elderly. Table 11.6 shows a rise in government measures officially sanctioning this practice.

There is reason to be seriously concerned with the "social irresponsibility" of such decisions in the face of transgenerational evidence of behaviors being

Table 11.6   Legalization of Assisted Suicide and Active Euthanasia

Country	Euthanasia legal	Assisted suicide legal
Finland, Denmark	No	No
France, Canada, Russia	No	No
Great Britain	No (bill to legalize it 2004)	No
United States	No	No (yes in Oregon)
Australia	No	No (yes in NT state)
Germany	No	Yes
Switzerland	No	Yes
Spain	No	Yes
Colombia, Japan	Yes	Yes
The Netherlands, Belgium	Yes	Yes

passed from one generation to the next. Before implementing measures that call into question the fundamental respect for life, of one's own life, ethical considerations need to be taken into account:

- first, evidence should be gathered and research conducted on the consequences of the posterity of older persons committing assisted suicide;

- second, legalizing assisted suicide without consulting society as a whole seems to give the message that decisions on the value and conception of life do not need a democratic approach. An urgent social and moral debate is needed on this issue, including families, all generations and health professionals, but also academics and religious leaders. As demonstrated earlier, the interdependency of individual behavior in matters of life and death reaches far beyond the person only;

- third, taking this first step in allowing the right to kill oneself with assistance is a very dangerous move toward allowing the right to kill oneself at any age and even to kill in general. Respect for life is the foundation for a peaceful life in the family, in society, and in the nation. Therefore, "dying with dignity" in full respect for the context of culture and beliefs would need to be addressed in family policies throughout the world;

- and fourth, the taboo surrounding the discussion of death and the process of dying might be overcome or at least moderated in favor of a frank dialogue on the reality of death, and more importantly on respect for the dignity of dying for each individual, which will impact future generations. Today, serious debates concerning the "process of dying" and the ethical perspective linked to it have started to enter the highly evidence-based arena of medicine. A recent example is the new mention of the "principles of a good death" in the most preeminent medical journals:
  - To know when death is coming, and to understand what can be expected
  - To be able to retain control of what happens
  - To be afforded dignity and privacy
  - To have control over pain relief and other symptom control
  - To have choice and control over where death occurs (at home or elsewhere)
  - To have access to information and expertise of whatever kind is necessary
  - To have access to any spiritual or emotional support required
  - To have access to hospice care in any location, not only in the hospital
  - To have control over who is present and who shares the end
  - To be able to issue advance directives that ensure wishes are respected
  - To have time to say goodbye and control over other aspects of timing

○ To be able to leave when it is time to go, and not to have life prolonged pointlessly
(Smith, British Medical Journal, 2000).

On the one hand, the older generation has a social and family responsibility in setting an example in the model of a righteous and wise life up to and including death. On the other hand, all generations and the family owe to the elderly respect and dignity, honoring their contributions and their role in the family and society.

Older people can be a key to preventing violence and to the promotion of a culture of peace, first, by the legacy they leave both to future generations collectively and to younger individuals personally through their implicit or explicit "moral testimony"; second, by the simple fact that, throughout their lives, they participated in and witnessed history at a personal level as well as at the levels of the family and society. In living the history of their own nation, older generations have experienced the profound impact of war and violence on society and on their families. Canadian General Romeo Dallaire, who witnessed the genocide in Rwanda and lived with post-traumatic syndrome for years, delivers speeches today to call for a nonviolent society where older generations have a duty to stop war and violence (see quotation in the box below). He reckons that the massacre of more that one million Tutsi by the Hutu people in three months was the consequence of the development of hate transmitted from generation to generation from the time of the Belgian occupation, which tended to give more privileges to the Tutsi people (see Silver, S. (film), *The Last Just Man*, 2002). Restoring and healing collective memories is thus of paramount importance for societies. The way in which the collective memory of war, violence, and the peace process is transmitted to the following generations is a powerful and undeniable factor of social transformation:

(i) either by encouraging a spirit of forgiveness and of reconciliation within society (political) and/or within the family (socio-genealogical) and within the self (psychological);

(ii) or by increasing hatred and the will for revenge from one generation to another, through daily attitudes, behaviors and words—e.g. through informal education of war, but also through behavior patterns that implicitly or explicitly teach violence as an acceptable norm.

Generations of Peace—Importance of the Elders of Today

We cannot continue to believe that war is the ultimate dimension of discipline and of destruction of the world....The elders of the world cannot accept that the youth of the world is being sacrificed and trained to self destruction, be abused in war, being instruments of war, soldiers, that they are targets of a new era of conflict. The elders can coalesce and bring to an end the intolerable use and abuse of younger generations. Elders can build the power, the lobby, to bring it all to an end. Elders today have to keep up with our youth, to be credible to our youth.

—Lieutenant General Romeo Dallaire, former commander of the United Nations
Observer Mission in Uganda and Rwanda during the Genocide, Speech given at the
World Congress on Gerontology in Vancouver (July 2001)

The beliefs—including false beliefs—passed from one generation to
another can without any doubt be a source of individual or collective violence
or a warranty of peace in the nation and in the world. One avenue for over-
coming discord, hatred, and violence is through the commitment of ageing
individuals to become conscientious role models and to embody and model
key values of forgiveness, reconciliation and peace. The elders have the choice
to conscientiously address their responsibility towards youth: (i) to leave the
fruits of their work and achievement behind them, a world of peace or a
world of destruction, for the following generations, (ii) to leave a model of
the way to live and die that will influence their peers and descendants positively, and (iii) more specifically, to transmit through their attitudes and
behaviors a "mental imprint" of living in peace with the self, the family, and
the nation.

Conclusion

This chapter demonstrates first, that human and family development
includes all generations and the entire living genealogy of a family; second,
that the family and time dynamics of generations make us interdependent
on one another during each unique individual life course; and third, that the
values we express during our life through behavior and value transmission
do have an impact on the younger generations' growth and development, as
well as on the family and nation as a consequence.

Thus, when addressing material development without the contextual systemic human development perspective, nations run the risk of approaching
developmental goals only on a short term basis, thereby only increasing family and social imbalance and therefore ultimately failing in the development
they seek. On the positive side, the findings of social science demonstrate that
each generation has an impact on future generations through its behavior,
through its pattern of attachment, and by its approaches to problem solving.
However, more investigations are needed in this area. It can be supposed that
just as disruptive or violent patterns of behavior are perpetuated in subsequent generations, these patterns can be reversed, thereby allowing peaceful patterns of behavior to be perpetuated in generations to follow. The
reversal point and measurement means and tools remain to be discovered
and utilized.

The decisive influence of one generation upon another in matters of inner
and outer peace and conflict calls for moral responsibility of older generations
with regard to younger generations, but more so for role models in the form
of political, religious, and spiritual leaders. In this respect, and in the world
context of increasing levels of migration and consequent mixing of cultures
and religions, the establishment of universal standards and objectives

applicable to all nations is a key to sustainable worldwide development, but great care must be taken to resist the temptation to do too much, to micromanage, or to use such standard setting to advance causes and ideologies that may ultimately be destructive rather than constructive, as no ethical framework had been discussed or been established in a consensual way. Religions today need to be involved with the development of the universal values to be promoted in global agendas such as the United Nations Millennium Developmental Goals. Religions are today frequently consulted in high-level economic fora (WEF 2001; WFDD), but there is still no consensus on fundamental universal human rights regarding reproductive health, education, environmental protection, extended family concepts, right to die, etc.). The United Nations has come up with Principles for Older Persons in 1991, but much remains to be done in the UN texts to recognize, make decisions, provide funding and legislation dealing adequately and respectfully with the older refugee, the older war and violence victim, the older epidemic survivor, the older poor, the older worker, but also the older helper, activist, humanistic advocate, environmental protection promoter, etc. The UN is also making very slow progress in mainstreaming ageing compared to its efforts on gender issues (Stuckelberger 1999; NGO committee on ageing 2003).

In conclusion, the question for further debate is what duty and responsibility older generations have towards younger generations and vice versa. No one can dispute that older generations have shaped the world we now live in and therefore bear a certain responsibility for the state of the world today. It is the older generation that sets the standard, the reference, and is a model or "anti-model" of not only a successful life but more importantly a valuable life and noble death. Elders are essential to the cohesion of society. Not only are elders transmitters of tacit knowledge, of life experiences, of history, and of life crisis management, they are also the "roots of our society." Thus, in order to find our "true common values for peace and justice," it is of paramount importance to restore the role and dignity of the elderly in society and to build a cohesive and inclusive common vision for the future.

Aboriginal cultures throughout the world have long woven into their cultures a special respect for their elders and for their ancestors, recognized as the builders and guides of all decisions. Oral traditions among some Native American tribes requires chiefs to consider the impact of their decisions for the next seven generations.

If an elder African dies, it is a whole Library that is burning.
                                        —Hampatê Ba, famous African writer from Mali

For a *United Nations Principles for Older Persons* document, see Appendix.

Presented at the European Dialogue, Geneva, Switzerland, August 2004.

Bibliography

Allard, M., Lèbre, V., and Robine, J.M. (1994). *Les 120 ans de Jeanne Calment, doyenne de l'humanité*. Paris, France: Le Cherche Midi Ed.

Attias-Donfut, C., Lapierre, N., and Segalen M. (2002). *Le nouvel esprit de famille*. Paris: Editions Odile Jacob.

Back, K. (1995). Generations. In G.L. Maddox (Ed.), *The Encyclopedia of Ageing* (2nd ed., pp. 395–396). New York: Springer Publishing Co.

Baltes, P.B., and Smith, J. (1995). Developmental Psychology. In G.L. Maddox (Ed.), *The Encyclopedia of Ageing* (2nd ed., pp. 267–270). New York: Springer Publishing Co.

Baltes, P.B., Smith, J., and Staudinger, U.M. (1992). Wisdom and successful ageing. In T. Sonderegger (Ed.), *Nebraska Symposium on Motivation* (Vol. 39, pp. 123–167). Lincoln: University of Nebraska Press.

Baltes, P.B., and Staudinger, U.M. (1993). The search for a psychology of wisdom. *Current Directions in Psychological Science, 2,* 1–6.

Bandura, A. (1977). *Social learning theory.* Englewood Cliffs, NJ: Prentice-Hall.

Bengtson, V.L., Cutler, N.W., Mangen, D.J., and Marshall, V.W. (1985). Generations, cohorts, and relations between age groups. In R. Binstock and E. Shanas (Eds.), *Handbook of aging and the social sciences* (2nd ed., pp. 304–338). New York: van Nostrand Reinhold.

Bowlby, J. (1988). *A secure base. Clinical applications of attachment theory.* London: Routledge.

Butler, R.N. (1995). Ageism. In G.L. Maddox (Ed.), *The encyclopedia of aging* (2nd ed., p. 35). New York: Springer Publishing Co.

Casper, L.M., and Bryson, K.R. (1998). Co-resident grandparents and their grandchildren. Paper prepared for the 1998 annual meeting of the Population Association of America, Chicago.

Central Census Steering Committee. (1999). *The 1999 Census of Vietnam at a Glance, Preliminary Results.* Hanoi, Viet-Nam: Thé Gioi Publishers.

Cutler, S.J. (1995). Crime against and by the elderly. In G.L. Maddox (Ed.), *The Encyclopedia of Ageing* (2nd ed., pp. 243–244). New York: Springer Publishing Co.

Dallaire, R. (2001, July). Transmitting fundamental values to younger generations through the healing of painful memories. Contribution to the Symposium convened by A. Stuckelberger and C. Taillon, Empowering Future Generations for Peace: The Elder's Role, World Congress of Gerontology, Vancouver, Canada.

Demetriou, A., Doise, W., and van Lieshout, C. (Eds.) (1999). *Life-span developmental psychology.* London: Wiley.

Erikson, E.H. (1959). Identity and the life cycle. *Psychological Issues, 1,* 18–164.

Erikson, E.H. (1982). *The life cycle completed.* New York: Norton.

Farkas, A.J., Distefan, J.M., Choii, W.S, Giulpin, E.A., and Pierce, J.P. (1999). Does parental smoking cessation discourage adolescent smoking. *Preventive Medicine, 28,* 213–218.

Fuller-Thomson, E., and Minkler, M. (2001). American grandparents providing extensive child care to their grandchildren: Prevalence and profile. *The Gerontologist, 41*(2), 201–209.

Höpflinger, F., and Stuckelberger, A. (1999). *Demographisches Älterung und individuelles Altern.* Zürich: Editions Seismo

Gillion, C., Turner, J., Bailey, C., and Latulippe, D. (2000). Social security pensions, development and reform. Geneva: International Labour Office.

Jung, C.G. (1971). The stages of life. In J. Campbell (Ed.), *The portable Jung* (pp. 2–22). New York. Viking.

Kaës, R., Faimberg, H., Enriquez, M., and Baranes, J.-J. (1993). *Transmission de la vie psychique entre générations.* Paris: Dunod.

Kinsella, K., and Velkoff, V.A. (2001). An Ageing world: 2001. International Population Reports. Washington, DC: U.S. Census Bureau.

Kohli, M. (16 November 1998). Intergenerational transfers of assets. Conference Report, Expert Conference "Ageing in Europe: Intergenerational Solidarity— A Basis of Social Cohesion," Vienna.

Lawton, P. (2001). Quality of life and end of life. In James E. Birren and Werner K. Shaie (Eds.), *Handbook of the Psychology of Ageing* (5th ed., ch. 24, pp. 592–616). New York: Academic Press.

Lehr, U. (16 November 1998). From the three-generation to the four-and five-generation family. Conference Report, Expert Conference "Ageing in Europe: Intergenerational Solidarity—A Basis of Social Cohesion," Vienna.

Mead, M. (1970). *A study of the generations gap.* New York: Doubleday and Co.

Mead, M. (1971). *Le fossé des générations (A Study of the Generations Gap).* Paris: Editions Denoël.

Mendel, G. (1963). *Les conflits des générations.* Paris: Presses universitaires de France.

Mendel, G. (2002). *Une histoire de l'autorité, Permanences et variations.* Paris: La Découverte.

Miller, P.H. (1993). *Theories of Developmental Psychology* (3rd ed.). New York: Freeman.

Myers, G.C. (1992). Demographic aging and family support for older persons. In H.L. Kendig, A. Hashimoto, and L.C. Coppard (Eds.), *Family support for the elderly* (pp. 31–68). Oxford: Oxford University Press.

NGO Committee on Ageing (2003, April). Older persons and human rights: Life long human rights—Generation and ageing perspective. Panel Report done for the NGO Committee on Ageing during the Human Right Commission. United Nations Geneva.

Ogburn, W.F. (1922). *Social Change.* New York: Huebsch.

Palmore, E. (1979). Predictors of successful ageing. *Gerontologist, 19,* 427–431.

Pargament, K.I. (1997). *The psychology of religion and coping, theory, research, practice.* New York: Guilford.

Parkes, C.M., Stevenson, Hinde J., and Morris, P. (1991). *Attachment across the life cycle.* London: Routledge.

Perls, T.T. (1995, January). The oldest old. *Scientific American, 272,* 70–75.

Quinn, K.M., and Tomita, S.K. (1997). *Elder abuse and neglect: Causes, diagnosis and intervention strategies* (2nd ed.). New York: Springer Publishing Company.

Roux, P., Gobet, P., Clémence, A., and Höpflinger, F. (1996). Generationenbeziehungen und Altersbilder. Ergebnisse einer empirischen Studie, Lausanne/Zürich (Switzerland): NFP 32.

Rowe, J.W., and Kahn, R.L. (1998). *Successful Ageing: The MacArthur Foundation Study.* New York: Pantheon Books.

Silver, S. (2002). *The Last Just Man* (documentary film).

Skinner, B.F. 1976. *About Behaviorism.* New York: Vintage.

Smith, K. (2000). Who's minding the kids? Child care arrangements: Fall 1995, U.S. Census Bureau Current Population Reports P70-70. Washington, DC: Government Printing Office.

Smith, R. (2000). A good death. Editorial. *British Medical Journal, 320,* 129–130.

Soldo, B.J. (1996). Cross Pressures on Middle-Aged Adults: A broader view. *Journal of Gerontology, Social, Sciences, 51B*(6), S271–273.

Sperling, M.B., and Berman, W.H. (Eds.). (1994). Attachment in adults, on individual difference. New York: The Guilford Press.

Sternberg, R.J., and Lubart, T. (2001). Wisdom and creativity. In James E. Birren and Werner K. Shaie (Eds.), *Handbook of the Psychology of Ageing* (5th ed., ch. 20, pp. 500–522). New York: Academic Press.

Stuckelberger, A. (July–August 1997). Men and women age differently. In *World Health "Active Ageing,"* 4, 8–9. WHO: Geneva.

Stuckelberger, A. (1999). Human Rights and Older Persons. Document prepared for the UN International Year of Older Persons 1999. Geneva: United Nations.

Stuckelberger, A. (2000). Vieillissement et état de santé subjectif: déterminants et mécanismes différentiels hommes femmes, Etude transversale de la population genevoise. Thèse de doctorat en psychologie, Université de Genève. Suisse.

Stuckelberger, A. (2002). Population ageing & world peace. Empowering future generations. Older persons role and responsibility. *Journal of Psycho-Social Intervention,* Contributions of the Psychology on Ageing: Towards a Society for All Ages. Special Issue for the 2nd World Assembly on Ageing in Madrid, Spain (pp. 29–75).

Stuckelberger, A., and Höpflinger, F. (1996). *Vieillissement différentiel: hommes et femmes.* Zürich: Editions Seismo.

Stuckelberger, A., and Höpflinger, F. (1998). Dynamics of ageing in Switzerland from a gender perspective. *Ageing International,* 62–84.

Toulemon, L. (2001). Combien d'enfants, combine de frères et sœurs depuis cent ans?, Population et Sociétés, Bulletin mensuel d'information de l'Institut national d'études démographiques, no 374, Paris.

Tribune de Genève (7 March 2002). De plus en plus de parents demandent qu'on leur retire la garde de leurs enfants [More and more parents request that their custody right be withdrawn] (p. 21). Geneva, Switzerland.

UN Press Release (6 March 2002). Secretary-General Urges Leaders to Act in Middle East. New York: UN News. http://www.un.org/News/ossg/sg/index.shtml.

UNAIDS (December 2001). UNAIDS Annual Report. Geneva: UNAIDS.

UNFPA (1999). 6 Billion: A Time for Choices. The State of the World Population 1999. New York: United Nations.

UNFPA (2001). Population Issues. Briefing Kit 2001. United Nations Population Fund, New York.

United Nations (1991). United Nations Principles for Older Persons. New York: United Nations.

United Nations (2001). We the peoples. The role of the United Nations in the 21st Century. The Millennium Report. New York: United Nations.

United Nations Population Division (2000). World Population Prospects: The 2000 Revision.

U.S. Census Bureau (2001). An Ageing world: 2001. International Population Reports. Washington, DC, USA.

U.S. Congressional Public Health Summit, 2000. Joint Statement on the Impact of Entertainment Violence on Children. http://www.aap.org/advocacy/releases/jstmtevc.htm

Van Ijzendoorn, M.H. (1995). Adult attachment representations, parental responsiveness, and infant attachment: A meta-analysis on the predictive validity of the adult attachment interview. *Psychological Bulletin, 117,* 387–403.

Vaupel, J.W., and Jeune, B. (1995). The emergence and proliferation of centenarians. In B. Jeune and J.W. Vaupel (Eds.). *Exceptional Longevity: from prehistory to the present monograph on population aging* (no. 2). Odense: Odense University.

WEF (2001). Concluding Statement of the Meeting of Religious Leaders, World Economic Forum Annual Meeting, Davos, Switzerland.

WEF (2004). Initiative for dialogue, action and understanding between the Western and Islamic World. World Economic Forum Annual Meeting, Switzerland.

WFDD (World Faiths and Development Dialogue), www.wfdd.org.uk/

WHO (1999). Suicide rates in the World. Geneva: WHO.

Wilber, K.H., and McNeilly, D.P. (2001). Elder abuse and victimization. In James E. Birren and Werner K. Shaie (Eds.), *Handbook of the Psychology of Ageing* (5th ed., ch. 23, pp. 569–591). New York: Academic Press.

Appendix: United Nations Principles for Older Persons

(1991—http://www.un.org/esa/socdev/iyop/iyoppop.htm)

The General Assembly:

Appreciating the contribution that older persons make to their societies,

Recognizing that, in the Charter of the United Nations, the peoples of the United Nations declare, inter alia, their determination to reaffirm faith in fundamental human rights, in the dignity and worth of the human person, in the equal rights of men and women and of nations large and small and to promote social progress and better standards of life in larger freedom,

Noting the elaboration of those rights in the Universal Declaration of Human Rights, the International Covenant on Economic, Social and Cultural Rights and the International Covenant on Civil and Political Rights and other declarations to ensure the application of universal standards to particular groups,

In pursuance of the International Plan of Action on Ageing, adopted by the World Assembly on Ageing and endorsed by the General Assembly in its resolution 37/51 of 3 December 1982,

Appreciating the tremendous diversity in the situation of older persons, not only between countries but within countries and between individuals, which requires a variety of policy responses,

Aware that in all countries, individuals are reaching an advanced age in greater numbers and in better health than ever before,

Aware of the scientific research disproving many stereotypes about inevitable and irreversible declines with age,

Convinced that in a world characterized by an increasing number and proportion of older persons, opportunities must be provided for willing and capable older persons to participate in and contribute to the ongoing activities of society,

Mindful that the strains on family life in both developed and developing countries require support for those providing care to frail older persons,

Bearing in mind the standards already set by the International Plan of Action on Ageing and the conventions, recommendations and resolutions of the International Labour Organization, the World Health Organization and other United Nations entities,

Encourages Governments to incorporate the following principles into their national programmes whenever possible:...

Independence

1. Older persons should have access to adequate food, water, shelter, clothing and health care through the provision of income, family and community support and self-help.

2. Older persons should have the opportunity to work or to have access to other income-generating opportunities.

3. Older persons should be able to participate in determining when and at what pace withdrawal from the labour force takes place.

4. Older persons should have access to appropriate educational and training programmes.

5. Older persons should be able to live in environments that are safe and adaptable to personal preferences and changing capacities.

6. Older persons should be able to reside at home for as long as possible.

Participation

7. Older persons should remain integrated in society, participate actively in the formulation and implementation of policies that directly affect their well-being and share their knowledge and skills with younger generations.

8. Older persons should be able to seek and develop opportunities for service to the community and to serve as volunteers in positions appropriate to their interests and capabilities.

9. Older persons should be able to form movements or associations of older persons.

Care

10. Older persons should benefit from family and community care and protection in accordance with each society's system of cultural values.

11. Older persons should have access to health care to help them to maintain or regain the optimum level of physical, mental and emotional well-being and to prevent or delay the onset of illness.

12. Older persons should have access to social and legal services to enhance their autonomy, protection and care.

13. Older persons should be able to utilize appropriate levels of institutional care providing protection, rehabilitation and social and mental stimulation in a humane and secure environment.

14. Older persons should be able to enjoy human rights and fundamental freedoms when residing in any shelter, care or treatment facility, including full respect for their dignity, beliefs, needs and privacy and for the right to make decisions about their care and the quality of their lives.

Self-fulfillment

15. Older persons should be able to pursue opportunities for the full development of their potential.

16. Older persons should have access to the educational, cultural, spiritual and recreational resources of society.

Dignity

17. Older persons should be able to live in dignity and security and be free of exploitation and physical or mental abuse.

18. Older persons should be treated fairly regardless of age, gender, racial or ethnic background, disability or other status, and be valued independently of their economic contribution.

For more information—see following Web site: http://www.un.org/esa/socdev/ageing/

12

Living Arrangements of the Elderly and Family Change in Japan

Hirofumi Tanada (Japan)
Professor of Human Sciences
Waseda University, Tokyo, Japan

In the second half of the twentieth century, we have faced population aging while also experiencing modernization, industrialization, and urbanization. Population aging might even be viewed as a kind of population modernization brought about by declining fertility and prolonged longevity. Although population aging is accelerating in developed countries, some Asian countries like Korea, Taiwan, and Singapore, where fertility has declined dramatically in recent years, will be confronted with serious population aging in the first quarter of the twenty-first century. Population aging is a demographic phenomenon of the age composition of a population. However, it also helps explain other changes in social structures such as changes in life-style, living conditions, family structure, and value systems of people.[1]

The aim of this chapter is to provide a brief overview of living arrangements of the elderly and related changes in the families and households in Japan, as well as to present the preliminary results of our "Living Arrangements" survey in Tokorozawa city near metropolitan Tokyo, conducted in January and February 2004.

This chapter consists of five parts. The first part deals with population aging in Asia and Japan. The second part and third part deal with marriage and birth, then households in Japan, respectively, and illustrate changes in fertility. The fourth and fifth parts discuss survey results concerning living arrangements in Tokorozawa city. The feelings of the elderly in Tokorozawa regarding desirable living arrangements, their views on family, and on long-term care are discussed and compared to the type of household they are presently experiencing.

Population Aging in Asia and Japan

As of January 1, 2005, persons sixty-five years of age and older made up 19.6 percent of the total population of Japan, so Japan is one of "the oldest countries" in the world.[2] The aging of the population has been progressing rapidly in Japan and other Asian societies. In Japan, especially, the speed of population aging has been very rapid; only about twenty years were required to shift from 10 percent elderly (in 1985) to 20 percent. Reviewing recent research trends on aging in Asian societies, "family structure and living arrangements" should be considered as one of the most important research topics.[3]

Generally, opinions about the social impact of modernization on family support systems can be roughly divided into two groups.[4] One opinion holds that modernization tends to degrade the family support system, forcing family members to limit or eliminate their support activities to aged family members. According to this view, a strong public support system is required to prevent serious deterioration in the living standards of the elderly.[5] The other argument asserts that the family support system in Asian societies should be discussed separately from those in Western societies, since Asian societies are inherently different from Western societies in terms of cultural, social, and economic backgrounds. This camp therefore suggests that future changes in family support systems in Asian societies will not be the same as those already experienced by Western societies.[6]

In fact, it is likely that in Asian societies many elderly will continue to live with their children and that this coresidence will continue to fill important functions for both the elderly and their children in terms of support activities. Thus, we should better understand the factors influencing peoples' "living arrangements" and any current or potential changes to them. Actually, during the past ten years, the issue of the living arrangements of the elderly has received more attention than ever before.[7]

First, we provide a general overview of population aging. According to a recent report on population increase in Asia, the rates of population increase have been declining sharply in every region (see Figure 12.1). In the near

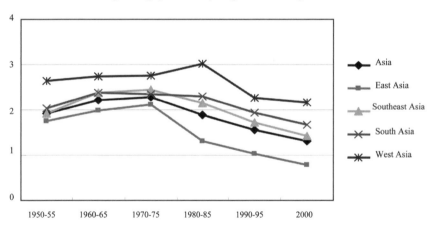

Figure 12.1   Population Increase Rate in Asia

Source: United Nations, *World Urbanization Prospects, The 2002 Revision,* 2003

future, all regions of Asia except West Asia will continue to experience a gradual drop in the rate of population growth. After completing this demographic transition, most Asian societies will be confronted with aging populations. Population aging is already progressing rapidly in East Asia at present. Southeast Asian countries are aging nearly as fast as East Asia, followed by South Asia and then West Asia. However, in West Asia, for example, Saudi Arabia and Yemen still have very high fertility rates, so it will take West Asian countries longer to become aging or aged societies.[8]

It is said that we are in the "Age of Global Aging." Most industrialized countries are aged societies, that is, societies in which the proportion of persons sixty-five years and older is more than 14 percent of the total population. Also, most developing countries will soon enter the preliminary stage of population aging. As shown in Figure 12.2, Japan is the front-runner in the race

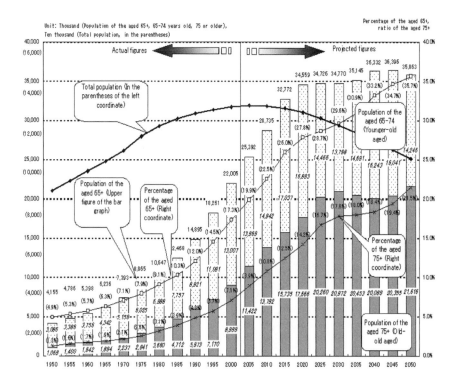

Figure 12.2 Total Population of Japan 1920–2050

Source: Up to 2000: Statistics Bureau, *Population Census of Japan,* various years. After 2005: National Institute of Population and Social Security Research, *Population Projections for Japan,* 2002. Note: In 1955, Okinawa's statistics divided the population of persons 70+, 23,328, into two age groups, 70–74 and 75 or older, based on the ratio of the population 75+ to the population 70+ in earlier and later years. (Cited from http://www8.cao.go.jp/kourei/english/annualreport/2004/1-1.html)

toward population aging. In 2004, 19.5 percent of total population was at least sixty-five years old, and the number of the elderly was 24.8 million.

We now take a closer look at the total population and population aging in Japan. In 2000, the total population of Japan was 126.93 million. According to the estimate by the Institute of Population and Social Security Research, the total population will start to drop in 2006. In 2050, the total population of Japan will be 100.59 million, about 25 million less than in the year 2000. Accordingly, the age composition of the population will change significantly. The population pyramid of Japan in Figure 12.3 shows the significant change of projected future shape of the Japanese population pyramid.

Marriage and Birth in Japan

The main influences affecting these dramatic demographic changes relate to birth and death. One such factor, for example, is longer life expectancy, now seventy-eight years for males, and eighty-five years for females. Another factor in these changes is the decline in fertility and the decrease in births. As shown in Figure 12.4, after World War II (WWII) the total fertility rate (TFR) was over 4 and in 1973 Japan's TFR had a second peak at 2.14. After 1973,

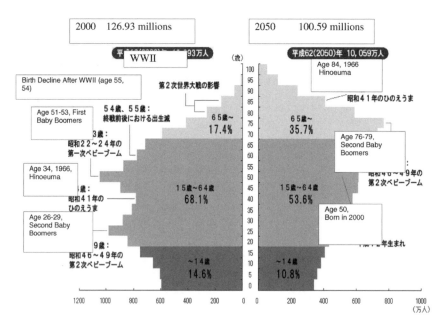

Figure 12.3   Population Pyramid of Japan 2000 and 2050

Source: Up to 2000: Statistics Bureau, *Population Census of Japan,* various years. After 2005: National Institute of Population and Social Security Research, *Population Projections for Japan,* 2002. [Cited from http://www.ipss.go.jp/syoushika/seisaku/html/111a2.htm (in Japanese) and revised in English.]

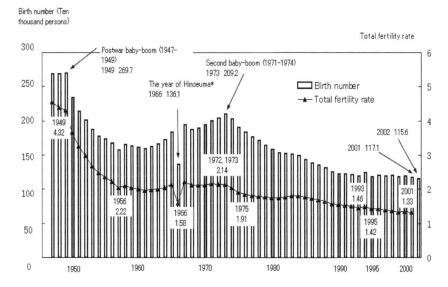

Figure 12.4   Birth Number and Total Fertility Rate in Japan 1947–2002

Source: Ministry of Health, Labour and Welfare, *Vital Statistics,* various years. Note 1: The birth number in 2002 is an estimated figure. Note 2: Okinawa Prefecture is excluded in data before 1972. **The year Hinoeuma:* The old superstition says that women born in the Year of Hinoeuma are not suitable as wives. The superstition still has some influence. (Cited from http://www8.cao.go.jp/kourei/english/annualreport/2004/1-1.html.)

the TFR began to decline gradually. In 2002, the TFR was far below replacement level at 1.32. In 2004, Japan announced a TFR of 1.28, the lowest rate since WWII. The total number of births has dropped accordingly. These recent changes in TFR and birth numbers have also resulted in changes in Japanese marriage patterns.

Recent marriage statistics in Japan (Figure 12.5) describing the mean age of first marriage from 1960–2001 show that the age at first marriage has been rising for both husband and wife. In 2001, it was 29.1 years old for husbands, and 27.4 years old for wives.

One more significant change in marriage is that the rate of never married persons is rising. Figure 12.6 shows the rate for the female cohort to be twenty-five to twenty-nine years old, and the male cohort thirty to thirty-four years old. In 2000, about half of males and females in these cohorts had never yet married. Also, the rate of people never married during their lifetime has been rising. Currently, more than 10 percent of males never marry in their lifetime.

Household and Family in Japan

The "living arrangements" and family structures of the elderly in Japan have seen dramatic changes in recent years. The causes for these changes

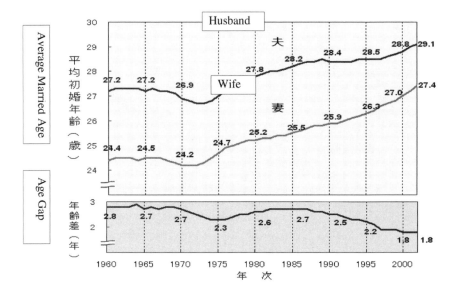

Figure 12.5　Mean Age of First Marriage in Japan 1960–2001

Source: Ministry of Health, Labour and Welfare (MHLW), *Vital Statistics,* various years. [Cited from http://www.ipss.go.jp/syoushika/seisaku/html/112a1.htm (in Japanese) and revised in English.]

can be broadly classified into two primary factors: internal factors influencing the elderly on an individual level, and external socioeconomic macro-level factors. Changes in values and lifestyles brought on by the modernization of Japanese society are often cited as internal factors. The most significant of these changes is the shift in views on the parent-children relationship, coresidence, and family support, which are closely tied to the general acceptance of lifestyles valuing independence in the elderly. The population factors mentioned above play a central role as the external factors.[9]

The total number of households was 46.782 million in 2000, broken down into relatives' households (72 percent), single (one person) households, and nonrelative households. See Figure 12.7.

Households with persons age sixty-five years and over are described in Figure 12.8, showing the types of households from 1975 to 2003. The total number of households containing elderly age sixty-five years and over was 7.118 thousand in 1975 and 17.273 thousand in 2003. These data indicate that the number of elderly households has more than doubled during this period of twenty-eight years.[10] Dramatic changes in household composition occurred during these twenty-eight years. In 1975, three-generation family households accounted for 54 percent of all households. In 2003, however, only 24 percent of households included three generations, and single (one person) households and couple-only households had come to account for about 50 percent of the total households in Japan.

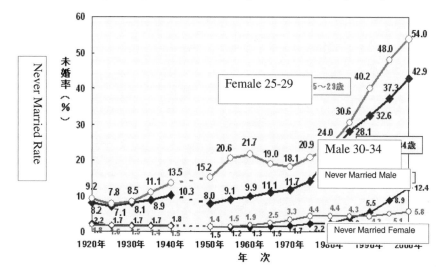

Figure 12.6   Percentage of Never Married in Japan 1920–2000.

Source: Statistics Bureau, *Population Census,* various years. [Cited from http://www.ipss.go. jp/syoushika/seisaku/html/112a2.htm (in Japanese) and revised in English.]

Figure 12.9 illustrates the living arrangements of the individual elderly. Forty-eight percent of elderly persons live with their children, while 37 percent of the elderly live alone.

Survey Results about Living Arrangements in Tokorozawa City

In January to February 2004, we conducted a "Living Arrangements" survey of current status and views of Japanese elderly. The survey was

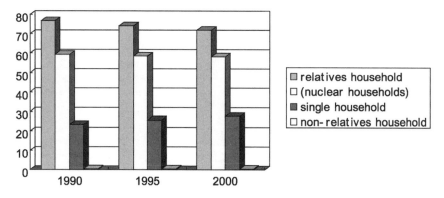

Figure 12.7   Types of Households in Japan 1990–2000

Source: Statistics Bureau, *Population Census,* various years. Note: Relatives' households include nuclear households.

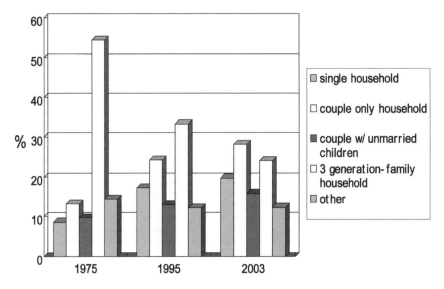

Figure 12.8   Households with Persons Age 65 and Over by Type in Japan 1975–2003

Source: MHLW, *Comprehensive Survey of Living Conditions of the People on Health and Welfare,* 2003.

conducted in Tokorozawa City, located in central Japan. Details of the survey are shown in Table 12.1.

According to the survey results, "Living Arrangements" of the elderly in Tokorozawa are as follows, compared with the data for Japan. Total

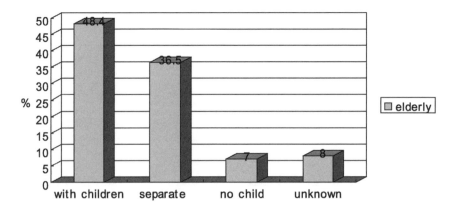

Figure 12.9   Distribution of Elderly by Living Arrangements, 2001, Japan

Source: MHLW, *Comprehensive Survey of Living Conditions of the People on Health and Welfare,* 2001.

Table 12.1   Tokorozawa Survey on Living Arrangements

Research topic	Intergenerational living arrangements
Purpose	Survey of current status and consciousness of elderly about living arrangements
Period	January to February 2004
Survey area	Tokorozawa City
Age of respondents	60 years old and over
Sample	590
Valid sample	261 (44%)
Sampling method	Random sampling
Method of survey	Interview with questionnaire

elderly households in the Tokorozawa survey were divided into four categories: single households, 11.9 percent; couple-only households, 37.5 percent; living-with-children households, 46.7 percent; and other, 4.2 percent. Living-with-children households were broken down further into living-with-unmarried-children households, 29.1 percent, and living-with-married-children households, 17.6 percent. This latter category equates to three-generation family households (Figure 12.10).

A part of the survey results shows the elderly's views on living arrangements, including intergenerational exchange, family life, and life satisfaction.

We asked, "In general, which living arrangement with children is desirable for the elderly?" The survey found that elderly who prefer to live in the same house with their children account for 29.1 percent, same housing site 14.2 percent, same neighborhood 38.7 percent, and same town 3.4 percent (Figure 12.11).

We questioned them about daily intergenerational exchanges between elderly and their children. About 50 percent of the elderly and their children often make phone calls to each other. However, 50 percent of the elderly will give money to their children, but only 10 percent of children give money to their elderly parents. Regarding the sharing of food, consulting about crucial problems, and so on, elderly also do so more than the children. With regard to medical support and transport to the hospital, children do more than the elderly. So we can say that cooperating and helping each other in daily life issues is widely observed.

How do the elderly view family and their relation with children? We asked about opinions and present six selected statements here: first, "When parents become old, their children should provide for their living expenses." Almost 20 percent of the elderly agree with this statement. Second, "Parents should take care of their grandchildren, if their children desire it." Just over 64 percent of the elderly agreed with this statement. Third, "When children have their own families, parents should try not to live in the same house."

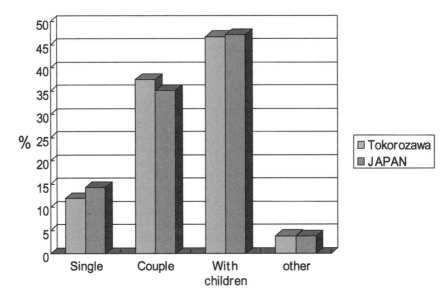

Figure 12.10   Living Arrangements of Elderly, Tokorozawa vs Japan

Source: For Tokorozawa: Waseda University, *Preliminary Results of Tokorozawa Survey,* forthcoming. For Japan: MHLW, *Comprehensive Survey of Living Conditions of the People on Health and Welfare,* 2003. Note for "With children": Tokorozawa, 17.6% + 29.1% (married + unmarried children); Japan, 26.1% + 20.9% (married + unmarried children).

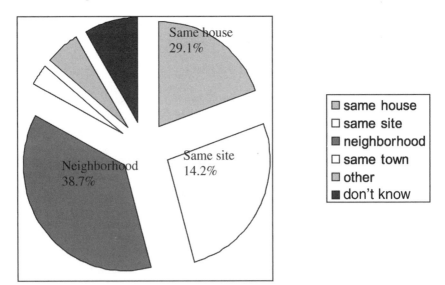

Figure 12.11   Preferences of the Elderly in Living Arrangements

Source: Waseda University, *Preliminary Results of Tokorozawa Survey,* forthcoming.

Fifty-two percent of the elderly agreed with this statement. Fourth, "Elderly people should be economically independent, rather than depending on their children." We found 85.5 percent of the elderly in agreement with this statement. So, the elderly become and want to be more independent from their children in terms of family life. But contrary to these responses, 40.6 percent of the elderly agreed with the statement that "the eldest son has a special role in family." Finally, "It is best to place priority on the family first." Just over 90 percent of elderly agreed with this statement.

With regard to life satisfaction, we found that 31 percent of the elderly answered "satisfied" and 59 percent of elderly answered "fairly satisfied" (moderately) (see Figure 12.12).

According to the "Five Nations Survey"[11] conducted by the Cabinet Office every five years, other nations demonstrate very similar results, as shown in Figure 12.13.

Other results from the "Five Nations Survey" show the difference between Asian societies and Western societies in terms of views on living arrangements for the elderly. As examined by the nationwide survey results in Figure 12.8, the number of elderly single households is increasing rapidly in Japan. According to the "Five Nations Survey," single households account for about 10 percent of all households, but in Western countries the rate is between 35 and 40 percent, as indicated in Figure 12.14.

The "Five Nations Survey" also asks a question about intergenerational exchange, "How do you keep company with children or grandchildren in

Figure 12.12   Life Satisfaction of Elderly

Source: Waseda University, *Preliminary Results of Tokorozawa Survey,* forthcoming.

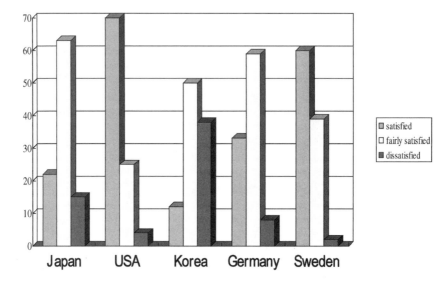

Figure 12.13　Life Satisfaction of Elderly (Five Nations Survey)

Source: Cabinet Office, *Report of International Comparative Survey on the Daily Life and Opinion of the Elderly,* 2001.

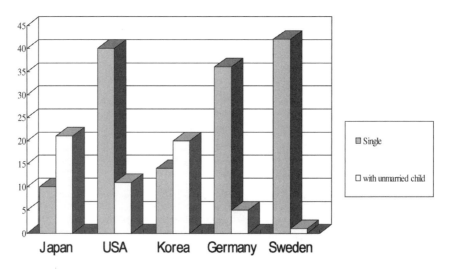

Figure 12.14　Living Arrangements of Elderly (Five Nations Survey, partial results)

Source: Cabinet Office, *Report of International Comparative Survey on the Daily Life and Opinion of the Elderly,* 2001.

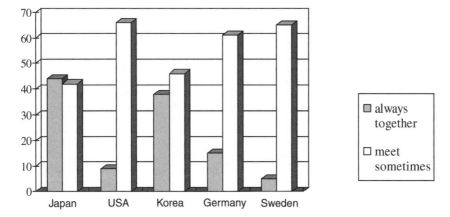

Figure 12.15   How to Keep Company with Child or Grandchild (Five Nations Survey, partial results)

Source: Cabinet Office, *Report of International Comparative Survey on the Daily Life and Opinion of the Elderly,* 2001.

daily life?" In Western Countries, a small number of the elderly agreed with the option of "stay or live together always" (Figure 12.15). According to the survey results cited here, despite the similarity in socioeconomic features between Japanese and Western countries, their views on living arrangements of the elderly are significantly different.

Living Arrangements Survey Analysis—Dual Scaling Method

This section utilizes the dual scaling method to examine the relationship between the actual living arrangements of the elderly and their values and views on family and long-term care. The results are shown in tables and by plotting maps of each variable. The relative distance between variables signifies the strength of the relationship between them.

Regarding a desirable living place, the category of living with married children households is equated to the variable "same house." Single households and couple only households were considered equivalent to the categories of "neighborhood" and "same city/town" (Table 12.2 and Figure 12.16).

As for the views of the elderly on the parent-child relationship, we asked seven questions on the subjects shown on the right side of Figure 12.17. The number in parentheses is the variable number in the plotting map shown as Figure 12.17 (with Table 12.3. For better context and conceptualization, Figure 12.17 also presents the statements mentioned above in connection with Figure 12.11.

First, "When parents become old, their children should provide for living expense": 19.6 percent of the elderly agreed with this statement. Second,

Table 12.2 Solution by Dual Scaling Method / Actual Living Arrangements and Desirable Living Arrangements (see Figure 12.16 for mapping of variables)

Solution	Same house	Same town	Different region
Correlation ratio	0.3608	0.0321	0.0013
Max. correlation ratio	0.6007	0.1793	0.0357
Contribution	91.53	8.15	0.32
Cumulative contribution	91.53	99.68	100.00

"Parents should take care of their grandchildren, if their children desire it": 64.3 percent of the elderly agreed with this statement. Third, "When children have their own families, parents should try not to live in the same house": to which 52.1 percent of elderly agreed. Fourth, "Elderly people should be economically independent, rather than depending on their children": 85.5 percent of elderly agreed. Fifth, "It is best to place priority on the family first": 90.4 percent of the elderly agreed with this statement. Sixth, "In general, family ties are becoming less strong these days": 68.6 percent of the elderly agreed. So, in total, the elderly have become more independent from children in terms of family life, but on the other hand, 40.6 percent of the elderly agreed with the statement that "The eldest son has a special role in

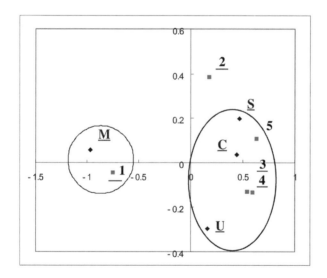

Figure 12.16 Desirable Living Arrangements for the Elderly

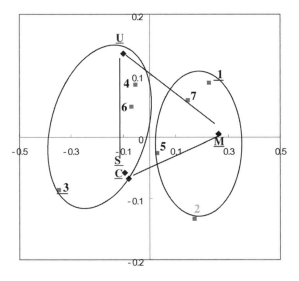

1 child should expense
2 care of grandchild
3 not in the same house
4 economic independent
5 family first
6 family ties are weak
7 first son has the role

Figure 12.17   Attitude to Parent-Child Relationship

family." According to these frequencies of response and the analysis by the dual scaling method, the elderly in the living-with-married-children household regard the parent-child relationship as most important, but the elderly in other types of households have more of an attitude of independence and/or self-help (see Figure 12.18 and Table 12.4).

In Japan, as in most aged countries in the world, the problem of caring for the elderly is an important policy agenda item. According to our survey results, the elderly in living-with-married-children households still hope to be cared for by their sons' wives.

Table 12.3   Solution by Dual Scaling Method / Actual Living Arrangements and Attitude to Parent-Child Relationship (see Figure 12.17 for mapping of variables)

Solution	Same house	Same town	Different region
Correlation ratio	0.0240	0.0063	0.0011
Max. correlation ratio	0.1550	0.0793	0.0326
Contribution	76.56	20.05	3.39
Cumulative contribution	76.56	96.61	100.00

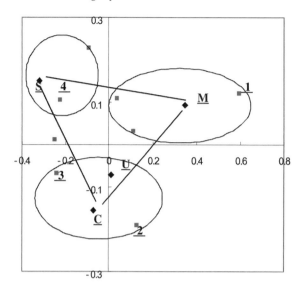

1 son's wife
2 spouse
3 home care
4 institutional care

Figure 12.18　Who is best suited to be in charge of "Long Term Care" for the Elderly?

Conclusion

We conclude with a note concerning the living arrangements of the elderly in Japan and Asia. In accordance with the population aging perspective in Japan, there has been and will continue to be great changes in living arrangements. The average size of household in Japan is shrinking and, for the elderly, single (one person) households and couple-only household sizes are increasing. One of the main factors in these changes is the internal shift in social values and views on family and parent-child relationships. The other factor is an external, demographic one, corollary to the first. Population aging and the low birth rate as well as the increase of delayed or never married persons have and will continue to affect the living arrangements of families in Japan.

Table 12.4　Solution by Dual Scaling Method / Actual Living Arrangements and Views on Long-term Care (see Figure 12.18 for mapping of variables)

Solution	Same house	Same town	Different region
Correlation ratio	0.0565	0.0152	0.0086
Max. correlation ratio	0.2378	0.1231	0.0927
Contribution	70.41	18.88	10.71
Cumulative contribution	70.41	89.29	100.00

Not only in Japan, but also in other Asian countries, there will be further changes in the living arrangements of the elderly, as the effects of industrialization and urbanization continue into the future. Researchers, therefore, need to continue to study the factors related to household changes and living arrangements to better understand which households or living arrangements will improve the quality of life for the elderly.

As for Japan, a very large age-cohort called "Dankai-no-Sedai," the Baby Boomers, will be over sixty-five years of age after 2015. Their impact on Japanese society will be great. Their views and values will be new and different from those of today's elderly, because they were born after WWII and were educated under the new school system of democratic Japan after WWII. We may have to deal with unexpected social changes in the near future. Therefore, we must conduct more social research relating to the family and the elderly in order to contribute positively to family and population policy and to truly realize "Family First Societies" in Japan and Asia.

Presented at the Asia-Pacific Dialogue
Kuala Lumpur, Malaysia, October 2004.

Endnotes

1. H. Sagaza, *The Determinants and Consequences of Population Ageing in Asia,* Comparative Studies on Ageing in Asia, Research Paper Series no. 4, Waseda University, 2004.

2. Statistics Bureau (Japan), http://www.stat.go.jp/data/jinsui/tsuki/index.htm (accessed 10 February 2005).

3. G.R. Andrews, "Research Directions in the Region: Past, Present and Future," in *Ageing in East and South-east Asia,* ed. D.R. Phillips (London: Edward Arnold, 1992).

4. T. Usui, *Approaches and Issues for International Comparative Research on the Households of the Elderly,* Comparative Studies on Ageing in Asia, Research Paper Series no. 1, Waseda University, 2004.

5. K. Tout, *Ageing in Developing Countries* (New York: Oxford University Press, 1989).

6. A. Chan, "The Social and Economic Consequences of Ageing in Asia." Special Issue, *Southeast Asian Journal of Social Science, 27,* no. 2 (1999).

7. United Nations, *Living Arrangements of Older Persons: Critical Issues and Political Responses,* New York. See also Advanced Research Center for Human Sciences, *A Bibliography of the Intergenerational Living Arrangements and the Quality of Life among Older Persons in East and Southeast Asia,* Waseda University, Tokyo, 2003.

8. H. Tanada, "Population Problem in Greater Asia" (in Japanese), *AJIA SHINSEIKI [Asia's New Century],* Vol. 8 (Tokyo: Iwanami Shoten, 2003).

9. H. Sagaza, *Changes in Living Arrangements and Households of the Elderly in Japan,* Comparative Studies on Ageing in Asia, Research Paper Series no. 2, Waseda University, 2004.

10. H. Sagaza, "Living Arrangements of the Elderly in Japan," in *Aging in Japan 2003,* Japan Aging Research Center, 2003. The author included the latest data for 2003.

11. Cabinet Office, *Report of International Comparative Survey on the Daily Life and Opinion of the Elderly,* 2001.

Bibliography

Bongaarts, J. "The End of Fertility Transition in the Developing World." *Policy Research Division Working Papers (Population Council),* 161 (2002).

Chan, A., and J. DaVanzo. "Ethnic Differences in Parents' Coresidence with Adult Children in Peninsular Malaysia." *Journal of Cross-Cultural Gerontology, 11,* no. 1 (1996).

Davanzo, J., and A. Chan. "Living Arrangements of Older Malaysians: Who coresides with their adult children?" *Demography, 31,* no. 1 (1994).

East-West Center, *The Future of Population in Asia.* Honolulu: East-West Center, 2002.

Ngin, C., and J. DaVanzo. "Parent-Child Coresidence and Quasi-Coresidence in Peninsular Malaysia." *Southeast Asian Journal of Social Science, 27,* no. 2 (1999).

Phillips, David R. (ed.). *Ageing in the Asia-Pacific Region.* London: Routledge, 2000.

Sagaza, H. "Koureika to Seisakutektaiou" (in Japanese) ["Ageing and Administrative Policy"]. N. Ishi and Y. Hayase (eds.). *Ajiano Jinkou Mondai [Population Problem in Asia].* Tokyo: Taimeidou, 2000.

Seetharam, K.S. "Half a Century of Unparalleled Demographic Change: the Asia-Pacific Experience." *Asia-Pacific Population Journal, 17,* no. 4 (December 2002).

United Nations, *World Population Prospects. The 2000 Revision,* vols. 1,2,3, 2001.

United Nations, *World Urbanization Prospects. The 2001 Revision,* 2002.

United Nations, *World Population Prospects. The 2002 Revision,* vols. 1,2, 2003.

13

Sex Differences: Nature's Signposts to a Good Marriage

Steven E. Rhoads (USA)
Professor of Politics
University of Virginia, Virginia, USA

Introduction

Although my topic is marriage, I want to look first at infancy and childhood. At those stages of life we can observe male and female differences before socialization may have created them, and thus we get some sense of what differences are innate. These deep-rooted differences will in turn reveal issues in marriage.

My comments will focus on *most* girls and *most* women, *most* boys and *most* men. There are, of course, exceptions to my generalizations. An important theme of my recent book (Rhoads 2004) is that the exceptions are particularly important for understanding females.

Compared to most women, a minority of women is more ambitious about careers, more assertive, and less interested in babies. They are more interested in sex. On average this group of women has been exposed to higher than average amounts of testosterone *en utero,* and they have higher levels of testosterone as adults as well (Rhoads 2004, 29–32). The very assertiveness of this subgroup of women gives them disproportionate influence in public debates about what women want. But in this chapter they must remain in the background. I focus here on what most women and men are like and on how those tendencies affect marriage.

Sex Differences in Children and Youth

In his book, *The Essential Difference,* Simon Baron-Cohen notes that one-day-old baby girls look longer at a picture of a human face, whereas boys look longer at an oval shape with weird alien-like features. Similarly, one-day-old female infants cry longer than male infants when they hear the sound of other crying infants (Rhoads 2004, 197). Baron-Cohen marshals many other kinds of evidence suggesting that females have an empathizing brain. They are more attuned to other people. To take another example, at just twelve months baby girls "respond more empathetically to the distress of other people, showing greater concern for others through more sad looks, sympathetic vocalizations, and comforting behavior" (Baron-Cohen 2003, 31). Grown women also comfort strangers more and are more likely than men to report that they share the emotional distress of friends.

Girls like cooperation more than boys do and competition less. They care about playmates' feelings more than boys do, and they can read others' emotions better than boys. Girls like one-on-one relationships, and they say sweet, affirming things to friends and put their arms around them. They bond through confiding talk. Girls play house, and their pretend play involves "more cooperative role playing" (Baron-Cohen, 460)—for example, with one person playing the mommy and the other the child. Their fantasy play often involves being a bride (Rhoads, 21).

Boys are more self-centered. They have a harder time learning to share; they act up more and are less likely to be team players in school. Boys develop strong passions for particular things, and the passions seem to arise out of nowhere. They are not necessarily based at all on parents' interests—and they change through time. A boy might be unable to get enough of cars, trucks, or tractors, and then of dinosaurs, soccer, music, or computers. A boy might learn the names of and collect cars and tractors, then pore over all the minutiae of soccer or baseball statistics, and later begin to compile pop music charts (Baron-Cohen, Chaps. 2, 4, 6).

Boys' interactions with others are based on activities that each values. They travel in packs, and there are frequently attempts to assert dominance. Boys have a clearer idea of who is dominant in their group. In summer camp, boys who would be leaders will often jump on and insult other boys right away to assert dominance. Girls at summer camp will build friendships for a week before subtly asserting dominance by verbal put-downs. Though social dominance is a goal for girls, it is not allowed to get in the way of intimacy with friends. Boys' dominance hierarchies tend to last all summer, whereas girls are more fluid, with girls often breaking up into groups of two or three who talk among themselves in an intimate way (Baron-Cohen, 38–42).

When boys and girls reach puberty, they begin to interact more, and the sex differences in mixed groups become less apparent. Boys, for example, learn that girls do not like to trade insults as boys do, so in mixed company sex differences can be hidden. After all, we men do not get to see how all female groups interact, nor do women get to see how all male groups behave. But scholars can observe and compare, and the differences can be striking. Whenever researchers separate the sexes, the differences become starker. For example, male prisons tend to develop "hierarchies of power and coercion," while in female prisons the women often form make-believe families in which prisoners are designated father, mother, aunt, daughter, son, and the like (Rasche 1991, 46; Mishra 1997; Dabbs and Dabbs 2000, 79). This is a particularly striking example of the female need for bonding and connection.

Surveys also show the female desire for connection and intimacy. When you ask *unmarried, childless* women what is most important to their happiness, they are five times more likely to cite personal relationships with their mothers (31 percent) or friends (24 percent) than they are to cite their careers (11 percent) (Pew Research Center Survey 1997; Bowman 1998, 24).

When you put it all together, it is hard to avoid the conclusion that females care most about emotionally close relationships (Baron-Cohen, 38–42).

Sex

When boys and girls start to interact more after puberty, they have very different orientations. Increases in estrogen and other female hormones make girls more social. They begin to spend more time with other people. On the other hand, Theresa Crenshaw, coauthor of a leading text on sexual pharmacology says that testosterone has a "loner profile." As boys reach puberty, they begin to spend more time alone (Rhoads, 50).

When girls go through puberty, the combination of hormones and their long-standing desire for strong intimate relationships often leads them to be boy crazy. As preteens, girls often spend hours reading romantic fiction or playing board games about dating and boys.

The girls are interested in relationships that may lead to physical contact, whereas boys are more interested in sex, frequently with a variety of partners. They are less interested in relationships and commitment.

The analysis to this point is more than sufficient to suggest that pubescent girls should be taught to be wary about boys' intentions. Several studies have noted the precipitous rise in depression rates in young teenage females. Research suggests that the depression is often preceded by the breakup of a sexual relationship that the girl, at least, saw as romantic (Joyner and Udry 2000; Meier, forthcoming).

Sexual restraint protects pubescent girls from depression, but it is also self-protective for young teens and women in their twenties and thirties. College coeds may experiment with casual sex these days, but despite their sexually liberated *attitudes,* in time they almost always find that their emotions make casual sex unattractive. They come to feel used, hurt, and demeaned after sleeping with men uninterested in relationships (Rhoads 2004, 102–105).

Women who cohabit are also vulnerable. For example, one study reveals that "women tend to see [living together] as a step toward marriage, while men regard it more as a sexual opportunity without the ties of long-term commitment" (Rhoads, 112–113).

When teenage girls come to realize that what they thought were relationships were for boys just sexual opportunities, and when twenty-something women go through cohabitations that do not lead to the expected marriages, they become hardened. In my book I discuss evidence for the proposition that since the sexual revolution women are more likely to think poorly of men (Rhoads, 118–120). These changes in women's outlooks and attitudes will have an impact on marriage. Women loaded with this kind of emotional *baggage* are not so likely to become loving wives.

And there is a more important reason why female sexual restraint can make stronger marriages. Premarital restraint builds trust, and the old-fashioned courtship dance involves a pledge of mutual fidelity. Writer Mary Elizabeth Podles explains this well:

> In serious courtship, a man conveys to a woman that if she is worth all this trouble to court, she must be worth more than any other mate in the world, and shall henceforth be The One Woman. On her part, the woman promises that if she was this hard for him to get, surely she will, as his wife, be impossible for others to get. The courtship dance is the unspoken pledge of future fidelity—the best of all bases for a happy marriage (Podles 1997; Buss 1994, 116).

The Problems Sex Differences Pose for Marriage

Marriage, then, brings together two very different kinds of creatures. Young women really "get" marriage. They have always been more attracted to people than to things. They love strong, long-term relationships. The marital ideal—one man and one woman bound in body and soul—sharing, comforting, and communicating through good times and bad is very appealing. This vision includes romantic and committed sex along with children, to whom most women have been drawn since childhood and who seem even more precious once pregnancy and breast-feeding bathe women in hormonal pleasure (Rhoads 2004, chaps. 2, 8).

Young men, on the other hand, are used to seeing human interactions in competitive terms. They are more single-minded, which makes them more selfish and less attuned to the needs of others (Baron-Cohen 2003, chap. 4; Rhoads, chap. 2). In our culture we have made things worse because men are used to getting sexual access without any courtship. Courtship—taking a date out for dinner or a movie, entertaining her—is a way of making a man less selfish. To be successful at courting, a man has to pay attention to what his date likes.

We have abandoned not just courtship but chivalry and good manners. Feminists who seek an androgynous world have cheered these developments on. Men used to stand when women came in the room. They held doors and chairs for their dates or their wives. They always made sure that their date had a drink before they got one. At least that is how my mother told me I should behave. Now feminists have long railed against occupational patterns: the men are the bosses; the women are their secretaries. The men are the doctors; the women are the nurses. Why, some feminists ask, are men primary while women are helpers?

Courtship, however, involved customs that made women primary and men their servants. But feminists did not like this either. I have had very nice young women tell me that they can open their own doors and ask, if opening doors is a courtesy, why they should not be able to show it to men. The effect is, however, that men stop opening doors because they do not know if women want them to do so. We lose another opportunity to get men to be less selfish by paying attention to other people's needs and desires.

Because so much of women's happiness is dependent on strong, loving connections to others, they are more vulnerable when trouble arises in marriages. One study of full-time dual-career couples finds that problems at work increase psychological distress equally for men and women, but that problems in the marriage lead to much more distress for women than for men. Women's vulnerability affects their physical health as well as their mental health. When wives perceive that their family and marriage are not going well, their blood pressure goes up. When husbands perceive trouble, their blood pressure does not increase, but the husband's perception of trouble will send his wife's blood pressure up. Similarly, after having an argument with her spouse, a woman's immune function decreases much more than a man's, and changes persist for at least twenty-four hours (Rhoads, 255).

No wonder women are more likely to be the peacemakers in families. Researchers who put recorders in dining rooms find that mothers are the most likely to deflect an unpleasant quarrel during family meals and that daughters are the next most likely to serve this role (Thompson and Walker 1989, 849). Teresa Crenshaw explains as follows: "mellowing [females] are their relatively high levels of serotonin compared to the male, oxytocin in abundant supply, and estrogen, a gentle, ordinarily soothing antidepressant hormone" (Crenshaw 1996, 184).

Feminists on Marriage

Now, to this point, the picture of marriage that I have painted is not terribly pretty. Maybe we should look again at the reasons why feminists have been so critical of marriage. They say that marriage is all about patriarchy and male power. Men have constructed an institution in which women will not be happy unless they are the ones who submit within the family. Feminists say that women must come to realize that they can be equal only if they equal men's power in the market place. In the feminist journal *Ms.* one family therapist sets forth her golden rule of marriage: "Whoever has the gold makes the rules" (Rhoads 2004, 261).

The feminists may have spotted a problem, but they surely have not pointed us to the solution. In fact, more earned income does not necessarily equal more power in a marriage. One review article reports that, at home, wives with high-achieving careers, especially the younger ones, "attempt to be especially attractive and sexual for their husbands, and they report indulging husbands' whims and salving egos" (Thompson and Walker 1989, 857).

Even if higher income were the recipe for greater marital power, research shows that wives are especially unhappy in wife-dominated marriages (Gray-Little and Burks 1983; Weisfeld et al. 1992). The dominated husband often just tunes out and focuses on other things. Since the marriage is so important to the wife's happiness, she becomes miserable. Evidently marriage cannot be seen as a struggle for power or economic influence in which the winner gains happiness.

Taking Sex Differences Seriously

Let us take another look at marriage and male power within marriage. First, it is not so clear that women resent their mate's power. Women want a man who shows strength in the outside world. They want a man who can provide for them and protect them. They also want a strong man for their intimate partner. One researcher on sexuality has noted that the

> intense desire for contact and cuddling seems so much stronger in women than in men. [When being held by your mate] you feel completely content, safe and sound. There is submission and dependence, born of trust. Allowing yourself to be held requires dropping all pretense, relaxing, and becoming vulnerable (Crenshaw 1996, 113, 116).

Alice Rossi, a prominent feminist and sociologist, says she suspects that "even the most ardent feminist, in her innermost heart, would feel more positive about being comforted with her head on the shoulder of a male than she would about comforting a man whose head was on her shoulder" (Rossi 1995, 186–187). Another female author believes that "women don't want to be dependent on men considered as a group," but they "feel it is sexy to be dependent on the particular man they have chosen" (Marlowe 2000).

Women want to tame the male competitiveness and strength and channel it; they do not want to wipe it out. The romance novel, the most popular of all mass market genres, shows this process in book after book (Rhoads 2004, 68). Male competitiveness and toughness can protect families and help civilize sons, so its attractions to women are not just atavistic, even in this enlightened age.

Second, taming and channeling really can work, and they start with the wedding bells. Testosterone is associated with aggressiveness. But when men marry, their testosterone levels go down; when married men have children, their levels go down again (Booth et al. 2000, 1027, 1029; Parke and Brott 1999, 20; Gallagher and Waite 2000, 53–55; Daly and Wilson 1999, 14). And when men have children, they come to care about them, and this makes them more social. Problems with school quality or drug use among teens no longer seem so abstract. The Parent and Teacher Associations (PTA's) at their kids' schools have new attractions.

Third, though women are harmed more by troubled marriages, they seem to gain more from good ones. One study asked couples to do three things: talk for five minutes about a situation that brought them closer together; then watch a romantic video; then give each other a big hug. The study found that women's oxytocin rose much more than that of their male partners (Ellas 2004).

Oxytocin tends to make one healthier and happier. It makes one less anxious, more calm and relaxed. It lowers levels of the stress hormone norepinephrine, and it lowers blood pressure. Sarah Hrdy, author of a landmark 700-page book on mothers and infants, calls oxytocin "the kindest of natural opiates" (Rhoads, 197–202).

Since women seem to gain more from good marriages and lose more from bad ones, they may have a little more at stake in making them good ones. So they tend to work harder at them. But really, as we have seen above, women work harder at *all* relationships because emotionally close relationships are the secret to their happiness.

In her book *Sex on the Brain,* Deborah Blum reports on the views of Ellen Frank, a researcher at the University of Pittsburgh:

> Women are genetically preprogrammed to be more affiliative. Interpersonal attachment is a bigger deal for women than men, and that's true in all cultures and times. It has an adaptive significance for the survival of the species. If women didn't attach, babies wouldn't survive.…If we have one half of the human race that's more preprogrammed for attachment, then that's the half that's going to be more vulnerable (Blum 1997, 217).

Feminists are right that women are more vulnerable, but as Frank notes, it is nature that makes them so, not men or patriarchy.

The modern marriage of two professionals can be relatively androgynous. The routines and concerns of husband and wife can be similar. But all this changes once pregnancy and babies enter the picture. In many ways pregnancy and babies make women vulnerable, and it was not patriarchy that determined that females would have the babies.

A Mother's Vulnerability: How Children Change Marital Dynamics

There are not many professionals who do not face stress at the office, and there is preliminary but accumulating evidence that stress is not good for the fetal brain (Rhoads 2004, 213; Olbermann 2005). Moreover, working leads to more exposure to germs, which can lead to respiratory infections like the flu. For pregnant women, flu can increase the risk to the fetus of developing devastating conditions. Children whose mothers had a respiratory infection during the middle three months of pregnancy, for example, have double the risk of developing schizophrenia, a condition affecting about 1 percent of the population (Rhoads, 214).

The effects of mothers' mental and physical health on their developing fetuses are just beginning to become widely known. But pregnant women do not need to be told that they are themselves more vulnerable. Women in the midst of a normal pregnancy are subject to a number of maladies. One obstetrics text calls nausea and vomiting, backache, and heartburn "common conditions." Fatigue is even more commonplace, affecting about three-quarters of all pregnant women. Postpartum fatigue is equally normal.

Two different studies have found that at six months postpartum more than 75 percent of mothers have not achieved full functional status. One study specifically asked about daily activities that were limited because the mother was "tired or felt poorly"; 40 to 50 percent of mothers responded that six months after giving birth, they were "accomplishing less than usual," "not performing as carefully as usual," "limiting work or other activities," and "requiring extra effort to perform work and activities."

The studies that specifically focus on working women with babies at home reach strong conclusions. One finds that more than 75 percent of the women who were back at work did not feel they were functioning at full capacity. A second study finds that employed women have "diminished levels of well-being...approximately 7 months after childbirth." A third study finds that "women who had taken more than 24 weeks maternity leave had better mental health outcomes at 9 and 12 months postpartum. Mental outlook was also brighter for women who spent fewer hours at their job" (Rhoads, 212–216).

After they have kids most women would prefer not to work or to work only part time (Rhoads, 248–250; Erickson and Aird 2005). They are typically less willing than men to spend whole days away from their children. They want to see the first steps and hear the first words, and they feel guilty and anxious if they spend ten-hour days away from their young children.

Of all the moving stories I encountered in researching my book, none are more poignant than those related by prominent politicians who are also mothers and who reflected on their dual roles. Madeleine Kunin, governor of Vermont, tells a fascinating political story in her autobiography. But Kunin says she was tormented at being governor while she was the mother of four children. "At least once a day," Kunin remembers, "I would feel a stab in my chest, thinking I should be at one place when I was at another." There was no cure for the anxiety; all she could do, she says, was "not to let it overwhelm me, not to let it pull me down, but to carry it as gracefully as I could."

Kunin's pain was not just from anxiety and guilt. It was also from longing to be at home for special occasions. During a campaign she came home to find that her family had already blown out her child's birthday candles. She had them do it over again so she could participate (Rhoads, 234, 237).

This long discussion of women, pregnancy, and babies is prologue to my fourth point about marriage. Feminists hate the idea that women need paternalistic protection. But they do. A pregnant woman needs to avoid stress; a postpartum woman needs time to fully recover and to nurse; and a mother wants and needs lots of time to spend with her children. She cannot do these things without a husband who will help take care of her so that she can be a healthy and happy mother.

Women who become mothers know that things have changed and that they are now dependent on their husbands in a way that they never were before. Second-wave feminist Naomi Wolf describes how pregnancy and childbirth transformed her. "The ways in which the hormones of pregnancy affected me called into question my entire belief system about 'the social construction of gender.'" Wolf admits to feeling clingier, weepier, and "stupidly domestic." She felt a "childlike surge of need for repetitive, utterly simple affirmations that I was—that we, the baby and I, were—not going to be abandoned" (Wolf 2002, 115–16).

When I read this passage in a talk at a convention, a University of Pennsylvania medical student sent me an e-mail saying,

> Reluctantly, I agreed that your work has merit. Scenarios flashed like bad cinema before my eyes, i.e. looking out the window, waiting for the appearance of one's husband to return home from work was a behavior worthy of my contempt...before my first baby was born.

If loyal, loving, and providing fathers go to work and come home every day, wives can be happy. If fathers are not loyal and loving, and if they refuse to provide, mothers' lives will be dramatically worse. Because mothers love and need their husbands, they typically work hard at making marriages work. They often act vulnerable, and their immune function and blood pressure respond accordingly because they are, in fact, vulnerable. Any creatures who get their happiness from intimate connection to other human beings are necessarily vulnerable because their well-being is dependent on the character, good fortune, and good will of those they love.

The Route to Happier Marriages

Feminists grasp the principal marital problem that needs solving—unchecked male dominance. But they do not have a clue about how deep its roots go or about how to solve it. If you ask men how they would like to be described, they use words like *dominant, assertive, independent.* Women asked the same question say *loving, generous, sensitive* (Rhoads 2004, 18–19). If marriage means bringing together one person with a taste for assertion and another with a taste for generosity, unchecked male dominance is a worrisome possibility.

But the problem is best solvable when women are true to their natures. An unmarried man in his late twenties is incomplete. His cronies are married off and moving away. Without shared activities with them he can be very lonely. Most important, he needs a purpose. Women may need a good marriage, but men need almost any kind of marriage. Their health and happiness rise with marriage; even their sex life improves.

Women need to make men slow down and give time a chance to turn their lust into love. And men will respond if loving, generous, and sensitive women—feminine women—are willing to show the vulnerability that the birth of their children later make clear to them. When a man sees vulnerability or neediness in a woman he loves, he can come riding to the rescue. He has found his purpose.

Institutions can help turn men into good fathers. One way to get men to dominate less and be open to their wives' influence is to create what Brad Wilcox calls "soft patriarchs." Such figures can be found in conservative

Protestant churches, which urge husbands to be "servant leaders" who attend to their wives' needs for communication and affection as well as to the family's needs for economic wherewithal and moral leadership (Wilcox 2004). While the emotional work of marriage may not be inherently pleasurable or come naturally to men, it can become central to their lives if it is seen as a duty or as intrinsic to a mission. (Men hate to iron, but even a Marine, who typically loves risk-taking and excitement, can take to ironing his dress uniform with attentive skill) (Moir and Moir 1999, 251).

The Protestant churches that Wilcox describes appeal to men by giving them a sense of importance and reminding them of their sacred obligation to use their familial power to serve their families. They appeal to the male sense of honor by encouraging the husband to imagine himself in a central, heroic role. Just as Christ sacrificed himself for the sake of others, husbands must be ready to sacrifice themselves for their wives and children. By making the male role in marriage vital, these churches make it more attractive to men, and by condemning extramarital sex, they make alternatives to marriage less attractive and less available.

A more secular approach might challenge men by pointing to the importance of biological fathers to the healthy development of children. Civilization needs family-oriented men. If we took sex differences seriously, we would not be looking for new ways to weaken the historic role of men in the family. By challenging the titular familial leadership of the male and undermining the centrality of his role as provider for his family, modernity has reduced the number of men to whom marriage seems desirable. But the titular familial leadership of the male survives. The Census Bureau used to ask, "Who is the head of the household?" Perhaps they expected to get less patriarchal answers when they changed the question to a nearly incomprehensible "Who is the 'family householder?'" (Presser 1998; Carlson 2003). In 1994, nevertheless, 91 percent of American couples said it was the husband.

Wives doubtful about whether to grant titular household leadership to husbands should realize they may not have to give up much more than the title. Some studies have shown that husbands overestimate their decision-making power, while wives underestimate theirs. Yet an early study "found that the most satisfied husbands were those who believed they had the greater decision-making power even where there was no independent evidence of it" (Weisfeld et al. 1992).

Men cannot be happy if their wives are overwhelmed as they scramble to cope with both work and family. Frantic wives tell husbands they are failing as providers and protectors. If I am right about what women value most—emotionally close relationships—they give up less than feminists claim when they cut back on or abandon their careers when their children are young.

One 1997 national survey of women by the Pew Research Center found that 93 percent of mothers regard their children as a source of happiness all or most of the time; 90 percent say the same about their marriage. Meanwhile, only 60 percent of working women find their careers to be a source of happiness all or most of the time. On a 10-point scale, 86 percent of mothers rate their children a 10 for their importance to personal happiness; just 30 percent of employed women rate their job as a 10 (Pew Research Center Survey 1997; Bowman 1998, 24).

A brilliant paper by my colleagues Brad Wilcox and Steve Nock (2006) shows that feminists get female marital happiness almost exactly wrong. Wives' marital happiness is not dependent on their marketplace income but on their husbands' "emotion work." When wives report that they are happy with the love, affection, and understanding shown by their husbands, wives report happiness with their marriages. The wives happiest with the love and affection shown by their husbands do not work outside the home. Moreover, wives who make more than 33 percent of total household income report lower marital happiness.

It seems that women with no income of their own do *not*, in fact, get pushed around by dominance-seeking men. Instead, they create happy men who feel needed and who cherish their wives. Despite their physical strength and assertive natures, men in marriage do not have all the power in marriage. They often do not even have most of the power. It is still quite common to hear of small, feminine women who have their strong, masculine husbands "wrapped around their little fingers." Happy women usually rule indirectly. They can rule because their husbands love and want to please them. They can also rule because, as positron emission tomography scans of male and female brains have demonstrated, women can read men better than men can read women (Rhoads, 262).

I once heard the University of Chicago law professor Richard Epstein give a talk in which he explained that his father made all the big decisions in his family. He decided, for example, what the family's position would be on going to war in Korea or on the United States joining the UN. His mother only made the little decisions—where the family would live, where the kids would go to school, where the family would go on vacation—small stuff like that. When I ask my classes who makes these "little" decisions in their families, most of them report that their mothers do.

In most single earner families women have lots of power. For example, they usually have more freedom to organize their days than do their working husbands (Graglia 1998, 57, 89, 112–113). Unlike their husbands, they do give up workplace power. But for most men this does not amount to a whole lot. Most men answer to some boss every working day of their lives.

Besides, most women do not care so much about workplace power and status (Rhoads, 61–66). They tend to warm to a subtle kind of female power— "the force that creates relationships, binds families and builds societies" (Moir and Jessel 1989, 129)

Androgynous feminists focus on a quantifiable marital power. They assume that men and women are alike and thus should share housework and child care equally. But, as we have seen, they are not alike. Mothers are loaded with estrogen and oxytocin, which draw them to young children and help induce them to tend to infants. Men are loaded with testosterone, and high levels of testosterone are associated with less interest in babies. If dads were as tormented as moms by prolonged absence from their children, we would have more unhappiness and more fights over which parent gets to spend time with the children. By faithfully working at often boring jobs to provide for their families, dads make possible moms who can do less paid work and thereby produce less stressed and happier households. Dads should surely help with the kids, but they deserve a lot of credit for simply making mom's nurturing possible.

In my class last year a good student who was a strong feminist declared near the end of the term that feminism had left her incapable of love. She was always asking herself if her partner was doing half of everything. She never looked at him appreciatively and gave him the benefit of the doubt. Such a chip-on-the-shoulder attitude is not likely to lead to women who can report satisfaction with the love and affection shown by their husbands.

At the deepest level, androgynous feminists simply do not like women. This is a strong statement but an accurate one. I hope that I have persuaded you that women care most of all about connection—strong intimate relationships. As argued above, these goals bring with them dependency and vulnerability.

Androgynous feminism's overarching goal is an end to female vulnerability and dependency. Feminists make statements like "If you believe you need a man [in your life] you won't pursue your own goals," and "Don't let your children define you" (Crittenden 1999, 61, 64). Feminists make a religion out of personal autonomy and self-reliance (Morse 2003, 58–60). At their core, however, most women want connection, not autonomy. A recent poll found that nearly 81 percent of mothers said that mothering is the most important thing they do (Erickson and Aird 2005). Even feminists sometimes sense their desire for connection and dependency. Katie Roiphe has said:

> I live alone, pay my bills, and fix my stereo when it breaks down. But it sometimes seems like my independence is in part an elaborately constructed facade that hides a more traditional feminine desire to be protected and provided for (Crittenden, 65).

We all learn to put up with the self-absorption of teenagers, but feminism would make self-absorption the essential characteristic of thirty-year-old women as well. Feminists would make women whose commitment to others reflects their natures and brings them great joy come to believe that to be entangled in dependent relationships is to be not fully human.

Shortly before he became Pope, Cardinal Joseph Ratzinger issued a letter to the Bishops of the Catholic Church that emphasized the crucial importance of feminine love for the well-being of children and families. While supporting women's rights to equality in the workplace, the Vatican letter argued that the interrelationship between family and work has, for women, "characteristics different from those in the case of men." It warned that women who work should not have a schedule that forces them to relinquish their family life or endure "continual stress, with negative consequences for [their] own equilibrium and the harmony of the family" (Ratzinger 2004).

Interestingly, the Vatican letter suggested that all family members, husbands as well as children, learn to love by seeing how women love within the home. In support of this understanding, three separate studies have concluded that father-son attachments are less secure "when non-maternal care is initiated on a full- or near-full-time basis in the first year [after birth]" (Belsky 2001). This suggests that men's paternal love is strengthened by observing the example of maternal love. In other words, in addition to naturally loving their babies, mothers facilitate the entrance of new love into the world.

"Do unto others as you would have them do unto you." It is a difficult standard for women as well as for men. But since women care so much about strong relationships with other people, they probably come closer to meeting the standard. Noticing and caring about what others want comes more naturally to women than to men. They can thus take the lead in providing "the force that creates relationships, binds families and builds societies." Such activity is hardly shameful; it is worthy of emulation.

Presented at the World Family Policy Forum, Provo, Utah, July 2005.

Bibliography

Baron-Cohen, Simon. 2003. *The Essential Difference.* New York: Basic Books.

Belsky, Jay. 2001. Developmental Risks (Still) Associated with Early Child Care. *Journal of Child Psychology and Psychiatry* 42(7): 845–860.

Blum, Deborah. 1997. *Sex on the Brain.* New York: Viking Press.

Booth, Alan, Karen Carver, and Douglas A. Granger. 2000. Biosocial Perspectives on the Family. *Journal of Marriage and the Family* 62(4): 1018–1034.

Bowman, Karlyn. 1998. Poll Pouri: Listen to Mom. *The Women's Quarterly* (Spring).

Buss, David M. 1994. *The Evolution of Desire.* New York: Basic Books.

Carlson, Allan. 2003. The Curious Case of Gender Equality. *The Family in America,* (November): 1–17.

Crenshaw, Theresa. 1996. *The Alchemy of Love and Lust.* New York: G.P. Putnam's Sons.

Crittenden, Danielle. 1999. *What Our Mothers Didn't Tell Us: Why Happiness Eludes the Modern Woman.* New York: Simon and Schuster.

Dabbs, James McBride, and Mary Godwin Dabbs. 2000. *Heroes, Rogues, and Lovers: Testosterone and Behavior.* New York: McGraw-Hill.

Daly, Martin, and Margo Wilson. 1999. Machismo. *Scientific American* 10(2).

Ellas, Marilyn. 2004. Hugs Can Do a Heart Good Especially for Women, Who Get More of a Protective Hormone, Study Finds. *USA Today,* 8 March.

Erickson, Martha Farrell, and Enola G. Aird. 2005. *The Motherhood Study: Fresh Insights on Mothers' Attitudes and Concerns.* Institute for American Values. The Motherhood Project.

Gallagher, Maggie, and Linda Waite. 2000. *The Case for Marriage.* New York: Random House, Inc.

Graglia, F. Carolyn. 1998. *Domestic Tranquility*. Dallas, TX: Spence Publishing Company.

Gray-Little, Bernadette, and Nancy Burks. 1983. Power and Satisfaction in Marriage: A Review and Critique. *Psychological Bulletin* 93(3): 513–516, 531–535.

Joyner, Kara, and J. Richard Udry. 2000. You Don't Bring Me Anything But Down: Adolescence Romance and Depression. *Journal of Health and Social Behavior* 41 (December): 369–391.

Marlowe, Anne. 2000. Wages of Sin: A Review of *4 Blondes*. http://www.salon.com/books/feature/2000/09/22/bushnell

Meier, Ann. (2006). "Adolescent First Sex and Subsequent Mental Health." Working Paper, University of Minnesota, Department of Sociology.

Mishra, Raja. 1997. Jessup's New Warden Lets Prisoners Know Who's Boss. *The Washington Post*, 22 November.

Moir, Anne and Bill. 1999. *Why Men Don't Iron*. New York: Citadel Press.

Moir, Anne, and David Jessel. 1989. *Brain Sex*. New York: Delta.

Morse, Jennifer Roback. 2003. The Limits of Equality. *Thomas Jefferson Law Review* 26, no. 1: 58–60.

Olbermann, Keith. Interview with Rachel Yehuda. *Countdown*. MSNBC. 4 May 2005.

Parke, Ross D., and Armin A. Brott. 1999. *Throwaway Dads: The Myths and Barriers That Keep Men from Being the Fathers They Want to Be*. Boston: Houghton Mifflin Company.

Pew Research Center for the People and the Press Survey. *As American Women See It; Motherhood Today—A Tougher Job, Less Ably Done (State of the Union Mother's Day Poll)*. Pew Research Center for the People and the Press Survey (cited 9 May 1997). http://people-press.org/dataarchive/#1997

Podles, Mary Elizabeth. 1997. Courtship and The Rules. *The American Enterprise* (March/April): 24–25.

Presser, Harriet B. 1998. Decapitating the U.S. Census Bureau's "Head of Household": Feminist Mobilization in the 1970's. *Feminist Economics* 4: 145–158.

Rasche, Christine E. 1991. *Special Needs of the Female Offender: A Curriculum Guide for Correctional Officers*. Tallahassee, FL: Florida State Department of Education.

Ratzinger, Joseph. 2004. Letter to the Bishops of the Catholic Church Regarding the "Collaboration of Men and Women in the Church and in the World." 31 July. Rome: Congregation for the Doctrine of the Faith.

Rhoads, Steven. 2004. *Taking Sex Differences Seriously*. San Francisco: Encounter Books.

Rossi, Alice S. 1995. A Plea for Less Attention to Monkeys and Apes, and More to Human Biology and Evolutionary Psychology. *Politics and the Life Sciences* (August): 185–188.

Thompson, Linda, and Alexis J. Walker. 1989. Gender in Families: Women and Men in Marriage, Work and Parenthood. *Journal of Marriage and the Family* 51: 845–871.

Weisfeld, Glenn E., R.J.H. Russel, C.C. Weisfeld, and P.A. Wells. 1992. Correlates of Satisfaction in British Marriages. *Ethology and Sociobiology* 13: 125–145.

Wilcox, W. Bradford. 2004. *Soft Patriarchs, New Men.* Chicago: University of Chicago Press.

Wilcox, W. B., and Nock, S. 2006. What's Love Got To Do With It?: Equality, Equity, Commitment and Women's Marital Quality. *Social Forces* 94, no. 3: 1321–1345.

Wolf, Naomi. 2002. *Misconceptions.* New York: Doubleday.

14

Global Maternal Mortality: Contributing Factors and Strategies for Change[1]

Lynn Clark Callister (USA)
Professor of Nursing[2]
Brigham Young University, Provo, Utah, USA

Worldwide, every minute of every day a woman dies as a result of pregnancy or childbirth; this is more than half a million women a year worldwide. This chapter, based on this author's invited talk to the United Nations, explores the topic of global maternal mortality. It describes the most common causes of maternal death (hemorrhage, infection, unsafe abortion, pregnancy induced hypertension, and obstructed labor), explains why maternal mortality remains so high in developing countries, and also invites the readers to look beyond the statistics and to visualize the faces of women and listen to the individual stories of women's lives. The author argues that a model for reduction of global maternal mortality should be based on the knowledge, skills, and health care practices of the woman, her family, the community, and health care delivery systems.

Globally, levels of maternal mortality have remained stable since 1995 (World Health Organization [WHO], 2001). Why do women continue to die during pregnancy and childbirth when we have the knowledge, skills, and technology to prevent these deaths? The purpose of this chapter is to provide a definition of terms and a statistical profile of global maternal mortality, discuss the challenges in the accurate measurement of maternal mortality, review the causes of global maternal mortality, present data on what factors are associated with reduction in maternal mortality, and describe innovative strategies currently being implemented that can meet identified needs, need little technology, are relatively inexpensive, and are sustainable.

While conducting cross-cultural studies over the past nearly two decades, I have sat cross-legged on the floor in a home in a Palestinian refugee camp in Jordan. I have been to the stick-walled homes of Mayan women in the rural highlands of Guatemala. I have interviewed women in health care facilities in Finland where women enjoy the lowest maternal mortality rates in the world. I have talked to Chinese women giving birth to their first and most likely only child. I have been to a birthing center staffed by direct entry or lay midwives in Texas where women in active labor walk across the border from Mexico, seeking to make a better life for their children. I have listened to the voices of Orthodox Jewish women living in Canada who espouse a deeply spiritual lifestyle. I have seen that these women have wisdom inherent in their traditional cultures, a strong commitment to the well-being of their children and families, tremendous strength and resilience, and wonderful resourcefulness. In spite of women's incredible strengths, however, maternal deaths continue to be a significant concern across the globe.

The global maternal mortality rate is estimated to be 400 per 100,000 live births (WHO 2000), or more than half a million women a year worldwide dying due to pregnancy or childbirth (Stevens 2000). While it is important to understand the statistics, we can never forget that these are human beings who are dying. For women living in Malawi African villages, for instance, 40 percent to 52 percent of study participants in an intervention study personally knew three or more women who had died of pregnancy-related complications (Gennaro, Thyangathyana, Kershbaumer, and Thompson 2001).

Lewis (2003, 35) has said that "each woman's death is an individual personal and family tragedy." These childbearing women who die leave at least 1 million motherless vulnerable children who are themselves at increased risk for mortality and morbidity (Katz et al. 2003; United Nations International Children's Emergency Fund [UNICEF], 2003). The World Health Organization estimates that "nearly two thirds of the 8 million infant deaths that occur each year result largely from poor maternal health and hygiene, inadequate care, inefficient management of childbirth, and lack of essential care of the newborn" (WHO 1999, 1).

The problems facing these women include lack of trained birth attendants, lack of appropriate medications and blood products, large numbers of pregnancies with little interpregnancy spacing, no contraception, societal pressures for childbearing, and lack of available treatment for HIV. The woman may be a child bride, physically not yet sufficiently developed to safely bear children, but struggling to give birth to a first baby, far from professional help in a remote rural area; or the woman may still be childbearing in her 40s, struggling to clothe and feed and care for her burgeoning family. I invite you to look beyond the statistics and to visualize the faces of women and listen to the individual stories of women's lives (WHO 2004).

Some Women's Stories

Maria Elena gave birth to her fifth child in her home in the Guatemalan highlands with the village midwife as the birth attendant. Placental fragments were retained, and because she was severely anemic, she experienced profuse hemorrhage and died within four hours of giving birth. The village woman who told me this story said she always sought the help of God in childbirth, because "many women die." The harsh realities of bearing children was articulated by another Mayan woman with whom I spoke: "Having a lot of children is very difficult. It is a miracle that one comes out alive. Only God can save your life at that time [of birth]. It's hard" (Callister and Vega 1998, 292).

Zukiswa, a twenty-four-year-old Xhosa woman living in a squatter's village in East London, South Africa, is HIV positive. She previously lost two children through perinatal transmission of the AIDS virus. When she found out she was pregnant with this child, she used plant toxins without success to try to end her life and that of her unborn child. Another African woman refused injectable contraception (Depo-Provera) because she heard rumors that it would not only make her infertile but also contained the AIDS virus.

Jehad, a devout Moslem woman living in Camp Baqa, a Palestinian refugee camp in Jordan, continues to bear many children because she feels strongly it is her religious obligation to perpetuate the Palestinian bloodline. Her strong beliefs mean modern family planning measures are not used and her children are not spaced (Khalaf and Callister 1997).

Himba tribal women living in northern Namibia must walk many kilometers to access prenatal care and are required to wash off their tribal markings before they are seen by health care providers who do not speak their native dialect. Is it any surprise that they do not receive adequate prenatal care?

An impoverished Pakistani woman refuses to use contraception because her social status is increased by bearing many sons; she lives every day with the societal pressure to have male children (Winkvist and Akhtar 2000). How effective would our teaching about contraception be?

Natalia, a woman in Russia who unexpectedly became pregnant in graduate school, was urged to have an abortion because she was single and poor. In the Russian Federation, for every ten births, there are nearly twenty-four abortions (Meyers 2003). Natalia declined to have an abortion and ultimately gave birth at home attended by a midwife because she felt the services in the public hospital were less than optimum.

Roxanna, a Mexican immigrant woman, explained why she considers health care during pregnancy important: "It's just my way of thinking—that pregnant women have one foot in life, and one foot in death. And that's why if you don't care for yourself, you can die" (Callister, 2006).

Definition of Terms and Statistical Profile of Global Maternal Mortality

Measures of pregnancy-related mortality include the ratio (the number of pregnancy-related deaths per 100,000 live births) (Stanton et al., 2001) and the rate (the number of pregnancy-related deaths per number of women of childbearing age) (WHO and United Nations International Children's Emergency Fund [UNICEF], 1996).

The International Classification of Diseases (ICD 10) defines a maternal death as "the death of a woman while pregnant or within forty-two days of termination of pregnancy, irrespective of the cause, duration, or site of the pregnancy, from any cause related to or aggravated by the pregnancy or its management but not from accidental or incidental causes" (WHO 1992, 5).

Pregnancy-related death is the death of a woman while pregnant or within forty-two days of termination of pregnancy, irrespective of the cause of death.

Late maternal death is the death of a woman from direct or indirect obstetric causes more than forty-two days but less than one year after the termination of the pregnancy (WHO 1992).

The following are some sobering statistics on global maternal mortality:

- Less than 1 percent of maternal deaths occur in the more developed regions of the world, while 90 percent occur in developing countries (WHO 2003).

- Maternal mortality is the health indicator with the greatest disparity between wealthy and poor countries.

- Maternal mortality is highest in Africa, second highest in Asia, third highest in Oceania, and fourth highest in Latin America and the Caribbean. It is lowest in the developed world (WHO 2001).

- Thirteen countries account for 67 percent of all maternal deaths. In order of the highest estimated number they are India, Nigeria, Pakistan, Demographic Republic of Congo, Ethiopia, the United Republic of Tanzania, Afghanistan, Bangladesh, Angola, China, Kenya, Indonesia, and Uganda (WHO 2001).

- In some developing countries, one in eleven pregnant women may die of pregnancy-related complications, compared to one in 5,000 to 10,000 in developed countries.

- With the exception of Afghanistan and Haiti, the countries with the highest risk per birth are in sub-Saharan Africa. A woman's risk of dying during the course of her lifetime from pregnancy related causes is one in sixteen, compared with one in 2,800 in developed countries (WHO 2001).

- Even in developed countries, demographic trends are changing the profile of childbearing. Women who chose not to bear children in the past are now making the conscious choice to become mothers, including first-time mothers who are bearing children in their forties, women with metabolic disorders and disabilities electing to have children, and first-generation "graduates" of newborn intensive care units reaching childbearing age whose own long-term health outcomes have yet to be determined (Williams and Mittendorf 2000).

- Maternal mortality is of particular concern in countries with a high prevalence of HIV/AIDS, such as sub-Saharan Africa (AbouZahr and Wardlaw 2001; United Nations Joint Program on HIV/AIDS 2002). In this area of the world, 67 percent of the population who are fifteen to twenty-six years of age and infected with HIV are female (United Nations Family Planning Agency 2003). Late-stage HIV infection may be aggravated by childbearing. HIV infection is pandemic among African childbearing women with the risk of vertical perinatal transmission and is a major public health problem currently coming to the forefront of the global community (Tabi and Frimpong 2003).

- In addition to maternal mortality, 7 million more women suffer serious health problems related to childbearing, and 50 million suffer adverse health effects (Cook and Dickens 2002; Geller et al. 2004; Hutchins, Grason, and Handler 2004; WHO 1999; WHO 2003). These numbers are considered to be a serious underestimation (Germain 2004).

Challenges in Measuring Maternal Mortality

Measuring rates of maternal mortality is actually a very complex task. Reliable estimates of maternal mortality are not generally available, and therefore assessing progress toward its reduction is difficult. In fact, "The absence of good information on the extent of the burden of maternal ill-health has resulted in its relative neglect by the international health community for many years. Maternal deaths are too often solitary and hidden events that go uncounted" (AbouZahr 2003, 1).

Underreporting by as much as 50 percent and misclassification are endemic, with wide margins of uncertainty (AboZahr and Wardlaw 2001; Stanton et al. 2001; WHO 2001; WHO and UNICEF, 2003). Murray (1999, 152) speaks of this as "piecing together the jigsaw." The World Health Organization and UNICEF (1996, 2–3) said: "It is extremely difficult to assess levels of maternal mortality at the national level. Assessment requires knowledge about deaths of women of reproductive age (15–49), the cause of death, and also whether or not the woman was pregnant at the time of death or had recently been so. Yet few countries count births and deaths; even fewer register the cause of death; and fewer still note pregnancy status on the death form."

Cross-country comparisons should be treated with considerable caution and scrutiny, because different strategies are used to derive estimates in different countries (AbouZahr 2003; World Bank 2000; WHO 2001; Yayla 2003). Verbal reports (also called verbal autopsies) and/or death certificates may be the only source of information on the causes of maternal deaths when women give birth at home (Sloan, Langer, Hernandez, Romero, and Winikoff 2001). This method does not identify deaths occurring early in pregnancy, deaths occurring late after the pregnancy, and indirect causes of maternal death such as malaria and HIV/AIDS (WHO 2001).

One inexpensive method of determining maternal mortality is the "Sisterhood Method" in which women are interviewed on the survival of all their adult sisters, and whether or not any deaths were related to childbearing. Used in 17 percent of countries, the method's accuracy is limited since it measures only maternal mortality during a ten- to twelve-year period and is not current. These data cannot be used, therefore, as an outcome measure of the success of interventions (Murray 1999; WHO 1997b; WHO 2001).

Complete vital record registration, either with good or uncertain/poor attribution of the cause of death, is the source of data in only fifty-nine, or 34 percent, of countries, covering 13 percent of births globally. Thirty-six percent of countries, constituting 27 percent of births globally, have no national data on maternal mortality. In these countries, a regression model is used, and the maternal mortality rates are obtained by dividing the number of maternal deaths by an estimate of the number of live births derived from United Nations projections (WHO 2001).

Causes of Maternal Mortality

Maternal mortality is classified as either (1) direct obstetric death that results from obstetric complications of pregnancy, accounting for 80 percent of all maternal deaths or (2) indirect causes that result from previous existing disease exacerbated by pregnancy or disease developed during pregnancy (WHO 1999).

It is estimated that approximately 25 percent of maternal deaths are caused by hemorrhage, 15 percent by infection, 13 percent by unsafe abortion, 12 percent by pregnancy-induced hypertension, 8 percent by obstructed labor (dystocia), and 8 percent by other direct causes. Twenty percent are ascribed to indirect causes, including malaria and iron deficiency anemia (Starrs 1998; WHO 1997a, 1999, 2000).

The majority of maternal deaths occur in the postpartum period. Postpartum hemorrhage is the most important single cause of maternal death, with 88 percent of deaths due to hemorrhage occurring within four hours of giving birth (WHO 1998). The true cause of death, however, may not be reflected even if there is a death certificate. This is explicated by Lewis (2003, 29):

> For example, a woman dying from hemorrhage may not have understood the need to seek care, may not have had the money or access to transport, may have been deterred from seeking help by inappropriate traditional practices, may have received inadequate clinical care or may have been treated in a facility without access to blood products.

Reducing Maternal Mortality

The World Health Organization has stated that "it is estimated that more than 80% of maternal deaths could be prevented or avoided through actions that are proven to be effective and affordable, even in resource-poor countries" (WHO Regional Office in Africa 2002). Sloan and associates (2001) remind us that there are no simplistic or single solutions to reduce maternal mortality, but there are some factors that are common to maternal mortality in many countries. Maternal health services may be the key to the reduction of maternal mortality rates (Frankenberg and Thomas 2001; Fransen 2003; Koblinsky, Campbell, and Heichelheim 1999; WHO 2004; WHO 2001). In cross-national regressions, having trained attendants for childbirth was significantly correlated with lower maternal mortality rates across sixty-four countries.

Robinson and Wharrad (2001), using a database of 155 countries, found that three variables could explain 87 percent of maternal mortality: lack of trained birth attendants, low gross national product (GNP), and low number of physicians per 1,000 population. Researchers concluded that maternal deaths could be substantially reduced if a high proportion of births are attended by health professionals, an aseptic birth environment is ensured, maternal/fetal/neonatal complications are identified, and transport services for childbearing women to higher level health centers are made available (Robinson and Wharrad 2001). Factors also implicated in maternal mortality included access to clean water and sanitation services, adequate and appropriate nutrition, and spacing of births. In the most comprehensive assessment reported to date, Bulatao and Ross (2001, 2002, 2003) conducted cross-national regressions for maternal mortality in forty-nine developing countries, using indices of the adequacy of maternal health services derived from ratings by at least ten experts in each country. Two important predictors of the reduction of maternal mortality were per capita GNP and the adequacy of access to maternal health care services. These results are similar to those of Shiffman (2000) and Sloan and associates (2001) in confirming the effect of maternal health services on maternal mortality rates. "The implication is that maternal mortality responds not just to a single intervention but to a range of services" (Bulatao and Ross 2003, 720).

If maternal health services are important in the reduction of maternal mortality, what are the essential components of such services? Factor analysis identified four essential components of maternal health services' program functions: (1) education and health promotion; (2) health facility capacity to provide maternal health services; (3) adequacy of maternal care women receive; and (4) the proportion of childbearing women with access to services. The provision of a broad range of high-quality health care services to childbearing women is essential to reduce maternal mortality rates (AdouZahr and Wardlaw 2001).

The World Health Organization's new document, *Beyond the Numbers: Reviewing Maternal Deaths and Complications to Make Pregnancy Safer* (2004), is a landmark step in planning, implementing, and evaluating strategies to help reduce maternal mortality and morbidity worldwide. The Initiative for Maternal Mortality Program Assessment (IMMPACT) (2003) was established in 2002 to strengthen the evidence available to guide safe motherhood initiatives.

Innovative Interventions

The United Nations millennium development goals include improving maternal health by reducing the maternal mortality rate by 75 percent by 2015 (United Nations 2004). Progress will be assessed by maternal mortality rates and the proportion of births attended by skilled health personnel. This is an ambitious goal to be achieved in just over ten years, especially since maternal mortality rates have not declined for more than a decade.

Interventions to reduce maternal mortality should be based on the following assumptions:

- The accuracy of measurement of maternal mortality should be increased to document progress in reducing maternal mortality (AbouZahr and Wardlaw 2001). Consideration should be given to the use of national population census as a means of measurement in developing countries (Stanton et al. 2001).

- Global health research priorities should focus on the disease burden in the developing world (Labonte and Spiegel 2003).

- Women bear children within their sociocultural context. Cultural beliefs such as gender roles and traditional practices have a significant impact on the health-seeking behaviors of women. For example, Kenyan adolescent women, some of whom are betrothed by age six, may be reluctant to use birth control because of the importance of "proven fertility" (Ehlers 1999). Women's health should be viewed from a cultural rather than a reproductive model (Meleis 2003) as we promote the optimal spiritual, physical, mental, and emotional health of women across the life span (Akukwe, 2000). For example, Mexican women immigrating to the United States who are less acculturated or first generation have better perinatal outcomes (such as fewer low birth weight infants) than those who are more acculturated (Callister and Birkhead 2002). There is evidence that these women bring with them cultural prescriptions for self-care to ensure healthy outcomes for themselves and their newborns, which may be lost as they become increasingly acculturated (Callister, Birkhead, Crookston, and Vega 2004).

- The lived experiences of women profoundly influence their responses to health, illness, and life challenges. This has been documented in cross-cultural studies of the cultural meanings of childbirth conducted with international nursing colleagues (Callister 2004).

- Culturally sensitive interventions are more effective than generic interventions and should be integrated in collaboration with traditional healers and health care providers demonstrating respect for cultural health practices as feasible (Bruce 2002).

- A model for reduction of maternal mortality should be based on the knowledge, skills, and health care practices of the woman, her family, the community, and health care delivery systems. Maternal mortality may be reduced when critical elements are addressed during preconception, pregnancy, birth, and postpartum. Factors that need consideration include intendedness of pregnancy, the knowledge of women and their families about pregnancy, the warning signs of complications, and the need to seek health care; the timeliness of women recognizing problems and taking action; the accessibility and acceptability of health care; the cultural competence and communication skills of health care providers; and the woman's adherence to health care counsel/interventions (Centers for Disease Control 2001; Peters 2000; WHO 2002).

- A model for maternal survival should include both a "tool kit" of personal health promotion/risk reduction/disease prevention practices and selected interventions, for example, evidence-based guidelines from the World Health Organization's Integrated Management of Pregnancy and Childbirth (IMPAC) tools, which can be adapted to a variety of local circumstances (http://www.who.int/reproductive-health/index.htm).

- Interventions should be tailored to meet the particular needs of those targeted based on assessment, implementation, and outcomes evaluation. Exemplary strategies include education of women across the life span, promising technologies, preconception health care, and care across the childbearing year.

Education of Women

The International Council of Nurses (ICN) has developed the ICN Girl Child Project, currently underway in Sweden and Botswana. In addition to capturing the voices of young girls, this educational intervention supports the healthy development of the girl child, including the promotion of literacy (International Council of Nurses 2004). Egypt has reportedly experienced a 50 percent decrease in maternal mortality over the past decade by improving the quality of obstetric care, increasing access to family planning, educating women and families about seeking health care for childbearing complications, and educating *dayas* (traditional birth attendants) about referring women with complications (WHO 2000). Nicaraguan women view the signs and symptoms of pregnancy-induced hypertension (PIH) as positive because they associate them with smaller babies and rapid births (Murray 1999). Appropriate education regarding the dangers of untreated PIH should be provided to overcome such misconceptions.

Gennaro and colleagues at the University of Pennsylvania (2001) developed a "train the trainer" intervention in fifteen villages in Chimutu, Malawi, Africa. This is a remote area with poor access to health care; 30,000 people have only one health center. Fifty-seven women completed an intensive educational program and were designated as health educators. Four years after training, over 20,000 people received some instruction from these village trainers. The content focused on safe motherhood. Complications that can occur during childbearing were identified, with a focus on those that are preventable or easily treatable. Because of low literacy rates, educational methods included drama, storytelling, role-playing, songs, and visual aids. As an incentive, each trainer was given fabric for an outfit, as well as an umbrella, and a bag for teaching supplies with the National Safe Motherhood logo imprinted on it. Results of this program included an increase in the percentage of women giving birth in clinics and district hospitals, an increase in the percentage of women receiving postpartum care, and improved understanding of the importance of adequate nutrition for childbearing women. The intervention was subsequently replicated in Rubanda, Uganda. Outcomes evaluation demonstrated an increase in health decision making by women and an increase in women receiving postpartum care (Gennaro, Dugyi, Doud, and Kershbaumer 2002). Such exemplary interventions meet identified community needs, are low cost with minimal use of technology, and are sustainable (Regional Prevention of Maternal Mortality Network 2004).

Application of Promising Technologies

A number of underused and promising technologies are relatively simple and inexpensive and can be used by health personnel in more remote areas (O'Heir 2004). These include measures to treat postpartum hemorrhage in addition to teaching the woman and those caring for her to massage the fundus to help the uterus contract, to put the baby to the breast as soon as possible to release oxytocin, and to use the oxytocin Uniject, a prefilled injection device (now available for a cost of 30 cents in U.S. dollars) (Tsu, Sutanto, Vaidya, Coffey, and Widjaya 2003). Wider availability of magnesium sulfate for PIH is proving helpful (Duley, Gulmezoglu, and Henderson-Smart 2003). Teaching traditional birth attendants techniques to manage obstructed labor is also essential. Birthing kits produced by Latter-day Saint charities are now being distributed in refugee camps by Mercy Charities. Developing a simple system of emergency transportation and communication in remote rural areas without electricity can be creatively and inexpensively achieved (Tsu 2004). The cost of these technologies is relatively low and the outcomes are significant.

Preconception Care

The provision of micronutrients (iron, folic acid, vitamin A, zinc) for women of childbearing age may be the most cost-effective intervention available to maximize the health of women before and during pregnancy and beyond (Black 2003). Data from China suggest that preconception folic acid supplementation is feasible and makes a significant difference in the reduction of neural tube defects in the unborn child (Berry et al. 1999).

Care Across the Childbearing Year

Prenatal care objectives include establishing contact with the woman and identifying and managing current and potential risks and problems. Appropriate prenatal care should include assessment of maternal health, detection and management of complications, observation and recording of clinical data, maintenance of maternal nutrition, health education, and prevention of major diseases including provision of micronutrients.

Care During Childbirth

It is widely documented in research conducted throughout the world that labor support makes an important difference in outcomes. However, in many countries in the developing world, women labor without support, sometimes in open wards with no space between beds, where family members are not allowed, and where no nurses are available to provide support. Simply increasing labor support is an intervention that should be encouraged. Lifesaving skills modules have been developed by the American College of Nurse

Midwives (2004) and are being used in such countries as Ghana, Uganda, Nigeria, Indonesia, and Vietnam to assist traditional birth attendants to recognize and respond to complicated births appropriately.

Success stories about improved care in childbirth are described in the *Safe Motherhood Newsletter* (WHO Making Pregnancy Safer Initiative 2003). One of these stories is of a sixteen-year-old Filipino primigravida, Mayrose, who lived in a remote hillside village. When her labor began, her mother sent for the hilot, or traditional birth attendant, living one kilometer away and a health worker living two kilometers away. After attending Mayrose for nearly twelve hours, they sent a note with some schoolchildren to the house of the rural midwife. She arrived and determined after two hours that Mayrose should be referred to the hospital, a three-hour journey by road. Neighbors used a hammock provided by the Safe Motherhood Project to carry Mayrose a few kilometers to the road, where she was transported by jeep to the hospital. As a member of the local Health Savings group, Mayrose's mother borrowed PHP 1,000 (equivalent to U.S. $18) to pay for transport and hospital care. Mayrose gave birth in the hospital, with positive maternal and neonatal outcomes. "Mayrose's story shows how strong community spirit, committed community health workers, a midwife's knowledge, an effective referral system, transport, and a health funding program all contribute to safe motherhood" (WHO Making Pregnancy Safer Initiative 2003, 16)

Conclusion

William Callaghan (Centers for Disease Control 2001, 53) has poignantly asked, "Whose faces are behind the numbers? What were their stories? What were their dreams? They left behind children and families. They also left behind clues as to why their lives end so early." Reflecting on this thought, "each maternal death or case of life-threatening complications has a story to tell and can provide indications on practical ways of addressing its causes and determinants" (Lewis 2003, 27).

Reduction of maternal mortality has a great potential for simultaneously improving the health of children, families, and communities. Khmer childbearing women living in Cambodia speak about giving birth as "crossing the river" (*chlong tonlee*) because navigating the Mekong River is often dangerous, just as giving birth is considered fraught with potential challenges (White 2002). The traditional African phrase, "A pregnant woman has one foot in the grave" unfortunately reflects the continuing challenges of maternal mortality, particularly in the developing world (Lewis 2003).

> The footprints of a family leading a child across an African mud flat more than a million years ago are the oldest known fossil footprints. What better testimony could there be of the universal and timeless recognition of the special needs of the family, women and children for care and attention? (Kadandara 1994, 12).

Presented at the Meetings of the International Commission
on the Status of Women, United Nations, 6 March 2004, New York City.

Endnotes

1. As the 2004 Fulbright Scholar to the Russian Federation, Dr. Callister was asked to give this address at the Meetings of the International Commission on the Status of Women, United Nations, 8 March 2004, New York City. It was later printed in the May/June 2005 issue of the *American Journal of Maternal Child Nursing* and is reprinted here with the permission of MCN's publisher, Lippincott, Williams and Wilkins. Funding for this work was from Brigham Young University College of Nursing, Kennedy Center for International Studies, and the World Family Policy Center.

2. Lynn Clark Callister is a Professor, Brigham Young University College of Nursing, Provo, UT; a 2004 Fulbright Scholar to the Russian Federation; and a member of MCN's Editorial Board.

Bibliography

AbouZahr, C. (2003). Global burden of maternal death and disability. *British Medical Bulletin, 6,* 1–11.

AbouZahr, C., and Wardlaw, T. (2001). Maternal mortality at the end of a decade: Signs of progress? *Bulletin of the World Health Organization, 79*(6), 561–573.

Akukwe, C. (2000). Maternal and child health services in the 21st century: Critical issues, challenges, and opportunities. *Health Care for Women International, 21,* 641–653.

American College of Nurse Midwives. (2004). ACNM Department of Global Outreach. Retrieved 27 January 2005, from http://www.midwife.org/dgo/.

Berry, R.J., Li, Z., Erickson, J.D., Li, S., Moore, C.A., Wang, H., et al. (1999). Prevention of neural-tube defects with folic acid in China. *New England Journal of Medicine, 341,* 1485–1490.

Black, R. (2003). Micronutrient deficiency—An underlying cause of morbidity and mortality. *Bulletin of the World Health Organization, 81*(2), 79.

Bruce, J.C. (2002). Marrying modern health practices and technology with traditional practices: Issues for the African continent. *International Nursing Review, 49,* 161–167.

Bulatao, R.A., and Ross, J.A. (2001). *Dimensions of ratings of maternal and neonatal health services: A factor analysis.* Chapel Hill: University of North Carolina. Retrieved 27 January 2005, from http://www.cpc.unc.edu/measure/publications/workingpapers/wp0140.pdf

Bulatao, R.A., and Ross, J. A. (2002). Rating maternal and neonatal health services in developing countries. *Bulletin of the World Health Organization, 80,* 721–727.

Bulatao, R.A., and Ross, J.A. (2003). Which health services reduce maternal mortality? Ratings of maternal health services. *Tropical Medicine and International Health, 8*(8), 710–721.

Callister, L.C. (2004). Making meaning: Women's birth narratives. *Journal of Obstetric, Gynecologic, and Neonatal Nursing, 33*(4), 508–518.

Callister, L.C. (2006). Mexican immigrant childbearing women: Social support and perinatal outcomes. In R. Crane and E. Marshall (Eds.), *Families in poverty: An interdisciplinary approach*. Thousand Oaks, CA: Sage.

Callister, L.C., and Birkhead, A. (2002). Acculturation and perinatal outcomes in Mexican immigrant childbearing women. *Journal of Perinatal and Neonatal Nursing, 16*(3), 22–38.

Callister, L.C., Birkhead, A., Crookston, L.M., and Vega, R. (2004). Perinatal outcomes in Mexican immigrant women giving birth in Utah. In press.

Callister, L.C., and Vega, R. (1998). Giving birth: Guatemalan women's voices. *Journal of Obstetric, Gynecologic, and Neonatal Nursing, 27*, 289–295.

Centers for Disease Control, Division of Reproductive Health, Safe Motherhood Initiative. (2001). *Strategies to reduce pregnancy-related deaths: From identification and review to action*. Atlanta, GA.

Cook, R.J., and Dickens, B.M. (2002). Human rights to safe motherhood. *International Journal of Gynecology and Obstetrics, 76*(2), 228–235.

Duley, L., Gulmezoglu, A.M., and Henderson-Smart, D.J. (2003). Magnesium sulfate and other anticonvulsants for women with pre-eclampsia (Cochrane Review). In *The Cochrane Library*, 2003(4). Chichester: John Wiley and Sons.

Ehlers, V. (1999). Women and population control in African countries. In L. Fernandez-Heber and T. George (Eds.), *International perspectives on women, health, and culture* (pp. 81-86). Snow Hill, England: Quay Books.

Frankenberg, E., and Thomas, D. (2001). Women's health and pregnancy outcomes: Do services make a difference? *Demography, 38*, 253–265.

Fransen, L. (2003). The impact of inequality on the health of mothers. *Midwifery, 19* (2), 79–81.

Geller, S.E., Rosenberg, E., Cox, S.M., Brown, M.L., Simonson, L., Driscoll, C.A., et al. (2004). The continuum of maternal morbidity and mortality. *American Journal of Obstetrics and Gynecology, 191*, 939–944.

Gennaro, S., Dugyi, E., Doud, J.M., and Kershbaumer, R. (2002). Health promotion for childbearing women in Ruwanda, Uganda. *Journal of Perinatal and Neonatal Nursing, 16*(3), 39–50.

Gennaro, S., Thyangathyanga, D., Kershbaumer, R., and Thompson, J. (2001). Health promotion and risk reduction in Malawi, Africa village women. *Journal of Obstetric, Gynecologic, and Neonatal Nursing, 30*, 224–230.

Germain, A. (2004, January 3). Reproductive health and human rights. *The Lancet, 363*. Retrieved 27 January 2005, from http://www.thelancet.com

Hutchins, E., Grason, H., and Handler, A. (2004). FIMR and other mortality reviews as public health tools for strengthening maternal and child health systems in communities. *Maternal and Child Health, 8*, 259–269.

Initiative for Maternal Mortality Program Assessment (IMMPACT). (2003). *IMPACT Annual Review 2003*. Aberdeen: University of Aberdeen. Retrieved 27 January 2005, from http://www.abdn.ac.uk/dugaldbairdcentre/immpact.

International Council of Nurses. (2004). *The Girl Child Project*. Retrieved 27 January 2005, from http://www.fnif.org/girlproject.htm

Kadandara, J. (1994). *Women's health: A must for development*. Geneva: World Health Global Commission on Women's Health.

Katz, J., West, K.E.P., Kahtry, S.K., Christian, P., Le Clerq, S.C., Pradhan, K., et al. (2003). Risk factors for early infant mortality in Sariahi district, Nepal. *Bulletin of the World Health Organization, 81,* 717–725.

Khalaf, I., and Callister, L.C. (1997). Cultural meanings of childbirth: Muslim women living in Jordan. *Journal of Holistic Nursing, 15,* 373–388.

Koblinsky, M.A., Campbell, O., and Heichelheim, J. (1999). Organizing delivery care: What works for safe motherhood? *Bulletin of the World Health Organization, 77,* 399–406.

Labonte, R., and Spiegel, J. (2003). Setting global health research priorities. *British Medical Journal, 326,* 722–723.

Lewis, G. (2003). Beyond the numbers: Reviewing maternal deaths to make pregnancy safer. *British Medical Bulletin, 6,* 27–37.

Meleis, A. (2003). Theoretical considerations of health care for immigrant and minority women. In P.F. Hill, J.G. Lipson, and A.I. Meleis (Eds.), *Caring for women cross-culturally* (pp. 1–10). Philadelphia: FA Davis.

Meyers, S.L. (2003). Russia retreats from fifty years of permissive law. *International Herald Tribune,* 26 August 2003. Retrieved 27 January 2005, from http://www.iht.com/articles/107657.html

Murray, S.F. (1999). Maternal mortality: Piecing information together. *RCM Midwives Journal, 1999,* 152–154.

O'Heir, J. (2004). Pregnancy and childbirth care following conflict and displacement: Care for refugee women in low-resource settings. *Journal of Midwifery and Women's Health, 49*(4), 14–18.

Peters, M. (2000). Safe Motherhood beyond the year 2000: A global perspective. *Midwifery, 16*(1), 2–7.

Rana, A., Pradhan, N., Gurung, G., and Singh, M. (2004). Induced septic abortion: A major factor in maternal mortality and morbidity. *Journal of Obstetrics and Gynecology, 30*(1), 3–8.

Regional Prevention of Maternal Mortality Network. (2004). *Objectives of the Regional Prevention of Maternal Mortality Network.* Retrieved 27 January 2005, from http://www.rpmm.org/objectives.htm

Robinson, J.J.A., and Wharrad, H. (2001). The relationship between attendance at birth and maternal mortality rates: An exploration of United Nations' data sets including the ratios of physicians and nurses to population, GNP per capita and female literacy. *Journal of Advanced Nursing, 34*(4), 445–455.

Shiffman, J. (2000). Can poor countries surmount high maternal mortality? *Studies in Family Planning, 31,* 274–289.

Sloan, N.L., Langer, A., Hernandez, B., Romero, M., and Winikoff, B. (2001). The etiology of maternal mortality in developing countries: What do verbal autopsies tell us? *Bulletin of the World Health Organization, 79*(9), 805–810.

Stanton, C., Hobcraft, J., Hill, K., Kodjogbe, N., Mapeta, W.T., Munene, F., et al. (2001). Every death counts: Measurement of maternal mortality via a census. *Bulletin of the World Health Organization, 79*(7), 657–664.

Starrs, A. (1998). *The Safe Motherhood Action agenda: Priorities for the next decade.* New York: Family Care International.

Stevens, R.D. (2000). Safe motherhood: An insight into maternal mortality in the developing world. *Health for the Millions, 26*(3), 34–37.

Tabi, M.M., and Frimpong, S. (2003). HIV infection of women in African countries. *International Nursing Review, 50,* 242–250.

Tsu, V.D. (2004, January 3). New and underused technologies to reduce maternal mortality. *The Lancet, 363,* 75–76. Retrieved 27 January 2005, from http://www.thelancet.com

Tsu, V.D., Sutanto, A., Vaidya, K., Coffey, P., and Widjaya, A. (2003). Oxytocin in pre-filled Uniject injection devices for managing third-stage labor in Indonesia. *International Journal of Gynecology and Obstetrics, 83,* 103–111.

United Nations. (2004). *Millennium development goals.* Retrieved 27 January 2005, from http://www.un.org/milleniumgoals.com

United Nations Family Planning Agency. (2003). *State of world population, 2003: Investing in adolescents' health and rights.* New York.

United Nations International Children's Emergency Fund (UNICEF). (2003). *Africa's orphaned generations.* New York. Retrieved 27 January 2005, from http://www.unicef.org/media/files/orphans.pdf

United Nations Joint Program on HIV/AIDS (UNAIDS). (2002). *Sub-Saharan Africa: Fact sheet 2002.* Retrieved 27 January 2005, from http://www.unaids.org

White, P.M. (2002). Crossing the river: Khmer women's perceptions of pregnancy and postpartum. *Journal of Midwifery and Women's Health, 47*(4), 239–246.

Williams, M.A., and Mittendorf, R. (2000). Maternal mortality. In M.G. Goldman and M.C. Hatch (Eds.), *Women and health* (pp. 171–195). San Diego, CA: Academic Press.

Winkvist, A., and Akhtar, H.Z. (2000). God should give daughters to rich families only: Attitudes toward childbearing among low-income women in Punjab, Pakistan. *Social Science and Medicine, 51,* 73–81.

World Bank. (2000). *World development indicators database.* Retrieved 27 January 2005, from http://www.worldbank.org/data/databytopic/GNPPC.pdf

World Health Organization. (1992). *International statistical classifications of diseases and related health problems. Tenth Revision.* Geneva.

World Health Organization. (1997a). *Regional and global incidence of and mortality due to unsafe abortion.* Retrieved 27 January 2005, from http://www.who.int/reproductive-health/publications/MSM_97_16/MSM_97_16_chapter5

World Health Organization. (1997b). *The sisterhood method for estimating maternal mortality: Guidance notes for potential users.* Geneva.

World Health Organization. (1998). *Postpartum care of the mother and newborn: A practical guide.* Geneva. Retrieved 27 January 2005, from http://www.who.int/reproductivehealth/publications/MSM_98_3/msm_98_3_4.html

World Health Organization. (1999). *Reduction of maternal mortality: A joint WHO/UNFPA/UNIEF World Bank statement.* Geneva.

World Health Organization. (2000). *Safe motherhood.* Geneva. Retrieved 27 January 2005, from http://www.who.int/reproductivehealth/publications/interagency_manual_on_RH_in_refugee_situations/ch3.pdf

World Health Organization. (2001). *Maternal mortality in 2000: Estimates developed by WHO, UNICEF, and UNFPA.* Geneva.

World Health Organization. (2002). *World health report 2002—Reducing risk, promoting healthy life.* Geneva. Retrieved 27 January 2005, from http://ww.who/reproductive-health/publications/maternal_mortality_2000/tables.html

World Health Organization (2003, October 20). *Maternal mortality report.* Geneva.

World Health Organization (2004). *Beyond the numbers: Reviewing maternal deaths and complications to make pregnancy safer.* Geneva.

World Health Organization and United Nations International Children's Emergency Fund. (1996). *Revised estimates of maternal mortality: A new approach by WHO and UNICEF.* Geneva.

World Health Organization Making Pregnancy Safer Initiative. (2003). Success stories. *Safe Motherhood Newsletter, 30*(1), 1–16.

World Health Organization Regional Office for Africa. (2002). *Reducing maternal deaths: The challenge of the new millennium in the African region.* Congo. Retrieved 27 January 2005, from http://www.afro.who.int/drh/index.html

Yayla, M. (2003). Maternal mortality in developing countries. *Journal of Perinatal Medicine, 31*(5), 386–391.

15

Women and Abortion

Selena Ewing (Australia)
Research Officer, Southern Cross Bioethics Institute, Adelaide
Founding Director, Women's Forum Australia

This chapter evaluates recently published research (within the past fifteen years except where evidence is scant) on aspects of abortion related to women's health and well-being in Australia and other developed countries in which abortion is legal or extensively practiced. Its purpose is to generate informed debate about how abortion is practiced and other issues faced by pregnant women in Australia in hopes that recommendations may be developed that enable recognition of potential abortion-related health risks to women and, more broadly, address structural conditions that impact a woman's ability to make a free and fully informed decision.

Motives Underlying Abortion Decisions

> Reasons women give for why they seek abortion are often far more complex than simply not intending to become pregnant.[1]

Abortion decisions are not random occurrences. Differences in demographic and social patterns are observable between women who have abortions and women who do not.[2,3,4] These patterns provide clues as to how to address and relieve pressures that can bias a decision in favor of abortion.

Evidence demonstrates that "unintended" pregnancy is not the simple cause of abortion. Women's decisions are not independent of their circumstances and the influences of people around them. Research suggests that abortion is considered by women because of lack of freedom to pursue motherhood, lack of emotional and financial support, and other barriers to giving birth. Specified medical conditions, fetal abnormality, and rape are "hard cases" that motivate relatively few abortions.[1,5] Notwithstanding the difficulties and challenges involved in all of these situations, the vast majority of abortions are performed on healthy mothers and babies.

A 1995 Australian research project involving women presenting at an abortion clinic[6] suggests that women primarily have abortions because they perceive that having a baby would jeopardize their future, they believe they could not cope with a baby, they do not want others to know they are pregnant, or they cannot afford to have a baby.[6] For women of all ages, relationship problems are an important factor in abortion decision making. Table 15.1 summarizes some of these findings.

A lack of support features prominently in this list: "could not cope," "cannot afford financially," "do not have support to continue," and "relationship at risk if continue." Other reasons are related to lack of self-confidence: "could not cope" and "would not be a good mother." Note that from a cognitive behavioral perspective, some of these statements may not be true facts, though this does not, of course, invalidate the woman's perception of them as true: "know termination of pregnancy safe, simple" and "pregnancy has no real form yet." Other statements may also represent beliefs or fears—"too old," "too young"—relating to the individual's circumstances and feelings rather than being objectively true across the population (others of the same age may not seek abortion). Coercion, explicit and implicit, is also evident: "others say should terminate," "result of forced sex," "relationship at risk if continue," "do not want others to know pregnant," and "partner could not cope."

It is noteworthy that all twenty women seeking abortion believed that giving birth would jeopardize their futures. This belief, however, is not an inevitable outcome; rather, it is a subjective assessment of how pregnancy and motherhood, to the best of her knowledge, might fit with a woman's hopes, dreams, and aspirations. On the other hand, few women were aware of the potential harm of the abortion itself, demonstrating the critical importance of fully informing a woman before she proceeds with abortion about all the possible effects of abortion on her health and well-being, as well as on all the options and alternatives available to her.

"Unwanted," "Unplanned," and "Unintended" Pregnancies

Pregnancy "intendedness" is a notion that cannot be used accurately in discussions of abortion.[7] Much research literature uses the terms "planned," "unplanned," "intended," "unintended," "wanted," "unwanted," and the concept of "planning" as self-evident and unproblematic.[8] But for a growing number of researchers, the concept of *pregnancy intendedness* is in transition: it is no longer thought correct or useful to assume that becoming pregnant is a rational activity based on planning and forethought.[9] For this reason, a simplistic focus on contraception and sex education to reduce the unintended pregnancy rate, and therefore to reduce the abortion rate, is unlikely to be successful on its own.

For example, in one empirical study, the intendedness of a woman's pregnancy and her adjustment to, and happiness with, her pregnancy did not appear to be closely linked.[10] In a 2002 study of UK women who had either given birth or had an abortion, most did not use the terms "planned," "unplanned," "intended," "unintended," "wanted," or "unwanted" to classify their pregnancies. Only thirteen of the forty-seven women interviewed used these terms at all. Three women used the term "intended"; all were

Table 15.1   Endorsement of "Pro-Terminate" Items of Balance Sheet (*n* = 20)

Statement	True for situation (%)	Considered (%)	Considered very much (%)
Continuing jeopardize future	100	100	80
Believe my right to choose	100	90	60
Know termination of pregnancy (TOP) safe, simple	95	75	60
Could not cope	90	90	70
Not want others to know pregnant	85	60	35
Cannot afford financially	75	70	60
Know women who aborted, did well	75	70	40
Pregnancy has no real form yet	75	70	45
Important others would suffer	65	55	35
Partner could not cope	65	55	25
Would be a single mother	55	40	35
Too young	45	45	24
Relationship unstable or new	45	45	30
Do not have support to continue	45	40	20
Worried not be a good mother	40	40	35
Relationship at risk if continue	35	25	10
Others say should terminate	35	20	15
Really scared of childbirth	35	25	20
Coped well with previous TOP	30	25	10
Health would suffer	20	15	10
Do not ever want (more) children	20	15	10
Too old	15	15	10
Not want involvement with partner in conception	5	0	0
Result of forced sex	5	5	5
Worried about health of pregnancy	5	5	5
Not want others to know had sex	5	5	5

married, over thirty, and held university degrees. Eight women used the terms "unplanned" or "unintended." These women varied in age from seventeen to thirty-seven, varied in education, and had pregnancies that were either carried to term or terminated. The researchers conclude that these terms are not spontaneously used by women. Many women found it difficult to define a "wanted" pregnancy, and the term "unwanted" provoked a strong emotional reaction and disagreement among women.[8]

Only eight of the forty-seven women applied the term "unwanted" to their pregnancies, some with reservation. All were terminating. Eleven of the nineteen women having abortions chose *not* to apply the term "unwanted." One woman expressed it thus: "It's not that I don't want the baby, it's that I can't have it...well not 'can't,' that's another word I should put in, but it's not within my means to have it, and I think it's for the baby's best. But I think 'unwanted'...it's not that I don't want it at all. I love it just as much because, you know, if I could have it, and I would love to be able to have it, so I think 'unwanted' is a bit of a kind of harsh word in my head." Barrett and Wellings noted that "women's reluctance to apply the term 'unwanted' is interesting in light of the way in which the term 'unwanted' is often used as a euphemism for pregnancies ending in abortion in the medical literature."[8] They concluded that the women in their study expected four criteria to be met for a pregnancy to be "planned":

(1) they all stated they had a clear intention to become pregnant;
(2) they had not used contraception in order to become pregnant;
(3) they had discussed and agreed with their partners that they would try to conceive;
(4) they had all made wide lifestyle preparations or reached the right time in their lives.

They also found that some women did not want to plan pregnancy—they wanted it to be a surprise. Evidence of resistance to family planning among some women was noted.

A U.S. study from 2001 is useful because of its unique approach—it considered women's retrospective attitudes towards their children's births.[11] Over time the women's attitudes changed, more often toward more favorable reports (15 percent more positive versus 10 percent more negative). The author found a "disturbingly high frequency (from the point of view of consistency)—19 percent for last pregnancies and 27 percent for next-to-last pregnancies—of women whose pregnancy was reported as 'unwanted' who said they reacted to the event by being happy, thrilled or glad, or by thinking how nice it was." The results suggest that women were likely to reclassify their unintended or unwanted pregnancies later as wanted or intended. Women rarely reclassified their originally intended pregnancies. The authors conclude that "it suggests considerable inconsistency between prospective and retrospective measures of the same event, either in the form of rationalization of the result, or in widespread changes of intention." Some studies have also found that many women do not use any method of birth control despite their lack of conscious or stated intention for pregnancy.[12]

Ambivalence in Decision Making During Pregnancy

Many researchers have found that the decision to abort is marked by a high degree of ambivalence (being unsure or "in two minds").[6,13,14,15] This is normal in almost all major life decisions, of which abortion is one.[16] However, ambivalence within the abortion decision-making process should still be of concern to policy makers and service providers because of the solid evidence of potentially severe effects of abortion for women who were unsure about their decision. It also highlights the need for women to be fully informed about abortion and all alternatives before making a decision.

Ambivalence is common in early pregnancy, even for many women whose pregnancies are specifically planned or wanted. Women's attitudes towards the pregnancy and the baby appear to change over time, even during pregnancy.[17] Some researchers report: "Of particular concern is the finding that women who reported their pregnancies as mistimed or unwanted were so much more likely to change their reports over time (to report the pregnancy as wanted) than were women who initially said that their pregnancies had been well timed."[11]

A Swedish study found that nearly a third of women seeking abortion reported contradictory feelings, both positive and negative, towards their pregnancy. Nearly half (46 percent) of all the women seeking abortion expressed a conflict of conscience about it.[18] Among 1,446 women applying for abortion in Sweden, almost one in ten changed their minds.[19] Another Swedish study, involving 854 women one year after abortion, found that 19.8 percent were still undecided as to whether they had made the right decision.[20]

One large study found a decreasing level of decision satisfaction over a two-year period after abortion. However, the study achieved only a 50 percent retention rate over two years. (Other research suggests that women who withdraw from postabortion studies are likely to experience the most distress; therefore studies with low retention rates may underestimate the negative effects of abortion.)[21] At one month postabortion 10.8 percent of women were dissatisfied and felt they had made the wrong decision, and 10.5 percent were neutral about their decision. At two years, 16.3 percent of women were dissatisfied and felt they had made the wrong decision. Nineteen percent of women said they would definitely not or probably not have the abortion again if they had to make the decision over, and 12 percent were undecided.[22]

In a Swedish study, women who were ambivalent about their decision more often stated that their decision might have been different under alternative personal circumstances, for example, if the partner had wanted the baby or if finances had been better. Among these women, ambivalence about the abortion decision was associated with pressure from other people, particularly the male partner, and a negative attitude towards abortion.[23] Another study showed that personal finances, housing conditions, and pressure from a partner were significant reasons for abortion among ambivalent women.[13] Another Swedish study found that women who changed their minds about abortion (i.e., applied for abortion but did not go through with it) were most often initially motivated to have an abortion because their partner did not want the baby.[19] Among 196 women who had a termination for fetal abnormality in The Netherlands, 8 percent reported feelings of regret and 10 percent reported feelings of doubt about their decision.[24] Among eighty-three women having abortion for fetal malformation in Germany, eight expressed retrospective doubts about the decision, and one felt she had made the wrong decision.[25]

Ambivalence among pregnant women is common and should inform considerations about abortion service delivery. It is a concrete indicator of the complexity of decisions made during pregnancy, underscoring the need for information, accessible counseling, and professional support to aid a woman's decision making by presenting alternative strategies that address external coercive factors such as finances, housing options, or lack of support. Moreover, a substantial evidence base shows that ambivalence and difficulty arriving at the decision to abort are risk factors for long-term psychological distress following abortion.[20,26,13,27,24] A Dutch study showed that women who reported feelings of doubt about their decision were overrepresented in the group with post-traumatic stress symptoms. The authors of this study emphasized the importance of adequate psychological support and guidance from the caregiver during the decision-making process "in order to avoid impulsive and not fully internalized decisions."[24]

Moral Position on Abortion

Interestingly, evidence suggests that a substantial number of women have abortions despite being personally opposed to abortion.[28,6,29,30] In an Australian study, five of the twenty women interviewed (all of them attending a clinic for an abortion) stated that "abortion is against my beliefs."[6] In a Norwegian study, 13 percent of women undergoing abortion were opposed to the law allowing abortion on demand.[28] It is, therefore, reasonable to assume that there were other powerful influences in these women's lives that motivated them to seek abortion, rather than abortion being a free, uncoerced choice or a straightforward and preferred option. Attention should be given to the pressures causing women to seek abortion, particularly for those women for whom abortion conflicts with their moral beliefs.

Finances

Research suggests that one of the most common motivations for abortion is financial concerns, that is, the reality or perception by the mother that she cannot afford to raise a baby.[3,31,6] This might be related to the costs of raising a child or to lost earnings or both. In New South Wales, in a study of 2,249 women having abortions in 1995, 60 percent gave the reason "cannot afford a baby now," by far the most common motivation.[3] In Australia and overseas, older women are more likely to cite completed family, work (pressures of work, or necessity to earn an income), and problems in their relationships with the partner as reasons for abortion.[3,32] This may indicate that women feel they cannot have as many children as they want, frequently on affordability grounds. Anecdotal evidence from abortion providers suggests that increasing numbers of partnered women over thirty in Australia are choosing to limit their family size by terminating pregnancies for economic reasons.[33]

The high cost of housing can affect women's options for caring for children in developed countries. One Swedish study showed that women living in crowded housing situations chose abortion more than twice as often as women living in spacious conditions.[28] The high cost of housing may force women to work when they would rather have children or care for their families at home. It may also force women to live in smaller homes than they would like or need. In Scotland, a retrospective study sought to identify women who were at risk of repeat abortion. The authors found that, apart from age and parity, which tend to be confounded, deprivation was the most important predictor of repeat abortion.[34]

Study and Work

The desire to study and work is often a reason given for abortion,[31] suggesting that many women feel that pregnancy and motherhood are not compatible with study and work. This could be because structural barriers prevent them from achieving both, or that women want to devote most or all of their time to their family when they have one.

All twenty of the women interviewed in an Australian study (who were attending for abortion) agreed with the statement "continuing the pregnancy would jeopardize my career, study or future plans."[6] Younger women are more likely to cite youth, career, single parenthood and changes to lifestyle as a reason for abortion,[3,32] perhaps reflecting a preference for abortion over childbearing. Alternative interpretations might include: schools, universities, workplaces, and careers may not be welcoming of mothers; relationship instability, including the threat of abandonment by men; young women's fear of an unknown future, dramatic changes to lifestyle, and the perceived "loss of self" as a mother.

Wanting the Best for Their Children

International research shows that some termination decisions are motivated by the desire to provide children with a safe and positive environment. If a woman is poor, or in a dysfunctional or violent domestic situation, she may seek abortion because she does not feel able to provide her child with an ideal upbringing.[35,36,14] There is evidence that women do not want to raise children as a single mother, whether because of potential practical, financial, or emotional difficulties, or stigmatization.[18,37] Evidence suggests that women believe their children have a right to be wanted and loved by both parents and raised in a caring environment.[18] Again, these findings may relate to a lack of emotional, financial, and community support for mothers, suggesting frequent abandonment of women by men in communities economically and professionally structured such that single motherhood seems too difficult to pursue and that women feel inadequate if they provide less than the perceived ideal.

Domestic Violence and Abuse

Abortion, particularly repeat abortion, has a strong established relationship with domestic violence in many countries.[35,38,39,40,41,42] Female victims of domestic violence may have an abortion for various reasons related to the abuse:[26]

- current or past pregnancies precipitated increased violence;
- she has fear that the fetus will be harmed by violence;
- there is coercion from an abuser;
- the pregnancy resulted from rape;
- she has a lack of desire and/or fears about having a child with an abuser.

Research has found that pregnant abused women may not want their children to suffer in the same abusive domestic situation and thus seek abortion, or that abused women are more likely to experience coerced sex or coercion to seek abortion, or all of these at once. The same English study found that almost 2 percent of requests for termination may have been due to forced sex.[41]

In an Australian study, 1,014 women were interviewed during pregnancy and followed up after delivery. Women reporting past abuse or abuse during pregnancy were compared with nonabused women. The study found that abused women had a higher incidence of two or more pregnancy terminations.[43] Another recent study of 14,784 Australian women aged eighteen to twenty-three years found that pregnancy loss, whether miscarriage or termination, was associated with the experience of violence. The authors recommend that when young women present with pregnancy, health providers should inquire about violence and be prepared to offer support.[39]

A sample of 486 women seeking abortion in the United States found the prevalence of self-reported abuse at 39.5 percent. Women with an abuse history were more likely than nonabused women to cite relationship issues as a reason for seeking termination. This study also found that women were much more likely to identify themselves as "abused" when given a paper survey compared with being asked directly, a relevant finding for screening and intervention programs. The authors suggest that past or present abusive relationships influence women's decisions to seek abortion.[38] Several researchers recommend systematic identification of abuse history among women seeking abortion, with concurrent provision of information about interventions, safety, and referral for counseling.[38,40,41,44]

A Canadian study investigated the possibility of universal screening for domestic violence in an abortion clinic and found it to be feasible but challenging.[45] The authors note that simply asking questions about abuse is an intervention because this communicates that domestic abuse is an important issue. This study found some difficulties in universal screening at the abortion clinic. Staff compliance with the policy was low, with staff asking the questions of only 254 of the 499 women attending for abortion. About half the reasons given for not asking were "patient centered," such as poor English skills, the partner being present, or the woman being too emotionally distraught. About half the reasons were counselor related, such as the counselor feeling rushed during the session or feeling that rapport was not established. In some cases, counselors "ran out of energy" to ask the questions. Nevertheless, the counselors found that, overall, women were receptive to the screening.[45]

Others recommend routine prenatal visits as opportunities for building trust between women and health care professionals and therefore counseling and intervention for those who disclose abuse.[46,47] However, the presence of a male partner at preabortion interviews may present an insurmountable problem for women in disclosing abuse or coercion, as may the lack of a trusted relationship with the abortion provider.[47]

A recent major Australian report on the social, economic, and safety needs of women during pregnancy provides a detailed picture of the extent, level, and nature of violence against women during pregnancy. The author cautions against careless implementation of screening programs in the context of pregnancy health care services. Her research and experience suggests that women will discuss violence only in the context of a trusted relationship (unless the violence is severe and the woman has already sought help). Hence, routine screening may or may not create the appropriate safe environment for women to speak freely about abuse.[48]

Dr. Angela Taft wrote a major paper on violence against Australian women in pregnancy and after childbirth in 2002. She states that 4–9 percent of pregnant women experience domestic violence and that a higher proportion of abused women than nonabused women seek abortion. She argues, however, that "we do not have the evidence to recommend partner abuse screening as policy at present" (referring to health services in general, not specifically to abortion services). This recommendation is based partly on evidence suggesting that most women do not disclose abuse, and if the response from a health professional is unsupportive or judgmental it may discourage the woman from seeking help for a long time.[49]

Relationships and Abortion
Problems with the quality of intimate relationships, including lack of commitment from a male partner or physical, psychological, and sexual

violence, appear to be a major contributor to abortion in Australia and over-seas.[14,31,19,35] A major factor in a woman's decision about her pregnancy is the influence of the people closest to her, especially her partner. Research shows that in making the decision, women assess the likely level of emotional and financial support from their partners. If the partner does not want the pregnancy, or will give no financial support, the woman is more likely to view her pregnancy as "unwanted."[50] Research suggests that the male partner has a direct influence on a woman's desire for pregnancy and childbearing and on a woman's attitude towards an unplanned pregnancy.[51]

An Australian study of teenagers' pregnancy resolution decisions found that most young women, whether choosing abortion or childbirth, reported that they arrived at the decision entirely on their own. However, the authors stated that these decisions clearly were occurring within the context of family and partner relationships, which in reality were external factors influencing the teenagers' decisions. Most significant was direct influence from the partner.[52]

A Swedish study found that women who changed their minds about abortion (i.e., applied for abortion but did not go through with it) were most often initially motivated to have an abortion because their partner did not want the baby,[19] this suggesting that these women were at first prepared to have an abortion because of lack of support, or perhaps a request or demand, from their partners. However, given time, the women decided not to accede to this pressure. Another Swedish study found that, among 103 women undergoing termination, "partner relationship" was the most common reason given. This included a relationship with no future or viewed as too recent, the ambivalence of the partner towards a pregnancy, his noncommitment to paternity, or a preexisting situation of crisis such as separation or divorce.[53]

Relationships can also influence a woman's perspective on whether her pregnancy was planned or unplanned. A U.S. study of pregnancy intendedness found that

> those who had been unmarried at both interviews were more likely to shift their reports from intended to unintended than were women who were married at both interviews. This may be the result of disappointed expectations regarding the stability of the relationships out of which the babies were born.[11]

The strength and quality of women's relationships are important factors in the abortion decision. An Australian study found that 30 percent of women having an abortion had considered, as an argument against having an abortion, that the partner relationship was stable and caring. Feeling that her partner could cope with a baby was also an important argument against abortion. This Australian study is extremely useful in identifying correlates between women's feelings about motherhood and the realities of their lives. In relation to their own present decision to have an abortion, the statement "I could not cope" was strongly related to "I do not have emotional and practical support." Eighteen of the twenty women said their inability to cope with a baby was an important reason for having an abortion.[6]

Depressed Mood during Pregnancy

Depressed mood during pregnancy is common, although often temporary, and is related to hormonal changes during pregnancy as well as the stresses of pregnancy, impending birth, and other coincidental life events. Bonari et al. cite estimates of prevalences ranging from 10 percent to 25 percent of pregnant women (who did not seek abortion).[54] Marcus et al. found that one in five pregnant women (not seeking abortion) experience depressed mood, yet few are diagnosed with clinical depression or seek treatment.[55] Evans et al. studied a population of 14,541 pregnant women in England and found depressive symptoms in 11.8 percent at eighteen weeks and 13.5 percent at thirty-two weeks gestation. The rate of depressive symptoms after childbirth was lower than during pregnancy.[56] In a study of women undergoing second-trimester abortion for fetal abnormality, there was a high rate of depression at enrollment in the study (61.9 percent of women electing surgical termination, and 53.8 percent of women electing medical termination). At four months post-abortion the prevalence was 23.5 percent for surgical versus 14.3 percent for medical, and 27.3 percent for surgical versus 20 percent for medical at twelve months.[57]

Ross et al. propose a biopsychosocial model of depression during pregnancy and the postpartum period, suggesting that "variance in depressive symptoms can be best accounted for by the indirect effects of biological risk factors on psychosocial variables and anxiety. These biological variables could alter sensitivity to environmental stressors, such as lack of social support, and in this way, determine the threshold for developing symptoms of depression or anxiety during pregnancy."[58] Depression and other types of mental illness can be related to cognitive distortions that may affect decision-making capacity.[54] It is therefore highly relevant to consider the possibility of undetected and untreated depression amongst women seeking abortion. There are effective nonpharmacological interventions for depression, including counseling, physical activity, and support services. Antidepressants may benefit pregnant women with severe depression.[56]

Academics and health professionals are considering and proposing routine screening for depression in prenatal clinics.[55] In Australia, this includes the *Beyond Blue* Postnatal Depression Program, which is conducting trials of a simple screening tool to identify pregnant women at risk of antenatal and postnatal depression.[59] Similar research might also be beneficial if directed towards women considering abortion.

Abortion for Disability or Disease in the Fetus

Abortion for congenital abnormality or other health indications in the fetus comprise relatively few of state and national totals. Nonetheless, these occurrences are worthy of research attention and consideration of more supportive and beneficial policies and practices. Currently, research and women's experiences highlight the routinization and expectations of participation in prenatal screening and abortion,[60,61] a lack of information for women undergoing screening or who have received positive results,[62,63,64] subtle and not-so-subtle pressure on women to choose abortion if their baby has suspected disability or disease,[63] and a commonly noted lack of support for families and individuals living with disability in our community.

This growing body of evidence suggests that the reasons for women's choice of abortion in these situations are more complex than simply not wanting to have a child with that particular disability. Some research has questioned whether women feel that abortion for suspected abnormality is even a free choice. A Netherlands study involved interviews with thirty women who underwent abortion at twenty-four weeks or later (compared with thirty women who underwent induced delivery resulting in perinatal death). Of the abortion group, eighteen reported that this was the outcome of a decision process, while twelve (40 percent) reported that they "had no choice."[65]

Significant pressures on women exist apart from personal preference to avoid bearing children with disease or disability. New prenatal testing technologies mean that women can now make the decision to give birth or not. It is therefore reasonable to predict that women will be increasingly seen as *responsible* for the births of children with disability or disease. Furthermore, if children have an illness that is perceived to be "preventable," they may be considered less worthy of help by health professionals and others.

A multinational study has already provided evidence of this. Marteau et al. explored the idea of *attribution* (the tendency to seek an explanation for an unexpected event) in relation to the birth of disabled children. Specifically, "attribution theory predicts that more help will be given when dependency is attributed to . . . lack of ability on the victim's part (internal but uncontrollable cause) than . . . a lack of effort on the victim's part (internal and controllable cause)."[66] Marteau's study involved hypothetical case studies by three groups: pregnant women, men and women from the general community, and geneticists from Germany, Portugal, and the United Kingdom (also included were obstetricians from the United Kingdom). In all three countries, and for all study groups, the mother's history of prenatal screening was the single most important factor influencing attributions of control and blame following the birth of a child with Down Syndrome. These results suggest that both health professionals and lay people make judgments about women's roles in the birth of children with disabilities. The authors conclude that "the results of the current study would suggest that less help will be given to parents who decline testing because the outcome, giving birth to a child with a condition for which prenatal screening and selective termination are available, is seen as preventable."[66]

Lippman has similarly argued that "the provision of prenatal testing for fetal abnormality and selective termination of affected fetuses will result in mothers being blamed for giving birth to children with disabilities."[67] As genetic research and prenatal screening technology develops, the range of available prenatal tests will expand. Women will therefore be faced with more decisions about what, if any, testing should be undertaken on their children and whether or not to proceed with an abortion in the case of detected or suspected abnormality.

Rape, Incest, and Coerced Sex

While abortion for rape or incest is relatively uncommon, sexual coercion is alarmingly common in Australia. In a recent representative sample of Australian women, 21.1 percent of women had experienced sexual coercion (i.e., were forced or frightened into unwanted sexual activity) and 10.3 percent had been coerced when aged sixteen or younger.[68] A Swedish study found that 12 percent of women seeking abortion had become pregnant in a situation where they had felt pressured or threatened by the man.[18] However, it is premature to assume that a woman pregnant through rape and incest will benefit from abortion. There is currently no evidence that it heals the woman's pain or provides any other benefits.

Overall, there is very little research on this topic, perhaps due to an assumption that abortion is the best option for a woman pregnant through rape. There is also little documentation of the experiences of women who have become pregnant as a result of rape and have chosen either abortion or birth. However, one book documents the experiences of almost 200 women who were raped and became pregnant, including women who continued the pregnancy as well as some who underwent abortion. Nearly all the women interviewed said they regretted aborting their babies conceived through rape or incest. On the other hand, among the women who carried their pregnancies to term, not one expressed regret. Reardon writes that

> many women report that their abortions felt like a degrading form of "medical rape"....Abortion involves a painful intrusion into a woman's sexual organs by a masked stranger....For many women this experiential association between abortion and sexual assault is very strong. Women with a history of sexual assault are likely to experience greater distress during and after an abortion than are other women.[69]

There is some evidence from India that abortion as an option facilitates and perpetuates the continuation of rape and violence in intimate relationships.[70]

Effects of Abortion (Physical and Psychological)

The published research on the outcomes of abortion for women is enormously varied in quality and scope. One must be alert to researcher bias, poor methodologies, and use of nonstandardized measures. The Australian NHMRC's (National Health and Medical Research Council) *General Guidelines for Medical Practitioners on Providing Information to Patients* identifies types of information that doctors should discuss with patients which are relevant to women considering abortion: the expected benefits; common side effects and material risks of any intervention; other options for investigation, diagnosis, and treatment; the degree of uncertainty about the therapeutic outcome; any significant long term physical, emotional, mental, social, sexual, or other outcome that may be associated with a proposed intervention.[71] The Guidelines state that "doctors should give information about the risks of any intervention, especially those that are likely to influence the patient's decisions. Known risks should be disclosed when an adverse outcome is common even though the detriment is slight, or when an adverse outcome is severe even though its occurrence is rare."

An Australian study suggests that while women have been told, and apparently believe, that abortion is a safe and simple procedure, many (eight of twenty) intuitively worry that it might damage them emotionally or physically and many others (ten of twenty) are "really scared" of the abortion procedure.[6] Women need objective and unbiased information in order to make fully informed decisions about pregnancy and birth.

Physical Harm

The risks of abortion vary according to the method used and the gestation at which the procedure occurs. Early abortions are generally considered to be very safe. However, any complications must be considered in light of the fact that abortion is a procedure almost always performed on a healthy woman, with no proven therapeutic benefit for her.

Death

A risk of death exists with all methods of termination. Additionally, more deaths from all causes, including suicide, follow abortion compared with childbirth, although this research has not confirmed causality.[72,73,74] There is also some evidence that deaths from abortion are unlikely to be identified as resulting from the abortion.[75,76]

A 1996 study in Finland linked suicides with the Finnish birth, abortion, and hospital discharge registry to examine the relationship between suicide and a woman's pregnancy status the year before death. The authors found that the suicide rate after an abortion was three times the general suicide rate and six times that associated with birth. Among women who committed suicide after abortion, divorced women and women of low social class (based on the woman's occupation) were overrepresented. Women who had given birth had half the suicide rate of women who had not been pregnant the year before death.[74]

U.S. researchers carried out a similar study using data from the Californian state-funded health insurance system, Medi-Cal. A major difference in this study was that the authors sought to examine the effects of pregnancy over a longer period. Primary analysis showed that deaths from all causes in the eight years after the first known pregnancy outcome were significantly higher among women with a history of abortion. After stratifying by cause of death, it could be seen that women who had had abortions and no births had the highest death rates for both natural and violent causes. When comparing women who had births only with women who had abortions only, during the eight-year period after the first pregnancy, women who aborted were 62 percent more likely to die from all causes. The researchers conclude that childbirth without any pregnancy loss may have a protective effect against death; conversely, abortion without any childbirth may increase risk of death.[72]

The U.S. authors pose several potential explanations. The first possibility is that women who have children may be less likely to take risks and may take better care of their own health. Second, abortion may be associated with other stress factors that increase the risk of death. The third possibility is that a higher death rate after abortion may be caused by psychological stresses resulting from the abortion such as unresolved guilt, grief, or depression, and perhaps substance abuse.

A recent systematic review found that there is no standardized method used to identify pregnancy at the time of a woman's death or close to the time of a woman's death.[75] Death certificates may not mention that the woman was or has recently been pregnant. For example, the Finnish study mentioned above found that in only 11 percent of the identified cases was an ended pregnancy also reported on the death certificate. In addition, cause of death may be misclassified or miscoded. Therefore, underreporting of pregnancy-associated mortality is inevitable, including among homicide and suicide victims. Two case-controlled studies show a much higher rate of both homicide and suicide among women who have an abortion compared with women who carry to term.[72,77] These findings "deserve careful analysis and replication. In particular, confounding factors should be examined such as higher rates of abuse or diagnoses such as depression or post-traumatic stress."[78]

Premature Delivery in Future Pregnancies

Women with a history of abortion have an increased risk of premature[79,80,81] as well as very premature[82,83] delivery in future pregnancies. Henriet et al. studied 12,432 women who had a singleton live birth during one week in France and found that previous induced abortion was associated with a 40 percent increased risk of premature birth. Risk of premature birth increased with the number of previous abortions. The association was unrelated to the stage of pregnancy at which the abortion occurred or to the abortion technique used. The authors propose some possible causal mechanisms.[84] A multicenter, case-controlled study in France found that women with a history of induced abortion were at higher risk of very preterm delivery than women with no history of abortion, an association that persisted after controlling for maternal characteristics and history of preterm delivery. This risk increased with the number of past abortions. A history of abortion significantly increased the risk of very preterm delivery due to premature rupture of the membranes and placenta previa, as well as idiopathic spontaneous preterm labor and fetal growth restriction.[82]

In 2004, Ancel et al. aimed to estimate the risk of premature birth associated with a history of first-trimester abortion using data from a large multicenter case-controlled survey in Europe, with a specific focus on complication during pregnancy leading to premature birth. Analysis included 2,938 cases of premature birth and 4,781 controls who gave birth at full term. After adjustment for potential confounding (maternal age, marital status, social class, smoking during pregnancy, and parity), the risk of premature birth was significantly higher in women with a history of abortion than those without, in countries with high and intermediate rates of abortion. In countries with a low rate of induced abortion, the increased risk was not statistically significant. A history of abortion was significantly associated with premature delivery following rupture of membranes, idiopathic premature labor, placenta previa, and other forms of intrapartum hemorrhage. The associations may have been underestimated because the authors could not rule out underreporting of abortions.[80] Researchers suggest that potential causal mechanisms could include infection following abortion (including intra-amniotic infection), cervical incompetence due to mechanical dilatation, and endometrial damage, which increases risk of placenta previa. Infertility has also been caused, although rarely, by fetal bones remaining after midtrimester abortion.[85]

Infection and Uterine Perforation

Infection is a well-known and frequently disclosed risk for women undergoing abortion procedures. Infection can cause infertility,[86] a particularly relevant risk when abortion is performed on women with existing genital infections, since they are at high risk of ascending upper genital tract infection.[87,88] The significant risks associated with untreated chlamydia are even greater for women who have had a termination.[88] A large study in Denmark, involving 12,972 women, found an excess risk of stillbirth among women who had an induced abortion complicated by infection.[89] The authors suggest further studies to confirm this result.

In contrast, uterine perforation is uncommon, but serious and potentially life-threatening. Hysterectomy may be required. A long-term complication may be rupture of the uterus in future pregnancies. Previous abortion and other gynecological surgery increase the risk of perforation during subsequent abortions.[90]

Placenta Previa, Miscarriage, and Low Birth Weight in Later Pregnancies

A recent review article found that previous abortion is a risk factor for placenta previa.[91,92] Placenta previa occurs when a low lying placenta partially or completely obstructs the cervical opening, sometimes requiring birth by caesarean section. Bleeding is a symptom of placenta previa, and if the placenta becomes detached as stretching of the lower part of the uterus occurs during later pregnancy, severe, life-threatening bleeding can occur.

An earlier U.S. case-controlled study of 486 women found that women with a history of one or more induced abortions were 28 percent more likely to have placenta previa in a subsequent pregnancy.[93] A retrospective case-controlled study of 2,002 pregnancies with placenta previa, compared with 1,004 randomly selected controls, found that risk of placenta previa was significantly increased after one abortion.[94] Another study of 192 cases and 622 controls found that the risk of placenta previa was increased by sharp curettage abortion in a dose-response manner. Placenta previa was not associated with vacuum aspiration.[95]

Research has suggested that abortion is a risk factor for miscarriage in later pregnancies.[96,97] Several causal mechanisms may explain these associations: cervical trauma from forced mechanical or rapid dilatation during the abortion procedure;[84,97] cervical and uterine adhesions due to curettage (suggested also by the relationship between abortion and placenta previa),[84] infection (either existing before the abortion or due to the procedure),[84,97] and delayed implantation possibly from minor trauma to the uterus during abortion.[97] Some studies suggest low birth weight in later pregnancies.[98] Other researchers find only a weak association.[84]

Breast Cancer

Recent research and commentary has raised a reasonable possibility that abortion may be a risk factor for breast cancer. The etiology of breast cancer suggests a close relationship to reproductive events, although current knowledge of risk factors can explain only a small percentage of cases.[99] Early age at first birth and increasing parity are both related to lifetime reduction in breast-cancer risk.[100] It is also well-established that a first pregnancy carried to full term has a protective effect in relation to breast cancer.[101] This information is noncontroversial and is important for women considering abortion.

Most women who have an abortion do not get breast cancer, and most women who have breast cancer have not had an abortion. However, the possible relationship between abortion and breast cancer should be highlighted because abortion may be one of the few avoidable risk factors for breast cancer. The hypothesis under examination is very specific and relates to the level of estrogen in a woman's body: when a woman has an abortion early in her first pregnancy at a time when her breast tissue is undergoing major change, the sudden halting of the process may leave her more susceptible to cancer.

Miscarriage, or spontaneous abortion, is not thought to be linked with breast cancer because low estrogen levels are usually implicated in miscarriage. Thus, researchers assessing this risk need to study women aborting their first pregnancies in the first trimester, or the hypothesis will not be tested. For example, a study of 267,040 Chinese women found no relationship between abortion and breast cancer. However, Chinese women rarely abort their first baby.[102] Similarly, a large registry study in Massachusetts failed to distinguish between abortion and miscarriage. Thus, neither study tested the hypothesis.[103]

A meta-analysis including twenty-eight published studies found that abortion was a significant independent risk factor, albeit a relatively low increase in risk, for breast cancer.[104] A case-controlled study of 1,302 women found that, among women who had ever been pregnant, breast cancer risk in those with one or more abortions was 20 percent higher. Higher risks were observed when the abortion occurred before eighteen years of age or at thirty years of age or older. No increased risk of breast cancer was associated with miscarriage.[105] A 1996 study found that, among women who had been pregnant at least once, the risk of breast cancer in those with a prior induced abortion was 20 percent higher than in women with no history of abortion. This association was present mostly among women who had never given birth and whose abortions occurred prior to nine weeks' gestation.[106]

A frequently quoted paper is *The Lancet's* meta-analysis of breast cancer and abortion, which reported no increase in risk.[107] The reviewers excluded all research that relied on retrospective self-reporting of abortion, claiming that such research was biased. This idea was based on a 1994 paper that claimed to show underreporting of abortions by women who did not have breast cancer, compared with women who did,[108] based on their finding that 27 percent of women claimed they had had abortions that were not recorded in the national abortion registry. However, this claim was later retracted by the authors in a published letter, acknowledging that the abortions may not have been recorded in the registry they used.[109]

There is disagreement about the proposed phenomenon of bias attributed to under- and overreporting of abortions: a statistician who regularly analyzes abortion statistics in South Australia writes that "it has been a constant finding that women tend to underreport their induced abortions."[110] A U.S. case-controlled study of 225 cases of women with breast cancer and 303 controls without, found no significant difference in the reporting of abortion history between women with and without cancer.[111] Interestingly, the authors of a recent major study on abortion and premature delivery stated that they expected more underreporting of abortion among cases than controls, resulting in an underestimation of the association.[82] A record-linked survey in the United States found that underreporting of abortion was significantly associated with race and also with positive attitudes towards childbearing and negative attitudes towards abortion.[112] Another record-linked survey found that underreporting could be predicted by race and education; additionally, as time passed, women became less likely to report their abortions.[113]

The process by which studies were selected for *The Lancet* meta-analysis has also been heavily criticized. For example, it has been suggested that many studies suggesting a link between abortion and breast cancer were excluded for unscientific reasons, some invalid studies whose flaws had been documented in the scientific literature were inappropriately included, and some valid studies whose data had been published were simply not mentioned at all. Furthermore, the majority of studies reviewed were unpublished. The control group selected for comparison was arguably inappropriate: Beral et al. selected studies comparing women who had induced abortions with women who had never been pregnant, while the better control group may have been women who carried pregnancies to full term.

At present, there are many studies showing an increased risk of cancer after abortion and other studies that show no increased risk. More research is warranted, and it is still best to assess each study individually. Not enough evidence exists to reassure women that no increased risk of breast cancer associated with termination of a first pregnancy exists; however, women can be told with certainty that carrying a first pregnancy to full term provides a degree of protection against breast cancer—highly relevant information for a woman considering abortion.

Psychological Harm

Recent research has provided new evidence, and confirms previous research, that for some women abortion results in mild, moderate, or severe psychological and emotional harm. Abortion is usually experienced as a stressful event; thus women tend to experience relief and a reduction in stress immediately after the abortion. However, there is relative consensus among postabortion psychology researchers that at least 10–20 percent of women who have had an abortion suffer from severe negative psychological complications.[26] With at least one in four Australian women undergoing abortion over a lifetime, this relates to a large subgroup of the Australian population.[114] Even higher proportions of women experience lesser degrees of emotional distress after abortion.

Causality is difficult to establish, since psychological morbidity can also be a risk factor for abortion. However, anecdotally many women identify their previous abortion as the cause of their suffering, strongly suggesting abortion as a causal factor in those cases. For example, retrospective data from 331 Russian and 217 American women who had experienced one or more abortions revealed that many women attributed negative outcomes to their abortions, including "felt badly" (53.9 percent U.S. and 47 percent Russian women), "thoughts of suicide" (36.4 percent, 2.8 percent), "feelings of sadness and loss" (55.8 percent, 38.6 percent), "guilt" (77.9 percent, 49.8 percent), "increase in alcohol or drugs" (26.7 percent, 4.4 percent), "felt part of me died" (59.5 percent, 33.6 percent), "relationship ended with partner" (19.8 percent, 7.8 percent), "unable to forgive self" (62.2 percent, 10.9 percent), and "need help to deal with this loss" (29 percent, 8.4 percent).[115] In a number of cases, women may take some time to identify the abortion as the source of their symptoms.

Research in postabortion psychology is increasing, indicating that researchers and funding bodies see the area as worthy of investing time and money. However, this area of research is still problematic for many reasons. Most importantly, it is ethically and practically unacceptable to conduct a randomized controlled trial of abortion versus motherhood and adoption. Also, existing studies suffer several methodological problems. One is nonparticipation. Many studies are compromised by low participation rates and high numbers of participants lost to follow-up. For example, one frequently quoted study had a retention rate of only 50 percent at two years, the end of the follow-up period.[22] A Swedish study found that nonparticipants in a retrospective interview study were associated with sociodemographic factors related to increased vulnerability and morbidity in other areas of health research. Nonparticipation was also associated with an increased level of childbearing over the following two years,[21] perhaps an indication of the phenomenon of replacement pregnancy (the desire to replace the pregnancy that has been terminated, often within three to six months after the abortion, and perhaps motivated by the conscious or unconscious need to undo the abortion).

Emotional Distress

Emotional distress is common immediately after abortion and in the months following. All women undergoing abortion in one particular Swedish town were invited to participate in a follow-up study, and 66.5 percent accepted, only 2.8 percent of whom had second-trimester abortions. Women were interviewed approximately one year after the abortion. "Slight emotional distress" was defined as mild depression or remorse, guilt feelings, tendency to cry for no reason, discomfort on meeting children, and recurrent fantasizing about the aborted baby's gender or appearance. "Serious emotional problems" included women who needed help from a psychologist or psychiatrist or who could not work because of depression.[20]

Of the 854 women who participated, 42 percent reported no psychological reaction at all, 55 percent experienced remorse or emotional distress of shorter or longer duration, 16.1 percent had slight emotional problems at the one-year point, and 3.9 percent had deeper depression, with 2.3 percent experiencing depression that persisted for a long time. Of the 854, only 13.3 percent reported no emotional distress, said they would consider abortion if they got pregnant again, and were sure they had made the right decision. The authors note that their study might have underestimated emotional distress after abortion, because a previous analysis of the nonparticipants showed that women who refused to participate tended to have characteristics associated with increased vulnerability to postabortion problems.

Depression and Anxiety

Both short-term and long-term studies, including record-linked studies that take into account a woman's preabortion psychiatric history, suggest that women are at higher risk of depression after abortion than after giving birth. At present these studies cannot establish direct causal relationships, although causal link is strongly suggested by case studies, interview studies of women about their abortion experiences, and women's own claims that their depression and anxiety are directly related to their past abortions. Strong associations between abortion, depression, and anxiety have been demonstrated, independent of the woman's psychiatric or psychological history, and independent of several other key factors for which some analyses control.

Several studies compare women who had abortions with women who carried pregnancies to term. Two important studies are particularly contentious at present, with the respective authors disputing methodological approaches and interpretation of data. The first was published in the *British Medical Journal* in 2002.[116] The authors, Reardon and Cougle, analyzed data from the National Longitudinal Survey of Youth (an interview-based cohort started in 1979 in the United States) and found that, among women with unintended pregnancies, married women were at higher risk of clinical depression after abortion compared with giving birth. In 2005, Schmiege and Russo published a paper in the same journal.[117] Although they claimed to replicate the above analysis, Schmiege and Russo did not provide analysis stratified by marital status, and they coded the same data differently, as they believed the 2002 coding methods were flawed. They concluded that, among the groups of women they selected for analysis, abortion did not raise the risk of depression. Their results did not contradict the original analysis, since they did not, in fact, replicate the original analysis. Interestingly, their results do contradict earlier research by Russo et al. showing that, among 2,525 women, those who had experienced abortion had significantly more depression, suicidal ideation, and lower life satisfaction than other women.[118]

Reardon has criticized the new methods of coding.[119] For example, Schmiege and Russo excluded women from the abortion group who said that their aborted pregnancies were at any point wanted. This exclusion must be questioned because research shows clearly that ambivalence is common during pregnancy, including among women who ultimately choose abortion. It is also a known risk factor for emotional and psychological problems resulting from abortion. Schmiege and Russo also excluded women who carried their first pregnancies to term but aborted subsequent pregnancies, including women in the control group who had experienced abortion. Reardon also points out that Schmiege and Russo identified 38 percent fewer cases of women classified as having experienced depression than his original analysis, thereby reducing the statistical power of their study to detect significant differences.

Underreporting of abortion is a constant problem for all postabortion research. Reardon points out that compared with national (U.S.) average abortion rates, only 40 percent of the expected number of abortions are reported to interviewers in surveys. Both studies would have suffered from this problem, diluting the observed effect of abortion compared with women's real experiences. The data set simply does not provide this information. Schmiege and Russo sought to address this problem by comparing women who filled out and returned an abortion history card with women who did not. They assumed that only women who did not return the card were likely to be concealing past abortions and drew the conclusion that underreporting is unlikely to dilute the researchers' ability to observe the effect of abortion on depression. They also assumed that women who conceal past abortions are less likely to experience depression. Reardon questions both assumptions and notes that neither have an evidence base. This recent dispute highlights many of the problems with research on abortion: the classification of pregnancy "wantedness," the diagnosis and categorization of mental illness, decisions about appropriate comparison groups and exposures, the concealment of abortion histories, and the potential effect of researchers' philosophical perspective on abortion.

Schmiege and Russo's paper erroneously claimed that "well-designed studies have not found that abortion contributes to an increased risk of depression." In fact, many studies have established a strong association between the two. For example, the same data set from the National Longitudinal Survey of Youth used by Schmiege and Russo was used in a separate analysis to assess women's risk of depression after either abortion or childbirth. All 1,884 women who experienced their first pregnancy between 1980 and 1992 were included, and researchers used data for an average of eight years following the pregnancy event. After controlling for age, race, education, income, marital status, history of divorce, and locus of control (an indicator of pre-pregnancy psychological state), results indicated that a history of abortion was associated with a greater risk of depression: In the abortion group, 27.3 percent had a high score on the depression scale, compared with 21.4 percent of women in the birth group. This finding was statistically significant.[120]

From a population-based sample of 4,161 women aged thirty-six to forty-five was taken a subset of 332 women who met the criteria for past or current major depression and a control group of 644 women with no past or current major depression. Through interviews, the researchers gained a detailed history of reproductive events and menstrual cycles from the beginning of menstruation. Depression was not associated with any number of miscarriages. However, compared to women with no abortion history, women with two or more abortions were two to three times more likely to have a lifetime history of major depression independent of age, education, or history of marital disruption. When the researchers considered only the cases of depression that came after abortion events, they found that women who had multiple abortions were at substantially increased risk of depression, but women with only one were not at greater risk. This study was unable to assess preexisting psychosocial factors interacting with reproductive decisions. They also note the confounding interactions of abusive relationships, depression, and abortion.[121]

A different U.S. study found that the cohort of women had, overall, a higher rate of depression before the abortion (26 percent) than after the abortion (20 percent), although both were much higher than the average rate of depression over the same time period among U.S. women overall. However, this study achieved only a 50 percent retention rate over two years.[22]

Anxiety has also been implicated as being related to abortion. A prospective study of 103 women undergoing termination in Switzerland found that some women had persisting sexual dysfunction six months after their abortion, which the researchers attributed to new symptoms of anxiety and depression following the procedure. After their abortions, women described feelings of fatigue (39 percent), guilt (35 percent), sadness (34 percent), and anxiety (29 percent).[122] While not clinically measured, women's reports of anxiety signal the need for more investigation of the relationship between abortion and anxiety disorders.

At least one longitudinal interview study, the U.S. National Survey of Family Growth, was used to investigate women's risk of anxiety disorders after abortion or childbirth, specifically among those women who reported their first pregnancy as unintended. Women reporting their first period of anxiety before or at the same time as their first pregnancy were excluded, so the final sample included 1,813 women delivering their first pregnancy and 1,033 women aborting their first pregnancy. Therefore, this study controlled for any prior history of anxiety. Among all women with unintended pregnancies, those who aborted had significantly higher rates of anxiety.[123]

Post-traumatic Stress Disorder

Researchers have observed that, for a small proportion of women, abortion triggers or causes post-traumatic stress disorder (PTSD) or related symptoms. The relationship between abortion and PTSD was investigated in 331 Russian and 217 American women using retrospective data from a study on pregnancy loss. Analysis showed that 65 percent of American women and 13.1 percent of Russian women experienced multiple symptoms of PTSD: increased arousal, reexperiencing, and avoidance. When women were asked about symptoms that they themselves attributed to their abortions, 14.3 percent of American and 0.9 percent of Russian women met the full diagnostic criteria for abortion-related PTSD. This suggests that cultural factors may play a role in how stress is experienced and reported and in how abortion is perceived by the wider public.[115]

Major et al. reported that, among women having a first-trimester termination, 1 percent developed PTSD within two years after the abortion.[22] Again, this study achieved only a 50 percent retention rate over two years. Other research suggests that low retention rates in such studies may lead researchers to underestimate the negative effects of abortion on women's psychological health.[21] Broen et al. found that, of eighty women undergoing abortion, 18.1 percent met diagnostic criteria for PTSD after two years. Most of these women experienced avoidance of thoughts and feelings related to the abortion. This may be a high estimate, since another important PTSD symptom —intrusive thoughts relating to the abortion—was found to be low. It was also found that mental health before the termination did not influence women's psychological stress responses.[124]

Among 196 women in The Netherlands undergoing terminations for fetal abnormality, 17.3 percent had pathological post-traumatic stress scores. This was significantly explained by level of education (highest scores in low-educated women), by the experience of pressure from family or significant others during the abortion decision, and by feelings of doubt and regret.[24]

Other Psychiatric Disorders

Large studies have found that aborting women suffer from more psychiatric problems, including bipolar disorder, neurotic depression, depressive psychosis, and schizophrenia. This association may be related to a lack of social support for women who have abortions compared with those who give birth, or women's responses to the abortion, or to common risk factors among mentally ill women and those who have abortions.

One large study in the US was designed to avoid the typical methodological problems of postabortion research, i.e., small sample sizes, concealment of abortion history, biased sampling, low participation and retention rates, lack of appropriate comparison groups, and short time frame.[125] This Californian study used record linkage involving 14,297 women who had a first abortion, compared with a control group of 40,122 women with at least one live birth and no abortions. All women were eligible for Medi-Cal assistance. (Medi-Cal is publicly funded health care, implying that these women had low incomes.) Psychiatric history for one year prior to the abortion was examined. Records of psychiatric treatment for up to four years following the abortion or birth were analyzed. Results were controlled for age, prior psychiatric history from twelve to eighteen months before the pregnancy, number of pregnancies, and months of eligibility for Medi-Cal assistance.

The study found that women in the abortion group had a significantly higher rate of psychiatric outpatient treatment than women in the birth group at 90 days, 180 days, one year, and two years after pregnancy. Aborting women had significantly higher rates of treatment within the specific categories of adjustment reactions (21 percent higher), bipolar disorder (92 percent higher), neurotic depression (40 percent higher), and schizophrenic disorders (97 percent higher). In the categories of anxiety states and alcohol and drug abuse (16 percent higher), the abortion group had higher rates that approached statistical significance (14 percent and 16 percent higher, respectively). There were no differences in single episodes of depressive psychosis, recurrent depressive psychosis, depression not otherwise classified, nonorganic psychoses, psychalgia, and acute stress reaction. These results suggest that, compared with a birth experience, abortion is associated with greater risk for psychological disturbance among low-income women. These psychological disturbances were sufficiently serious to require professional intervention.

The relationship between abortion and psychiatric admissions was investigated in a record-based study of 56,741 U.S. women eligible for Medi-Cal who either had an abortion or gave birth during 1989, excluding women with any psychiatric admissions during the year before the pregnancy. Women who had an abortion were found to be at significantly higher risk of psychiatric admission compared with women who delivered. Results may have been diluted by the inclusion of some women in the childbirth group who may have had a history of abortion.[126]

A prospective study by Gilchrist et al. of 13,261 women with an unplanned pregnancy in the United Kingdom found that the rate of total psychiatric disorders reported by general practitioners (GPs) following abortion was similar to that in women who gave birth. The exception was deliberate self-harm (DSH)—women after abortion were significantly more likely to engage in DSH than women who gave birth (among women with no history of DSH).[127]

Interestingly, the authors note that differences in the timing of admission and the past psychiatric history for women giving birth compared to undergoing abortion suggests that the psychiatric illness experienced by the two groups had different underlying mechanisms. However, according to the authors, the rate of psychosis among women giving birth was almost certainly inflated because of systematic miscoding by GPs. Another consideration: by the end of the study, only 34.4 percent of the abortion group and 42.4 percent of women not requesting abortion were still under observation. Also this study may suffer from reporting bias, since the general practitioner who provided the follow-up records of psychiatric health was the same GP who referred the woman for abortion or otherwise. The rate of psychiatric illness for women who gave birth was artificially inflated because doctors were using the term "puerperal psychosis" in a wide range of cases.

In a prospective study of 150 women seeking first and repeat terminations in Scotland, 42 percent of those undergoing repeat abortions reported that they suffered significant psychological problems as a consequence of their past abortions.[128]

Deliberate Self-harm, Including Substance Abuse

As described above, a study of 13,261 women with an unplanned pregnancy in the United Kingdom found that, among women with no history of self-harm, the rate of deliberate self-harm was significantly higher after abortion than after childbirth. Other studies have identified an increased risk of substance abuse, particularly during subsequent pregnancies. One study examined substance abuse during pregnancy with regard to reproductive history using survey data from a sample of 607 women from the National Pregnancy and Health Survey in the United States. Women with a history of abortion were significantly more likely to use marijuana (odds ratio of 10.29), various illicit drugs (odds ratio 5.60), and alcohol (odds ratio 2.22) during their next pregnancy. No difference was detected in the use of cigarettes.[129,130]

Another recent study used data from women in the National Longitudinal Survey of Youth whose first pregnancy was unintended and used data from women with no pregnancies as a control group. Use of alcohol, marijuana, cocaine, and behaviors suggestive of alcohol abuse were studied over an average of four years after the target pregnancy among women with prior histories of delivering an unintended pregnancy (535 women), abortion (213 women), or those with no history of pregnancy (1,144 women). Results were controlled for age, race, marital status, income, education, and pre-pregnancy self-esteem and locus of control. The data showed that the way in which women resolved unintended pregnancies was significantly associated with substance abuse during subsequent pregnancies. Compared to women who carried an unintended first pregnancy to term, those who aborted were significantly more likely to report use of marijuana and more likely to report using cocaine (this result approached statistical significance). Women with a history of abortion also reported more frequent drinking than those with a history of delivering an unintended pregnancy. The authors suggest that a history of abortion may be a useful marker for identifying women who might benefit from counseling for substance abuse.[131]

The relationship between substance abuse during pregnancy and past perinatal loss, including miscarriage, stillbirth, and abortion, was examined in a study of 1,020 women who gave birth in Washington, DC, during 1992. Substances examined were marijuana, cigarettes, alcohol, cocaine, and any other illicit drug. After controlling for various sociodemographic variables (age, race, marital status, income, years of formal education, and number of people living with the respondent), the data showed that a history of one induced abortion was significantly associated with an elevated risk for substance abuse except for alcohol during pregnancy of all types. Other forms of perinatal loss were not systematically related to substance abuse during pregnancy.[132] Two speculative interpretations are offered by the researchers. One is that women who use substances are more likely to abort and continue their usage into subsequent pregnancies, perhaps because women who abuse substances fear that they have harmed the fetus prior to discovering the pregnancy. Another is that women with a history of abortion have unresolved negative emotions relating to their past losses, and are more likely to use substances to deal with their feelings.

Negative Emotional Responses and Replacement Pregnancies

Research has shown that many women experience a range of emotions after abortion, including sadness, loneliness, shame, guilt, grief, doubt, and regret.[27,18,124,133,24] Major and Cozzarelli et al. found that, during the two years after abortion, women's reports of negative emotions increased ("sad," "disappointed," "guilty," "blue," "low," and "feelings of loss") while relief and other positive emotions ("happy," "pleased," and "satisfied") decreased.[22]

Among U.S. college students (including women who had had an abortion and men whose partners had had an abortion), almost one-third of women and almost half of the men were not comfortable with their decision. The same proportions expressed a sense of regret, and many felt sad when thinking of the abortion. A third of both men and women said that they sometimes felt a sense of longing for the aborted fetus. More than half the women and a quarter of the men reported an increase in depression after the abortion and just under one-sixth of both groups experienced increases in anxiety post-abortion. The only predictor of increased anxiety after abortion for women was a lack of comfort with the decision. Men who experienced a sense of connection to the aborted fetus were most likely to experience anxiety.[134]

Kero et al. carried out a prospective study of sixty-five women (66 percent of those asked to participate) with interviews four and twelve months after abortion, with fifty-eight women (58 percent) completing the study at twelve months. At one year, one woman regretted the abortion, and another spoke of it as a mistake. Fifty women regarded the abortion as a form of taking responsibility. Most women experienced the abortion as a relief, although half also expressed concurrent feelings such as grief, emptiness, and guilt. Women's retrospective reports of their emotions immediately after the abortion indicated that 62 percent experienced no emotional distress, 17 percent had mild/moderate distress, and 21 percent had severe emotional distress. Nearly all women with mild/moderate distress also reported relief in concurrence with sadness, loneliness, shame, guilt, emptiness, and regret. Twelve women (18.5 percent) suffered severe emotional distress; their decision had been full of conflict and difficult to make. Three clearly stated that they wanted to give birth, and five others were ambivalent about the decision. Ten saw their abortion as "a necessity or a sacrifice." At one year follow-up, two of these women had already given birth to another child.[27]

Some evidence exists for the "replacement pregnancy" phenomenon. For example, among 14,297 low-income U.S. women aborting their first pregnancies, and a control group of 40,122 women giving birth, the abortion group experienced more subsequent pregnancies. Possible explanations have been that it may help the woman reexperience the earlier pregnancy with the hope of resolving grief and stress about her abortion, or that the woman perceived her abortion as a personal failure and was driven to become pregnant again to succeed in carrying to term. The woman also may feel that her abortion was a mistake and that she actually desired to have a child.[125]

Harm Resulting from Abortion for Disability or Disease in the Fetus

For women who abort because of disability or disease in the fetus, the procedure and years after an abortion can be extremely traumatic, characterized by grief and guilt.[135] A Scottish study of women's reactions to second-trimester abortion for fetal abnormality found that, despite its acceptance in the community, the procedure "remains an emotionally traumatic major life event for both the father and mother," involving turmoil, ambiguity, and reticence. Particularly vulnerable groups were found to be young and imma-ture couples, women with secondary postabortion infertility, or those with a reproductive conflict, as well as those with vulnerable personalities and those who were unsupported. The authors recommended that all of these require early identification and support.[30]

This study also found that after abortion for fetal abnormality, a majority of women and men had negative emotional feelings and somatic complaints related to the abortion. Thirty percent of women felt relief. But women also tended to experience sadness (95 percent), depression (79 percent), anger (78 percent), fear (77 percent), guilt (68 percent), failure (61 percent), shame (40 percent), vulnerability (35 percent), isolation (27 percent), numbness (23 percent), panic spells (20 percent), crying (82 percent), irritability (67 percent), lack of concentration (57 percent), listlessness (56 percent), sleep-lessness (47 percent), tiredness (42 percent), loss of appetite (31 percent), and nightmares (24 percent). Women reported recurrent nightmares about the pro-cedure. Couples experienced changes in their sexual relationships: 50 percent reported they engaged in sexual intercourse less frequently and 24 percent rarely engaged in sexual intercourse at all (as compared to before the abortion). All couples experienced emotional distress, but 40 percent of the women reported coping problems lasting more than twelve months. Thirteen couples refused to participate, mostly because the subject was still too painful to dis-cuss, so the true percentage of adverse sequelae may be 53 percent.

Davies et al. studied thirty women undergoing first- and second-trimester abortion for ultrasound-detected fetal anomaly.[136] The women were assessed at six weeks, six months, and twelve months after the abortion, using a quali-tative interview as well as four standardized self-completed questionnaires that had been validated by many other researchers for use in community or hospital populations. Sixty-seven percent screened positive for post-traumatic stress at six weeks, 50 percent at six months, and 41 percent at twelve months. Emotional distress was experienced by 53 percent at six weeks, 46 percent at six months, and 43 percent at twelve months, and grief by 47 percent at six weeks, 31 percent at six months and 27 percent at twelve months. Depression was diagnosed in 30 percent at six weeks, 39 percent at six months and 32 percent at twelve months. Compared with first-trimester abortion, women undergoing second-trimester abortion had significantly greater levels of post-traumatic stress symptoms at six weeks, but not at six or twelve months. Other measures of psychological morbidity were generally similar between the two groups. The small sample size of this study should be taken into consideration as well as the loss of follow-up of women in the second-trimester group, such that women "with higher levels of psychologi-cal distress early on were more likely to be lost to follow-up."

Elder and Laurence tested the effects of a support program for women undergoing second trimester termination for fetal abnormality in the United Kingdom. Describing women's reactions to the procedure, they found that 78 percent in one group (detection at ultrasound or early blood test) and

90 percent in a second group (detection at amniocentesis) experienced an acute grief reaction. Five women from the second group had prolonged periods of grief lasting up to two years. The authors conclude that abortion for fetal abnormality in the second trimester "should be regarded as no less serious than a stillbirth and that acute grief reactions by the parents must be expected," bearing in mind that this will be compounded by feelings of guilt for having chosen the procedure.[137]

Moreover, recent studies arising from the Christchurch Health and Development Study, a longitudinal cohort study dating back to 1979 in New Zealand, have found significantly elevated rates of suicidal behaviors, depression, substance abuse, anxiety, and other mental health concerns in young women following abortion, even after controlling for preexisting prepregnancy differences in mental health. The researchers concluded that abortion itself is a strong contributing factor in these outcomes.[138]

Dutch researchers found that, among 196 women aborting for fetal abnormality, grief and post-traumatic symptoms did not decrease between two and seven years after the event. In their cross-sectional sample, with a relatively high response rate of 79 percent, pathological post-traumatic scores were found in 17.3 percent of participants. Advanced gestational age was associated with more psychological distress. Grief and regret were reported by 8 percent and 10 percent of participants, respectively. The authors emphasize the importance of "adequate psychological support from the caregiver during the decision-making process in order to avoid impulsive and not fully internalised decisions."[24]

A metasynthesis of qualitative research involving women who had experienced abnormal prenatal tests found that couples chose to terminate their pregnancies for reasons including "the availability and acceptability of termination and the perceived certainty of fetal death." Factors contributing to the choice to terminate included ambivalence about the ability to parent an impaired child and altruistic concerns about the fetus, other children, and marriage and family life. The authors note that "no matter what they ultimately chose to do, couples felt pulled to make the opposite decision and justify it to themselves, to close and distant members of their social network, and to health care providers. Couples continuing their pregnancies felt pressure from providers to terminate their pregnancies, and all couples felt the need to explain or explain away their choices." They found that the intimate links between choice and loss involved in prenatal testing and abortion created a paradoxical situation that did not support a simplistic notion of "choice."[139]

Kersting et al. conducted a detailed analysis of three women's experiences of termination for fetal abnormality. The authors conclude that this event is to be seen as a severe trauma, which may entail a pathological grieving process, and that health professionals should be aware of the varying responses and coping methods.[140] The same researchers investigated eighty-three women terminating due to fetal malformation, comparing them with women terminating for nonmedical reasons and women giving birth. They found that termination of pregnancy due to fetal malformation is an emotionally traumatic major life event that leads to severe post-traumatic stress response and intense grief reactions that are still evident two to seven years after the procedure. Contrary to expectations, women's experiences of traumatic stress four years after the procedure were not significantly different from women's experiences fourteen days afterwards.[25]

Sandelowski and Barroso note that "positive prenatal diagnosis was devastating for women as it—and its aftermath—were embodied experiences for women, that is, prenatal testing, quickening, the continuation or termination of a pregnancy with an impaired fetus, and postpartum leaking of breast milk happen in women's bodies."[139] They also state that "couples experienced selective termination as a technologically induced, historically unique, and paradoxical form of suffering entailing the intentional loss of a desired pregnancy and killing to care....Couples, health care providers, family and friends underestimated the intensity and duration of feelings of loss following selective termination." They concluded that "couples experienced selective termination as traumatic, regardless of the prenatal test revealing the fetal impairment or stage in pregnancy in which the termination occurred."

In a 1993 study, Zeanah et al. concluded that "women who terminate pregnancies for fetal anomalies experience grief as intense as those who experience spontaneous perinatal loss, and they may require similar clinical management. Diagnosis of a fetal anomaly and subsequent termination may be associated with psychological morbidity."[141] Similarly, a 1997 study on the long-term effects of abortion for fetal disability concluded that "the long-term psychological stress response in women to pregnancy termination following ultrasonographic detection of fetal anomalies does not differ from the stress responses seen in women experiencing perinatal loss."[142]

Prenatal diagnosis and abortion of fetuses with disease or disability has been assumed beneficial for women, but the psychological consequences of these procedures has been a neglected area of research.[143] In particular, recent research (Davies et al.) questions the assumption that early detection and termination of fetal anomaly has better outcomes for women in psychological terms.[136]

Case Studies and Women's Stories

Clinical case studies and many stories written and told by women themselves confirm the research that shows abortion is associated with negative emotional and psychological outcomes for some.[144,145,146,147] In-depth surveys with seventeen women who had experienced abortion demonstrated the complexity, depth, and long-term nature of emotions relating to abortion. These women spoke of their immediate reactions to abortion as relief, sadness, and remorse. But in the long term (from six to thirty-one years postabortion) the women talked about flashbacks, anniversary-related depression, denial, emotional repression, fantasizing about the aborted fetus, and triggering of painful emotions by significant events many years later. Several women rode an "emotional roller coaster" for decades and thought constantly about their aborted children.[133]

The author notes that the research interview was, in itself, a therapeutic intervention for many of the women. She makes several recommendations for postabortion clinical practice, including the following:

- Take an extensive reproductive history of the pregnant woman, thus creating an atmosphere where she feels free to tell you about previous abortion(s) without feeling condemned or ashamed.

- Observe women during subsequent labor and immediate postpartum situations for postpartum depression, detachment from newborn, and unnatural grief.

- Help women work through grief for both miscarriage and previous abortion (s), acknowledging the losses.

- Assist perimenopausal and menopausal women who wish to make a life appraisal to be open about their abortion history and work through any unresolved feelings.

- Make appropriate referrals for spiritual, emotional, and/or psychiatric care.

Risk Factors for Psychological Harm and Emotional Distress

Some research has identified particular risk factors among women seeking abortion as predictive of negative psychological and emotional outcomes of abortion. Swedish researchers found that women are more likely to suffer both psychologically and emotionally from abortion if they live alone, have poor emotional support from family and friends, experience adverse postabortion change in relationship with their partner, have underlying ambivalence or adverse attitudes towards abortion, or are actively religious.[20] In one Swedish study, an absence of emotional distress immediately after the abortion was reported by women who had made the decision without conflict of conscience and without pressure.[27] Other researchers have found that ambivalence about the abortion and difficulty with the decision are predictors of postabortion psychological harm.[13,26] Clinicians should note that delaying the decision is a marker for ambivalence.[26]

Abortion for fetal abnormality is known to be associated with psychological morbidity. Relationship violence also predicts particularly negative responses to abortion.[20,118] In a study of abortion and post-traumatic stress disorder in Russian and American women, more negative responses to abortion in American women were related to being younger, having a history of divorce, not having been employed full-time, having more years of education, having bonded to the fetus, not believing in a woman's right to have an abortion, not being counseled before the abortion, having felt pressured into the decision, and having experienced more abortions. Among Russian women, negative responses were associated with having bonded to the fetus, not believing in a woman's right to have an abortion, having a partner who desired the pregnancy, experiencing health complications, feeling pressured into the decision, having experienced ambiguity surrounding the decision, not having received counseling before the procedure, and being further along in the pregnancy.[115]

Pre-pregnancy history of depression consistently predicted poorer post-abortion mental health and more negative abortion-related emotions and evaluations. Furthermore, younger women evaluated their abortion more negatively, as did women who had more children at the time of abortion.[22] A study of 13,261 women with an unplanned pregnancy in the United Kingdom found that women with a history of psychiatric illness were found to have higher rates of such illness after both abortion and childbirth (although in this study, psychiatric disorders after childbirth were found to be artificially inflated by poor coding). As noted earlier, however, the rate of deliberate self-harm was found to be significantly higher after abortion than after childbirth among women with no history of self-harm.[127]

A recent comprehensive review of the psychology of abortion summarizes research on "mediators in psychological processes." This means "how characteristics of the individual or experiences are able to partially or fully explain relations between specific predictor variables and outcomes."[26] The reviewers found evidence of several mediators in current postabortion psychology literature:

- *Self-efficacy*— the woman's judgment, taking into account her knowledge and her confidence, that she has the ability to successfully execute various life tasks.

- *Attribution of blame*—the degree to which the woman feels the situation was modifiable.

- *Subsequent reproductive events*—including another abortion or other forms of perinatal loss, such as miscarriage or stillbirth, difficulty conceiving, problems with a desired pregnancy, and giving birth.

Counselors, doctors and abortion practitioners need to be particularly alert to women who are seeking abortion yet express some enjoyment in being pregnant or a desire to have the child.

Chemical Abortion

Chemical abortion is increasingly promoted in many countries as a simple, convenient, and less invasive alternative to surgical abortion. Many women choose chemical abortion because they want to avoid a surgical procedure.[148] However, the procedures require more intervention and visits to the clinic than a surgical abortion. Chemical abortion involves the use of drugs to soften the cervix and cause the uterus to contract, expelling the fetus and placenta. It may take twelve to forty-eight hours, and even up to several days.[149] About 60 percent of women abort within twenty-four hours, but for 20 to 30 percent it may take three or more weeks.[150] Currently there is little evidence that the method is in any way preferable to surgical abortion. A Cochrane Review (of medical versus surgical methods for first trimester termination of pregnancy) found that the trials available for review were relatively small and that inadequate evidence existed to compare the acceptability and side effects between the two methods.[151]

Chemical abortion requires active patient participation and women are more aware of the physical aspects of the process, such as bleeding and cramping. On the other hand, chemical abortion offers a completed abortion without surgery or anesthesia, apparently similar to a "natural miscarriage," and a more private patient experience.[148] During second trimester abortion, women undergoing chemical abortion are more likely to require surgical intervention for missed abortion (29 percent of women undergoing chemical abortion compared with 4 percent undergoing surgical abortion).[152]

Misoprostol and methotrexate are used off-label in Australia for chemical abortion. Mifepristone is an oral antiprogestin. It blocks progesterone receptors and causes breakdown of the implantation site. It also causes local prostaglandin release to increase, causes the uterus to become more sensitive to prostaglandins, and softens the cervix. Methotrexate is an antimetabolite and interferes with DRNA synthesis, preventing the continuation of implantation. Misoprostol is a prostaglandin analog that causes the uterus to contract when administered orally or vaginally. The simple explanation is that the first drug prevents the embryo or fetus from continuing to implant, while the second medication causes cramping and therefore expulsion of the embryo or fetus.[148] In 2 to 10 percent of cases, surgical abortion is required to complete the abortion.[148]

A 1998 study in England compared women having surgical abortions with women having chemical abortions. The researchers found that women having chemical abortions rated the procedure as more stressful and painful, and they experienced more post-termination physical problems and disruption to their lives. Women may not expect, or are not told, that they may see the fetus, which was associated with nightmares, flashbacks, and unwanted thoughts related to the procedure. Of the chemical abortion group, 53 percent said they would choose the same procedure again, compared with 77 percent of the surgical group.[153] Another study by the same authors found similar results—chemical abortion was more stressful. This was related to the physical and emotional aspects of the process, seeing or feeling the fetus, waiting times during the procedure, and the process itself.[154]

These researchers also note that seeing the fetus is particularly distressing for women—it can "bring home the reality of the event and may influence later emotional adaptation."[154] Another researcher explains that the patient may expel the fetus at home and that some are curious about what it looks like and may benefit from seeing a photograph of an embryo/fetus of the appropriate age.[148] However, a recent study finds that during second trimester, chemical abortion was not significantly different from surgical abortion in relation to depression and grief (although this study had a very high attrition rate, with only fourteen of forty-nine subjects completing the study). The authors hypothesize that women who have contact with their dead fetus may have something tangible to grieve.[57]

Chemical abortion may result in the delivery of a live fetus, as alleged in a recent prosecution of a doctor in Sydney.[155] The psychological damage of such an experience is unknown, but should not be underestimated, and women need to know about this possibility. They also need to know that some drugs used in chemical abortion can cause serious birth defects in babies if the pregnancy continues. First-trimester exposure to misoprostol has been associated with skull and limb defects. Clinicians must stress the need to confirm the abortion and strongly advise a surgical procedure should the chemical abortion fail.[148]

Currently identified contraindications for chemical abortion include:[148]

- indecision about having an abortion;
- pregnancy beyond the gestational age limits;
- unwillingness to have a surgical abortion if the medical method fails;
- lack of telephone or beeper access;
- inability to return for follow-up visits;
- difficulty in completing all the steps of the protocol;
- inability to give consent.

Benefits of Abortion

The vast majority of studies have looked at potential negative effects of abortion. So far few, if any, benefits of abortion have been established. Studies consistently show that many women report relief immediately after abortion and in the months following, yet relief is often experienced in concurrence with negative emotions such as grief, guilt, and shame. A retrospective study of U.S. and Russian women who had experienced abortion found that 13.8 percent of U.S. women and 6.9 percent of Russian women felt relief after the abortion attributed to the abortion. The statement "felt more in control of my life" was given by 3.7 percent and 1.6 percent of U.S. and Russian women, respectively. In contrast, much higher percentages of women attributed negative outcomes to their abortion such as thoughts of suicide, guilt, substance abuse, relationship problems, sadness and loss, and expressions such as "felt part of me died" and "unable to forgive self."[115]

A prospective study of forty women after miscarriage and eighty women after abortion in Norway found that aborting women were significantly more likely to have feelings of relief as well as guilt and shame. Some women after miscarriage also reported relief.[124] In research to date, "relief" is generally undefined. Some researchers suggest a variety of interpretations: "Women who state they felt relief following an abortion may variously mean that they were relieved that they would not have the responsibility of a child to care for, relief that they had made it beyond the stressful day of the abortion, relief that they were no longer being pressured by others, relief that there was no longer a risk of their parents discovering the pregnancy, relief that the physical symptoms of pregnancy were over, relief that they did not experience any complications from the surgery, or numerous other forms of relief."[26]

Relief appears to be a short-term effect of abortion. Indeed, there are no studies indicating that relief continues to be experienced by women many years after their abortions. Major and Cozzarelli et al. found that relief was the most frequent emotion reported by women immediately after their abortion. However, among the women remaining in the study at two years (50 percent retention rate), reports of relief and other positive emotions had declined, and negative emotions had increased.[22]

A U.S. study of ninety-seven women used interviews at three stages: thirty minutes after the abortion, one week later, and one month later. Quality of life functions were measured by a Quality of Life questionnaire (originally designed for cancer patients), which contained items for physical, emotional, cognitive, and social functioning. The questionnaire also asked about fatigue, nausea, vomiting, and other gastrointestinal disturbances relevant to both cancer patients and pregnant women. Not surprisingly (since the baseline interview was held at a particularly emotionally distressing time immediately after the abortion) the women reported significant improvements in quality of life over one month. Symptoms of pregnancy were gone, although pain and physical functioning were worse at one week.[156] This study is widely cited as evidence that abortion generally improves women's well-being, despite its relatively small sample size and short time frame.

Abortion is sometimes conceptualized as a maturing or growth experience for women, giving an increased sense of control over one's life,[27] due to a process of intense introspection often associated with consideration of abortion that brings women to a state of greater self-understanding.[26] However, there is no evidence that maturation or growth is greater for those who abort relative to those who do not. Some studies report on women's self-assessed sense of well-being after abortion without providing a reference point of well-being before the abortion.[157, 158] Major et al. asked 438 women with abortion experience to rate their agreement or disagreement with the statement "I think the abortion has had a positive effect on me" on a scale of 1 (strongly disagree) to 5 (strongly agree), with an average response of 3.1.[22]

Russo and Zierk found higher self-esteem among women who had abortions than women who had given birth, and slightly higher than all women in the study. However, after controlling for contextual factors, which they called "childbearing and resource variables"—employment, income, and education—this effect disappeared. They concluded that, when examined in the context of childbearing and coping resources, the experience of abortion does not appear to have an independent relationship to women's well-being. They suggest that "abortion's positive relationship to well-being may come through its contribution to reducing women's total number of children rather than through a psychological effect of feeling empowered by having an abortion experience."[159] However, this hypothesis was not tested in their research.

Kero et al. question whether painful feelings after abortion are always to be considered problematic or threatening. Their study (discussed above under "negative emotional responses and replacement pregnancies") expressed a degree of mixed results, but more than half of the women reported only positive experiences such as maturity, deeper self-knowledge, strengthened self-esteem, and "identity of the abortion process." Other positive effects included maternal feelings, knowing they were fertile, and specific female experiences. Bad or mixed experiences were related to emotional and mental suffering, bad treatment at the hospital, or a disturbed sex life.[27] More research is needed to identify whether tangible long-term benefits of abortion exist for women.

Teenage Girls

Abortion is often promoted as a good option for pregnant teenagers. Again, evidence of benefits is lacking. On the contrary, strong evidence suggests that, once pregnant, choosing to give birth can have better outcomes for young women, or at least that giving birth is not a harmful choice. The National Longitudinal Study of Adolescent Health (U.S.) collected data on approximately 19,000 U.S. adolescents.[160] Adolescent females who had abortions were the *most* likely to report that they had wanted to become pregnant (79.3 percent of girls who had abortions reported their pregnancies as "wanted," 9.5 percent reported "undecided," 11.2 percent reported "unwanted"). The authors note the likelihood that parental input played an important role in these decisions, so the extent to which adolescents' preferences are reflected in their pregnancy outcomes is unknown.

Ever-pregnant girls (who had been pregnant at least once) had higher rates of delinquency than never-pregnant girls (who had never been pregnant). The highest rates of juvenile delinquency were among (1) those who gave babies up for adoptions (caution: small sample size), (2) those who had abortions, and (3) those who had miscarriages. Girls who kept their babies had delinquency rates the same as never-pregnant girls. Multivariate analysis of the data reveals that "the prevalence of delinquent behaviour is strongly dependent on the form of pregnancy resolution. Specifically, girls who have abortions or give their babies up for adoption have substantially higher rates of juvenile delinquency than those who keep their babies."

Other research has found that young mothers often demonstrate greater maturity than their childless peers and are especially unlikely to consume alcohol or spend time with friends who drink, and young fathers have especially high rates of participation in socially productive work.[160] Before pregnancy, girls in the "keep baby" group had significantly higher rates of smoking and marijuana use than girls in the "never-pregnant" group. After pregnancy, they had substance use rates about 45 percent lower than their never-pregnant peers. Adolescent pregnancy is linked to a complex range of problem behaviors, but the nature of those links depends on the outcome of the pregnancy. In addition, a 2005 study found that perceived quality of life in teenage mothers does *not* appear to be lower than the quality of life in teenagers without children or than that of adult women.[161]

Women with Mental Illness

It is sometimes claimed that only psychologically vulnerable women have emotional or psychological problems after abortion. This claim is not supported by the available evidence. It is true, however, that preexisting psychological problems are a risk factor for postabortion psychological problems.[26,22] This evidence calls into question the assumption that abortion will benefit women with doubtful mental health.

Some recent studies have included controls for prior psychological difficulties, and results suggest that abortion is associated with an increased risk for inpatient and outpatient treatment for various psychological problems, depression, and suicide.[125,120,72,126] A Norwegian prospective study of eighty women having induced abortion found that mental health before the termination did not influence women's psychological stress responses.[124] An important corollary is whether the experience of motherhood is harmful to women with serious mental illness. In a study of women with bipolar disorder, the authors wrote that "similar proportions of women perceived that pregnancy had a positive influence on their illness course and overall well-being (47%, 16 of 34) as those who reported negative effects (53%, 18 of 34). One-half reported that becoming a mother had bolstered their self-esteem."[162]

In the United States, a large number of women with major psychiatric disorders abort their pregnancies compared to the general population. Among a sample of ninety-three such women, abortion was associated with being a victim of sexual abuse and the experience of physical assault. Repeat abortions were prevalent. Women with reproductive losses were at greater risk for rehospitalization than the women who had no children.[163] There is an institutionalized bias against motherhood for women with mental illness. According to this research, "approximately one-half of the 70 respondents had been advised against pregnancy by a psychiatrist, primary care physician, obstetrician, or family members, suggesting widespread bias against pregnancy for such women."

Among women with major psychiatric disorders, "one or more extreme negative emotional responses regarding abortion occurred in one-third of the present study's participants. These extreme feelings involve predominantly anger and shame and should not be minimized nor ignored when they occur and, for some, may be unexpectedly intense. Obviously, there is no painless way to cope with an abortion."[164] It is possible that women with mental illness feel abortion is their only choice because psychiatric patients who give birth are at high risk of losing custody of their children.[164] Regrettably, there is little research on mental illness and pregnancy to inform women and clinicians in decision making.

Conceptualization of Abortion

Interpretation of the Harm of Abortion

The harm experienced by women who undergo abortion is a highly controversial and sensitive topic. The body of research on women's psychological and emotional responses to abortion is constantly expanding, yet it is easy to rely on a select few studies or reviews that may, in isolation, suggest that abortion is a benign experience for women. In fact, the breadth of women's experiences cannot be described by a single study. Women live with their reproductive decisions for a lifetime, and the long-term effects are perhaps more important than the short-term. Even if a minority (10 to 20 percent) of women experience severe responses to abortion, these half million or so Australian women are worthy of consideration in research and public policy.

Australian pro-choice researchers note that "fear of sabotaging the case for women's right to choose abortion has meant that the distress and ambivalence experienced by women facing a problem pregnancy and abortion has been understated or disregarded by some writers despite clinicians' and researchers' ready observation of its prevalence."[6] A feminist perspective that supports abortion might interpret the potential harm as something that women must accept if they are to have the right to choose. Others might assert, contrary to the evidence, that women suffering psychological anguish and harm after abortion are simply experiencing a continuation of suffering from previously existing conditions. Others believe that "being forced to choose between giving birth to a child or having an abortion seems impossible, but it can also be seen as part of the difficulty inherent in life.... The fact that we have to choose creates the anguish."[14]

Much research is carried out in the context of abortion service delivery. In such cases, many of the researchers support abortion and may feel compelled to evaluate their findings in a number of ways that maintain this support. First, the experience of a crisis or a difficult decision, or grief and loss, and even the experience of being pregnant temporarily, is conceptualized as beneficial because it results in maturity, growth, and improved understanding of others.[29,27] Second, the interpretation of "relief" varies according to the ideological perspective of the researcher. Third, the grief and mourning that the woman goes through is perceived as necessary and normal, and therefore unproblematic. One interpretation is that negative reactions "can be best understood within the framework of a normal stress response."[156] However, some researchers find that "although it has been suggested that emotional distress following abortion should be considered a normal stress reaction, our results do not support this view" because of the indications of regret and ambivalence among many women one year after the procedure.[20]

The reason for postabortion grief—the loss of something of value to the woman—often remains unexamined. Some researchers do not consider that the woman could have avoided such grief and pain by avoiding the abortion. It is also not considered whether the woman expected or was warned that she might experience such feelings. Kero and Lalos note that "the fact that women and men choose to have an abortion despite simultaneously feeling that they are relinquishing something that has a positive value is seldom emphasized in research. Feelings of ambivalence are an indication that abortion has a price, which implies that it is a more or less painful solution to the unwanted pregnancy."[29]

Regardless of how the harm of abortion is interpreted, women must be told about these potential harms if they are to have real choice. Also, since abortion is offered to women by the medical profession, the benefits ought to outweigh the harms or at least be established by evidence. This is not the case with abortion. Hence, more research and debate is necessary.

Abortion as a Perinatal Loss

Abortion is a perinatal loss, even when it is chosen, despite a widely held assumption that women do not grieve after abortion because they do not want the baby. It is assumed that miscarriage creates a problem for a woman who wants the baby, while abortion solves a problem for the woman who does not. Evidence suggests that reality is not so straightforward. One study showed that depression after miscarriage was associated with ambivalence towards the fetus.[165] Other studies found that psychological reactions to miscarriage were not related to whether or not the pregnancy was desired.[166,167]

Miscarriage is an emotionally traumatic experience for many women. After miscarriage, women's losses "consist not of an embryo or a foetus, but their child....A feeling of utter emptiness occurs after the little living creature who was there no longer exists."[168] Previous studies suggest that 48 to 51 percent of women who experience miscarriage will suffer psychiatric morbidity and that 22 to 44 percent of women will show clinically significant levels of depression and anxiety.[169]

The Norwegian study, Broen et al. discussed earlier, showed that women's responses after abortion compared with miscarriage were, in fact, quite similar, except that women after abortion had more feelings of guilt, shame, and relief and were more likely to experience avoidance of thoughts about the event, a common symptom of post-traumatic stress disorder. Towards the end of the follow-up period, two years after the procedures, feelings of loss and grief were similar between women who had had abortions compared with women who had miscarried.[124] Yet abortion is not widely discussed, and women do not publicly grieve their loss. Research suggests that a lack of grief reaction after abortion may increase the risk of later depression.[124]

It is widely believed that most women undergoing abortion do not want the baby. But in an Australian study, a significant minority of women who were attending an abortion clinic had expressed fantasies about the baby and maternal attachment to their fetus (for example, patting her tummy affectionately or talking to the baby) and had imagined what kind of mother she might be or what the baby might be like.[15]

Conclusion

This chapter is an evaluation of recent international research on the impact of abortion on women. What have emerged are myriad factors that influence a woman's decision making in pregnancy and the potential physical and psychological effects, in both the short- and long-term, of abortion on women. Further research is required to better understand the pressures influencing women to decide to undergo termination of pregnancy and how those pressures can be addressed and ameliorated, but existing research appears to be converging on the conclusion that abortion has significant detrimental effects on women.

For those concerned about women's well-being and freedom, the negative impacts of abortion on significant numbers of women underscores the need for public policy and structural and cultural changes to enable women to make informed decisions without undue external pressures. Notwithstanding the methodological difficulties inherent in abortion research and the controversies involved, comprehensive consideration of the available evidence also provides an important opportunity to develop creative public policy and community initiatives that address the real needs of women.

Submitted to the Papers of the Doha International Conference for the Family.

Endnotes

1. Bankole, A., Singh, S., and Taylor, H. (1998). Reasons why women have induced abortions: evidence from 27 countries. *International Family Planning Perspectives, 24*(3).

2. Söderberg, H., Andersson, C., Janzon, L., and Sjöberg, N.O. (1993). Sociodemographic characteristics of women requesting induced abortion. A cross-sectional study from the Municipality of Malmö, Sweden. *Acta Obstetrica et Gynecologica Scandinavica, 72,* 365–368.

3. Adelson, P., Frommer, M., and Weisberg, E. (1995). A survey of women seeking termination of pregnancy in New South Wales. *Medical Journal of Australia, 163,* 419–422.

4. Smith, A.M.A., et al. (2003). Sex in Australia: Reproductive experiences and reproductive health among a representative sample of women. *Australian and New Zealand Journal of Public Health, 27*(2), 204–9.

5. Parliament of South Australia. 33rd Annual Report of the Committee Appointed to Examine and Report on Abortions Notified in South Australia for the Year 2002. Published 2004.

6. Allanson, S., and Astbury, J. (1995). The abortion decision: reasons and ambivalence. *Journal of Psychosomatic Obstetrics and Gynaecology, 16,* 123–136.

7. Pulley, L., Klerman, L.V., Tang, H., and Baker, B.A. (2002). The extent of pregnancy mistiming and its association with maternal characteristics and behaviours and pregnancy outcomes. *Perspectives on Sexual and Reproductive Health, 34* (4), 206–211.

8. Barrett, G., and Wellings, K. (2002). What is a "planned" pregnancy? Empirical data from a British study. *Social Science and Medicine, 55,* 545–557.

9. Klerman, L.V. (2000). The intendedness of pregnancy: a concept in transition. *Maternal and Child Health Journal, 4*(3), 155–162.

10. Sable, M.R., and Libbus, M.K. (2000). Pregnancy intention and pregnancy happiness: are they different? *Maternal and Child Health Journal, 4*(3).

11. Williams, L., Piccinino, L., Abma, J., and Arguillas, F. (2001). Pregnancy wantedness: attitude stability over time. *Social Biology, 48*(3), 212–233.

12. Petersen, R., et al. (2001, September/October). How contraceptive use patterns differ by pregnancy intention: implications for counselling. *Women's Health Issues, 11*(5), 427–435.

13. Törnbom, M., et al. (1999). Decision-making about unwanted pregnancy. *Acta Obstetrica et Gynecologica Scandinavica, 78,* 636–41.

14. Alex, L., and Hammarström, A. (2004). Women's experiences in connection with induced abortion—a feminist perspective. *Scandinavian Journal of Caring Sciences, 18,* 160–8.

15. Allanson, S., and Astbury, J. (1996). The abortion decision: fantasy processes. *Journal of Psychosomatic Obstetrics and Gynaecology, 17,* 158–167.

16. Singer, J. (2004). Options counselling: techniques for caring for women with unintended pregnancies. *Journal of Midwifery and Women's Health, 49,* 235–242.

17. Poole, V.L., et al. (2000). Changes in intendedness during pregnancy in a high-risk multiparous population. *Maternal and Child Health Journal, 4*(3), 179–182.

18. Kero, A., Hogberg, U., Jacobsson, L., and Lalos, A. (2001). Legal abortion: a painful necessity. *Social Science and Medicine, 53,* 1481–1490.

19. Söderberg, H., et al. (1997). Continued pregnancy among abortion applicants: A study of women having a change of mind. *Acta Obstetrica et Gynecologica Scandinavica, 76,* 942–947.

20. Söderberg, H., Janzon, L., and Sjöberg, N.O. (1998). Emotional distress following induced abortion. A study of its incidence and determinants among abortees in Malmö, Sweden. *European Journal of Obstetrics and Gynecology and Reproductive Biology, 79,* 173–8.

21. Söderberg, H., et al. (1998). Selection bias in a study on how women experienced induced abortion. *European Journal of Obstetrics and Gynecology, 77,* 67–70.

22. Major, B., et al. (2000). Psychological responses of women after first-trimester abortion. *Archives of General Psychiatry, 57,* 777–784.

23. Husfeldt, C., et al. (1995). Ambivalence among women applying for abortion. *Acta Obstetrica et Gynecologica Scandinavica, 74,* 813–817.

24. Korenromp, M.J., et al. (2005). Long-term psychological consequences of pregnancy termination for fetal abnormality: a cross-sectional study. *Prenatal Diagnosis, 25,* 253–260.

25. Kersting, A., et al. (2005, March). Trauma and grief 2–7 years after termination of pregnancy because of fetal anomalies—a pilot study. *Journal of Psychosomatic Obstetrics and Gynecology, 26*(1), 9–15.

26. Coleman, P.K., Reardon, D.C., Strahan, T., and Cougle, J.R. (2005). The psychology of abortion: a review and suggestions for future research. *Psychology and Health, 20*(2), 237–271.

27. Kero, A., Högberg, U., and Lalos, A. (2004). Wellbeing and mental growth —long-term effects of legal abortion. *Social Science and Medicine, 58*, 2559–2569.

28. Skjeldestad, F.E. (1994). When pregnant—why induced abortion? *Scandinavian Journal of Social Medicine, 22*(1), 68–73.

29. Kero, A., and Lalos, A. (2000). Ambivalence—a logical response to legal abortion: a prospective study among women and men. *Journal of Psychosomatic Obstetrics and Gynecology, 21*(2), 81–91.

30. White-Van Mourik, M.C.A., Connor, J.M., and Ferguson-Smith, M.A. (1992). The psychosocial sequelae of a second-trimester termination of pregnancy for fetal abnormality. *Prenatal diagnosis, 12*, 189–204.

31. Larsson, M., Aneblom, G., Odlind, V., and Tyden, T. (2002). Reasons for pregnancy termination, contraceptive habits and contraceptive failure among Swedish women requesting an early pregnancy termination. *Acta Obstetrica et Gynecologica Scandinavica, 81*, 64–71.

32. Sihvo, A., Bajos, N., et al. (2003). Women's life cycle and abortion decision in unintended pregnancies. *Journal of Epidemiological and Community Health, 57*, 601–605.

33. Karvelas, Patricia, and Hart, Cath. (2004, 10 November). Age emerges as abortion factor. *The Australian.*

34. St. John, H., Critchley, H., and Glasier, A. (2005). Can we identify women at risk of more than one termination of pregnancy? *Contraception, 71*, 31–34.

35. Fisher, W.A., et al. (2005, March 1). Characteristics of women undergoing repeat induced abortion. *Canadian Medical Journal, 172*(5), 637–41.

36. Phillips, S. (2005, March 1). Violence and abortions: what's a doctor to do? *Canadian Medical Journal, 172*(5), 653–4.

37. Skjeldestad, F.E., Borgan, J.K., Daltveit, A.K., and Nymoen, E.H. (1994). Induced abortion: effects of marital status, age and parity on choice of pregnancy termination. *Acta Obstetrica et Gynecologica Scandinavica, 73*, 255–260.

38. Glander, S., Moore, M., Michielutte, R., and Parsons, L. (1998). The prevalence of domestic violence among women seeking abortion. *Obstetrics and Gynecology, 91*, 1002–6.

39. Taft, A.J., Watson, L.F., and Lee, C. (2004). Violence against young Australian women and association with reproductive events: a cross-sectional analysis of a national population sample. *Australian and New Zealand Journal of Public Health, 28*(4), 324–9.

40. Hedin, L.W., and Janson, P.O. (2000). Domestic violence during pregnancy: the prevalence of physical injuries, substance use, abortions and miscarriages. *Acta Obstetrica et Gynecologica Scandinavica, 79*, 625–630.

41. Keeling, J., Birth, L., and Green, P. (2004). Pregnancy counselling clinic: a questionnaire survey of intimate partner abuse. *Journal of Family Planning and Reproductive Health Care, 30*(3), 165–8.

42. Leung, T.W., et al. (2002). A comparison of the prevalence of domestic violence between patients seeking termination of pregnancy and other general gynecology patients. *International Journal of Gynecology and Obstetrics, 77,* 47–54.

43. Webster, J., Chandler, J., and Battistutta, D. (1996, February). Pregnancy outcomes and health care use: effects of abuse. *American Journal of Obstetrics and Gynecology, 174*(2), 760–7.

44. Woo, J., Fine, P., and Goetzl, L. (2005). Abortion disclosure and the association with domestic violence. *Obstetrics and Gynecology, 105,* 1329–34.

45. Wiebe, E.R., and Janssen, P. (2001, September/October). Universal screening for domestic violence in abortion. *Women's Health Issues, 11*(5), 436–441.

46. Saltzmann, L.E., et al. (2003, March). Physical abuse around the time of pregnancy: an examination of the prevalence and risk factors in 16 states. *Maternal and Child Health Journal, 7*(1), 31–43.

47. Webster, J., Sweett, S., and Stolz, T.A. (1994). Domestic violence in pregnancy: a prevalence study. *Medical Journal of Australia, 161,* 466–470.

48. Walsh, D., and Weeks, W. (2004, August). *What a Smile Can Hide.* A report prepared for *The Support and Safety Survey: The social, economic and safety needs of women during pregnancy,* Women's Social Support Services, Royal Women's Hospital, Brisbane.

49. Taft, A. (2002). Violence against women in pregnancy and after childbirth: Current knowledge and issues in health care responses. *Australian Domestic and Family Violence Clearinghouse Issues Paper 6.*

50. Kroelinger, C.D., and Oths, K.S. (2000). Partner support and pregnancy wantedness. *Birth, 27*(2), 112–119.

51. Stanford, J.B., et al. (2000). Defining dimensions of pregnancy intendedness. *Maternal and Child Health Journal, 4*(3), 183–189.

52. Evans, A. (2001). The influence of significant others on Australian teenagers' decisions about pregnancy resolution. *Family Planning Perspectives, 33*(5), 224–230.

53. Bianchi-Demicheli, F., et al. (2003). Contraceptive practice before and after termination of pregnancy: a prospective study. *Contraception, 76,* 107–113.

54. Bonari, L., et al. (2004). Perinatal risks of untreated depression during pregnancy. *Canadian Journal of Psychiatry, 49*(11), 726–735.

55. Marcus, S.M., Flynn, H.A., Blow, F.C., and Barry, K.L. (2003). Depressive symptoms among pregnant women screened in obstetric settings. *Journal of Women's Health, 12*(4), 373–380.

56. Evans, J., et al. (2001, 4 August). Cohort study of depressed mood during pregnancy and after childbirth. *British Medical Journal, 323,* 257–260.

57. Burgoine, G.A., et al. (2005). Comparison of perinatal grief after dilation and evacuation or labor induction in second trimester terminations for fetal anomalies. *American Journal of Obstetrics and Gynecology, 192*(6), 1928–1932.

58. Ross, L.E., Sellers, E.M., Gilbert Evans, S.E., and Romach, M.K. (2004). Mood changes during pregnancy and the postpartum period: development of a biopsychosocial model. *Acta Psychiatrica Scandinavica, 109,* 457–466.

59. http://www.beyondblue.org.au/index.aspx?link_id=4.65

60. Press, N., and Browner, C.H. (1997). Why women say yes to prenatal diagnosis. *Social Science and Medicine, 45*(7), 979–989.

61. Markens, S., Browner, C., and Press, N. (1999). "Because of the risks": How us pregnant women account for refusing prenatal screening. *Social Science and Medicine, 49,* 359–369.

62. Abramsky, L., Hall, S., Levitan, J., and Marteau, T.M. (2001, 24 February). What parents are told after prenatal diagnosis of a sex chromosome abnormality: Interview and questionnaire study. *British Medical Journal, 322,* 463–466.

63. Dunne, C., and Warren, C. (1998). Lethal autonomy: The malfunction of the informed consent mechanism within the context of prenatal diagnosis of genetic variants. *Issues in Law & Medicine, 14*(2), 165–202.

64. Brookes, A. (1994). Women's experience of routine prenatal ultrasound. *Healthsharing Women, 5*(3&4), 1–5.

65. Hunfeld, J.A., Wladimiroff, J.W., and Passchier, J. (1994, February). Pregnancy termination, perceived control, and perinatal grief. *Psychological reports, 74* (1), 217–8.

66. Marteau, T., and Drake, H. (1995). Attributions for disability: the influence of genetic screening. *Social Science and Medicine, 40*(8), 1127–1132.

67. Lippman, A., cited in Marteau, T., and Drake, H. (1995). Attributions for disability: the influence of genetic screening. *Social Science and Medicine, 40*(8), 1127–1132.

68. De Visser, R.O., and Smith, A.M.A., et al. (2003). Sex in Australia: Experiences of sexual coercion among a representative sample of adults. *Australian and New Zealand Journal of Public Health, 27*(2), 204–9.

69. Reardon, D., Makimaa, J., and Sobie, A. (eds). (2000). *Victims and Victors: Speaking Out About their Pregnancies, Abortions and Children Resulting from Sexual Assault.* San Francisco: Acorn Books.

70. Sundari Ravindran, T.K., and Balasubramanian, P. (2004). "Yes" to abortion but "No" to sexual rights: the paradoxical reality of married women in rural Tamil Nadu, India. *Reproductive Health Matters, 12*(32), 88–99.

71. National Health and Medical Research Council. (2004). *General Guidelines for Medical Practitioners on Providing Information to Patients* (p. 11). Canberra: Australian Government.

72. Reardon, D.C., et al. (2002, August). Deaths associated with pregnancy outcome: a record linkage study of low income women. *Southern Medical Journal, 95* (8), 834–841.

73. Gissler, M., et al. (2004). Pregnancy-associated mortality after birth, spontaneous abortion, or induced abortion in Finland, 1987–2000. *American Journal of Obstetrics and Gynecology, 190*(2), 422–7.

74. Gissler, M., Hemminki, E., and Lönnqvist, J. (1996). Suicides after pregnancy in Finland, 1987–94: register linkage study. *British Medical Journal, 313,* 1431–4.

75. Strahan, T. (2003). Incomplete or inaccurate reporting of information on 47 death certificates of U.S. women who died from confirmed or suspected legal abortion: 1972–1992. *Research Bulletin of the Association for Interdisciplinary Research in Values and Social Change, 17*(4).

76. Horon, I.L. (2005). Underreporting of maternal deaths on death certificates and the magnitude of the problem of maternal mortality. *American Journal of Public Health, 95*(3), 478–82.

77. Gissler, M., Kaupplia, R., Merilainen, J., et al. (1997). Pregnancy-associated deaths in Finland 1987–1994—definition problems and benefits of record linkage. *Acta Obstetrica et Gynecologica Scandinavica, 76*, 91–97.

78. Shadigian, E.M., and Bauer, S.T. (2005, March). Pregnancy-associated death: a qualitative systematic review of homicide and suicide. *Obstetrical and Gynecological Survey, 60*(3), 183–190.

79. Zhou, W., et al. (1999). Induced abortion and subsequent pregnancy duration. *Obstetrics and Gynecology, 94*(6), 948–53.

80. Ancel, P.Y., et al. (2004). History of induced abortion as a risk factor for preterm birth in European countries: results of the EUROPOP study. *Human Reproduction, 19*(3), 734–40.

81. Ekwo, E.E., Gosselink, C.A., and Moawad, A. (1993). Previous pregnancy outcomes and subsequent risk of preterm rupture of amniotic sac membranes. *British Journal of Obstetrics and Gynaecology, 100*(6), 536–41.

82. Moreau, C., et al. (2005). Previous induced abortions and the risk of very preterm delivery: results of the EPIPAGE study. *BJOG, 112*(4), 430–7.

83. Martius, J.A., Steck, T., Oehler, M.K., and Wulf, K.H. (1998). Risk factors associated with preterm (<37+0 weeks) and early preterm birth (<32+0 weeks): univariate and multivariate analysis of 106 345 singleton births from the 1994 statewide perinatal survey of Bavaria. *European Journal of Obstetrics, Gynecology, and Reproductive Biology, 80*(2), 183–9.

84. Henriet, L., and Kaminski, M. (2001). Impact of induced abortions on subsequent pregnancy outcome: the 1995 French national perinatal survey. *BJOG, 108*(10), 1036–42.

85. Moon, H.S., et al. (1997, February). Iatrogenic secondary infertility caused by residual intrauterine fetal bone after midtrimester abortion. *American Journal of Obstetrics and Gynecology, 176*(2), 369–370.

86. Wallach, E.E. (1990). Fertility after contraception or abortion. *Fertility and Sterility, 54*(4), 559–573.

87. Smith, C.D., et al. (2001). Genital infection and termination of pregnancy: are patients still at risk? *Journal of Family Planning and Reproductive Health Care, 27*(2), 81–84.

88. La Montagne, D.S., et al. (2004, December). Management of genital chlamydial infections at termination of pregnancy services in England and Wales: where are we now? *BJOG, 111*, 1408–1412.

89. Zhou, W., and Olsen, J. (2003). Are complications after an induced abortion associated with reproductive failures in a subsequent pregnancy? *Acta Obstetrica et Gynecologica Scandinavica, 82*, 177–181.

90. Pridmore, B.R., and Chambers, D.G. (1999). Uterine perforation during surgical abortion: a review of diagnosis, management and prevention. *Australian and New Zealand Journal of Public Health, 39*(3), 349–53.

91. Ananth, C.V., Smulian, J.C., and Vintzileos, A.M. (1997). The association of placenta previa with history of cesarean delivery and abortion: a metaanalysis. *American Journal of Obstetrics and Gynecology, 77*(5), 1071–8.

92. Faiz, A.S., and Ananth, C.V. (2003, March). Etiology and risk factors for placenta previa: an overview and meta-analysis of observational studies. *Journal of Maternal Fetal Neonatal Medicine, 13*(3), 175–90.

93. Taylor, V.M., Kramer, M.D., Vaughan, T.L., and Peacock, S. (1993, July). Placental previa in relation to induced and spontaneous abortion: a population-based study. *Obstetrics and Gynecology, 82*(1), 88–91.

94. Tuzović, L., et al. (2003). Obstetric risk factors associated with placenta previa development: case-control study. *Clinical Sciences, 44*(6), 728–733.

95. Johnson, L.G., Mueller, B.A., and Daling, J.R. (2003). The relationship of placenta previa and history of induced abortion. *International Journal of Gynecology and Obstetrics, 81,* 191–198.

96. Infante-Rivard, C., and Gauthier, R. (1996). Induced abortion as a risk factor for subsequent fetal loss. *Epidemiology, 7,* 540–542.

97. Sun, Y., et al. (2003). Induced abortion and risk of subsequent miscarriage. *International Journal of Epidemiology, 32*(3), 449–54.

98. Zhou, W., Sørensen, H.T., and Olsen, J. (2000). Induced abortion and low birthweight in the following pregnancy. *International Journal of Epidemiology, 29,* 100–106.

99. Dumitrescu, R.G., and Cotarla, I. (2005, January–March). Understanding breast cancer risk – where do we stand in 2005? *Journal of Cellular and Molecular Medicine, 9*(1), 208–21.

100. Veronesi, U., et al. (2005, May). Breast cancer. *Lancet, 365*(9472), 1727–41.

101. Verlinden, I. et al. (2005, April). Parity-induced changes in global gene expression in the human mammary gland. *European Journal of Cancer Prevention, 14*(2), 129–37.

102. Ye, Z., et al. (2002). Breast cancer in relation to induced abortions in a cohort of Chinese women. *British Journal of Cancer, 87,* 977–981.

103. Lash, T.L., and Fink, A.K. (2004). Null association between pregnancy termination and breast cancer in a registry-based study of parous women. *International Journal of Cancer, 110,* 443–448.

104. Brind, J., Chinchilli, V.M., Severs, W.B., and Sunny-Long, J. (1996). Induced abortion as an independent risk factor for breast cancer: a comprehensive review and meta-analysis. *Journal of Epidemiology and Community Health, 50,* 481–96.

105. Daling, J.R., Malone, K.E., Voigt, L.F., White, E., and Weiss, N.S. (1994). Risk of breast cancer among young women: relationship to induced abortion. *Journal of the National Cancer Institute, 86*(21), 1584–92.

106. Daling, J.R., et al. (1996, August 15). Risk of breast cancer among white women following induced abortion. *American Journal of Epidemiology, 144*(4), 373–80.

107. Collaborative Group of Hormonal Factors in Breast Cancer. (2004). Breast cancer and abortion: collaborative reanalysis of data from 53 epidemiological studies, including 83,000 women with breast cancer from 16 countries. *Lancet, 363,* 1007–16.

108. Lindefors-Harris, B.-M., Eklund, G., Adami, H.-O., and Meirik, O. (1991). Response bias in a case-control study: analysis utilizing comparative data concerning legal abortions from two independent Swedish studies. *American Journal of Epidemiology, 134,* 1003–8.

109. Meirik, O., Adami, H.-O., and Eklund, G. (1998). Letter re: Relation between induced abortion and breast cancer. *Journal of Epidemiology and Community Health, 52,* 209–12.

110. Chan, A., and Keane, R.J. (2004, 1 March). Prevalence of induced abortion in a reproductive lifetime. *American Journal of Epidemiology, 159*(5), 475–80.

111. Tang, M.C., Weiss, N.S., Daling, J.R., and Malone, K.E. (2000, June). Case-control differences in the reliability of reporting a history of induced abortion. *American Journal of Epidemiology, 151*(12), 1139–43.

112. Jagannathan, R. (2001). Relying on surveys to understand abortion behaviour: some cautionary evidence. *American Journal of Public Health, 91*(11), 1825–1831.

113. Udry, J.R., et al. (1996). A medical record linkage analysis of abortion underreporting. *Family Planning Perspectives, 28*(5), 228–231.

114. Pregnancy Outcome Unit. (2003, November). *Pregnancy Outcome in South Australia 2002* (p. 45). Department of Human Services.

115. Rue, V.M., Coleman, P.K., Rue, J.J., and Reardon, D.C. (2004). Induced abortion and traumatic stress: a preliminary comparison of American and Russian women. *Medical Science Monitor, 10*(10), SR5–16.

116. Reardon, D.C., and Cougle, J.R. (2002). Depression and unintended pregnancy in the National Longitudinal Survey of Youth: a cohort study. *British Medical Journal, 324,* 151–2.

117. Schmeige, S., and Russo, N.F. (2005, 28 October). Depression and unwanted pregnancy: longitudinal cohort study. *British Medical Journal,* doi:10.1136/bmj.38623.532384.55

118. Russo, N., Denious, J.E. (2001). Violence in the lives of women having abortions: Implications for policy and practice. *Professional Psychology Research and Practice, 32,* 142–150.

119. Reardon, D. (2005, 1 November). Study fails to address our previous findings and subject to misleading interpretations. *British Medical Journal Rapid Responses.*

120. Cougle, J., Reardon, D.C., and Coleman, P.K. (2003). Depression associated with childbirth: a long-term analysis of the NLSY cohort. *Medical Science Monitor, 9,* CR105–112.

121. Harlow, B.L., et al. (2004). Early life menstrual characteristics and pregnancy experiences among women with and without major depression: the Harvard study of moods and cycles. *Journal of Affective Disorders, 79,* 167–76.

122. Bianchi-Demicheli, F., et al. (2002). Termination of pregnancy and women's sexuality. *Gynecologic and Obstetric Investigation, 53*(1), 48–53.

123. Cougle, J.R., Reardon, D.C., and Coleman, P.K. (2005). Generalized anxiety following unintended pregnancies resolved through childbirth and abortion: a cohort study of the 1995 National Survey of Family Growth. *Journal of Anxiety Disorders, 19*(1), 137–42.

124. Broen, A.N., et al. (2004). Psychological impact on women of miscarriage versus induced abortion: a 2-year follow-up study. *Psychosomatic Medicine, 66,* 265–271.

125. Coleman, P.K., Reardon, D.C., Rue, V., and Cougle, J. (2002). State-funded abortions vs deliveries: a comparison of outpatient mental health claims over four years. *American Journal of Orthopsychiatry, 72,* 141–152.

126. Reardon, D.C., et al. (2003). Psychiatric admissions of low-income women following abortion and childbirth. *Canadian Medical Association Journal, 168*(10), 1253–6.

127. Gilchrist, A.C. et al. (1995). Termination of pregnancy and psychiatric morbidity. *British Journal of Psychiatry, 167* 243–8.

128. Tewari, S.K., et al. (2001, May). Understanding factors influencing request for a repeat termination of pregnancy. *Health Bulletin (Edinb), 59*(3), 193–7.

129. Coleman, P.K. (2005). Induced abortion and increased risk of substance abuse: a review of the evidence. *Current Women's Health Review, 1*(1), 21–34.

130. Coleman, P.K., Reardon, D.C., Rue, V.M., and Cougle, J.R. (2002). A history of induced abortion in relation to substance use during subsequent pregnancies carried to term. *American Journal of Obstetrics and Gynecology, 187,* 1673–8.

131. Reardon, D.C., Coleman, P.K., and Cougle, J.R. (2004, May). Substance use associated with unintended pregnancy outcomes in the National Longitudinal Survey of Youth. *American Journal of Drug and Alcohol Abuse, 30*(2), 369–83.

132. Coleman, P.K., Reardon, D.C., and Cougle, J.R. (2005). Substance use among pregnant women in the context of previous reproductive loss and desire for current pregnancy. *British Journal of Health Psychology, 10,* 255–268.

133. Hess, R.F. (2004). Dimensions of women's long-term postabortion experience. *MCN, 29*(3), 193–198.

134. Coleman, P.K., and Nelson, E.S. (1998). The quality of abortion decisions and college students' reports of post-abortion emotional sequelae and abortion attitudes. *Journal of Social and Clinical Psychology, 17*(4), 425–442.

135. Kolker, A., and Burke, B.M. (1993). Grieving the wanted child: ramifications of abortion after prenatal diagnosis of abnormality. *Health Care Women International, 14*(6), 513–26.

136. Davies, V., et al. (2005). Psychological outcome in women undergoing termination of pregnancy for ultrasound-detected fetal anomaly in the first and second trimesters: a pilot study. *Ultrasound in Obstetrics and Gynecology, 25,* 389–392.

137. Elder, S.H., and Laurence, K.M. (1991). The impact of supportive intervention after second trimester termination of pregnancy for fetal abnormality. *Prenatal Diagnosis, 11,* 47–54.

138. Fergusson, D.M., Horwood, L.J., and Ridder, E.M. (2006). Abortion in young women and subsequent mental health. Journal of Child Psychology & Psychiatry 47(1): 16–24.

139. Sandelowski, M., and Barroso, J. (2005, May/June). The travesty of choosing after positive prenatal diagnosis. *JOGNN, 34,* 307–318.

140. Kersting, A., et al. (2004, June). Grief after termination of pregnancy due to fetal malformation. *Journal of Pyschosomatic Obstetrics and Gynecology, 25*(2), 163–169.

141. Zeanah, C., et al. (1993). Do women grieve after terminating pregnancies because of fetal anomalies? a controlled investigation. *Obstetrics and Gynecology, 82,* 270–5.

142. Salvesen, K.A., et al. (1997, February). Comparison of long-term psychological responses of women after pregnancy termination due to fetal anomalies and after perinatal loss. *Ultrasound in Obstetrics and Gynecology, 9* (2), 80–5.

143. Leithner, K., et al. (2004, March). Affective state of women following a prenatal diagnosis: predictors of a negative psychological outcome. *Ultrasound in Obstetrics and Gynecology, 23,* 240–246.

144. Bianchi-Demicheli, F., Lüdicke, D., and Chardonnens, D. (2004). Imaginary pregnancy 10 years after abortion and sterilization in a menopausal woman: a case report. *Maturitas: The European Menopause Journal, 48,* 479–481.

145. Tankard Reist, M. (2000). *Giving Sorrow Words: Women's stories of grief after abortion.* Sydney: Duffy and Snellgrove.

146. Butler, C. (1996). Late psychological sequelae of abortion: questions from a primary care perspective. *Journal of Family Practice October, 43*(4), 396–402.

147. Brockington, I. (2005, May). Post-abortion psychosis. *Archives of Women's Mental Health, 8*(1), 53–4.

148. Breitbart, V. (2000). Counselling for medical abortion. *American Journal of Obstetrics and Gynecology, 183*(2)(Suppl.), S26–S33.

149. Hedley, A., et al. (2004, December). Accounting for time: insights from a life-table analysis of the efficacy of medical abortion. *American Journal of Obstetrics and Gynecology, 191*(6), 1928–33.

150. Goldberg, A.B., Carusi, D.A., and Meckstroth, K.R. (2003). Misoprostol in gynecology. *Current Women's Health Reports, 3,* 475–483.

151. Say, L., Kulier, R., Gulmezoglu, M., and Campana, A. (2005, 25 January). Medical versus surgical methods for first trimester termination of pregnancy. *Cochrane Database System Review* (1), CD003037.

152. Autry, A.M., Hayes, E.C., Jacobson, G.F., and Kirby, R.S. (2001). A comparison of medical induction and dilation and evacuation for second-trimester abortion. *American Journal of Obstetrics and Gynecology, 187,* 393–7.

153. Slade, P., Heke, S., Fletcher, J., and Stewart, P. (1998). A comparison of medical and surgical termination of pregnancy: choice, emotional impact and satisfaction with care. *British Journal of Obstetrics and Gynaecology, 105,* 1288–1295.

154. Slade, P., Heke, S., Fletcher, J., and Stewart, P. (2001). Termination of pregnancy: patients' perceptions of care. *The Journal of Family Planning and Reproductive Health Care, 27*(2), 72–77.

155. Doctor charged with manslaughter. (2005, 10 August). *Courier-Mail.*

156. Westhoff, C., Picardo, L., and Morrow, E. (2003). Quality of life following early medical or surgical abortion. *Contraception, 67,* 41–47.

157. Major, B., Zubek, J.M., Cooper, M.L., Cozzarelli, C., and Richards, C. (1997). Mixed messages: implications of social conflict and social support within close relationships for adjustment to a stressful life event. *Journal of Personality and Social Psychology, 72,* 1349–1363.

158. Cozzarelli, C., Sumer, N., and Major, B. (1998). Mental models of attachment and coping with abortion. *Journal of Personality and Social Psychology, 74,* 453–467.

159. Russo, N., and Zierk, K. (1992, August). Abortion, childbearing, and women's well-being. *Professional Psychology Research and Practice, 23*(4), 269–280.

160. Hope, L.T., Wilder, E.I., and Watt, T.T. (2003, Fall). The relationships among adolescent pregnancy, pregnancy resolution, and juvenile delinquency. *Sociological Quarterly, 44*(4), 555–576.

161. Wrennick, A.W., Schneider, K.M., and Monga, M. (2005). The effect of parenthood on perceived quality of life in teens. *American Journal of Obstetrics and Gynecology, 192,* 1465–8.

162. Viguera, A.C., et al. (2002). Reproductive decisions by women with bipolar disorder after prepregnancy psychiatric consultation. *American Journal of Psychiatry, 159,* 2102–2104.

163. Thomas, T., Tori, C.D., and Scheidt, S.D. (1996). Psychosocial characteristics of psychiatric inpatients with reproductive losses. *Journal of Health Care for the Poor and Underserved, 7*(1), 15–23.

164. Thomas, T., and Tori, C.D. (1999). Sequelae of abortion and relinquishment of child custody among women with major psychiatric disorders. *Psychological Reports, 84,* 773–790.

165. Beutel, M., Deckhardt, R., von Rad. M., and Werner, H. (1995). Grief and depression after miscarriage: their separation, antecedents, and course. *Psychosomatic Medicine, 67,* 517–26.

166. Neugebauer, R., Kline, J., Shrout, P., et al. (1997). Major depressive disorder in the first six months after miscarriage. *JAMA, 277,* 383–8.

167. Neugebauer, R., Kline, J., O'Connor, P., et al. (1992). Determinants of depressive symptoms in the early weeks after miscarriage. *American Journal of Public Health, 82,* 1332–9.

168. Adolfsson, A., Larsson, P.G., Wijma, B., and Berterö, C. (2004). Guilt and emptiness: women's experiences of miscarriage. *Health Care for Women International, 25*(6), 543–60.

169. Athey, J., and Spielvogel, A.M. (2000). Risk factors and interventions for psychological sequelae in women after miscarriage. *Primary Care Update for Ob/Gyns, 7,* 64–69.

16

The Abortion–Breast Cancer Connection

Joel Brind (USA)
Professor of Human Biology and Endocrinology
Baruch College, City University of New York, USA

The reputation of abortion as safe for women—which claim is explicitly part of the *Roe v. Wade* decision—has rightfully come under serious question for many reasons over the years since *Roe*. One of the reasons that "safe abortion" has come under question is the evidence linking abortion to an increased risk of breast cancer (ABC link). The ABC link has been an issue that has been in and out of the limelight in recent years. It is an issue that has stubbornly refused to go away despite recurrent pronouncements from high places of its nonexistence.

A recent example is a 2004 article in the prestigious British medical journal *The Lancet*.[1] The paper was promoted by the mainstream media as "a full analysis of the current data."[2] According to the byline on the paper, the results of all these studies were compiled into a "collaborative reanalysis," by the "Collaborative Group on Hormonal Factors in Breast Cancer," a group of authors too numerous to list. However, a small print footnote reveals that the study was actually put together by a group of five scientists at Oxford University, headed by prominent British epidemiologist Valerie Beral. The Beral study's conclusion is unequivocal: "Pregnancies that end as a spontaneous or induced abortion do not increase a woman's risk of developing breast cancer."[3] This conclusion is remarkably reminiscent of the National Cancer Institute's (NCI) statement given on its "Cancer Facts" Web page on "Abortion, Miscarriage, and Breast Cancer Risk," carried on the NCI Web site since the spring of 2003.[4] On this "fact sheet," the NCI concludes that "having an abortion or miscarriage does not increase a woman's subsequent risk of developing breast cancer."

The trouble is, to accept this conclusion, one needs to dismiss almost half a century's worth of data that do show a significant link between abortion and an increased risk of breast cancer. Beral et al. suggest that those previous studies "yielded misleading results,"[5] and that one should trust the largest, most recent studies (i.e., those that show no ABC link). Such apparently knowledgeable pronouncements seem just a bit too self-assured in an age when concerns about women's health reign supreme.

If one can be certain of anything about the ABC link, it is surely that the question of its very existence is important enough for a careful evaluation, given the millions who choose abortion and the tens of thousands who die of breast cancer each year. This chapter, therefore, examines the ABC link in some historical and scientific detail, offering a perspective on an issue that is at the center of a long-running public policy debate that, having been sucked into the maelstrom of the "abortion wars," plays out in legislatures, courtrooms, and newspaper editorials, as well as in scientific and medical journals.

Early History of the ABC Link

Neither the ABC link nor the efforts to suppress it are new; the first published study to document it occurred almost half a century ago. Over the years, denial of the ABC link has become the party line of all major governmental agencies [including the World Health Organization (WHO)],[6] mainstream medical associations (including the American College of Obstetricians and Gynecologists[7] and Royal College of Obstetricians and Gynaecologists),[8] and the most prestigious medical journals (including the *New England Journal of Medicine*).[9]

A 1957 nationwide study in Japan (published in the English language *Japanese Journal of Cancer Research*) reported that women who had breast cancer had a threefold higher frequency of pregnancies that had ended in induced abortion.[10] As abortion was neither legal nor common in many places, however, such studies were few and far between. But in 1970, a very high profile, multinational WHO study, based at Harvard and published in the WHO's own *Bulletin,* reported a disturbing trend "in the direction which suggested increased risk associated with abortion—contrary to the reduction in risk associated with full-term births."[11] The WHO study findings were not based specifically on induced abortion, including both induced abortions and miscarriages, but it is interesting that they came out just about the time when, in the United States and elsewhere, the question of legalization of induced abortion was being widely considered. The fact that the WHO findings never entered the debate reveals a disturbing—and continuing—disconnect between the so-called women's health advocates pushing for legalized abortion, and any genuine concern for women's health.

The first epidemiological study on American women to consider the ABC link specifically was published in the *British Journal of Cancer* (*BJC*) by Malcolm Pike and colleagues[12] of the University of Southern California in 1981. Since abortion had been legal in the United States for scarcely a decade by then, the only appropriate candidates for the study were women diagnosed with breast cancer by their early thirties. In other words, the subjects needed to have been young enough to have been exposed to legal abortion. The results of the Pike study made headlines: women who had an abortion before they had any children were at a 2.4-fold (i.e., 140 percent) increased risk for breast cancer.

The response of the scientific community to the Pike study was dichoto-mous: reflective of responsible concern from some quarters, and of active denial from others. Exemplifying the former was a 1982 review in the presti-gious journal *Science* by Willard Cates, Jr., of the Centers for Disease Control and Prevention.[13] Writing on the overall, roughly decade-long history of the safety of legal abortion in the United States, Cates expressed his concern: "There is some concern about...possibly higher risks of breast cancer in cer-tain women." Exemplifying the effort to deny the ABC link, however, was a 1982 study published in the *BJC* by a group from Oxford University (interest-ingly, with overlapping authorship with the 2004 Oxford [Beral] "collabora-tive reanalysis").[14] The 1982 Oxford study targeted Pike's study specifically and claimed greater credibility for its much larger number of patients (1,176 compared with 163 in the Pike study) and much greater age range (up to age fifty, compared with a maximum age of thirty-two in the Pike study). The Oxford group's conclusion was as noteworthy for its emotional tone as for its contrary result: "The results are entirely reassuring, being, in fact, more compatible with protective effects than the reverse." Scientifically, it is a sim-ple matter to explain the Oxford group's negative result: It was based almost entirely on miscarriages, as so few of the women in the study had been young enough to be exposed to legal induced abortion. The biological differences between these two events are clear and are discussed in some detail a bit later on in this chapter. It was also particularly telling that, in a paper based entirely on quantitative data, the only quasiquantitative expression in the entire text (or tables) for the number of women in the study who had actually undergone an induced abortion was "only a handful of women." Clearly, this Oxford "study" was little more than a fabrication of apparently negative data, designed to "reassure" the public about the safety of abortion.

The Biology behind the Statistics

One would think, especially given the overwhelmingly elective nature of induced abortion, that the precautionary principle would prevail, if not in terms of legal regulation, then at least in terms of recommendations by medi-cal societies and public health agencies. That is to say, even one or two studies showing a significant association between induced abortion and future breast cancer risk would surely raise some red flags about the procedure's safety. Yet not only was a statistical connection showing up in the vast majority of stud-ies that had examined the issue, but, by the early 1980s, a clear picture of the physiological events explaining that connection was beginning to emerge.

One important line of evidence providing biological support for the ABC link came from the field of reproductive endocrinology (the study of the hor-mones of reproduction). Only during the 1970s did laboratory methods for measuring such hormones as estradiol (the main active form of estrogen) and progesterone easily and cheaply become widely available. In 1976, a landmark study by two Swiss obstetricians, Kunz and Keller, was published in the *British Journal of Obstetrics and Gynaecology*.[15] The Kunz and Keller study documented a clear difference between the enormous rise of estrogen and progesterone in the first trimester of viable pregnancies and the stunted and short-lived rise of these hormones during pregnancies destined to abort spontaneously (miscarry). These findings dovetailed perfectly with the patterns of differences in breast cancer risk following different pregnancy outcomes that was now clearly emerging from the epidemiological data.

During the same period of the late 1970s, key experimental research on laboratory rats was providing another avenue of verification of the ABC Link. Jose and Irma Russo, a prominent husband-and-wife research team at the Michigan Cancer Foundation in Detroit (they are now at Fox Chase Cancer Center in Philadelphia) conducted a landmark study in which rats were exposed to standard, cancer-producing doses of a known chemical carcinogen after different pregnancy outcomes.[16] Almost 80 percent of rats who had undergone surgical abortion developed breast cancer (similar to rats not allowed to become pregnant at all), while those allowed a full-term pregnancy were completely protected from developing the disease.

Not only do experimental animals provide verification of epidemiological data, but their bodies can be examined microscopically during and after the experiment. In this way, the Russos have been major players in the discovery of the changes that take place in the mammalian breast before, during, and after pregnancy. In Figure 16.1, lobules type 1 (LOB 1) represent those very primitive structures present in the breast at birth. Lobules type 2 (LOB 2, not pictured) are present in greatest number after puberty, but before any pregnancy. Only toward the end of a full-term pregnancy (about thirty-two weeks gestation in the human species) do most lobules become lobules type 3 (LOB 3; see Figure 16.2), which are much denser and elaborate and capable of lactation. Lobules type 4 are those that are actively producing milk. The progression from type 1 to type 3 requires an enormous amount of cellular multiplication. Lobules type 3 are also terminally differentiated, meaning the cells' ability to multiply has switched off. Part of the development process in the breast, and in most types of tissue generally, is this terminal differentiation. Cancer, whether of the breast or any other tissue, is a disease wherein cellular multiplication or proliferation is out of control. Therefore, it is only those cells that are still capable of proliferation, such as the cells in lobules type 1 and type 2, which are vulnerable to the effects of carcinogens. Carcinogens can cause cancer by causing mutations in the cellular DNA. Such abnormal cells, if they are then stimulated to proliferate, can ultimately progress to malignancy.

Knowledge of the development of breast lobules thus provides a coherent explanation of the experimental results obtained in the rats treated with carcinogens. In rats not allowed to complete a pregnancy, most of the lobules would be type 2, in which most cancers are known to arise due to lack of full differentiation. Treating these rats with a carcinogen therefore resulted in most developing breast cancer. In contrast, rats allowed to bear a full-term litter of pups were resistant to the carcinogen, since most of their breast lobules

Figure 16.1   Primative lobule structures present in breast at birth.

had developed into types 3 and 4. In other words, the carcinogen would have caused just as many mutations, but any abnormal cells that may have been generated were incapable of proliferation, and therefore incapable of becoming cancerous.

The facts about lobular development in the breast also provide a clear explanation of the epidemiological data. That is, the completion of a full-term pregnancy provides some level of permanent protection against breast cancer, because it leaves a woman with fewer vulnerable, undifferentiated cells that can give rise to cancer. The younger a woman is when she has her first full-term pregnancy, the greater the protection, since it means there would be less time overall during which her breasts contained a large percentage of such vulnerable cells. The breast cell situation with induced abortion is that not only are the cells not yet differentiated, but because of the growth stimulation of pregnancy hormones—mainly estradiol—during the incomplete pregnancy, there are more of those cancer-vulnerable cells in the

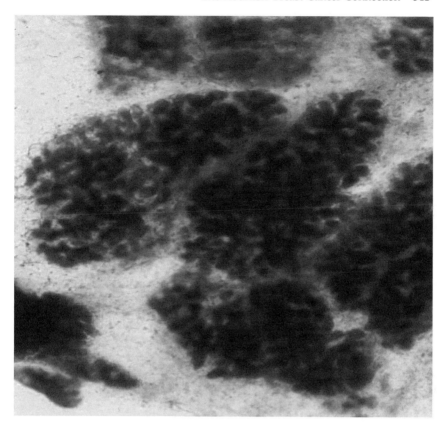

Figure 16.2   Primative lobule structures present in breast at birth.

breasts than were there at the start of the pregnancy. Consequently, most epidemiological studies have shown higher risks in women who have had an induced abortion than in those who had not become pregnant at all.

Knowledge of the actions of estrogen and progesterone in terms of their effects upon breast growth completes the coherent picture of induced—but not spontaneous—abortion and breast cancer risk. As long as some progesterone is present (called a "permissive hormone" in this situation), estradiol (which, recall, is a form of estrogen) is a strong promoter of cellular proliferation in the breast. The greatest growth stimulation occurs by far in the first and second trimesters of a normal pregnancy. Importantly, estrogen is implicated in most known risk factors for breast cancer: everything from taking artificial estrogens in the form of birth control pills or postmenopausal estrogen replacement therapy to beginning menstruation at an early age and/or having menopause at a later age (both of which cause a greater lifetime exposure to estrogen). Even nonreproductive risk factors such as postmenopausal obesity and chronic alcohol consumption are explained in terms of such women having higher chronic circulating levels of estrogen (because fat cells actually make estrogen and alcohol impedes the liver's ability to degrade estrogen).

Epidemiological Data Continue to Accrue

During the 1980s and early 1990s, as various researchers studied older and older populations of women who had been exposed to legalized abortion, study after study—in Japan,[17] Europe,[18] and the United States[19]—continued to report significantly increased breast cancer risk in women who had had an induced abortion. By 1994, six epidemiological studies out of seven in the United States, on women of both black and white ethnicity, had reported increased risk with induced abortion.[20] It should be noted that most of these data reflected the standard of comparing the effects of having a pregnancy which was ended by induced abortion versus the effects of not having had that pregnancy (as opposed to versus continuing that pregnancy to childbirth). Yet, even with the issue of breast cancer having had more media exposure, and achieving major publicity with a "National Breast Cancer Awareness Month," which highlighted that it had about 200,000 victims per year, abortion—which was emerging as the most preventable of cancer causes—received no attention whatsoever.

That changed abruptly at the end of October 1994, with the publication of a study by Janet Daling and colleagues of the Fred Hutchinson Cancer Research Center in Seattle, Washington.[21] The Daling study could hardly avoid a high profile, as it was published in the *Journal of the National Cancer Institute (JNCI)*. The Daling team's overall finding was of a statistically significant, 50 percent increase in the risk of breast cancer among women who had chosen abortion. Even the *New York Times* carried the story with the headline "New Study Links Abortions and Increase in Breast Cancer Risk."[22] But forces were already set in motion to make sure the news was short-lived. For one thing, the Daling study was accompanied by a most unusual *JNCI* editorial.[23] It was unusual because most medical journal editorials, written by a scientist who has peer-reviewed the study, are published by the journal in order to highlight the importance of a major study on a subject of wide public interest. Such editorials typically make it easy for reporters—usually nonscientists working on short deadlines—to glean the major points of a study and render it understandable to the general public. Instead, Dr. Lynn Rosenberg, of Boston University School of Medicine, took the opportunity to write an editorial that sandbagged the Daling study, concluding—among other things—that "…the overall results as well as the particulars are far from conclusive, and it is difficult to see how they will be informative to the public." Rosenberg did offer a possible explanation for drawing the inferences that she did, introducing the idea that "reporting bias" could well have generated a false positive result. Since "reporting bias" (also known as "response bias" or "recall bias") continues to be employed as the main reason to dismiss the ABC link, it is discussed in some detail below.

But first, there are other aspects to the Daling study and its treatment in the professional and popular media that need to be aired. In the study itself, it was ominous enough that it showed that women in general suffered a 50 percent increased risk of getting breast cancer after choosing abortion. However, there were other findings yet more ominous. The risk was far more—more than a 100 percent increase—for women who had an abortion prior to age eighteen or after age thirty. The risk was also compounded for women who had any family history of breast cancer—even a grandmother or aunt. That is, when women with a family history of breast cancer and an abortion were compared with women with a family history of breast cancer and no abortion, they were found to have an 80 percent increased risk, rather than a 50 percent increased risk. As for women with the three risk factors combined, that is, abortion before age eighteen with a positive family history of breast cancer, the relative risk was actually reported as infinite. It should be admitted that this last statistic was based on only twelve women; i.e., all twelve women who had such a reproductive and family history were found among the 845 breast cancer patients, and none of them were found among the 961 healthy control women to whom they were compared. Could any other medical or surgical intervention—especially one chosen by over a million healthy patients each year—that raised such a specter of mortal danger in a major, peer-reviewed study, continue unabated, and still be touted as safe?

Most assuredly not. But the number of abortion's apologists and promoters, within the ranks of science and medicine as well as politics and the media, is prodigious. Rosenberg's "poison pill editorial" in the *JNCI* gives us a hint, and ensuing events were even more revealing. For example, the article in the *New York Times,* while attracting attention by headlining Daling's conclusion of overall increased risk, was as dismissive as Rosenberg's editorial. While it is appropriate to cut reporters some slack for their being misled by the medical journal itself, it should be noted that the author of the *Times* story, Dr. Lawrence Altman, was a seasoned epidemiologist in his own right who worked for many years in the Centers for Disease Control. He should certainly have known better. It turns out that Altman was later dragged through the professional mud in July 1995, when an article in *Science* berated him for giving the Daling study a credible headline.[24] Daling herself was treated even worse, having her study belittled in the professional and lay media alike for several months following its publication, although she continued to stand by her findings.

As for the editorialist Rosenberg, she could hardly claim any degree of objectivity. Her editorial clearly misrepresented the Daling study, an act that by itself satisfies most definitions of scientific misconduct. Rosenberg has also shown herself to take a stance that appears to go beyond "pro-choice" (as Janet Daling has described herself), and that is radically pro-abortion. In 1999, for example, she served on behalf of a group of Florida abortion clinics as an expert witness in their (ultimately successful) facial challenge of a new parental notification law in Florida for minors seeking abortion.[25] Such minimal restrictions on abortion are supported by the vast majority of even pro-choice citizens, but not by the likes of Rosenberg. Other strange events bear her fingerprints. For example, a study on breast cancer in South Australian women was published in the *American Journal of Epidemiology (AJE)* in 1988,[26] when Rosenberg was an associate editor.[27] Only seven years later, in the *British Journal of Cancer,* did a small review appear that revealed that abortion—which had been omitted entirely as a variable in the 1988 *AJE* paper (the data about abortion in that study were kept unpublished)—was the strongest and most significant risk factor identified in the 1988 study.[28] Specifically, the 1988 data showed that South Australian women who had had an induced abortion experienced a statistically significant, 160 percent increased risk of breast cancer.

The Reporting Bias Canard

Of course, Rosenberg's dismissive editorial that accompanied the Daling study seemed plausible enough to the untrained reader, and she did offer a reason why Daling's results could not be trusted. What she wrote in this particular regard was: "A major concern, especially because the observed effect was small, is the possibility of reporting bias."[29] This attribution of an observed ABC link to reporting bias (aka "response bias" or "recall bias") refers to a potential weakness in any epidemiological study that relies on a retrospective data collection method. What "retrospective" refers to is collecting data through interviews and/or questionnaires from cancer patients and healthy control subjects who have been identified for the study. Such studies rely, therefore, on the subjects' ability and/or willingness to recall or report their history of exposure to the variable in question. What the term "bias" refers to in this context is a difference in the reporting accuracy between the cases and the controls. If—the argument goes—breast cancer patients are more likely to remember and report a history of abortion than are control subjects, then abortion would appear more often among the patient population, even if no more of them had had an abortion than the control women. This discrepancy would translate, in turn, to an increased risk (i.e., a relative risk > 1.0) of breast cancer associated with abortion, but it would not be a real result.

This reporting bias hypothesis seems all the more plausible because abortion is such a sensitive subject for women to talk about. In fact, the under-reporting of abortion history is well documented in the literature. The real question is whether or not there is a difference in reporting accuracy between cases and controls. The hypothesis of such a bias is certainly testable and worthy of testing. The problem with the hypothesis, however, is that it has repeatedly been tested, and the bias found not to exist.

Actually, the first paper that articulated the reporting bias argument in ABC research, and claimed to have found such evidence, was a 1991 paper by a group headed by Olav Meirik of the WHO.[30] However, a closer look at that claim reveals just how far beyond the breaking point some are willing to stretch scientific credibility in order to reach a politically correct conclusion. The Meirik group had previously performed a study in the late 1980s (published in *The Lancet*)[31] on reproductive risk factors for breast cancer, based on retrospective interviews with women in Sweden and Norway. The Swedish women in that study had also had their abortions recorded at the time they took place (in addition to recalling them for the later study interview), so in the 1991 *AJE* study, Meirik compared these prospective medical records with the responses the women had given in the earlier study.[32] Meirik's group found a significant difference between the interview responses and the medical records, that is, "between underreporting of previous induced abortions among controls [those who did not develop breast cancer] relative to overreporting among cases [those who did develop breast cancer]."[33] This peculiar term, "overreporting," actually is intended to mean what it says; that is, that women who reported having had an abortion of which the computer had no record were deemed to have imagined the event. Without such a preposterous assumption, the Meirik group could produce no significant evidence of reporting bias. Under some published peer pressure—from both Daling's group and my own—Meirik et al. quietly retracted the claim of "overreporting" in a published letter in 1998.[34] However, they did not retract the hypothesis of reporting bias in ABC research, and reporting bias continues to be cited as fact by the NCI and all the other "mainstream" sources of public health information.

Yet, not only is there no credible evidence for the existence of reporting bias in ABC research, but there is ample credible evidence to prove its nonexistence by any reasonable standard. Even going back to the early days of ABC research, a 1968 study published in Japan reported an increased risk of over 50 percent in women who had had an abortion.[35] In this case, the fact that the control subjects were also cancer patients—stomach cancer patients, rather than healthy controls—is evidence against reporting bias. More recently, a 1989 study performed by the New York State Department of Health, which was based on fetal death records—not retrospective interviews—reported a 90 percent increase in risk among women who had had an induced abortion (relative risk = 1.9).[36] In a more recent study in 2000, Daling's group did something similar to what Meirik et al. had done.[37] They compared retrospective interview responses with responses given by the same women several years earlier, at the time of a prenatal interview, long before anyone could have known who would end up with breast cancer. Their result was also unequivocal: "The authors' data do not suggest that controls are more reluctant to report a history of induced abortion than are women with breast cancer."[38]

Though false, the reporting bias argument was—and still is—sufficient to keep the ABC link as a credible scientific finding out of the public consciousness. As long as the public keeps faith in government agencies such as the NCI, some voluntary organizations such as the American Cancer Society, and the major medical journals and societies, and so long as these agencies send a clear unified message, then it does not matter whether the message is true or false: the public will believe it. The only effective counterweight to such unified enforcement of the party line (in this case, "safe abortion") is an independent media. Importantly, the mainstream media's tendency to lean in the pro-choice direction is well known, and it reinforces their tendency to view the mainstream scientific and medical authorities as authoritative. The mainstream media is therefore not the prime mover in the ongoing effort to deny the reality of the ABC link.

Comprehensive Review Refocuses Public Attention

This influence of the mainstream media became clear with the October 1996 publication of the "comprehensive review and meta-analysis" on the ABC link, which I wrote in conjunction with Vernon Chinchilli, Walter Severs, and Joan Summy-Long of the Pennsylvania State College of Medicine, and published in the British Medical Association's (BMA) epidemiology journal, the *Journal of Epidemiology and Community Health (JECH)*.[39] I had deliberately chosen this journal in order to get a fair shake at publishing it without substantive change. Moreover, we did not wish to have our study misrepresented and discounted in a *JNCI* editorial, as had happened to the 1994 Daling study. (As it happens, in December the *JNCI* did publish an editorial that misrepresented and discounted our paper, but at least we had two months for our message to gain some traction.)[40]

Our paper was both a narrative review and quantitative compilation of every published study we could find (there were twenty-three) that had reported data on the ABC link. We also enumerated the studies that reported data on spontaneous abortion and those that did not distinguish between induced and spontaneous abortion. Our conclusion was a statistically significant, overall 30 percent increase in the risk of breast cancer among women who had had an induced abortion, and no significant link with spontaneous abortion. Importantly, the comparison criterion for induced abortion was—as it has always been—"not having had that pregnancy," rather than the childbirth choice. We also included an extensive discussion of the theory and the evidence that form the biological basis of an ABC link.

Fortunately, the institutions involved in the publication of the meta-analysis paper—Baruch College, Penn State Medical College, and the BMA—made efforts to draw media attention, and the news was reported widely around the world. Unfortunately, but not surprisingly, the backlash from "mainstream" science and medicine was swift and unrelenting.

Just three months after the publication of our meta-analysis, a new paper that was widely hailed as the definitive disproof of the ABC link appeared in what is arguably the most prominent and prestigious medical journal in the world, the *New England Journal of Medicine (NEJM)*.[41] Although this was a study only of women in Denmark, and authored by Mads Melbye and colleagues of the Statens Serum Institut in Copenhagen, it was largely funded by the U.S. Department of Defense and heralded by a *NEJM* editorial written by Patricia Hartge, a senior NCI scientist. Hartge's editorial conclusion was: "In short, a woman need not worry about the risk of breast cancer when facing the difficult decision of whether to terminate a pregnancy."[42] This followed quite naturally from the Melbye group's conclusion: "Induced abortions have no overall effect on the risk of breast cancer."[43]

Just how, one may reasonably ask, could one single study's result nullify almost half a century's data from dozens of studies? The answer given was basically a two-pronged argument: strength in numbers, and use of prospective medical records, which eliminates the possibility of reporting bias. In regard to the former, the Melbye study is no doubt the largest study on the ABC link, comprising every woman born in the state of Denmark between 1935 and 1978 (over 1.5 million women), over 300,000 abortions, and over 10,000 cases of breast cancer. The null result (relative risk = 1.00) was stated with very tight statistical limits (i.e., very high confidence). In the public mind, the Melbye study pretty much did settle the issue, even though scientifically it was a complete travesty.

What was hailed as the Melbye study's greatest strength actually turned out to be its greatest weakness. That is, while its reliance on medical records does indeed preclude the possibility of reporting bias, the flaws in the compilation of the data were breathtaking. For starters, the study included records of induced abortions dating back to 1973. Melbye's justification for this seems straightforward enough: "In 1973, the legal right to an induced abortion through 12 weeks' gestation was established for women with residence in Denmark."[44] The implication here, of course, is that Denmark had the equivalent of *Roe v. Wade* in 1973, before which time elective abortion was not legal. In fact, induced abortion has been legal (and on record) in Denmark for reasons other than medical necessity since 1939 and was only most recently liberalized in 1973.[45] Consequently, some 60,000 of the oldest women in the Melbye study cohort—the part of the population with the most cases of breast cancer—who had had an abortion before 1973, were misclassified as not having had an abortion, because their abortions had not been entered into the computerized registry.[46] This is a very crucial point. It is not necessarily very consequential if records are missing for many patients, providing these patients are thus excluded from the analysis. But it is quite another matter when these patients are included in the study as subjects, thus representing their abortion history as different than it actually was.

Yet the Melbye study embodies still more egregious violations of proper scientific methodology. Most glaring was the inclusion of breast cancer diagnoses dating back to 1968. This actually violates the most fundamental rule of all in scientific inquiry, i.e., temporality: cause must precede effect. Yet here, Melbye was measuring the effect—breast cancer—from 1968, five years before beginning the collection of data in 1973 on the potential cause: induced abortion. Despite these glaring gaps and flaws, the calculation of Melbye's raw numbers resulted in a 44 percent increase in breast cancer risk with induced abortion, an increase that did not appear in print in the study, and which was made to disappear with statistical adjustment.[47] Even then, the Melbye study still reported—but not as a "conclusion"—a statistically significant trend of increasing breast cancer risk with gestational age at abortion. Thus, women who had aborted at more than eighteen weeks' gestation were at more than double the risk of breast cancer, compared to women who had aborted at less than seven weeks gestation. Clearly, the Melbye study was purely a political exercise in the guise of a scientific study, designed to shore up the reputation of abortion as safe for women.

While the Melbye study was generally quite effective in keeping the ABC link out of public awareness, the issue kept rearing its head around the United States as state after state considered abortion informed consent laws that mandated that ABC link warnings be given by abortion practitioners to women seeking abortion. Many such bills got as far as enactment into state law in the 1990s, specifically, those in Mississippi, Montana (enjoined by a state court in 1999), Louisiana, and Kansas. Texas and Minnesota followed in 2003. Over a dozen more states continue to debate such legislation perennially. But the stubborn persistence of the issue has been tested with a continuing program of denial from high places, most notably from the National Cancer Institute.

Since the publication of the Daling study in 1994, the NCI has maintained a "Cancer Facts" fact sheet devoted to abortion and breast cancer on its Web site. Until early 1997, the message was generally dismissive of the ABC link, calling the evidence for it "inconsistent and inconclusive."[48] In 1997, however, shortly after the publication of the Melbye study, the NCI ratcheted up the rhetoric of denial, claiming that "there is no convincing evidence of a direct relationship between breast cancer and either induced or spontaneous abortion."[49] The inclusion of spontaneous abortion here serves to confuse the issue, since the difference between induced and spontaneous abortion in terms of pregnancy hormones and breast cancer risk had long been resolved. But most outrageous about the new version of the NCI fact sheet was the addition of the following sentence: "The scientific rationale for an association between abortion and breast cancer is based on limited experimental data in rats, and is not consistent with human data." This, of course, was exactly contrary to reality, as the scientific rationale was based on many lines of evidence (as discussed above), and the ABC link is entirely consistent with the overwhelming majority of studies on women.

Fortunately, there were some members of Congress who knew better, and were also in a position to exercise their constitutional oversight authority to rein in the NCI. Most notable was Dr. Tom Coburn (R-OK), an obstetrician as well as a congressman, who managed to ask some hard questions of NCI representative Dr. Edison Liu at a 1998 congressional subcommittee hearing in the House Commerce Committee. Within months after a pointed follow-up letter was sent to the NCI Director from the Chairman of the Commerce Committee, Tom Bliley (R-VA),[50] there was a substantial modification of the language of the NCI's Web site fact sheet. Thus, "no convincing evidence" morphed into "evidence of a direct relationship...is inconsistent." Most importantly, the most offensive and untruthful statement about the "scientific rationale" and the data's "not [being] consistent with human data" was completely expunged.[51]

With the NCI forced to take at least a noncommittal stance, the ABC link continued to emerge around the United States as a state issue in terms of informed consent legislation.

A Slew of Large New Studies

Between the years 2000 and 2003, several new studies were published on women from the United Kingdom, China, and Scandinavia, studies that, yet again, were trumpeted as definitively disproving the ABC link. When subjected to close scrutiny, however, the validity of their findings again runs into serious trouble.

The 2001 UK study was authored by Oxford epidemiologist Michael Goldacre et al., and published in the *JECH*.[52] Interestingly—and it would seem hardly by coincidence—the Goldacre study had overlapping authorship with both the 1982 Oxford study[53] and the 2004 "collaborative reanalysis."[54] The Goldacre study was widely considered to be very strong because, like the 1997 Melbye study, it involved a very large number of women (over 350,000), over 28,000 of whom had developed breast cancer. Also like the Melbye study, the Goldacre study relied entirely upon medical records of abortion, from the (UK) National Health Service (NHS) hospital records. The results actually showed a statistically significant 17 percent decrease in breast cancer risk among women who had had any induced abortions. However, also like the Melbye study, many missing abortion records resulted in the misclassification of abortion-positive women as abortion-negative. But even more egregiously than in the Melbye study, more than 90 percent of abortion-positive women were misclassified in this way. This could be quite easily determined, since the Goldacre study was based on all the women who had been admitted to NHS hospitals in the Oxford area for any reason. A simple perusal of statistics on induced abortion in the United Kingdom reveals that at least 15 percent of those women were abortion-positive,[55] yet the records upon which the Goldacre study relied indicated that only just over 1 percent of the cancer patients—300 of them, to be exact—had an induced abortion on record. Such a massive gap in the database renders any study of the ABC link in this population statistically meaningless.[56]

China, on the other hand, comprising a population under very tight control and in which abortion is very common, would seem to offer a very good place to do ABC link research. Between 2000 and 2002, three published reports of two studies on overlapping populations of female textile workers in Shanghai appeared in the *American Journal of Epidemiology*,[57] the *International Journal of Cancer*,[58] and the *British Journal of Cancer*.[59] These studies were quite large, reflecting a study population of over 260,000 total, and the Ye study was based on prospective data—that is, women had filled out questionnaires when they entered the study, before any of them developed breast cancer. The Sanderson study was based on retrospective interviews, and the results of both studies were essentially null; that is, no significant effect on breast cancer risk was found associated with induced abortion. The main problem with the Chinese studies is that abortion is so common (over 50 percent of the study population in both the Sanderson and Ye studies). In addition (and contrary to the usual pattern in the United States and the United Kingdom), almost all abortions are done after the birth of a woman's first (and usually only) child. Thus, the women in the study who had not had an abortion at a given age were not typical. These women were either childless or they had their first child at an older age, characteristics that are both risk factors for breast cancer. In other words, the women who had an abortion were being compared to what amounts to a high-risk subgroup of women, rather than to a group of women who are truly typical of the population, and the risk-increasing effect of abortion was therefore masked.[60] This difficulty is inherent in the nature of epidemiology, and it arises when the exposure in question—in this case, induced abortion—has become the rule rather than the exception within the population under study.

In Scandinavia, a study by Erlandsson et al. appeared in the *International Journal of Cancer* in 2003.[61] This study was reasonably large—almost 1800 case-controlled pairs, which made it about twice as large as the 1994 Daling study. As in most of the other large recent studies discussed above, the data were collected prospectively, and the study was widely viewed as more credible for that reason. However, as in the Melbye and Goldacre studies, the Erlandsson study ran into the misclassification problem resulting from huge gaps in the database. The subjects were all Swedish women who had had at least one live birth during the study period, because in Sweden a record is automatically created at an antenatal interview. In the antenatal record, each woman gives a detailed history, including any abortions. The registry of antenatal record data was linked by Erlandsson et al. to the breast cancer registry in order to find any connection between induced abortion and breast cancer. Similar to the Goldacre study, Erlandsson et al. found a 20 percent decrease in risk of breast cancer with women who had had abortions, with a borderline significance to that decrease. The problem here is that the typical pattern of induced abortion in Sweden is more like that in China than the United States or the United Kingdom; that is, abortion is used more often to limit family size than to delay first childbirth. What that means for the Erlandsson study is quite simply that most of the induced abortions in the study population happened sometime between the antenatal interview (when all the abortion data were collected) and the time of breast cancer diagnosis, and were therefore missing from the record. Here again, then, we find a database that is simply unsuitable for obtaining a valid result regarding the ABC link because most of the women who had had an induced abortion were misclassified as not having had one.[62]

A final note regarding these large recent studies is in order. In the authors' discussions of their findings in the text of the papers, all misrepresent the published record of previous articles involving research on ABC. Specifically, all omit any mention of the 1989 New York State study, a study which—prominently published in the *International Journal of Epidemiology*—found an unequivocal ABC link using a rock-solid prospective database.[63] The most glaring example of this misrepresentation appears in the Goldacre study: "None of the cohort or record linkage studies have shown a significant increase in breast cancer risk after exposure to induced abortion."[64]

More Changes on the NCI Fact Sheet

The rash of new, large studies that showed no ABC link set the stage for a major change in the tone of the NCI fact sheet on the link. The change was set to coincide with the arrival of new leadership in Washington, following the election of Republican President George W. Bush. Just over a year into his first term, in early March 2002, his appointee for NCI Director, Andrew von Eschenbach, took the agency's helm. When he arrived at his new office, Dr. von Eschenbach found the proposed text of the new ABC link fact sheet on his desk, waiting for his signature.[65] Two days later, the NCI's message on the ABC link no longer referred to evidence of the ABC link as "inconsistent." Instead, the text read: "The current body of scientific evidence suggests that women who have had either induced or spontaneous abortions have the same risk as other women for developing breast cancer."[66] This presented a more conclusive tone than previous versions. The new fact sheet was also shorter, the description of the 1994 study by Janet Daling and colleagues having been eliminated entirely.

The net result was that the single most influential worldwide authority on what causes cancer and what does not was firmly in denial of the ABC link. At the same time, the underlings who orchestrate NCI policy had managed to tie what amounted to an endorsement of "safe abortion" to the new conservative antiabortion administration in Washington. The effect of the NCI policy change was chilling for those engaged in the effort to raise public awareness of the ABC link. At the time the change was made, there were two lawsuits in progress—one in North Dakota[67] and one in California[68]—which accused abortion providers of engaging in false advertising by denying the ABC link. Armed with the new NCI fact sheet, judges in both cases ruled against the plaintiff. In the North Dakota case, the judge actually permitted the outrageous claim—made by the defendant—that there was "no evidence" of the ABC link to stand. In California, the judge dismissed the suit summarily.

Politically, conservative voices in Washington were soon heard by the Bush administration. Late in April, the National Physicians Center for Family Resources, based in Birmingham, Alabama, sent Dr. von Eschenbach a detailed critique of the NCI fact sheet. Among other flaws, the critique cited the NCI's "overall tone of denial," its "misrepresentation of the published medical literature on the ABC link," and its "inclusion of inaccurate statements."[69]

Then, in early June, a letter was sent to the Secretary of Health and Human Services (HHS, the federal department that includes the NCI), Tommy Thompson, by U.S. Congressmen Chris Smith (R-NJ), Joseph Pitts (R-PA), and twenty-six other representatives, asking "that the fact sheet be reevaluated for accuracy and bias and that it be removed from the Department website until that review is completed." They based this request on their stated belief that the "fact sheet" "is scientifically inaccurate and misleading to the public."[70]

On July 1, 2002, the NCI removed the fact sheet, an action that prompted predictable outrage from "safe abortion" advocates. A letter to HHS originating from the office of Representative Henry Waxman (D-CA) and signed by eleven of his fellow pro-choice colleagues referred to the ABC link as a "popular myth" and asked for the restoration of the latest fact sheet.[71] Predictably, the pro-choice print media rallied to Waxman's cause, accusing the Bush administration of political meddling with "objective" science. One newspaper, the *Star-Ledger* (NJ), went so far as to compare President Bush to Joseph Stalin as one out to control information and hide the truth from the American people.[72]

In late November, the removed fact sheet was replaced—sort of—with a statement on "Early Reproductive Events and Breast Cancer." The new statement reverted to calling the data on the ABC link "inconsistent" and announced an NCI workshop to be conducted shortly to help determine the current state of knowledge and the direction of future research.[73]

The NCI Workshop

In January 2003, the NCI announced its "workshop" on "Early Reproductive Events and Breast Cancer" to be held in late February. It was billed as a three-day workshop at which all the data on the ABC would be subject to "scientific scrutiny" and "comprehensive review." However, it was obvious from the start that the workshop was a scam. First, the meeting lasted barely two days—not three days, as it began with Monday evening introductory addresses by Dr. von Eschenbach and two other speakers, presentations of data on Tuesday morning, breakout sessions (off the record) on Tuesday afternoon, and a wrap-up and presentation of summary findings by midday Wednesday.[74]

Second, as if the time were not short enough, discussion of the ABC link was severely limited, diluted by inclusion of animal research and basic reproductive hormone and genetic research, as well as human reproductive research unrelated to induced abortion. Even some of the invited experts who had published important work on the ABC link, such as Janet Daling and the Russos, were invited to present data only on breast cell and tumor genetics, and not on induced abortion. In fact, most of the invited experts were not experts on the ABC link at all and were unaware of the fact that eradicating the ABC link was really the sole purpose of the meeting. I myself was invited only at the eleventh hour, and only to have a seat in the audience —not to make a presentation of any sort.

Third, it was particularly telling that the only experts who were invited to present on the ABC link were publicly known to be on the side of discrediting it. There was only one full-length, on-the-record lecture on the subject, given by Leslie Bernstein of the University of Southern California,[75] and there were two off-the-record short presentations of "late-breaking results," one of them given by Mads Melbye. There was neither any comprehensive review of extant published data nor any opportunity to review any of the new data, of which the audience was given only a "sneak peek."[76] I had no podium, but only the opportunity to ask a few questions. One question I did ask was for access to Dr. Bernstein's new data, and I was told that she would not make it available until after it was published. At least this verbal exchange was on the record.[77] Interestingly, one of Bernstein's studies, which was in press at the time of the workshop, was published a month later;[78] however, the journal that published it took the unprecedented action of refusing to publish a letter critical of the study from our group[79]—even though our group has standing in the field of ABC link research.

If the NCI's experts really wanted to settle the matter of the ABC link once and for all, to debunk the extant published evidence and relegate it to the scrap heap of epidemiological history, this was their chance to do so. The lone "crusader" (yours truly) was there, armed with all the data and opinion ever published in the peer-reviewed literature on the subject. I could have been set up to present my analysis of it to the assemblage, with the opportunity for all of them to take their best scientific shots at it for as long as they liked. But they missed their chance. They played out a political charade, just waiting to re-post on the NCI's Web site a year later the conclusion that "the best evidence" indicates "no overall association" between abortion and breast cancer. It was an exercise of brute political force, backed by the power of the purse (our tax dollars), and any potential dissenters among the gathered NCI grantees would assuredly have been held to account.

That brings up the fourth important point: the inherent conflict of interest between the NCI career scientists, who make the highly competitive grant funding decisions for the agency that funds most of the cancer research in the United States (and much of it elsewhere), and the supposedly independent research scientists who receive those grants, who dare not break with the party line.

It is also noteworthy that political forces outside the NCI were keeping up maximal pressure for the agency to arrive at the politically correct conclusion. A month prior to the workshop, a heavy-handed *New York Times* editorial said it all: "If the experts at the meeting agree that there is no link between abortion and breast cancer, the institute will have no excuse to suppress the information. It will have to issue a new fact sheet or admit it can no longer provide objective guidance on matters that inflame social conservatives."[80] As for von Eschenbach himself, his willingness to play along with the NCI career scientists bent on discrediting the ABC link may come as a surprise, because he was appointed by President Bush. However, at the time of his appointment he was national president-elect of the American Cancer Society (ACS), an organization with the same "safe abortion" bias as the NCI. The ACS itself has engaged in a vigorous campaign against the ABC link, including attempts to silence the free speech of the independent, nonprofit Coalition on Abortion/Breast Cancer through legal intimidation.[81]

Almost immediately after the workshop, the NCI posted its "summary findings."[82] The finding relevant to the ABC link reads: "Induced abortion is not associated with an increase in breast cancer risk (1)" [the "(1)" means that this conclusion is accorded the highest quality of evidence rating, i.e., "well established"]. Interestingly, this "epidemiologic finding" was only the sixth out of ten, with the first three relating to the "long-term risk reduction" in breast cancer risk attributable to childbirth. The simplicity of connecting the proverbial dots to show that interrupting a pregnancy in progress therefore leaves a woman at higher long-term breast cancer risk, compared to not interrupting it, is exceeded only by the temerity of deliberately disconnecting the dots.

As an invited participant to the NCI workshop, I felt compelled to file a "minority report."[83] One would think that, were the workshop not a sham, this report would be posted on the NCI Web site. Instead, a brief excerpt is posted as a "Minority Dissenting Comment," without identifying the author or providing any means to obtain the full text.[84]

With the NCI giving its highest stamp of disapproval to the ABC link, convincing the public of its reality has been made difficult, to say the least. For example, two informed consent laws enacted in 2003, one in Texas[85] and the other in Minnesota,[86] mandated that information on the ABC link be given to women considering abortion. However, in 2004 the ABC link information was removed from the state Web site by the governor of Minnesota under pressure from the state medical association.[87] Subsequently, the commissioner of health of Louisiana removed ABC link information[88] that had been in that state's mandated booklet since 1995.[89]

It certainly did not help matters when, in March 2004, Beral's "collaborative reanalysis" appeared in The Lancet.[90] Not only did the Beral "reanalysis" arrive at essentially the same conclusion as the NCI workshop, but it also claimed to be a thorough review of the extant data. Another important similarity—revealed by close scrutiny—shows the reanalysis to be every bit as disingenuous as the workshop.

Although the group of "fifty-three epidemiological studies" (actually, fifty-two with data specifically relating to induced abortion) comprising the reanalysis seems impressive, it is not what it appears to be. With a total of forty-one studies extant in the published literature, one naturally assumes that the reanalysis therefore included data from eleven additional studies. However, this is far from the truth. What Beral et al. actually did was exclude seventeen published studies and add data from twenty-eight that were previously unpublished. Two of the excluded studies were excluded for appropriate scientific reasons; i.e., they had not ascertained the occurrence of abortion directly in cases and controls. But eleven of the studies were excluded for entirely unscientific reasons, specifically, that "principal investigators... could not be traced," or "original data could not be retrieved," or "researchers declined to take part in the collaboration," or "principal investigators judged their own information on induced abortion to be unreliable." Four other studies were excluded by simple omission, without any mention at all. The reader will hardly be surprised that ten of these fifteen excluded studies had reported a statistically significant ABC link. In fact, a compilation of all fifteen excluded studies reveals an overall 80 percent risk increase among them. It is therefore hardly surprising that the Beral group's conclusion shows no significant risk increase, especially considering that twenty-eight of the fifty-two studies on which they relied had not been previously published. Moreover, Beral et al. did include the large prospective studies of the Melbye, Goldacre, and Erlandsson groups, studies which—as enumerated above—should have been excluded on purely scientific grounds.[91]

A Serious Methodological Flaw

Another important aspect of the Beral reanalysis is that it provides a particularly clear example of a standardized methodological flaw peculiar to ABC link research, one that masks the most obvious connection between abortion and breast cancer. In looking at the key data summary table in that study, it is important to note the comparison that produced the overall negative result. The title of the table unequivocally states: "Relative risk of breast cancer, comparing the effects of having a pregnancy that ended as an induced abortion versus effects of never having had that pregnancy." The artificiality of this comparison is striking, for "never having had that pregnancy" is not an option for a woman already pregnant. In terms of any reasonable standard of informed consent, the potential harm of any given medical or surgical procedure must be weighed against the alternative of not having the procedure. In the case of induced abortion—especially since this procedure is overwhelmingly performed on healthy women—that would mean the childbirth alternative. As far as breast cancer is concerned, the risk-reducing effect of full-term pregnancy (FTP) has been well-known literally for centuries and is universally acknowledged.

It is even acknowledged explicitly in the introduction to Beral's reanalysis: "Pregnancies that result in a birth are known to reduce a woman's long-term risk of breast cancer." It is hardly difficult to connect the dots here: Having an induced abortion leaves a woman with a higher long-term risk of breast cancer, compared to not having the abortion, i.e., compared to childbirth. Even ABC link nemesis Lynn Rosenberg was forced to admit this under oath in cross-examination in court: "Question: So in other words, a woman who finds herself pregnant at age fifteen will have a higher breast cancer risk if she chooses to abort that pregnancy than if she carries the pregnancy to term, correct?" Answer: "Probably, yes."[92]

It is therefore unequivocal that one aspect of the ABC link has long since been proven beyond a reasonable doubt, but it has been hidden by a standard peculiarity of epidemiological methodology. Yet even more telling is that this peculiarity reflects a double standard, for it seems to apply only to abortion, while a more reasonable standard is applied when evaluating other potential risk factors for breast cancer. This double standard is exemplified most clearly when evaluation of the ABC link is compared to evaluation of another risk factor in the news lately, i.e., postmenopausal hormone replacement therapy (HRT). In fact, the parallel to HRT is really quite striking, since FTP has effects similar to menopause on a woman's long-term breast cancer risk. In particular, both FTP and menopause lower a woman's breast cancer risk, and the younger the woman is when either event occurs, the more her risk is lowered (i.e., the greater the protective effect).

Beral's own collaborative group at Oxford actually helped to establish HRT as a risk factor with their "Million Woman Study" on women in the United Kingdom, published in *The Lancet* in 2003.[93] In conducting the study, the Beral group sent questionnaires to women aged fifty through sixty-four. Importantly, not all women in that age group have gone through menopause. It has also long been established that women who go through menopause at a later age are at higher risk of breast cancer, due to longer exposure to the cancer-promoting hormone estrogen. In fact, the "million woman" study reproduced this very finding among all the nonusers of HRT: "The relative risk of breast cancer also varied substantially according to menopausal status; for example, among never users of HRT the relative risk of invasive breast cancer was...0.63 (0.58–0.68) for postmenopausal, compared with premenopausal women." (In other words, menopause reduced the risk of breast cancer by a statistically significant 37 percent, compared to premenopausal women of the same age.) Therefore, including premenopausal women in the HRT analysis would have only confounded the results. That is, comparing postmenopausal HRT users to premenopausal women of the same age would make it look like HRT was *not* a risk factor, because the risk among the premenopausal women is elevated in the same manner by their bodies' own estrogen production.

Accordingly, the Beral group restricted their analysis of the effect of HRT in an appropriate way: "To keep confounding by factors associated with the menopause to a minimum, the main analyses of the risk of breast cancer in relation to use of HRT were restricted to postmenopausal women with a defined time since menopause." The result? Current users of HRT were found to be at higher risk of breast cancer than nonusers by between 30 percent and 100 percent (average = 66 percent), depending upon the particular type of hormonal formulation taken. Just as it is only appropriate to compare postmenopausal women who choose to take HRT to postmenopausal women who choose not to take HRT, it is only appropriate to compare pregnant women who choose abortion to pregnant women who choose not to have an abortion. This would clearly yield a scientifically correct—but politically incorrect—result.

Doing the Right Thing

Despite the worst efforts of scientists, doctors, politicians, journalists, and judges to quash public knowledge of the ABC link, the fact that published evidence of it abounds would make it a daunting task to convince a jury of its nonexistence, given a well-presented case. Along these lines, two recent medical malpractice cases give cause for optimism. Both were filed by young women against abortion providers for failure to warn about the risk of breast cancer and psychological complications. Both were filed in reference to abortions that were obtained when the women were minors, and were filed in politically liberal jurisdictions. Importantly, both were also filed by women who did not have breast cancer. The first, in Philadelphia, Pennsylvania, was settled late in 2003 for an undisclosed but substantial amount, when the case was on the brink of jury selection.[94] The second was adjudicated in January 2005 in Portland, Oregon.[95] Importantly, this was not a settlement, but rather was a judgment of liability following the entry of the equivalent of a plea of no contest by the abortion clinic. It also involved an undisclosed but substantial cash award to the plaintiff. All indications are that this is only the beginning of what may become a legal avalanche.

It is indeed unfortunate that—even assuming the truth will eventually win out—it may not occur until the issue is forced into the courtroom. We have estimated that upwards of 10,000 cases of breast cancer each year presently, and up to over 25,000 per year in twenty or thirty years hence, are or will be attributable to induced abortion.[96] How many thousands of women will be subjected to the pain and suffering of this horrible life-threatening disease, only because the doctors, the public health agencies, the media, and even the voluntary anticancer organizations are under the thumb of the "safe abortion" lobby?

But there is more to challenge the "safe abortion" mythology. Even as politically correct studies have been promulgated to neutralize the data proving the ABC link, even stronger data have emerged in recent years that firmly link abortion to premature births in subsequent pregnancies (which in turn raise the risk of breast cancer in the mother and cerebral palsy in the prematurely born children), and to suicide and other forms of premature death in women.[97]

Many adjectives may be used to properly describe induced abortion, but "safe" is assuredly not one of them. The day will surely come when this is common knowledge, and for every day sooner that this happens, thousands of lives may be saved.

Reprinted with the kind permission of the National Catholic Bioethics Center.

Endnotes

1. Collaborative Group on Hormonal Factors in Breast Cancer, "Breast Cancer and Abortion: Collaborative Reanalysis of Data from 53 Epidemiological Studies, Including 83,000 Women with Breast Cancer from 16 Countries," *The Lancet* 363.9414 (27 March 2004): 1007–1016.

2. David Wahlberg, "Study: Breast Cancer Not Tied to Abortion; Group Backs Up Institute's Earlier Findings," *Atlanta Journal-Constitution* (GA), 26 March 2004, A9.

3. Collaborative Group, "Breast Cancer and Abortion," 1007.

4. National Cancer Institute, "Abortion, Miscarriage, and Breast Cancer Risk," http://cis.nci.nih.gov/fact/3_75.htm

5. Collaborative Group, "Breast Cancer and Abortion," 1007.

6. World Health Organization, "Induced Abortion Does Not Increase Breast Cancer Risk," Fact Sheet No. 240 (June 2000), http://www.who.int/mediacentre/factsheets/fs240/en/

7. American College of Obstetricians and Gynecologists, "ACOG Finds No Link Between Abortion and Breast Cancer Risk," news release, July 31, 2003, http://www.acog.org/from_home/publications/press_releases/nr07-31-03-2.cfm

8. Royal College of Obstetricians and Gynaecologists, "RCOG Statement on Abortion and Breast Cancer," January 28, 2004, http://www.rcog.org.uk/press_releases.asp?PageID=33&PressReleaseID=82

9. Patricia Hartge, editorial, "Abortion, Breast Cancer, and Epidemiology," *New England Journal of Medicine* 336.2 (9 January 1997): 127–128.

10. M. Segi et al., "An Epidemiological Study on Cancer in Japan," *GANN (Japanese Journal of Cancer Research)* 48, Suppl. (1957): 1–63.

11. B. MacMahon et al., "Age at First Birth and Breast Cancer Risk," *Bulletin of the World Health Organization* 48.2 (1970): 209–221.

12. M.C. Pike et al., "Oral Contraceptive Use and Early Abortion as Risk Factors for Breast Cancer in Young Women," *British Journal of Cancer* 43.1 (January 1981): 72–76.

13. W. Cates, Jr., "Legal Abortion: the Public Health Record," *Science* 215.4540 (26 March 1982): 1586–1590.

14. M.P. Vessey et al., "Oral Contraceptive Use and Abortion before First Term Pregnancy in Relation to Breast Cancer Risk," *British Journal of Cancer* 45.3 (March 1982): 327–331.

15. J. Kunz and P.J. Keller, "HCG, HPL, Oestradiol, Progesterone and AFP in Serum in Patients with Threatened Abortion," *British Journal of Obstetrics and Gynaecology* 83.8 (August 1976): 640–644.

16. J. Russo and I.H. Russo, "Susceptibility of the Mammary Gland to Carcinogenesis," *American Journal of Pathology* 100.2 (1 August 1980): 497–512.

17. F. Nishiyama, "The Epidemiology of Breast Cancer in Tokushima Prefecture" [in Japanese], *Shikoku Ichi [Shikoku Medical Journal]* 38 (1982): 333–343.

18. L. Lipworth et al., "Abortion and the Risk of Breast Cancer: A Case-Control Study in Greece," *International Journal of Cancer* 67.2 (10 April 1995): 181–184.

19. H.L. Howe et al., "Early Abortion and Breast Cancer Risk among Women under Age 40," *International Journal of Epidemiology* 18.2 (June 1989): 300–304; A. E. Laing et al., "Breast Cancer Risk Factors in African-American Women: The Howard University Tumor Registry Experience," *Journal of the National Medical Association* 85.12 (December 1993): 931–939.

20. The six studies that reported a positive association are the following: M.C. Pike et al., "Oral Contraceptive Use and Early Abortion as Risk Factors for Breast Cancer in Young Women," *British Journal of Cancer* 43.1 (January 1981): 72–76; L.A. Brinton et al., "Oral Contraceptives and Breast Cancer Risk among Younger Women," *Journal of the National Cancer Institute* 87.11 (7 June 1995): 827–835; L. Rosenberg et al., "Breast Cancer in Relation to the Occurrence and Time of Induced and Spontaneous Abortion," *American Journal of Epidemiology* 127.5 (May 1988): 981–989; H.L. Howe et al., "Early Abortion and Breast Cancer Risk among Women under Age 40," *International Journal of Epidemiology* 18.2 (June 1989): 300–304; A.E. Laing et al., "Breast Cancer Risk Factors in African-American Women: The Howard University Tumor Registry Experience," *Journal of the National Medical Association* 85.12 (December 1993): 931–939; A.E. Laing et al., "Reproductive and Lifestyle Factors for Breast Cancer in African-American Women," *Genetic Epidemiology* 11 (1994): 300. The one study that reported no association was M. Moseson et al., "The Influence of Medical Conditions Associated with Hormones on the Risk of Breast Cancer," *International Journal of Epidemiology* 22.6 (December 1993): 1000–1009.

21. J.R. Daling et al., "Risk of Breast Cancer among Young Women: Relationship to Induced Abortion," *Journal of the National Cancer Institute* 86.21 (2 November 1994): 1584–1592.

22. Lawrence K. Altman, "New Study Links Abortions and Increase in Breast Cancer Risk," *New York Times,* 27 October 1994, A24.

23. L. Rosenberg, "Induced Abortion and Breast Cancer: More Scientific Data Are Needed," *Journal of the National Cancer Institute* 86.21 (2 November 1994): 1569–1570.

24. C.C. Mann, "Press Coverage: Leaving Out the Big Picture," *Science* 269.5221 (14 July 1995): 166.

25. *North Florida Women's Health and Counseling Services, Inc., et al., v. State of Florida et al.,* Circuit Court, Second Judicial District, Leon County, FL, No. 99-3202 (1999).

26. T.E. Rohan, A.J. McMichael, and P.A. Baghurst, "A Population-Based Case-Control Study of Diet and Breast Cancer in Australia," *American Journal of Epidemiology* 128.3 (September 1988): 478–489.

27. Rosenberg was an associate editor of the journal during the period 1987 to 1991.

28. N. Andrieu et al., "Familial Risk, Abortion and Their Interactive Effect on the Risk of Breast Cancer—A Combined Analysis of Six Case-Control Studies," *British Journal of Cancer* 72.3 (September 1995): 744–751.

29. L. Rosenberg, "Induced Abortion and Breast Cancer," 1569.

30. B.M. Lindefors-Harris et al., "Response Bias in a Case-Control Study: Analysis Utilizing Comparative Data concerning Legal Abortions from Two

Independent Swedish Studies," *American Journal of Epidemiology* 134.9 (1 November 1991): 1003–1008.

31. Olav Meirik et al., "Oral Contraceptive Use and Breast Cancer in Young Women: A Joint National Case-Control Study in Sweden and Norway," *The Lancet* 2.8508 (20 September 1986): 650–654; H.-O. Adami et al., "Absence of Association between Reproductive Variables and the Risk of Breast Cancer in Young Women in Sweden and Norway," *British Journal of Cancer* 62.1 (July 1990): 122–126. Both papers report the results of the same study, from somewhat different perspectives and using somewhat different statistical treatments of the data.

32. B.M. Lindefors-Harris et al., "Response Bias in a Case-Control Study."

33. Ibid.

34. Olav Meirik, Hans-Olav Adami, and Gunnar Eklund, letter to the editor, "Relation between Induced Abortion and Breast Cancer," *Journal of Epidemiology and Community Health* 52.3 (March 1998): 209. See also Joel Brind et al., Reply to "Relation between Induced Abortion and Breast Cancer," *Journal of Epidemiology and Community Health* 52.3 (March 1998): 209–211.

35. H. Watanabe and T. Hirayama, "Epidemiology and Clinical Aspects of Breast Cancer" [in Japanese], *Nippon Rinsho* 26.8 (August 1968): 1843–1849.

36. H.L. Howe et al., "Early Abortion and Breast Cancer Risk Among Women Under Age 40."

37. Mei-Tzu C. Tang et al., "Case-Control Differences in the Reliability of Reporting a History of Induced Abortion," *American Journal of Epidemiology* 151.12 (15 June 2000): 1139–1143.

38. Ibid.

39. Joel Brind et al., "Induced Abortion as an Independent Risk Factor for Breast Cancer: A Comprehensive Review and Meta-Analysis," *Journal of Epidemiology and Community Health* 50.5 (October 1996): 481–496.

40. D.L. Weed and B.S. Kramer, "Induced Abortion, Bias, and Breast Cancer: Why Epidemiology Hasn't Reached Its Limit," *Journal of the National Cancer Institute* 88.23 (4 December 1996): 1698–1700.

41. Mads Melbye et al., "Induced Abortion and the Risk of Breast Cancer," *New England Journal of Medicine* 336.2 (9 January 1997): 81–85.

42. Hartge, "Abortion, Breast Cancer, and Epidemiology."

43. Melbye et al., "Induced Abortion and the Risk of Breast Cancer," 81.

44. Ibid., 82.

45. M. Osler et al., "Family Planning Services Delivery: Danish Experience," *Danish Medical Bulletin* 37.1 (February 1990): 95–105.

46. *Befolkningens bevaegelser* [*Vital Statistics*] *1994* (Copenhagen: Danmarks Statistik, 1996), 56–62.

47. Joel Brind and Vernon M. Chinchilli, letter to the editor, "Induced Abortion and the Risk of Breast Cancer," *New England Journal of Medicine* 336.25 (19 June 1997): 1834–1835.

48. National Cancer Institute, "Abortion, Miscarriage, and Breast Cancer Risk," fact sheet 3.75 (October 1996), formerly found at http://cancernet.nci.nih.gov/clinpdq/risk/Abortion_and_Breast_Cancer.html (This fact sheet is no longer available online, but a copy may be obtained from Dr. Brind on request.)

49. National Cancer Institute, "Abortion, Miscarriage, and Breast Cancer Risk," fact sheet 3.75 (February 1997), formerly found at http://cancernet.nci.nih.gov/clinpdq/risk/Abortion_and_Breast_Cancer.html. This fact sheet is no longer available online, but a copy may be obtained from Dr. Brind on request.

50. Tom Bliley to Richard Klausner, January 12, 1999. A copy of this letter may be obtained from Dr. Brind on request.

51. Joel L. Brind, "NCI's New ABC 'Facts': Fewer Lies," *Abortion-Breast Cancer Quarterly Update* 3.3 (Fall 1999): 1–2.

52. M.J. Goldacre et al., "Abortion and Breast Cancer: A Case-Control Record Linkage Study," *Journal of Epidemiology and Community Health* 55.5 (May 2001): 336–337.

53. Vessey et al., "Oral Contraceptive Use."

54. Collaborative Group, "Breast Cancer and Abortion."

55. Office for National Statistics (UK), "Report: Legal Abortions in England and Wales, 2000," *Health Statistics Quarterly* 10 (Summer 2001): 57. As the overall induced abortion rate in England and Wales averaged more than 1 percent per year during the study period (1968–1998), it is conservatively estimated that approximately 15 percent of the women in the cohort underwent an induced abortion in their lifetime.

56. Joel L. Brind and Vernon M. Chinchilli, letter to the editor, "Abortion and Breast Cancer," *Journal of Epidemiology and Community Health* 56.3 (March 2002): 237–238.

57. M. Sanderson et al., "Abortion History and Breast Cancer Risk: Results from the Shanghai Breast Cancer Study," abstract of presentation at the Society for Epidemiological Research Annual Meeting, *American Journal of Epidemiology* 151.11 (1 June 2000): 151.

58. M. Sanderson et al., "Abortion History and Breast Cancer Risk: Results from the Shanghai Breast Cancer Study," *International Journal of Cancer* 92.6 (15 June 2001): 899–905.

59. Z. Ye et al., "Breast Cancer in Relation to Induced Abortions in a Cohort of Chinese Women," *British Journal of Cancer* 87.9 (21 October 2002): 977–981.

60. Joel L. Brind and Vernon M. Chinchilli, letter to the editor, "Breast Cancer and Induced Abortions in China," *British Journal of Cancer* 90.11 (1 June 2004): 2244–2246.

61. G. Erlandsson et al., "Abortions and Breast Cancer: Record-Based Case-Control Study," *International Journal of Cancer* 103.5 (20 February 2003): 676–679.

62. Joel L. Brind and Vernon M. Chinchilli, letter to the editor, "Abortions and Breast Cancer: Record-Based Case-Control Study," *International Journal of Cancer* 109.6 (10 May 2004): 945–946.

63. Howe et al., "Early Abortion and Breast Cancer Risk among Women under Age 40."

64. Goldacre et al., "Abortion and Breast Cancer: A Case-Control Record Linkage Study," 337.

65. A. von Eshenbach, opening address at NCI Workshop on Early Reproductive Events and Breast Cancer, Bethesda, MD, 24 February 2003. Video record available at http://videocast.nih.gov/PastEvents.asp?c=1&s=91

66. National Cancer Institute, "Abortion, Miscarriage, and Breast Cancer Risk," fact sheet 3.75 (March 6, 2002), formerly found at http://cancernet.nci.nih.gov/fact/3_53.htm. This fact sheet is no longer available online, but a copy may be obtained from Dr. Brind on request.

67. *Amy Jo Mattson v. MKB Management Corp., dba Red River Women's Clinic,* District Court, East Central Judicial District, County of Cass, State of North Dakota, Civil No. 9-3734.

68. *Agnes Bernardo et al. v. Planned Parenthood Federation of America et al.,* Superior Court of the State of California, County of San Diego, Case No. GIC 772552.

69. National Physicians Center for Family Resources, "National Cancer Institute Fact Sheet Analysis: The Abortion-Breast Cancer Connection (ABC Link)," fact sheet, April 2002. A copy may be obtained from Dr. Brind on request.

70. Jocelyn Kaiser, "Cancer Risk: Nudge from Congress Prompts NCI Review," *Science* 297.5579 (12 July 2002): 171.

71. Office of Henry Waxman to Tommy Thompson, 21 October 2002, http://www.house.gov/waxman/news_files/pdfs/news_letters_thompson_hhs_websites_10_21_02.pdf

72. Editorial, "Political Science," *The Star-Ledger* (NJ), January 3, 2003, 16.

73. National Cancer Institute, "Early Reproductive Events and Breast Cancer," http://cancer.gov/cancer_information/doc.aspx?viewid=8cf78b34-fc6a-4fc7-9a63-6b16590af277

74. National Cancer Institute, "Early Reproductive Events and Breast Cancer: Workshop Agenda, February 24–26, 2003," http://cancer.gov/cancerinfo/ere-workshop-agenda

75. Leslie Bernstein, address given at NCI Workshop on Early Reproductive Events and Breast Cancer, Bethesda, MD, 25 February 2003. Video record available at http://videocast.nih.gov/PastEvents.asp?c=1&s=91

76. Ibid.

77. Joel L. Brind, Q&A regarding Bernstein address, ibid.

78. Maya Mahue-Giangreco et al., "Abortion, Miscarriage, and Breast Cancer Risk of Young Women," *Cancer Epidemiology Biomarkers & Prevention* 12.3 (1 March 2003): 209–214.

79. Joel Brind and Vernon M. Chinchilli, letter to editor, "Re: Induced Abortion, Miscarriage, and Breast Cancer Risk of Young Women," submitted to *Cancer Epidemiology Biomarkers & Prevention,* 10 July 2003.

80. Editorial, "Abortion and Breast Cancer," *New York Times,* Late Edition-Final, 6 January 2003, A20.

81. Coalition on Abortion/Breast Cancer, "Society's Legal Eagles Harass the Coalition," http://www.abortionbreastcancer.com/american_cancer_society.htm

82. National Cancer Institute, "Summary Report: Early Reproductive Events and Breast Cancer Workshop," http://www.nci.nih.gov/cancerinfo/ere-workshop-report

83. Joel Brind, "Early Reproductive Events and Breast Cancer: A Minority Report," 10 March 2003, http://bcpinstitute.org/nci_minority_rpt.htm

84. National Cancer Institute, "Minority Dissenting Comment Regarding Early Reproductive Events and Breast Cancer Workshop," http://cancer.gov/cancer_information/doc.aspx?viewid=15e3f2d5-5cdd-4697-a2ba-f3388d732642

85. *Woman's Right to Know Act* (1 September 2003), Texas Health & Safety Code, Chapter 171, subchapter A (Texas Legislative Council, 2004). Available under "Chapter 171. Abortion" at http://www.capitol.state.tx.us/statutes/hs.toc.htm

86. *Women's Right to Know Act* (14 April 2003), Minnesota Statutes 2004, Chapter 145, sections 4241–4249 (Minnesota Office of the Revisor of Statutes, 2004). Available under "145.4241" and subsequent section numbers at http://www.revisor.leg.state.mn.us/stats/145/

87. Dr. Robert Meiches, chief executive officer, Minnesota Medical Association, to Minnesota Governor Tim Pawlenty and Diane Mandernach, Minnesota commissioner of health, 9 December 2003. A copy of this letter may be obtained from Dr. Brind on request.

88. Louisiana Department of Health and Hospitals, *Abortion: Making a Decision* (Baton Rouge, LA: Louisiana Department of Health and Hospitals, n.d.), http://www.dhh.state.la.us/offices/publications/pubs-1/Abortion-MakingaDecision04.pdf; Associated Press, "Women Wrongly Warned Cancer, Abortion Tied," 9 November 2004, http://abcnews.go.com/Health/wireStory?id=239655

89. Louisiana Department of Health and Hospitals, *Abortion: Making a Decision* (Baton Rouge, LA: Louisiana Department of Health and Hospitals, 1995), 17. The 1995 version of this document is no longer available from the Louisiana Department of Health and Hospitals, but a copy may be obtained from Dr. Brind on request.

90. Collaborative Group, "Breast Cancer and Abortion."

91. Breast Cancer Prevention Institute, "Fact Sheet: Abortion and Breast Cancer, Re: 'Collaborative Reanalysis of Data' Published in *Lancet* 3/25/05," http://bcpinstitute.org/beralpaperanalysis.htm

92. *North Florida Women's Health and Counseling Services, Inc., et al., v. State of Florida et al.*, official transcript of videotape deposition of Lynn Rosenberg, Sc.D., for purposes of trial testimony, 18 November 1999, 77.

93. Million Woman Study Collaborators, "Breast Cancer and Hormone-Replacement Therapy in the Million Woman Study," *The Lancet* 362.9382 (9 August 2003): 419–427.

94. *Stephanie Carter v. Charles E. Benjamin and Cherry Hill Women's Center*, Philadelphia Court of Common Pleas, April Term, 2000, No. 3890.

95. Dave Andrusko, "Plaintiff Wins Suit against Abortion Clinic," *National Right to Life News* 32.2 (February 2005): 15.

96. Brind et al., "Induced Abortion as an Independent Risk Factor for Breast Cancer."

97. John M. Thorp, Jr., Katherine E. Hartmann, and Elizabeth Shadigian, "Long-Term Physical and Psychological Health Consequences of Induced Abortion: Review of the Evidence," *Obstetrical and Gynecological Survey* 58.1 (January 2003): 67–79.

17

Should Voluntary Euthanasia be Legalized?

John Keown (USA)
Rose F. Kennedy Professor of Christian Ethics
Kennedy Institute of Ethics
Georgetown University Medical School, Washington, DC, USA

Definitions

Much unnecessary confusion has been generated in the euthanasia debate as a result of differences in terminology. It is therefore important to be clear what we mean by "euthanasia" and what we do not mean. There is, unfortunately, no agreed definition of the word. This chapter adopts the following definitions.

"Euthanasia" will be used to connote the *intentional* shortening of a patient's life *by a doctor* because the doctor believes that the patient would be *better off dead.* (Current proposals for legalization would authorize only doctors to perform euthanasia, and implicit in those proposals is the notion that death would benefit the patient, typically by bringing an end to severe suffering.)

When performed at the request of the patient, euthanasia is "voluntary." When performed on a patient who is incapable of requesting it (such as an infant or an adult with advanced dementia) it is "nonvoluntary." When performed on a patient who is capable of requesting it but does not want it, euthanasia is involuntary.

Euthanasia may be either "active" or "passive." It is "active" when the doctor intentionally shortens life by an act (such as by injecting potassium chloride) and "passive" when the doctor intentionally shortens life by withholding or withdrawing treatment (or tube feeding).

From the definitions just offered it will be clear that what characterizes euthanasia is the doctor's *intention (purpose)* to shorten life. If the doctor does not intend to shorten life (whether by act or omission), then the doctor does not commit euthanasia (whether active or passive). Therefore, if a doctor injects a patient with potassium chloride with intent to shorten the patient's life, and thereby hastens death, the doctor commits euthanasia. By contrast, if a doctor injects a dying patient with morphine solely with the intention of alleviating the patient's pain, and the doctor merely foresees that the patient will, as a side effect of the drug, die sooner than would have been the case without the morphine, the doctor does not commit euthanasia.[1]

Similarly, if a doctor withdraws a patient's tube feeding with intent to shorten the patient's life, and succeeds in hastening death, then the doctor commits (passive) euthanasia. By contrast, if a doctor withdraws a patient's treatment (or even tube feeding) on the ground that it is futile (that is, offers no reasonable hope of therapeutic benefit) or because it is too burdensome to the patient (as involving, say, a degree of pain the patient finds too taxing), and with no intent to shorten life, then the doctor does not commit euthanasia. In sum, the essence of euthanasia is the *intentional* shortening of life.

The current debate about whether the law should be relaxed centers on the legalization of *voluntary, active euthanasia* (VAE), which therefore provides the focus for this chapter. Before outlining the ethical arguments for and against relaxing the current law against VAE, it may be helpful to summarize the existing law in one representative jurisdiction, England, not least because of the global influence it has historically exercised.

English Law

In English law a doctor who actively and intentionally accelerates a patient's death commits the crime of murder. This is so whether or not the patient asks to be killed, whether or not the patient is suffering gravely, whether or not there are alternative means to alleviate any such suffering, and whether or not the patient is close to death.

If a doctor does not shorten the patient's life but rather intentionally facilitates the patient's suicide, then the doctor commits the offense of assisting suicide. Although suicide was decriminalized in 1961, the offense of assisting suicide was preserved.

English law draws a clear distinction, tracking the distinction in the definitions offered in Part I, between VAE and palliative care. It holds that a doctor may administer palliative drugs in order to alleviate a dying patient's pain even if the doctor foresees that the drugs may, as a side effect, hasten death. Indeed, the law holds not only that a doctor may do so, but that it is the doctor's duty to do so. Advocates of VAE want the law to go much further. They want the law to permit doctors not only to kill the pain but to kill the patient. What are the main arguments these advocates deploy?

Ethical Arguments and Counterarguments

There are at least five arguments commonly advanced in favor of legalizing VAE. We state each and, in turn, sketch corresponding counterarguments.

A Right to Suicide?

The starting point of the first argument is the observation that in several countries, like England, it is not an offense to kill oneself. This shows, the argument runs, that these countries recognize there is a right to commit suicide. And if there is a right to commit suicide, it is illogical to prohibit assisted suicide. If there is a right to kill oneself, why should it be illegal to help someone to exercise that right?

The counterargument is that the mere fact that suicide is not a crime does not show it is therefore a right. Although suicide was decriminalized in England in 1961, the government made it clear that decriminalization did not signal condonation. On the contrary, the government stated that it continued to regard suicide as gravely wrong. The decriminalization of suicide was, rather, a recognition that the suicidal needed psychiatric help rather than criminal punishment and that the criminal penalty attached to suicide not only compromised this goal but also stigmatized the relatives of those who killed themselves. The fact that decriminalization was not intended to condone suicide, let alone confer a right to suicide, is further illustrated by the fact that the same legislation which decriminalized suicide maintained the prohibition on assisting another to commit suicide.

Euthanasia and Palliative Care: Morally Equivalent?

Another argument runs that there is no moral difference between, on the one hand, administering palliative drugs that one foresees will hasten the patient's death and, on the other hand, administering a lethal drug with intent to hasten the patient's death. And as the former is widely condoned both in medical ethics and by law, why not the latter?

The counterargument is that there is not only a conceptual difference between intending and merely foreseeing a consequence but that there can also be an important moral difference. That foresight is not the same as intent is a widely accepted truth. One may intend a consequence without foreseeing it will occur: one may buy a lottery ticket intending to win the prize without foreseeing that one will do so. Conversely, one may foresee a consequence as certain without intending it: one may foresee that as a result of chemotherapy for cancer one's hair will fall out without intending it should.

That there can be an important moral difference between intending death and merely foreseeing death is also clear. When General Eisenhower ordered the allied forces to invade Normandy on D-Day, he doubtless foresaw that many allied troops would be killed, but he hardly intended that they should die. Had he done so he would not be regarded as an honorable but as a dishonorable commander. Similarly, the doctor who intentionally ends the life of a patient makes a judgment that the patient would be better off dead and acts on that judgment. The doctor who, by contrast, administers drugs solely to ease the pain of a dying patient, merely foreseeing that the patient will die sooner as a side effect of that palliative treatment, makes no such judgment.

Autonomy

An argument at the forefront of the case for legalizing VAE is the claim that each person has a right to self-determination, a right to make his or her own decisions, especially about important personal matters as when and how to die. To forbid patients from choosing euthanasia or assisted suicide, the argument runs, is an unwarranted interference with their autonomy.

There are a number of responses to this argument. First, how many requests in practice are likely to be *truly* autonomous? Is there not a real risk that the autonomy of many patients will be compromised by the effects of their illness and medication, by pressure applied by others, as well as by a lack of expert information on alternatives such as palliative care?

Second, even if a particular request were truly autonomous, this would not by itself justify compliance with it. Sound ethics is about choosing what is right, not about a "right to choose" disconnected from true human well-being. The value of autonomy lies in enabling us to make choices that help us and others to flourish as human beings. Such choices clearly merit respect. But a choice that is contrary to the good of the patient, such as one that intends to put an end to the patient's life, merits no respect. This is not to say a doctor must prolong the patient's life against the patient's wishes—the doctor may, for example, be too busy treating those who want their lives prolonged—but it *is* to say that doctors should not comply with patients' requests to be killed, requests which show that the patients have, for whatever reason —whether from suffering or from a sense of abandonment—lost sight of their ineliminable dignity.

Third, we do not live in a vacuum but in society. Our choices often have implications for others. And a choice to be killed is a choice that, if endorsed by medical ethics and law, would profoundly affect the doctor, other patients, and society generally. For example, by intentionally killing the patient the doctor would be undermining a disposition essential to the healing vocation of medicine: a disposition to respect the fundamental equality in dignity of each patient and never to judge that the lives of certain patients are no longer worth living.

Beneficence

A fourth argument is that doctors have a duty to alleviate the suffering of their patients. How can it be consistent with that duty to allow patients to suffer when the doctor has the means to bring their suffering to a swift end? If pet owners have a duty not to cause unnecessary suffering to their animals, and to put them down when they are suffering without prospect of recovery, how much greater is the duty of doctors to not prolong the suffering of their patients?

A counterargument is that, just as respect for patient autonomy has always been understood to be subject to limits, not least the doctor's duty never intentionally to kill, so too the doctor's duty to alleviate suffering has always been understood to be similarly circumscribed. The reason that we put down animals but not patients is that, unlike animals, human beings possess an ineliminable dignity simply by virtue of their humanity. This inalienable dignity has long been recognized in declarations of human rights, such as the International Declaration of Human Rights and the European Declaration on Human Rights. Put more bluntly, doctors should not treat patients like dogs. Simply to assert that euthanasia is justified by respect for individual autonomy, and/or by the doctor's duty to alleviate suffering, is to beg the question.

Nor does a rejection of VAE leave the doctor helpless in the face of a suffering patient. The relief of suffering is an important, and too often neglected, dimension of the medical vocation. Advances in palliative care now allow the bulk of suffering to be alleviated. And, in the rare cases of intractable suffering, there is always the option of total sedation where the patient can be rendered completely unconscious.[2]

"Abuse"

In the quiver of arguments for reform, one that has recently been gaining increasing prominence is the argument that VAE is already being practiced, albeit illegally, and that it would be preferable, by legalizing it, to "bring it out into the open." Legalization, it is claimed, would end the current "abuse" of the law and would ensure regulation and control.

There are several counterarguments. First, there appears to be little cogent evidence that VAE is currently practiced at all frequently. Second, even if such evidence did exist, is it not an odd argument that because a crime is committed to a certain extent the law should permit it? Speeding is common yet that is hardly an argument for abolishing speed limits. Third, if VAE is currently practiced to a certain extent, so too is nonvoluntary euthanasia (NVAE). Would advocates of VAE therefore urge that NVAE also be permitted? Fourth, proposals for the legalization of VAE typically contain procedural requirements (such as a requirement for doctors to report cases of VAE to the authorities), which, it is claimed, would ensure that only VAE was permitted and that the law was no longer abused. However, such procedures are essentially geared toward the *monitoring* of VAE and would do little or nothing to prevent or punish the practice of euthanasia in circumstances *not* permitted by the legislation. In other words, the opportunities for doctors to practice unauthorized euthanasia, such as NVAE, would continue much as at present.

Fifth, it is highly likely that legalization would bring in its train more, not less, abuse of the law. This is because of the danger of a "slippery slope" from VAE to NVAE, and from euthanasia as a "last resort" in cases of "unbearable suffering" to its use in cases of less serious suffering and where there were alternatives.

Such a slide is likely to happen because *practically* safeguards to prevent it could not be made effective. For example, how could vague concepts such as "unbearable suffering" be defined, and how could what transpires beneath the confidential carapace of the doctor-patient relationship be effectively policed?

But the slide is also likely to happen because the argument for VAE is also *logically* an argument for NVAE. No responsible doctor would kill a patient just because the patient autonomously requested death (any more than a responsible doctor would remove a patient's kidney merely because the patient autonomously requested it). The doctor decides whether the patient's request for death is justified, whether death would, in fact, benefit the patient. But, if the doctor is willing to make this judgment—that the patient would be better off dead—in the case of a patient who requests death, why can the doctor not make the same judgment in relation to a patient who is unable to request it? Put another way, if death is a benefit in certain circumstances, why should it be granted to those who request it but denied to those who cannot? In short, the case for VAE is, at bottom, also a case for NVAE. The fact that many philosophers who support the former also support the latter illustrates the logical link between the two.

The inevitable tendency to slippage is also apparent in the internal tension between the two major arguments for reform: respect for autonomy and relief of suffering. If doctors are under a duty to alleviate suffering, even to the extent of intentionally dispatching their patients, why should this duty not extend to incompetent patients? And, if doctors are under a duty to respect their patients' autonomy, why should they not kill patients who request death even if they are not suffering?

The steepness of the "slippery slope" should not be underestimated. If VAE were legalized in certain cases, it would likely precipitate a paradigm shift in medicine, family relations, and society. There is every reason to believe that VAE would become less of an exception limited to infrequent "hard cases" and more of an expectation in a wide range of circumstances. Put more pointedly, the "right to die" might well become a duty to die. One commentator, Professor Patricia Mann, has written perceptively about how cultural expectations about death are likely to be transformed by legalization. She observes:

> [M]any doctors will adjust their practices, and gradually their values, as well . . .Insofar as assisted suicide is a cost-efficient means of death, doctors are also likely to be rewarded by healthcare companies for participating in it. As institutional expectations and rewards increasingly favor assisted suicide, expectations and rewards within the medical profession itself will gradually shift to reflect this. Medical students will learn about assisted suicide as an important patient option from the beginning of their training. We may expect that a growing proportion of doctors will find themselves sympathetic to this practice, and will find themselves comfortable with recommending it to their patients.

Turning to the likely impact on family relations, she comments:

> Once assisted suicide ceases to be illegal, its many advantages to busy relatives will become readily apparent. More than merely an acceptable form of

ending, relatives and friends may come to see it as a preferred or praise-worthy form of death.

In the changed cultural climate heralded by legalization, a "lingering death may come to seem an extravagance, a frivolous indulgence."

She goes on, "We can be relatively certain that our views of dying will change quite radically if and when assisted suicide is legalized," and remarks, "Strong social expectations are likely to develop for individuals to choose assisted suicide as soon as their physical capacities decline to a point where they become extremely dependent upon others in an expensive, inconvenient way."[3]

This is not scaremongering by an avowedly pro-life campaigner; her essay expresses no personal opinion against voluntary euthanasia in principle and appears in a book edited by a leading advocate of VAE. And lest such a paradigm shift be dismissed as speculative, it would be as well to recall the profound changes in medicine, family relations, and society that have been effected by the legalization of abortion. Lord Habgood, the former Archbishop of York and a member of the House of Lords Select Committee on Medical Ethics, which examined the euthanasia question in depth, has commented

> Legislation to permit euthanasia would in the long run bring about profound changes in social attitudes towards death, illness, old age, and the role of the medical profession. The Abortion Act has shown what happens. Abortion has now become a live option for *anybody* who is pregnant. This does not imply that everyone who is facing an unwanted pregnancy automatically attempts to procure an abortion. But because abortion is now on the agenda, the climate of opinion in which such a pregnancy must be faced has radically altered.[4]

Moreover, the reality of the "slippery slope" (and its steepness) can clearly be seen in the experience of the Netherlands.

The Netherlands

VAE has been legally approved and widely practiced in the Netherlands for some twenty years. The law requires that the patient make a voluntary request for euthanasia, that euthanasia be a last resort to alleviate "unbearable suffering," and that a doctor consults with another doctor before performing euthanasia and reports it to the authorities (formerly to the medical examiner, but now to an interdisciplinary review committee) after carrying it out. Advocates of VAE often point to the Netherlands as a model to be followed. They claim that the guidelines for VAE are "precise" and "strict" and that the Dutch have successfully controlled its practice. The Dutch have carried out three major empirical surveys into end-of-life decision making in the Netherlands (into practice in the years 1990, 1995, and 2001). What light have these surveys cast on the extent of compliance with the three core guidelines?

First, were any patients killed without making a voluntary request? Exposing a disturbing incidence of NVAE, the surveys have disclosed that in each year around 1000 patients were killed even though they had not made an explicit request for euthanasia. Second, has euthanasia been confined to patients who were "suffering unbearably" and for whom euthanasia was a last resort? The surveys have revealed that many patients were euthanized not because they were in unbearable pain but because of a "loss of dignity," and that in many cases palliative care would have offered an alternative but was simply refused. Third, were all cases duly reported? The surveys have shown that a large majority of cases have, in fact, been improperly covered up by doctors, often simply to avoid inconvenience. In 1990 over 80 percent went unreported. In 1995 some 59 percent were covered up. Only in 2001 was a majority of cases, 54 percent, reported.[5] So much, then, for legalization of VAE "bringing it out into the open."

In short, the evidence illustrates the bite of the *practical* "slippery slope" argument. The Dutch law has signally failed effectively to control VAE. The incidence of NVAE speaks for itself. So, too, does the widespread failure of doctors to report. (It should also not be assumed that, in the relatively few cases in which doctors did file a report claiming that they had complied with the law, their actions did, in fact, meet the legal requirements.)

But the Dutch experience also illustrates the force of the *logical* "slippery slope" argument. For it shows that NVAE is not only practiced but is in certain circumstances actually approved, and also that the notion of "unbearable suffering" has been stretched to breaking point.

When the first survey disclosed that 1000 patients had been killed without having made a free and explicit request, the government-appointed committee that had commissioned the survey reacted to the finding not with condemnation but with condonation. The committee sought to justify the bulk of these cases on the ground that it had been the doctor's duty to alleviate suffering. Also illustrating the swift Dutch slide from condonation of VAE to NVAE, two Courts of Appeal have declared it lawful for doctors to administer lethal injections to disabled babies in certain circumstances.

Just as the requirement of a voluntary request has been compromised, so has the notion of "unbearable suffering" been diluted. In 1989 I interviewed a prominent Dutch practitioner of VAE. I put to him the hypothetical case of an elderly man who requested VAE because his family wanted him dead so that they could inherit his estate. I asked the doctor whether he would rule out VAE in such circumstances. The doctor replied that he would not.

A real case decided by the Dutch Supreme Court five years later concerned a woman who was assisted in suicide because of her grief at the death of her two sons. The Court held that "unbearable suffering" did not need to arise from a physical, let alone terminal, illness and could, as in this case, be purely mental. In 2004, the Minister of Justice cited this precedent in approving a decision not to prosecute a doctor who had assisted in suicide a patient who was only in the early stages of dementia: the patient's mere *fear* of the progression of the disease was held to qualify as "unbearable suffering." The implications of this decision seem quite open-ended. Hardly less strikingly, the former Dutch Minister of Health has called for suicide pills to be made available to the elderly, who could take them if they simply felt "tired of life."

In the light of the wealth of disturbing evidence, much of it helpfully generated by the Dutch themselves, it is not surprising that bodies such as the UN Committee on Human Rights have expressed their concern about the situation in the Netherlands.

Expert Bodies

The case for the legalization of VAE or physician-assisted suicide has in recent years been considered by a number of expert bodies. For example, in 1994 a Select Committee of the House of Lords produced a report in which it rejected calls for relaxation of the law. A delegation from the Committee visited the Netherlands and concluded that to allow VAE would be wrong in principle and unsafe in practice. It observed that the prohibition on intentional killing was "the cornerstone of law and of social relationships" and protected "each one of us impartially, embodying the belief that all are equal." The Committee was also concerned about the dangers of the "slippery slope." It concluded: "It would not be possible to frame adequate safeguards against non-voluntary euthanasia....It would be next to impossible to ensure that all acts of euthanasia were truly voluntary, and that any liberalization of the law was not abused."[6]

In the same year, the report of another expert body appeared. The New York State Task Force concluded that, although its members differed on the issue of VAE in principle, they were unanimously opposed to legalization because of the adverse social consequences it would produce.

> [T]he Task Force unanimously concluded that the dangers of such a dramatic change in public policy would far outweigh any possible benefits. In light of the pervasive failure of our health care system to treat pain and diagnose and treat depression, legalizing assisted suicide and euthanasia would be profoundly dangerous for many individuals who are ill and vulnerable. The risks would be most severe for those who are elderly, poor, socially disadvantaged, or without access to good medical care.[7]

Further, the argument that there is a right to physician-assisted suicide has been rejected by the Supreme Court of Canada, the Supreme Court of the United States, the House of Lords, and the European Court of Human Rights. Finally, the World Medical Association has consistently maintained its opposition to VAE.

Conclusions

Whether the law should be relaxed to permit VAE is one of the most important debates in the modern world. The way in which societies answer this question is sure to have to profound ramifications for patients, doctors, families, and society generally. This chapter suggests that the case for relaxation of the law is unpersuasive.

The House of Lords Select Committee and the New York State Task Force recommended not that the law be relaxed but that the availability of palliative care be improved. As this wise recommendation shows, the problems facing the dying are susceptible of more positive solutions than VAE, solutions that will strengthen, rather than undermine, the interests of patients, doctors, families, and society.

Presented at the Asia-Pacific Dialogue, Kuala Lumpur, Malaysia, October 2004.

Endnotes

1. The belief that morphine administered to alleviate pain shortens life lacks a sound clinical basis. *See* Robert Twycross, *Where there is hope there is life: a view from the hospice, in* Euthanasia Examined 141, 162 (John Keown ed., Cambridge University Press 1995).

2. *See generally* Robert Twycross, *supra.*

3. Patricia S. Mann, *Meanings of Death,* in Physician-Assisted Suicide 11, 21–25 (Margaret Battin ed., Routledge 1998).

4. Rt. Rev. J.S. Habgood, *Euthanasia—A Christian View* 3 Journal of the Royal Society of Health 12, 126 (1974). Original emphasis.

5. The third survey also disclosed thousands of cases in which patients had died as a result of "terminal sedation." It is not clear how many of these may have been cases of VAE disguised as terminal sedation so as to avoid compliance with the guidelines for VAE.

6. *Report of the House of Lords Select Committee on Medical Ethics* (Paper 21-I of 1994), paras. 237–238.

7. The New York State Task Force on Life and the Law, When Death Is Sought: Assisted Suicide and Euthanasia in the Medical Context (1994), ix.

18

The Effects of Pornography on Marriage: Dealing with a Spouse's Sexually Addictive and Compulsive Behaviors

Jill C. Manning (Canada)
Marriage and Family Therapy Graduate Programs
Brigham Young University, Provo, Utah, USA

Introduction

The field of sexual addictions and compulsivities is relatively new. In 1983, Patrick Carnes's groundbreaking work, entitled *Out of the Shadows,* brought forth a theoretical basis for sexually addictive behavior and sparked widespread debate, investigation, and recognition of sexual addictions as a clinical construct (Carnes, 1983; Delmonico and Carnes, 1999). Though not included in the diagnostic classifications of sexual disorders in the Diagnostic and Statistical Manual of Mental Disorders (DSM IV), sexual addictions and compulsivities are increasingly being encountered by mental health professionals, and the field of sexual addictions is gaining wider acceptance (Delmonico and Carnes, 1999; Garos, 1997).

Research into the field of sexual addictions is also growing as organizations such as The Society for the Advancement of Sexual Health and the *Sexual Addiction and Compulsivity Journal,* now in its ninth year of publication, gain recognition and popularity (Delmonico and Carnes, 1999). This professional and academic growth is helping clinicians and policy makers respond to the estimated 6 percent of the U.S. population (Wildmon-White and Young, 2002), or approximately 17,600,900 people (U.S. Census Bureau, 2004) who are struggling with a sexual addiction of some kind.

The rapid growth of Internet usage has been identified as the primary reason for the exponential increase in sexual addictions and compulsivities (Schneider, 2000a; Schneider, 2000b; Cooper and Griffin-Shelley, 2002). Regarding the influence of the Internet on sexuality generally, Cooper, Boies, Maheu, and Greenfield (1999) poignantly contend, since its inception, the Internet has been associated with sexuality in a kind of synergistic dance, each fueling the transformation of the other. The influence of the Internet on sexuality is likely to be so significant that it will ultimately be recognized as the cause of the next "sexual revolution" (519). Many agree this influential interplay between the Internet and sexuality has been fueled to a large extent by what Cooper (1998) coined as the Internet's "Triple-A Engine" effect of accessibility, affordability, and perceived anonymity (Cooper, Delmonico, and Burg, 2000; McCarthy, 2002; Schneider, 2000a; Schneider, 2000b).

According to current Internet traffic statistics for North America, there has been a 109.5 percent increase in Internet usage since 2000, with Internet accessibility now penetrating 69.3 percent of the North American population (Internet World Stats: Usage and Population Statistics, 2004). According to Nielsen//NetRatings (2004), in the U.S. alone 35,183,000 unique users accessed adult entertainment Web sites during the *month* of April 2004. In light of the burgeoning growth and increasing accessibility of the Internet, and the fact that a seemingly infinite array of subjects may be searched via the World Wide Web, it is both interesting and significant that "sex" is the most frequently searched topic on the Internet, and "porn" is the fourth most frequently searched topic (Engel, 2001).

It has been suggested that the expanding Internet serves many adaptive and healthy purposes in the area of human sexuality. For example, the Internet enables marginalized or disenfranchised groups such as the disabled, rape survivors, and gay or lesbian communities to share information with each other on topics of mutual interest (Cooper, Boies, Maheu, and Greenfield, 1999). Newman (1997) heralded the educational potential of the Internet as something that would spark greater understanding and more candid discussions about sex because information about safe sexual practices, sexual dysfunctions, reproduction, contraception, and sexually transmitted diseases would be more accessible. The Internet is also becoming an increasingly popular avenue to find romantic partners (Cooper, Boies, Maheu, and Greenfield, 1999) for traditional and nontraditional relationships (i.e., courtship versus casual sexual partners). In addition, the Internet provides a relatively safe avenue for people to experiment with risky behaviors that, if enacted in real life, may put them at risk for disease or criminal consequences (Delmonico and Carnes, 1999; Cooper, Boies, Maheu, and Greenfield, 1999).

While the Internet is having many positive effects on human sexuality, others argue this modern phenomenon is fostering serious consequences and risks. Cooper, Delmonico, and Burg (2000), for example, suggest on-line sexual pursuits are "…a hidden public health hazard exploding, in part because very few are recognizing it as such or taking it seriously" (25). In the research conducted by Young (1996, 1997) and Cooper, Scherer, et al. (1999), clear warnings are given regarding the dangers of excessive Internet use for sexual gratification due to the correlations between the amounts of time spent on-line and negative consequences such as poor academic and professional performance, and sexual compulsivity and distress. Although there is research to support the fact that the majority of people who pursue sexual pursuits on-line do not experience life difficulties (Cooper, Delmonico, and Burg, 2000), Delmonico and Carnes (1999) argue that, despite this fact, there is a significant minority who need research and clinical attention.

Research shows the majority of people struggling with sexual addictions and compulsivities involving the Internet are married, heterosexual males (Cooper, Delmonico, and Burg, 2000). Women who are married to these men are directly impacted by this problem (Schneider, 2000b). For instance, marriages in which a sexual addiction or sexual compulsivities exist are commonly pervaded with diminished intimacy and sensitivity, anxiety, secrecy, isolation, relationship dysfunction, and decreased temporal security due to the risk of job loss or related debts (Carnes, 1992; Wildmon-White and Young, 2002; Schneider, 2000a). Clearly, the impact of sexual addictions and compulsivities is not limited to the consumer.

Although there is research on many issues relating to wives of sex addicts, the database searches conducted for this literature review (PsycINFO Web-SPIRS, PsycINFO EBSCO, Family & Society Studies Worldwide BioLine, and Social Work Abstracts WebSPIRS) revealed no research findings that address the kinds of support women find most beneficial when dealing with a spouse's sexual addiction or sexually compulsive behaviors. The research that is available, however, provides insight into the following: (1) the effects of Internet pornography and cybersex addictions on wives and families (Schneider, 2000a; Schneider, 2000b); (2) the profiles of women married to sex addicts (Wildmon-White and Young, 2002; Wildmon-White, 2002); (3) the common recovery issues and phases these women encounter (Milrad, 1999); and (4) the effects of couple therapy when combined with individual twelve-step meetings designed for sex addicts and family members (Schneider and Schneider, 1996; Milrad, 1999).

Recent studies (Wildmon-White, 2002; Wildmon-White and Young, 2002; McCarthy, 2002; Corley, Schneider, and Irons, 1998) refer to the lack of empirical research that has focused exclusively on the wives of sexually addicted and compulsive men, and have encouraged a breadth of controlled studies of this kind. In light of the fact that one of the most important determinants of successful recovery from sexual addiction is for the wife to receive treatment as well (Carnes, 1991; Schneider, 1991), researching how this population may best be supported is not only beneficial for augmenting the wife's well-being, but also the sex addict's treatment course and prognosis, and subsequently family stability.

Review of Relevant Literature

Having only emerged as a field of study within the last twenty years, the voids in sexual addiction literature are understandable as sexual addictions are a relatively new research undertaking, and, as with research in all areas, it takes time for researchers to recognize who and what needs attention. The present voids in the sexual addiction literature also highlight the need for more research in this area, especially when one considers the context of the problem previously described and the following research findings.

Spousal Effects of Sexual Addiction and Compulsivities

Sexual addictions and compulsivities directly impact spouses in diverse ways (Schneider, 2000a; Schneider, 2000b; Wildmon-White, 2002). In two studies on the effects of sexual addictions and compulsivities on the family, it was found that sexual addictions and compulsivities are a predictor of decreased marital satisfaction and martial intimacy and are a major contributing factor to separation and divorce of the couples surveyed (Schneider, 2000a; Schneider, 2000b).

Emotionally speaking, women in such marriages commonly report feeling "hurt, betrayal, rejection, abandonment, devastation, loneliness, shame, isolation, humiliation, jealousy,...anger...loss of self-esteem" (Schneider, 2000b, 252), and in some cases suicidal (Schneider, 2000a). The heightened sense of insecurity both emotionally and temporally (due to the risk of job loss or related debts) also increases the levels of anxiety experienced by this population. These women report that a major source of distress is the lies told to them repeatedly by their partners and that they "overwhelmingly felt that online affairs were as emotionally painful to them as live or off-line affairs" (Schneider, 2000b, 252). Wives of sex addicts also report comparing themselves unfavorably to the women featured in pornographic images or the sex service industry and feel hopeless about being able to measure up to or compete with such women for their partners' attention (Schneider, 2000b). Many even blame themselves for their husbands' problem and believe they have the power to stop it (Wildmon-White and Young, 2002). This erroneous self-attribution drives many wives to become hypervigilant of their husband's actions and engage in "detective behaviors" (Milrad, 1999).

In terms of sexual relations, Schneider's (2000a) study revealed that 68 percent of couples directly impacted by "cybersex," or on-line sexual activity, had lost interest in relational sex and many had had no relational sex in months or years. These findings are congruent with other research that reveals these women often feel sexually inadequate, question their own attractiveness and sexuality, and are prone to experiencing chronic anxiety and depression (Wildmon-White and Young, 2002; Schneider, 2000c), symptoms that can impact sexual functioning in and of themselves.

In regard to social effects, women in these marriages tend to experience loneliness and isolation because they are vulnerable to getting entangled in secret keeping (Matheny, 1998). As well, they fear they will not be understood if they do speak out or fear the potential risks, ridicule, and consequences of sharing information (Wildmon-White and Young, 2002). The shame, shock, disgust, and embarrassment many women describe also affect the manner in which they reach out or withdraw from support.

Many women experience physiological effects such as fatigue, changes in appetite and libido, and other signs and symptoms of depression. Laaser (1996) points out that wives of sexually addicted or compulsive men have often been coerced physically by being forced or pressured into sexual practices they experienced as abusive such as sex with multiple partners or sadistic practices (Wildmon-White and Young, 2002).

In light of the relational, emotional, sexual, social, and physical effects, it can be inferred that women married to men with sexually addictive or compulsive behaviors need various forms of support, including therapeutic care.

Characteristics of Women Married to Sex Addicts

Because there has been relatively little research that has focused exclusively on the wives of sex addicts, much of the information regarding characteristics of this population is postulated rather than being empirically supported. Experts in the field of sexual addictions have observed some of the following characteristics in these women:

(1)...loss of a sense of self (Matheny, 1998), (2) preoccupation with the addict (Schneider, 1988; 2000c), (3) depression (Schneider, 1988), (4) low self-esteem and attempts to control the sexual addict (Schneider, 1988; 2000c; Weiss and DeBusk, 1993), (5) relationship dependency (Schaef, 1989; Schneider, 1989; 2000), (6) a history of sexual abuse and neglect in their families-of-origin (Carnes, 1991; Kasl, 1989), and (7) unmet emotional needs in their family-of-origin, emotional turmoil, and feelings of hyper-responsibility (Carnes, 1991). (Wildmon-White and Young, 2002, 264).

Others have found that wives of sexually compulsive men often come from families in which addictions to alcohol, drugs, food, and work were present (Wildmon-White and Young, 2002; Crawford, Hueppelsheuer, and George, 1996; Schneider and Schneider, 1996). As a result of these family-of-origin addictions, these women often have difficulty setting healthy boundaries. This pattern is frequently compounded by histories of sexual, physical, or emotional abuse that these women commonly bring to their marriages (Wildmon-White and Young, 2002; Crawford et al., 1996). In combination with one another, these characteristics are thought to play a role in both the formation and maintenance of the marital relationship between the wife and the sex addict (Wildmon-White and Young, 2002).

Several researchers and clinicians have postulated that women involved in marriages where a sexual addiction is occurring share characteristics with women in chemically dependent relationships (Schneider and Schneider, 1996; Schwartz and Brasted, 1985). Extensive research has been conducted with wives of chemically dependent men. Family-of-origin characteristics for this group include:

(1) Feelings of rejection and abandonment (Kitchens, 1991; Woititz, 1983); (2) a lack of acceptance and rigid, inflexible, nonadaptive family environments (Kitchens, 1991); and (3) being raised in an emotionally deprived and repressed home (Wegscheider-Cruse, 1985; Woititz, 1983). (Wildmon-White and Young, 2002).

Wildmon-White's (2002) doctoral research looked at the relationship between relational attachment, learned helplessness, and the construct of sexual addiction among conservative Christian women who were married to men involved in a range of sexually compulsive behaviors. Wildmon-White (2002) was the first to provide empirical evidence that characteristics such as fear of abandonment, relational dependency, and learned helplessness that are commonly found in wives of chemically dependent husbands were similar to those of wives of sexually addicted husbands. This was done by demonstrating a systematic relationship between scores on the *Sexual Addiction Screening Questionnaire—Spousal* and the instrument's two subscales, "Depend" and "Helplessness." Women who scored low on the "Depend" subscale, which measures one's sense of being able to depend on others when they are needed, reported higher levels of sexually addictive behaviors in their husbands. Women who scored high on the "Helplessness" subscale, which measures one's feeling of being unable to control circumstances in important relationships and life, also reported more sexually addictive behaviors in their husbands. Wildmon-White (2002) therefore concluded that wives of sexually addicted men tend to exhibit unhealthy dependence on others, feel helpless to change their circumstances, and share many key characteristics with women in chemically dependent relationships.

In terms of cognitive characteristics, Schneider (2000c) found that wives of sexually compulsive men commonly hold four core dysfunctional beliefs that may unwittingly enable or exacerbate the problematic sexual behaviors of their husbands, namely: (1) I am not a worthwhile person; (2) no one would love me for myself; (3) I can control other people's behavior; and (4) sex is the most important sign of love.

Women as "Customers for Change"

Some may contend that researching individual women's perspectives is not congruent with marriage and family therapy research that tends to be relational and systemic in nature. From a systemic point of view, however, the axiom of the system theory or concept of interconnectedness readily applies to this issue. The axiom of the system theory suggests that a change in any one part of a system will affect all other parts of the system (Nichols and Schwartz, 1998, 127–128). In the field of sexual addictions, this assumption is supported by psychologists and physicians who encourage women to receive individual treatment (Carnes, 1991; Schneider and Schneider, 1996) in order to increase the health of the individuals and the marital relationship affected by the sexual addictive or compulsive behaviors.

Furthermore, women are considered an appropriate focus of research because they are often the most motivated for change when their husbands' sexually addictive or compulsive behaviors are disclosed or discovered. Working with the person most motivated for change within a family system is often the only respectful therapeutic option available, as well as the best therapeutic leverage for influencing the family member with the "problem" if they are refusing help.

Although the term "customer for change" was first introduced by Steve de Shazer in 1988, both the Mental Research Institute and Solution-Focused models of therapy emphasize the importance of clarifying who the customer for change is within a family or client system (Nichols and Schwartz, 1998, 366). A "customer for change" is defined as the person most motivated for things to change and is often not the person with the problem (Nichols and Schwartz, 1998, 366).

The argument that women are often customers for change is supported by recent research findings. Doss, Atkins, and Christensen (2003) found the largest differences in the process of seeking marital therapy were gender differences. Out of 147 couples, wives were the first to recognize the problem, consider treatment, and seek treatment in 67 percent to 73 percent of the time according to the husbands and wives, respectively.

Furthermore, earlier research suggests wives play a critical role in their husbands seeking therapy. Horwitz (1977) concluded that when husbands did seek individual therapy, their wives were the only person they spoke to regarding the problem, and their wives more readily identified the problem. Saunders (1996) further concluded that at every stage of seeking professional help, husbands were more likely than wives to report receiving help from their spouse. In short, when there is marital problem wives initiate therapy and help motivate their husbands to seek help as well.

Women's General Preferences for Support

Research on coping and support seeking styles reveals significant and consistent gender differences. For example, according to Kunkel and Burleson (1999), when compared to men,

> women are more willing and likely to provide emotional support to others (e.g., Trobst, Collins, and Embree, 1994), to seek support (e.g., Ashton and Fuehrer, 1993), to produce feeling-centered and emotion-focused supportive messages (e.g., Barbee, Gulley, and Cunningham, 1990), to produce qualitatively more sensitive comforting messages (e.g., Burleson, 1982), and to value comforting skill as more important for the maintenance of interpersonal friendships (e.g., Burleson, Kunkel, Samter, and Werking, 1996). (307–308).

Generally speaking, women prefer distress-reducing strategies and utilize social support, while men tend to prefer active behavioral methods including high-risk coping behaviors such as substance use (Rao, Moudad, and Subbak-rishna, 2000).

According to Barbee, Gulley, and Cunningham (1990), both men and women prefer talking to their same-sex rather than opposite-sex friends about relationship and task problems. The same researchers also found that, when women turned to female friends for support, they expected them to use more problem-solving and support behaviors in response to relationship problems, and they expected their male friends to use more dismiss and escape behaviors in response to problems. In a similar study, Vingerhoets and Van Heck (1990) found men tend to use problem-focused coping, talk problems down, and look on the bright side, while women tend to prefer emotion-focused coping, expressing their emotions, seeking social support, and blaming themselves.

In a recent study on women's mental health that was conducted in a gynecological clinic, 59 percent of the women who reported being psychologically distressed expressed interest in talking with a trained professional and reported that they would prefer individual therapy over group therapy (Glover, Novakovic, and Hunter, 2003). Twenty-nine percent of the women in the study, however, said they felt adequately supported by their friends and family (Glover, Novakovic, and Hunter, 2003).

An earlier study that was also set in a gynecology clinic found that the "vast majority" of women were interested in receiving some form of professional mental health support, and that individual therapy and psychoeducational classes were the top choices (Alvidrez and Azocar, 1999). Alvidrez and Azocar (1999) found that women were less interested in supports that involved group therapy and medication.

Summary

Based on these research findings, it could be suggested that women married to men with a sexual addiction may benefit from a range of supports in light of the relational, emotional, social, and physical symptoms and characteristics they commonly present with. What these supports are and how they would work in tandem or exclusively can only be hypothesized at this time. Because women tend to initiate therapy and seek help before their husbands, understanding how these women prefer to be supported could provide clinicians with valuable information for helping create a context for change for the entire family system, as well as for the individual woman. In light of research that has looked at women's general preferences for support, it could be postulated that individual therapy, female friendships, and emotionally focused outlets may be supports this population would benefit from and prefer.

Submitted to the Papers of the
Doha International Conference for the Family.

Bibliography

Alvidrez, J., and Azocar, Francisca. (1999). Distressed Women's Clinic Patients: Preferences for mental health treatments and perceived obstacles. *General Hospital Psychiatry, 21*(5), 340–347.

Ashton, W.A., and Fuehrer, A. (1993). Effects of gender and gender role identification of participant and type of social support resource on support seeking. *Sex Roles, 28*, 461–476.

Barbee, A.P., Gulley, M.R., and Cunningham, M.R. (1990). Support seeking in personal relationships. *Journal of Social and Personal Relationships, 7*(4), 531–540.

Burleson, B.R. (1982). The development of comforting communication skills in childhood and adolescence. *Child Development, 53*, 1578–1588.

Burleson, B.R., Kunkel, A.W., Samter, W., and Werking, K.J. (1996). Men's and women's evaluations of communication skills in personal relationships: When sex differences make a difference—and when they don't. *Journal of Social and Personal Relationships, 13,* 201–224.

Carnes, P.J. (1983). *Out of the shadows.* Minneapolis, MN: CompCare Publishers.

Carnes, P.J. (1991). *Don't call it love.* New York, NY: Bantam Books.

Carnes, P.J. (1992). *Out of the shadows.* Center City, MN: Hazelden.

Cooper, A. (1998). Sexuality and the Internet: Surfing into the new millennium. *CyberPsychology & Behavior, 1*(2), 181–187.

Cooper, A., Boies, S., Maheu, M., and Greenfield, D. (1999). Sexuality and the Internet: The next sexual revolution. In F. Muscarella and L. Szuchman (Eds.), *The psychological science of sexuality: A research based approach* (pp. 519–545). New York: Wiley.

Cooper, A., Delmonico, D.L., and Burg, R. (2000). Cybersex users, abusers, and compulsives: New findings and implications. *Sexual Addictions & Compulsivities, 7,* 5–29.

Cooper, A., and Griffin-Shelley, E. (2002, November/December). A quick tour of online sexuality: Part 1. *Annals of the American Psychotherapy Association,* 11–13.

Cooper, A., Scherer, C., Boies, S.C., and Gordon, B. (1999). Sexuality on the Internet: From sexual exploration to pathological expression. *Professional Psychology: Research and Practice, 6*(2), 23–35.

Corley, M.D., Schneider, J.P., and Irons, R. (1998). *Disclosure: A cornerstone for healing.* Paper presented at the meeting of the National Council on Sexual Addiction and Compulsivity.

Crawford, P., Hueppelsheuer, M., and George, D. (1996). Spouses of incest offenders: Coaddictive tendencies and dysfunctional etiologies. *Sexual Addiction and Compulsivity, 3,* 289–312.

Delmonico, D.L., and Carnes, P.J. (1999). Virtual sex addiction: When cybersex becomes the drug of choice. *CyberPsychology & Behavior, 2*(5), 457–463.

Doss, B.D., Atkins, D.C., and Christensen, A. (2003). Who's dragging their feet? Husbands and wives seeking marital therapy. *Journal of Marital & Family Therapy, 29*(2), 165–177.

Engel, M. (2001, 14 February). Alexa Research finds "sex" popular on the Web. *Business Wire.* Retrieved 18 May 2004, from http://home.businesswire.com and http://www.alexaresearch.com/rd/rd31.php

Garos, S. (1997). *The Garos Sexual Behavior Index: A measure of addictive sexual behavior.* Unpublished doctoral dissertation, Arizona State University, Arizona.

Glover, L., Novakovic, A., Hunter, M.S. (2003). Women's needs and preferences for psychological help and support in a gynecological outpatient service. *Journal of Reproductive and Infant Psychology, 21*(3), 195–206.

Horwitz, A. (1977). The pathways into psychiatric treatment: Some differences between men and women. *Journal of Health and Social Behavior, 18,* 169–178.

Internet World Stats: Usage and Population Statistics. (2004). *Internet usage stats for America.* Retrieved 27 May 2004, from http://www.internetworldstats.com/stats2.htm

Kasl, C.D. (1989). *Women, sex and addiction.* New York: Ticknor and Fields.

Kitchens, J. A. (1991). *Understanding and treating codependency*. Englewood Cliffs, NJ: Prentice-Hall.

Kunkel, A. W., and Burleson, B. R. (1999). Assessing explanations for sex differences in emotional support: A test of the different cultures and skill specialization accounts. *Human Communication Research, 25*(3), 307–340.

Laaser, M. (1996). *Faithful and true: Sexual integrity in a fallen world* (2nd ed.). Grand Rapids, MI: Zondervan.

Matheny, J. C. H. (1998). Strategies for assessment and early treatment with sexually addicted families. *Sexual Addiction and Compulsivity, 5*(1), 27–48.

McCarthy, B. W. (2002). The wife's role in facilitating recovery from male compulsive sexual behavior. *Sexual Addiction & Compulsivity, 9,* 275–284.

Milrad, M. (1999). Coaddictive recovery: Early recovery issues for spouses of sex addicts. *Sexual Addiction & Compulsivity, 6,* 125–136.

Newman, G. (1997). The use of online services to encourage exploration of ego-dystonic sexual interests. *Journal of Sex Education and Therapy, 22*(1), 45–48.

Nichols, M. P., and Schwartz, R. C. (1998). *Family therapy: Concepts and methods* (4th ed.). Boston: Allyn and Bacon.

Nielsen//NetRatings. (2004). Retrieved 27 May 2004, from http://www.nielsen-netratings.com/

Rao, K., Moudad, S., and Subbakrishna, D. K. (2000). Appraisal of stress and coping behavior in college students. *Journal of the Indian Academy of Applied Psychology, 26*(1–2), 5–13.

Saunders, S. M. (1996). Applicant's experience of social support in the process of seeking psychotherapy. *Psychotherapy, 33,* 617–627.

Schaef, A. W. (1989). *Escape from intimacy*. New York: Harper Collins.

Schneider, J. P. (1988). *Back from betrayal: A ground breaking guide to recovery for women involved with sex-addicted men*. Center City, MN: Hazelden.

Schneider, J. P. (1989). Rebuilding the marriage during recovery from compulsive sexual behavior. *Family Relations, 38*(3), 288–294.

Schneider, J. P. (1991). How to recognize the signs of sexual addiction. *Postgraduate Medicine, 90*(6), 171–182.

Schneider, J. P. (2000a). Effects of cybersex addiction on the family: Results of a survey. *Sexual Addiction & Compulsivity, 7,* 31–58.

Schneider, J. P. (2000b). A qualitative study of cybersex participants: Gender differences, recovery issues, and implications for therapists. *Sexual Addiction & Compulsivity, 7,* 249–278.

Schneider, J. P. (2000c). Compulsive and addictive sexual disorders and the family. *CNS Spectrums, 5*(10), 53–62.

Schneider, J. P., and Schneider, B. H. (1996). Couple recovery from sex addiction/coaddiction: Results of a survey of 88 marriages. *Sexual Addiction & Compulsivity, 3,* 111–126.

Schwartz, M. F., and Brasted, W. S. (1985). Sexual addiction. *Medical Aspects of Human Sexuality, 19,* 103–107.

Trobst, K. K., Collins, R. L., and Embree, J. M. (1994). The role of emotion in social support provision: Gender, empathy and expressions of distress. *Journal of Social and Personal Relationships, 11,* 45–62.

U.S. Census Bureau. (2004). U.S. and World Population Clocks—POPClocks. Retrieved 27 May 2004, from http://www.census.gov/main/www/popclock.html

Vingerhoets, A.J., and Van Heck., G.L. (1990). Gender, coping and psychosomatic symptoms. *Psychological Medicine, 20*(1), 125–135.

Wegscheider-Cruse, S. (1985). *Choice-making: For codependency, adult children and spirituality seekers.* Pompano Beach, FL: Health Communications.

Weiss, D., and DeBusk, D. (1993). *Women who love sex addicts.* Fort Worth, TX: Discovery Press.

Wildmon-White, M.L. (2002). *Validation of the construct of sexual addiction through an analysis of relational attachment and learned helplessness among married conservative Christian women.* Unpublished doctoral dissertation, Mississippi State University.

Wildmon-White, M.L., and Young, J.S. (2002). Family-of-origin characteristics among women married to sexually addicted men. *Sexual Addiction & Compulsivity, 9,* 263–273.

Woititz, J.G. (1983). *Adult children of alcoholics.* Pompano Beach, FL: Health Communications.

Young, K.S. (1996, August). *Internet addiction: The emergence of a new clinical disorder.* Paper presented at the 104th annual convention of the American Psychological Association, Toronto.

Young, K.S. (1997, August). *Internet addictions: What makes computer-mediated communication habit forming?* Paper presented at the 105th Annual convention of the American Psychological Association, Chicago, IL.

About the Editors and Contributors

Joel Brind is a biochemist who, since 1972, has specialized in reproductive steroid hormones and their links to human diseases. A graduate of Yale College in 1971, he earned his Ph.D. in basic medical science from New York University in 1981. Since 1986, Dr. Brind has been a Professor of Human Biology and Endocrinology at Baruch College of the City University of New York.

Since 1992, Dr. Brind has devoted most of his research efforts to studying and promoting awareness of what has come to be known as the "ABC link" (Abortion-Breast Cancer). In 1996, with colleagues from the Pennsylvania State College of Medicine, Dr. Brind coauthored a "comprehensive review and meta-analysis" on the ABC link in the British Medical Association's epidemiology journal. In 2003, he was appointed to a federal advisory committee of the Centers for Disease Control and Prevention (CDC) on the early detection and control of breast and cervical cancer. His most recent paper, which critically reviews ABC-link research published over the past decade, appears in the winter 2005 issue of the *Journal of American Physicians and Surgeons* (http://www.jpands.org/vol10no4/brind.pdf).

Don Browning is Alexander Campbell Professor of Religious Ethics and the Social Sciences, Divinity School, University of Chicago, Emeritus. For twelve years he was Director of the Religion, Culture, and Family Project funded by the Division of Religion of the Lilly Endowment. He is most recently the author of *Marriage and Modernization* (2003), *Christian Ethics and the Moral Psychologies* (2006), and coeditor of *Sex, Marriage, and Family in the World Religions* (2006). He is presently involved in the project on the Child in Law, Religion, and Society based at the School of Law of Emory University.

Samantha Callan is the Senior Consultant Researcher for Care for the Family, a major UK charity that aims to promote strong family life and to help those hurting because of family breakdown. As well as acting as a research consultant to other voluntary sector organizations, she advises politicians and policy-makers on family issues. She currently chairs the Family Breakdown Working Group of the UK Conservative Party's Social Justice Policy Commission.

An honorary research fellow at Edinburgh University, she is engaged in primary research into long term marriage and committed relationships. Working from a background in Social Anthropology and Islamic Studies, she holds Master's degrees from the Universities of Cambridge and Nottingham and a Ph.D. from the University of Loughborough. Her doctoral research analyzed cultural change in organizations as a result of implementation of family-friendly policies, and she acts as a consultant to firms that are addressing issues of work-life balance.

Lynn Clark Callister, RN, Ph.D., FAAN, is a professor in the Brigham Young University College of Nursing as well as an adjunct professor in the School of Family Life. She has conducted cross cultural studies of child-bearing women in North and Central American, the Peoples Republic of China, Scandinavia, the Middle East, and the Russian Federation. Dr. Callister is a Fellow in the American Academy of Nursing and has received Excellence in Education and Excellence in Research awards from the Association of Women's Health, Obstetric, and Neonatal Nursing. She was a Fulbright Scholar to the Russian Federation in 2004.

Jason S. Carroll, Ph.D., is an assistant professor in the School of Family Life at Brigham Young University. Dr. Carroll has published in several leading academic journals and recently coauthored the book, *Premarital Prediction of Martial Quality or Break-up: Research, Theory, & Practice.* He is a past recipient of the Award of Excellence from Family Process for the Best Manuscript by a Professional in Training. Dr. Carroll's recent scholarship focuses on the development of marital competence during the impact of emerging adulthood on early marriage and the effectiveness of premarital education programs.

William J. Doherty, Ph.D., is Professor of Family Social Science and Director of the Marriage and Family Therapy Program at the University of Minnesota. He is past-President of the National Council on Family Relations. He has authored or edited fourteen books, including *Soul Searching: Why Psychotherapy Must Promote Moral Responsibility,* and three books for the lay public: *Take Back Your Kids: Confident Parenting in Turbulent Times; Take Back Your Marriage: Sticking Together in a World That Pulls Us Apart;* and *Putting Family First: Successful Strategies for Reclaiming Family Life in a Hurry-Up World.* He has received the Significant Contribution to the Field of Marriage and Family Therapy Award and the Margaret Arcus Award for Outstanding Contribution to Family Life Education. He speaks nationally and internationally to professional and lay audiences about how families can join together to create a healthier environment for our marriages and our children.

Selena Ewing is Research Officer at Southern Cross Bioethics Institute, an independent, nonsectarian, autonomous institution committed to research into important bioethical issues (www.bioethics.org.au). She is also a Founding Director of Women's Forum Australia, an independent women's think tank that undertakes research, education, and public policy development about social, economic, health, and cultural issues affecting women (www.womensforumaustralia.org). She holds a Bachelor of Health Sciences degree and has worked in public health research and health promotion. She is married with three small children and lives in Adelaide, Australia.

Scott FitzGibbon is a graduate of the Harvard Law School (J.D.), where he was an Articles Officer of the Harvard Law Review, and of Oxford University (B.C.L.), where he studied legal philosophy. He is a professor at Boston College Law School, a member of the American Law Institute, and a member of the International Society of Family Law. One of his interests is corporate and securities law. He practiced in that area for five years at the law firm of Ropes and Gray in Boston and is the author of several articles on related subjects and of the leading treatise on legal opinions in financial transactions (with Donald Glazer). His most recent publication in this area is an article entitled "True Human Community: Business Company Structure and Catholic Moral Theology" (*St. Louis University Law Journal*, 2001).

His other major interest is jurisprudence and legal philosophy, with special attention to friendship and marriage in the Aristotelean tradition. He is the author of "Marriage and the Good of Obligation" (*American Journal of Jurisprudence,* 2002) and of "Marriage and the Ethics of Office" (*Notre Dame Journal of Law, Ethics, and Public Policy,* 2004). His most recent talks on philosophical topics include "A City Without Duty, Fault or Shame" (Cambridge, Massachusetts, 14 October 2004); "The 'Beautiful City' of Plato's *Republic:* How the Legal and Social Promotion of Divorce and Same-Sex Marriage Contravenes the Philosophy and Undermines the Projects of the Universal Declaration of Human Rights" (Geneva, Switzerland, August 2004 (printed in theses volumes)); "Divorce and the Decline of Obligation: Towards a Recovery of the Philosophy of Marital Fidelity" (Beijing, China, 19 July 2004); and "The Seduction of Lydia Bennet and the Jurisprudence of the Juristic Society" (Salt Lake City, Utah, July 2005).

Maggie Gallagher is president of the Institute for Marriage and Public Policy (www.marriagedebate.com) whose mission is research and public education on ways that law and public policy can strengthen marriage as a social institution. She is a nationally syndicated columnist with Universal Press and the coauthor (with University of Chicago Professor Linda J. Waite) of *The Case for Marriage: Why Married People Are Happier, Healthier, and Better Off Financially.* National Journal named her to its list of the "most influential" Americans in the same-sex marriage debate.

Norval D. Glenn, Ph.D. (University of Texas at Austin), is Ashbel Smith Professor in Sociology and Stiles Professor in American Studies at the University of Texas at Austin. His main research interests relate to family relations in modern societies and aging and the life course. A former editor of *Contemporary Sociology* and the *Journal of Family Issues,* he has served on the editorial boards of such journals as the *American Sociological Review,* the *Journal of Marriage and Family,* the *Public Opinion Quarterly,* and *Demography.* His recent publications have dealt with such topics as variations in marital success among different segments of the American population, changes in the institutional means of mate selection, age at marriage and marital success, and the characteristics of the "children of divorce" as young adults. He is the chair of the Research Advisory Group for the Texas Healthy Marriage Initiative and a member of the RAG for the Oklahoma Marriage Initiative.

Thomas B. Holman is a Professor in the School of Family Life at Brigham Young University. He is also Chair of the Board of Directors of the RELATE Institute, a research and outreach consortium of scholars and practitioners. Dr. Holman received his Ph.D. in Family Studies at Brigham Young University in 1981 and taught at the University of Wisconsin–Stout before returning to BYU in 1985. His numerous research publications have been largely in the areas of understanding marital formation and the early years of marriage.

John Keown graduated in law from the University of Cambridge before taking a doctorate at the University of Oxford. After being called to the Bar he lectured in the law and ethics of medicine at the University of Leicester and then at the University of Cambridge, where he was a Fellow of Queens' College and of Churchill College. In 2003 he was elected to the Rose F. Kennedy Chair of Christian Ethics in the Kennedy Institute of Ethics at Georgetown University. His other publications (which have been cited by bodies including the U.S. Supreme Court and the House of Lords) include *Abortion, Doctors and the Law* (1988), *Euthanasia Examined* (1995), and *Euthanasia, Ethics and Public Policy* (2002), all published by Cambridge University Press.

Daniel Lapin a noted rabbinic scholar, president of Toward Tradition and host of the *Toward Tradition Radio Show,* is one of America's most courageous and eloquent voices fighting institutions of secular fundamentalism that foster anti-Semitism and anti-Christianism, harm families, erode wealth, divide the nation, and ultimately jeopardize the future of America. In addition to his frequent television and radio appearances, Rabbi Lapin is a noted writer and lecturer. His articles have appeared in the *Wall Street Journal, National Review, Commentary, The Jewish Press, The American Enterprise, The Washington Times, Crisis,* and other publications. His first book, *America's Real War,* was a national best seller and his second book, *Buried Treasure; the Secrets for Living from the Lord's Language,* was published early in 2001. His third book, *Thou Shall Prosper; The Ten Commandments for Making Money,* was published by John Wiley in 2002. He speaks frequently at universities, schools, synagogues, and churches throughout the country.

Before immigrating to the United States in 1973 and becoming a proud naturalized citizen, Rabbi Lapin had studied Torah, physics, economics, and mathematics in Johannesburg, London, and Jerusalem. Lapin is well known for his outspoken views that America has become history's most successful engine of tranquility, prosperity, and power because of its traditional Judeo-Christian culture. He insists that these traditional values are vital for our nation's survival. As he says, *"The more things change, the more you must depend upon those things that never change."*

Lapin was the founding rabbi of the Pacific Jewish Center, an Orthodox synagogue in Venice, California, where he implanted the community's mission of demonstrating the relevance of traditional faith to modern life. He and his family relocated to Washington State in 1992 to develop Toward Tradition, a national movement of Jewish and Christian cooperation in the areas of family, fortune, and faith.

A. Scott Loveless, J.D., Ph.D., was appointed Executive Director of the World Family Policy Center at the J. Reuben Clark Law School at Brigham Young University in 2001. In addition to his law degree (1978), he completed a Ph.D. in Family Studies from BYU in April 2000. Prior to receiving his Ph.D., he served for several years as an attorney in the federal government in the natural resources arena. After observing the adverse consequences of divorce among both parents and children within his circle of acquaintances in the Washington, DC, area, he became concerned with the high national divorce levels and decided to pursue graduate study in the field of marriage and the family. His research interests center on the human-relational effects of philosophy and the similar effects of policy on human society. He and his wife, Cheri, are the grateful parents of eight children and five grandsons, so far.

Jill C. Manning, Ph.D., is a Marriage & Family Therapist who specializes in research and clinical work related to pornography and problematic sexual behavior. Dr. Manning was selected to be a visiting Social Science Fellow at The Heritage Foundation in Washington, DC, and, as a result of her research there, testified before a Senate subcommittee on the harms of pornography. She has been featured in several television programs and radio talk shows, and has authored numerous chapters and articles on the subject of pornography. A native of Calgary, Alberta, Canada, she currently resides in Colorado with her husband.

Elizabeth Marquardt is director of the Center for Marriage and Families at the Institute for American Values in New York City. She holds an M.Div. and an M.A. in international relations from the University of Chicago, and a B.A. in history and women's studies from Wake Forest University, is the author of *Between Two Worlds: The Inner Lives of Children of Divorce* (Crown, 2005), and is a principal investigator of reports on the future of parenthood and the hook up culture on college campuses. Her writings have appeared in the *New York Times, Washington Post, Los Angeles Times,* and elsewhere. She lives near Chicago with her husband and their two children.

Steven L. Nock is Professor of Sociology and Psychology at the University of Virginia, and Director of the Marriage Matters project. He is the author of many books and articles about the causes and consequences of change in the American family. He has investigated issues of privacy, unmarried fatherhood, cohabitation, commitment, divorce, and marriage. His book, *Marriage in Men's Lives,* won the William J. Goode Book Award from the American Sociological Association for the most outstanding contribution to family scholarship in 1999.

He focuses on the intersection of social science and public policy concerning households and families in America. He is an advisor to the Oklahoma Marriage Initiative and several national projects that are part of President Bush's Healthy Marriage Initiative. He is currently serving as an advisor to the Assistant Secretary for Planning and Evaluation (U.S. Department of Health and Human Services).

Charles J. Reid, Jr., holds degrees in canon law and American law from the Catholic University of America and a Ph.D. in medieval history from Cornell University. He has served on the research faculty of Emory University School of Law and is now Associate Professor of Law at the University of St. Thomas in Minnesota. He has written extensively on the history of marriage, both medieval and modern. His book-length treatment of the medieval origins of the conjugal debt and marital rights ("Power Over the Body, Equality in the Family," Eerdmans, 2004), has been well-received by reviewers. Dr. Reid is currently working on a book on the nineteenth-century American Protestant Establishment and the development of the law of marriage and domestic relations. He has spoken at a number of American and foreign locations on the subject of the history of marriage.

Steven E. Rhoads received his A.B. degree cum laude from Princeton University in 1961 and an MPA degree cum laude from Cornell University in 1965. He received the Ph.D. from Cornell with a concentration in American government and political theory in 1972. He is the recipient of Bradley, Earhart, Olin, National Endowment for the Humanities, and Sloan Foundation fellowships. He has taught public policy in the Politics Department at the University of Virginia for over thirty years. For the past fifteen years, Professor Rhoads has focused his studies on sex differences and their importance for an understanding of many contemporary cultural and policy issues. His most recent book, *Taking Sex Differences Seriously,* reflects these interests, focusing in particular on sex differences with regard to sex itself, nurturing the young, and aggression. His essays have appeared in the *New York Times,* the *Los Angeles Times,* and the *Public Interest* among other publications. Over the past year or two, Steve has discussed sex differences and their implications on the *Today Show,* PBS, C-Span's book TV, NPR, and many commercial radio shows.

Astrid Stuckelberger is a gerontologist and internationally recognized expert in aging. She is currently a lecturer and researcher at Geneva School of Public Health of the Faculty of Medicine of the University of Geneva. She holds a doctorate in psychology from the University of Geneva and has published more than 100 articles and reports and several books.

As a representative to the UN in Geneva of both the International Association of Gerontology and Geriatrics (IAGG) and the Society for Psychological Study of Social Issues (SPSSI), she was nominated as a chair of the NGO Committee on Aging where she advocates in particular for a human rights framework for older persons. She conducted several scientific expertises and reports for the Swiss government, the European Commission, and several United Nations specialized agencies and programmes. She is a permanent member of the WHO Ethical Review Committee (ERC).

During the past decade, as Deputy-Director of the Swiss National Research Programme on Aging, she created with WHO and AARP, the Geneva International Network on Ageing (GINA). After organizing numerous events for the 1999 UN International Year of Older Persons for the UN in Geneva and the Swiss authorities (i.e., the UN Open House Day), she received an Award from the UN Secretary-General. She also contributed to the UN "Research Agenda on Aging for the XXIst Century," the Plan of Action, and the NGO Forum declaration at the 2nd UN Assembly on Aging in Madrid in 2002.

Hirofumi Tanada is professor of sociology at the Faculty of Human Sciences, Waseda University, and director of Institute for Multi-ethnic and Multigenerational Societies, Waseda University in Tokyo, where he also completed his graduate training and Ph.D. His publications (in Japanese and English) on urban sociology and sociological studies of Asian societies include *Low Fertility, Ageing and Socio-economic Development in Asia* (edited, 2005), "Urbanization and Ageing in Malaysia" (2003), "Population of Islamic Societies in the Future" (2002), *Urban Society in Egypt* (1999), *Aging People in Transition* (coauthored, 1997), and "Survey of Migrant Associations in Cairo Metropolitan Society" (1996). He is currently conducting survey research on "Muslims in Japan," and "Low fertility in East Asia."

Linda J. Waite is Lucy Flower Professor of Sociology and Director of the Center on Aging at the University of Chicago. Her research focuses on the family, from the youngest to the oldest ages. She is the author, with Frances Goldscheider, of *New Families, No Families?: The Transformation of the American Home* (University of California Press, 1991), winner of the Duncan Award from the American Sociological Association. She is also author, with Maggie Gallagher, of *The Case for Marriage: Why Married People are Happier, Healthier and Better Off Financially* (Doubleday, 2000), which won the 2000 Outstanding Book Award from the Coalition for Marriage, Family and Couples Education. One current project examines the role of the social context in the etiology of loneliness and stress, and the biological and physiological mechanisms through which loneliness and other psychological states affect health and well-being at older ages. She is also Principal Investigator of *The National Social Life, Health and Aging Study,* which focuses on the relationship between social networks, intimacy, physical health, emotional well-being, and cognitive function at older ages. Both of these studies include researchers and research perspectives from a range of social sciences, and both include a substantial focus on biological and physiological measures of functioning. She is listed in *Who's Who in Economics,* 4th Edition.

Richard G. Wilkins, J.D., is the Managing Director of The Doha International Institute for Family Studies and Development, Doha, Qatar. Her Highness Sheikha Mozah Bint Nasser Al-Missned, Consort of His Highness the Emir of Qatar, established the Institute at the conclusion of the 2004 Doha International Conference for the Family. The Institute conducts interdisciplinary international family research and outreach. It assists local, national, and international actors to develop and implement sound family policy. Professor Wilkins chaired the NGO Working Committee during the 2004 Doha Conference, which collected the scholarship published in these volumes. He is the Robert W. Barker Professor of Law and Managing Director of the World Family Policy Center at Brigham Young University (on leave) and has written extensively on United States constitutional law, international law, and family law. He is married to Melany Moore Wilkins, M.S.W., C.S.W. They have four children and four grandchildren.

Camille S. Williams, Administrative Director of the Marriage & Family Law Research Grant, BYU Law School, is an Assistant City Attorney, and has practiced family law, taught family law for undergraduates, and has participated in professional seminars on family law. She has authored articles in law journals dealing with planned parent-deprivation strategies of same-sex couples, state marriage amendments and the nonessential woman, family norms in adoption law, and why a federal marriage amendment may be a necessary condition for women's equality (forthcoming). She has also authored chapters in *The Silent Subject: Reflections on the Unborn in American Culture* (1996) and *The Bill of Rights: A Bicentennial Assessment* (1994).

Index